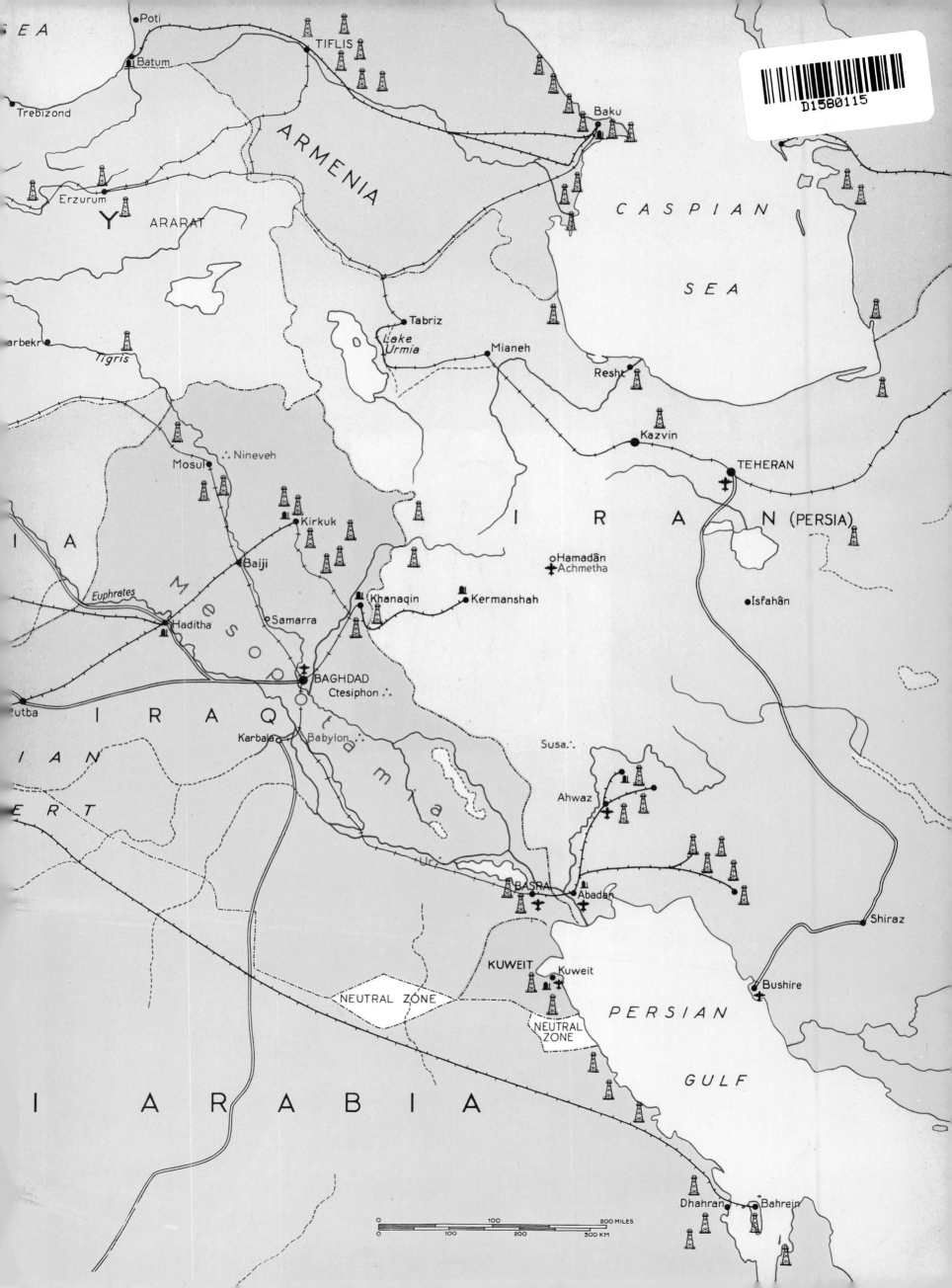

IN ARDUIS AUDAX

ATLAS
OF THE BIBLE

L. H. GROLLENBERG O.P.

ATLAS
OF THE BIBLE

TRANSLATED AND EDITED BY

JOYCE M. H. REID B.A.

AND

H. H. ROWLEY M.A., B.LITT., D.D., LL.D., F.B.A.
PROFESSOR OF HEBREW LANGUAGE AND LITERATURE
UNIVERSITY OF MANCHESTER

FOREWORD BY

W. F. ALBRIGHT PH.D., LITT.D., D.H.L., TH.D., LL.D.
PROFESSOR OF SEMITIC LANGUAGES, JOHNS HOPKINS UNIVERSITY

AND

H. H. ROWLEY

PREFACE BY

ROLAND DE VAUX O.P.
DIRECTOR, FRENCH SCHOOL OF BIBLICAL AND ARCHAEOLOGICAL
STUDIES AT JERUSALEM

NELSON

1957

THOMAS NELSON AND SONS LTD
LONDON AND EDINBURGH

THOMAS NELSON AND SONS
NEW YORK

THOMAS NELSON AND SONS
(CANADA) LTD
TORONTO

THOMAS NELSON AND SONS LTD
JOHANNESBURG
MELBOURNE

SOCIÉTÉ FRANÇAISE D'ÉDITIONS NELSON
PARIS

First published in this edition October 1956
Reprinted 1957

★

Originally published as
ATLAS VAN DE BIJBEL
(Amsterdam - Elsevier)

FOREWORD

IT IS A pleasure to introduce Father Grollenberg's ATLAS to English readers on both sides of the Atlantic, and there is little need to add to what Father R. de Vaux says in praise of the work. The eye of anyone who opens it must be caught immediately by the abundance of the illustrations and by their striking character. These alone would give a high value to the book as an aid to the reader of the Bible, since they are so admirably calculated to invest with a new meaning many of the passages he knows so well. They bring before him man's creations, both large and small, which have survived from the ancient Near East to our own day; but beyond that they enable him to picture the scenes described in the Bible, since not a few of them are photographs, taken from the ground and from the air, of the land of the Bible as it is today. Many of them will live in the mind and will prove more illuminating than long pages of description.

An Atlas of the Bible by its very title offers a collection of maps. Here we have a large number of them, so arranged that they illustrate the different periods of Biblical history; they are therefore not too crowded with names, and they bear descriptive comments which in themselves summarise much of the history. It will be only by long and careful use that the reader will discover how much information is given on these maps, and how much labour and research have gone into their preparation. For it is no simple matter to identify many of the Biblical sites, and Father Grollenberg seeks neither to bewilder the reader by giving all the alternative identifications that have been proposed, nor to mislead him by unjustified certainty, where caution is wiser. Hence by an ingenious system of signs he indicates the degree of probability attaching to the identifications here offered.

If we leave till last the text of the book which the author has written, this is not because it is of less worth than the pictures and the maps. In a graphic, but brief, narrative he presents the reader with a summary of the course of Biblical history. He has avoided the temptation to over-burden it with detail, yet he writes as a scholar who is well acquainted with all the problems attaching to the subject. On many questions there is, and must be, diversity of view, and if Father Grollenberg offers his readers guidance — as an author should do — it is the responsible guidance of one who speaks with the caution born of knowledge.

While this ATLAS is written primarily for the general reader, and is likely to be treasured in great numbers of Christian homes, it will be used by readers at all levels, and there is none who will not learn from it. To students and teachers it will offer a mine of information, and all who are charged with expounding the Scriptures will turn to it again and again with profit. Its author is one who knows and loves the land of the Bible, but who even more knows and loves the Bible and its enduring spiritual message.

W. F. Albright
Professor of Semitic Languages, Johns Hopkins University

H. H. Rowley
Professor of Hebrew Language and Literature
University of Manchester

PREFACE

THE BIBLE is an eternal book, the common heritage of men through the ages. Moreover, because of its constant use by the Church, the Bible has been instrumental, together with the legacy of Greece and Rome, in building Western civilisation. It has nurtured our thinkers and saints, it has inspired our poets and artists. For the believer, the Bible is the Sacred Book, which embodies God's message to mankind, the progressive revelation of His nature and His works and the authoritative statement of the condition and destiny of man. It unfolds the great design of saving grace which was manifested from the Creation down to the Coming of Christ, and which continues from the foundation of the Church until its consummation in the heavenly Jerusalem. The Bible contains the Alpha and the Omega, the Beginning and the End; it bears the Word of God, which endures for ever.

But this ever-topical book was in fact written in certain definite periods and places; this revelation addressed to all mankind has its setting in the history of a chosen people, living at a given time, subject to specific cultural influences, and established in a particular geographical environment. These human factors have coloured the divine message and made it more accessible, while in no way weakening its force. When we know the material circumstances in which it was proclaimed and to which it alludes, we are better able to understand its rich resources; we apprehend it more vividly and more nearly. A knowledge of this 'Biblical History' and this 'Biblical Land' is therefore of supreme importance for an understanding of the Scriptures.

No-one who has travelled in the East or made a pilgrimage to the Holy Land will ever forget his excitement on stepping ashore at Haifa, at the foot of Mount Carmel, with all its memories of Elijah, his joy on beholding the changeless horizons of Galilee and the Lake of Tiberias, the principal scene of the ministry of Jesus, or his deep emotion on reaching Jerusalem, the City of David, the city of the Crucifixion and the Resurrection. Every step in the Holy Land stirs a Biblical memory: Hebron recalls the Covenant with Abraham; the shores of the Dead Sea, the cursing of Sodom; Jericho, the epic of the conquest; Samaria, the invective of the prophets; Nazareth, the Annunciation; Bethlehem, the birth of Jesus. Nothing can quite take the place of this personal experience; but every serious reader of the Bible, whether or not he has had the good fortune to visit the East, feels the need to elucidate his text by reference to history, to situate a place or an event on a map, to examine or re-examine the picture of a site, a monument, or an object, which evokes the scene, the circumstances, or merely the atmosphere of the Biblical story.

It is to meet this need that the Reverend Father L. H. Grollenberg, O.P., has compiled his ATLAS OF THE BIBLE, whose French edition I had the honour and pleasure to introduce. The immediate success of the original edition, which was published in Holland in 1954, testifies to the soundness of the plan and the merit of its execution. The author is not only a Biblical scholar by profession; he has profited by several long visits to Jerusalem, he has travelled all over Palestine, and he has visited the neighbouring countries: we can have every confidence in him.

His ATLAS makes use of three media in close conjunction: maps, illustrations, and text. Not only do the maps indicate relief, political frontiers, and the sites of towns mentioned in the Bible; by a system of colours, symbols, and over-printed legends, they succeed in expressing the events which took place in this geographical setting; they spring to life and each becomes a page of history.

The illustrations consist mainly of uniformly excellent photographs, many of them the work of Father Grollenberg himself. They have been chosen for their documentary interest, and still more for their evocative power. A photograph may be faithful and yet inanimate; these are eloquent and living. To study them is to be transported to an actual geographical and human setting and to breathe its very atmosphere. This is true not only of landscapes, but of monuments, details of sculpture, and single objects. All the formidable might of Assyria is evoked in a few bas-reliefs; two or three pictures suffice to illustrate the perfection of Egyptian culture, or the ascendancy of Rome in the East.

The text serves to link the maps and the illustrations. It organises all this material and, by means of references to the books of the Bible, weaves it into a broad history extending from the nomad origins of the chosen people to 'the fullness of time', marked by the Coming of Christ and the expansion of His Church.

This is a book which the reader will delight to dip into. It is also a book which he will study, making conjoint use of all the facilities which it provides. Bible-readers, now happily numerous, will not only derive great pleasure from it; they will be helped to a better understanding of the Book of books, and this, I believe, is the sole reward which the author sought.

R. de Vaux, O.P.
Director of the French School of Biblical
and Archaeological Studies at Jerusalem

TABLE OF CONTENTS

The Hebrew prophets habitually regarded their people as a person; from this personification our Atlas takes its plan.

In such a work as this, the Author is very conscious of what he owes to the labours of such eminent scholars as Abel, Albright, Alt, Noth, De Vaux, Vincent, and others. This debt he gratefully acknowledges. Particular thanks are due to Dr A. van Deursen, Lecturer in Geography at Groningen, who kindly made available his wide knowledge of Biblical Geography.

THE SPELLING OF BIBLICAL NAMES

Our modern languages show little uniformity in the spelling of Biblical names for the obvious reason that, in many cases, they habitually attach different sound-values to any given letter of the Latin alphabet. To mention only two examples, the letter *u* has various values in our Western idioms, and there are three ways of representing the unvoiced guttural occlusive: *c, k, q.*

These divergences are already very marked between related languages, such as Greek, Latin, and the Western languages. They become even more serious when we are obliged to write down the sounds of a non-Indo-European language such as Hebrew, the language of the Bible, which belongs to the Semitic group.

The alphabets of the Semitic languages contain only consonants, the vowels being indicated by various diacritics. Hebrew has a total of twenty-two consonants, including, unfortunately, several which are polyphonic. There are, for example, only three letters to represent four distinct sibilants. Arabic, with its twenty-eight consonant signs, is much better equipped to represent the wide variety of sounds which occur in Semitic speech.

When European scholars wish to reproduce Semitic words in their own alphabet, they are obliged to resort to various expedients. These are all inadequate, and, to make matters worse, they differ from country to country. For Arabic names, the English system of transliteration (already adopted for the Dutch and French editions of this Atlas) has the advantage of brevity, and is therefore steadily gaining ground.

In the case of Hebrew names, the position has been greatly complicated by historical events and long-standing traditions. Four stages may be distinguished in the history of their graphic representation:

(*a*) In ancient Israel only the consonants were written down.

(*b*) The Greek-speaking Jews, such as the translators of the Septuagint and the authors of the New Testament, found that the Greek alphabet did not contain letters corresponding to all the Hebrew consonants. They therefore adopted the easiest solution, and omitted certain consonants altogether. They also introduced vowels corresponding to the Hebrew pronunciation of their own time. Finally, they added grammatical terminations designed to fit the words into declensional categories. These Hellenised forms became the accepted usage of the Early Church, and St Jerome's Latin translation of the Bible made no important changes in this respect.

(*c*) Towards the ninth century A.D., certain rabbis (the Massoretes) provided the Hebrew text of the Bible with vowel points to indicate what they believed to have been the ancient Hebrew pronunciation.

(*d*) During the Reformation, many Protestant translators adhered as closely as possible to the Massoretic spelling, which was regarded as that of the original Hebrew text.

For example, in the name of Solomon's son, *rhb'm*, the second and fourth consonants (the latter represented here by the apostrophe) were very difficult to pronounce for speakers of Greek, and were omitted in writing. But letters could be introduced to represent the vowel sounds which they heard, and the Hellenised Jews therefore wrote: *Roboam*, a form which stands in the Gospel of St Matthew (1:7) in the Greek and also in the Authorized (King James) Version of the English Bible and in all Catholic Bibles. But the Massoretes, in accordance with their principles, wrote the vowels of this name as follows: a weak *e*, an *o* (same sign as for *a*), an *e* still weaker than the first, and an *a*, *Rehabeam* or *Rehobeam*, which becomes *Rehoboam* in the Protestant Old Testament. The Catholic Bibles, however, have the Hellenised form *Roboam* also in the Old Testament.

As a result of these historical developments, there is in certain countries so great a difference between the Protestant and Catholic translations that the names are often difficult to recognise. We find, for example, the variants Hezekiah and Ezechias, Ahaziah and Ochozias, Jesse and Isai, etc. Neither Protestants nor Catholics, however, have chosen a uniform system of transliteration.

The spelling adopted for this Atlas is that of the Revised Standard Version of the Bible and the Revised Version of the Apocrypha, but cross-references to most of the variant forms in the Authorized Version and the Douay and Knox versions have been included in the Index, and it should therefore be possible to use the Atlas with any English translation of the Bible.

BIBLICAL ABBREVIATIONS

Old Testament			
Gn	= Genesis	Ezk	= Ezekiel
Ex	= Exodus	Dn	= Daniel
Lv	= Leviticus	Hos	= Hosea
Nu	= Numbers	Jl	= Joel
Dt	= Deuteronomy	Am	= Amos
Jos	= Joshua	Ob	= Obadiah
Jg	= Judges	Jon	= Jonah
Ru	= Ruth	Mic	= Micah
1 S, 2 S	= 1 and 2 Samuel	Nah	= Nahum
1 K, 2 K	= 1 and 2 Kings	Hab	= Habakkuk
1 Ch, 2 Ch	= 1 and 2 Chronicles	Zeph	= Zephaniah
Ezr	= Ezra	Hag	= Haggai
Neh	= Nehemiah	Zec	= Zechariah
Est	= Esther	Mal	= Malachi
Job			
Ps	= Psalms	*Apocrypha*	
Pr	= Proverbs	To	= Tobit
Ec	= Ecclesiastes	Jth	= Judith
Ca	= Song of Solomon (Canticles)	Wis	= Wisdom
Is	= Isaiah	Sir	= Sirach or Ecclesiasticus
Jer	= Jeremiah	Bar	= Baruch
La	= Lamentations	Bel	= Bel and the Dragon
		1 Mac, 2 Mac	= 1 and 2 Maccabees

New Testament	
Mt	= Matthew
Mk	= Mark
Lk	= Luke
Jn	= John
Ac	= Acts
Ro	= Romans
1 Co, 2 Co	= 1 and 2 Corinthians
Gal	= Galatians
Eph	= Ephesians
Ph	= Philippians
Col	= Colossians
1 Th, 2 Th	= 1 and 2 Thessalonians
1 Ti, 2 Ti	= 1 and 2 Timothy
Tit	= Titus
Philem	= Philemon
He	= Hebrews
Ja	= James
1 P, 2 P	= 1 and 2 Peter
1 Jn, 2 Jn, 3 Jn	= 1, 2, and 3 John
Jude	
Rev	= Revelation

N.B. 1. All other abbreviations are listed at the beginning of the Index (p. 140).

2. The numbers in the margins of the text refer to relevant illustrations. Important Biblical references are also indicated in the margins.

3. The illustrations are numbered from left to right and from top to bottom of the page.

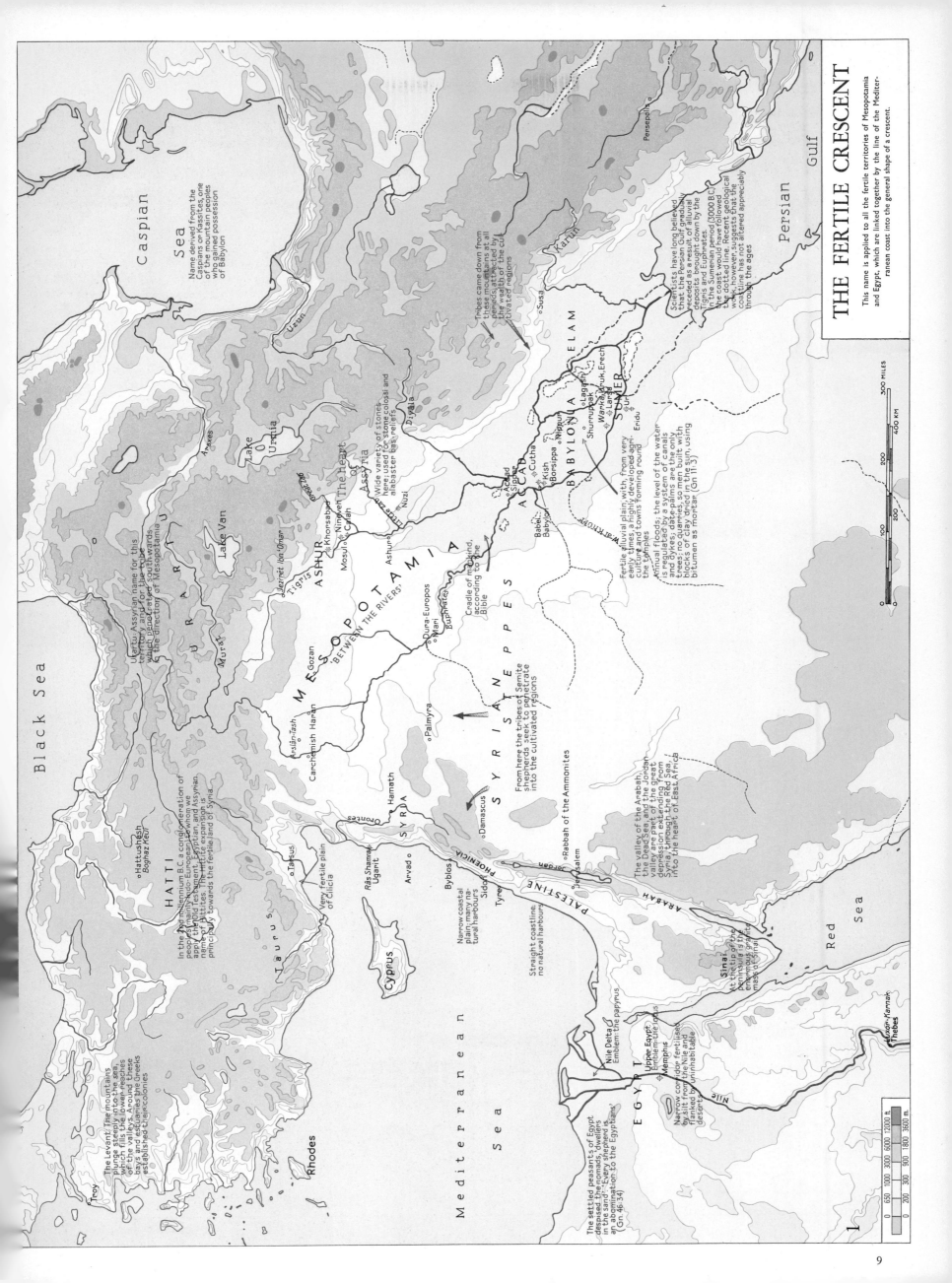

THE FERTILE CRESCENT

This name is applied to all the fertile territories of Mesopotamia and Egypt, which are linked together by the line of the Mediterranean coast into the general shape of a crescent.

Black Sea

Mediterranean Sea

Caspian Sea

Persian Gulf

Red Sea

Rhodes

Cyprus

Troy

HATTI

Hattushésh
Boghaz-Keui

Taurus

Tarsus

Very fertile plain of Cilicia

Rás Shamra
Ugarit

Arvad

Byblos

Sidon

Tyre

PHOENICIA

Arslan-Tash

Carchemish Harran

Gozan

URARTU

Lake Van

Murat

Araxes

Lake Urmia

M E S O P O T A M I A
'BETWEEN THE RIVERS'

Mosul
Nineveh Calah
Khorsabad

ASSYRIA

ASHUR

Tigris

Jezirat ibn 'Omar

Nuzi

Ashur

Diyala

Dura-Europos
Mari

Euphrates

Cradle of mankind, according to the Bible

SYRIA

Orontes

Hamath

Damascus

Palmyra

S Y R I A N   S T E P P E S

PALESTINE

Jerusalem

Jordan

Rabbah of the Ammonites

ARABAH

Sinai

EGYPT

Nile Delta:
Emblem: the papyrus

Memphis

Upper Egypt
Emblem: the lotus

NILE

Luxor Karnak
Thebes

Accad Sippar
ACCAD
Cutha
Kish
Babel Borsippa Nippur
Babylon
BABYLONIA
Shurrupak
Larsa
Warka, Uruk, Erech
Ur
SUMER
Eridu

ELAM

Susa

Karun

Persepolis

Wâdi-Khabur

0 200 400 600 900 1800 3600 m.
0 650 1000 3000 6000 12000 ft.

0   100   200   300   400 500 MILES
0   200   400 KM

In the 2nd millennium B.C. a conglomeration of peoples (mainly Indo-European, to whom we apply the Old Testament Egyptian, and Assyrian name of Hittites. The Hittite expansion is principally towards the fertile land of Syria.

Urartu: Assyrian name for this territory and for the tribe which penetrated southwards in the direction of Mesopotamia.

Name derived from the Caspians or Kassites, one of the mountain peoples who gained possession of Babylon.

Tribes came down from these mountains at all periods, attracted by the wealth of the cultivated regions

The Levant: The mountains plunge steeply into the sea, which fills the lower reaches of the valleys. Around these bays and estuaries the Greeks established their colonies.

Wide variety of stones here; used for stone colossi and alabaster bas-reliefs

Fertile alluvial plain, with, from very early times, a highly developed agriculture and towns forming round the temples

Annual floods; the level of the water is regulated by a system of canals and dykes; date-palms are the only trees; no quarries, so men built with blocks of clay dried in the sun, using bitumen as mortar. (Gn 11:3)

Scientists have long believed that the Persian Gulf gradually receded as a result of alluvial deposits brought down by the Tigris and Euphrates. In the Sumerian period (3000 B.C.) the coast would have followed the dotted line. Recent geological work, however, suggests that the coastline has not altered appreciably through the ages

From here the tribes of Semite shepherds seek to penetrate into the cultivated regions

The valley of the Arabah, the Dead Sea, and the Jordan valley are part of the great depression extending from Syria, through the Red Sea, into the heart of East Africa

Sinai. At the tip of the peninsula is the enormous granite mass of Sinai

Narrow coastal plain; many natural harbours

Straight coastline; no natural harbours

Narrow corridor fertilised by the Nile and flanked by desert

The settled peasants of Egypt despised the nomads, dwellers in the sand: 'Every shepherd is an abomination to the Egyptians'. (Gn 46:34)

9

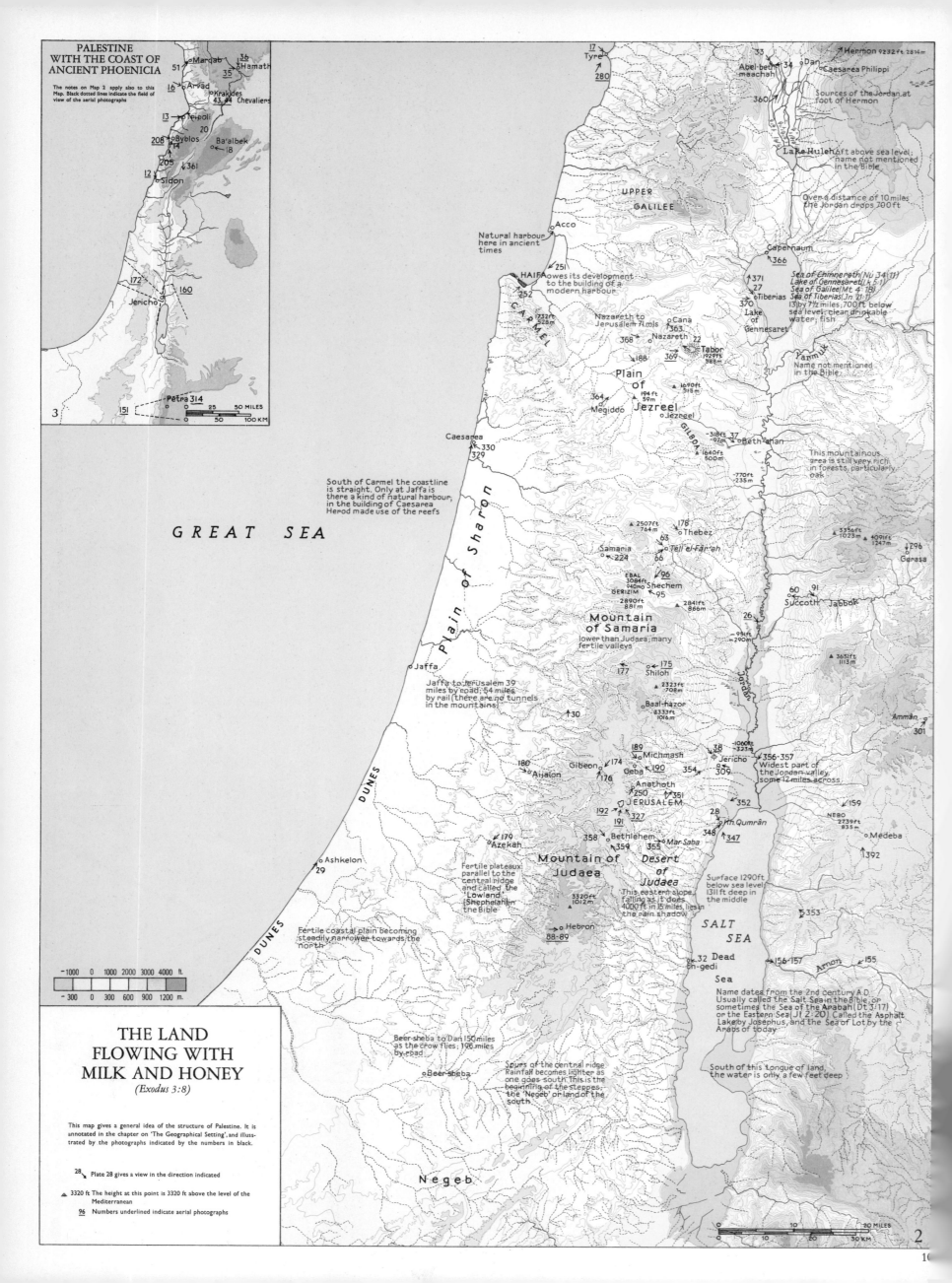

THE LAND FLOWING WITH MILK AND HONEY (Exodus 3:8)

1 / *Caravan in the Arabian Desert.* Direct trade between southern Mesopotamia and Egypt across the waterless steppes became possible only when man learned to employ the camel, which can go without water for several days.

[Map 1, p. 9]

THE GEOGRAPHICAL SETTING

Little more than a century ago, all that was known of the ancient Near East came from information contained in the writings of Herodotus and historians who followed him, from the fifth century B.C. onwards. Biblical history alone provided details of a more remote past, and only the solitary figure of Abraham lit the darkness of these distant ages. All this was changed when, in 1822, after brilliant research over many years, Jean-François Champollion discovered the key to the mysterious hieroglyphs covering the walls and columns of the Egyptian ruins, and when other scholars succeeded in deciphering the numerous clay tablets and the inscriptions sent to Europe following early excavations in Mesopotamia. Since then, a galaxy of archaeologists and philologists have succeeded in rolling back the veil of darkness to a period well before Abraham. Today, we contemplate with wonder the civilisations which flourished in Egypt and Mesopotamia more than a thousand years before the ancestor of Israel left Ur of the Chaldees. We now know that, in this setting, Israel was a comparatively young people which, during a period of political upheaval, had managed to establish itself upon a narrow coastal belt between the two ancient civilisations of Egypt and Mesopotamia. Numerous features in the language, customs, and religion of Israel, formerly considered to be exclusively Biblical, are now seen to be part of the common property of the Ancient East, and it is clear to us today that the political history of the Hebrew people was very largely determined by the interplay of relations between the powers established at the two extremities of the corridor it inhabited. If we wish to understand the milieu in which the books of the Bible had their origin we must therefore, before all else, form a clear idea of the central position of Palestine in relation to the ancient civilisations. And since these civilisations were greatly influenced by the country and climate in which they first arose, our Atlas must begin with a map of the Near East (Map 1, p. 9).

The Nile valley and delta and the alluvial plains of the Tigris and Euphrates make up, together with the fertile coastal belt of the Mediterranean, a vast semicircle, usually called the 'Fertile Crescent'. Its left tip is formed by the Nile, one of the longest rivers in the world. When it enters the region of the cataracts (cf. Map 10, p. 44), the Nile has already covered the greater part of its course. And yet it has still at five further points to carve a channel through walls of rock (cataracts or rapids) before it can come down freely towards the Mediterranean, covering a distance of 560 miles from *Assuân*, the *Sewêne* of the Hebrew text of the Bible (Syene in the Greek period). Rainfall is scanty, and, but for the Nile, this long valley would be as inhospitable as the Sahara. But in its annual floods, caused by torrential rains in the Abyssinian uplands, the river spreads a fertilising silt over the land bordering its banks. (As the colours on Map 1 indicate relief and not the nature of the soil, see Map 9 (p. 44), on which fertile areas are shown in green. It will be seen that the land is cultivable only close to the river and within the Delta.) In this fertile region, which amounts to only 3½% of the present area of Egypt, live 99½% of its population. In ancient times the situation was much the same. The country was like a long corridor teeming with life, hemmed in between vast deserts of death. In the south, the region of the cataracts cut across this corridor. It was here that Egypt ended, as the visitor to *Assuân* still perceives today. Farther south began Africa proper, Negro Africa, known to the ancient Egyptians as 'the land of gold' (*neb*, from which comes 'Nubia'). The broad fan of the Delta was regarded as a different land: Egypt could flourish only if the 'two lands' were united under the rule of a strong Pharaoh. On a statue of Rameses II, in the great forecourt at Luxor, are seen two figures which are linking the emblems of the 'two lands', the lotus and the papyrus, to an object which expresses the idea of 'union' in the language of hieroglyphs. The two figures are the gods of the Nile, portrayed in evocative fashion with a man's beard and a woman's breast. Other representations of the same scene add a Negro and an Asiatic, who symbolise the fact that Egypt lay open to her only two neighbours: the world of the Negro to the south, and Syria and Palestine to the east. But it was not until the sixteenth century B.C. that Egypt began to take an interest in these neighbouring peoples, when, after the defeat of the Hyksos, the Pharaohs of the Eighteenth Dynasty extended their power deep into Asia and Africa. By that time, however, the Egyptian character had long since been formed, and was not to be affected by foreign influences. 40

Shut away in his valley, the Egyptian gratefully and happily enjoyed the favour of gods who seemed to him reasonable and benevolent and in no way capricious or arbitrary. For did he not see the radiant sun, the bearer of life, rise each morning in the east? And each year when its rays grew too hot for the parched land, the Nile began to rise and again covered the fields with a fertile layer of silt. This was the time for repairing the dykes and canals; one must sow, plant, and use the precious water in the most effective way. This work called for common effort and sacrifice, a strong authority, and a fair distribution of tasks. But the Egyptian could rely upon his gods. He lived in a kindly world. In a land where the dark night was invariably followed by a brilliant day, where the rising of life-bearing waters always vanquished the deadly threat of drought, man could not envisage, after the trials of his old age and the shadows of death, anything but a new and glorious life. These happy men built their own houses from the clay beneath their feet. This they fashioned into bricks baked in the heat of the sun; that is why 132 practically nothing has been recovered of their dwellings, and why palm-trees now sway upon the site of the famous city of Memphis. But they built their 8 'eternal homes' of a much more durable material. They carefully worked great blocks of limestone rock which came from the mountains in the desert to the east and west of their valley and, from the granite mountains near *Assuân*, they hewed 263 great stones, which were transported on the Nile to the site of their tombs. In burial chambers which defy the hand of time they placed mementos or 124 representations of their occupations and former delights, while by means of a 140 steadily-improving technique they contrived to preserve flesh and bones from decomposition.

In Mesopotamia, the inhabitants were equally dependent upon the rising of the rivers. But here the floods were less regular and sometimes suddenly transformed a blessing into catastrophic destruction. Great winds might spring up and sweep before them all that man had built and planted. And there were other destructive forces against which the country was defenceless. Sometimes marauding tribes descended from the mountains in the east and swarmed over the fields, orchards, and towns, spreading chaos where the work of centuries had established order. To the west stretched endlessly the mysterious steppes, which time and again poured forth hordes of nomads who fell greedily upon the riches of the old civilisation. Is this why the ancient gods of Mesopotamia were unreasonable and sometimes capricious? And why their Underworld, where the shades were gathered together to spend a grey and joyless eternity, was so dismal a place?

While the civilisation of ancient Egypt retains the same characteristics for a

11

2 / *The Euphrates*. One of the many meanders on the lower course of this river, which is 1,700 miles long. 3 / *The Tigris*, emerging from the mountains near *Ibn 'Omar;* for 95 miles it forms the frontier between Turkey and Syria and then flows into Iraq. 4 / *Dura-Europos*, the Pompeii of the Euphrates: founded about 300 B.C. on the site of an Assyrian fortress (*dûr*) by the Macedonians, who called it after the town where their king Seleucus I was born (Europos in Macedonia); engulfed by sand in the 3rd century A.D., it was discovered and excavated in 1921. 5 / *Mari*, a little further south, on the banks of the Euphrates; for centuries a flourishing centre of trade; destroyed by Hammurabi about 1700 B.C.; discovered in 1933 by poor nomads who were digging a grave. 6, 7 / *The Khâbûr* (Habor in the Bible), a tributary of the Euphrates; there are many tells along its banks.

[*Map 1, p. 9*]

8–11 / *Egypt, Memphis, and Thebes*. 10: An aerial view of Egypt: a strip of cultivable land between deserts white in the sunlight. Memphis stood at the beginning of the Delta; today palm-trees grow on the site of the palaces of the Pharaohs of the Old Empire. Only their 'eternal homes', at the edge of the desert to the west of the Nile, still bear witness to their art and power (8: the stepped pyramid of Zoser, 2600 B.C.). 375 miles to the south, Luxor (9) and Karnak watch over the famous ruins of Thebes; the rugged mountain standing on the west bank of the Nile made the building of pyramids unnecessary: the Pharaohs of the New Empire erected their mortuary temples at its foot (Pls. 185, 186) but carved out their tombs in the 'Valley of the Kings' (11: entrances to the graves of Rameses II (1), Rameses VI (2), and Tutankhamon (3); in the top right-hand corner is the Nile, flowing northwards). [*Maps 1, p. 9; 8, p. 43*]

12 / *Saïda*, on the site of Sidon, one of the most ancient and important cities in Phoenicia; on a rocky islet is a fortress of the Crusaders (ca A.D. 1230).
13 / *Tripolis*, so called since Hellenistic times, because each of the three towns of Sidon, Tyre, and Arvad had its own walled quarter in this centre of trade. In the background, the snow-covered mountains of the Lebanon. **14** / *The narrow coastal plain* (see Pl. 205) with the mouth of the *Nahr el-Kelb* (the 'river of the dog'), seen from the projecting rock on which Rameses II, Shalmaneser III, and other commanders after them, recorded their victories. **15, 16** / *Ruâd*, the Arvad of the Bible, with the ruins of huge ramparts. **17** / *Sûr*, the ancient Tyre: in Old Testament times it was an island like Arvad; Alexander the Great joined it to the mainland by a causeway built for the siege (see Pl. 280).
[*Map 3, p. 10*]

18

period of more than twenty centuries and while the main outlines of the political history of this closed land are easy to follow, the geographical position of the Land of the Two Rivers results in its history being characterised by a diversity of dynasties and cultures, so that it is difficult to take it in at a glance. The reader will be aware of this when he observes the number of maps needed to illustrate Mesopotamia's ever-changing historical situation. Moreover, the history of Israel from the foundation of the monarchy to the rise of Alexander the Great was more closely affected by what happened in Mesopotamia than by events in Egypt, which was more isolated and in decline. This was in part due to the geographical situation of Palestine, which belongs to the belt of country (shown in its entirety on Map 4, p. 29) between the Syrian Desert and the Mediterranean.

This coastal strip, comparatively fertile owing to an abundant winter rainfall, attracts the desert nomads; moreover, by reason of its situation and structure, it forms a line of communication between Mesopotamia and Egypt, and is also in touch with the world around the Aegean Sea through numerous ports strung along the coast to the north of Carmel. The objects and texts discovered since 1929 in the ruins of *Râs Shamra* (the ancient city of Ugarit) show clearly that the culture of the Canaanites was a mixture of Babylonian, Hurrian, Hittite, Aegean, and Egyptian elements. At Byblos, a little further south, though the two last-named elements predominate, the others are also represented; and the same is true of the sister-cities of Arvad, Sidon, and Tyre.

This elongated area, with Palestine forming its southernmost end, is really a mountainous belt, made up of two ridges with a deep channel running between them. The geographical structure shows up very clearly in the central sector, dominated by the Lebanon, the 'white mountain'. In ancient times the Lebanon was entirely covered with mighty cedars and was one of the greatest attractions of

Canaan for the kings of Egypt and Mesopotamia. The Lebanon is separated from the other ridge, the Anti-Lebanon, by the majestic valley of the Beqa' famous today for the ruins of Ba'albek. The traveller who, after crossing the Lebanon by the Beirut-Damascus high-road, surveys the wide valley sees to his left the Anti-Lebanon and to his right its southern continuation, the imposing mass of Mount Hermon. The Jordan rises at the foot of Hermon and flows down towards the south with capricious détours, following the continuation of the Beqa', into which it plunges ever more deeply. On Map 2 (p. 10) the course of the Jordan completely dominates the picture of Palestine. Plates 26 and 160 give some idea of why this great rift in the earth's surface inevitably captured the imagination of all who dwelt by it or crossed over it.

340–
345

360–
361

The mountainous region to the east of the Jordan is intersected by three deep clefts. The most northerly is not named in the Bible, but, in the time of Jesus, the torrent which here comes down from the mountain was certainly called the Yarmuk, a name found in the *Natural History* of Pliny (A.D. 24–79). The plateau north of the Yarmuk, which falls away in a steep slope towards the Sea of Galilee, is composed of a fertile mixture of tufa and red-brown earth, where, a little enviously, the Israelites saw the fat kine of Bashan at pasture. To the south, between the Yarmuk and the next cleft, mentioned in the Bible as the river Jabbok, lies a mountainous area, heavily wooded to this day. A transverse section of our map at this point would show the same basic features as a section across the Lebanon and the Anti-Lebanon, for here also we have a channel bounded by two ridges: the Syrian steppe, on the east side of our map, lies about 2,000 feet above sea level, and the Jordan valley some 800 feet below sea level; between the two are peaks sometimes rising to more than 3,000 feet, forming the eastern ridge (the western ridge is dealt with below). The third cleft is formed by what some translations

370

Am 4:1

19
20
21

18 / *The Lebanon seen from Ba'albek.* Pl. 13 shows the same ridge seen from the SW. Here it is viewed from the east, from the wide valley of the *Beqa'*, parallel to the coast. This plain is well-known for the impressive ruins of *Ba'albek*, seen here in the foreground (Pls. 340–345). The word *Lebanon* derives from the Semitic root *lƀn*, 'to be white'; several of its summits, nearly 10,000 feet high, are always white with snow. **19–21** / *The Cedars of Lebanon.* In ancient times the slopes of the mountains were covered with these majestic trees, whose fine timber attracted both the Pharaohs, building in Egypt, and the kings of Assyria (2 K 19:23) and Babylon (Is 14:8). After forty centuries of spoliation, there are only a few isolated plantations left today; the most beautiful of these, carefully walled in, is at a height of 6,300 feet, where it is greatly admired by tourists and skiers. [Map 3, p. 10]

of the Bible call 'the brook of Arnon'. Anyone who gazes from the brink of this gorge down into the depths below, or is prepared to follow the tumultuous torrent down to where it enters the Dead Sea, realises how ill-chosen is the word 'brook'. A more appropriate term would be 'canyon'. To the south of the Arnon stretches the land of the Moabites, bounded in the south by an equally imposing canyon, that of the Zered, 'the brook of the willows'.

The Jordan valley is a phenomenon unique in the geography of our planet: it is farther below sea-level than any other valley in the world. It must in prehistoric times have been the bed of a very extensive lake, which has disappeared through evaporation, leaving only three stretches of water at its deepest points (Lake Huleh, the Sea of Galilee, and the Dead Sea). The northern part of the valley is luxuriant. In springtime, the well-watered plain around little Lake Huleh and, above all, the western shores of the magnificent Sea of Galilee are a veritable garden with flowers of every hue stretching as far as the eye can see; a deep blue sky above, and the white splendour of Hermon on the horizon complete the glittering picture. The two lakes abound in fish, and one may drink freely of their crystal-clear water without fear of infection. Towards the south, the valley, which varies in width from 2½ to 12 miles, grows less and less fertile. Below the confluence with the Jabbok, it may be described as a desert; vegetation is restricted to the vicinity of the springs and forms sporadic green areas seen from the air as dark patches.

The Dead Sea fully justifies its name. Owing to the high mineral content of its water (sodium chloride, magnesium chloride, calcium chloride, bromides, etc., a total of six times the salt content of the ocean), all the fish brought down by the Jordan die within a few moments. The enormous quantities of water carried in each day by the swiftly-flowing Jordan and other rivers quickly evaporate under the fierce heat of the sun, concentrated between the precipitous sides of the great lake. If, coming from the cruel desert of Judah, one encamps on the parched banks of this dead water and recalls the chapter of Ezekiel describing the stream of living water which issued from the Temple, one is filled with admiration for such deep faith in the creative power of God. One understands also why the members of a sect, living in the time of Jesus, chose to withdraw to the shores of this sea for a life of penitence and contemplation. For this imposing landscape, bathed in an ever-changing light, is most conducive to a state of reflection and meditation amid evident signs of a power greater than man's.

To the west of the Jordan valley, the other ridge is formed by a mountain chain running north and south, which is perhaps geologically the continuation of the Lebanon. To the northwest of the Sea of Galilee, the peaks rise to more than 3,500 feet; the ridge falls away in the direction of Nazareth, where it finally descends to the fertile plain of Jezreel. The most striking sight in this region is Mount Tabor, which, though not very high, dominates the surrounding country so impressively that an old rabbi used to remark: 'Our fathers would have built the Temple of God on that mountain if He had not Himself designated Mount Moriah'. After the plain of Jezreel, the ridge reappears, rising progressively on its way south and, after reaching a height of 3,320 feet (near Hebron), descends steadily to the arid Negeb. The western slopes catch the rain, so that eastern Judaea lies in the rain-shadow and is therefore desert (cf. Map 4, p. 29).

In the south, between the straight coastline and the central mountain ridge, are situated, from west to east: a narrow belt of dunes, a very fertile coastal area, and a series of gently-sloping hills. This last region, known as the Shephelah, grows narrower towards the north, disappearing opposite Jerusalem; and the coastal plain also narrows before being crossed, in the north, by Mount Carmel, which sweeps right down to the sea. The undulating country linking Mount Carmel to the central ridge is not very high and, at a point near Megiddo, permitted the passage of the ancient highway securing communications between Egypt and Mesopotamia.

The limestone plateau of the Negeb, extending south from Beer-sheba to the desert of Sinai and the Gulf of 'Aqaba, is today dry and barren, though in former times the northern part was populous. Its name, from a Hebrew word meaning 'dry', has, from its position relative to Judah, acquired the general significance of 'south'. Here Solomon had rich copper mines, and from Elath ('Aqaba) his fleet sailed for Ophir.

22 / *The Hills of Galilee* seen from the flat top of Mount Tabor; Nazareth is hidden among the distant hills in the centre (see Pl. 368, taken from the opposite direction). **23** / *The Plain of Jezreel*, bounded to the SE by the mountains of Gilboa; Transjordan can be seen to the left (Pl. 188). **24** / *Judaea*. Characteristic view of the central hill-country. **25** / *The Desert of Judah* between Bethlehem and the Dead Sea. *Opposite*, **26** / *'The Pride of the Jordan'*. The river twists and turns capriciously in the lowest valley in the world; vegetation is almost tropical. Lions once roamed in this jungle, which only the bravest dared enter (Jer 12:5). [Map 2, p. 10]

27, 28 / *The Two Biblical Lakes.* To the left, the Sea of Galilee with Tiberias (founded in the youth of Jesus). The surface of the water is 695 feet below the level of the Mediterranean. Hidden behind the hill on the right is the point where the Jordan leaves the lake to follow a winding course of 220 miles to the Dead Sea (28), which lies 1,290 feet below the level of the Mediterranean. *Khirbet Qumrân* is seen beside the archaeologists' tents (see Pls. 347–350); in the background, the rugged slopes of the mountains of Moab. **29** / *The Palestinian Coast* near the ruins of Ashkelon. **30** / *In the Mountains of Ephraim*. **31** / *The Negeb*, the 'southern land' of Judah, SW of the Dead Sea, looking east. The Dead Sea is just visible to the left of the mountain; to the right is the broad valley of the Arabah. **32** / *En-gedi*, seen from the shores of the Dead Sea, looking west.   [Map 2, p. 10]

33
34

33, 34 / *Abil el-Qamh*, a village on the slopes of *Tell Abil*. This tell covers the ruins of Abel-beth-maacah, a fortified town in the extreme NW of the plain which extends northwards from little Lake Huleh. This lake lies in the haze in the far distance on the left-hand plate. [*Maps 2, p. 10; 15, p. 66*]

THE TECHNIQUE OF BIBLICAL GEOGRAPHY

In order to produce an historical atlas of a region, it might appear sufficient to give a competent scholar some such order as: 'We are sending you as many maps as there are periods in the history of the country. Please indicate on each of these maps the places and frontiers which play a part in the corresponding period.' For a country of Western Europe, the task is relatively easy. But this does not apply to the ancient Near East in general, nor to Palestine in particular. In this region the difficulties facing such an enterprise multiply to an alarming degree, and specialised knowledge of many kinds must be pressed into service if a satisfactory result is to be achieved.

Anyone who obtains a detailed map of present-day Palestine in order to look up the places he meets in his Bible will be disappointed. No doubt he at once locates a few well-known cities, such as Jerusalem, Bethlehem, Hebron, or Jericho, but, among the hundreds of other names, hardly one recalls any episode in the Old or New Testament. If he buys a Biblical Atlas, he finds, on the contrary, nothing shown on the maps but names mentioned in the Scriptures, and all the difficulties disappear – for as long, at least, as he has no occasion to compare his new Atlas with a work of the same kind by a different author. Should he make such a comparison, he is astonished to find that, in the different atlases, the same town may appear in different parts of Palestine, and is sometimes followed by a question-mark.

These difficulties are due to the fact that the majority of the towns and villages of the Bible have been transformed into unrecognisable heaps of ruins, and that their identification calls for a special technique. The earliest inhabitants of Palestine, with its lack of water (it hardly ever rains between April and October), preferred to settle in the vicinity of the springs; and there were, moreover, other factors which influenced the choice of a site for the towns, such as a good strategic position, or the existence of natural lines of communication. For the building of houses, there was an inexhaustible supply of stones strewn over the fissured limestone surface. The walls were made of a double line of uncut stones; in the cavity were piled small pebbles and damp earth. In most cases, stones were not used for the upper walls; the builders made shift with earth, shaped and moulded into bricks and then dried in the sun. The roof consisted of reed canes, supported by beams and covered with a layer of earth. The floor was simply of beaten earth, sometimes coated with lime, with a flat stone placed here and there to support an upright.

When a cluster of such houses was ravaged by pestilence, famine, or war (usually by a combination of all three), and emptied of its inhabitants, only the lower part of the walls remained standing, and even that disappeared beneath canes and earth from the roof, beneath the clay and the stones and the half-charred beams. If a later generation, attracted by the favourable position, re-occupied the site and built houses on it, using the same technique as their ancestors, they erected them upon a mass of earth and stones levelled by wind and time. They were glad to make use of portions of wall protruding here and there; the beaten earth floor of the new houses then lay only a foot or two above the earlier floor. In the course of centuries this process was repeated several times, and, ultimately, many towns were literally heaped one on top of the other. If a site remained uninhabited after devastation, it retained the appearance of an artificial hill: in the ancient Semitic languages it was called a *tell*, a word still in use today. If traces of wall are visible, the Arabs also use the term *chirbe*, which is found with a slight difference of vowels in the Bible. (We adopt the normal transcription of this term, *khirbeh*, before a proper name *khirbet*.)

If the earliest settlement already had a name, this may have been preserved, in a more or less corrupt form, down to the present day, since place-names are usually very constant in the East, and may designate a mound of ruins uninhabited for centuries past. On the other hand, where present-day villages or towns have grown up near the ancient site, they have sometimes taken over the old name, and the tell has then acquired a different name. Thus the modern town of *Hama* 35 on the Orontes encircles in picturesque fashion the tell of the famous ancient city, which appears in the Bible under the name of Hamath. The imposing *Tell* 36 *el-Hosn* is formed by the accumulation of more than twenty settlements. These 37 were called Beth-shan, a name well-known in the Bible and preserved in that of the neighbouring village, *Beisân*. The name of Jericho, so rich in associations for 38 readers of the Bible, remains attached to the small Arab village of *Rîha*. Just outside this village stands the tell of the ancient town which, for some reason, bears the fine name of *Tell es-Sultân*, the 'tell of the Sultan'.

Other names have been forgotten, and were replaced centuries ago by new ones; or else they have been so badly corrupted as to be unrecognisable in the modern Arabic name for the tell or the neighbouring village. Finally, there are in Palestine a few extensive tells and a large number of small ones which the Arabs have named according to their shape, their colour, the animals which live there, or in memory of some former sheikh who is buried there. In these cases all information about the former name is lacking, and the archaeologist and geographer must then look elsewhere for their evidence for identification.

The geographer possesses, on the one hand, an impressive list of Biblical towns and villages which he must locate as accurately as he can, and on the other, a very detailed map of present-day Palestine, on which, during the period of the Mandate, British surveyors carefully marked the majority of the mounds, and recorded in each case the name they had heard in use among Arabs of the locality. Armed with these two kinds of information, the geographer must endeavour to identify the towns, asking himself: 'What name in the Bible corresponds to this tell?' The reply is far from easy. For Palestine is strewn with ruins, as the reader will appreciate if he looks at the map on page 105. This is a fragment of the large map of Palestine on a scale of 1 to 100,000; it covers an area of 11 by 12 kilometres (about 7 by 7½ miles), to the north of Hebron; and, in this tiny space alone, the surveyors recorded forty-eight ruined sites! The problem which such complexity presents to the investigator is at once obvious.

To solve this problem, the cartographer will first ascertain whether the Bible itself does not contain information about the position of the town in question. For example, from all that took place at Shechem, it appears that the town was situated in the centre of the country, at an important crossroads, and between two 95 mountains, like the 'back of a neck' (the meaning of the Hebrew word) between 96 two high, broad shoulders. Consequently, it can only be located near a particularly noticeable saddle, in the middle of Palestine. There is, in fact, a tell which meets these requirements. Its name, like that of the nearby hamlet, is *Balâta*, which 100 means 'land covered with stones' and is therefore not very helpful: nor are 101 any clear traces of the ancient name to be found in the vicinity. Yet the identification of this tell with the Biblical town of Shechem, already made by early Christian tradition, is quite certain; all doubts have been removed by modern excavations on the spot. Unfortunately, however, not all identifications are so clear or are accepted with such unanimity.

Megiddo is mentioned in the book of Judges together with other towns on ^{Jg 1:} the great plain of Jezreel which the Israelites did not succeed in wresting from the Canaanites: the town did not fall until the time of David.   Towards the end of last ^{I K 4} century, an English scholar believed he had detected the name of this town at the foot of the mountain of Gilboa, southwest of Beth-shan, in a ruin called *Khirbet el-Mujadda'* by the local Arabs.   But the identification encountered serious difficulties: could this name, with its final guttural, have derived from the Hebrew *Megiddo*, and was the tiny ruin so ancient?   Furthermore, the Bible several times mentions Megiddo in company with the town of Taanach.   Now, the modern *Tell Ta'annak* ^{Jg 5:} puts the location of the latter town beyond dispute, and Biblical accounts suggest a similar situation for Megiddo, on the southwestern edge of the great plain dominated by Mount Tabor, at the point where it is crossed by the only road ³⁶⁴ running from Egypt to the north.   Further light is thrown on these facts by the illustrated account which the Pharaoh Thothmes III had carved on the wall of a temple at Karnak, following his victory at Megiddo a little after 1480 B.C.   There is, in fact, an imposing tell on the edge of the plain, which the Arab population calls *Tell el-Mutesellim*, 'the tell of the governor'.   There is no trace of the ancient name, Megiddo; but the location is certain and has been confirmed beyond doubt by excavations.

Sometimes the text of the Bible does not provide sufficient information about the situation of a town; the geographer then searches elsewhere, in documents contemporary with, or later than, the Biblical accounts.   The records of Egyptian campaigns in Palestine and Syria are an important source of information.   They contain lists of captured towns, diligently compiled by chroniclers who accom- ⁴¹ panied the Pharaohs of the New Empire on their expeditions.   Thothmes III ³⁹ caused a list of 118 towns of Canaan to be carved three times in the temples of ⁴⁰ Karnak.   Rameses II had a list of the same kind recorded on the base of his statue at Luxor.   Another Pharaoh, Sheshonq (Shishak), also deserves special mention here: after his campaign against Judah, described in the Bible, he handed down ^{1 K 14:} to posterity the names of 156 Israelite cities.   The Assyrian conquerors were also ²⁴ accompanied by scribes, and their annals provide a further source of information on this subject.   In order to make use of these lists and records, the Biblical geographer obviously needs a thorough knowledge of the Egyptian and Assyrian languages, and a close acquaintance with the principles adopted by the chroniclers for transcribing foreign names.

In addition, a great deal of information about the geography of Canaan and Israel is to be found in documents of all kinds: archives of cuneiform tablets, commemorative stelae like those of Merneptah and Mesha, fragments of ancient ¹³ records of travels, historical descriptions and geographical treatises by profane ²² authors, Greeks, Romans, and others.   The Jewish writer Flavius Josephus (*ca* A.D. 37–100) deserves mention: he lived more than thirty-five years in Palestine, taking a keen interest in the history of the country and its people, and, in the exercise of his military and political duties, was able to bring together in his works a great deal of geographical information.   After him, it is above all the early Christian writers who, in their commentaries on the books of the Bible, pass on various ancient traditions, later forgotten, concerning Biblical sites.   These were systematically collected by the learned Bishop Eusebius of Caesarea (A.D. 263–339), who wrote several works on the geography of the Holy Land and later compiled an alphabetical Index of all the names of towns mentioned in the Scriptures; in it he recorded the name in use in his own time and the distances between Biblical towns and other towns better known to his contemporaries (e.g. the distance of Lachish from Eleutheropolis).   Fortunately, this Index was not lost like the other geographical works of Eusebius.   In his monastery at Bethlehem, St Jerome (*ca* A.D. 345–420), the first great Biblical scholar in the modern sense of the term, translated the Index into Latin and enriched it with much explanatory material.   Thus, for centuries to come, he provided the western world with a guide to the lands of the Bible.

Information may also be found here and there in rabbinical writings and in the works of the early Arab geographers.   Some medieval scholars profited by the Crusaders' conquest of the Holy Land to study the country.   The most important work, entitled *A Description of the Holy Land* (1283), is by the Dominican Burchard.   He knew all the earlier *onomastica* and descriptions and had a complete command of the Arabic tongue; he made many journeys on foot through Biblical country, and in this way greatly contributed to our knowledge of Palestine.   There was no book of equal merit until that of Adriaan Reland (1676–1718).   He never visited Palestine, but, in his study in Utrecht, he collected together almost everything which had been published in the way of geographical documentation and set it forth critically and systematically in a Latin work in two volumes (1714), which appeared in Dutch five years later, under the title: *New Light on Palestine, or the Geographical Situation of the Land of the Jews, based on the Commemorative Documents of the Ancients, Demonstrated and Proved according to Sounder Principles than Heretofore.*

If, after studying all these sources, one knows the exact region in which a given town must be situated, one is then confronted with numerous mounds to be examined.   This work can only be done on the spot, and must begin with the exact

35, 36 / *Hama on the Orontes*, encircling the tell of a very ancient town called Hamath in the Bible.   **37** / *The Impressive Tell el-Hosn*, covering the Biblical town of Beth-shan; the nearby village has inherited this name in the form *Beisân*.   **38** / *Tell es-Sultân*, the Biblical Jericho; a tell of 330 by 175 yards, beside the fountain of Elisha (see arrow).   Left, amid palm-trees, the modern village of *Rîha*.   In the background, the Dead Sea.   [*Maps 2, 3, p. 10*]

39
40

41
42

39–42 / *Lists of Place-names in Egyptian Temples.* Temple inscriptions, in which the Pharaohs of the New Empire recorded their military expeditions in Asia, are very important for the geography of Canaan. Rameses II erected a colossal statue of himself among the buildings which he added to the temple of Luxor (39; also in the centre of Pl. 9); on the base he had carved, in graphic style, the list of occupied regions (40); each name is enclosed in a ring, with projections symbolising the ramparts and their towers; above each is the torso of a Semite with arms bound, tied to the others by a rope around his neck (42). 41: Above three rows of names, Thothmes III, a predecessor of Rameses, strikes down a group of vanquished Asiatics. [*Maps 7, 8, p. 43*]

43
44

45
46
47

48
49
50

43–50 / *Fortress of the Crusaders*. Ruins of the Crusaders' strongholds are to be found everywhere, from the Taurus to the Red Sea. Above are views of the well-preserved 'Krak des Chevaliers', a fortress of the Knights Hospitallers commanding the road from Hama to Tripolis. Protected on its northern flanks by steep cliffs (44), it is joined to the mountain on the south (43), where the ramparts are specially strengthened, and the inner wall with its bastions appears impregnable (46, 48: the figures give an idea of its size). Along broad passages, cleverly built for defence (47), knights on horseback could ride up to the living quarters, where there were Gothic halls and courtyards in the Western style (45, 50). *Opposite*, **51** / *The Fortress of Marqab*, overlooking a bay on the Phoenician coast.

[*Map 1, p. 9*]

51

determination of the name given to the ruins by the local population. A superficial resemblance between one of these names and a Biblical term is not, however, a sufficient proof of their identity, since Hebrew words adopted by Arabic are modified in accordance with phonetic laws which must be taken into account, and guesswork based on resemblances of sound or spelling plays no part in the equating of ancient town and modern tell. Once the modern name of the tell is established, archaeological investigation proper begins.

Sometimes a methodical and more or less complete excavation is undertaken; this we shall discuss in the next chapter. Sometimes investigation is confined to the surface, and the expert carefully scrutinises the fragments of pottery scattered all over the sides of the tell. If these date exclusively from the Byzantine or Arab period, he can be practically certain that the site was not inhabited in Biblical times. If, on the contrary, the fragments provide evidence of occupation in these times, then the identification of the tell with a Biblical town becomes possible.

It is not surprising that there should be different degrees of certainty about the identification of Biblical sites. A very strong probability is established when all the data agree: the Biblical evidence, the extra-Biblical documents and the *onomastica*, the resemblance between the present name and the ancient name, and, finally, the evidence from potsherds collected on the tell. If some of these elements are lacking, one can assert only that the identification does not appear impossible. Moreover, it is obvious that, as a result of laying greater or less emphasis on one or other of these factors, scholars may differ among themselves. As time passes, however, tentative agreement is becoming possible in an increasing number of doubtful cases.

We have avoided the use of question-marks on the maps in this Atlas, since they are irritating to the reader. But we do not wish to imply certainty where only a slight probability exists. For this reason, on some maps (Nos. 11, 12, 13, pp. 59 and 60) we have clearly distinguished between the doubtful locations and those which are certain, and in the Index we show the degree of certainty for every Biblical site marked on the maps.

52
|
59
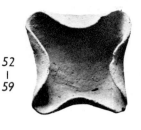   

EXCAVATIONS IN PALESTINE

The popular conception of the archaeologist too often tends to be somewhat vague and tinged with romanticism, as if he were an adventurer in the midst of suspicious Orientals, who runs all manner of risks and at last succeeds in 'digging a hole', from which he produces treasures of antiquity. It is not sufficiently realised that the work of excavation calls for manifold studies and a protracted technical training.

We have seen how tells were formed in Palestine. The process was obviously different on the alluvial plain around the edges of the Persian Gulf, where clay bricks had to be used for building instead of stone, and in Egypt, where the houses were of clay, though natural stone, plentiful on the fringes of the desert, was used for temples and funerary monuments. Here we are concerned only with Palestine, where, moreover, the extent to which traces of antiquity are preserved varies according to place and circumstance. The earliest settlements, entirely surrounded by a wall many feet thick, are naturally better preserved than the unfortified Israelite villages of the uplands, whose ruins were often washed away, at least in part, by the winter rains.

The ideal procedure for investigating a tell is to begin on the surface and analyse the remains of each occupation separately: to 'peel' the tell, as it were, layer by layer. This method requires great caution, for though the work of clearing the ground must begin with pick and spade, trained eyes are needed to distinguish between the remains of the original walls and loose stones which have fallen down from upper levels, and between the original floor of trodden earth and the equally solid débris. While a great many labourers are needed for the heavy digging and for carrying the rubble and stones to a predetermined place alongside the tell, trained overseers are equally necessary for the constant supervision of the work. Finally, after the remains of the outer walls, the streets, and the houses of the upper level have been laid bare, the archaeologist must, as it were, destroy his own work, so as to be able to examine the level beneath. Now the interests of science and, in these days, the governments of the countries in whose territory the tells are situated, demand that nothing of what has come to light should be destroyed before it has all been carefully recorded and described, so that the progress and results of the excavation may later be reconstructed in their entirety. A surveyor must therefore make a detailed plan of all that has been uncovered, recording the different levels, and a photographer must complete the documentation with photographs taken from numerous angles. The objects recovered will already have been photographed *in situ* at the time of their discovery and their position scrupulously marked on the surveyor's map, which also shows numbers for all the walls and rooms in the houses.

The study of pottery in Palestine has made such progress in the last few decades that an experienced archaeologist is able, often at a glance and without much hesitation, to assess the age of an isolated fragment to within a few centuries, and that of an intact pot or dish to within a century. Pottery is thus of the highest importance for dating the level in process of excavation. That is why every excavation must have at least one competent ceramist to examine all the pottery discovered in each room or house. There must also be on the site a workshop for temporary repairs to the pots, so that the archaeologists may know their shape without delay. Finally a complete register of all discoveries must be kept.

When one remembers that some tells cover more than twenty superimposed towns beneath their extensive surface, one can appreciate that a complete excavation calls for a great deal of time and money. The archaeologist must have a competent team at his disposal (surveyor, photographer, ceramist, draughtsman, secretary to keep the register, and, in addition, cook, quartermaster, etc. . . .), several able supervisors, and a great many workmen. He is also obliged to publish a scientific report on his work, a very costly undertaking on account of the multiplicity of maps, photographs, and drawings. One of the few complete excavations thus far undertaken is that of the ancient Phoenician town of Byblos, where work has been going on since 1919, in an unbroken series of seasons. There, the excavators are not only going down from one archaeological level to the next over the whole surface of the tell: to give their report a mathematical objectivity, they are each time removing a layer exactly 10 inches thick. M. Maurice Dunand, who is directing these excavations, hopes to complete the work in a few years' time. We are indebted to him for the magnificent aerial photograph of Byblos which appears in this Atlas. This work at Byblos could never have been achieved without a Government subsidy. For lack of time and money, the method of partial excavation is usually employed. After the digging of a few trial trenches, a particular section of the tell is selected and exposed layer by layer. This is the method adopted for the extensive *Tell el-Fâr'ah*, about seven miles northeast of Shechem, of which we show some photographs opposite. (The author of this book worked there for four seasons.)

On what principles does one select a tell and engage in such costly work upon it? The decision is invariably based on several considerations. First of all, one wants the tell to have much to offer, i.e. to contain the ruins of settlements which have been important in different periods of history. Sometimes this is assured *a priori* in the case of a large town which has retained its ancient name, or whose identity is, for other reasons, certain; such are the ancient city of David at Jerusalem, Jericho, Shechem, Beth-shan, Megiddo, etc. The director of the

60
61

52–59 / *Evolution of the Oil Lamp.* Today the scholar can assess the age of pottery by its shape and composition. Here, for example, is a series of lamps. The first three date from the three periods of the Bronze Age (3000–2000, 2000–1600, and 1600–1200 B.C.). The fourth is Israelite; the foot (invisible in the photograph) spoils the elegant shape of the shell. The lip grows narrower, and the fifth – of the 4th century B.C. – clearly foreshadows the last three, which are Hellenistic, Roman, and Byzantine. **60** / *Tell Deir 'Alla*, in the Jordan valley; generally believed to be the Biblical Succoth, but not yet excavated. **61** / *Tell Nebi-Mend*, 125 miles farther north, in the same geological depression, is the ancient city of Kadesh on the Orontes. [Maps 1, p. 9; 2, p. 10]

62–69 / *Tell el-Fâr'ah* lies in a vast bowl open only to the SE, and linked to the Jordan valley by a broad wâdi (63). The tell stands on a natural plateau (62) between two springs (1 and 2 on Pls. 63 and 66; 66 also shows the field of vision in 62). Fragments of pottery found on the surface suggested occupation from about 3000 to 700 B.C. The French Dominican School at Jerusalem began the excavation in 1946. As it was impossible to excavate the whole site, the work was confined to carefully chosen spots: one part (66a) was examined layer by layer during the seasons 1946 and 1947 (64, 65); another (66d) in 1950, 1951, 1954, and 1955. 67: An Israelite storage pit. 68: Grave pottery found in a cave near by (*ca* 3000 B.C.). 69: A grave found on the tell.   [*Map 2, p. 10*]

excavations is more easily successful in raising the necessary funds for a town known to every reader of the Bible. In other cases, the choice is influenced by the size of the tell, its situation relative to ancient highways, and the potsherds found on its summit and sides. In any case, before finally deciding to excavate one can experiment with one or more trial trenches. The choice is equally influenced by purely practical considerations, which sometimes favour one tell rather than another, such as location near a modern main road, near drinking water, or near a village which can provide labour. Thus, for example, work has been carried out on tells in the southern part of the coastal zone, which has long been traversed by the high road to Egypt (*Tell el-'Ajjûl, Tell Jemmeh*). The great *Tell Beit Mirsim*, some twelve miles southwest of Hebron, was selected, among other reasons, because the levels corresponding to the centuries immediately before and after the occupation of Canaan by Joshua appeared interesting and well preserved. The mounds on the east bank of the Jordan, a few miles north of the Dead Sea (*Teleilât el-Ghassûl*), were investigated because it was hoped that they would settle the question of the earliest habitation in the Jordan valley, and equally that of the traditions concerning Sodom and Gomorrah. The French Dominican School at Jerusalem began work upon *Tell el-Fâr'ah* because this particularly extensive area of ruins, at the head of the wâdi of the same name, was very favourably situated between two springs and promised a rich harvest. Here and there, on the surface, protruded traces of walls which could not be later than the seventh century B.C. Even at the top level, one would therefore plunge straight into Biblical history. Furthermore, the potsherds found there and an experimental excavation revealed that, with a few interruptions, there had been an important town on the site as far back as the third millennium B.C.

While engaged in the arduous but invariably interesting work of excavation, in the heat and dust and amid the cries of workmen and the noise of wheelbarrows and trucks, one is occasionally surprised by the arrival of a visitor, who has turned aside from the normal pilgrim routes and is anxious to see archaeologists at work. After looking round the site and refreshing himself with a cool drink in the tent, he asks to see what has been found. He is led past the draughtsman's table, the surveyor's papers and instruments, and the ceramist's workshop, to a corner of the tent where the finds are laid out. These always prove a disappointment to him, for the Palestinian archaeologist has nothing spectacular to offer. The visitor sees nothing but pots, which are usually broken and vary in size, shape, technique, and decoration; or small ornaments, like bone and bronze pins;

oxydised lance-heads; scarabs and seals, sometimes with an inscription; and, very occasionally, a clay tablet or potsherds with characters inscribed upon them. The visitor can make nothing of these plans and unimpressive discoveries. But the excavators can read in them the history of the civilisation of a town. And the archaeologist who, in the coolness of his study, assembles and examines the voluminous reports of all the seasons of excavation can form an idea both of the history of the country and of the succession and mutual influences of the different civilisations.

Having seen all over the site, the visitor sometimes asks if the excavation has helped to prove the truth of the Bible. The director of the investigation will perhaps reply that this truth has no need of the corroborative evidence which he finds on his tell. But the visitor will certainly be told, emphatically and with conviction, that the arduous work carried out on the site, and the many months later spent in preparing the scientific report on the excavation, play their part in confirming the picture of Biblical antiquity which Palestinian archaeology has drawn for us, and which it is filling in with every day that passes. Today there could be appended to each book of the Bible an archaeological commentary, showing how many obscure points have been elucidated as a result of excavation. Every season of excavation adds its quota of facts to the ever-growing total – facts slowly and patiently deduced from remains which, to the untutored eye, are but cryptic fragments. Now, as the history of more and more towns and fortresses, known to us from ancient records, documents, and annals, becomes clear, the Bible reader who avails himself of the results of modern research has before him a picture of the early civilisations of the Middle East which may in many respects be clearer and fuller than that known to the later generations of Egyptians, Hebrews, Assyrians, and Persians. The discoveries and theories mentioned in these pages, numerous and impressive though they are, represent only a fraction of the immense jig-saw which is being assembled piece by piece by scholars all over the world, as reports flow in from excavations on hundreds of sites, large and small, in all parts of the Middle East.

Because of the great expense involved, international co-operation is essential in the field of archaeology; and nearly all the excavation thus far undertaken has been carried out by scientific institutes of the United States and of most of the countries of Europe. Thanks to them, a great deal of work has already been completed. But still more remains to be done; and it is to be hoped that, in the years to come, many scholars may be able to dedicate themselves to this highly important task.

Level I	A.D. 600–300 Remains of an early Christian church of the first centuries A.D.
Level II	A.D. 300–64 B.C. Village of the time of St Paul
Level III	64–500 B.C. Colony of the time of the Persian Empire
Level IV	500–1000 B.C. Layer dating from the period of the Syro-Hittite Empire
Level V	1000–1200 B.C. Traces of pottery of the 'Peoples of the Sea'
Level VI	1200–1600 B.C. Period of the migration of peoples; pottery from many different regions, particularly Cyprus
Level VII	1600–1800 B.C. Links with the East; clay statues of the Mother-Goddess type
Level VIII	1800–2000 B.C. Painted pottery similar to that of the Hyksos period
Level IX	2000–2400 B.C. Use of bronze for weapons and axes
Level X	2400–2600 B.C. Evidence of commercial relations with northern Mesopotamia
Level XI	2600–3100 B.C. Importation of cylinder seals from Ur, the city of Abraham
Level XII	3100–3400 B.C. Beginning of the widespread use of metal
Level XIII	3400–3800 B.C. Pottery shaped by hand, as beautiful in form as that of later periods
Level XIV	3800–4500 B.C. Earliest traces of a Syrian village

70 / *Experimental Excavation in Northern Syria.* Before deciding to excavate a tell, either over its whole surface (as with Byblos, Pl. 208), or in part (*Tell el-Fâr'ah*, Pl. 66), archaeologists often make a limited investigation to determine whether interesting periods are sufficiently represented to justify the very heavy expense of excavation. Above is an instructive photograph of an experimental trench on *Tell Judeideh* in northern Syria, near the ancient town of Alalakh. The various levels are easily distinguished; the right-hand column shows how pottery and other objects serve to establish the different periods. (After Edward Chiera, *They Wrote on Clay*, by kind permission of the Oriental Institute of Chicago.)   [Map 4, p. 29]

71
72
73
74

THE CHARACTER OF BIBLICAL HISTORY

In the translations of the Bible in use today, the books of the Old Testament are not arranged as they are in the Hebrew text. The latter keeps to the order already used in the time of Ben Sira and attested in the Gospels. At this period three kinds of writings were distinguished: the *Law* (later sub-divided into five books – the Pentateuch); the *Prophets*, 'former' (Joshua, Judges, Samuel, Kings) and 'latter' (Isaiah, Jeremiah, Ezekiel, and the book of the 'Twelve Prophets'); and lastly the *Writings*, comprising, after the Psalms, Proverbs, and Job, a certain number of shorter texts and a few others of a later date. As a result of Graeco-Latin influence, this order, which appears to have evolved in the course of history, was replaced by the more logical division which we find in our Bibles today: first, the *historical* books, then the *didactic* books, and lastly the *prophetic* writings. The texts of the New Testament may be classified according to the same plan (facts, teaching, and prophecies).

It is debatable whether this division, a product of the Western mind, has helped us to understand the intention of the authors of the Bible any better. We of the Western world expect an historian to give us, first and foremost, a faithful account of the facts: he may, indeed, examine their inter-relations, but only provided that he bases himself upon the objective data. Once certain Biblical writings had been classified as 'historical', people unconsciously began to judge their content according to the standards expected of a work of history. Faith in their divine origin gave rise to the belief that the books of the Bible met the requirements of objectivity more completely than any other writings. Each one of the Bible stories must needs be the faithful presentation of a firm and substantial fact. These events, guided by God, clearly had a meaning; but this meaning was of secondary importance and presupposed that the fact related 'had really happened'. Thus the literary genre 'Biblical history' was evolved: the historical books told the history of the world from the Creation to the death of St John the Apostle, in a way which was essentially identical with, for example, the history of Rome to be found in a profane author.

It was gradually realised that this approach did not correspond with reality. This is not the place for a lengthy analysis of how the Western mind attained to a more accurate appreciation of the intention of the authors of the Bible. Suffice it to say that it gradually became clear how wide a variety of literary genres were used in each book of the Bible: folk tales, proverbs and poems, prophetic admonitions in narrative form, annals, etc. It was also realised that the ancient Israelite did not reason according to our system of logic and did not make use of abstraction, severing the essence of things from their substance. He thought in a concrete and dynamic way. He did not speculate about the Being of God, but spoke of His will, His purpose, and His interventions in the world of men. He judged things with reference not to their beauty but to their utility. And he did not consider that a fact or event was worth recording for its own sake. A fact was the expression of a desire or a plan; it was a spur to action and suggested a line of conduct. When an Israelite related history he moralised, and when he moralised he told a story. He never talked in abstractions. Thus, when Jesus used parables so widely in His teaching, He remained in the tradition of the prophets and teachers of Israel. In short, what interested an ancient Israelite was *the meaning of the event related*; the question of exactly what happened in reality seemed to him somewhat strange and irrelevant.

The very delicate task of making a literary analysis of the books of the Bible is being increasingly assisted by the discovery of texts in the Near East. New parallels with the literary genres employed in the Bible are constantly coming to light. The serious gaps in our knowledge of the Ancient East are gradually being filled in, and gradually, too, fresh material is enabling us to establish the objective course of the events from which the Bible draws its teaching. With each new discovery, the Bible is seen to be ever more deeply rooted in the life of the Ancient East; but, for this very reason, the peculiar character and unique features of the spiritual heritage of Israel equally emerge.

The scientific study of the Bible in the light of these discoveries in the Ancient East is still in its infancy and remains at the mercy of many fortuitous circumstances. We know, for example, how the tell of Ugarit was accidentally found in 1928 by a peasant who, after running against a tombstone with his ploughshare, was honest enough – a rare occurrence! – to report his discovery in the proper quarter. Elsewhere, in 1933, Bedouin engaged in digging a grave for one of their number unearthed the statue which was the starting point of the excavations at Mari; they did not take the figure to the antique market, but dutifully notified the authorities. Ugarit and Mari have been only partially investigated. Yet they have already yielded information of considerable importance, not least for the study of the Old Testament. The work continues, and there is no reason why further discoveries should not be made. At any rate, the fortuitous nature of these two discoveries justifies the hope that there may be other such pleasant surprises in store for us.

In such circumstances, it would be rash and unwarranted to expect these studies – and consequently, a Biblical Atlas – to provide final solutions for every problem. On the contrary, many answers are only provisional and are subject to later revision, should fresh facts come to light. Nevertheless, the horizon of this field of study has widened so strikingly in recent years that it is desirable to attempt to provide Bible readers with a convenient résumé of the present state of our knowledge of Biblical geography. This the present volume tries to do, and Maps and Index taken together summarise the views of the scholars of today.

75
76
77

71–77 / *Cylinder Seals from Mesopotamia.* As early as prehistoric times, the inhabitants of the 'Land between the Two Rivers' used small stone cylinders on which figures were engraved. By rolling them they stamped the lids of their provision jars while they were still moist and, later, their clay tablets before they were dried in the sun. The designs, nearly always religious (mythological) in character, are an important source of knowledge which is studied by a special branch of archaeology, known as glyptics. Above are a few of the thousands of examples discovered. 71–74: Impressions of seals bearing religious representations: figures by the 'tree of life' and (in the middle) two 'ziggurats'. 75–77: Cylinder of green stone, with rings of shell and a silver knob. The motif suggests that it belonged to a priest in charge of a temple herd. [Map 1, p. 9]

78

78 / *Nomads with Donkeys and Flocks* at a watering-place recently created on the western fringe of the Syro-Arabian steppes. For centuries water has been the key to the existence of the nomadic tribes of the Near East. Generation after generation, these families move their tents, flocks, and other possessions from grazing ground to grazing ground and from water-hole to water-hole.
[*Map 1, p. 9*]

WANDERING ARAMAEANS

No people has retained in its national tradition so clear a picture of its origins as the people of Israel. Chapters 12–50 of the book of Genesis contain masterpieces of narrative art, and the figures of the patriarchs are full of life and character. We learn how it was at God's command that Abraham left his tribe, with which he had come from Ur of the Chaldees as far as Haran. In obedience, he set out with his immediate family towards the land which God had promised to him and to his seed for ever, and we see him journeying, with his flocks and herds, across the Palestinian uplands. The accounts refer to three places in particular: a tree near the town of Shechem where a deep well keeps alive the memory of the patriarch Jacob; a place of sacrifice between Bethel and Ai, from which a great part of the Jordan valley can be seen; and finally Hebron, whose present Arabic name still movingly recalls the sojourn of the 'Father of Believers', for does not *El-Khalîl* mean 'the friend' and reveal that Islam also recognises the title of honour which Jews and Christians have bestowed upon Abraham, the 'Friend of God'?

The negotiations between Abraham and the inhabitants of Hebron, after the death of Sarah, are typically Eastern in character. They concern the purchase of a field with a cave which is to serve as a family burying-place. We have no reason to doubt that the magnificent outer wall later erected by Herod, which may still be seen today, does actually shelter the family tomb, in which were laid, after Sarah and Abraham, Isaac, Rebekah, Jacob, and Leah. Abraham used to pitch his tents near the 'tree of Mamre'. It is no easy matter to discover where this tree, an oak or a terebinth, was situated, because the indications in Genesis are confused and the name Mamre does not occur anywhere outside that book. It is thought that the ancient Israelites worshipped their God near this tree where He had appeared to Abraham. Later, in the time of the prophets, it was considered sinful to worship under 'oaks, poplars, and terebinths'; for this reason, later religious literature may have avoided mentioning the tree of Mamre and scrupulous revisers may have removed all definite indications of locality in Genesis. As a result, however, of a study of the earliest traditions and of archaeological explorations of the area, scholars are now able to mark the site of Mamre at a point 2¼ miles north of Abraham's tomb. Here are still to be seen the ruins of a Christian sanctuary, standing on a height which bears the Arabic name of *Râmet el-Khalîl*, the 'hill of the friend'.

Abraham and his sons also wandered in the Negeb, where they acquired rights in the use of watering-places. Elsewhere they bought fields. They were therefore semi-nomadic, a transitional stage between complete nomadism and a settled existence. The patriarchs, moreover, always thought of themselves as foreigners amidst the people of Canaan. They had no desire to marry there, and kept in touch with their relations still living near the trading centre of Haran. Abraham sent his servant into these northern regions to look for a wife for Isaac, and it was there that Jacob fathered eleven of his sons. But when the winter rains were not sufficiently abundant, when the fields were parched and the wells dry, they turned instead towards the south, to the unfailing pastures of Egypt. At the close of the fascinating story of Joseph, we find all the descendants of Abraham through Jacob settled for years to come in a region to the east of the Nile Delta, 'in the land of Rameses'.

The Bible thus shows us the ancestors of Israel in their relations, first with Mesopotamia and particularly with its northwestern part, called Aram in the Bible; then with Egypt, first as occasional visitors in search of corn and later as settled inhabitants; and lastly, though not without misgivings, with the Canaanites, whose women bore sons for Judah.

But when, in later years, the head of a Hebrew family, surrounded by his children and neighbours, told the epic story of his ancestors, he had no thought of drawing a picture of Israel's earliest relations with the great civilisations. The subject did not interest him. A few generations after Joseph, most Hebrews probably still knew the name of the Pharaoh who, thanks to his intelligent vizier, had established them in his country. But his name was soon blotted out from the memory of Israel. Who governed Canaan in the days of Abraham? Was it thickly populated? What was the political situation in Mesopotamia and Syria at this time? What language did the patriarchs speak? Could they read and write? We look in vain for a reply to such questions in the accounts of the origins of Israel. The sole aim of their authors is to show how, from a single ancestor, a people was created under the guidance of God. In this connection, births, deaths, marriages, and inheritances are more important than politics and culture.

But if our historical problems are outside the compass of the sacred authors, they delight in answering the questions asked by the people, such as: how did Beer-sheba get its curious name, and why is a town in the Jabbok called the 'Face of God'? Why does the Dead Sea smell of sulphur, and who set up those strange pillars of salt on its shores? How is it that the tribes of Moab and Ammon, although related to Israel, can yet behave so unpleasantly towards her? What fascinates the Israelite in the stories of his ancestors is precisely such explanations and popular etymologies, which are often of little interest to us today, especially when we read them in translation. But for the sacred authors all these things are often no more than incidental ornamentation or a means of expressing more profound truths; of the stories they heard from the lips of their fathers, it is primarily the didactic content which they prefer to pass on to the young Hebrews seated at their feet; and they use their skill as story-tellers to illustrate in concrete terms the tenets of the faith of Israel. The principle of election appears in Abraham, whose steadfast faith and heroic obedience become examples for Israel. With Jacob, we are shown how God is completely free in His choice; He prefers the younger son to the elder, embodies a reprehensible trick in His plans and remains favourable to the man who is to be called Israel because he has 'striven with God'. All the peoples of the earth are involved, for, in His choice of one people, the God of Israel had in mind the salvation of all.

The points briefly outlined above are impressively illustrated in the narrative of Genesis. In relating the history of their forebears, the patriarchs and leaders of Israel have succeeded in expressing their creed in a concrete and universally accessible form. That is why the reader of the later books must constantly turn back to Genesis.

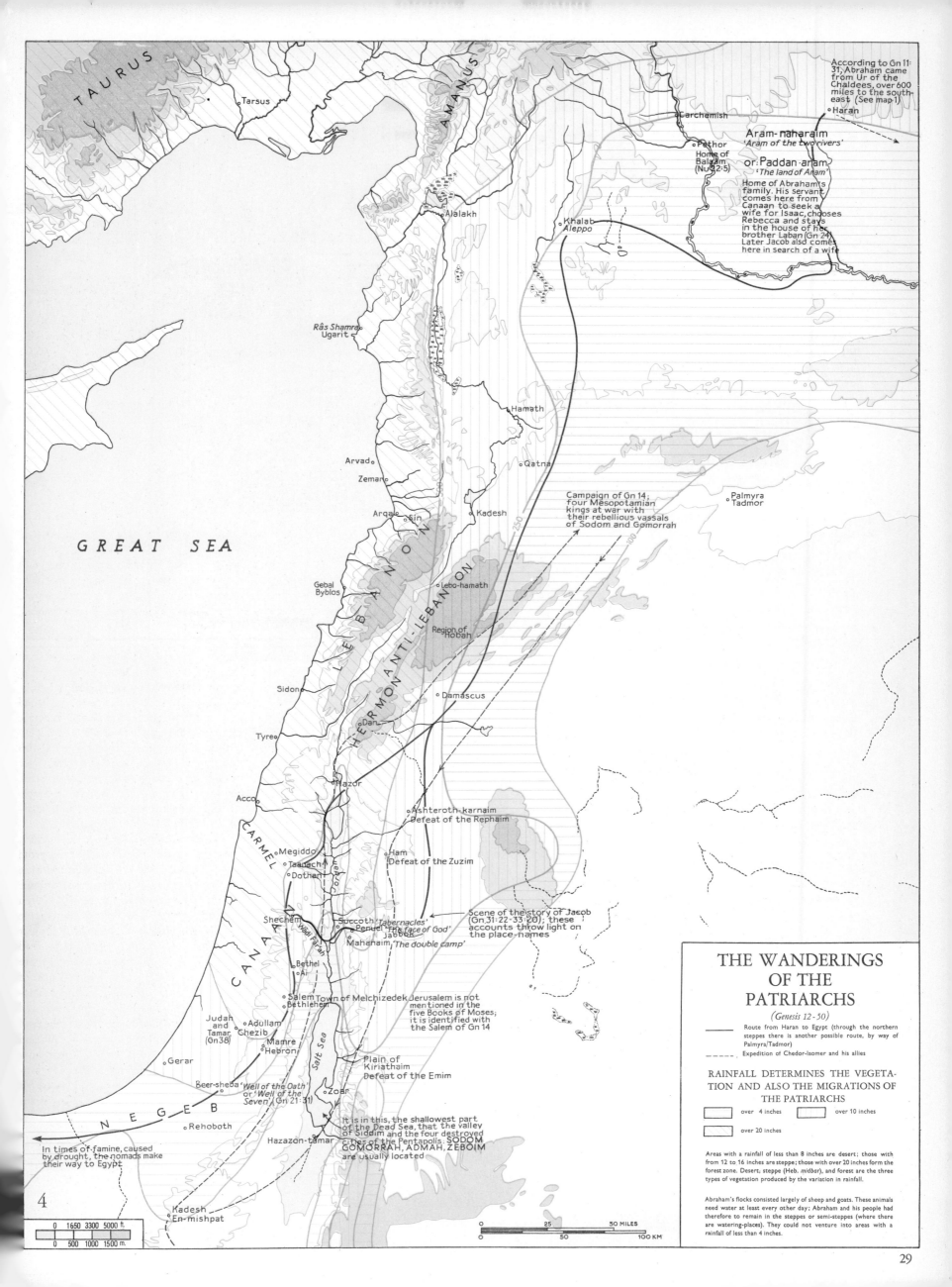

TAURUS

Tarsus

AMANUS

Carchemish

According to Gn 11:
31, Abraham came
from Ur of the
Chaldees, over 600
miles to the south-
east (See map 1)

Haran

Pethor
Home of
Balaam
(Nu 22:5)

Aram-naharaim
Aram of the two rivers

or: Paddan-aram
The land of Aram

Home of Abraham's
family. His servant
comes here from
Canaan to seek a
wife for Isaac, chooses
Rebecca and stays
in the house of her
brother Laban (Gn 24)
Later Jacob also comes
here in search of a wife

Alalakh

Khalab
Aleppo

Râs Shamra
Ugarit

Hamath

GREAT SEA

Arvad

Zemar

Qatna

Palmyra
Tadmor

Arqa   Sin

Kadesh

Campaign of Gn 14:
four Mesopotamian
kings at war with
their rebellious vassals
of Sodom and Gomorrah

Gebal
Byblos

LEBANON

Lebo-hamath

ANTI-LEBANON

Region of
Hobah

HERMON

Sidon

Damascus

Tyre

Dan

Hazor

Acco

Ashteroth-karnaim
Defeat of the Rephaim

CARMEL

Megiddo

Taanach

Ham
Defeat of the Zuzim

Dothan

Shechem

Succoth *Tabernacles*
Penuel *'The face of God'*
Mahanaim *'The double camp'*

Wadi Far'ah

Jabbok

Scene of the story of Jacob
(Gn 31:22-33:20): these
accounts throw light on
the place-names

CANAAN

Bethel
Ai

Salem Town of Melchizedek Jerusalem is not
mentioned in the
Bethlehem
five Books of Moses;
it is identified with
the Salem of Gn 14

Judah
and
Tamar
(Gn 38)

Adullam
Chezib

Mamre
Hebron

Salt Sea

Plain of
Kiriathaim
Defeat of the Emim

Gerar

Beer-sheba *'Well of the Oath'*
or 'Well of the
Seven' (Gn 21:31)

Zoar

NEGEB

Rehoboth

It is in this, the shallowest part
of the Dead Sea, that the valley
of Siddim and the four destroyed
cities of the Pentapolis, SODOM
GOMORRAH, ADMAH, ZEBOIM
are usually located

In times of famine, caused
by drought, the nomads make
their way to Egypt

Hazazon-tamar

4

Kadesh
En-mishpat

0   1650 3300 5000 ft.

0   500 1000 1500 m.

THE WANDERINGS
OF THE
PATRIARCHS

(Genesis 12-50)

Route from Haran to Egypt (through the northern
steppes there is another possible route, by way of
Palmyra/Tadmor)

----- Expedition of Chedor-laomer and his allies

RAINFALL DETERMINES THE VEGETA-
TION AND ALSO THE MIGRATIONS OF
THE PATRIARCHS

over 4 inches   over 10 inches

over 20 inches

Areas with a rainfall of less than 8 inches are desert; those with
from 12 to 16 inches are steppe; those with over 20 inches form the
forest zone. Desert, steppe (Heb. *midbar*), and forest are the three
types of vegetation produced by the variation in rainfall.

Abraham's flocks consisted largely of sheep and goats. These
animals need water at least every other day; Abraham and his people had
therefore to remain in the steppes or semi-steppes (where there
are watering-places). They could not venture into areas with a
rainfall of less than 4 inches.

0   25   50 MILES

0   50   100 KM

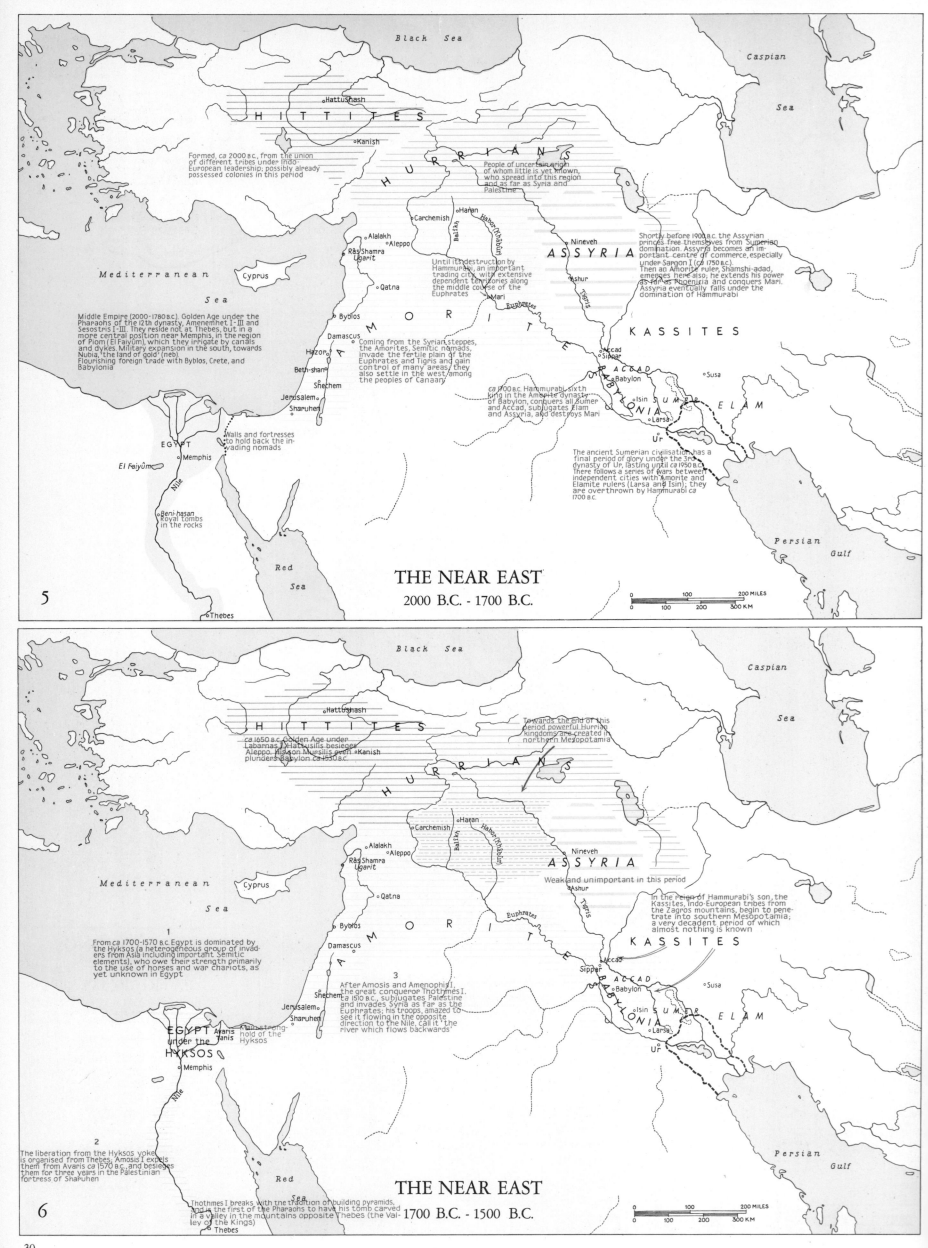

Black Sea

Caspian Sea

HITTITES

○Hattushash

○Kanish

HURRIANS

Formed, ca 2000 B.C., from the union of different tribes under Indo-European leadership; possibly already possessed colonies in this period

People of uncertain origin of whom little is yet known, who spread into this region and as far as Syria and Palestine

○Carchemish

○Haran

Balikh

Habor (Khabur)

○Nineveh

ASSYRIA

Shortly before 1900 B.C. the Assyrian princes free themselves from Sumerian domination. Assyria becomes an important centre of commerce, especially under Sargon I (ca 1750 B.C.). Then an Amorite ruler, Shamshi-adad, emerges here also; he extends his power as far as Phoenicia and conquers Mari. Assyria eventually falls under the domination of Hammurabi

○Alalakh

○Aleppo

○Ràs Shamra
Ugarit

Mediterranean Sea

Cyprus

○Qatna

Until its destruction by Hammurabi, an important trading city with extensive dependent territories along the middle course of the Euphrates

Euphrates

Tigris

○Ashur

AMORITES

KASSITES

○Byblos

○Mari

Middle Empire (2000-1780 B.C.). Golden Age under the Pharaohs of the 12th dynasty, Amenemhet I-III and Sesostris I-III. They reside not at Thebes, but in a more central position near Memphis, in the region of Piom (El Faiyûm), which they irrigate by canals and dykes. Military expansion in the south, towards Nubia, 'the land of gold' (neb).
Flourishing foreign trade with Byblos, Crete, and Babylonia.

○Damascus

○Hazor

○Beth-shan

○Shechem

○Jerusalem

○Sharuhen

Coming from the Syrian steppes, the Amorites, Semitic nomads, invade the fertile plain of the Euphrates and Tigris and gain control of many areas; they also settle in the west, among the peoples of Canaan

○Accad
○Sippar

ACCAD
BABYLON

○Babylon

○Susa

ca 1700 B.C. Hammurabi, sixth king in the Amorite dynasty of Babylon, conquers all Sumer and Accad, subjugates Elam and Assyria, and destroys Mari

SUMER
ELAM

○Isin

○Larsa

○Ur

EGYPT

○Memphis

El Faiyûm

Nile

Walls and fortresses to hold back the invading nomads

The ancient Sumerian civilisation has a final period of glory under the 3rd dynasty of Ur, lasting until ca 1950 B.C. There follows a series of wars between independent cities with Amorite and Elamite rulers (Larsa and Isin); they are overthrown by Hammurabi ca 1700 B.C.

○Beni-hasan
Royal tombs in the rocks

Persian Gulf

Red Sea

THE NEAR EAST

2000 B.C. - 1700 B.C.

5

○Thebes

0   100   200 MILES

0   100   200   300 KM

Black Sea

Caspian Sea

HITTITES

○Hattushash

ca 1650 B.C. Golden Age under Labarnas I; Hattusilis besieges Aleppo. Hyksos? Mursilis even plunders Babylon ca 1530 B.C.

○Kanish

HURRIANS

Towards the end of this period powerful Hurrian kingdoms are created in northern Mesopotamia

○Carchemish

○Haran

Balikh

Habor (Khabur)

○Alalakh

○Aleppo

○Ràs Shamra
Ugarit

○Nineveh

ASSYRIA

Mediterranean Sea

Cyprus

○Qatna

Weak and unimportant in this period

○Ashur

AMORITES

Euphrates

Tigris

In the reign of Hammurabi's son, the Kassites, Indo-European tribes from the Zagros mountains, begin to penetrate into southern Mesopotamia; a very decadent period of which almost nothing is known

○Byblos

○Damascus

KASSITES

1

From ca 1700-1570 B.C. Egypt is dominated by the Hyksos (a heterogeneous group of invaders from Asia including important Semitic elements), who owe their strength primarily to the use of horses and war chariots, as yet unknown in Egypt

○Accad
○Sippar

ACCAD
BABYLON

○Babylon

○Susa

○Shechem

3

After Amosis and Amenophis I, the great conqueror Thothmes I, ca 1510 B.C., subjugates Palestine and invades Syria as far as the Euphrates; his troops, amazed to see it flowing in the opposite direction to the Nile, call it 'the river which flows backwards'

SUMER
ELAM

○Isin

○Jerusalem

○Sharuhen

○Larsa

○Ur

EGYPT under the HYKSOS

Avaris
Tanis

Main stronghold of the Hyksos

○Memphis

Nile

2

The liberation from the Hyksos yoke is organised from Thebes; Amosis I expels them from Avaris ca 1570 B.C., and besieges them for three years in the Palestinian fortress of Sharuhen

Persian Gulf

6

Red Sea

Thothmes I breaks with the tradition of building pyramids, and is the first of the Pharaohs to have his tomb carved in a valley in the mountains opposite Thebes (the Valley of the Kings)

THE NEAR EAST

1700 B.C. - 1500 B.C.

0   100   200 MILES

0   100   200   300 KM

ABRAHAM IN HISTORY

The Bible records that Abraham was seventy-five years old when he left Haran (Gn 12:4), and a hundred years old when his son Isaac was born (Gn 21:5), that Isaac was forty years old when he married Rebekah (Gn 25:20), and sixty years old when Esau and Jacob were born (Gn 25:26). In Egypt, Pharaoh asks Jacob: 'How many are the days of the years of your life?' And Jacob replies: 'The days of the years of my sojourning are a hundred and thirty years' (Gn 47:8f.). Later we are told that the Israelites spent four hundred and thirty years in Egypt (Ex 12:40), and that in the four hundred and eightieth year after they came out of Egypt Solomon began to build the Temple of Jerusalem (1 K 6:1). If we use these Biblical figures to calculate the duration of the sojourn of the patriarchs in Canaan, we arrive at a total of 215 years (25 + 60 + 130): exactly half of 430 years, the length of time their descendants sojourned in Egypt.

According to the texts we have quoted, 1,200 years separate the birth of Abraham and the erection of the Temple of Solomon. If the Bible were a work of modern Western history, it would be possible, calculating from the year the Temple was built and using the above data, to work out very accurately the most important dates in the history of the patriarchs of Israel. But as every reader of the Bible knows, the figures in this ancient book are not always intended to establish the exact number of things, but often indicate one of their inherent qualities or connote their spiritual significance. Thus the number 7 indicates plenitude, and 12 is usually the number of the elect (as in Israel, made up of twelve tribes, and the church, founded on the twelve apostles). The figure 40, originally a round number indicating the span of a generation, frequently characterises periods which lead up to a fresh stage in the history of man's salvation; we have only to think of the 40 years in the desert before the entry into the Promised Land, of Elijah's journey of 40 days before he came to the mountain of God, of the 40 days of solitary fasting which followed the baptism of Jesus, and the 40 days leading up to the Ascension.

After dwelling among His people in a sanctuary which was carried from place to place, God chose for Himself the site of a permanent abode in Jerusalem. In the eyes of the devout priests, it was for this Temple of Solomon that all the ancestors had yearned since the Exodus from Egypt. A permanent dwelling-place in a land of their own had always been the dream of the people of Israel; for the priests, this dream was not completely realised until the day when God exchanged His tabernacle for a fixed abode. On the basis of their reckoning of the generations, they assigned to this intermediate period between the Exodus and the building of the Temple the figure of 480 (40 × 12) years, which could be interpreted: preparation (40) for a new election (12). Between the birth of Abraham, the first of the elect, and the construction of God's permanent dwelling in the place designated by Him, was to elapse a period whose innermost meaning was conveyed by the sum of 12 times 100 (1,200). It is at once obvious that in using figures of this kind to calculate the exact dates of events, we misinterpret the intentions of the writers. The Bible has therefore no direct answer to the question: in what century did Abraham live? We could answer it if we knew the length of the sojourn in Egypt and had some information about the date of the Exodus. But, unfortunately, there is no absolute certainty on these two matters.

1 K 6:1

In addition to the figure of 430 years for the sojourn in Egypt, given in the passage quoted from Exodus (12:40), we find in other texts 400 years (Gn 15:13), and in one place 450 years. The ancient text which gives 400 years refers, a few verses later, to four generations, which in the Bible usually means a period of about 160 years (4 × 40). Elsewhere, the sojourn in Canaan appears to be included in this 430 or 400 years, so that the years in Egypt must be reduced by 215. Serious scholars believe the figure of 400 years to be that most firmly rooted in tradition. Those who place the Exodus at the beginning of the thirteenth century B.C., thus calculate the entry into Egypt at around the year 1700 B.C., and the youth of Abraham in the region of the year 1850 B.C.

Such chronological calculations, however tentatively advanced, would have been dismissed with a polite smile by Biblical scholars of a generation ago. In their opinion the patriarchs were figures created by the fertile imagination of the people of Israel; to assign a date to them was as naïve and unsound as to attempt to establish the year of Cinderella's birth. During the nineteenth century acute critical minds had striven to draw from the discovery of the composite character of the books of the Bible, and especially of the Pentateuch, conclusions which would illustrate a particular evolutionary theory. As a result of this discovery, each of the documents identified in the five books of Moses, divided into four groups, was assigned to a separate period in the history of the people of Israel. The oldest group was believed to comprise those passages in which the name Yahweh is used for God, and which are chiefly remarkable for their simple and graphic narrative style. These documents, the work of one or more so-called

79
80
81

79–81 / *The Code of King Hammurabi.* For the history and importance of this document, see the text. 80: Parts of paragraphs 17 and 25, almost actual size. An example of cuneiform writing; each sign represents a syllable. By spelling out the eight lower columns (beginning at the top right), one obtains: *shum-ma i-na bît a-wi-lim / i-sha-tum / in-na-pi-ikh-ma / a-wi-lum / sha a-na bu-ul-li-im / il-li-ku / a-na nu-ma-at / be-el bîtim /*; which means: 'If in a man's house / a fire / has broken out / and if some person / who in order to put it out / has gone there / on the property / of the master of the house . . .' and the text continues, 'has cast his eyes, and has taken the property of the master of the house, that man shall be cast into this same fire.' Paragraph **17** concerns a runaway slave.

[Map 5, p. 30]

82
83

84
85

86
87

82 / *Ur of the Chaldees*. Since 1918 *Tell el-Muqaiyar* has been systematically excavated over a number of seasons. Three times undisputed mistress of its region (ca 2700–1900 B.C.), the town was for centuries afterwards a religious centre, particularly for the cult of the moon-god Sin. **83–85** / *Near the Modern Harrân* are the ruins of the Biblical Haran where Abraham left part of his family. In 83, the chief tell is seen to the left, behind the small houses characteristic of northern Syria. 84: Animals round a well; to the left, archaeologists are looking for a temple of the god Sin, whose cult flourished here also. On the neighbouring tell (*Sultantepe*, 85), a 'library' of Assyrian tablets was discovered in the winter of 1950–1951. **86, 87** / *The Ziggurat of Ur*. The figure at its foot gives an idea of the scale. Only the lowest step remains. [Map 5, p. 30]

88
89

90
91

92
93
94

88–90 / *Hebron*. In the time of Abraham, Hebron stood on the hill of *er-Rumeideh* (90), now covered with olive-trees; the ruins of *el-Arba'in* on this hill preserve the memory of the old name of the town, Kiriath-arba (Gn 23:2, etc.). Abraham bought the cave of Machpelah (Gn 23:19), to the east of this hill, for a family tomb. Herod erected a fine outer wall around this holy place (Pls. 331, 332) and a church was added in Christian times. The houses of Hebron were later grouped around the sanctuary. **91** / *The Jabbok*, with the black tents of the nomads; here Jacob fought with the angel of God (Gn 32). **92, 93** / *Lot's Wife*, a curious column of rock-salt, about 50 feet high, associated from time immemorial with the story of Lot. **94** / *Grotesque Rock-Salt Formations* in the *Jebel Usdum* (SW coast of the Dead Sea), a name recalling that of Sodom.
[*Map 4, p. 29*]

33

95

96

95, 96 / *Situation of Shechem and Jacob's Well.* The tell of Shechem blocks the entrance of the pass which bisects the N-S line of the central hills of Palestine. To the east of the mountains of Gerizim and Ebal (1 and 2) stretches a small fertile plain (96, photograph taken at harvest-time, mid-June 1953). Above 3 is the tell, near the modern village of *Balâta*; near 4 is the walled enclosure of Jacob's Well (Pl. 101); 5 shows the direction in which 95 was photographed; 6–9 indicate roads towards the four points of the compass: 6 to Jerusalem; 7 to Beth-shan and Galilee; 8 to the coast; 9 to the Jordan valley. The patriarchs passed through Shechem, and it was there that Abimelech determined to become king (Jg 9). Jesus also stopped there on His way from Jerusalem to Galilee (Jn 4). The woman of Samaria pointed to Mount Gerizim and He afterwards spoke of the fields 'already white for the harvest'. [*Maps 4, p. 29; 14, p. 65; 34, p. 116*]

97
98
99

Yahwistic authors, were thought to have originated in the period after David (tenth or ninth century B.C.), the classical era of narrative art. A second group of documents, called Elohistic because they are characterised by the use of the more general name Elohim for God, was believed to have been written in the Northern Kingdom at some later date. Next was placed a document constituting the greater part of the present book of Deuteronomy, which clearly reflects the views of the great prophets, particularly Jeremiah, to whom there is also a marked resemblance in style. It was therefore assigned to the seventh century B.C., and held to be identical, either in whole or in part, with the book of the Law found in the Temple of Jerusalem in the reign of Josiah. The remaining parts of the Pentateuch showed a strong similarity to the views and style of Ezekiel, and also reflected the interests of the priesthood, which dominated the life of the Jewish community for several centuries after the return from Babylon; these documents, consisting mainly of laws, were therefore brought together under the name of the Priestly Code.

In advancing these theories, nineteenth-century Biblical historians broke with the ancient tradition which had accepted Moses as the author of the books bearing his name. They believed that, like every other living organism, the religious beliefs peculiar to Israel must have been the product of a lengthy evolution, and could not possibly have been recorded in such a mature form by one man, especially at a period before Israel had really emerged as a nation. Since the Yahwistic documents, regarded as the oldest in the Pentateuch, were assigned to the period after David, and in the other books of the Bible only a few poems, such as the 'Song of Deborah', were held to be of still earlier date, it naturally followed that the Biblical accounts of events said to have taken place before the time of the Judges were a concretisation of certain ideas rather than a record of historical facts. Many of these Biblical historians did not think it possible to go back before the time when the tribes of Israel settled permanently in Canaan; they were therefore sceptical about the story of the mass Exodus from Egypt; they accepted, almost without question, the conclusion that the patriarchs, as described in Chapters 12 to 50 of Genesis, were not historical figures, and some even doubted whether Moses himself had ever actually existed. For them the only question really at issue was how the Israelites of the tenth century B.C. had come to regard their ancestors in this particular manner. When they settled in Canaan, did these former nomads raise some of the local deities to the status of tribal ancestors? Or were the adventures of these fictitious persons a graphic portrayal

of the collective experiences of one or more of the tribal groups? On the former view Abraham and Sarah would have been deities of the region of Hebron, venerated at Mamre and Machpelah respectively; on the latter view the embrace of Jacob and Esau would indicate a peace treaty between two tribes.

Gn 33:4

Today even the most critical scholars take a different view of these problems. The views outlined above proceeded from a rather hasty application of the evolutionary pattern, and were based too exclusively upon textual criticism. Thanks to the work of the archaeologist, the modern scholar is in closer contact with the actual world in which Israel had its roots. He now knows the names of some of the presumed deities of Canaan. None of them is called Abraham; but, on tablets of the nineteenth century B.C., this name occurs as that of ordinary mortals. The names Isaac and Jacob accord well with the nomenclature of the now familiar Amorite world, the latter having been borne by several persons. The information obtained from the Code of Hammurabi about the manners, customs, and legal system of Mesopotamia before 1700 B.C. has now been supplemented by the discovery of Sumerian, Hittite, Assyrian, and Babylonian legal codes; and the documents found near *Kirkuk*, in the ruins of ancient Nuzu (Nuzi), including various contracts concerning family and business affairs, court records, etc., have enabled us to form a clear picture of daily life in northern Mesopotamia about 1500 B.C. Now, the patriarchs of Israel would fit admirably into this cultural setting; while, on the other hand, many of their customs were certainly no longer current among the Israelites of the tenth century B.C. Today, in consequence, many scholars feel a renewed confidence in the skilful narrators of Chapters 12 to 50 of Genesis. Oral tradition is strong in the East, and it is felt that the stories of the patriarchs must be based on historical memories.

As we cannot establish the date of Abraham with any certainty, we have not attempted historical correlations with non-Biblical sources on the map showing the wanderings of the patriarchs (Map 4, p. 29). Maps 5 and 6 (p. 30) provide a broad outline of the political situation in the Fertile Crescent during the first half of the second millennium B.C. If we place the patriarchs in the eighteenth century B.C., they must have known the situation shown on Map 5; Terah and his people must have gone up from Ur of the Chaldees to Haran through the territory of the important town of Mari; and Jacob and his sons must have heard of the great king, Hammurabi, who held sway over all ancient Mesopotamia. This ruler personally organised the works of irrigation on the river-beds and canals, so vital

100
101

97-99 / *Solitary Trees.* The old stories about the patriarchs and the judges often mention certain trees (usually called oaks or terebinths in our translations) which were specially venerated and served as meeting-places for the nomads ('the oak of Moreh' near Shechem, 'the Diviners' Oak', 'the palm of Deborah', etc.). 97: An old oak near Mahanaim in Transjordan, with a nomad encampment in the background. 98: the 'oak of Abraham' near Hebron. 99: A terebinth, still venerated today. **100,101** / *A Closer View of Shechem.* 100: The tell and the village of *Balâta* at the entrance to the pass; *upper left,* the slopes of Mount Ebal round which runs the road to the north. 101: View of the tell and village taken from the slopes of Mount Ebal; in the background can be seen the unfinished church over Jacob's Well, and, at top right, the road to Jerusalem. [*Maps 2 p. 10; 4, p. 29*]

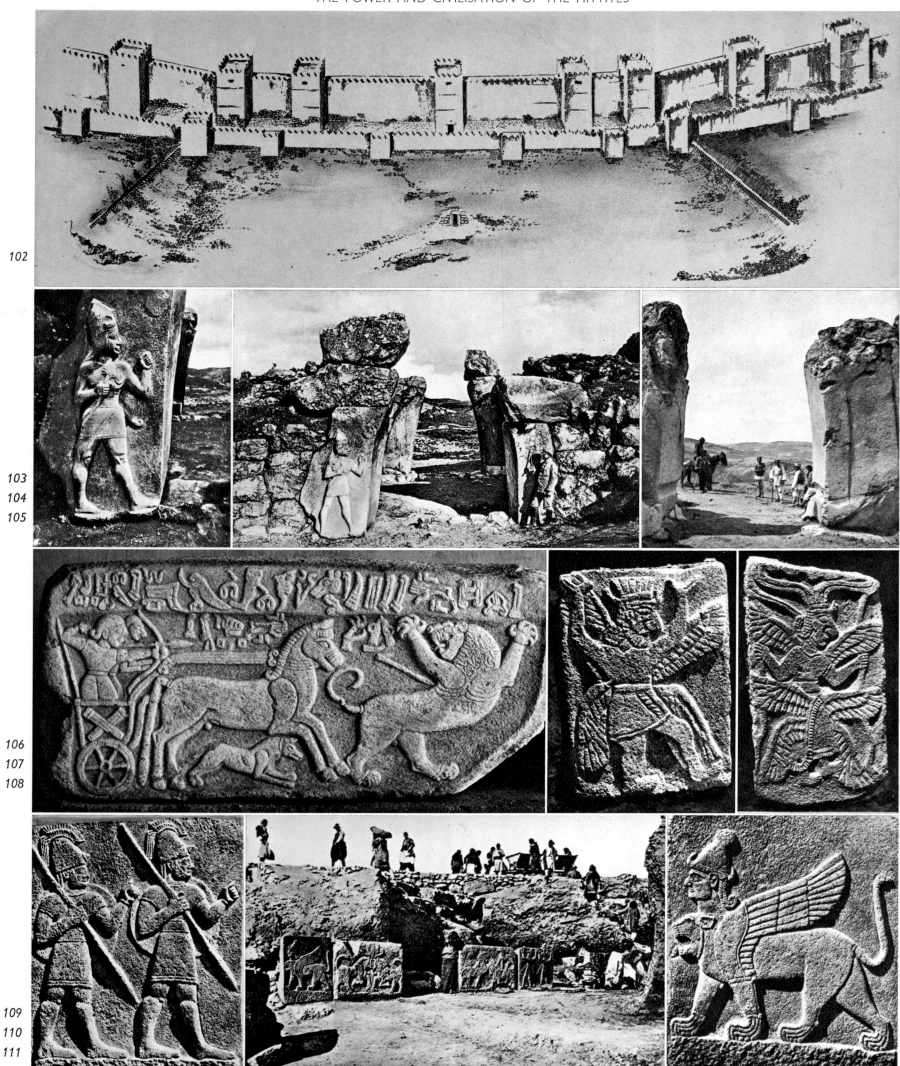

102 / *The Capital of the Hittites.* Ruins near the Turkish village of Boghaz-Keui, in the heart of Asia Minor, first found in 1834, have been methodically excavated since 1906. Discoveries here include archives containing 16,000 tablets, which have brought to life a vanished civilisation. The Hittites excelled in military architecture, as can be seen from the exact reconstruction of the outer wall of their capital, Hattushash. **103–105** / *Two Gates of Hattushash: left,* the 'Royal Gate' with its famous bas-relief; *right,* the equally imposing 'Gate of the Lions'. **106** / *Hittite Bas-relief* of a lion hunt, with a specimen of the Hittite hieroglyphic script, only recently deciphered. **107, 108** / *Two Winged Spirits;* that on the right recalls the seraphim of Is 6:2. **109–111** / *Excavations at Carchemish*, the most important city of Hittite Syria.
[*Maps 5–8, pp. 30, 43*]

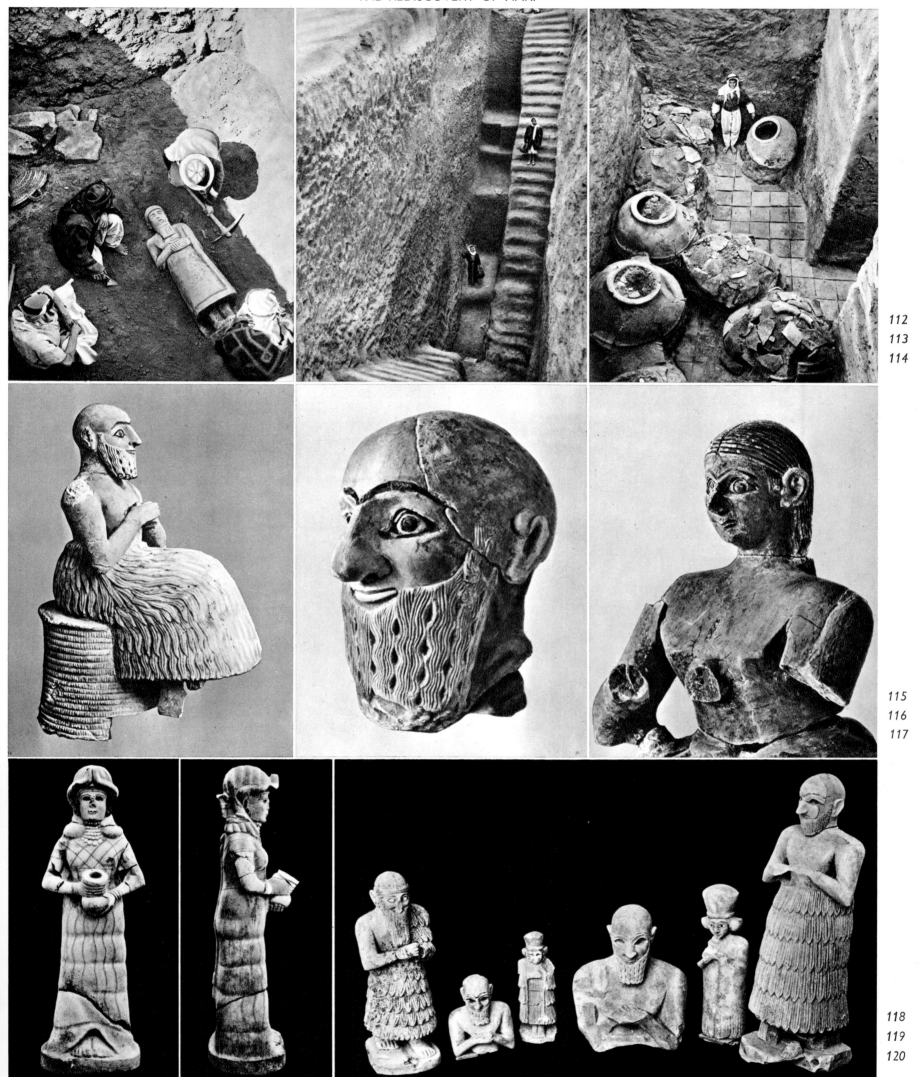

112
113
114

115
116
117

118
119
120

112 / *Discovery of the Statue of Ishtup-ilum*, who governed Mari in the 19th century B.C. **113** / *Deep Trench in the heart of the Ziggurat*. **114** / *Provision Chamber in the Royal Palace*. A number of jars have been smashed by falling masonry. **115** / *A High Official* seated in an attitude of respectful adoration before Ishtar, from whose temple this alabaster statuette, 21 inches high, was recovered. **116** / *Head of an Official;* from the same temple, plaster, 5½ inches high, before 2500 B.C. **117** / *The Singer Ur-nanshe;* detail from a seated statuette, plaster, 10 inches high, same period. **118, 119** / *Goddess of Fertility* holding a vessel which poured forth water, 18th century B.C. **120** / *Votive Statues from the Temple of Ishtar*, before 2500 B.C. (All the above photographs are taken from the magnificent volume of M. André Parrot, *Mari*, Editions Ides et Calendes, Neuchâtel and Paris.)

[Maps 1, p. 9; 5, p. 30]

121

121 / A Group of Semitic Nomads appears before an Important Egyptian Official. Wall painting from the tomb of Chnumhotep at *Beni-hasan* (the bottom panel should be placed to the left of the upper one). [*Map 5, p. 30*]

for the fertility of the country. He also administered justice in person and, by an ingenious system of government, strove to unite closely all the subject peoples, with Accadian as the official language. His famous code, found in 1902 at Susa, whither it had been carried as a trophy by an Elamite conqueror about 1200 B.C., bears witness to his endeavours: it does not embody a new legal system, but is rather the methodical codification of the public and private law which had long been in force.

The Egypt which Abraham and his family visited when there was famine in Canaan was the Egypt of the Middle Empire, considered by later Egyptians as the golden age in their history, and by modern experts as the zenith of Egyptian civilisation. (This is reflected in the extraordinary delicacy of the hieroglyphs from a temple pillar, seen on the opposite page.) The beautiful fresco reproduced above shows a party of Semites, probably Amorites, arriving in Egypt to trade in cos-

metics. The inscription (reading from right to left) means: 'Arrival of black paint for the eyes, brought to him by 37 Asiatics'. An Egyptian who presents the party to the governor, Chnumhotep, drawn on a much larger scale, holds a papyrus on which can be read, *inter alia*, the date, 6th year of Sesostris II. There follows another Egyptian; then comes the leader of the foreigners, making a respectful gesture with his right hand and holding in his left a tame ibex on a cord. Between the beast's horns can be seen the traditional crook, characteristic for the Egyptians of a Bedouin prince. In front of the leader is his name, 'the chieftain Ibsha' (a name which we later meet with in the Bible as Abishai). The multi-coloured clothing (reminiscent of Joseph's coat), the bows and arrows, lances and sticks carried by the men, the eight-stringed lyre played by the penultimate figure, the shoes, the leather bottles, and the asses' burdens are all details which help us to form a concrete picture of Abraham and his sons.

122

122 / Small Temple of Sesostris I. Built *ca* 1950 B.C.; demolished by Amenophis III *ca* 1400 B.C. to make way for the famous hall of columns of Karnak. The limestone blocks were discovered and reassembled in 1937–1938. The arrow shows the panel reproduced on the opposite page (Pl. 123).

THE HIEROGLYPHS REPRODUCED ON THE OPPOSITE PAGE (about 1/4 actual size) were cut in limestone seven centuries before the time of Moses. They illustrate the artistry with which the Egyptians could use their writing as a decorative motif. At the foot of the panel, the Pharaoh Sesostris is seen offering a sacrifice to Amon-Min, the god of male fertility. The top is framed by the wings of the sun-god. The part of the text which relates to the god begins at the top of the second column from the left. We give a translation, after Dr J. Janssen, with a few explanatory notes in parentheses:

'Words spoken by Amon-Re, Lord of the Throne [three seats] of the Two Lands [two horizontal bars, since Egypt is a plain; the throne means the temple of Amon at Karnak]: I have given all life, stability and health to [the text continues in the first column on the left] my son [a goose] Kheper-ka-Re [royal name of Sesostris I, inscribed in a cartouche], and I have given him all command [or 'provisions'; in the absence of determinatives either rendering is possible] that is with me.'

The two signs at the bottom of the column, to the left of the god's plumes, mean 'endowed with life' and doubtless belong to his name, carved in front of the plumes in slightly smaller characters: 'Amon-Re'. Opposite, in front of the king's crown, are three signs, also of the smaller type: 'May he be endowed with life'. Above the king, in the right-hand columns, is a selection from the five names of the royal titulary. The text begins in the second column from the right, with the falcon immediately below the winged sun:

'Horus, Who repeats births, King of Upper and Lower Egypt [lotus shoot and insect], Kheper-ka-Re [again in a cartouche], Lord of the Two Lands.'

And in the extreme right-hand column:

'The Two Matrons, Who repeats births, Sesostris [in a cartouche] like Re, for ever.'

We see that the artist has arranged his text symmetrically within the framework and that the animals in the two halves are facing each other. There is an exception to this in the group of three signs above the sacrificial offerings tendered by the king (observe the characteristic representation of the hands): the horned serpent, the sign for the 3rd person masculine singular, faces towards the king. This is to make it clear that these smaller signs, which admirably fill the blank space, are not part of the text proper. The same is true of the signs of Amon-Re, the first of which (the vertical feather) also serves to prolong the line separating the columns.

IN THE LAND OF RAMESES

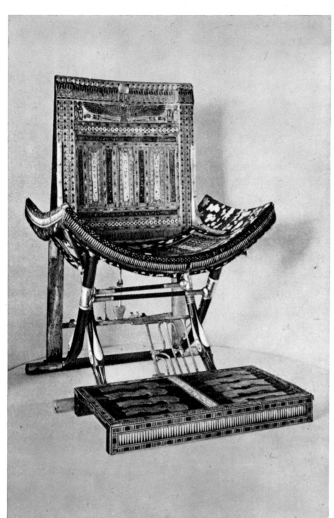

124

125

124, 125 / *Throne of Tutankhamon* in his function as supreme religious authority in Egypt. The footstool (125), bearing a representation (inlaid with cedar, ivory, and gold) of the nine traditional enemies of Egypt, is as magnificent as the throne itself. We are reminded of Psalm 110:1: 'Till I make your enemies your footstool.'

Everyone knows the beautiful story of the magnanimity of the young Joseph. Sold into slavery by his brothers, he rose to be master of the Egyptian royal household, and sent for his entire family, consisting of seventy persons, to join him. Do the numerous Egyptian documents now known to us provide any clear indications concerning the brilliant career of Joseph and the vicissitudes of his family, which so soon became a nation? If we insist on the word 'clear', the answer must be 'No'. But Egyptologists have brought to light a number of facts that go to form a background consonant with the Biblical stories.

The division of Egyptian history into thirty dynasties is known to go back to Manetho (*ca* 280 B.C.), a priest and archivist of the great temple of Heliopolis. A Hellenist to the finger-tips, it was his ambition to achieve a synthesis of the Egyptian and Greek cultures: to this end he compiled a monumental history of his country, in imitation of Herodotus who had written 170 years earlier, and doubtless also with the intention of correcting the latter's erroneous views concerning the land of the Nile.

Unfortunately the text of this work has been lost, probably because it had too strong a national flavour to appeal to the Greeks, and failed to arouse the minimum of interest then necessary to ensure the regular copying of a book. Something of Manetho's work has, however, come down to us, partly through the industrious historians of the early Christian period (such as Julius Africanus, *ca* A.D. 220, and Eusebius, *ca* A.D. 327), who reproduced the lists of dynasties and kings from copies still extant in their day; and partly through the Jewish historian Josephus, who quoted from Manetho anything which seemed to him important for the early history of his people.

According to Manetho, Egypt was ruled during the fifteenth and sixteenth dynasties by Hyksos kings, a term which he interprets as meaning 'shepherd-kings'. He tells of the appalling havoc wrought by these shepherd-kings in their conquest of Egypt. His actual words on the subject are preserved by Josephus, who accepts, not without pride, the identification of the Hyksos with the Hebrews which had already been proposed in the Ptolemaic period. He ought to have realised, however, that the peaceful arrival of the seventy members of Joseph's family, expressly invited to Egypt, hardly agreed with the devastating invasion described by Manetho. Today we hold a different view of the relationship between the Hyksos and the Hebrews.

The word *hyksos* appears in fact to be a corruption of an Egyptian expression meaning 'chieftain of a foreign land', or in the plural, 'chieftains of foreign lands'. In the golden age of the Middle Empire, under the eleventh and twelfth dynasties, this expression was already being applied to the chieftains of the nomadic tribes who visited Egypt. (The hieroglyph used for it is seen on Plate 121, above the horns of the ibex which the chieftain Ibsha is respectfully offering to the governor Chnumhotep. The lower sign represents mountain country, characterising a foreign land for the inhabitants of the flat plain of the Nile.)

It has been established from a whole series of documents and discoveries that Egypt, seriously weakened under the insignificant kings of the thirteenth and fourteenth dynasties, was overwhelmed about 1700 B.C. by a wave of foreigners from Palestine, who settled in the Delta of the Nile and completely dominated the country until about 1570 B.C. Unfortunately it is extremely difficult to draw a picture of these Hyksos and their reign. Egyptian architecture did not flourish in this period when all creative work was paralysed. In addition, the climate of the Delta is less favourable to the preservation of ancient remains than the dry conditions in Upper Egypt. And finally, after the liberation from the Hyksos yoke, later Egyptians fanatically destroyed everything which reminded them of the hated conquerors.

This migration of peoples appears to have been associated with invasions in the north, where, from the beginning of the second millennium B.C., Hurrian tribes with an Indo-European ruling class had penetrated into northern Mesopotamia and Syria (Map 5, p. 30). It is possible that, under the influence of these invasions, the already very mixed population of Canaan began to migrate. In any event, according to the names deciphered on scarabs of the Hyksos period, the Semitic element was well represented – we even find the name Jacob. These invaders were tactically stronger than the Egyptians because of horses and war chariots, both still unknown in Egypt. Avaris, their capital, they established in the east of the Delta, and from it their kings dominated Palestine also. Excavation provides evidence of a type of fortification based on the use of the horse and chariot, and also bears witness to the high level of their material civilisation. Before long, however, they adopted all kinds of habits and customs of the Pharaohs and emulated their religious zeal in constructing temples; and, a little later, the New Empire in Egypt was to reciprocate by borrowing from the Hyksos their use of horses and war chariots, and also by using a vocabulary of Semitic origin to describe them.

It is uncertain how far south the effective sway of the 'shepherd-kings' extended, but it seems probable that Upper Egypt, though paying tribute to the reigning king in Avaris, nevertheless enjoyed considerable autonomy. The Hyksos probably remained a feudal military ruling caste, few in numbers compared with the subject Egyptians. After over-running the country and crushing any resistance, they probably withdrew to the Delta, from which, by means of their superior military strength, they dominated the country.

There is a growing conviction that the settlement of Jacob's family in Egypt is linked with his Hyksos domination. Naturally the writers of Israel always confined their attention to the vicissitudes of this one family; the broader historical setting remains outside their purview, and in the later form of the stories direct traces of it are no longer to be found. Nevertheless, the migration of Jacob and his people does probably represent one trickle in the flood which submerged Egypt. The promotion of a Hebrew to supreme office under a Pharaoh is not improbable if the Pharaoh was himself a Semite; and we can also understand why the story seems to take place exclusively in the Delta. If we are able to illustrate many of the details of the story of Joseph with what we have learned about the manners of the inhabitants and the customs of the court from authentic Egyptian art and documents, it is because, under the Hyksos kings, life went on as before and because the kings themselves soon fell under the influence of the superior civilisation of ancient Egypt.

Barely a hundred years after their invasion, the Hyksos were expelled by strong chieftains from the region of Thebes; but the Delta seems to have remained largely occupied by Semitic peoples. We may

126

surmise that the little community of Hebrews still dwelt almost unnoticed in the territory which had been assigned to them. The 'land of Goshen' probably lay to the north of the fertile valley which links the region of the Nile to the Bitter Lakes and which is now called *Wâdi Tumilât*. There they doubtless followed their former way of life, possibly now a little less nomadic, but still drawing their main livelihood from their flocks. As Palestinian archaeology demonstrates ever more clearly that the tribes of Israel did not settle in Canaan before the middle of the thirteenth century B.C., the opinion which places the Exodus about the middle of this century gains more and more adherents. According to this hypothesis, the sojourn in Goshen did actually last for the four centuries mentioned in the Biblical traditions. But nothing has come down to us from these four centuries: Biblical history jumps from the death of Joseph to the events leading up to the Exodus. The most probable explanation of this silence is that nothing occurred in which the people recognised the special providence of God, or which led to a significant enrichment of the spiritual heritage of Israel.

From their remote land the Hebrew shepherds witnessed the birth of the New Empire. They heard tales of how the last of the Hyksos stubbornly held out for three years in the Palestinian fortress of Sharuhen. Not far from their territory there passed the armies which Thothmes I led in victorious progress to the banks

of the Euphrates. And when a Hebrew who had become a trader in a town or had made his mark as an interpreter at court, came home to see his family he would fascinate them for hours on end with descriptions of the wealth and luxury of Thebes, the distant capital (Map 6, p. 30).

More than sixteen times the armies of Thothmes III passed this way, until, by the close of his reign, ambassadors from every part of the known world came to seek the favour of this Pharaoh who held sway over a territory extending for 2,000 miles. About 1400 B.C. there followed the peaceful reign of Amenophis III, during which Egypt enjoyed her prosperity. But his hold over Asia weakened, and, under his son and successor, Amenophis IV, conditions became chaotic in this part of the Empire. A man of deep religious feeling, this ruler devoted all his energies to spreading the cult of the god Aton, changing his own name to Akhenaton. His general, Horemheb, struggled desperately to hold together the crumbling world empire, and on several occasions he passed not far from Goshen with his Asiatic captives. After the death of Akhenaton's weak son-in-law, Tutankhamon, the forceful Horemheb seized the throne, and so inaugurated at the close of the fourteenth century B.C. a final period of greatness (Map 7, p. 43). The might of Egypt then threatened to crush the descendants of Abraham, and at this point the Bible takes up the story once again.

127
128

126–128 / *Bas-reliefs from the Tomb of Horemheb*. These fragments of the tomb which the future Pharaoh Horemheb caused to be built in the necropolis at Memphis (Pl. 8), while he was still campaigning as a general in Asia, are among the most beautiful exhibits in the Museum of Antiquities at Leiden. On one wall of the tomb he is depicted receiving marks of distinction from the Pharaoh. Behind him, one above the other, are three rows ('registers') of officers and captives. 126 shows the well-preserved central register (a detail of which is enlarged in 127); the officers, with their wigs and pleated aprons, may be distinguished from the captives, who are bareheaded, in long robes, and tightly manacled. One can recognise Semites in the realistic group of 128 (see also Pl. 184). *Overleaf*, **129** / *Statues of the Pharaohs at Karnak*. [Map 7, p. 43]

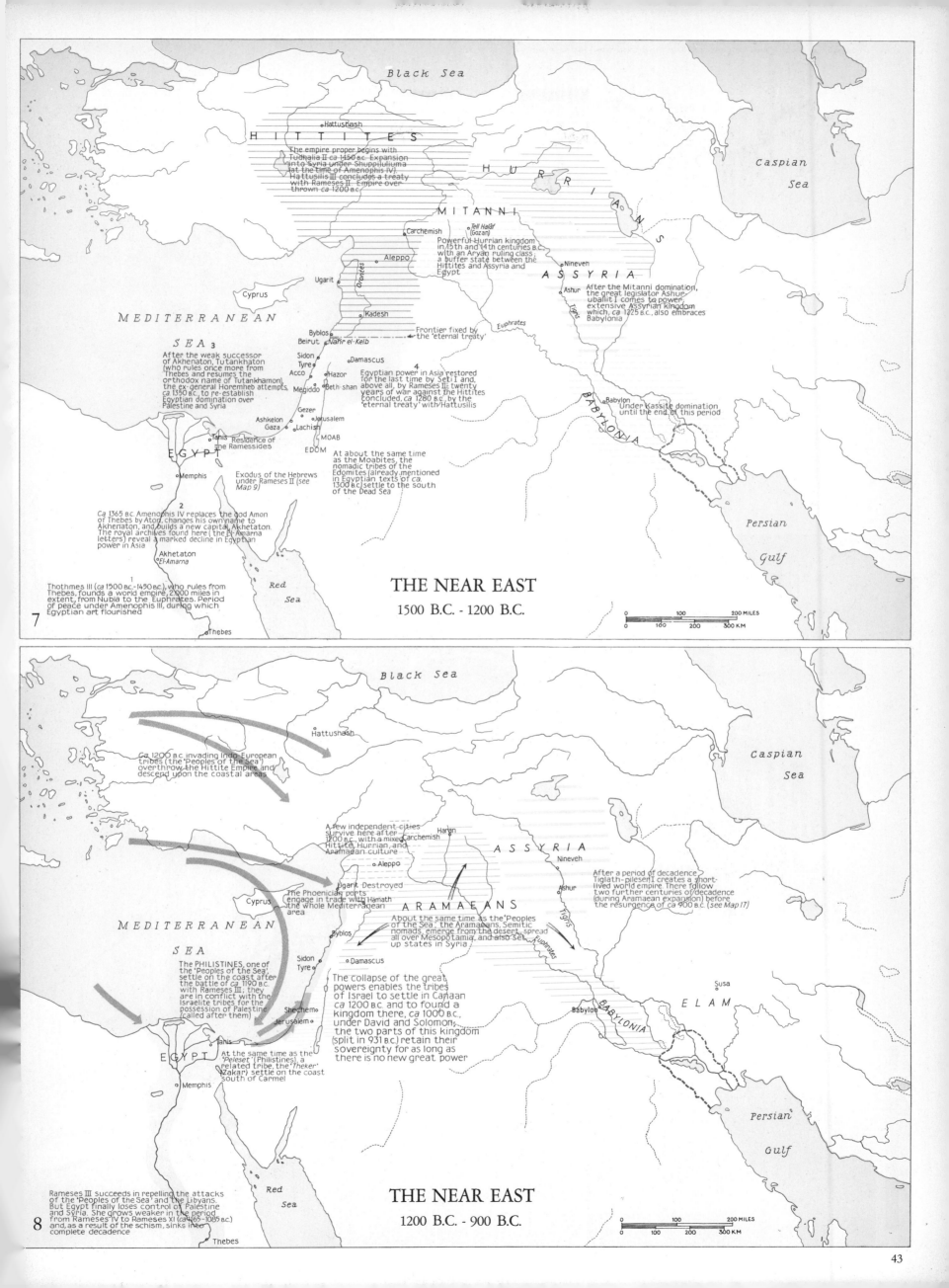

Map 7

Hattushash

HITTITES

The empire proper begins with Tudhalia II ca 1450 B.C. Expansion into Syria under Shuppiluliuma (at the time of Amenophis IV). Hattusilis III concludes a treaty with Rameses II. Empire overthrown ca 1200 B.C.

H U R R I A N S

Carchemish

Tell Halâf (Gozan)

Aleppo

M I T A N N I

Powerful Hurrian kingdom in 15th and 14th centuries with an Aryan ruling class; a buffer state between the Hittites and Assyria and Egypt

Nineveh

ASSYRIA

After the Mitanni domination, the great legislator Ashuruballit I comes to power; extensive Assyrian kingdom which, ca 1225 B.C., also embraces Babylonia

Ugarit

Cyprus

M E D I T E R R A N E A N

Kadesh

S E A ₃

After the weak successor of Akhenaton, Tutankhaton (who rules once more from Thebes and resumes the orthodox name of Tutankhamon), the ex-general Horemheb attempts, ca 1350 B.C. to re-establish Egyptian domination over Palestine and Syria

Byblos
Beirut · *Nahr el-Kelb*

Sidon
Tyre · Damascus
Acco
Hazor
Megiddo · Beth-shan

Frontier fixed by the 'eternal treaty'

Euphrates

Ashur

B A B Y L O N I A

Babylon

Under Kassite domination until the end of this period

4
Egyptian power in Asia restored for the last time by Seti I and, above all, by Rameses II; twenty years of war against the Hittites concluded, ca 1280 B.C. by the 'eternal treaty' with Hattusilis

Gezer
Ashkelon · Jerusalem
Gaza · Lachish
MOAB
EDOM

E G Y P T
Tanis · Residence of the Ramessides

Memphis

Exodus of the Hebrews under Rameses II (see Map 9)

At about the same time as the Moabites, the nomadic tribes of the Edomites (already mentioned in Egyptian texts of ca 1300 B.C.) settle to the south of the Dead Sea

2
Ca 1365 B.C. Amenophis IV replaces the god Amon of Thebes by Aton, changes his own name to Akhenaton, and builds a new capital, Akhetaton. The royal archives found here (the El-Amarna letters) reveal a marked decline in Egyptian power in Asia

Akhetaton
El-Amarna

Persian Gulf

1
Thothmes III (ca 1500 B.C.-1450 B.C.), who rules from Thebes, founds a world empire, 2,000 miles in extent, from Nubia to the Euphrates. Period of peace under Amenophis III, during which Egyptian art flourished

Red Sea

THE NEAR EAST
1500 B.C. - 1200 B.C.

7

Thebes

0 — 100 — 200 MILES
0 — 100 — 200 — 300 KM

Map 8

Black Sea

Ca 1200 B.C. invading Indo-European tribes (the 'Peoples of the Sea') overthrow the Hittite Empire and descend upon the coastal areas

Hattushash

Caspian Sea

A few independent cities survive here after 1200 B.C. with a mixed Hittite, Hurrian, and Aramaean culture

Harran
Carchemish

A S S Y R I A

Nineveh

After a period of decadence Tiglath-pileser I creates a short-lived world empire. There follow two further centuries of decadence (during Aramaean expansion) before the resurgence of ca 900 B.C. (see Map 17)

Aleppo

Ugarit Destroyed

The Phoenician ports engage in trade with the whole Mediterranean area

Hamath

A R A M A E A N S

Ashur

Cyprus

M E D I T E R R A N E A N

S E A

Byblos

About the same time as the 'Peoples of the Sea', the Aramaeans, Semitic nomads, emerge from the desert, spread all over Mesopotamia, and also set up states in Syria

Sidon
Tyre · Damascus

The PHILISTINES, one of the 'Peoples of the Sea', settle on the coast after the battle of ca 1190 B.C. with Rameses III; they are in conflict with the Israelite tribes for the possession of Palestine (called after them)

Euphrates

Tigris

Susa

The collapse of the great powers enables the tribes of Israel to settle in Canaan ca 1200 B.C. and to found a kingdom there, ca 1000 B.C., under David and Solomon; the two parts of this kingdom (split in 931 B.C.) retain their sovereignty for as long as there is no new great power

E L A M

Shechem
Jerusalem

Babylon

B A B Y L O N I A

Tanis

E G Y P T

At the same time as the 'Peleset' (Philistines), a related tribe, the 'Theker' (Zakar) settle on the coast south of Carmel

Memphis

8
Rameses III succeeds in repelling the attacks of the 'Peoples of the Sea' and the Libyans. But Egypt finally loses control of Palestine and Syria. She grows weaker in the period from Rameses IV to Rameses XI (ca 1165-1085 B.C.) and, as a result of the schism, sinks into complete decadence

Red Sea

Persian Gulf

THE NEAR EAST
1200 B.C. - 900 B.C.

Thebes

0 — 100 — 200 MILES
0 — 100 — 200 — 300 KM

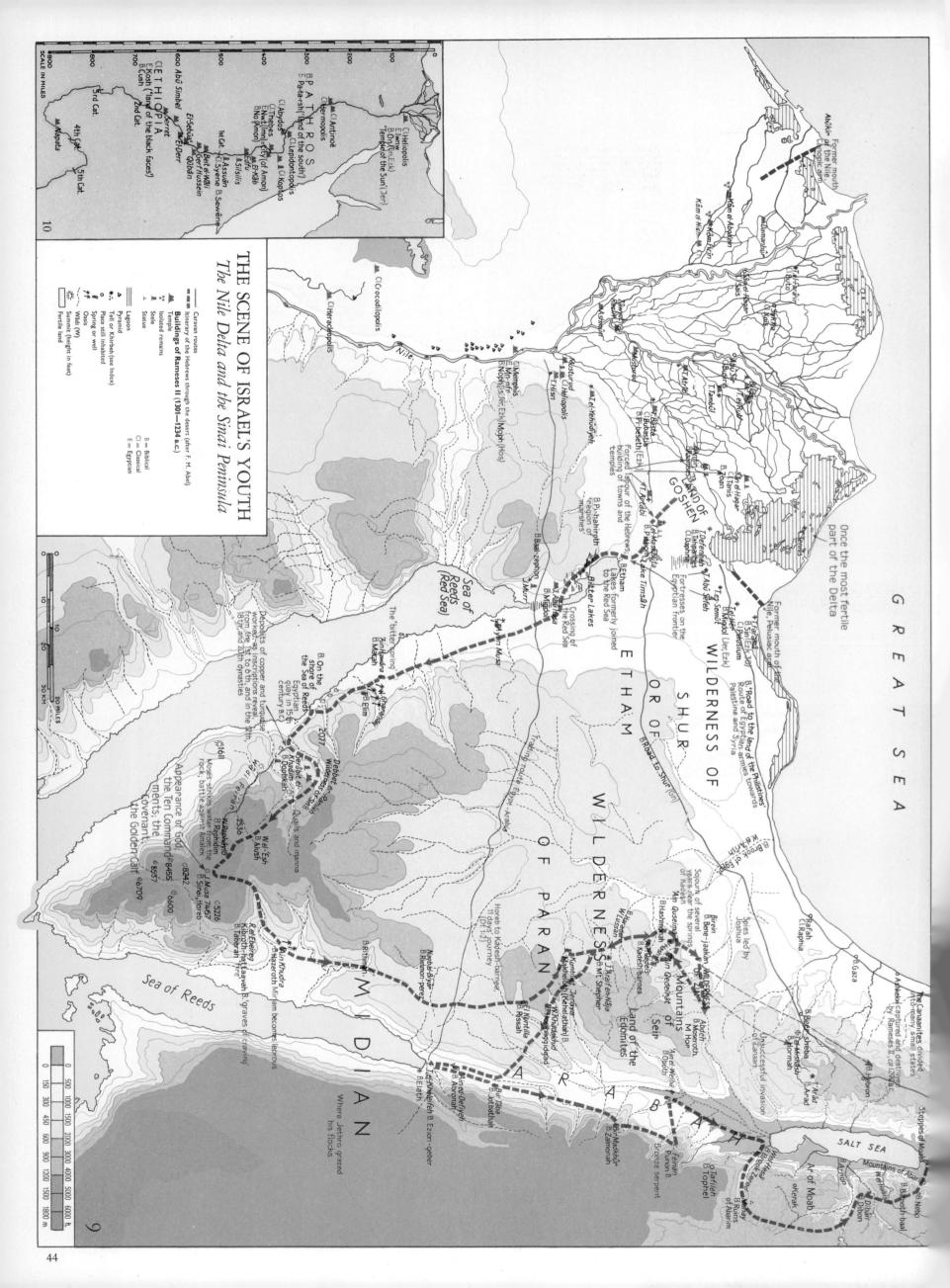

THE SCENE OF ISRAEL'S YOUTH
The Nile Delta and the Sinai Peninsula

Buildings of Rameses II (1301—1234 b.c.)
Itinerary of the Hebrews through the desert (after F. M. Abel)
Caravan routes

B = Biblical
Cl = Classical
E = Egyptian

- ⌂ Isolated remains
- ⊥ Stele
- ▲ Statue
- ⚑ Temple
- △ Pyramid
- ◉ Tell or Khirbeh (see Index)
- ○ Place still inhabited
- ✢ Spring or well
- ☼ Oasis
- Lagoon
- Wadi (W)
- ▲ Summit (height in feet)
- Fertile land

GREAT SEA

Once the most fertile
part of the Delta

WILDERNESS OF GOSHEN
LAND OF

OR OF SHUR

ETHAM

WILDERNESS OF PARAN

WILDERNESS OF SHUR

MIDIAN

Sea of Reeds

Sea of Reeds
(Red Sea)

SALT SEA

ARABAH

44

THE DELIVERANCE FROM PHARAOH

When the Israelite peasant came to offer the first fruits of his field to God he had solemnly to declare before Him: 'A wandering Aramaean was my father; and he went down into Egypt and sojourned there, few in number; and there he became a nation, great, mighty, and populous. And the Egyptians treated us harshly, and afflicted us, and laid upon us hard bondage. Then we cried to the Lord the God of our fathers, and the Lord heard our voice and saw our affliction, our toil, and our oppression; and the Lord brought us out of Egypt with a mighty hand and an outstretched arm, with great terror, with signs and wonders; and he brought us into this place and gave us this land, a land flowing with milk and honey. And behold, now I bring the first fruit of the ground, which Thou, O Lord, hast given me.'

Dt 26: 5-10

To the Israelite these words were the expression of his deepest faith, founded on the historical fact of God's intervention in the life of his people. When they sought to remind Israel of the true nature of her situation, the great prophets always appealed in the first instance to this fundamental fact. 'When Israel was a child, I loved him, and out of Egypt I called my son ... I am the Lord your God from the land of Egypt ... For I brought you up from the land of Egypt, and redeemed you from the house of bondage ... The covenant which I made with their fathers when I took them by the hand to bring them out of the land of Egypt'. From all their experiences the people of Israel had learned to envisage their God as a liberator, a conception which lies at the root of their belief that they belonged in a special sense to God. 'What other nation on earth is like thy people Israel, whom God went to redeem to be his people ...?'

Hos 11:1
Mi 6:4
Hos 13:4
Jer 31:32

2 S 7:23

A father, when his son asked him about the reason for the laws, commandments, and precepts, was bound to answer him with the story of the miraculous Exodus. Every year these prodigious events were symbolically re-lived through the rites of the Passover, and it was impossible to praise the love and glory of God in psalms and hymns without once again celebrating the great deliverance. The exuberant confidence of the exiles in Babylon, expressed in the lyrical chapters of Isaiah 40–55, is based entirely upon the sure belief that what Yahweh did in former times, He would do again today; that as with a strong hand He led their fathers out of Egypt, so would He lead them out of Babylon.

Generation after generation, the story of the miraculous Exodus from Egypt was tirelessly related with a confidence born of deep faith, with the result that the guiding theme of the story, namely the divine intervention, was increasingly emphasised and amplified, while the factual details gradually became blurred. The Bible shows us only the last stages of this evolution. It had already begun before the date of the first written accounts preserved in the Scriptures. The earliest narrative is found in the first fifteen chapters of the book to which it gives its name, Exodus, and, as with Genesis, there are many indications of its composite character. Even the Yahwistic version of the story is already markedly epic in quality and conveys an impression of almost liturgical solemnity. The separation of the vital fact from its attendant circumstances has already been carried to such lengths that the name of the Pharaoh who strove to prevent the Children of Israel leaving Egypt is not recorded, and it is impossible to establish from the Biblical text the exact scene of the miraculous crossing of the Red Sea, or even to understand the precise sequence of events. There is consequently a divergence of opinion on these matters among Biblical scholars.

130 / *Rameses II*, a larger than life-size granite statue now at Turin. On his helmet is the serpent Uraeus and in his hand the sceptre, the symbols of his authority. **131** / *The 'Stele of Israel' of Merneptah*. The almost symmetrical tableau is a double representation of the god Amon, presenting a sickle-shaped sword to the king, above whose helmet is the disc of the sun. On the extreme right is the falcon-headed god Horus (cf. Pl. 291); on the extreme left Mut, wife of Amon and goddess of Thebes.

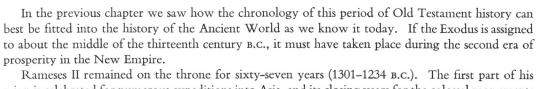

In the previous chapter we saw how the chronology of this period of Old Testament history can best be fitted into the history of the Ancient World as we know it today. If the Exodus is assigned to about the middle of the thirteenth century B.C., it must have taken place during the second era of prosperity in the New Empire.

Rameses II remained on the throne for sixty-seven years (1301–1234 B.C.). The first part of his reign is celebrated for numerous expeditions into Asia, and its closing years for the colossal monuments he erected. His father, Seti I, had already attempted to regain the territories lost in Palestine and Syria, and traces of his campaigns have been brought to light by excavations in these areas. Rameses II continued these operations, and on the shores of the Mediterranean, in an incomparably beautiful place near the present *Nahr el-Kelb* (the 'river of the dog'), he had two stelae cut out in the rock; this was the frontier of Egypt! But there he was checked, and an Egyptian army was never again to cross the Euphrates; for the Hittites were pushing southwards. During Rameses' fifth campaign in Syria the Egyptian troops (four metropolitan divisions and a large force of auxiliaries) came to grips with the Hittites near Kadesh on the Orontes. This famous battle, sung by the poets and pictured on many a temple wall (showing the same distinction between the Hittite national and auxiliary troops as was made in the Egyptian army), had no decisive outcome, and even the town of Kadesh was not captured. Rameses was often to return to Palestine to check the Hittite incursions and quell local rebellions; the fall of Ashkelon was one episode in these encounters. Finally, about 1280 B.C., the long struggle was ended by an agreement, the famous 'eternal treaty', of which we now know both the Egyptian and the Hittite versions. This agreement, sealed by the marriage of Rameses to a Hittite princess who became his chief consort, stabilised the situation in Palestine and Syria for several decades. Hittite campaigns were henceforth confined to Asia Minor; and Rameses' son and successor, Merneptah, dispatched corn to Anatolia to help to combat famine there.

137
139

154B

Rameses' numerous campaigns in Asia, though they were probably by no means the resounding victories which he delighted to portray in his official records, greatly enhanced the importance of the eastern part of the Delta, which was crossed and recrossed by his armies and their trains of captives. Moreover, Rameses' family probably originated from the neighbourhood of Avaris, the former capital of the Hyksos and the centre of the cult of the god Set, after whom his father was called. Rameses built a new capital in this region and made it his principal seat. Where was this 'town of Rameses', known in classical times as Tanis and called Zoan in the Bible? The name of Rameses is met with on numerous ruined sites in the eastern part of the Delta; and though many scholars identify his capital with the remains situated near the fishing village of *Sân el-Hagar*, others believe that it should be located at the modern *Qantir* (this hypothesis has been adopted on Map 9, opposite). In any event, Thebes, the wealthy and powerful city of Amon, could not fail to lose its political importance, although

130

131

133-
139

it remained a great religious centre. There also, Rameses built on a large scale; indeed, one can truthfully declare that there is not a town or a temple which does not bear witness to his strange predilection for the colossal. But the mass-produced work of an army of artists must, in the nature of things, be less perfect than that of the individual craftsmen of the past; and often, from the sheer clumsiness with which the hieroglyphs of Rameses' name are cut on a finely worked statue, we can recognise that he has appropriated an earlier work.

130

By the time Rameses II died, several of his seventy-nine sons and fifty-nine daughters had predeceased him, and he was succeeded by his thirteenth son, Merneptah. During the reign of this king, Libyan tribes penetrated into the western part of the Delta; this was the prelude to the great migrations in the eastern basin of the Mediterranean, set in motion by what are usually called the 'Peoples of the Sea'. Merneptah defeated the Libyans and commemorated his

131

victory on a huge basalt stele. The other side of the stele had already been used for an inscription of Amenophis III, which indicates that the royal house was impoverished, no doubt by the cost of Rameses II's buildings. But Merneptah's inscription is of vital importance for us. It is actually a triumphal chant composed of a series of short poems; the first poems celebrate the victory over the Libyans, while the last proclaims:

> The kings yield and cry, 'Peace!'
> All the vanquished are bowed down.
> Libya is devastated and the land of the Hittites pacified;
> Despoiled is Canaan and all her wickedness.
> Ashkelon is fallen; Gezer is conquered; Yenoam is destroyed.
> Israel is ravaged and her seed annihilated.
> Philistia stands widowed before Egypt.
> All the lands are pacified.
> All the nomads are in chains.
> Benire, beloved of Amon, son of Re, Merneptah,
> Blest, like Re, with life every day.

The 'cry' of the kings is the Canaanite and also the Biblical word for 'peace' (sh-l-m). Ashkelon, Gezer, and possibly Yenoam are mentioned in the Bible. Philistia, which is Palestine (in Egyptian the word resembles that for 'widow'), is stated to have no men left to defend her against Egypt. It should also be noted that the name of Israel is not accompanied by the hieroglyph signifying 'country', as are Canaan, Ashkelon, Gezer, and Yenoam, but by the one which, when attached to a name, normally means a 'people'. If we set aside the reading 'Yizreel' for 'Israel', proposed by a Dutch scholar, we may conclude that about 1230 B.C., in the fifth year of Merneptah's reign, an Israelite community was living in the land of Canaan.

By placing the departure from Egypt in the first half of the thirteenth century

B.C., on the basis of these data, we furnish the scant information in the Biblical account with a background as colourful as it is appropriate. The Hebrews had to build for Pharaoh 'store cities, Pithom and Raamses'. The first name may be a corruption of the Egyptian *pr-Itm*, 'house of Atum', which is one of the names of the sun god. This town must have been situated in the *Wâdi Tumilât*, the tongue of fertile land mentioned earlier, which links the Delta to the present Bitter Lakes. Two extensive ruined sites, nine miles apart, both claim the distinction of being the Pithom mentioned in the Bible. Excavations have proved that in both places Rameses erected buildings (both of limestone and of brick) and that there was a cult of the god Atum. The name Raamses no doubt designates the new royal residence, whose magnificence is praised in a stele from Beth-shan and in several other texts. One of these specifically refers to a temple of Ashtarte. This fact and a growing number of other indications prove that the extensive semitisation of the eastern part of the Delta did not end with the expulsion of the Hyksos. Besides Ashtarte, the deities Anat, Baal, and Horon were also worshipped there, associated or even fused with purely Egyptian deities like Nephthys, Isis, Set, and Horus. The new capital, close to the frontier between Egypt and Canaan, became the centre of a cosmopolitanism hitherto unknown in the ancient world. It may be assumed that Canaanite was as widely spoken as Egyptian, rather like French and Flemish in Brussels today. For diplomatic correspondence, a Semitic language, Accadian, was already being used in the previous reign, and no doubt a knowledge of this language was a prerequisite for important posts.

Around the cosmopolitan capital with its fertile countryside, there lived, on the fringes of the desert, a great many semi-nomads, among them the Hebrews, who provided a welcome labour force for the vast projects of Rameses. The Bible refers in particular to work with clay and bricks, and one cannot fail to be struck by the fact that, in a pictorial record of this work, one of the labourers has a Semitic cast of countenance.

The pleasing story of the birth of Moses suggests the period of Rameses II, because the royal palace is supposed to be close to the territory inhabited by the Hebrews. Moses spent his early years in his father's house and was afterwards brought up at the court. The simple religion of his parents therefore made its impression upon him, but he had soon to attend the school of the royal children and there experience the harsh methods then practised to inculcate the wisdom of Egypt. As a young man he enjoyed the many-sided and colourful life of the capital.

Doubtless Moses did not feel the surprise which we today feel, when he found his teachers of philosophy combining elements which to us seem irreconcilable. In the course of the centuries, the pantheon of this conservative land had accumulated such a plethora of deities that the priests of the different sanctuaries strove in vain to reduce them to any sort of order. Religious practices were steeped in magic, and increasingly complicated burial rites were believed to

132 / The Making of Bricks in Ancient Egypt. In order to miss nothing of the colourful daily life of Egypt in the next world, Rekhmire, vizier of Thothmes III, had the walls of his tomb painted with a wide variety of scenes, *ca* 1460 B.C. The above reproduction gives the reader of the Bible some idea of the work required of the Hebrews in Egypt. *Top left:* two slaves draw water from a tree-fringed pool. The men next to them are working the clay, which is then carried in baskets to be pressed into wooden moulds. The blocks thus formed are dried in the sun *(top left)* and afterwards used for building. Overseers armed with sticks urge on the work. The kneeling slave in the middle of the upper register is obviously a Semite.   [*Map 9, p. 44*]

133–136 / *The Temple of Amon.* Above are a few of the many contributions made by Rameses II to this huge complex of buildings: one of the colossal statues (134) and the forty rams which line the processional way from the banks of the Nile to the sanctuary (135, 136). **133, 137–139** / *The Ramesseum.* On the west bank of the Nile, at the foot of the mountains where he had carved out his tomb (Pls. 9-11), Rameses built his mortuary temple. 133 shows the corner of a court with 3 of the 16 pillars of Osiris and, alongside, the head and shoulder of a granite statue which stood 56 feet high. On the wall behind the pillars is a huge relief of the battle of Kadesh. 137, a detail, the storming of Kadesh; 139, the Hittite armies (cf. Pl. 184). The figure (138) gives the scale. [*Map 10, p. 44*]

ensure a happy life in the next world. But, alongside these aberrations, there was nevertheless room for a very pure conception of the deity; the hymns to the sun god, the source of life, were still in use, and the young Moses must certainly have copied as a writing exercise the books of ancient wisdom enjoining man to open his heart to the one god, who could see into the secret places of the soul and required absolute righteousness of all men.

In addition, Moses was able to form a clear idea of the religious beliefs and practices in Canaan through his contact with officials working in Palestine and Canaanites who lived in the town of Rameses and sometimes held offices at the court. The picture was not an attractive one: sexual excesses of every kind, a repulsive cult of serpents, and human sacrifice were all included in the ritual.

When he came to visit his people, Moses saw the extent to which they were exploited and ill-treated. In his anger, he killed an Egyptian overseer and hastily took flight for fear of punishment. By way of the caravan route, dotted with watering-places, he came to the land of the wandering Midianites. There he met a daughter of the priest Jethro (Reuel) and married her. As a member of her tribe, Moses, the aristocrat brought up in the lap of luxury, came to know quite a different kind of life. This primitive existence, with all its deprivations, was a liberating experience for a man who had just come from the empty frivolities of an indolent and self-indulgent civilisation. This lonely and impressive setting helped to prepare him for the revelation on Mount Sinai. Here he found his vocation and had the decisive experience which gave him for the rest of his days a steadfast faith in his mission: he was to lead the Hebrew tribes out of Egypt and weld them into a nation belonging to Yahweh.

In the fascinating story of the encounters between Moses and Pharaoh and the
Ex 3: plagues which descended upon Egypt, the Bible emphasises the fact that the God
19-20 who had called Moses was more powerful than Pharaoh, and could summon all the forces of nature to compel the foreign ruler to release His people.

When the most terrible of the plagues had struck Egypt, the Hebrews left the land of Goshen. A few stopping-places are mentioned before their crossing of the Sea of Reeds or Red Sea, but they cannot be identified with any certainty from the data at present at our disposal. There are even several hypotheses as to which place the Hebrews called the 'Sea of Reeds'. The route shown on Map 9 (p. 44) is based on the most plausible theory, that advanced by Father F. M. Abel, O.P. (d. 1953), a professor at the French Dominican School in Jerusalem, who devoted his whole life to the study of Biblical geography and carried out several thorough explorations in the Sinai peninsula.

According to the text of Exodus, the Hebrews 'journeyed from Rameses to
Ex 12:37 Succoth' and from there to 'Etham, on the edge of the wilderness'; they then
Ex 13:20 encamped 'in front of Pi-hahiroth, between Migdol and the sea, in front of
Ex 14:2 Baal-zephon'. The trouble is that most of these terms are rather imprecise. The Hebrew word *sukkoth* means 'the tabernacles' and is more than once used as a place-name. *Etham* derives from an Egyptian term meaning 'wall' or 'rampart' and is equally vague, for the Egyptians had for centuries been constructing a series of fortifications (see Map 5, p. 30), roughly in a line along the present Suez Canal, which were intended to protect their country against the Asiatic hordes. *Pi-hahiroth* may mean 'house of the marshes', a name which also occurs

frequently in this region of lagoons and abundant papyrus. *Migdol* means 'fortification' in both Semitic and Egyptian of the period, and may therefore apply to any one of the fortifications. There remains *Baal-zephon*, which refers to a deity, the 'Baal of the North', i.e. of Canaan, whose sanctuary must have been somewhere along a road leading towards Palestine.

Geological investigation carried out to the north of Suez and archaeological information from various ruined sites suggest that, at the time of the Exodus, the Bitter Lakes were linked to the Gulf of Suez. There were consequently shallows; and this throws light upon the Biblical reference to 'a strong east wind' which sufficed to divide the waters. The expression 'Sea of Reeds' could have applied to both the Gulf of Suez and the arm of the sea which connected it to the Bitter Lakes. This is all the more plausible since Hebrew has only one word to designate both a 'sea' and a 'lake'.

Our map places Etham on the ruins of one of the Egyptian strong-holds: the Hebrews obviously found it impossible to pass through at this point. Migdol, then, may have been the Hebrew name of a fortress built by Seti I on the ruins of which a temple of Hathor (the goddess of the mines along the road to Sinai) has been found. Baal-zephon may also have lain somewhere in the same neighbourhood, as we find the expression 'migdol Baal-zephon' occurring in a later papyrus.

The steppe which the Hebrews entered after crossing the Sea of Reeds is called the desert of Etham or the desert of Shur (the Hebrew word *shur* meaning 'wall'). In their journey southwards, they took the road which had for centuries been used by mineworkers in the service of Egypt. (The western edge of the peninsula is rich in copper and all kinds of precious stones. In the two mining centres excavated in modern times, the ruins of a temple, a large number of stelae, and countless inscriptions dating from different dynasties were unearthed. Near by were found remarkable texts, attributed to Semitic slaves, and showing the earliest known attempt to simplify Egyptian writing and reduce it to an alphabetical system.) South of this region, the Hebrews were no longer in danger of meeting with companies of soldiers. Making their way from oasis to oasis, they penetrated deeply into the mountains until they came to the height where God revealed Himself to Moses.

Since ancient times, Christian tradition has placed Mount Sinai in the imposing granite range which lies at the southern end of the Sinai peninsula, with *Jebel Mûsa* (7,500 feet) as its highest peak. But this location has been contested by armchair scholars. Some of them would situate Mount Sinai in the land of Midian, or at least in northern Arabia. They maintain that the descriptions in the Bible suggest a volcanic site, and there is no evidence of volcanic activity in the peninsula. According to others, it must have been situated near Kadesh, or, again, in the vicinity of Petra. The latter site does in fact lie in a *Wâdi Mûsa*. But this name can be based only on comparatively recent Jewish traditions, which have associated several stories concerning Moses and Aaron with the region of the future capital of the Nabataeans. A visit to the traditional Mount Sinai suffices to dispel all these doubts. The huge granite formations are an awe-inspiring spectacle. The atmosphere, the light and the colours, the incredible stillness, all conspire to make the scene an unforgettable setting for the meeting of God with man.

140

140 / Egyptian Infantry. Wooden soldiers, about 6 inches high, from a tomb of 1800 B.C. Many details of the daily life of the Egyptians are known to us through their belief that, in the next world, the dead could enjoy everything which was actually present, or represented, or named in their tombs. They therefore drew up long lists of all kinds of choice foods and beverages and made detailed representations of the earthly life of the deceased. In their tombs we find costly objects (Pl. 124), and numerous bas-reliefs (Pls. 126-128 and 271), mural paintings (Pls. 121 and 132), and statuettes. From the above models we are able to form an idea of the companies of foot-soldiers whom the sons of Jacob must have encountered on the frontiers of Egypt as they attempted to pass into the Promised Land.

[Map 9, p. 44]

141, 142 / *The Syrian Desert*. The western fringes of the extensive steppes indicated in the middle of Map 1 (p. 9) do receive a certain amount of rain. There are wells, springs, and a scanty vegetation. Here the patriarchs wandered with their flocks. Pl. 142 cannot be used to illustrate the stories of Genesis, since, in all probability, the nomads of this region did not use the camel until about 1100 B.C. **143, 144** / *The Land of Midian*, east of the Gulf of Elath or 'Aqaba, where Moses married into the tribe of Jethro. The black tents of the nomads are dwarfed by their majestic surroundings. **145, 146** / *On the Road to Sinai*. The deeper we penetrate into the multi-coloured granite mountains of the peninsula, the wilder the valleys become; only occasionally does a luxuriant oasis reveal the presence of a spring.

[Maps 4, p. 29; 9, p. 44]

49

147
148

149

147–150 / *Mount Sinai.* After a long journey through wild ravines (Pl. 146), the traveller suddenly finds himself on the edge of a great plain. Beyond this rise the majestic mountain mass of red granite which, since early Christian times, has been regarded as the Sinai and Horeb of the Bible. 149: Travellers journeying across the plain to the famous monastery of St Catherine, whose cypresses are almost hidden in the shadow of the mountain mass. 147 was photographed from the opposite direction; the monastery is bathed in the light of the setting sun, which shines down over the saddle between the two mountains. The mountain with the three peaks towers 1,600 feet above the monastery. Behind lies the J. Mûsa, the mountain of Moses, 2,600 feet above the monastery (the leftmost summit in 149, and in 150, *opposite*). 148: View from the mountain of Moses across the saddle towards the three-peaked mountain, behind which lies the plain.

[Map 9, p. 44]

THE COVENANT AND THE LAW

After the dramatic accounts of the plagues of Egypt, the Exodus, and the appearance of God on Mount Sinai, the Bible begins upon a long enumeration of prescriptions and laws. The book of Exodus is followed by Leviticus, consisting entirely of laws, mainly relating to ritual. It is not until the tenth chapter of the following book, Numbers, that the story is taken up once again with the departure from Mount Sinai; but it is interrupted at every step by lists of ordinances. Nevertheless, by Chapter 22, the people of Israel have already reached 'the plains of Moab beyond the Jordan at Jericho'. There follow a few narrative passages, but Deuteronomy, the fifth part of the Pentateuch, is again devoted to legislation, with the exception of its closing chapters, which tell of the last words and death of Moses. The remaining books of the Old Testament contain no further ordinances and prescriptions in the strict sense: the whole legislative system of Israel seems, therefore, to have been fitted into the historical setting of the journey through the wilderness and associated with the figure of Moses.

The scholars who, at the end of last century, applied evolutionary theories to the history of Israel observed that both its social institutions and religious beliefs had evolved in the process of time. Their meticulous literary analysis of the Pentateuch showed it to be a patchwork of all kinds of laws, reflecting a variety of social conditions and religious ideas; and they deduced that these laws must consequently belong to different periods in the later history of Israel. Limited by their narrow conception of the evolution of religions, which they sought to apply to the faith of Israel, some of these scholars reached the conclusion that the background of the Sinaitic legislation could not be historical and that the figure of Moses was a figment of the creative imagination of later Hebrews; and they naturally held similar views on the settlement of the tribes 'in the land of Rameses' and their miraculous liberation.

When we are confronted with theories such as these, certain observations must be made. When set against the background of religious beliefs in the Near East, Yahwism is seen to be so very exceptional in its distinctive features that an evolution from inferior forms is unlikely. We can but speak of a creation. And since the whole tradition refers so explicitly to Moses, there can be no reason to doubt that this great figure played a part in its foundation. The many short narrative passages in Exodus, Numbers, and Deuteronomy portray this man who was at all times profoundly aware of both the transcendence and the nearness of the God who had taken possession of him and had charged him with the task of leading the Hebrew families of Goshen, 'a mixed multitude', out of Egypt and welding them into a nation. Moses is firm and forceful as well as gentle and forbearing; he is ready to sacrifice himself for the sake of his people, and he is also a determined leader who repeatedly triumphs over those who lose courage or rebel.

Although Moses himself was undoubtedly concerned in the origins of the legislation, it is equally certain that many of the laws in the Pentateuch were not formulated until a later date. The task of a legislator is to determine social relations and behaviour, either by codifying existing customs and usages or by creating new precepts to meet new situations. Now the Covenant of Mount Sinai created a new situation and therefore called for legislative action: the bond with Yahweh, more or less voluntarily accepted by the 'mixed multitude' under the leadership of Moses, could be expected to make a profound impression on the structure of their society. This community was dedicated for all time to the God who had just revealed Himself, the God who was wholly spirit, the master of men and events, who could see into the very depths of the heart, and to whom no form or dwelling-place could be assigned. It was Moses who formulated the obligations proceeding from this Covenant into a series of precepts, pertaining both to human relationships and to the worship of Yahweh.

The concrete forms of a legal system vary according to the conditions in which the society is living. The social relations of a people who live in permanent houses and till the soil differ from those of nomads who wander with their flocks from one grazing ground to another. The institutions of Israel in the post-Exilic period, when she was governed by priests and her life centred on the Temple, were

151

151 / *The Arabah.* The Jordan valley and the deep depression filled by the Dead Sea are prolonged to the south by a broad valley, 112 miles long, still called the Arabah. Here we are looking east (see the field of vision marked on Map 3, p. 10): in the foreground are the freakish limestone formations of the Negeb, through which the tortuous wâdis carve out their paths down to the valley. The eastern mountains are composed mainly of granite and porphyry; behind the dark ridges which can be discerned lies the 'rose-red city' of Petra (Pls. 311–317). Across this impressive desert the Hebrews journeyed from Ezion-geber towards the Promised Land. In after years Solomon subjugated the Edomites who lived in this region in order to secure free access to his naval base on the Gulf of Elath and to the neighbouring copper-mines.

[Map 9, p. 44]

152
153

necessarily different from those which obtained in the highly-organised state of Solomon.

Any attempt to date the laws in the Pentateuch must be based on a clear picture of the evolution of the people of Israel in the centuries which elapsed between Moses and Ezra. Unfortunately the Bible tells us extremely little about social and economic structure in the various periods. We are better informed about the phases of the religious evolution, owing to the special nature of the literature of Israel. Each of the prophets stressed one particular aspect of Yahwism, not only according to the dictates of his own character, but also according to the dangers which threatened religion in his day. It may be assumed that each prophet left the mark of his mind and style upon the legislation of the period of his spiritual ascendancy.

Nevertheless, the dating of these laws remains a delicate task. The Biblical scholar of today finds it less easy to reach definite conclusions than did his colleague of a generation ago. Not only does he live in a world which has seen the collapse of the sanguine judgments based on evolutionary theories; his work must also take account of the lessons of archaeology. For the archaeologist sometimes discovers a clay tablet recording, long before the time of Moses, customs which are also referred to in the laws of the Pentateuch, and which earlier scholars, wedded to the evolutionary theory, had assigned to the time of Ezekiel. It is therefore inevitable that many earlier ideas have to be reversed or modified.

The Ten Commandments appear in two forms which differ very little from each other. Their original form, which must have been shorter, is now generally attributed to Moses. The body of laws known as the 'Book of the Covenant' appears to suggest a semi-nomadic society in process of adopting a settled life; it is sometimes assigned to the last phase of the life in the wilderness, shortly before the entry into Canaan. Both the content and style of the Ten Words in Exodus 34 suggest the period of David and Solomon, while the collection of laws in Deuteronomy is universally believed to embody traditions from the Northern Kingdom, written down for the most part after the destruction of Samaria, and promulgated as laws in the reign of Josiah. The Law of Holiness appears to be a compilation of traditions current among the priestly circles of Jerusalem, traditions which have left their mark also on the mind of Ezekiel. The

experiences of the hard years of the Exile, when the faith of the people of Judah was so severely tested by the lack of a Temple and by the dazzling spectacle of the religious feasts of Babylon, may have formed the psychological background to the Priestly Code. Here a great body of laws is set in an impressive historical framework recording the principal blessings God has bestowed upon Israel and all mankind, beginning with the Creation. Although it is impossible to determine exactly how much of the Pentateuch derives from this source, it seems reasonably certain that we must attribute its division of the history and the chronological and genealogical framework to the compiler of this Priestly Code. Into this general setting have been inserted a great many detailed regulations concerning sacrifices, purity, and the ritual of feasts, and though their wording frequently reflects the spirit of the theocratic Jewish community of the post-Exilic period, the customs they embody are often very ancient.

Gn 10

The whole corpus of the varied legislation in the Pentateuch is attributed to Moses. Those who are acquainted with the general problems involved in the evolution of legal codes will see no lack of honesty in this. Today, for example, the name 'Napoleonic Code' is applied to a code containing a great many prescriptions which were not envisaged by the Emperor. Similarly, the generations of priests and wise men who contributed to the composition of the 'Books of Moses' saw nothing dishonest in attaching the formula 'And the Lord spake unto Moses' to a law of much later date. It might even be argued that they could not have acted otherwise; for they were entrusted with the task of regulating the conduct of Israel in accordance with the demands of the Covenant which had created a special relationship between Israel and God. It was God Himself who had chosen Moses as His mouth-piece and as the mediator of the Covenant; and in this capacity Moses had established for all time the basic pattern of behaviour. Changing circumstances called for a further definition of the fundamental attitude. But the later legislators were fully aware that they were not introducing radical changes. Nor had they any such intention. On the contrary, they sought to defend the ancient heritage and to protect Israel against new customs which were incompatible with the service of Yahweh and would have made her unfit to fulfil her true obligations under the Covenant. For this reason no law could be valid in Israel except as a law of Moses.

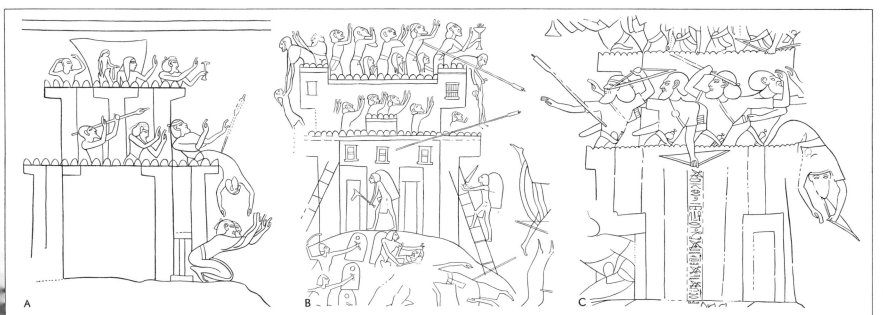

A   B   C

154

152, 153 / *The 'Wilderness of Kadesh'.* 153: The exhausted traveller resting in the shade of a broom bush recalls the story of Elijah (I K 19:4). **154**/*Fortresses of Canaan.* Egyptian bas-reliefs enable us to form an idea of the fortresses which prevented the Israelites from entering Canaan directly from the south. Observe the double walls; the inner wall is probably that of the citadel. 154A: Detail from a bas-relief in a temple of Rameses II at *Abû Simbel.* The defenders are yielding; behind the woman and child is the flag (shaped like a sail) of the city. 154B: Capture of Ashkelon by Rameses II. Outside the city, the Egyptians are killing the last of the soldiers; inside the city, one of whose gates is being broken in, the defenders beg for mercy, offering children as hostages or (*right*) burning incense as a sign of submission. 154C: Siege of Kadesh (Kedesh in Galilee?) by Seti I.   [*Maps 9 and 10, p. 44*]

155 / *The Arnon*. This photograph is intended to give the reader an idea of what the translations of the Bible sometimes describe as the 'brook' Arnon! It is in fact a deep gorge bisecting the highlands to the east of the Dead Sea. At the point south of Dibon where this photograph was taken, the gorge is about 2½ miles wide and the river-bed lies 1,650 feet below the top of the cliffs. We can understand why, in the Bible, the Arnon is nearly always mentioned as a frontier, usually as the southern frontier of Transjordan, sometimes with the majestic Hermon (Pl. 361) as the northern frontier (Dt 3:8). The boy is on the right bank, looking towards the land of the Moabites, whose king, Mesha, proudly recorded on his famous stele (Pl. 229) that he had built a road along the Arnon. **156, 157** / *The Arnon near its Entry into the Dead Sea*.

[Maps 11, p. 59; 14, p. 65]

160

158–160 / *Scene of the Entry of the Hebrews into Canaan.* 160: At bottom left the winding Jordan is still nearly 17 miles from the Dead Sea, which can be seen at top right as far as its salt peninsula. The arid valley of the Jordan is about 12 miles wide at this point. The dark patches are oases. The figure 4 marks the tell of Jericho (Pls. 38 and 172); 3 shows the vicinity of Gilgal, while the region around 2 on the opposite bank is called the 'plains of Moab' in the Bible. 1 indicates Mount Nebo, on the edge of the highlands; it is seen at closer range in 159. 158: A backwater of the Jordan, near the present *Tell ed-Dâmiyeh* (the Biblical Adam, Jos 3:16), formed some centuries ago when part of the steep marl bank, undermined by the swift current, collapsed into the river and blocked its course for several hours. [Map 14, p. 65]

161
I
166

0   10

THE SETTLEMENT IN CANAAN

After the events on Mount Sinai, Moses led his people to the north, towards the Promised Land. Chapter 33 of the book of Numbers summarises the whole of the journey through the wilderness, dividing it into forty stages, very much in the spirit of the Priestly Code which we have just been discussing (p. 53). This summary repeats part of an account already given in the preceding pages of the Bible; but for the final stages of the journey it contains a number of place-names which are not found elsewhere in the Bible. The majority of Biblical scholars consider that it is impossible to identify these places. Father Abel did, however, attempt to reconstruct the route from Mount Sinai to Kadesh-barnea, basing his hypothesis on information about natural stopping-places and the names applied to them by the nomads of today, which he and his colleagues of the French Dominican School in Jerusalem had collected in the course of their journeys in this region.

Whatever view we may take of these identifications, with Kadesh-barnea we are once again on firm ground: the situation of this oasis is beyond dispute. The name survives in that of the spring of '*Ain Qedeis*; and a short distance away there are two further springs, '*Ain Qedeirât* and '*Ain Quseima*. To the Israelites, who had journeyed down from the heart of the Sinai peninsula through the parched desert of Paran, this area of springs must have seemed a very attractive oasis.

From Kadesh, Moses appears to have attempted an invasion of the Promised Land; but the attack failed before Arad, a well-fortified town in the north of the Negeb. So the Israelites settled down in the region of the springs, where they appear to have spent several years. We may assume that they built huts near their tents and thus began to follow a settled way of life.

The geographical details of the next stages of the Exodus are not clear, and their interpretation is not agreed. The following would be a plausible sequence of events: the Edomites having refused to allow them to pass through their territory, the Hebrews must have made their way first in the direction of the Gulf of 'Aqaba and, from there, moved northwards along the broad valley of the Ara-

bah. On reaching the Dead Sea, they veered to the east, doubtless following the majestic canyon of the 'brook of the willows' (Zered). By-passing Moab, they then entered the area north of the Arnon, and finally (here all the texts are in agreement) 'encamped in the plains of Moab beyond the Jordan at Jericho'. The local rulers of the region between the Arnon and the Jabbok were defeated, and a few Israelite clans settled in their territory.

The Pentateuch closes with an unforgettable scene: at God's bidding, Moses ascends the slopes of Mount Nebo and, from the summit, he surveys the whole of the Promised Land. 'And the Lord said to him, "This is the land of which I swore to Abraham, to Isaac, and to Jacob, 'I will give it to your descendants'. I have let you see it with your eyes, but you shall not go over there." ' Then Moses dies, at the age of 120 years, but 'his eye was not dim, nor his natural force abated'.

The period which now follows is treated in the books of Joshua and Judges. We have already seen that the Jews classified these works among the prophetic writings (see p. 27). This means that their compilers assembled and worked over the documents with the idea of using this presentation of memorable events in the history of Israel as a vehicle for preaching the faith, and, from this point of view, few books of the Bible have so simple a structure.

The first of these works tells of the invasion of Canaan, the fall of Jericho, and the conquest of first the southern and then the northern part of the country. Joshua then apportions the land among the tribes and, his task accomplished, dies 'a hundred and ten years old'. It may be observed from a careful reading of this book, however, that the writers who determined its final shape had at their disposal a wide variety of documents belonging to different periods and milieux. They respected these documents, with no thought of the repetitions, or even the contradictions, that this might entail. For example, we are on several occasions told that Joshua conquered the whole country and utterly destroyed its people. But we subsequently learn that there were a number of places which the Israelites were unable to wrest from the Canaanites, who continued to occupy them until

167
168
169
170
171

161 / *Liver of an Animal (terracotta).* The liver, often referred to in the Bible as the seat of life and the emotions, was used for divination in Babylon (Ezk 21:21). The above model, found in Palestine, was no doubt used as an amulet. **162–166** / *Terracotta Statues of the Goddess of Fertility.* Such statues have been recovered from excavated sites all over Palestine, at the Israelite as well as at the earlier Canaanite levels. They throw light on the action of the prophets against Ashtoreth. The Egyptian coiffure of 163 and 164 and the lotus flowers of 164 and 165 reveal the composite character of the civilisation. **167–171** / *Bronze Idols.* After being cast in moulds, they were chased and sometimes covered with gold leaf (cf. Is 40:19, 'a goldsmith overlays it with gold'; and Jer 10:1–5). 167 and 171: Two views of the same idol; 168 and 170 are Phoenician Baals; 169 has an Egyptian coiffure.

a later period, when they were finally conquered and subjugated. Chapters 13 to 21 (the portions of the tribes; see pp. 58–61) record hardly a single Israelite town in the centre of Palestine; and there is no description of the conquest of this part of the Promised Land. Yet Joshua built an altar to Yahweh on Mount Ebal, and it was at Shechem that he reaffirmed the Covenant.

*Jos 8: 30
24*

The first chapter of the book of Judges provides a certain amount of information about the results of the conquest. After an introduction (Judges 2:6–3:6), there then follows a series of brief narratives which strike us, even at first reading, by their composite character and their diversity of style. The story of Gideon, for example, is manifestly made up of two accounts of the same facts. The exploits of Deborah and Barak are described first in prose and then in the famous 'Song of Deborah', believed to be the older of the two versions. The collection of various traditions about the six major Judges, and brief accounts of the six minor Judges, are presented in the framework of a religious history.

The delicate task of reconciling the mass of data embodied in the traditions of the books of Joshua and Judges with the results of excavation, in order to form a comprehensive picture, raises problems which are still the subject of controversy. Here we must confine ourselves to a broad outline of the sequence of events. With the capture of Jericho and Ai, Joshua established a bridge-head which was to afford the Israelites easy access into the mountains of Ephraim. Certain Biblical scholars believe that they found there some of their kinsmen, who had remained in the area after an earlier occupation of the region of Shechem by Hebrew clans. It is thought that traces of this occupation are preserved in the book of Genesis. The treaty with Gibeon and the neighbouring towns proves that Joshua did not take all the towns by force of arms, or destroy all their inhabitants. In any case, he was not the only military leader: the capture of Hebron is attributed to Caleb, and that of Debir, another important town in the south, to Othniel. Joshua himself fought against various coalitions of Canaanite kings, both in the southern mountains and in Galilee.

In any event, at the time of Joshua's death we cannot talk of a complete conquest. Between the mountains of Judah and those of Ephraim stood Jerusalem, the fortress of the Jebusites; and in the northwest of the region lived the Gibeonites and their allies. The northern tribes were separated from the rest by the plain of Jezreel and its well-fortified towns; the Israelites did not dare to enter the plain where the Canaanites could use their chariots, nor could they prevent the 'Peoples of the Sea' from occupying the coastal zone.

The period following the death of Joshua is presented in the Bible as a crucial time for Israel. The tribes were held together only by their faith in Yahweh and by the symbol of His presence, the Ark of the Covenant, venerated at Shiloh. This organisation has been rightly compared to the amphictyonies of Greece and Italy, which were formed by the religious confederation of a number of tribes (sometimes twelve) around a particular shrine, as at Delphi. The comparison is valid only on the sacral plane. Other features are peculiar to Israel: for example, the occasional emergence in periods of danger of outstanding figures, the Judges, who, by the special grace of God, re-established His rights through their victorious leadership of their tribe or clan.

The writer of the Epistle to the Hebrews gives the following description of the deeds of these leaders: 'And what more shall I say? For time would fail me to tell of Gideon, Barak, Samson, Jephthah, of David and Samuel and the prophets – who through faith conquered kingdoms, enforced justice, received promises, stopped the mouths of lions, quenched raging fire, escaped the edge of the sword, won strength out of weakness, became mighty in war, put foreign armies to flight'. Their activities could not be better summarised. For the word 'judge' is liable to be misleading; and we must beware of thinking of them as magistrates who exercised a well-defined authority. The term 'liberator-prophet' would perhaps come nearest to suggesting their rôle: they were, it is true, primarily military and political leaders, but in the process of defending the tribes against the Canaanites they became champions of the faith.

He 11: 32-34

Their influence remained purely local, however, even when they succeeded in uniting several tribes in the face of the enemy. In any case, these alliances did not always prove effective, as the 'Song of Deborah' complains: 'Why did you tarry among the sheepfolds, to hear the piping for the flocks?... Asher sat still at the coast of the sea, settling down by his landings.' Only under the threat of the Philistines did the tribes submit to a closer political bond.

Ju 5: 16-17

Palestinian archaeology places the destruction of the various Canaanite settlements at the close of the thirteenth century B.C. Thus, if the destructive Philistine attack at Aphek (ca 1050 B.C.; see p. 67) is regarded as marking its close, the period of the Judges must have lasted for nearly 200 years.

Map 14 (p. 65) shows only those places which figure in the Biblical traditions of the period of Joshua and the Judges. A complete historical map for these centuries would look extremely crowded and might confuse the ordinary reader of the Bible, for whom this Atlas is primarily intended.

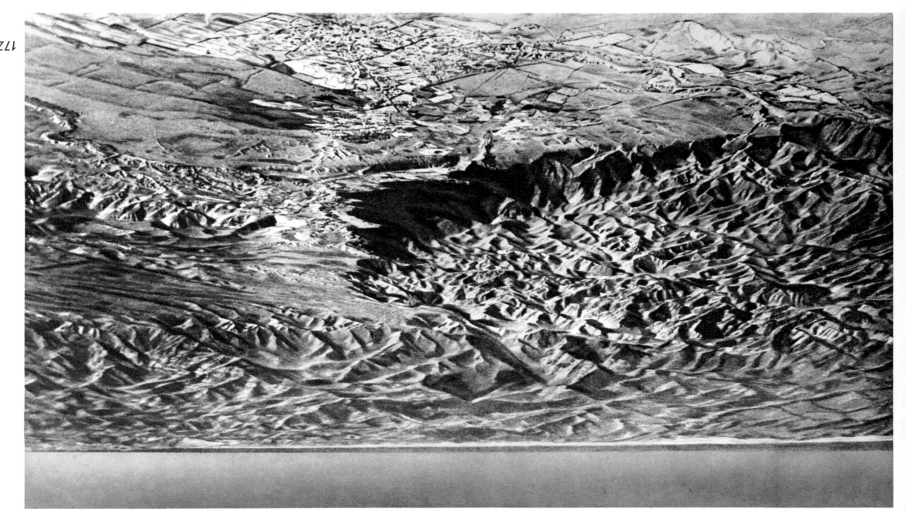

172 / View over the Whole Breadth of Palestine. An aerial photograph of about 1930 taken at a very great height. A comparison with Pl. 160 shows that aerial photography had not then reached its present technical perfection; it is hard to say exactly where truth ends and retouching begins. But it does, nevertheless, give us a striking impression of the Palestinian highlands: in the foreground is the western edge of the Jordan valley, with the houses, gardens, and roads of the present Jericho just above the dark oval mound of the *Tell es-Sultân* (Pl. 38). The steep mountain face shown on Pls. 309 and 310 can be clearly discerned; behind it, to the left, lies the desert of Judah. We can see why, as is indicated on Map 14, Joshua entered the mountains by a detour in order to reach Ai. In the distance is the Mediterranean, edged with dunes. [Map 14, p. 65]

JOSHUA 13—21: THE PORTIONS OF THE TWELVE TRIBES [MAPS 11, 12, and 13]

Even the most assiduous reader of the Bible will frankly admit that when he comes to Chapter 13 of Joshua he skips a few pages. Indeed, these interminable lists of apparently meaningless place-names hardly appear calculated to hold the reader's attention. But this passage is, none the less, an integral part of the Scriptures, and certainly no Biblical Atlas can afford to ignore the only chapters in the Bible which are expressly concerned with geography. We shall therefore attempt to introduce a little order into this mass of data and to make it easier for the reader to survey.

The compiler of the book of Joshua has recorded the territories and towns to which each tribe was entitled. After an introduction dealing with the regions still to be conquered, he recalls that, in Transjordan, Moses had already allocated to two tribes and to half of a third the lands which were to be theirs. He then passes to the division of Cisjordan, under the direction of Joshua, at first probably at Gilgal, where Judah and the descendants of Joseph cast lots for their portions, and afterwards at Shiloh where the remaining tribes were assembled. Finally comes the proclamation of the cities of refuge and the cities allotted to the Levites. This whole body of information may therefore most appropriately be described as a national register, or record, of the lands held by the twelve tribes.

For his very methodical survey the compiler has drawn upon a wide variety of documents. A glance at the map opposite, based *exclusively* on Chapters 13–21 of Joshua, shows that he had such a mass of detailed information about the territory allotted to Judah that, for greater clarity, it has been necessary to include a special map of this region (Map 13, p. 60). For Ephraim and Manasseh, on the other hand, he could give only approximate boundaries, and mentions no towns. For the

northern tribes, he worked sometimes from a list of towns, sometimes from records of boundaries, and sometimes from a more or less effective combination of the two.

For the reader's convenience, we give below a table of all the place-names in Joshua 13–21, arranged in their Biblical order. All the sites marked on Maps 11, 12, or 13 (pp. 59, 60) are printed *in italics*. It can thus be seen at a glance that the situation of many towns is still unknown. On the maps, when the location of a site is *certain* the name appears without an accompanying symbol. In the other cases a red ‡ or † warns the reader that the localisation is, respectively, *probable*, or no more than *possible*. These pages and maps are in themselves an illustration of the technique of Biblical geography (see pp. 19ff.). We have distinguished between tells and places which are still inhabited; and this serves to call attention to the fact that the majority of the Biblical towns still lie buried beneath the sand of centuries. At the same time, the infrequent appearance on these maps of the symbol indicating excavation shows how few tells have been systematically investigated. Both in the tables below and on the maps, we have indicated the places which played some part in Biblical history. The fact that these chapters are a record of the tribal portions is thereby further emphasised, while a comparison of the territories of the tribes thus indicated serves to show the main scenes of those events which the Israelite historians felt it their duty to record for future generations.

The translation of a number of the place-names – a very modest attempt – may suggest the memories they stirred in the minds of the Israelites, and also help to explain the recurrence of certain names in different places.

13:1–7: THE LAND WHICH REMAINS TO BE POSSESSED (MAP 12)

Now Joshua was old and advanced in years; and the Lord said to him, "You are old and advanced in years, and there remains yet very much land to be possessed. This is the land that yet remains: all the regions of the Philistines and those of the Geshurites (from the Shihor, which is east of Egypt, northward to the boundary of Ekron, it is reckoned as Canaanite; there are five rulers of the Philistines, those of Gaza, Ashdod, Ashkelon, Gath, and Ekron), and those of the Avvim, in the south, all the land of the Canaanites, and Mearah which belongs to the Sidonians,

to Aphek, to the boundary of the Amorites, and the land of the Gebalites, and all Lebanon toward the sunrising, from Baal-gad below Mount Hermon to the entrance of Hamath, all the inhabitants of the hill country from Lebanon to Misrephoth-maim, even all the Sidonians. I will myself drive them out before the people of Israel; only allot the land to Israel for an inheritance, as I have commanded you. Now therefore divide this land for an inheritance to the nine tribes and half the tribe of Manasseh."

13:15–23 PORTION OF REUBEN

▲ Aroer	▲ Jahaz	▲ Beth-peor
▲ Medeba	▲ Kedemoth	p ○ Beth-jeshimoth
▲ Heshbon	p ○ Mephaath	
p ○ Dibon	p ○ Kiriathaim	
▲ Bamoth-baal	p ○ Sibmah	
p ∅ Beth-baal-meon	+ Zereth-shahar	

13:24–28 PORTION OF GAD

▲ Jazer	+ Betonim	∅ Beth-haram
▲ Aroer	▲ Mahanaim	∅ Beth-nimrah
▲ Heshbon	+ Lidebir	▲ Succoth
+ Ramath-mizpeh	(= ▲ Lo-debar)	▲ Zaphon

13:29–31 PORTION OF HALF THE TRIBE OF MANASSEH

▲ Villages of Jair	▲ Ashtaroth	▲ Edrei

15 PORTION OF JUDAH (see p. 61)

16–17 PORTION OF EPHRAIM AND MANASSEH

Delimitation

▲ Jericho	▲ Ataroth-addar	+ Janoah
▲ Bethel (Luz)	▲ Upper Beth-horon	∅ Naarah
▲ Lower Beth-horon	+ Michmethath	× Tappuah
▲ Gezer	+ Taanath-shiloh	+ Brook Kanah

Towns in Issachar and Asher

▲ Beth-shan	▲ Dor	▲ Taanach
▲ Ibleam	▲ En-dor	▲ Megiddo

KEY TO THE SYMBOLS

▲ Figures in Biblical history

+ Mentioned only in Jos 13–21

× Mentioned only in Jos 13–21, but with variants

○ Mentioned only in Jos 13–21 and similar lists

∅ Mentioned in these lists, but with variants

p Mentioned only in Jos 13–21 and prophetic texts

18 PORTION OF BENJAMIN (see p. 61)

19:1–9 PORTION OF SIMEON

▲ Beer-sheba	∅ Bethuel	× Sharuhen
× Sheba (Shema)	▲ Hormah	∅ En-rimmon
○ Moladah	▲ Ziklag	∅ Ether
○ Hazar-shual	+ Beth-marcaboth	∅ Ashan
∅ Balah	∅ Hazar-susah	+ Baalath-beer
○ Ezem	× Beth-lebaoth	∅ Ramah of the
∅ Eltolad		Negeb

19:10–16 PORTION OF ZEBULUN

Delimitation and towns

+ Sarid (Shadud)	+ Japhia	+ Valley of Iphtahel
+ Mareal	▲ Gath-hepher	∅ Kattath
+ Dabbesheth	+ Eth-kazin	∅ Nahalal
○ Jokneam	∅ Rimmon	▲ Shimron
× Daberath	+ Neah	+ Idalah
× Chisloth-tabor	+ Hannathon	▲ Bethlehem

19:17–23 PORTION OF ISSACHAR

Delimitation and towns

▲ Jezreel	+ Rabbith	+ Beth-pazzez
× Chesulloth	+ Kishion	▲ Mt Tabor
▲ Shunem	+ Ebez	+ Shahazumah
+ Hapharaim	∅ Remeth	+ Beth-shemesh
+ Shion	+ En-gannim	
+ Anaharath	+ En-haddah	

19:24–31 PORTION OF ASHER

Delimitation and towns

+ Helkath	+ Shihor-libnath	+ Kanah
+ Hali	+ Beth-dagon	+ Ramah
+ Beten	+ Beth-emek	+ Hosah
▲ Achshaph	+ Neiel	∅ Mahalab (Hebel)
+ Allammelech	▲ Kabul	○ Achzib
+ Amad	∅ Ebron (Abdon)	▲ Ummah (Acco)
+ Mishal	○ Rehob	○ Aphek
▲ Mt Carmel	+ Hammon	

19:32–39 PORTION OF NAPHTALI

Delimitation and towns

+ Heleph	+ Ziddim	+ Edrei
+ Zaanannim	+ Zer	+ En-hazor
+ Adami-nekeb	× Hammath	+ Yiron
+ Jabneel	+ Rakkath	+ Migdal-el
+ Lakkum	▲ Chinnereth	+ Horem
+ Aznoth-tabor	▲ Adamah	○ Beth-anath
+ Hukkok	+ Ramah	○ Beth-shemesh
	▲ Hazor	
	▲ Kedesh	

19:40–48 PORTION OF DAN (see p. 61)

20:1–9 CITIES OF REFUGE

Kedesh in Galilee
Shechem in the hill country of Ephraim
Hebron in the hill country of Judah
Bezer in the wilderness
Ramoth-gilead
Golan in Bashan

21:1–45 LEVITICAL CITIES

JUDAH AND SIMEON:	DAN:	NAPHTALI:
Hebron	Eltekeh	Kedesh
Libnah	Gibbethon	Hammoth-dor
Jattir	Aijalon	(Hammath)
Eshtemoa	Gath-rimmon	Kartan (Rakkath)
Holon		
Debir	MANASSEH:	ZEBULUN:
Ashan (Ain)	Taanach	Jokneam
Juttah	Ibleam	Kartah
Beth-shemesh	Golan	Dimnah (Rimmono)
	Beeshterah	Nahalal
BENJAMIN:	(Ashtaroth)	
Gibeon		REUBEN:
Geba	ISSACHAR:	Bezer
Anathoth	Kishion	Jahaz
Almon	Daberath	Kedemoth
	Jarmuth	Mephaath
EPHRAIM:	En-gannim	
Shechem		GAD:
Gezer	ASHER:	Ramoth
Kibzaim	Mishal	Mahanaim
Beth-horon	Abdon	Heshbon
	Helkath	Jazer
	Rehob	

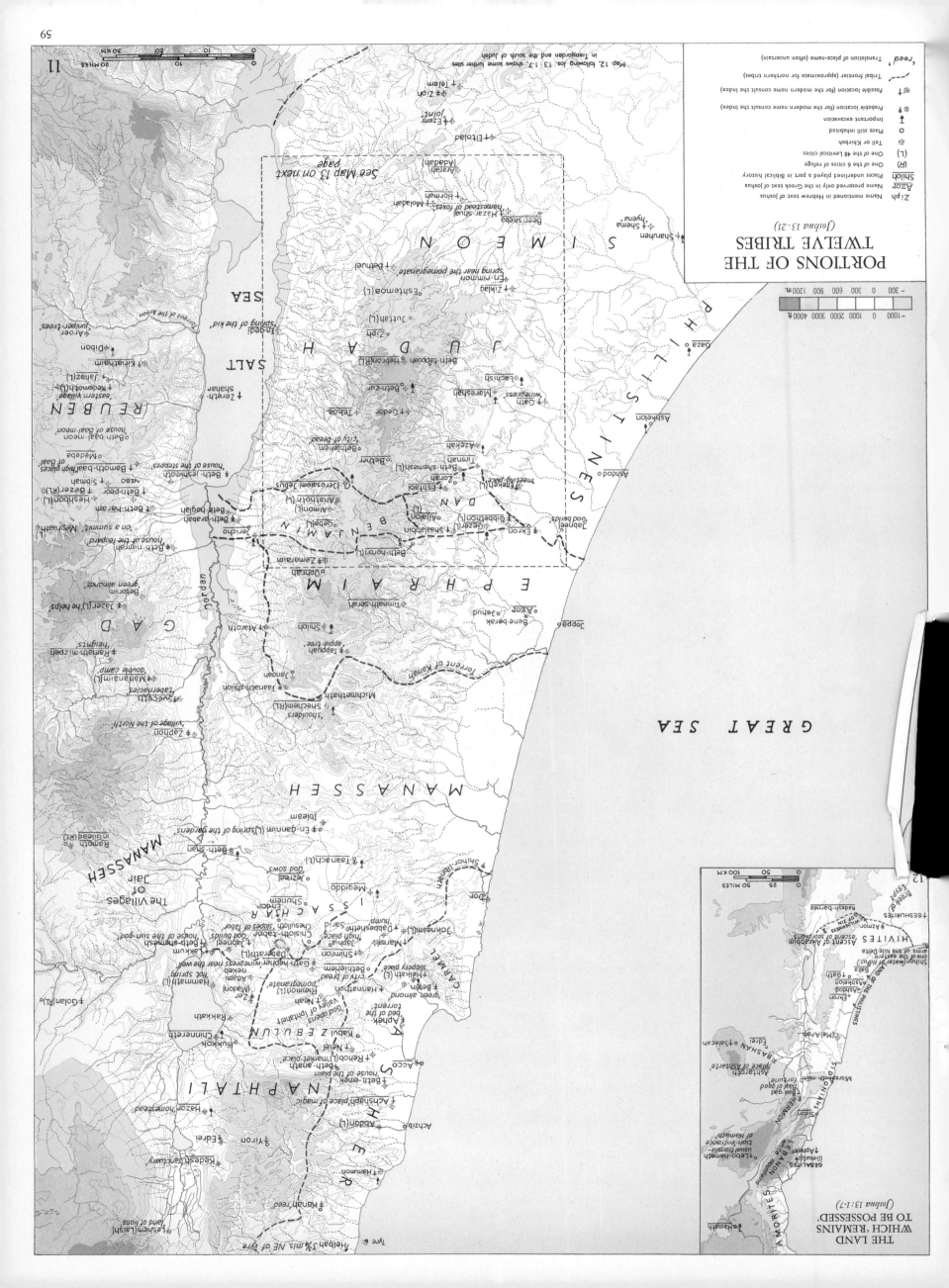

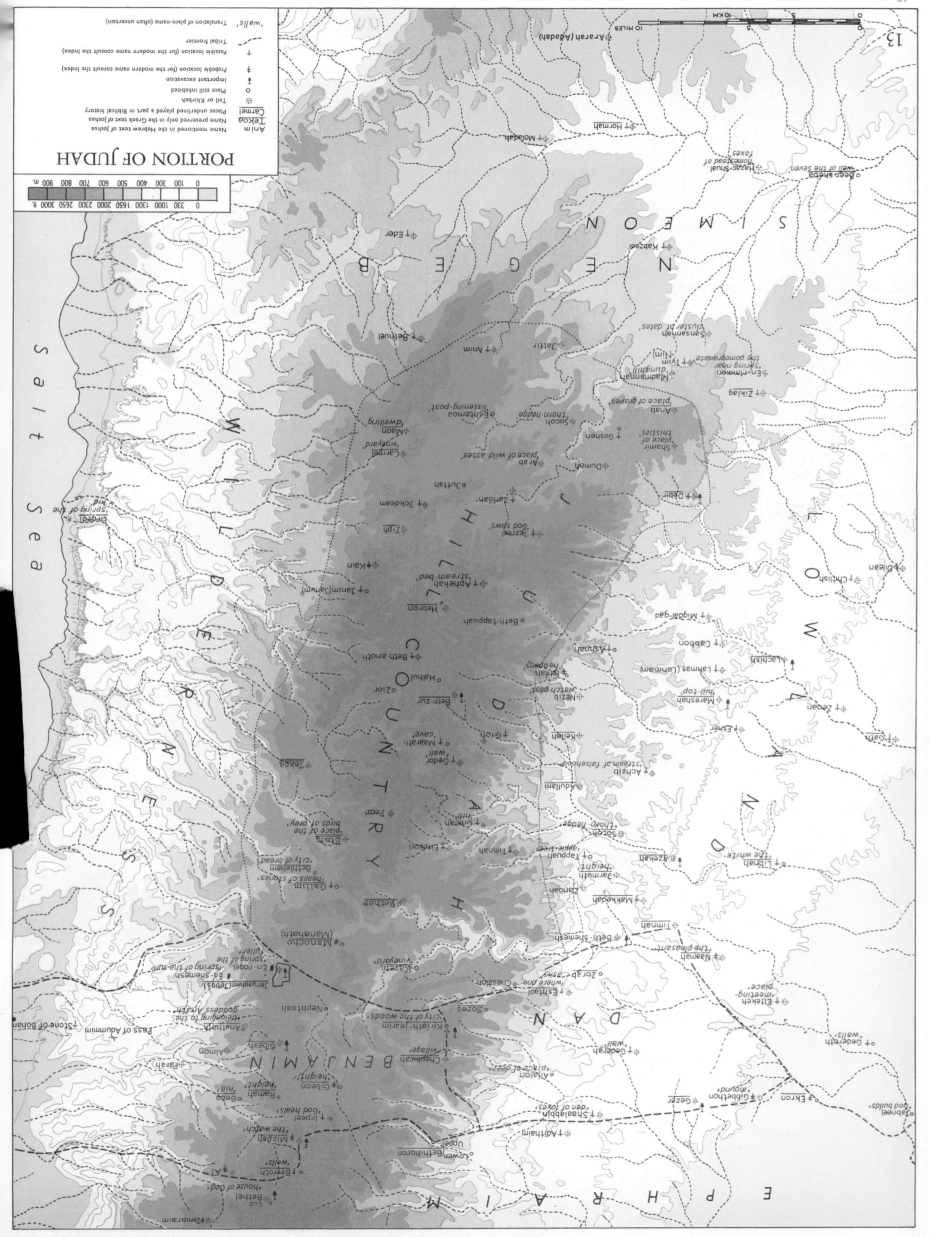

CONTINUATION OF THE PORTIONS OF THE TWELVE TRIBES [MAP 13]

PORTION OF JUDAH

Joshua 15:1–12: Frontiers

○ Ascent of Akrabbim × Gilgal
▲ Zin (wilderness) + Ascent of ▲ Baalah
▲ Kadesh-barnea Adummim (Kiriath-jearim)
+ Hezron + En-shemesh + Mt Seir
∅ Addar ▲ En-rogel + Chesalon
+ Karka ▲ Valley of the son ▲ Beth-shemesh
∅ Azmon of Hinnom ▲ Timnah
+ Beth-hoglah (Map 33, p. 115) + Ekron
+ Beth-arabah ▲ Jebus (Jerusalem) + Shikkeron
+ Debir + Waters of ▲ Mt Baalah
+ Stone of Bohan Nephtoah ▲ Jabneel
▲ Hebron

Joshua 15:21–32: Portion of Judah in the Negeb

▲ Kabzeel + Hazor-haddattah ∅ Baalah
+ Eder + Kerioth + Iyim (Iim)
+ Jagur + Hezron (i.e. ○ Ezem
+ Kinah Hazor) ∅ Eltolad
× Dimonah + Amam ∅ Chesil (Bethuel)
+ Adadah (Ararah, + Shema ▲ Hormah
Adanah) ○ Moladah ▲ Ziklag
▲ Kedesh (Kadesh- + Hazar-gaddah + Madmannah
barnea) + Heshmon + Sansannah
+ Hazor + Beth-pelet × Lebaoth
+ Ziph ○ Hazar-shual + Shilhim
+ Telem ▲ Beer-sheba ○ En-rimmon
+ Bealoth

Joshua 15:33–47: Portion of Judah in the Lowland

▲ Eshtaol + Gederothaim + Beth-dagon
▲ Zorah p Zenan + Naamah
+ Ashnah + Hadashah ▲ Makkedah
▲ Zanoah + Migdal-gad ▲ Libnah
+ En-gannim + Dilean + Ether
+ Tappuah + Mizpeh ∅ Ashan
+ Enam + Joktheel + Iphtah
▲ Jarmuth ▲ Lachish + Ashnah
▲ Adullam ▲ Bozkath + Nezib
▲ Socoh ▲ Eglon + Keilah
+ Azekah + Cabbon p Achzib
▲ Shaaraim + Lahmas (Lahmam) ▲ Mareshah
+ Adithaim + Chitlish ▲ Ekron
+ Gederah ▲ Gederoth ▲ Ashdod

Joshua 15:48–60: Portion of Judah in the Hill Country

+ Shamir + Eshan + Zanoah
▲ Jattir + Janim (Janum) + Kain
+ Socoh + Beth-tappuah + Gibeah
+ Dannah + Aphekah ▲ Timnah
▲ Kiriath-sannah + Humtah + Halhul
(i.e. Debir) ▲ Kiriath-arba ▲ Beth-zur
▲ Anab (i.e. Hebron) + Gedor
▲ Eshtemoh ▲ Maon p Maarath
▲ Anim ▲ Carmel + Beth-anoth
+ Goshen + Ziph + Eltekon
∅ Holon + Juttah ▲ Kiriath-baal (i.e.
▲ Giloh ▲ Jezreel Kiriath-jearim)
+ Arab + Jokdeam + Rabbah
+ Dumah

Joshua 15:61–62: Portion of Judah in the Wilderness

+ Beth-arabah + Secacah + City of Salt
+ Middin + Nibshan ▲ En-gedi

Joshua 15:59b according to the Septuagint

▲ Tekoa + Koulon + Gallim
▲ Ephrathah + Tatam + Bether
+ Peor + Sores + Manocho
▲ Etam ▲ Karem (Manahath)

Joshua 18:11–28 PORTION OF BENJAMIN

Delimitation

▲ Jericho ▲ Kiriath-baal ▲ En-rogel
▲ Beth-aven (i.e. Kiriath- + En-shemesh
-jearim)
▲ Luz (i.e. Bethel) + Waters of + Ascent of Adummim
+ Ataroth-addar Nephtoah + Stone of Bohan
▲ Upper Beth-horon ▲ Valley of the son + Beth-arabah
of Hinnom
(Map 33, p. 115)
▲ Lower Beth-horon ▲ Valley of + Beth-hoglah
Rephaim

Towns

▲ Jericho + Chephar-ammoni + Irpeel
+ Beth-hoglah + Ophni + Taralah
▲ Emek-keziz ▲ Geba + Zela ha-eleph
+ Beth-arabah ▲ Gibeon ▲ Jebus (Jerusalem)
▲ Zemaraim ▲ Ramah ▲ Gibeah
▲ Bethel ▲ Beeroth ▲ Kiriath (abb. of
+ Avvim (Ai) ▲ Mizpah Kiriath-jearim)
+ Almon ▲ Chephirah
▲ Anathoth + Mozah
▲ Parah + Rekem
▲ Ophrah

Joshua 19:40–48 PORTION OF DAN

▲ Zorah + Elon + Me-jarkon
▲ Eshtaol + Ithlah + Baalath
▲ Gezer (frontier) ▲ Timnah + Jehud
▲ Ir-shemesh ▲ Ekron (frontier) + Bene-berak
(=Beth-shemesh) + Eltekeh (frontier) ○ Gath-rimmon
▲ Shaalabbin ▲ Gibbethon + Rakkon
▲ Aijalon ▲ Joppa (frontier)
▲ Leshem (Laish)

KEY TO THE SYMBOLS

▲ Figures in Biblical history
+ Mentioned only in Jos 13–21
× Mentioned only in Jos 13–21, but with variants
○ Mentioned only in Jos 13–21 and similar lists
∅ Mentioned in these lists, but with variants
p Mentioned only in Jos 13–21 and prophetic texts

See also Maps 11 and 12, p. 59

A FRAGMENT OF THE FAMOUS MOSAIC MAP OF MADABA

173

The Salt Lake, which is also called the Asphalt Lake and the Dead Sea

Neapolis, where the well of Jacob is found (the long text quotes from Gn 49:25 and Dt 33:13)

Jericho

The Holy City of Jerusalem

Bethlehem

Jabneel which is also called Jamnia

The heritage of Dan 'Why did he abide with the ships?' (Jg 5:17)

The tomb of Jonah

A few notes have been translated in order to give the reader a general impression. Hellenists will notice that the diphthong OU is often indicated by a sign and that there are numerous abbreviations. There are also mistakes in spelling.

THE IDEA OF A BIBLICAL MAP OF PALESTINE with explanatory notes is not new. As early as the sixth century A.D., an artist had used the floor of a church to construct a map in mosaic. The church was destroyed by the Moslems, but the mosaic remained intact beneath its ruins. In 1890, however, when a new church was built on the site, a local mason, dignified by the high-sounding title of architect, ignorantly destroyed the greater part of the map.

To judge by the little that remains (most of which is reproduced opposite), this was an incalculable loss. The fragment extends from the Mediterranean at the bottom edge to the Dead Sea at the top. The north therefore lies to the left. The territories of the tribes are shown in red letters, often accompanied by a Biblical text. Many sites also carry an inscription of this kind. The size of the towns corresponds to their importance, and the map thus gives an idea of the actual order of precedence of the cities in the sixth century A.D. Jerusalem is particularly large. One can recognise its main street lined with columns, with the entrance to Constantine's basilica prominent in the centre, above Calvary and the Holy Sepulchre.

Each of the villages is portrayed in a different way, and colours are used to evoke the beauties of the Palestinian countryside, the mountains in dark tones and the valleys in light. The Jordan is full of golden fish, and the palms of Jericho are hung with red dates. A gazelle flees from a ferocious beast. Black tracery on the green water of the Dead Sea suggests a storm. But a ship is sailing upon it, and above the ship can be seen a wâdi coming down to the sea through the hill country.

Madaba (Biblical Medeba), the village where the map is to be found, lies to the east of the northern end of the Dead Sea, outside the area covered by the surviving fragments (cf. Map 2, p. 10; Pl. 392).

174/ *The Village of el-Jîb*, believed by many scholars to be the ancient Gibeon. On this assumption, the distant hill on the left, on which stands a mosque dedi-cated to Samuel *(Nebi Samwîl)*, would be the high place of Gibeon (2 S 21:6–9, etc.). 176: View of the village from this hill. **175**/ *Khirbet Seilûn*, with the ruins of ancient Shiloh. **177**/ *The Mountain of Ephraim*, looking west, with the Mediterranean just visible on the horizon. **178**/ *The Village of Tûbas*, which preserves the name of the Biblical Thebez, seen from the northwest. On the left is a hazy view of the Transjordanian plateau. Between the mountain ridges on the right runs the *Wâdi Fâr'ah* (Pl. 63). **179**/ *Tell Zakariyeh* in the Judaean hills, doubtless the Biblical Azekah. At the foot of the tell is part of the 'valley of the terebinth' where David slew Goliath. **180**/ *Yâlo*, formerly Aijalon, the gateway to the mountains of Judah. [*Maps 2, p 10; 14, p. 65*]

181
182

183
184

185
186

181–185 / *The Mortuary Temple of Rameses III*. At the foot of the walls of rock beyond which lies the valley of the royal tombs (Pl. 11), Rameses III erected his mortuary temple (*Medînet Habu*), slightly south of the famous terraced temple of Queen Hatshepsut (**186**). Above are drawings of the façade (182; showing the first pylon, 223 feet wide) and a corner of the first court (181); 185 shows the opposite corner of the court with the pillars of Osiris. The great area of wall-surface is decorated both with reliefs of a religious character and with scenes from Rameses' campaigns. The pictures of the captives are instructive; those in 184, from left to right, are: Libyan, Semite, Hittite, Philistine, and Semite. 183 shows eight Philistines who, according to the inscription, are begging the Pharaoh to spare their lives: 'Grant us breath for our nostrils, O King, son of Amon!'

[*Map 8, p. 43*]

'When I arrived at Byblos, the king sent me this message: "Get thee gone from my harbour! I am neither thy vassal, nor the vassal of him who sent thee to me."' About 1090 B.C. the Egyptian Wenamon was dispatched to Byblos to obtain cedar wood for use in the construction of the sacred boat of Amon-Re at Thebes. He left a very lively description, of which an almost complete copy has been found. The account of his dealings with the king of Byblos serves to demonstrate the decadence of Egypt more effectively than any theoretical argument; for it shows the contempt with which Pharaoh's servants were received in regions formerly ruled with an iron hand. Rameses III's victorious struggle against the 'Peoples of the Sea' (ca 1190 B.C.) was obviously his last great effort. The campaign is commemorated in his vast mortuary temple at *Medînet Habu*, with its impressive bas-reliefs. We reproduce below the famous picture of the naval battle, which is unique in the remains of Egyptian art. The panel measures approximately 20 by 40 feet. The ships on the left-hand side, with a lion's head at the prow, are Egyptian, and so is the one in the centre. The rest contain enemy troops: *Peleset* (Philistines), *Theker* (Zakar, who also later settled along the Palestinian coast south of Carmel) with their very curious helmets, and other representatives of the 'Peoples of the Sea'. The Egyptians are drawing their bows on the enemy, whose long lances leave them powerless to defend themselves. They grapple with the ships: one is about to founder; in another the sailors are surrendering. The survivors are being taken on board the ships and to the shore, where they are marshalled into long files of prisoners. The divine Pharaoh, standing on the heads of the vanquished, dominates the battle with a martial air. The text above his bow, reading from the top left-hand corner, means:

> The good god, Montu in Egypt, / powerful as Baal / in foreign lands, strong of arm, stout / of heart, magnanimous, skilful, / in his strength a bulwark / to protect Egypt so that no other country / can come to harm her, King of Lower and Upper Egypt / Lord of the Two Lands, / Weser-Maat-Re, beloved of Amon. (The names of the king appear in cartouches; cf. Plate 123.)

But the effort of withstanding the 'Peoples of the Sea', coupled with internal disorganisation, exhausted the country. The kings who followed Rameses III, all bearing the name of Rameses, lived at Tanis, whilst at Thebes the priests became increasingly influential. During the following dynasty, the 21st, Egypt was to be convulsed by a schism between north and south and to reach the nadir of her power.

If the Hebrew tribes had nothing to fear in Canaan from this quarter, neither were they threatened by any serious danger from the north. As a result of the long domination of the Kassites, who were a mountain people, the ingenious system of irrigation in southern Mesopotamia had been impaired. All regular cultivation, an essential prerequisite for material and political progress, therefore became impossible. Without meeting any resistance, the Aramaean tribes of the Syrian desert were able to penetrate into the region of Babylon, and extended their incursions as far as the upper reaches of the Euphrates and the Tigris. The Assyrian resurgence during the reign of Tiglath-pileser I (1112–1074 B.C.) was

short-lived and, under his weak successors, Assyria held only a restricted territory for the next two hundred years. Nor, after the collapse of the Hittite empire, was there a power of any importance in Asia Minor. The political climate of the Near East in the twelfth and eleventh centuries B.C. has therefore been very aptly described as 'a dead calm' (Map 8, p. 43).

This state of affairs made possible, in spite of some opposition, the creation of a strong and well-organised Israelite kingdom in Canaan. What actually impelled the tribes of Israel to close their ranks was the expansion of the Philistines, who emerged from their fertile coastal plain in an attempt to conquer the mountain country. In fact the Israelites merely followed the example of their kinsmen in the southeast, where monarchical régimes had already been established in Edom, Moab, and Ammon; and in the north, where the semi-nomadic Aramaeans had begun to follow a settled life and to create petty kingdoms.

This important period in the history of Israel is dealt with in the books of Samuel. Originally, these were in the form of a single volume, which may have been part of a larger whole. A careful reading of the lively and colourful stories in the first book quickly reveals a number of inconsistencies in their composition: in some cases there are two different versions of the same facts, and contradictory opinions on the institution of the monarchy are found side by side. On closer inspection, the work proves to be markedly composite in character. The compilers have included an early account of the fortunes of the Ark of the Covenant in the hands of the Philistines, followed by a cycle of stories about the prophet Samuel, who consecrates the kings in God's name, although according to another tradition he was opposed to the institution of the monarchy. Tales of the adventures of the young David, of his friendship with Jonathan, his difficulties with Saul, and his wandering life are juxtaposed without regard for logical sequence.

By contrast, the second book gives, from the ninth chapter onwards, a very well-arranged account of the rise of the dynasty of David in the face of all kinds of obstacles and family feuds. This narrative is set in a frame, as it were, between the birth of Solomon and his unopposed accession to the throne and could be called: 'How it befell that David was in the end succeeded by Solomon.' It is generally thought to be the work of an eye-witness, an author in David's retinue, who wrote in the reign of Solomon, soon after the happenings he describes. This section is probably the oldest written document in the books of Samuel. The episodes which concern Samuel, Saul, the youth of David, and the fortunes of the Ark were not written down until later, and the final compilation of the two books in their present form may be attributed to scribes of the Deuteronomic school.

The most important of the military operations can be followed on Map 15 (p. 66). After their defeat at Aphek, about 1050 B.C., the tribes which were attacked went to Shiloh to fetch the Ark of the Covenant and then, no doubt reinforced by other tribes, they ventured upon a second battle. This time they were decisively defeated, and the Ark fell into the hands of the Philistines. From then on, the story is devoted to the adventures of this sacred object and does not mention the consequences of the defeat. But excavation at Shiloh has established that at precisely this time the Israelite town was totally destroyed, and, as the Bible

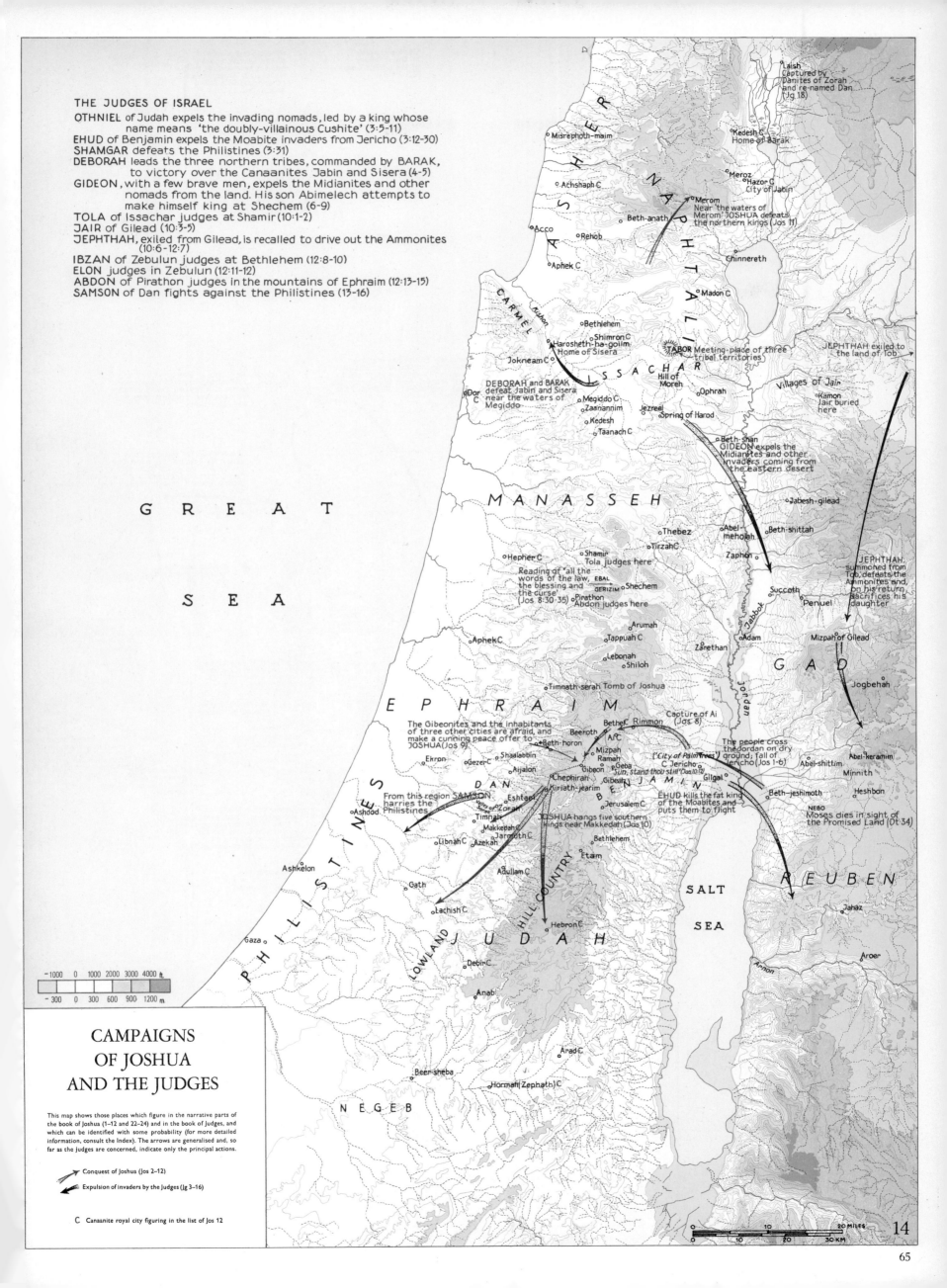

THE JUDGES OF ISRAEL

OTHNIEL of Judah expels the invading nomads, led by a king whose
  name means 'the doubly-villainous Cushite' (3:5-11)
EHUD of Benjamin expels the Moabite invaders from Jericho (3:12-30)
SHAMGAR defeats the Philistines (3:31)
DEBORAH leads the three northern tribes, commanded by BARAK,
  to victory over the Canaanites Jabin and Sisera (4-5)
GIDEON, with a few brave men, expels the Midianites and other
  nomads from the land. His son Abimelech attempts to
  make himself king at Shechem (6-9)
TOLA of Issachar judges at Shamir (10:1-2)
JAIR of Gilead (10:3-5)
JEPHTHAH, exiled from Gilead, is recalled to drive out the Ammonites
  (10:6-12:7)
IBZAN of Zebulun judges at Bethlehem (12:8-10)
ELON judges in Zebulun (12:11-12)
ABDON of Pirathon judges in the mountains of Ephraim (12:13-15)
SAMSON of Dan fights against the Philistines (13-16)

CAMPAIGNS
OF JOSHUA
AND THE JUDGES

This map shows those places which figure in the narrative parts of
the book of Joshua (1–12 and 22–24) and in the book of Judges, and
which can be identified with some probability (for more detailed
information, consult the Index). The arrows are generalised and, so
far as the judges are concerned, indicate only the principal actions.

➤ Conquest of Joshua (Jos 2–12)

➤ Expulsion of invaders by the Judges (Jg 3–16)

C Canaanite royal city figuring in the list of Jos 12

14

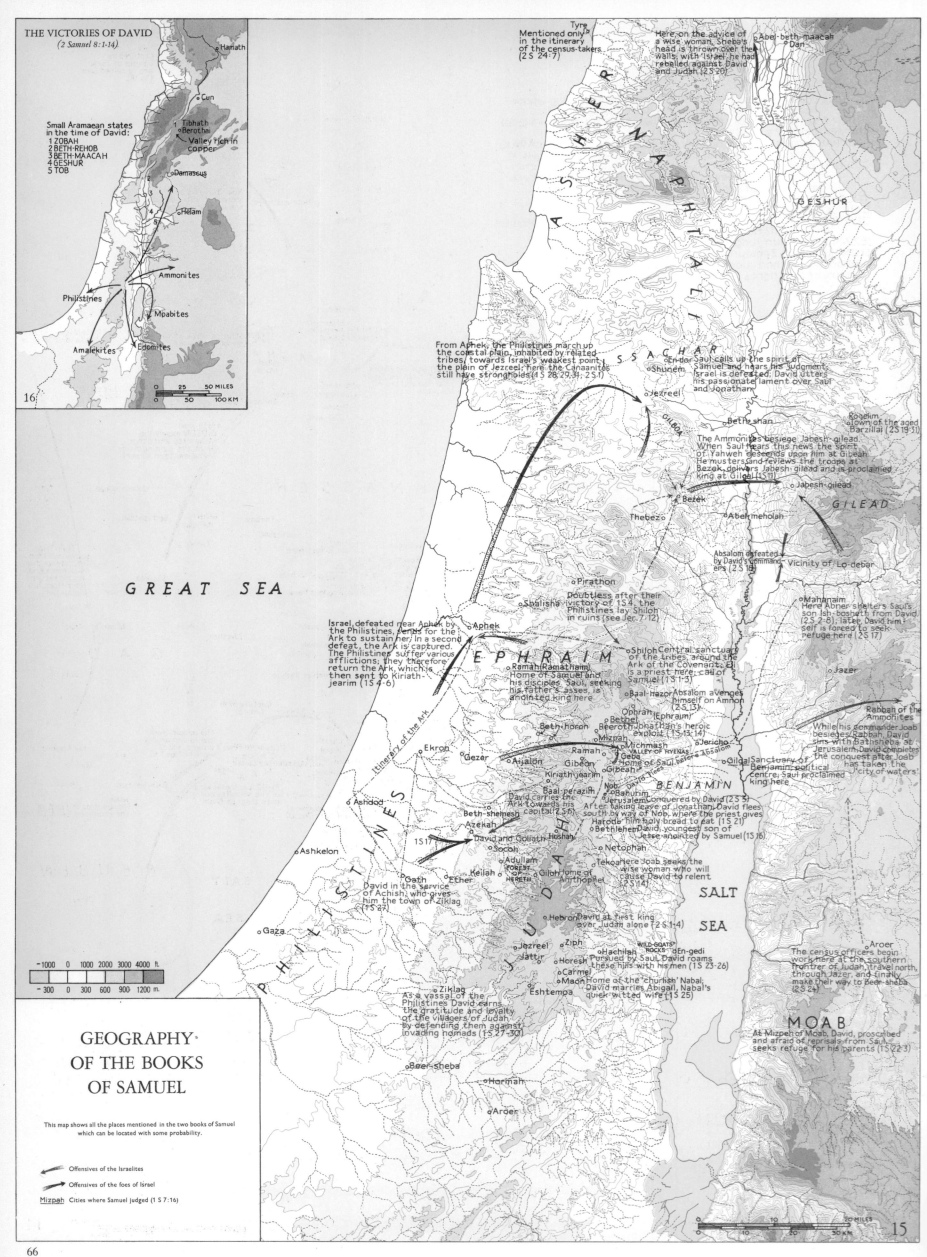

THE VICTORIES OF DAVID
(2 Samuel 8:1-14)

Small Aramaean states
in the time of David:
1 ZOBAH
2 BETH-REHOB
3 BETH-MAACAH
4 GESHUR
5 TOB

Hamath
Cun
Tibhath
Berothai
Valley rich in copper
Damascus
Helam
Ammonites
Philistines
Moabites
Amalekites
Edomites

0   25   50 MILES
0   50   100 KM

16.

GREAT SEA

Tyre
Mentioned only
in the itinerary
of the census-takers
(2 S 24:7)

Here, on the advice of
a wise woman, Sheba's
head is thrown over the
walls; with Israel, he had
rebelled against David
and Judah (2 S 20)

Abel-beth-maacah
Dan

ASHER

NAPHTALI

GESHUR

From Aphek, the Philistines march up
the coastal plain, inhabited by related
tribes, towards Israel's weakest point,
the plain of Jezreel; here the Canaanites
still have strongholds (1 S 28, 29, 31; 2 S 1)

ISSACHAR
Shunem

En-dor Saul calls up the spirit of
Samuel and hears his judgment;
Israel is defeated; David utters
his passionate lament over Saul
and Jonathan

Jezreel
GILBOA
Beth-shan
Rogelim
town of the aged
Barzillai (2 S 19:31)

The Ammonites besiege Jabesh-gilead.
When Saul hears this news the spirit
of Yahweh descends upon him at Gibeah.
He musters and reviews the troops at
Bezek, delivers Jabesh-gilead and is proclaimed
king at Gilgal (1 S 11)

Bezek
Thebez
Abel-meholah
Jabesh-gilead
GILEAD

Absalom defeated
by David's command-
ers (2 S 18)
Vicinity of Lo-debar

Pirathon
Shalisha

Doubtless after their
victory of 1 S 4, the
Philistines lay Shiloh
in ruins (see Jer. 7:12)

Mahanaim
Here Abner shelters Saul's
son Ish-bosheth from David
(2 S 2-6), later David himself is forced to seek
refuge here (2 S 17)

Israel, defeated near Aphek by
the Philistines, sends for the
Ark to sustain her; in a second
defeat, the Ark is captured.
The Philistines suffer various
afflictions; they therefore
return the Ark, which is
then sent to Kiriath-
jearim (1 S 4-6)

Aphek

EPHRAIM

Ramah (Ramathaim)
Home of Samuel and
his disciples. Saul, seeking
his father's asses, is
anointed king here.

Shiloh Central sanctuary
of the tribes, around the
Ark of the Covenant; Eli
is a priest here; call of
Samuel (1 S 1-3)

Jazer

Baal-Hazor Absalom avenges
himself on Amnon
(2 S 13)

Ophrah
(Ephraim)

Bethel
Beeroth Jonathan's heroic
exploit (1 S 13:14)

Beth-horon
Mizpah
Ekron
Gezer

Ramah
Michmash
Geba
Gibeon
Gibeah Home of Saul
Kiriath-jearim

VALLEY OF HYENAS
Jericho
Absalom
Gilgal Sanctuary of
Benjamin; political
centre; Saul proclaimed
king here

Rabbah of
the Ammonites

While his commander Joab
besieges Rabbah, David
sins with Bathsheba at
Jerusalem. David completes
the conquest after Joab
has taken the
'city of waters'

Aijalon

Nob David flees

BENJAMIN

Bahurim
Jerusalem conquered by David (2 S 5)
After taking leave of Jonathan, David flees
south by way of Nob, where the priest gives
him holy bread to eat (1 S 21)
Bethlehem David, youngest son of
Jesse, anointed by Samuel (1 S 16)

Ashdod

Baal-perazim
David carries the
Ark towards his
capital (2 S 6)

Beth-shemesh
Azekah

1 S 17

David and Goliath Hushah

Socoh

Netophah

Tekoa Here Joab seeks the
wise woman who will
cause David to relent
(2 S 14)

Ashkelon

Adullam
FOREST
Keilah
Ether
HERETH
Giloh Home of
Ahithophel

Gath

David in the service
of Achish, who gives
him the town of Ziklag
(1 S 27)

Gaza

Hebron David at first king
over Judah alone (2 S 1-4)

SALT
SEA

JUDAH

Jezreel
Jattir
Ziph
Hachilah
Horesh
Carmel
Maon Home of the 'churlish' Nabal;
David marries Abigail, Nabal's
quick-witted wife (1 S 25)
Eshtemoa

WILD-GOATS'
ROCKS
En-gedi
Pursued by Saul, David roams
these hills with his men (1 S 23-26)

The census officers begin
work here at the southern
frontier of Judah, travel north,
through Jazer, and finally
make their way to Beer-sheba
(2 S 24)

Aroer

Ziklag
As a vassal of the
Philistines David earns
the gratitude and loyalty
of the villagers of Judah
by defending them against
invading nomads (1 S 27-30)

MOAB
At Mizpeh of Moab, David, proscribed
and afraid of reprisals from Saul,
seeks refuge for his parents (1 S 22:3)

Beer-sheba

-1000 0 1000 2000 3000 4000 ft.
-300   0 300   600   900   1200 m.

GEOGRAPHY
OF THE BOOKS
OF SAMUEL

This map shows all the places mentioned in the two books of Samuel
which can be located with some probability.

Offensives of the Israelites

Offensives of the foes of Israel

Mizpah Cities where Samuel judged (1 S 7:16)

Hormah

Aroer

15

shows, four centuries later the memory of the disaster still lingered in men's minds (Jer 26:6). The Philistines obviously exploited their victory to the full. From scattered information in the Biblical account, we may conclude that they gained control of all the mountain region and established many garrisons and strong-points. We also know that they jealously guarded the secret of working in iron which they had learnt from Asia Minor, so that the Israelites found themselves dependent on the occupying power for both tools and weapons (1 S 13:19). This situation lasted for many years and came to an end only when the Ammonites, led by their king, Nahash ('the serpent'), took advantage of the exposed position of the Transjordanian tribes to launch a brutal attack against Jabesh, a city of Gilead. The men of Jabesh sent messengers across the Jordan to seek help. When they arrived in Gibeah, a violent frenzy seized the young peasant Saul. He called to arms all the able-bodied men of every tribe to raise the siege of Jabesh. After mustering at Bezek, they crossed the Jordan and routed the Ammonites; then, following the course of the river, the army marched towards the famous sanctuary of Gilgal, situated out of the reach of the Philistines, where Saul was proclaimed king. As the sole ruler of a people which was henceforward virtually united, he was to bring the struggle against the Philistines to a successful conclusion. But it is easy to discern from the Biblical accounts that the radical transformation of the sacral bond uniting the tribes aroused sharp differences of opinion. However, Saul soon had local successes to his credit and gathered around him a band of valiant warriors, like Jonathan, Abner, and David. We are not told that he established a system of administration, and the excavations at Gibeah have shown that his kingship was marked by little outward splendour.

The disagreements between Saul and Samuel demonstrate that the transition from the old order to the new was not easy. Everyone is familiar with the colourful episodes which resulted from the king's mounting exasperation with David and his attempts to suppress the young hero, who was as handsome as he was courageous and engaging. Saul's hatred led him to murder Ahimelech, the priest of Nob, who had given David the holy bread when he was making his escape to Judah. He then went even further: he massacred all the inhabitants of this little 'city of priests', where the surviving sons of Eli had taken refuge after the devastation of Shiloh. This violent action against the official priesthood may perhaps indicate a backsliding in his allegiance to Yahweh.

Saul's little company of picked men had been successful in its encounters with equally primitive armies, like those of the Ammonites and the nomadic Amalekites, but it was not strong enough to take the field against the well-organised armies of the Philistines. In due course these armies swept across the plain of Sharon, the home of other tribes of the 'Peoples of the Sea', into the valley of Jezreel. This valley, still for the most part held by the Canaanites, was a life-line between the Galilean tribes and the rest, and was the most vulnerable part of the Israelite territory. The Philistines encamped near Shunem, while the Israelite warriors pitched their tents on the slopes of Mount Gilboa. There the life of Saul reached its tragic climax. He realised that the saving power of the Lord of Hosts had been withdrawn from him. In despair, he disguised himself and, with only two companions, went by night to the village of En-dor, making a great détour round the Philistine camp. At En-dor there lived a woman who could summon up the spirits of the dead. She raised the spirit of Samuel, who solemnly confirmed what Saul had long known. The armies joined battle. Three of Saul's sons, including Jonathan, were killed before his eyes. And Saul fell upon his sword (1 S 28 and 31).

Meanwhile, David had gathered around him in the mountains of Judah a band of fearless men, with whom he had long been roaming the countryside, always eluding the pursuit of Saul. He had finally taken refuge with the Philistine king of Gath, who had given him the town of Ziklag. He there succeeded in winning both the confidence of his patron and the sympathy of the inhabitants of the Judaean villages, whom he protected against the incursions of the nomads from the southern desert. He skilfully contrived to extricate himself from the delicate situation in which his double dealing had placed him: he was not after all required to march with the Philistine army to do battle with Saul near Gilboa. His reaction to the news of the defeat (2 S 1:11 ff.) seems completely sincere. The compiler has inserted here David's lament for Saul and Jonathan, taken from the 'Book of the Upright', a collection of old national songs. This song is certainly the work of David: there are few corrupt readings in the manuscript tradition, which is elsewhere less reliable for the two books of Samuel than for most of the books of the Bible. The lament is clearly constructed and beautifully expressed. In a noble yet unpretentious style the young warrior tells of his genuine admiration for Saul and his tender affection for Jonathan:

> Thy glory, O Israel, is slain upon thy high places!
> How are the mighty fallen! . . .
> Ye daughters of Israel, weep over Saul,
> who clothed you daintily in scarlet, . . .
> I am distressed for you, my brother Jonathan . . .
> your love to me was wonderful,
> passing the love of women.

2 S
1:17-27

Although David's immediate reaction to the death of Saul was undoubtedly spontaneous and sincere, the downfall of his rival cannot have surprised him. For years he had been very shrewdly laying his plans. After their victory at Gilboa the Philistines not only regained control of the mountains, but also occupied the north, which was now entirely cut off. In addition, they were threatening Transjordan. Saul had failed to hold back the Philistines. Now a better king was needed, who would be able to free Israel from this menace for ever; and David saw to it that no Judaean should have any doubt who that king must be. When he went to Hebron with his wives and soldiers, immediately after the news of the defeat, he reaped the reward of his patient scheming. In this great city of the south, where the patriarchs were buried and near which the tree of Mamre was still venerated, the Judaeans proclaimed David king, their own king, a Judaean, who would give a better account of himself than the Benjamite Saul. 2 S 2:4

Meanwhile, Abner, one of the generals, who had fled across the Jordan with what remained of the army, caused Saul's only surviving son to be proclaimed king in the town of Mahanaim, recently identified with a tell on the southern side of the deep valley of the Jabbok. The new king was called Ish-baal, 'Baal's man', meaning that he owed allegiance to Yahweh; ba'al means 'lord' or 'master', and was a title given to Yahweh at this time. This explains why, in another text, Saul's son is called Ishvi, perhaps for Ish-yo, 'Yahweh's man'. Later, when the name Baal became restricted to the false heathen god, this element in the name Ish-baal was changed to bosheth, 'shame' (Ish-bosheth). There was now a king of 'Israel', whose territories were almost entirely in the hands of the Philistines, and a king of 'Judah'. The shadow of the future schism already lay over the land. The coming unification was to be superficial and short-lived. 2 S 2:8 1 S 14:49

188 / *The Plain of Jezreel and the Mountains of Gilboa.* A view over the plain, looking southeast from a hill south of Nazareth. At the extreme right are the mountains of Gilboa (Pl. 23 gives a closer view). To their left, the plain slopes down to the Jordan valley, and Transjordan can be seen in the distance. In this corridor, a little lower than the plain, lies the imposing tell of Beth-shan (Pl. 37). Towards the left is the J. Dahi, 'the hill of Moreh' which figures in the story of Gideon (Jg 7:1). Further left, outside the photograph, is Mount Tabor. Modern Jewish agricultural settlements can be seen in the foreground. At the foot of the mountains, in a line across the photograph, are the Biblical sites indicated by arrows, from right to left: *Zer'în*, the ancient Jezreel, which has given its name to the plain (corrupted in Greek to *Esdraelon*); *Sôlem*, the Shunem of the Bible; *Nein*, clearly visible, the Nain of the N.T.; and, at the extreme left, En-dor. [Maps 14, p. 65; 15, p. 66]

THE UNIFICATION UNDER DAVID AND SOLOMON

The early chapters of the second book of Samuel draw a colourful picture of the events which led up to the accession of David as king over all the tribes: fierce battles between the house of David and the house of Saul, Abner's quarrels with his weak master Ish-baal, followed by his secret negotiations with David and, finally, the murder of Abner and Ish-baal. The leaders of the northern tribes confer together. David has convinced the people that he was not responsible for the death of Abner and his brief and skilful lament for this hero circulates among them. No one believes he could have murdered Ish-baal / Ishbosheth either; for the dastardly Beerothite assassins have been punished in exemplary fashion. Meanwhile he has finally taken Saul's daughter Michal as a wife. Everything therefore points to him as Saul's successor on the throne. Envoys from 'Israel' come to Hebron. David accepts the kingship which they offer him. His will be the task of restoring the shattered unity of the confederated tribes, or rather of creating the much surer unity of an organised state.

2 S 3: 33-34

Immediately after these events, we are told how David captured Jerusalem. The compiler of Samuel appears to have found this episode in a different source and interpolated it here; for the text then mentions a Philistine offensive as the consequence of David's consecration as king of all Israel. This latter sequence of events seems probable. The princes of the allied Philistine cities would naturally be well pleased that their vassal of Ziklag should govern only the single tribe of Judah, since his regional authority divided and weakened the federation of the Israelite tribes. The same was true of the king of Mahanaim, whose territory was almost entirely in the hands of the Philistines. But the power which their intelligent and forceful vassal had now acquired over all the tribes seemed altogether too strong to the enemies of Israel, and we learn that a Philistine army at once appeared on the scene 'in search of David'. To this end, it marched into the plain of Rephaim, a broad valley to the west of Jerusalem, which city, in our view, was still held by the Jebusites. The journey from the north to the south of Palestine could be made only along the central mountain ridge, for its sides are broken by many transverse valleys which hinder the traveller's progress. By their manoeuvre the Philistines thus drove a wedge into the newly-formed kingdom. From it they might be able to capture David on the way to his new territories, or at least to prevent the passage of auxiliary troops from the northern tribes.

2 S 5:17

David went to meet them 'with his men', the brothers-in-arms of the long years in the mountains of Judah, whose number and battle strength he had certainly increased during his seven and a half years' reign at Hebron. He knew the military tactics of the Philistines at first hand. The battle ended in a victory for David, and, when shortly afterwards the enemy again took the field, David beat them a second time 'from Gibeon to Gezer', back to their own frontier. The way

2 S 5:21

1 Ch 14:16

in which the memory of these victories was preserved in tradition and the allusion to them in a text of Isaiah, written some three centuries later, prove their importance in the eyes of David's contemporaries, who saw them as a turning-point in the history of Israel. After this time there is no further mention of Philistine invasions. The remains of outer walls with casemates, unearthed at *Tell Beit Mirsim* and Beth-shemesh, and attributed by archaeologists to this period, show that a chain of fortresses was constructed. The battles mentioned in a later enumeration of the exploits of David's heroic men seem all to have taken place in Philistine territory. The initiative had thus passed to David, who was now free to organise his state.

Is 2

One of his first actions was to capture Jerusalem. The position of this old Canaanite city threatened the unity of his kingdom, and it had therefore to be rendered harmless. But David, who was a shrewd politician, also planned to make it his capital. Hebron certainly had a prior claim and could boast tangible relics of the sojourn of the patriarchs. Unfortunately it was situated too far to the south, and if David resided in the middle of the territory of Judah he could never hope to exert any influence over the other tribes. Shechem also had an ancient title to the honour and a unique situation in the geographical centre of the kingdom. But this choice would have displeased the Judaeans. It was unquestionably on account of the jealousy and latent hostility between North and South that David chose the 'neutral' fortress of the Jebusites, in a central position between the two halves of the kingdom, as his capital and place of residence. This was a very ancient city. Its name has been found on one of the potsherds which an Egyptian of about 2000 B.C. covered with the names of enemy cities and individuals; he would then have broken the clay to pieces in a sacred place and, by this magic rite, sealed the doom of cities and individuals alike. The name next occurs in some letters from the *El-Amarna* archives, in which the prince Abdi-Khipa ('servant of Khipa', the Hurrian goddess) reports to his Egyptian master Akhenaton on the political situation about 1365 B.C. He writes from his town of Urusalim 'which I did not receive from my father or my mother, but from thy hand'.

For a very long time people were mistaken about the exact situation of the old Jebusite city. A Christian tradition, which can be traced back to the second century, placed the upper room of the Last Supper and of the events of Pentecost on the southwestern hill of Jerusalem, the upper town of that time (Map 33, p. 115). This was thought to be the new Zion, in contrast to the old Zion which had borne the Temple and had now forfeited its rights. The basilica built in this place about the year A.D. 400 was thus given the name 'Sancta Sion'. It was the 'mother of all the churches', because it was from here that the Gospel spread throughout the world, as Isaiah had prophesied: 'Out of Zion shall go forth the law.' In

189

190

189, 190 / *Scene of Jonathan's Exploit.* Owing to the stability of place-names in the East, the scene of the story in 1 S 14 can be precisely located. About 6 miles NNE of Jerusalem are the villages of *Jeba'* and *Mukhmâs*, nearly 1½ miles apart and separated by a valley which, sloping down to the Jordan towards the east, quickly narrows to a wild gorge with almost vertical cliffs. The scene of the battle can be easily identified despite the disappearance of the names Bozez and Seneh, and the confusion in the textual tradition between Geba and the nearby Gibeah. 189 is a view taken from the NW; 190 was taken from the opposite direction (1 is Michmash, 2 is Geba, 3 is the pass). In the background of 189 is the desert of Judah. In the foreground of 190 is the desolate ravine in which the village of Parah was situated (Pl. 254).

[Map 15, p. 66]

191

192

191, 192 / *The Situation of the 'City of David'.* On the lower photograph, taken from the SW, the rocky spur (outlined by a white dotted line on 191) on which stood the fortress of the Jebusites can be clearly seen between the valley of the Kidron (1) and the Tyropoeon valley (2), formerly much deeper. We can observe how it is dominated by the terrace of the Temple to the north (cf. Pl. 381). The other numbers indicate: 3, Spring Gihon; 4, Garden of Gethsemane (cf. Pl. 326); 5, modern road to Jericho; 6, ancient road to Jericho; 7, Dominus flevit; 8, traditional site of Bethphage; 9, traditional scene of the Ascension; 10, German hospital on the site of Nob; 11, Bahurim; 12, Anathoth; 13, cupola of the Holy Sepulchre (cf. Pl. 373); 14, Citadel, site of Herod's palace (cf. Pl. 378); 15, Church of the Cenacle.

[Map 33, p. 115]

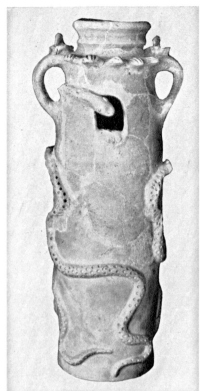

193
194
195

the twelfth century a tomb of David appeared there: after all, he had been buried in Zion! Enlightenment came only with the excavation of the southeastern hill, much lower than the one to the southwest, and outside the present city walls. This revealed that the original Zion must have stood on the southeastern hill.

191
192
327

By comparing the various aerial photographs in this Atlas with each other and also with Maps 24 and 33 (pp. 96, 115), one can form a clear idea of the relative positions of the city in David's time and the 'old city' (the walled area) of today: Jerusalem is seen to have shifted northwards. Although the spur (several times referred to in the Bible as Ophel, meaning 'swelling' or 'hump') on which the city of David stood is lower than the surrounding mountains, a strong town could be built there, thanks to the deep valleys on either side and the spring which rises at its foot; but its weakest point, the northern side, had to have very strong defences. This may have been the site of the sector of the defences called the Millo in the Bible. The Jebusites had sunk an almost vertical shaft into the limestone hill within their ramparts, so that in the event of a siege they could still obtain water from the spring, the normal approach to which was then walled up. The account of the capture of the town, which is somewhat garbled in the manuscript tradition, seems to imply that Joab crept up the shaft and took the Jebusites completely by surprise. At the beginning of the century, an English climber demonstrated on the spot that this unusual style of mountaineering must have called for extraordinary agility.

Ps 125:2

2 S 5:8

Jerusalem was thus in a good strategical position on this rocky spur, but there was no room for it to expand. Further, though it stood not far from the central

ridge along which all the north-south traffic of Palestine must pass, the city had no easy access to the Jordan valley or to the coastal plain. In this respect it was much less favourably situated than Shechem or, later, Samaria. It is therefore highly probable that David based his decision primarily upon political considerations. Shortly after the capture of the city, he sealed his choice by an action which was certainly of universal historic importance; with great ceremony he brought to Jerusalem the Ark of the Covenant, which had lain half-forgotten at Kiriathjearim during the turmoil of the recent years. In this way his capital supplanted Shiloh, which had been the sacral centre of the federated tribes for nearly two centuries. Thus it was that the ancient city of the Jebusites became the home of Yahwism and that this place, chosen by David, later saw the birth of Christianity.

David therefore began to reign in a city which he held in his own right, and to which none of the tribes could lay claim. Apart from the remaining Jebusites, no one lived there except men in the personal service of the king: members of the bodyguard, army officers, priests, and officials. The Ark alone did not belong to him; if one can speak of property in this connection, it was owned by all the tribes of Israel.

David's administration was unquestionably as skilful and successful as his preparatory plans had been. But the Bible is a religious document and, as such, touches only briefly on those aspects of government which hold so much interest for us today. Although the second book of Samuel is entirely devoted to David, at the ninth chapter it enters upon the masterly account we have already mentioned (p. 64), which deals only with the affairs of his family; for the promises

196
197

193 / *Vessel (incense-burner?) from the Canaanite Temple at Beth-shan.* One of the many indications of the worship of the serpent as an animal sacred to the deity who granted life and health (cf. the serpent near the tree of life in Pl. 74). **194** / *Laver on a Stand with Wheels,* found in a tomb in Cyprus (12th century B.C.; 15½ inches high). This object is very important for the interpretation of 1 K 7. Note the winged sphinxes, and the birds at the four corners. **195** / *Altar from Megiddo.* From this domestic altar, 21½ inches high, we can see what was meant by the 'four horns of the altar'. **196, 197** / *Canaanite Sanctuaries after Excavation.* 196: Temple of the 13th century B.C. discovered at Lachish. The altar stood at top left, in front of the platform. The offerings were probably deposited on the steps at top right. 197: Temple at Beth-shan, 14th century B.C. [Map 14, p. 65]

God made to David and his descendants invested the royal succession with a religious significance. It is only incidentally that we learn of his interest in the organisation, consolidation, and expansion of his kingdom.

He first of all put an end to the independence of a certain number of old Canaanite cities, such as Megiddo, Taanach, and Beth-shan, which he incorporated in his new-fledged state; he thus consolidated and completed the geographical unity of the tribal federation. Apart from a rather sketchy summary the Bible makes no mention of David's external wars. Only his campaign against the Ammonites is described in a little more detail, because it had a bearing on his family life: from his initially sinful union with Bathsheba his successor was to be born. Map 16 (p. 66) gives a broad outline of the expansion of the kingdom.

As a result of his many successes, David became the ruler of extensive domains. Around the greatly enlarged territory of the twelve tribes was grouped a ring of vassal states: in the north were a number of Aramaean provinces, administered in David's name by a governor; next came the kingdom of the Ammonites, of which he had himself proclaimed king; then Moab, which became a subject state after the Israelite troops had committed the most brutal atrocities there, but apparently kept its own king; and finally Edom, savagely devastated and completely subjugated by Joab. The Philistines were driven back into their own territory, and the whole coast, from below Joppa up to Mount Carmel, was controlled by David. A great part of the booty and the whole of the tribute was naturally sent to Jerusalem, where a great store of treasure was accumulated.

The Bible tells us equally little about internal organisation. A comparison of two lists of great officers of state, one for the time of David and the other for the reign of Solomon, shows that their number and functions steadily increased. A more detailed examination suggests that David modelled the administration of his state on the Egyptian system. He not only borrowed from it certain administrative offices; he also appears to have brought in Egyptians to fill them. The very high office of Secretary of State was held by a man whose name is variously spelt Seraiah, Shusha, Shisha, or Shavsha in the present text of the Bible. The form which must underlie these names (and which obviously puzzled the copyists) suggests that the man was an Egyptian. In the modern text his eldest son is called Elihoreph, for which it would be well to adopt the reading of the Septuagint, Elihaph, which means 'my god is Apis'. The father thus provided his son with a name whose first element was Hebrew, while the second expressed his fidelity to the religion of his Egyptian ancestors.

David's royal guard was largely composed of foreigners, in accordance with the practice of the Pharaohs and other rulers in the ancient world who wished to protect themselves against the intrigues of their own countrymen. In the Bible we meet with the Cherethites and the Pelethites, mercenaries who probably came from Philistine territory; there are also soldiers from Gath and Uriah the Hittite. These picked troops were David's personal army and, thanks to them, he was completely independent of all the tribes. In addition to these forces, there was, of course, an army made up of the able-bodied men of Israel; from time to time they also marched into battle, and sometimes they bore the Ark of the Covenant in their midst.

There can be no doubt that David was responsible for far-reaching measures in the religious sphere. The top of the hill, on whose southern spur stood the Jebusite fortress, was used as a threshing-floor. It was a high, exposed place where the slightest wind was sufficient to separate the chaff from the grain as it was tossed into the air. David entered into negotiations with the owner of the threshing-floor, whose Jebusite name is variously spelt in the texts (Araunah and Ornan), and bought the land in order to establish the national sanctuary on this hill-top to the north of the town. No doubt he prepared detailed plans which Solomon had only to carry out. He was also in part responsible for the organisation of worship (particularly for the temple music).

Yet, for all his great gifts as a king, David did not succeed in welding together the two parts of his kingdom. The earliest witnesses make no attempt to conceal the breach, since they refer to him as king of Judah and of Israel. Uriah speaks of 'the Ark and Israel and Judah', and the men liable for military service from the two halves of the kingdom were separately returned in the census. There is thus every justification for describing the state as a federal kingship or a union held together by one individual. The story of Absalom provides tragic evidence of this. By playing the part of the just king in opposition to his father, Absalom 'stole the hearts of the men of Israel'. When the dénouement of the drama came, it was David's personal troops who defeated the army of Israel and killed Absalom. On David's return, the two parties quarrelled over the king himself: 'The king . . . saved us from the hand of the Philistines', said Israel; 'The king is near of kin to us', said Judah to the men of Israel.

Perhaps a successor of equal stature might have succeeded in gradually healing the breach. It was David's tragic misfortune that he had no son of his own calibre. This may explain why he delayed the nomination of his successor, a choice which rested entirely with him in this kingship without traditions. On his death-bed he could see how in court and official circles, a world of his own creation, people were already plotting against Solomon and in support of

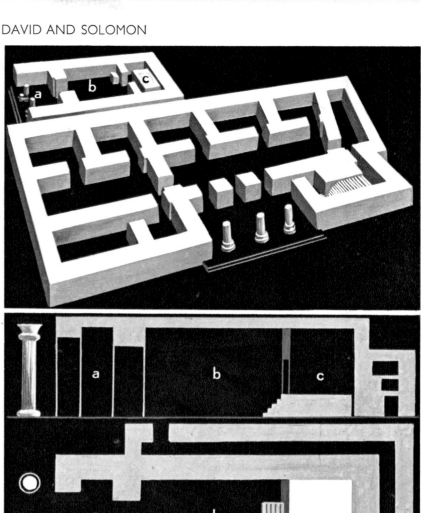

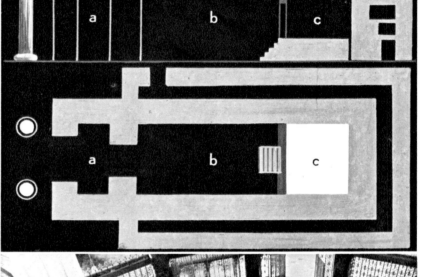

198 / *Royal Palace of Tell Tainat*, on the Orontes (9th cent. B.C.). This isometric drawing shows that the general plan of the royal chapel (about 82 by 39 feet) resembles that of the Temple of Yahweh. **199, 200** / *The Temple of Jerusalem*. Section and plan after R. de Vaux, O.P. It is divided into three parts: vestibule (a, *'ûlam*); principal chamber (b, *hêkal*); rear chamber (c, *debîr*). **201** / *Sacred Rock of the Temple*; now in the centre of the Mosque of Omar.

202

203

Adonijah, his fourth son. Solomon, however, was the favourite, probably more for the sake of Bathsheba, always the most dearly loved of David's wives, than for his own personal qualities. The dying ruler chose Solomon and at once had him anointed and publicly proclaimed king.

These events must have taken place about the year 965 B.C. The story of the succession to David, which occupies most of the second book of Samuel, is concluded in the opening chapters of the first book of Kings. The rest of this book is devoted to Solomon and the history of the two kingdoms of Israel and Judah, which continues in the second book of Kings, formerly included in a single volume with the first book. This work was also classified by the Jews among the prophetic writings and, compared with a work of history in the modern sense, it is very fragmentary and biased. Sometimes the author – if we may for the present refer to him in the singular – refers by name to his sources; sometimes a careful analysis of the texts reveals that other documents have also been used. It becomes quite clear that his aims were exclusively religious. The invasion of the Pharaoh Sheshonq (Shishak) appears to be recorded only because this ruler pillaged the Temple and carried away Solomon's shields of gold. Certain facts of very great military and political importance, now known to us from archaeological records, he did not consider worthy of mention. All we are told about the great Omri is that he built Samaria, and that without a single word of appreciation. It is the Temple of Jerusalem which chiefly interests the author. A great part of his record is devoted to the construction and dedication of this sanctuary, the repeated pillage of its treasures, and the ordinances relating to its maintenance, profanation, and purification. What made the Temple so important was that it was the centre of the legitimate cult as laid down in Deuteronomy. It is the legislative part of this book which is referred to as the 'Law of Moses', and this was probably the code discovered about 621 B.C., in the reign of Josiah. Deuteronomy repeatedly insists on the centralisation of worship and enjoins fidelity to the Covenant by constantly drawing attention to the inevitable consequences of transgression. The book of Kings was written to illustrate these principles from history. This approach is exemplified in the long reflective passage on the destruction of Samaria and, even more clearly, in Solomon's prayer on the occasion of the dedication of the Temple. It also influences the brief summary of each reign. Solomon's successes are a reward for his piety; his setbacks and the division of the kingdom are a punishment for his disobedience to Yahweh. All the kings of the Northern Kingdom are relentlessly condemned for persisting in the sinful practices of Jeroboam and for failing to suppress the unlawful worship at Bethel and Dan. The kings of Judah were the lawful heirs of David and their royal Temple the lawful sanctuary of Jerusalem. Nevertheless, there are only eight of whom the author speaks in terms of praise; they fought against heathen practices; they actively supported the Temple and, in general, showed that they were faithful to the ordinances of Yahweh. Yet this praise is usually qualified by a note of disapproval, because 'the high places were not removed'. The fact that these kings sanctioned the use of local sanctuaries outside Jerusalem cast a shadow over their reigns. Only two kings receive unqualified praise: Hezekiah, who abolished the high places throughout the land, and Josiah, who made the laws in Deuteronomy a universal rule of conduct. The greater part of the books of Kings must have been written while the Temple was still standing, and the description of Josiah's reform suggests a date prior to his death. But the story is carried down to the Exile, and we must therefore assume a later completion and revision of the work during the Exile. In any event, the books of Kings illustrate our earlier remarks (p. 27) on the nature of Biblical history and explain why the modern historian is glad to make use of information from archaeological sources in reconstructing the story of the period from Solomon to the Exile.

Solomon began his reign by ridding himself of his enemies. As we have said, the relevant chapter forms part of the long account of the succession to David and is probably a faithful account of the events. These are far from edifying! Solomon no doubt acted in part on the advice of his father. David himself had been great enough to come to power without such bloodshed; but perhaps he foresaw that his son would not be sufficiently strong to contend with the powerful members of the court. Whatever the reason, Solomon acted too drastically and showed himself a lesser man than his father. This is borne out by all that follows; for the account of Solomon's reign, for which the compiler has drawn upon the 'Book of the Acts of Solomon', is no more than a general outline (Solomon as sage, administrator, builder, merchant, and, finally, as a sinner incurring punishment), but is nevertheless full of unconnected details. There is no question of a well-constructed whole, and we receive no clear impression of Solomon himself. David's intelligence and humanity obviously won the hearts of his contemporaries and inspired a biographer to record the exciting story of the foundation of the dynasty. Solomon, on the contrary, seems to have dazzled men with his impressive projects, his love of luxury, and his clever sayings.

204

202 / *An Egyptian Scribe.* Since David was influenced by the administrative system of Egypt in the organisation of his newly-formed state (see the text), we include one of the countless statues of members of the important class of scribes, found in Egyptian tombs of all periods. This figure, now in Boston, belongs to the 5th Dynasty (ca 2400 B.C.). The scribe sits cross-legged, a roll of papyrus on his knees and his palette in his left hand. He wears a wig, and bends his head forward slightly, as if in attention. **203** / *Zither player from Canaan.* **204** / *Music and the Dance in Ancient Egypt.* For the light-hearted Egyptians, no feast was complete without music and dancing. After the conquests in Asia (15th century B.C.), the number of musical instruments considerably increased. Like young Israel, ancient Egypt also learned from the Canaanites, who were highly accomplished in the art of music. (Relief from a temple of Hatshepsut at Karnak.)

205
206
207

208

205 / *The Phoenician Coast.* Where the foothills of the Lebanon stretch almost to the sea, the fertile coastal plain is very narrow, but well provided with natural harbours. **206–208** / *Byblos.* The whole surface of the tell has now been excavated, layer by layer (208, which also shows the field of vision of 207). In ancient times it was a very important port called Gubla or Gebal, a form corrupted by the Greek merchants into *Bublos*. Long before 3000 B.C. the Egyptians, whose country was not rich in timber, were coming here to obtain cedars in exchange for their papyrus. This writing material was imported from here into the Greek world and came to be called *biblos*. The inhabitants, called Gebalites in the Bible, invented the alphabet. 206: Observe the characters of the inscription which King Elibaal of Byblos caused to be cut in the 10th century B.C. on a statue of the Pharaoh Osorkon I. [*Map 8, p. 43*]

209, 210 / The Stables of Megiddo. The photograph on the right shows the remains uncovered in 1928 (Pl. 364: the state of the site in 1951). The partial reconstruction on the left is based on a very careful study of the ruins of these stables, whose ingenious planning fills us with admiration. It has been estimated that the stables in this quarter of Megiddo provided accommodation for 300 horses.

[Map 17, p. 81]

Solomon was spared the necessity to go to war, and in this respect his reign matched his name, which suggests *sh-l-m*, 'prosperity, peace'. Egypt under the 21st dynasty was too weak to exert any influence in Asia; and in the reign of Solomon's insignificant contemporary, Tiglath-pileser II, the might of Assyria ebbed away. The Phoenicians had grown very prosperous but, from the island city of Tyre, they were turning towards the coasts of the Mediterranean; and, after the fall of the Hittite Kingdom, there was no powerful state left in Asia Minor. Solomon had therefore only to administer the territories conquered by David. The return of the Edomite prince, Hadad, shortly after David's death, does not appear to have led to the resurgence of Edom, for the Arabah, through which ran the important road to Ezion-geber, remained in Solomon's hands. More serious was the *coup d'état* of the Aramaean Rezon, who expelled from Damascus the governor appointed by David and had himself proclaimed king there. But it was not until later that this little state at the foot of the Anti-Lebanon became a real danger to Israel.

Solomon nevertheless created a permanent army which, according to the details in the books of Kings, numbered 1,400 war chariots and 12,000 horses. **1 K 10:26** This was a new departure: David had hamstrung all the horses captured from Hadadezer, with the exception of 100 chariot-teams which he had retained for civil and ceremonial purposes. His troops still fought on foot and he himself was content to ride a donkey. It was only his sons who sometimes rode abroad on horses or in chariots. Solomon's 'modern' army certainly contributed to his glory, even though it never fought a campaign. The Biblical figures were always held to be exaggerated until the excavations at Megiddo brought to light, at the level corresponding to this period, vast installations which can only have been **1 K 9:15** stables. Megiddo is, in fact, included in a list of the chariot and horse cities. The photograph (*top right*) was taken immediately after the discovery. When the reader reflects that these unimpressive ruins are the most important traces of Solomon's buildings so far discovered, he will appreciate the inadequacy of the information at our disposal for any illustration of the Biblical passages devoted to Solomon as a builder.

The same is true of his most important construction, the Temple of Jerusalem. Since the rock upon which the Temple stood is a holy place of Islam, now enshrined within the Mosque of Omar, it has never proved possible to excavate the site. Fortunately the detailed description in the Bible provides some measurements and other particulars of the main building; but, unhappily, we are not sure how to translate certain technical terms and difficult expressions. Apart from the information in the Bible, archaeologists have found a number of plans and details relating to the construction of other temples in Syria and Palestine, as well as decorative motifs which serve as a basis of **1 K 6:29** comparison. When we read that Solomon 'carved figures of cherubim and palm trees and open flowers', we can think of some of the motifs on the ivory carvings seen opposite. We now know of temples in Syria of the same period **198** as that of Solomon which are also divided into three parts (vestibule, nave or **191** Holy Place, and inner sanctuary or Holy of Holies). To form an idea of the whole **192** site we can study present-day aerial photographs. On Ornan's threshing-floor (where the Mosque of Omar stands) Solomon had probably created an artificial esplanade, like the present terrace which goes back to the time of Herod, but on **199** a smaller scale. The actual sanctuary, of which we show a plan and a section, **200** was built in the Semitic style with surrounding courtyards. Between the Temple and the city, Solomon erected the buildings of the royal palace, which took thirteen years to complete. These constructions greatly extended Jerusalem

towards the north, and seen from above, the city, which was several times longer than it was wide, must have looked like a narrow white line.

In contrast to his father, Solomon was increasingly to assume the rôle of the ostentatious monarch. Quite apart from the skilled architects and the building labourers brought from Phoenicia to work on the palace and the Temple, envoys from neighbouring countries and a host of foreign merchants were to be found in his capital. For Solomon engaged in commerce on a large scale; he sold horses from Cilicia (then called Que, Qewê in the Bible) to Egyptian purchasers, while the chariots made in Egypt were sold in Syria. The corn and oil from Palestine were bartered in Phoenicia for cedars of Lebanon. Excavation at Ezion-geber on the Gulf of Elath ('Aqaba) has brought to light ingeniously constructed blast-furnaces in which Solomon's workmen smelted the iron and copper ore extracted from the mountains on either side of the valley. This detail is missing from the Bible: Ezion-geber is, indeed, mentioned, but in connection with the fleet which Solomon built and manned, with the help of King Hiram of Tyre and his ship-builders and sailors, in order to trade with distant regions like Ophir (probably the southwestern coast of Arabia and the Somali coast opposite). Surrounded by his court, Solomon lived in magnificent style. His visitors were dazzled:

And when the queen of Sheba had seen all the wisdom of Solomon, the house that he had built, the food of his table, the seating of his officials, and the attendance of his servants, their clothing, his cup-bearers, and his burnt offerings which he offered at the house of the Lord, there was no more spirit in her. And she said to the king, "The report was true which I heard in my own land of your affairs and of your wisdom, but I did not believe the reports until I came and my own eyes had seen it; and, behold, the half was not told me; your wisdom and prosperity surpass the report which I heard."

But the people had to provide for the upkeep of this court. The king therefore divided the land of 'Israel' (Judah was probably exempted) into twelve districts in charge of twelve officials, who were responsible for collecting the levies in kind and for ensuring that there was no evasion of the forced labour.

It goes without saying that even in the life-time of David, and particularly during the reign of Solomon, the social structure of the people of Israel underwent great changes. The freedom-loving peasants were subjected to organisation. Their harvests were assessed by the tax collectors and every able-bodied man was obliged to work for the king. The cities annexed by David acquired great importance as administrative centres, while contacts were established with their pagan inhabitants and with all kinds of foreign merchants. As a result, a class distinction developed between those who succeeded and those who failed in the new society.

Meanwhile, partly under the influence of the court scribes, a written literature was being created. In addition to the ancient poems and stories handed down orally among the people from father to son, men began to set down religious traditions and to record past events. It was probably at this time that the frank and vivid story of David's family life and troubles, preserved in the second book of Samuel and the opening chapters of the first book of Kings, was composed.

Solomon's reign left behind a memory of greatness and magnificence. This is illustrated by a passage, possibly comparatively late in date, from the first book of Kings: 'And God gave Solomon wisdom and understanding beyond measure, and largeness of mind like the sand on the seashore, so that Solomon's wisdom surpassed the wisdom of all the people of the east, and all the wisdom of Egypt.' But the sequel to the story shows that, for all its glory, his reign ended in failure.

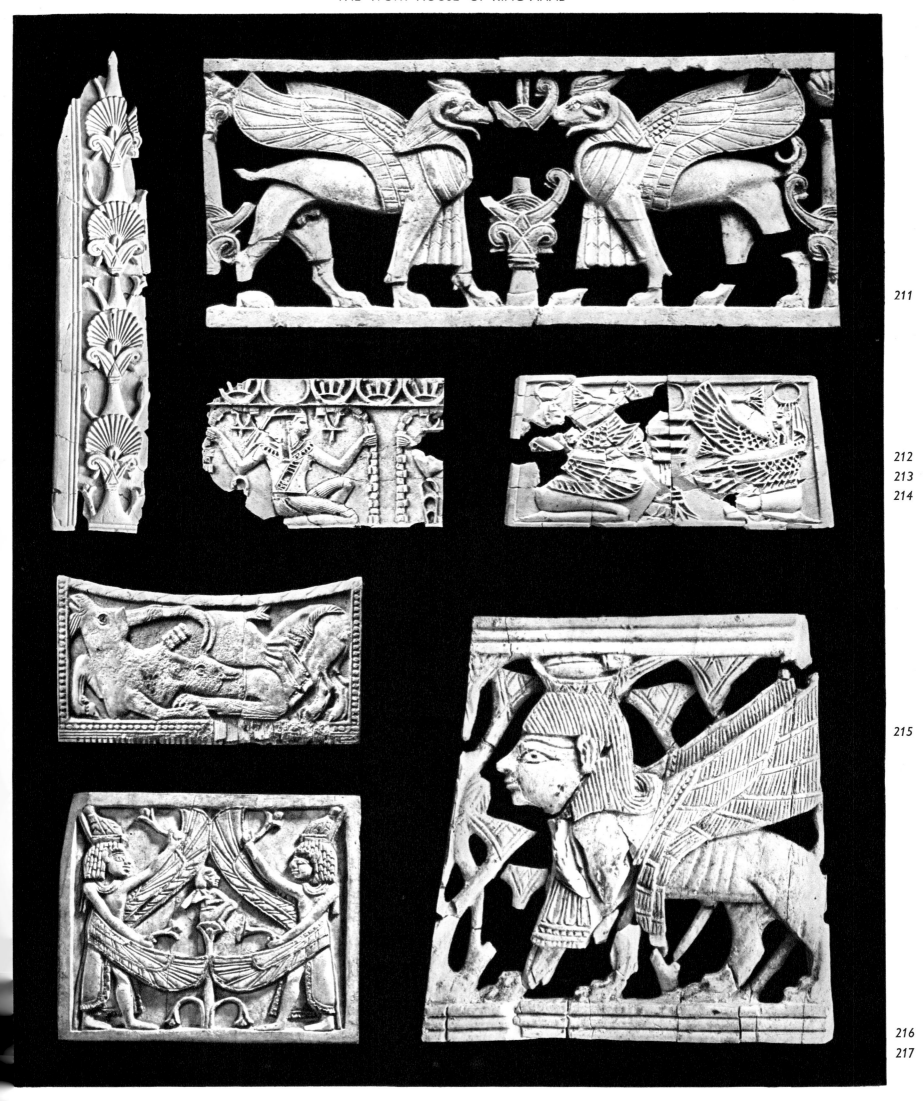

211

212
213
214

215

216
217

211–217 / *Ornamentation in Carved Ivory.* Excavation has revealed that the art of carving in ivory flourished in Syria during the period of the monarchy in Israel. To decorate wooden panelling, chairs, beds, divans, etc., small plaques of ivory were carved with all kinds of figures inspired by motifs from Egypt, Mesopotamia, Cyprus, and the Greek islands. (This fact is important for the interpretation of certain Biblical passages. See the text.) The beautiful palm-leaf border (212; 7⅛ inches long) comes from the palace of Ahab in Samaria. The winged creatures with rams' heads (211) belonged to the furnishings of Hazael's palace at Damascus (found at *Arslân-Tash*), as did also the carving shown in 216. The delicate reliefs of 213 and 214 (four-fifths actual size) were encrusted with gold and with blue pottery. The 'cherub' (217; just over 3 inches high) also came from Samaria, while the comb-handle ornamented with animals (215; actual size) was found at Megiddo.

THE DISRUPTION AND ITS CONSEQUENCES

Solomon's successor was not to have an easy task. At the beginning of this brilliant reign the people had certainly enjoyed all the advantages which proceed from a well-organised state. 'And Judah and Israel dwelt in safety, ... every man under his vine and under his fig tree ... they ate and drank and were happy.' But methodical organisation brought inevitable consequences in its train: there was no escape from all manner of taxes and payments in kind, or from forced labour which, as a result of Solomon's great projects, grew increasingly heavy. If the absence of the territory of Judah from Solomon's register of the districts may be taken as an indication that this tribe was exempted, we can but conclude that this was a very serious mistake on his part, especially as the highest offices at court and in the administration were almost exclusively held by Judaeans, when they were not filled by foreigners. David's efforts to weld together the two parts of the kingdom were not continued by his son who, imprudently, went rather in the other direction.

The most responsible religious leaders in Israel had grounds for deeper dissatisfaction with Solomon. He had delighted in imitating foreign monarchs and had striven to excel them. He wanted to possess a fleet like the king of Tyre, in order to sail to more distant seas than the Tyrians. He was anxious to have war chariots like the old-established and powerful Pharaohs of Egypt. His harem had also to be as large and varied as theirs. He hankered after seats of ivory, in the latest fashion; monkeys and peacocks; and the glitter of gold in every room. His parvenu craving for all the fine things that foreign lands could offer was consonant neither with the character of the Israelite people, nor with the spirit of the religion they had accepted at the foot of the majestic Mount Sinai and had practised at first in the barren wilderness. Solomon was capable and skilful, but not deeply religious. David, in his simple and direct communion with God, had been the model of what Israel should be. But such things were foreign to Solomon's character. For all his brilliant gifts and his fine sensibility, he was cold and worldly at heart, a man who scarcely knew either truss or faith.

The Judaeans had no difficulty in nominating his son Rehoboam as the obvious person to continue the royal line of David, and we learn of his arrival at Shechem, where Israel had gathered to proclaim him king. But the next verse reveals that the people of the North wished to recognise his kingship by means of a covenant, as had formerly been done at Hebron, when delegates from Israel came to conclude an alliance with David. But Rehoboam replied caustically to the proposals of Israel: 'My little finger is thicker than my father's loins'. The new king had no intention of lightening the heavy yoke which Solomon laid on the northern part of the kingdom. Instead of heeding the counsel of experienced men, he followed the advice of the young men who had grown up with him and were now in his service, petty despots in the making. He would replace the leather whips of the overseers by lashes tipped with iron. And then we again hear the cry already raised in the time of David when there was a danger of schism: 'What portion have we in David? We have no inheritance in the son of Jesse. To your tents, O Israel!' The representatives of the tribes placed themselves under the leadership of Jeroboam, a former controller of forced labour under Solomon, who had fled to Egypt after a clash with the king. He had earlier been designated in God's name as the future king by the prophet Ahijah of Shiloh. The division of the kingdom was now an accomplished fact: Israel had a king in the old tradition, a king who, like Saul, had been designated by a prophet and proclaimed by the people.

The dynastic table which appears on Map 17 (p. 81) serves to illustrate that the events we have just related are in many ways characteristic of the later history of the two parts of the kingdom. The straight line linking together the kings of Judah emphasises the unity and permanence of the dynasty: to the very end the throne of Judah will be occupied by a descendant of the house of David. By contrast, the line of the kings of Israel is broken, revealing the numerous dynastic changes.

This difference between Israel and Judah can, to some extent, be explained: David was a Judaean; for more than seven years he had reigned over Judah alone and had grown sufficiently influential to impose his choice of Solomon as his successor. He thereby made the monarchy hereditary. Though the people of Judah might in later years be dissatisfied with this or that king, they would never allow a usurper to reign in Jerusalem, which proudly called itself 'the city of David'. By reason of the very circumstances of its foundation, the monarchy in the North was much less firmly rooted in a tradition and a locality. In principle, the people could condemn the behaviour of a reigning monarch and, through the medium of a prophet, could incite a more suitable candidate to seize the throne, if necessary by force. This did in fact happen on several occasions in the years following the Disruption; and certain pretenders did not wait to be nominated by a prophet! Moreover, there was no obvious traditional capital, as was the case with Jerusalem in the South. Shechem had the best claim to the title (see p. 68), and Jeroboam did in fact reside there during the early years of his reign. But, for reasons which are unknown to us, he then moved to Penuel (Peniel), on the river Jabbok in Transjordan (this town, like Shechem, figured in the story of the patriarch Jacob). He finally established himself at Tirzah. Omri, the fifth of his successors, was to build Samaria, destined to remain the capital until the downfall of the Kingdom.

Jeroboam quickly realised that he had nothing to offer which could equal the religious importance of Jerusalem. For Jerusalem was the home of the Ark of the Covenant, the centre of the cult of Yahweh, and still drew worshippers from every corner of Palestine. It was the Ark, the reminder and symbol of the Sinaitic Covenant and the visible throne of Yahweh, rather than any artificial political bonds, which had held the tribes together under David and Solomon. Rehoboam, Jeroboam's rival, would thus continue to attract the best elements in the North to his capital. Jeroboam therefore resolved to create two new shrines of Yahweh, and to urge his people to worship the God of Israel there and so save themselves the journey to Jerusalem. His choice fell upon Bethel and Dan, and in each of these towns he set up a solid gold, or gold-cased, statue of a bull calf. These two cities were well chosen: Dan, which lay on the northern frontier of the Kingdom, at the foot of Mount Hermon near the source of the Jordan, had possessed, since the period of the Judges, a sanctuary of Yahweh served by a priesthood of its own. Israelites from the extreme north, who had always been somewhat isolated, could now go there to offer their sacrifices and gifts to Yahweh. Bethel had been a holy place of the Canaanites from time immemorial; it was there that Abraham built an altar to his God, and Jacob dreamed of angels ascending and descending a ladder between heaven and earth and received God's promise of further bounties. It was a much-visited sanctuary in the time of the Judges and of Samuel, when it served as a meeting-place for the tribes. The situation of Bethel, which lay less than ten miles to the north of

218 / *Ishtar*, goddess of love and war, standing on a lion; a stele from Mesopotamia, 8th century B.C. **219** / *The God Hadad*, standing on a young bull, with a thunderbolt in each hand; 7th century B.C., found at *Arslân-Tash*.

the Temple of Solomon, exactly suited Jeroboam's purpose. Pilgrims from the North were obliged to pass by it on their way to Jerusalem; weary of travelling, they would be easily persuaded to make their devotions in this holy place. The king accordingly consecrated his new sanctuary on the very day when the annual feast of consecration was being celebrated in Jerusalem The Bible also mentions that he installed at Bethel 'priests from among all the people' (Dan already had its own priesthood); he was apparently forced to take this action because, after the Disruption, the Levites settled in Judah.

Why does the compiler of the books of Kings deal at such length with these acts of Jeroboam? It is because they constituted his grave sin, the sin in which all the kings of Israel were to persist. But in what did his fault consist? From a cursory reading of the texts, one might interpret his action as an express reversion to idolatry. But this was not the case. Jeroboam did certainly propagate the faith with the cry: 'Behold your gods, O Israel, who brought you up out of the land of Egypt'. But the plural here either refers to the two statues, or, more probably, arises from the use of the name Elohim (a plural which attempted to express the all-embracing nature of the divine being). Moreover, the abandonment of the national God would never have been tolerated. Nor must we forget that Jeroboam gave his son the name Abijah, 'my father is Yah(weh)', and that when the child fell ill he sought the advice of a prophet. These facts prove his desire to be a servant of Yahweh. And, in later years, neither Elijah nor Jehu, who were both strongly opposed to strange gods, uttered a word of protest about the sanctuaries at Bethel and Dan. Jeroboam clearly believed that the golden calves could legitimately figure in the worship of the God who had delivered Israel out of the power of Egypt and had revealed Himself as Yahweh. Did he regard them as true representations of this God? We are by no means sure that he did. Excavation has brought to light stelae bearing the figure of a deity standing upon the back of the animal which is especially sacred to him; sometimes there is only a symbol on the back of the animal, and on occasion there is nothing at all: in the last case the animal is regarded as the throne upon which the unseen god is standing. The golden calves may well have had this significance, and it has been pointed out that there was a similar example in the Holy of Holies at Jerusalem, where Yahweh was invisibly enthroned upon two cherubim, resembling winged sphinxes.

Even if Jeroboam may be credited with this orthodox view, his sanctuaries none the less paved the way for a falsification of Yahwism. For the Canaanites associated the symbol of a vigorous young bull with Baal, the god of fertility. How were the ordinary people to distinguish the bull upon which the unseen Yahweh was seated from the bull which represented Baal? The prophets sometimes liken Yahweh to a lion, another animal which was then a symbol of divinity in the Near East, but they avoid any comparison with the bull. At Bethel and Dan, Jeroboam was leading his people into a perverted form of Yahwism; this is why he was sternly denounced even in his own lifetime, and yet more bitterly by later generations.

After this episode, the Bible proceeds with the parallel histories of the two Kingdoms. Judah, whose unproductive territory was little larger than an average English county, had a homogeneous population, steadfastly loyal to the dynasty of David and drawing spiritual sustenance from the Ark of the Covenant in the Temple of Jerusalem. Israel covered a much more extensive area, stretching as it did to the east of the Jordan, and its lands were, for the most part, fertile; but its population, which comprised several different tribes as well as the inhabitants of the old Canaanite cities, was united neither by an hereditary monarchy, nor by the authentic cult of Yahweh. In the political field, Israel was always to be the superior of Judah. Its economic situation was more favourable: it cultivated relations with Phoenicia and, at some periods, owned trading agencies in Damascus. But its people lacked spiritual backbone and, when deported to distant regions, were to disappear without trace in the foreign population. Judah, by contrast, was to retain her individuality in Babylon.

As was mentioned earlier, the compiler of the books of Kings examines this period from one particular angle. His accounts nevertheless impress the modern reader as being a genuinely 'historical' record, since they contain a seemingly accurate chronology. The reigns of the kings of Judah and Israel are synchronised. For each new king the same formula is repeated: 'In the ...th year of X, king of Judah (Israel), Y began to reign over Israel (Judah), and he reigned for ... years'. It is therefore theoretically possible to establish the dates of the reign of every king. Unfortunately there are inconsistencies in the original text and defects in the manuscript tradition which prevent scholars from reaching agreement. The only Biblical events which can be precisely dated are those which are also recorded in Assyrian documents; for, with the help of a very substantial collection of records and the calculations of astronomers, we are able to date, almost to the year, the Assyrian reigns of this period. In any case, what interests the compiler of the books of Kings is not the dates, but the attitude of the kings towards the Temple of Jerusalem. Time and again he says: 'If you wish to learn something of the political and military activities of this king, you must consult the 'Book of the Chronicles of the Kings of Judah (Israel)'.' Unhappily these 'Chronicles' are lost, and we are obliged to fill out the skeleton account in Kings with details gleaned from other parts of the Bible or from non-Biblical sources. These do not carry us very far and the sum total remains meagre.

Immediately after the schism, hostilities broke out between the two Kingdoms. Rehoboam wished to subdue the northern tribes by force. A prophet intervened to warn him that these events were ordained by God and that he must not interfere. Yet we are told that 'there was war between Rehoboam and Jeroboam continually'. This must be taken to mean fighting over the common frontier. Such conflicts were inevitable; for had not David chosen Jerusalem as his capital precisely because it was a neutral zone between the territory of Judah and that of the other tribes? Unless he chose to reside on the edge of his kingdom close to the frontier with Israel, Rehoboam had to annex part of the land of the Benjamites.

220 / *Fragment of Inscribed Pottery from Samaria.* Unfortunately this 'letter' scribbled by an Israelite of the 8th century B.C. is incomplete. Two lines begin with the name Baruch, the third with the equally Biblical name Imna. **221** / *Seals of the Royal Period.* 1: A scarab from Lachish, showing from l. to r., the upper side, the under side, and the impression: a winged scarab above the words 'of Ahimelech'. 2: A so-called scaraboid from Mizpah; above the fighting cock is the inscription 'of Jaazaniah / the servant of the king' (see 2 K 25:23). 3, *left:* A simple stamp, with the impression 'of Hilkiah'; *right:* the seal 'of Chaim', with the Egyptian sign for life and a crowned sphinx. 4: Between the paws of a similar sphinx is the name 'Chaman', below is a locust. **222, 223** / *Two Impressions of Seals on Jar Handles.* Below the figures (winged scarab and sun-god?) can be read 'Hebron' and 'Socoh' respectively.

224

225

224, 225 / *Samaria, Capital of the Northern Kingdom*. These photographs illustrate the reasons for Omri's choice (1 K 16:24). Entirely isolated amid fertile hills, at the junction of important roads, and provided with a natural acropolis, 'the hill of Shemer' was an exceptionally good site for a town, both strategically and economically. 224, a view from the ESE, gives a general idea of its situation. 225 suggests something of the gentle nature of the surrounding country, so different from the stern landscapes of Judaea. The little village on the eastern slope is *Sebastiyeh* (about 700 inhabitants; Samaria had a population of 30,000 in 721 B.C.!) When we read such texts as Is 28:1 ('Woe to the proud crown . . . which is on the head of the rich valley'), we should visualise this hill crowned (like Lachish, Pl. 233) with a double ring of walls built of yellowish limestone. [Map 17, p. 81]

226
227

228

226–228 / *Evidence of the former Glory of Samaria*. The excavations of 1908–10 and 1931–35 brought to light some remains from the different periods in the history of Samaria. 227: Fragment of a wall of the time of Omri, who brought from Phoenicia not only a wife for his son Ahab, but also the builders of his new capital. 226: Part of the basilica near the forum, built by Herod and later restored by the Romans. 228: Of the magnificent temple erected by Herod in honour of his deified benefactor in Rome (Augustus, who gave the town its Greek name of *Sebaste*), nothing remains but the imposing and monumental flight of steps. Behind *(left)*, deep excavation was necessary to uncover the palaces of Omri and Ahab, whose archives yielded many ostraca (Pl. 220).
[Maps 17, p. 81; 34, p. 116]

At this juncture, the Pharaoh Sheshonq (Shishak) invaded Palestine; Rehoboam began to build a chain of fortified towns around his territory; and Jeroboam transferred his capital to Penuel. The modern reader would like to know whether there was any connection between these events. Might not Rehoboam have abandoned his plan to conquer the Northern Kingdom because Jeroboam sought the aid of the Pharaoh, with whom he was personally acquainted? Was it in the face of this threat from the southwest that the king of Judah erected the ring of fortresses? In any event, it was only by offering Sheshonq the Temple treasures that Rehoboam was able to avert the devastation of Judah. Indeed, it is only because the Temple figured in the story that we are told anything at all about the Egyptian invasion.

The famous list of the towns (see p. 20) captured by Sheshonq, a Libyan who sought to raise Egypt from her weakness, suggests that the Northern Kingdom was also heavily plundered. But other inscriptions of the same Pharaoh reveal that, in his official records, he was actuated more by a desire to imitate the great Pharaohs of the past than by a regard for the truth. Is the list of towns reliable? It includes the name of Megiddo, where a commemorative stele of Sheshonq has, in fact, been found. Is this sufficient confirmation? We may at least ask ourselves whether by his appeal to Egypt Jeroboam did not bring in the Trojan horse, and whether it was not in fact in the face of this invader that he was obliged to withdraw from Shechem to Penuel, in Transjordan. This example illustrates how fragmentary is the information in the Bible and how tentative are our efforts to assemble it into a coherent whole.

We are once more indebted to the Temple treasures for definite information about the frontier warfare between the two Kingdoms. Baasha, the third king of Israel, began to fortify the little town of Ramah, some six miles to the north of Jerusalem, in order to block the communications of Asa, his southern rival. The latter bribed Ben-hadad, the king of Damascus, to intervene, using for the purpose what remained of the Temple treasures. Ben-hadad eagerly agreed to the proposal, invaded Israel, and captured the northernmost towns. When Baasha learned of this, he stopped the work at Ramah and returned to Tirzah. The king of Judah was then able quietly to take possession of Mizpah, which lay a few miles farther north from his capital, and with the help of the materials captured at Ramah, to turn it into a strong frontier post. He also fortified Geba with these same materials. In the seventh century B.C. the tribe of Judah will be said to stretch 'from Geba to Beer-sheba' (Geba was probably preferred to Mizpah because of the assonance); from which we may conclude that the northern frontier had not shifted since the time of Asa. This is not surprising, for Ben-hadad's invasion marked the beginning of a period of almost continuous warfare between Aram and Israel. Damascus was striving to gain possession of the fertile plains and ancient trading cities of northern Transjordan, which were part of the territory of Israel. Instead of engaging in frontier warfare with Judah, Omri and his sons therefore sought the help of the Southern Kingdom against the onslaughts of the Aramaeans. It was doubtless partly owing to the threat from Damascus that this great ruler Omri entered into close relations with the increasingly prosperous and powerful towns on the coast of Phoenicia, and sealed the bond by marrying his son Ahab to Jezebel, a royal princess of Tyre. When this queen came to Samaria, the luxurious new capital of Israel, she brought her own religion with her. The effect of this official cult of Baal upon a people who already worshipped Yahweh in the form of a bull calf at Bethel and Dan and even in Samaria itself could not fail to be disastrous. Orthodox Yahwism therefore reacted vigorously in the persons of Elijah and Elisha, and now the compiler of Kings can expand the meagre summaries of reigns with colourful stories of the deeds of these two prophets, clearly borrowed from an old collection. It is only because Elijah and Elisha played a part in them that some episodes in the struggle between Israel and Aram have been handed down to us; but since the compiler's interests were dominantly religious, we are not always able to identify the king concerned or to date the events.

These wars seriously weakened the Northern Kingdom. We have proof of this in the rebellion of the vassal state of Moab, which is briefly recorded in the second book of Kings: 'Now Mesha king of Moab was a sheep breeder; and he had to deliver annually to the king of Israel a hundred thousand lambs, and the wool of a hundred thousand rams. But when Ahab died, the king of Moab rebelled against the king of Israel.' This serves as an introduction to the account of a campaign against Moab which was originally part of the Elisha cycle and did not refer by name to the king of Judah (the name Jehoshaphat in our present text is a later insertion). The attack on Moab, made from the south by Joram of Israel with the help of Judah and Edom, was at first crowned with success, but appears to have ended in failure.

Our documentation of this incident is completed by the famous stele of Mesha, the Moabite Stone (reproduced opposite). We give a translation of the first eighteen lines. The last four lines are too damaged to be satisfactorily interpreted. Even in the translated portion there are a number of illegible characters and we are not sure of the meaning of certain words.

I am Mesha, son of Chemosh . . ., king of Moab, the Dibonite. My father reigned over Moab for thirty years and I reigned after my father. And I built this sanctuary to Chemosh at Qarhoh . . . because he delivered me from all the kings and caused me to triumph over all my enemies. Moab was long oppressed by Omri, king of Israel, for Chemosh was angry with his land. And his son (Ahab) succeeded him and he also said: I will oppress Moab. It was in my day that he spoke thus, and I have triumphed over him and his house and Israel has perished for ever. Now, Omri had taken possession of the land of Medeba and (Israel) dwelt there during all his days and for half the days of his son, for forty years. But Chemosh returned it (to us) again in my time. And I built Baal-meon and made the reservoir there. And I built Kiriathaim. Now, the people of Gad had dwelt in the land of Ataroth from ancient times and the king of Israel had built Ataroth. And I fought against the city, and I captured it and killed all the people of the city, a satisfaction (?) for Chemosh and for Moab. And I carried away from there the altar of his god and I dragged it before Chemosh at Kerioth. And I peopled it with men from Sharon and Maharath. And Chemosh said to me: Go! Capture (the city of) Nebo from Israel! And I went by night and I fought against it from the break of day until noon and I took it and I killed all the people, seven thousand men and boys, and women and girls and maid-servants, for I had sworn to Ashtar-Chemosh to destroy it and I took from there the . . . of Yahweh and I dragged them before the face of Chemosh . . .

Mesha then records the capture of Jahaz from the king of Israel and its annexation to Dibon; the building of Qarhoh ('I . . . caused the prisoners from Israel to dig the ditches . . .'), of Aroer, and of 'the road along the Arnon'; the rebuilding of Beth-bamoth and Bezer; and the building of Medeba, Beth-diblathaim, and Beth-baal-meon.

1 K
14:25f.

1 K
15:17-22

229

229 / *The Moabite Stone*, stele of Mesha, king of Moab in the time of Ahab. This stone (44 by 28 by 14 inches) was on the tell of Dibon and was examined with interest by a German missionary in 1868. After his departure, the Arabs, convinced that a European could only be searching for treasure, heated and shattered it. It was possible to piece together the fragments with the help of a plaster cast made before the stone was broken (Paris, Louvre).

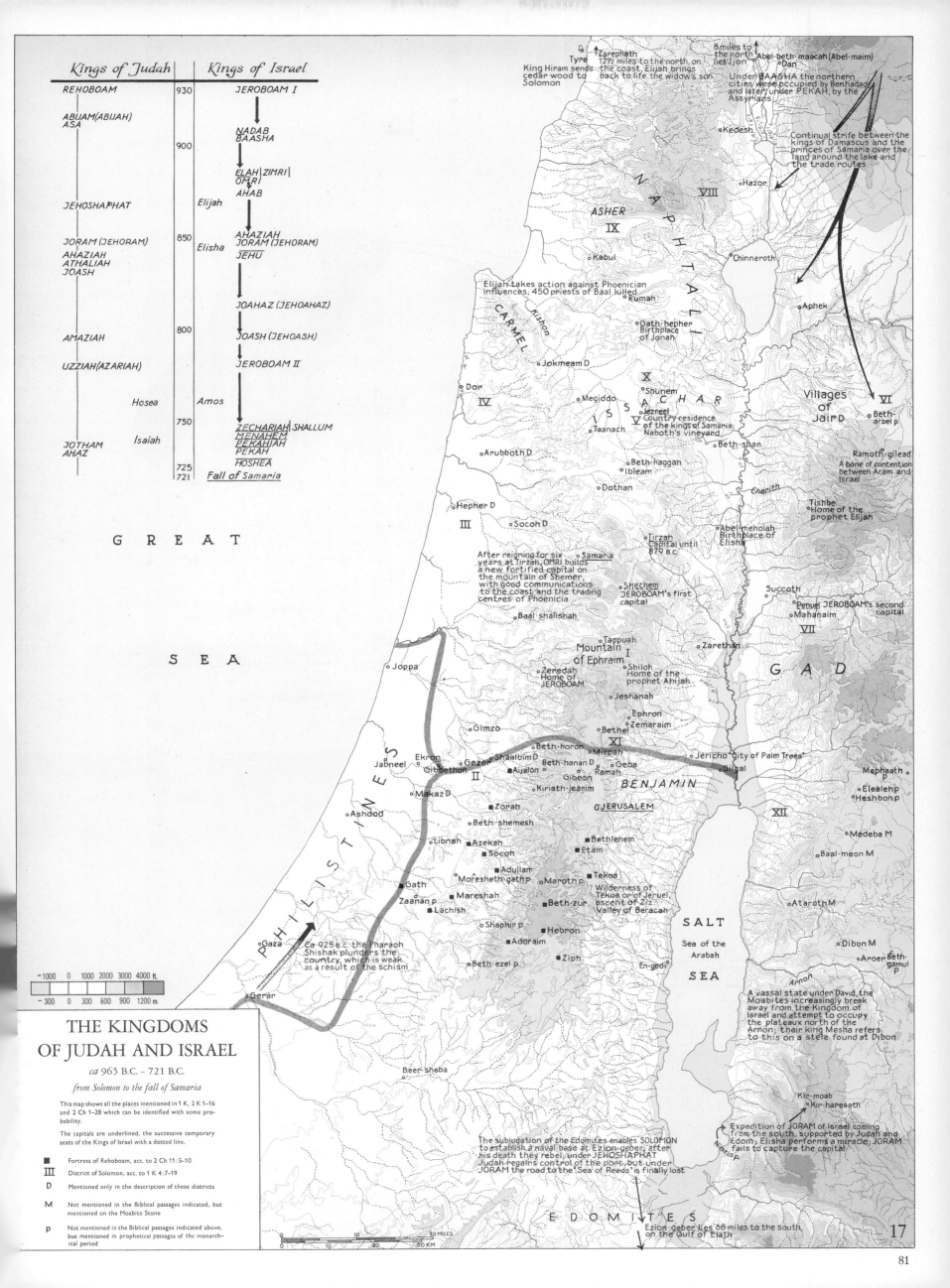

THE KINGDOMS
OF JUDAH AND ISRAEL

ca 965 B.C. – 721 B.C.

from Solomon to the fall of Samaria

This map shows all the places mentioned in 1 K, 2 K 1–16
and 2 Ch 1–28 which can be identified with some probability.

The capitals are underlined, the successive temporary
seats of the Kings of Israel with a dotted line.

■   Fortress of Rehoboam, acc. to 2 Ch 11:5–10

III   District of Solomon, acc. to 1 K 4:7–19

D   Mentioned only in the description of these districts

M   Not mentioned in the Biblical passages indicated, but
mentioned on the Moabite Stone

p   Not mentioned in the Biblical passages indicated above,
but mentioned in prophetical passages of the monarchical period

Kings of Judah | Kings of Israel

Kings of Judah		Kings of Israel
REHOBOAM	930	JEROBOAM I
ABIJAM (ABIJAH)		
ASA		NADAB
	900	BAASHA
		ELAH ZIMRI
		OMRI
JEHOSHAPHAT	Elijah	AHAB
		AHAZIAH
JORAM (JEHORAM)	850 Elisha	JORAM (JEHORAM)
AHAZIAH		JEHU
ATHALIAH		
JOASH		
		JOAHAZ (JEHOAHAZ)
AMAZIAH	800	JOASH (JEHOASH)
UZZIAH (AZARIAH)		JEROBOAM II
	Hosea Amos	
	750	ZECHARIAH SHALLUM
		MENAHEM
JOTHAM	Isaiah	PEKAHIAH
AHAZ		PEKAH
	725	HOSHEA
	721	Fall of Samaria

17

81

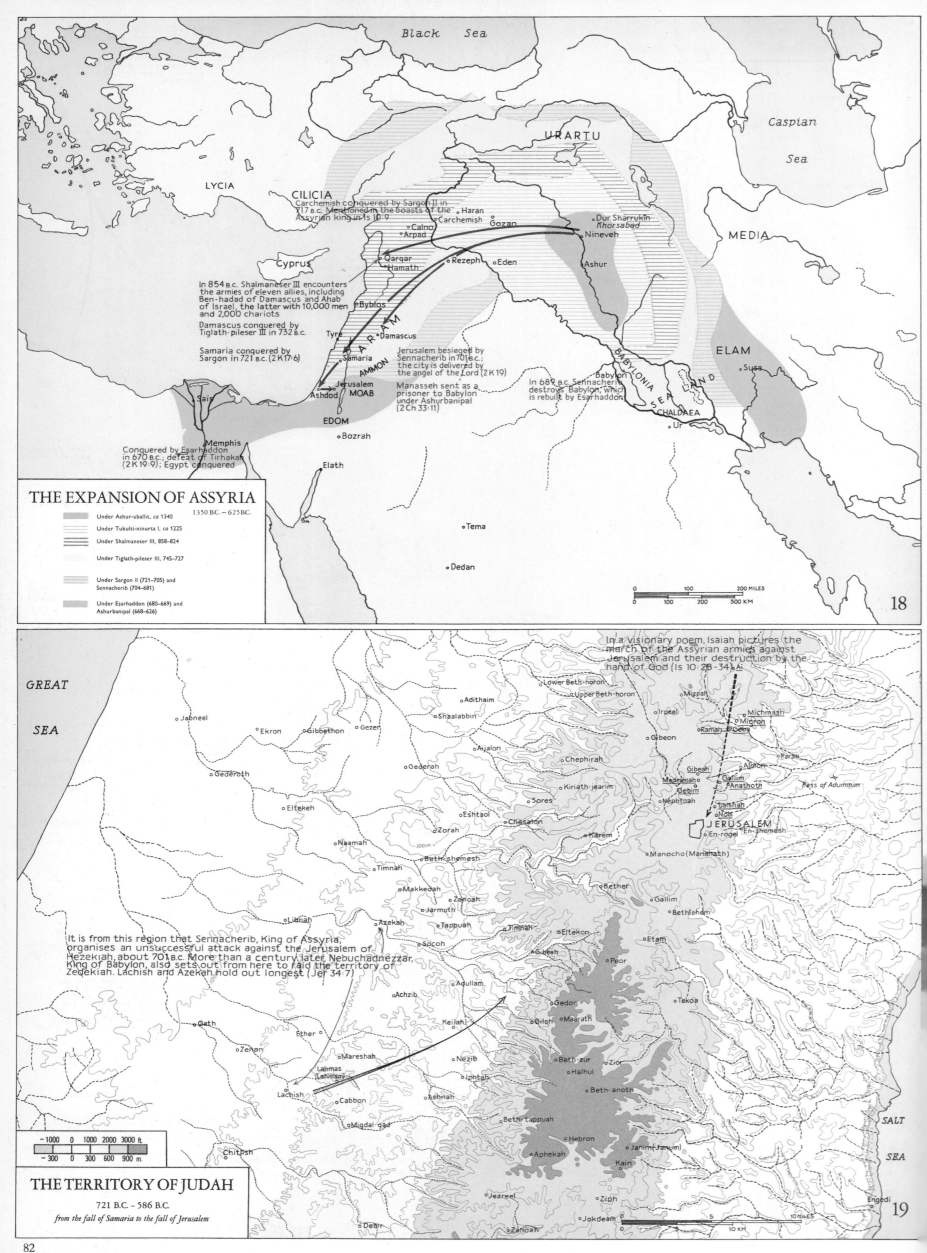

THE EXPANSION OF ASSYRIA

Black Sea

LYCIA

CILICIA

Carchemish conquered by Sargon II in 717 B.C. Mentioned in the boasts of the Assyrian king in Is 10:9

In 854 B.C. Shalmaneser III encounters the armies of eleven allies, including Ben-hadad of Damascus and Ahab of Israel, the latter with 10,000 men and 2,000 chariots

Damascus conquered by Tiglath-pileser III in 732 B.C.

Samaria conquered by Sargon in 721 B.C. (2 K 17:6)

Jerusalem besieged by Sennacherib in 701 B.C.; the city is delivered by the angel of the Lord (2 K 19)

Manasseh sent as a prisoner to Babylon under Ashurbanipal (2 Ch 33:11)

In 689 B.C. Sennacherib destroys Babylon, which is rebuilt by Esarhaddon

Conquered by Esarhaddon in 670 B.C.; defeat of Tirhakah (2 K 19:9); Egypt conquered

Cyprus

URARTU

Caspian Sea

MEDIA

Haran Gozan Dur Sharrukin Khorsabad
Calno Arpad Nineveh
Carchemish
Qarqar Rezeph Eden Ashur
Hamath
Byblos
Tyre Damascus
ARAM
Samaria AMMON
Ashdod Jerusalem MOAB
Sais EDOM
Bozrah
Elath
Memphis
Babylon
BABYLONIA
CHALDAEA Ur
ELAM
Susa

Tema

Dedan

THE EXPANSION OF ASSYRIA

1350 B.C. – 625 B.C.

- Under Ashur-uballit, ca 1340
- Under Tukulti-ninurta I, ca 1225
- Under Shalmaneser III, 858–824
- Under Tiglath-pileser III, 745–727
- Under Sargon II (721–705) and Sennacherib (704–681)
- Under Esarhaddon (680–669) and Ashurbanipal (668–626)

0 100 200 MILES
0 100 200 300 KM

18

In a visionary poem, Isaiah pictures the march of the Assyrian armies against Jerusalem and their destruction by the hand of God (Is 10:28–34)

GREAT SEA

Lower Beth-horon Ai
Upper Beth-horon Mizpah Michmash
Adithaim Irpeel Migron
Jabneel Ekron Gibbethon Gezer Shaalabbin Gibeon Ramah Geba
Aijalon Gibeah Parah
Gederoth Gederah Chephirah Madmenah Almon
Kiriath-jearim Gebim Gallim Anathoth Pass of Adummim
Eltekeh Sores Nephtoah
Eshtaol Laishah
Zorah Chesalon Nob
Naamah Karem JERUSALEM
En-rogel En-shemesh
Beth-shemesh Manocho (Manahath)
Timnah
Makkedah Zanoah Bether
Jarmuth Gallim
Libnah Azekah Tappuah Bethlehem
Socoh Timnah Eltekon
Gibeah Peor Etam
Adullam Gedor Tekoa
Achzib Maarath Etam
Keilah Qiloh
Gath Nezib Bath-zur Zior
Ether Mareshah Iphtah Halhul
Zenan Beth-anoth
Lahmas (Lahmam) Ashnah
Lachish Cabbon Beth-tappuah Hebron
Migdal-gad Janim (Janum)
Chitlish Aphekah Kain
Jezreel Ziph
Debir Jokdeam Zanoah
Engedi

It is from this region that Sennacherib, King of Assyria, organises an unsuccessful attack against the Jerusalem of Hezekiah, about 701 B.C. More than a century later, Nebuchadnezzar, King of Babylon, also sets out from here to raid the territory of Zedekiah. Lachish and Azekah hold out longest (Jer 34:7)

SALT SEA

-1000 0 1000 2000 3000 ft.
-300 0 300 600 900 m.

THE TERRITORY OF JUDAH

721 B.C. – 586 B.C.
from the fall of Samaria to the fall of Jerusalem

0 5 10 MILES
0 5 10 KM

19

231
232

DANGER FROM THE NORTH

Towards the middle of the ninth century B.C., the kings of the little states of Syria-Palestine were alarmed to hear the distant rumbling of thunder from the north. In the course of the previous two centuries, the flood of Aramaean invasions had reduced the territory of Assyria to a tiny area between the Tigris and the Zab. About the year 900 B.C., however, the old lust for conquest once more took possession of the Assyrian kings. Their armies began to move forward with aims which grew more ambitious year by year. Their god Ashur must reign over a world empire; and any tribe which challenged his claim must be ruthlessly overthrown. In the area between the Euphrates and the Tigris, Ashurnasirpal (883–859 B.C.) struck with the utmost brutality at every Aramaean group which might conceivably become a power of any importance. Those Aramaean states which lay to the west of the Euphrates and in northern Syria retained their independence during his reign. But for how long was this to last? Ashurnasirpal's kingdom was soon as extensive as the world empire of Tiglath-pileser I had been two centuries earlier. It was, however, more methodically organised and much more firmly united, being divided up into provinces, cantons, and districts, administered by a corps of well-trained officials. His son and successor, Shalmaneser III, built upon this basic political organisation and, with incredible energy, extended the god Ashur's domain both to the west and to the south. In northern Syria, the Aramaean states succumbed one after the other. He overran Cilicia and seized all its natural wealth, the silver mines in the Taurus and the inexhaustible supplies of timber. But when he turned to the south, Shalmaneser met with formidable opposition. The princes of central Syria

had been warned well in advance. In the military report for the sixth year of his reign (854 B.C.), Shalmaneser records an encounter between his troops and the armies of twelve allied kings at Qarqar, south of Hamath on the Orontes. In listing these enemies and their contingents, he mentions, among others, Hadadezer of Damascus (with 20,000 soldiers, 1,200 horses and 1,200 chariots), the king of Hamath, and also Ahab of Israel, who took the field with 2,000 chariots and 10,000 men. According to this report, Shalmaneser naturally carried the day! 'I dammed the Orontes with their dead.' Assyrian kings were always victorious.

The battle of Qarqar was clearly an important event for King Ahab, since he took part in it with such a large contingent. It is also of interest to us because the Assyrian account gives a date, the sixth year of Shalmaneser, which we can fix in our chronology as 854 B.C. But, unfortunately, the Bible does not even mention this battle, and our hopes of synchronising this date with a definite year of Ahab's reign are disappointed. All we can infer from the Assyrian record is first, that Ahab was still alive in 854 B.C., and secondly, that he had been wise enough to forget the hostility of Damascus for a space and to fight alongside the Aramaean king against the common enemy. The Bible may, indeed, contain a hint of this truce in its account of a treaty between Israel and Syria after Ahab's victory near Aphek. The compiler of Kings apparently included an account of this victory because an unnamed prophet played a part in it. The treaty concerned the restitution of towns and market rights, but we may guess that it was inspired by the common Assyrian danger.

233

Previous page, **230** / *Assyrian Troops destroy a Captured City.* Detail from a mural relief (actual size 37 by 25 inches). While the engineers are expertly demo ishing the outer walls, flames are already leaping from the towers of the inner defences and from the gate. The last soldiers, laden with booty, have ju emerged, followed by one of their comrades who is driving before him two inhabitants who were still in the city. Below, a glimpse of the camp; soldiers ar camp-followers carouse under the impassive eye of the sentry. **231** / *Hezekiah's Tunnel,* dug, in view of the danger from Assyria, to ensure a supply of wat in case of siege (see p. 93). **232** / *The Siloam Inscription* at the end of the tunnel (the lines are about 28 inches long). In the same 'common characters' Isai wrote the name of his son (Is 8:1). **233** / *Lachish.* For the walls and the gate this drawing follows the foundations discovered during excavation.

234

235
236

234–236 / *Assyrian Bas-reliefs.* Today, owing to the patriotic zeal of the first excavators in Mesopotamia, who were mainly looking for museum pieces, we are able to admire in the museums of London and Paris masterpieces of Assyrian art, carved on great plaques of alabaster which formerly adorned the walls of the palaces. 234: King Ashurbanipal, followed by two servants, hunts the wild ass; fragment of a bas-relief from his palace at Nineveh (the above portion measures 44 by 21 inches). 235: Soldier from the palace of Sargon II (over 9 feet high), of the type that conquered Samaria. Over his shoulder is a quiver and a bow with a bird's head at each end; in his belt is a sword and in his left hand a heavy club. 236: Ashurbanipal in his state chariot. The king stands under a canopy; his servants carry fans and weapons; all is equally ceremonious.　　　　　*[Map 18, p. 82]*

237
238
239

240
241

242
243

237–243 / *Hunting Scenes.* Besides religious and military scenes, there are also a great many hunting scenes on the alabaster facings of the walls of the Assyrian palaces. (The reliefs from Nineveh alone, placed end to end, would be almost two miles long.) *Top right:* Ashurnasirpal (883-859 B.C.) hunting lions. The artists have not yet attained the perfect mastery revealed in the relief on the previous page (Pl. 234: Ashurbanipal, 668–626 B.C.). In the other reliefs, all from Nineveh and now in the British Museum, we see how lions were kept in cages and excited by beaters (243; observe the controlled fury of the crouching lion, and the horse which has mastered its terror); we also see lions being shot by the king from his chariot, or run through at close quarters (237-239). After the chase, the king offers a libation (240, 241). 242: Detail from the same scene as Pl. 234.   [*Map 18, p. 82*]

244

But whenever there was a momentary lull in the Assyrian pressure, the struggle between Samaria and Damascus seems to have flared up once more. For the Bible tells us that shortly after this treaty Ahab met his death in a battle with Syria over that perpetual bone of contention between the two kingdoms, the city of Ramoth-gilead. The account of this event in Kings enters into some detail, because it forms part of a significant story which shows the false prophets of Ahab in contrast with Micaiah, who spoke the true word of Yahweh.

Ahab's ally in the battle at Ramoth-gilead, which cost him his life, was Jehoshaphat king of Judah. As we have seen, the Northern kings tried to maintain friendly relations with Judah in order to be strong against the Aramaeans. This alliance was also in the interest of Judah. Jehoshaphat had still controlled the Arabah with the road to Ezion-geber, as appears from the brief reference to the failure of his expedition to Ophir. But the few lines devoted to the reign of his son Joram (848–841 B.C.) show that he was faced with a rebellion in Edom by which that country regained its independence from Judah. Both the Northern and the Southern kingdoms were then having to fight for their territories. The political friendship between them was further cemented by the marriage of Joram of Judah to Athaliah, the daughter of Ahab and Jezebel. The new queen no doubt introduced the perverted religion of her heathen mother into the palace of Jerusalem, the heart of the Southern kingdom. We are not surprised to learn that the bloody revolution which ensued, inspired in large part by the reaction of orthodox Yahwism, struck at both royal houses with one savage blow.

The book of Kings gives a detailed account of Jehu's revolution and accession to the throne of Israel. This rising started in the camp before Ramoth-gilead, where, under the command of Joram (852–841 B.C.) and Ahaziah (841

B.C.), the allied troops of Israel and Judah were again fighting the Aramaeans. Joram was wounded in the battle and carried to Jezreel, where he was visited by Ahaziah. In their absence, a disciple of Elisha came to Ramoth-gilead and anointed Jehu, an Israelite commander, charging him on behalf of Yahweh with the destruction of the house of Ahab. The new king was at once acclaimed by the troops, and set out with a small escort for Jezreel. There followed the brutal murder of Joram and Ahaziah, the death of Jezebel, and the massacre of all the males of Ahab's family (including some kinsmen of the king of Judah). Finally, the priests and worshippers of the Tyrian Baal were slaughtered in his temple in Samaria. For this military *coup d'état* was primarily a violent reaction against Phoenician influences in Israel and their disastrous effects in the religious sphere. This is no doubt why so many details of the story remained current in Yahwistic circles in Israel and were recorded by the compiler of Kings, and why Jehu was supported by those fanatical devotees of Yahweh, the 'Sons of Rechab'. There are also signs that the greatly increased class of impoverished peasants, angered by the luxury of the court, may have welcomed the new king.

Behind these local events loomed the constant threat of Assyrian expansion. The Annals of Shalmaneser reveal that after the battle of Qarqar he again marched into Syria in the tenth, eleventh, and fourteenth years of his reign. During his last campaign he mentions receiving tribute from 'Jehu of Israel, son *(sic)* of Omri'. This act of submission must have seemed important to Shalmaneser, for it occupies a considerable part of his famous black obelisk. The Bible does not mention Jehu's tribute: apparently it had no religious consequences. Thanks to Shalmaneser's Annals, however, we can be certain that in 841 B.C., the fourteenth year of his reign, Jehu was already king of Israel.

245
246

244 / *Army Musicians with Two Horses.* Detail from a bas-relief in the Louvre which probably depicts a military celebration. The musicians, two playing stringed and two percussion instruments, seem to be moving backwards and forwards in time with the music. The carving of the horses demonstrates the artist's mastery of his medium; led by the bridle, they are apparently being taught to walk to the music. 245 / *The Storming of a Fortress* in the time of Tiglath-pileser III (relief from Calah); a battering-ram, propelled from inside by its crew, moves forward over an earthwork towards the fortifications (invisible in the photograph); an officer (in a long robe) and a soldier are in position behind a great shield; in the distance *(top left)* are three inhabitants impaled. 246 / *A File of Prisoners* (see Pls. 230 and 258); detail from the grand parade which Ashurbanipal is watching in Pl. 236. [Map 18, p. 82]

247 a

When there is talk of the great discoveries and inventions of the past century, our minds turn in the first place to practical things, to the wonderful uses of electricity, to television, to the jet aeroplane, or to nuclear fission. We easily overlook two discoveries which have enabled people today to examine the most important periods in their past history – the deciphering of the Egyptian hieroglyphs and of cuneiform writing. These achievements have brought to life for us the ancient civilisations of the Nile Valley and of Mesopotamia. Both these systems of writing developed from very simple drawings: for example, to indicate a head, one merely drew a head. The inhabitants of the peaceful valley of the Nile were able to make very life-like drawings on their soft limestone (see p. 39). In Mesopotamia, a handful of clay could be picked up almost anywhere, moulded into a tablet, and used for writing. But clay was a less suitable medium for the realistic representation of objects than the limestone of Egypt. Soon people began to conventionalise and to produce 'wedge-shaped' impressions with the aid of the stylus: their writing had then become cuneiform, and it was no longer possible, in the majority of cases, to recognise the original object from which the sign had been developed. The 'wedge-shaped' impression was formed by pushing the angular point of the stylus into the clay and then withdrawing it obliquely so as to score the clay lightly with a tapering line. Typical examples may be seen at the top and bottom of the illustration below. Each sign consisted of a combination of vertical, oblique, or horizontal 'wedges' of all sizes. Some signs still continued to indicate an object, while others eventually came to represent nothing but a syllable (cf. Pl. 80 and caption).

In the course of the eventful history of Mesopotamia (cf. p. 15), this system of writing was sometimes used for several different languages at once. The single sign for a head thus acquired a separate phonetic value in each language. The system was also used outside Mesopotamia, in Canaanite Palestine, in Asia Minor by the Hittites (in addition to their own hieroglyphic writing, cf. Pl. 106), in Elam, and in Persia. Moreover, the number of different signs multiplied into some thousands. In Elam the number was reduced to 113 syllabic signs, and the Persians cut this figure down to 41, thereby coming close to alphabetical writing. When the work of deciphering began, shortly after 1800, scholars therefore turned first to the relatively simple Persian system. The key to Assyrian, which was much more complicated, was not finally discovered until 1852, mainly as a result of the outstanding work of Sir Henry Rawlinson, who, between 1843 and 1847, transcribed and largely deciphered Darius' great trilingual inscription at Behistun, carved on the face of a precipice 500 feet above the surrounding countryside - a feat calling for considerable agility. The inscription covers an area of more than 1,200 square feet, and describes Darius' early victories. Since then our understanding of cuneiform writing has been increased by the patient labours of several generations of scholars.

The discovery of fresh documents is constantly enabling us to widen and deepen our knowledge of the ancient civilisations and their mutual relations. For example, many texts have thrown light upon the last great centuries of the Assyrian Empire. Because Assyria's bid to control Syria and Palestine brought her into contact with the two little kingdoms of Israel and Judah, we now possess an invaluable store of records which furnish a background to the fragmentary information in the Bible. As an illustration, we reproduce below part of a text which Sennacherib caused to be cut on a number of hexagonal prisms (cf. Pl. 248; translation after J. T. Nelis).

Sennacherib (1), the great king, the mighty king, the king of the universe, the king of Ashur, the king of the four quarters of the earth, the wise shepherd, the favourite of the great gods, defender of the right, lover of justice, he who gives help, who succours the orphans and devotes himself to good works, perfect hero, courageous man, first among all the princes, the mighty man who quells the rebels and strikes the wicked with his thunderbolts.

247 b

247a / *The Black Obelisk of Shalmaneser III*, from his palace at Calah and now in the British Museum. On the four sides of this black basalt stele, standing 6½ feet high and stepped at the top like a ziggurat, the great conqueror recorded a succinct but vividly illustrated account of the military successes which marked the 31 years of his reign. 247b / *King Jehu Offers his Tribute*. The four reliefs in the second row from the top are devoted to 'the tribute of Jehu, son of Omri', to quote the beginning of the text above the principal relief, which is reproduced here (half actual size). The king of Israel, wearing a pointed hat, bows low at the feet of Shalmaneser, who is offering a libation. Above are the winged sun and the star of Ishtar; on either side are servants with parasol, fan and sceptre. The cortège which follows in Jehu's train, bearing gifts, is visible in 247a.

Ashur, the great mountain (2), has granted me unrivalled kingship and has made my weapons more powerful than those of all the men who dwell in palaces. From the upper sea of the sunset, to the lower sea of the sunrise (3), every black head (4) is bowed at my feet and the most powerful princes fear to meet me in battle: they leave their lands and flee, like the owl in the cleft of the rock, to inaccessible places.

After this introduction, Sennacherib gives an account of his operations in 703 B.C. against Merodach-baladan, who is mentioned in the Bible; he then tells of the campaign which he led in 702 B.C. against the Kassites. The lower part of the second column of the prism (Pl. 248, left-hand column) and the third column (Pl. 248, central column) are devoted to an account of his expedition to the coastal regions of Syria-Palestine.

In my third campaign I went to Hatti (5). Luli, the king of Sidon, so feared the terrible splendour of my power that he fled far across the sea (6) and perished. Great Sidon, Little Sidon, Bit-zitti, Zaribtu, Mahalliba, Ushu (7), Achzib, Acco, his (8) fortified cities, fortresses with pastures and wells of water for his garrisons, the might of the weapons of Ashur, my Lord, overwhelmed them and they bowed at my feet. I placed Tuba'lu upon the throne to be their king and imposed upon him the tribute due to me as his overlord, to be paid faithfully each year. As to Menahem of Samsimuruna, Tuba'lu of Sidon, Abdili'ti of Arvad, Urumilki of Gebal (9), Mitinti of Ashdod, Buduilu of Beth-ammon, Kammusunabdi of Moab, Aiarammu of Edom, all the kings of Amurru, they brought me very costly presents and their fourfold gift of alliance and they kissed my feet.

As to Sidqa, the king of Ashkelon, who had not submitted to my yoke, the gods of his fathers, himself, his wife, his sons, his daughters, his brothers, all the descendants of his family, I deported and sent to Assyria. I installed Sharruludari, son of Rukibti, their former king, as governor over the people of Ashkelon and imposed upon him the tribute, the gifts which are due to me as his overlord – he bears the reins (10). During my campaign I besieged, captured, and sacked Beth-dagon, Joppa, Banai-barqa, Azuru, cities belonging to Sidqa, which had not immediately bowed at my feet. The hearts of the magistrates, nobles, and common people of Ekron who had imprisoned Padi, their king, bound by an oath to Ashur, and had given him as a prisoner to Hezekiah of Judah – who held him in prison in a criminal manner – [the hearts of the magistrates . . .] had begun to tremble. They had called upon the king of Egypt, upon the bowmen, chariots and horses of the king of Ethiopia, a host beyond counting, to lend them aid. Upon the plain of Eltekeh they drew up in battle formation against me and furbished their weapons. Trusting in Ashur, my Lord, I took the field against them and defeated them. I took prisoner alive with my own hands, in the heat of the battle, the commander of the chariots and the sons of the king of Egypt and the commander of the chariots of the king of Ethiopia. I besieged, captured, and sacked Eltekeh and Timnah. I attacked Ekron, put to death the magistrates and nobles who had caused the revolution and hung their bodies on gibbets around the city. The citizens who had committed crimes and other offences, I counted as spoil (11). The others, who were not accused of misbehaviour or crimes, who had done no wrong, I let go free. Padi, their king, I brought from Jerusalem, I placed him upon the throne as their lord and I imposed upon him the tribute due to me as his overlord. As for Hezekiah of Judah, he did not submit to my yoke: forty-six of his strong cities, fortresses, and countless small towns in the vicinity, I besieged and conquered by building earthworks, by bringing up siege-engines, with the help of assault troops, by breaches in the walls, by mines under the ramparts and onslaughts with the battering-ram. I deported from among them and counted as spoil 200,150 persons, young and old, men and women, and horses, mules, asses, camels, sheep and cattle, in countless numbers. Himself, I imprisoned in Jerusalem, his residence, like a bird in its cage. I surrounded him with earthworks in order to punish the temerity of any man who dared to come out of the city gate. His cities which I had sacked, I took away from his country and gave them to Mitinti, king of Ashdod, Padi, king of Ekron, and Sillibel, king of Gaza, and thus I diminished his country. To the former tribute which he was obliged to pay each year, I added a further tribute and the gifts of alliance due to me as my overlord.

Hezekiah himself was so terrified by the terrible splendour of my power that he sent to me at Nineveh, my royal city, the Urbi (12) and his excellent soldiers whom he had brought in to strengthen Jerusalem his residence and whom he had received as a reinforcement – with 30 talents of gold, 800 talents of silver, precious stones, stibium, great blocks of red stone, couches inlaid with ivory, as well as state chairs inlaid with ivory, elephant hides, elephant tusks, maple wood, yew wood, all kinds of precious treasures, and his daughters, his concubines, and male and female singers. To pay the tribute and to testify to his submission, he sent his ambassador to me.

248

NOTES

1. Sennacherib, Assyrian *Sin-achê-eriba*, 'may (the god) Sin increase my brothers'
2. cf. the name 'Rock' to designate Yahweh
3. The Mediterranean Sea and the Persian Gulf
4. Mankind
5. The region of the Hittite towns in northern Syria
6. ? to Cyprus
7. The mainland city of Tyre
8. i.e. Luli's
9. Byblos
10. i.e. of my yoke
11. i.e. made prisoners of war
12. ? Arabs

N.B. The names of well-known towns and persons which occur in the Bible are given here in their Hebrew form and transcribed according to the principles adopted for this Atlas.

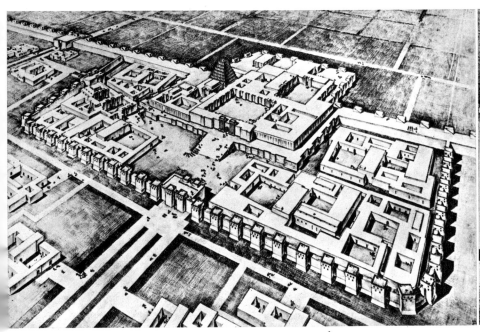

249a

249b

248 / *Hexagonal Prism of Sennacherib.* The example reproduced above is not the famous prism of Taylor, discovered at Calah, on which Sennacherib recorded his campaign against Hezekiah, but a prism with an almost identical text (see above) found at the end of 1952. Made of baked clay and inscribed with very small characters, it stands 14½ inches high and is now in the Museum of Baghdad; the above photograph is published by kind permission of the Museum authorities. **249a** and **b** / *Reconstruction of Dur Sharrukin,* the fortified residence built by Sargon II. His son Sennacherib again made Nineveh the capital, with the result that the 'citadel of Sargon' never became a living city. The work of Victor Place (about 1858) on the well-preserved ruins at Khorsabad was admirably resumed in 1931 by the Oriental Institute of Chicago, where these drawings were made.

[*Map 18, p. 82*]

250 / 'Anâta in the Evening Sun, looking NNE. In the centre is the village which preserves the name of the Biblical Anathoth, the home of Jeremiah. In the distance, the hills slope down to the Jordan valley. The highest point of the ridge is *J.el-'Asûr*, the Baal-hazor where Absalom killed his brother (2 S 13:23–29). The two villages of Geba and Michmash are just visible at the extreme left. [*Maps 15, p. 66; 17, p. 81*]

THE VOICE OF ISRAEL'S CONSCIENCE

2 K 9,10

After devoting nearly two entire chapters to the bloody revolution which installed the warrior Jehu on the throne of Israel, the books of Kings pass judgment on this ruler: he has destroyed the house of Ahab; this is well, in Yahweh's sight; in return his descendants will be privileged to retain the throne down to the fourth generation. But in spite of his 'zeal for the Lord, ... Jehu did not turn aside from the sins of Jeroboam the son of Nebat, which he made Israel to sin, the golden calves that were in Bethel, and in Dan'. During his reign, Yahweh therefore began to 'cut off parts' of the Northern Kingdom, and caused Hazael of Damascus to conquer all the land beyond the Jordan; for Jehu, faithful to the principles which had brought him to the throne, had severed all relations with Phoenicia, thereby depriving himself of the support which Omri and his immediate successors had found in that quarter.

2 K 10:16
2 K 10:29-32

The king of Damascus took advantage of this situation. Hazael's name appears, with that of Jehu, on the black obelisk of Shalmaneser III, while another text describes him as the successor of Hadadezer and 'son of a nobody', which means that he was a usurper and not the lawful heir. This is how he is presented in the Bible, in a passage linking him with the prophet Elisha. It was only during the first years of Hazael's reign that the kingdom of Damascus was subjected to the dangerous attacks of Shalmaneser. The Assyrian campaign of 838 B.C., during which Shalmaneser captured a number of towns, does not appear to have been followed by others. The closing years of his reign were, in fact, marked by rebellions in Assyria itself. Nor was his successor (Shamshi-adad V, 823–810 B.C.) able to organise a large-scale campaign in the west. The little states in Syria and Palestine could thus breathe more freely for a few decades. Hence the repeated attacks made by Hazael and his successors on a friendless Israel.

247

2 K 8:13

But the Assyrians once more recovered. In the Annals of Adad-nirari III (809–782 B.C.), we read of a campaign against Damascus which clearly spelt the beginning of the end for that city. The roll of states which paid tribute to the conqueror also includes the name of Israel. But Adad-nirari was unable to consolidate his Syrian victories: other regions were causing him too much anxiety, especially the mountain area in the northeast, where the Medes were growing rebellious. Nor could his three weak successors (781–746 B.C.) concern themselves with the west; and in the north they were powerless to prevent a decline in their authority over the peoples of Urartu. During this period Joash of Israel was consequently able to reconquer from a greatly weakened Damascus all the lost territories; and we learn that his son restored the original frontiers of the Northern Kingdom, 'from the entrance of Hamath as far as the Sea of the Arabah'. In the long reign of this king, Jeroboam II (*ca* 783–742 B.C.), the Kingdom knew a final period of glory.

2 K 14:25

Since both the faith and the Temple were threatened by Athaliah's activities in Judah, the compiler of the books of Kings includes a detailed account of her downfall after a reign of six years. Her grandson Joash, who had escaped her murderous designs, was placed on the throne by the Judaeans. After a long and rather uneventful reign, he died the victim of a conspiracy. A similar fate befell his son and successor Amaziah. But Judah remained loyal to the dynasty: after Amaziah, his son Azariah (also called Uzziah) was placed on the throne of David by 'all the people' (*ca* 781–740 B.C.). He was, therefore, the contemporary of Jeroboam II, and was on the throne for almost the same length of time. During his reign the Southern Kingdom flourished and grew prosperous. He, too, reconquered lost territories; he completely regained control of the Arabah and fortified the town of Elath, on the Gulf in the south. The compiler of Chronicles, drawing upon early records, mentions all kinds of measures to improve farming and stock-breeding, to extend and consolidate the ring of fortresses around Jerusalem, and to reorganise the army.

These last details should be noted. The shadow of Assyria lay over the sunny prosperity of the two Israelite states. The Assyrians had reduced the kingdom of Damascus to impotence for a time – and both Hamath and Israel, her northern and southern neighbours, had taken the opportunity to seize a large part of her territory. Since then the armies of Nineveh had not reappeared in Syria. The colossus appeared to be sleeping. But any day he might rouse himself and finally shatter the little states along the shores of the Great Sea.

That fateful day dawned even before the close of the reigns of Azariah and Jeroboam II. In 745 B.C., the throne of Assyria was seized by a man who confidently assumed the famous name of Tiglath-pileser. Having thus announced his programme, he proceeded to carry it out during the eighteen years of a reign which stamped him as the greatest of the Assyrian kings. In order to achieve his ambition of a world empire, he had to subdue the rebellious Aramaeans in the south and contrive to gain possession of the cultural and religious metropolis of Babylon; he had to contain the tribes of Urartu in the north; and, finally, he had to conquer Syria and Palestine in the west. This last operation was not only dictated by the wealth of these countries; it was primarily necessary because they stood at the gateway to Egypt and gave access to the western sea.

In the execution of these plans, Tiglath-pileser pursued a systematic policy of mass deportations. This was intended not only to destroy the national loyalties of the subject peoples, who had very strong local ties, but also to lay the foundations of a world empire in which all men could feel at home everywhere, knowing no masters save the representatives of the small, but proud, nation of Assyria. It was not until 738 B.C. that the conqueror began upon a series of campaigns in the west. The records of these events have survived only in an incomplete form, but they nevertheless provide us with an invaluable supplement to the information in the Bible.

Meanwhile, the death of Jeroboam II had heralded a period of fresh disturbances in Israel. After reigning for six months, his son Zechariah was assassinated by Shallum, who was in turn deposed by Menahem after only a month. Menahem reigned for seven years (743–737 B.C.) and, according to the Bible, he gave Tiglath-pileser a large sum of money 'to confirm his hold of the royal power'. In the Assyrian ruler's records, Menahem of Israel

251, 252 / *Mount Carmel and the Bay of Haifa.* Carmel, clothed in verdure (the name means a garden with vines and fruit trees), has been a holy mountain from time immemorial. The God of Israel was worshipped here; Elijah restored His altar in this place, and, on feast days, people would go up to see Elisha (1 K 18:30; 2 K 4:23). 251: The promontory, with the modern town of Haifa. 252: A view from Haifa over part of the bay and the fertile coastal plain; in the distance are the hills of Galilee. **253, 254** / *'Ain Fâra.* An abundant spring (from which drinking-water for Jerusalem is now pumped), 3¾ miles NE of Anathoth, near the meeting-place of the two ravines seen in Pl. 190. The little *Khirbet Fâra*, near the spring, is the Parah of Jos 18:23, and may also be the Perath of Jeremiah's dramatic action (Jer 13, where English versions have Euphrates). **255, 256** / *A Booth and a Watch-tower in the Fields.* [Maps 13, p.60; 17, p.81]

THE LACHISH LETTERS. In the spring of 1935, scholars who were excavating at Tell ed-Duweir, 'the tell of the little cloister', discovered a collection of eighteen fragments of pottery inscribed in ink. These fragments, together with hundreds of others which had become completely illegible, were found in the guard-room between the two walls of the town, near the gate. On three of the potsherds only a few characters can be distinguished; on a fourth there remain only two barely discernible lines on the outside, while the inscription on the inside has completely disappeared. The more important fragments reveal that these were letters written to a certain Yaôsh, who was without doubt the governor of the district whose capital stood on the tell. This capital was almost certainly the Biblical town of Lachish. It may be assumed that Yaôsh removed his 'archives' to the bastion at the town gate after his palace had been destroyed by Nebuchadnezzar in 597 B.C. The very high humidity has destroyed the papyrus documents and removed the ink from most of the potsherds. But the little that remains is full of interest for the student of the Bible. These letters were, in fact, written between 597 and 587 B.C. by Judaeans who must have had some knowledge, if only by hearsay, of the prophet Jeremiah; they spoke the same language as he did, and they used the same script as that in which Baruch recorded the prophecies of his master. The style of the letters is very similar to that of the contemporary Biblical texts and nearly all the personal names recur in the Scriptures.

Opposite is shown one of the fragments (No. 4 of the collection). It is inscribed on both sides. We append a translation of the French version of Father R. de Vaux, O.P. The strokes give a rough indication of the endings of the lines in the original. It opens with a classic epistolary formula (as do the other letters). From the end of the 7th line to the 9th the translation is uncertain:

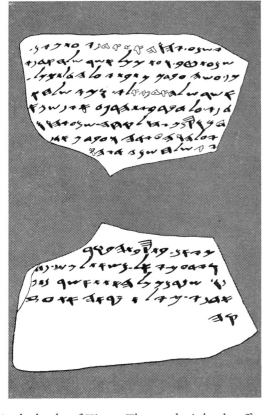

May Yahweh cause my lord to hear, this very day, | good tidings. And now according to everything that my lord hath written | thus hath thy servant done: I have inscribed upon the gate [?] in accordance with all | that thou hast written to me. Touching what my lord wrote | concerning Beth-haraphid, there is | no-one there; as for Semachiah, Shemaiah hath taken him and | brought him to the town [?Jerusalem]. Thy servant, my lord, | will write thither. Where is he, if not in the neighbourhood [of the town]? | Make an enquiry and [my lord] | will find that we are obeying the signals of Lachish | according to all the signs that my lord giveth, | for we do not see Azekah.

We may guess that the letters were written by the garrison commander of an outpost north of Lachish, after Azekah had fallen to the Babylonians and when it seemed that an attack on Lachish, the last Judaean stronghold except for Jerusalem (cf. Jer 34: 7), could not be long delayed. The fragments throw a dramatic spotlight on the death throes of Judah.

is in fact mentioned, together with Rezin of Damascus, among the kings who paid tribute. Two years after his accession, Pekahiah, the son and successor of Menahem, was assassinated and succeeded by one Pekah. This happened in 735 B.C., while Tiglath-pileser was up in the north administering a death-blow to the peoples of Urartu. Pekah took advantage of his absence to form a coalition against Assyria, and was immediately joined by Rezin of Damascus. But Ahaz of Judah refused to co-operate. The allies then marched on Jerusalem, bent on placing a puppet of their own upon the throne of David. They laid waste the land and prepared to besiege the capital. With the Temple treasure, Ahaz bought the intervention of the Assyrian conqueror. We learn from his Annals that, having crossed the territory of the Philistines, Tiglath-pileser first attacked Damascus, which he crushed once and for all in 732 B.C.; he then led an expedition against Israel and annexed her northern and eastern territories, after devastating virtually the whole country and deporting its inhabitants. Only the mountain of Ephraim, around Samaria, was spared. The following years saw the death-throes of the Northern Kingdom, which are reflected in the Bible. The end came in 721 B.C. The Kingdom of the Ten Tribes finally disappeared from the pages of history; the torch of the faith in Yahweh was to be borne by Judah alone.

The closing decades of the eighth century are dominated by the impressive figure of Isaiah. This fact emerges more clearly from the book of Isaiah itself, the first of those of the 'Latter Prophets' (cf. p. 27), than

257

257 / Stele of Esarhaddon. Among the symbols of the gods (top right), we see Hadad on his bull (see Pl. 219) and, below the crescent of the moon (Sin), the winged sun and the star of Ishtar (see Pl. 247b). The stele measures 10 feet 7 inches by 4 feet 5 inches.

from the meagre information in the books of Kings. The prophetic books offer us no more than fragments, passages drawn from a much larger body of teaching. The task of the prophets was to explain to Israel her rôle in relation to world events and to define for her the requirements of the Covenant with Yahweh in the light of ever-changing circumstances. As early as the time of Samuel, we met with prophets who had ecstatic experiences when possessed by the spirit of God; they would then perform wild dances, with or without musical accompaniment, sometimes wounding themselves and rending their clothing. Groups of the 'Sons of the Prophets' were attached to the old sanctuaries and appear to have constituted a special class, which was sometimes marked by a characteristic costume or other distinguishing features. The stories in which they figure prove that their activities were primarily directed to maintaining Yahwistic traditions. In the Northern Kingdom we find them taking part, under the leadership of Elijah and Elisha, in the struggle against the pagan policy of Ahab and the cult of Baal. They were consequently persecuted by the successors of Omri. Sometimes men consulted a prophet before making an important decision; on other occasions the prophet would himself intervene to proclaim the will of Yahweh. At the court of David and his successors we meet with official prophets. But priests or humble peasants also assumed the rôle of prophet in order to convey a message from Yahweh, and sometimes spoke contemptuously of the professional prophets.

We possess the teachings of only a few of the prophets, known as the 'writing prophets', which means that extracts from their works have been preserved in Scriptural tradition. We must not therefore imagine that these men themselves composed, in the strict sense of the word, the works which bear their names. Many of their utterances, sometimes couched in highly poetic language, probably circulated orally, or were originally recorded each on a separate potsherd or papyrus. Disciples also collected together the sayings and pronouncements of their masters, as Baruch did those of Jeremiah. These various materials were not brought together until later, when biographical details were sometimes added, and the whole was presented in accordance with certain definite ideas.

In the middle of the eighth century Amos and Hosea had prophesied in the Northern Kingdom. Despite all the prosperity of Jeroboam II's reign, they saw that the foundations of the national life were unstable, since the will of God was flouted in the life of the nation. Justice and humanity did not prevail amongst men, and ever-widening class distinctions separated them. Such a condition could only lead to disaster, which they foresaw as God's discipline of His people.

About the year 740 B.C., Isaiah witnessed the events which preceded the disappearance of the Northern Kingdom, crushed by the ruthless might of Assyria. He was deeply moved, and felt himself called to utter prophecies which are preserved in Chapters 1–33 of the book which bears his name. He proclaims that the course of world events is ordained by the will of Yahweh and that no earthly power can prevent the fulfilment of the mighty plans whose foundations He laid in making the Covenant with His people.

Therefore thus says the Lord, the Lord of hosts: "O my people, who dwell in Zion, be not afraid of the Assyrians when they smite with the rod and lift up their staff against you as the Egyptians did. For in a very little while my indignation will come to an end, and my anger will be directed to their destruction. And in that day his burden will depart from your shoulder, and his yoke will be destroyed from your neck."

258

258 / *Deportation of the Inhabitants of a Conquered City*. Bas-relief from the palace of Tiglath-pileser at Calah. The city stands on a hill; it is surrounded by an outer wall, fortified with towers and (*top left*) a citadel, whose arched gate can be seen. According to the inscription, this is Astartu, the Biblical Ashtaroth (east of the Sea of Galilee).   [*Maps 4, p. 29; 12, p. 59*]

JUDAH IN EXILE

One may ask why the compiler of Isaiah's prophecies did not place the account of the prophet's call at the beginning of his work. No-one can answer this question, for we have no definite information about the origins of this book, which doubtless took shape over a very long period. What is certain is that the inaugural vision has been given a most appropriate setting. In the present book of Isaiah, this impressive scene is placed in Chapter 6. The preceding prophecies are addressed to the inhabitants of Judah and consist mainly of bitter reproaches for their abandonment of Yahweh and their oppression of the weak. The broad political scene remains outside their purview. It is only at the very end of this section, immediately before the inaugural vision, that a short passage about the Assyrians is introduced. They are not mentioned by name, but they may be clearly recognised in these few lines, much of whose evocative force is unfortunately lost in translation. It is Yahweh Himself who has loosed the Assyrian flood and who has summoned from a far land the unerring archers and the swift horsemen. The heavy tramp of the armies, like the roaring and rumbling of an angry sea, is drawing near to Judah. The light of certainty and joy has departed. Terror and anxiety spread like heavy shadows over the land. After this dark picture, there follows Isaiah's description of the glory of the God whom he has been privileged to behold, Yahweh, the king of Heaven and earth, enthroned amid resplendent seraphim. The contrast with what precedes is striking.

Moreover, the passage is linked with equal care to the following scene, in which Isaiah appears before the king and utters the famous words concerning Immanuel. There, in contrast to the terrified men around him, he behaves with the calm assurance of a man who has looked upon Yahweh, the supreme arbiter of history. At that moment Rezin of Damascus and Pekah of Israel were marching on Judah to install an Aramaean on the throne of David in place of Ahaz, who had refused to join the alliance of the Palestinian states against Assyria. The book of Kings merely records that the two kings besieged Ahaz in Jerusalem, but could not defeat him. In the book of Isaiah we are given some details, doubtless at first hand. Ahaz need not be afraid of this attack on the dynasty of David. 'These two smouldering stumps of firebrands' may indeed intend to impose a foreign king; but there is nothing to fear, for 'thus says the Lord God: It shall not stand, and it shall not come to pass'. Behind these kings another danger was threatening – it had, in fact, been the cause of their attack on Judah. In verses of incomparable beauty, Isaiah prophesies that 'the waters of the River [Euphrates], mighty and many' will overwhelm the whole land of Judah. Yahweh has summoned them to punish the unfaithful people. He takes the Assyrians in His hand as a rod to chastise Judah.

It is clear from the book of Kings that Ahaz was not convinced by Isaiah's assuring words. For we are told that he attempted to rid himself of his enemies by buying, with the Temple treasure, the intervention of Tiglath-pileser. Here

he succeeded, and Rezin and Pekah were forced to withdraw. But, by his own action, Ahaz had made himself tributary to Assyria and had opened the door to Assyrian influences, even in the religious sphere, as is apparent from the detailed account in the book of Kings of the installation of a new altar in the Temple. Meanwhile, Tiglath-pileser was devastating a great part of the Northern Kingdom and deporting its inhabitants. This disaster forms the background to Isaiah's famous prophecy concerning the miraculous child who is to be born. A great light will dispel the darkness which now overshadows Galilee and the region of the Lake. Here again, we see how the reappearance of the Assyrian Empire is reflected in the visions of the prophet.

Is 9: 1-7 (Heb. 8:23-9:6)

Ahaz was succeeded by his son Hezekiah. We cannot establish the exact year of his accession, as the Biblical evidence is conflicting. But the Bible leaves us in no doubt that Hezekiah understood the lesson to be drawn from the destruction of the Northern Kingdom, and realised that it was foreign influences and religious degeneration which had led to its decay. He therefore made radical changes in his father's policy and, with the moral support of the prophets Isaiah and Micah, energetically engaged upon a number of reforms. He perceived that Judah's strength as a nation lay in the purity of her faith in Yahweh. This is why there is a fundamental connection between his religious reforms and his economic and military reorganisation.

The Bible mentions that Hezekiah 'made the pool and the conduit and brought water into the city'. These words must refer to the conduit which still carries water from the Spring Gihon through the rock of Ophel to a pool which then lay inside the walls. Our detailed knowledge of this conduit dates from 1880, when its southern end was found to bear the famous inscription in which the workmen describe how they began to tunnel from opposite ends and finally met 'pick to pick'. Water then began to flow from the spring to the pool 'over a distance of 1,200 cubits, the rock above the heads of the workmen being 100 cubits thick'. In the course of centuries a heavy calcareous deposit had formed. Now that this has been removed, the tunnel has been restored to its original width, which varies between 23 and 26 inches; its average height is about 5 feet. The course, with its amazing twists and turns, is shown on Map 33 (p. 115). The tunnel itself is 560 yards long, although the distance in a straight line from one end to the other is only 354 yards. One of the many possible reasons for this may have been the wish to avoid at all costs any interference with the royal tombs, which were quite deeply hewn into the rock on the eastern slope of Ophel.

2 K 20:20

231

232

Whatever the explanation, with the help of Map 33 we can fully appreciate the great strategic importance of this tunnel. Before the time of Hezekiah, there was already a conduit which brought water from the Spring Gihon to a pool in the most low-lying part of the city; but it was no more than a trench in the hillside, which ran outside the walls over most of its course and could therefore easily be blocked by a besieging army. Its course was later altered. In 1886,

a second conduit was discovered, partly cut through the rock and partly covered with flat stones, but this new channel was still outside the walls and could still be obstructed without difficulty. It was probably this conduit which Isaiah had in mind when he spoke to Ahaz of 'the waters of Shiloah that flow gently'. It is easy to visualise the frightened king, on a tour of inspection of the hasty improvements which were being made to this weak point in Jerusalem's defences, when Isaiah arrived to urge him to have faith in God. Hezekiah's tunnel is the best preserved Biblical 'monument' in Jerusalem. The tourist who does not mind wading for a third of a mile, knee-deep in the cool water which still flows gently through, should certainly visit this spot; he will otherwise be missing an unforgettable experience.

Hezekiah was indeed besieged by the Assyrians. After the death of Tiglath-pileser III, his son Shalmaneser V (726–722 B.C.) was obliged to undertake military expeditions in three successive years, in order to unite the regions conquered by his father more firmly to his empire. The kings of the small states in Syria and Palestine periodically refused to pay their annual levy, and this Assyria always regarded as rebellion. The kings were emboldened by the hope of support from Egypt who, weak though she was, could hardly allow Assyria to dominate southern Palestine. It was Shalmaneser who finally destroyed the Northern Kingdom, although his successor, a man who seized the throne by force and assumed the ancient name of Sargon, boasts in his Annals of having conquered Samaria and deported its inhabitants. This Sargon II (721–705 B.C.) is once mentioned by name in the Bible, in the introduction to one of Isaiah's prophecies. The historical background to this prophecy is also provided by Sargon's Annals. About the year 713 B.C., Yamani, king of the Philistine city of Ashdod, had attempted, with the promise of help from Egypt, to stir up Edom and Moab, as well as Judah, against Assyria. Sargon first placed another king on Yamani's throne, and when this puppet was assassinated by the people and replaced by an Ionian from Cyprus, he sent his general (tartân) to destroy the town.

We also gather from Isaiah's writings that envoys from Egypt regularly appeared in Jerusalem. The Egyptian throne was then occupied by an Ethiopian, whose nephew Tirhakah already held a high military post and was later to reign in his turn. Isaiah has a boundless admiration for these tall, dark-skinned Ethiopians from the distant land of many rivers. But he utters repeated warnings against the temptation 'to take refuge in the protection of Pharaoh, and to seek shelter in the shadow of Egypt', instead of trusting in the protection of Yahweh. 'The Egyptians are men, and not God; and their horses are flesh, and not spirit.' Egypt will not prove a match for Assyria, and then the statesmen of Judah 'shall be dismayed and confounded because of Ethiopia their hope and of Egypt their boast'.

During the disturbances which followed the death of Sargon in 705 B.C., Hezekiah ventured to rebel against Assyria. He did so in company with several neighbouring states. The arrival of envoys from Merodach-baladan, which is mentioned in the Bible, must also have been connected with the spirit of rebellion in Judah. It is in no way improbable that this tireless champion of Babylonian independence should have searched as far afield as Palestine for allies against the hated Assyrian Empire. It took Sennacherib (705–681 B.C.), the son and successor of Sargon, several years to suppress various revolts in other parts of his empire and to expel Merodach-baladan from Babylon. It was therefore not until 701 B.C. that he turned to Syria and Palestine. The account of his campaign has come down to us inscribed on several hexagonal cylinders of baked clay; a photograph of the most recently discovered example appears with a translation on pp. 88–89.

The Bible devotes nearly two chapters to the peril which threatened Jerusalem during these months and to the miraculous deliverance of the city. Isaiah, who had advised Hezekiah against joining an anti-Assyrian coalition, is now at his side and declares: 'He [Sennacherib] shall not come to this city or shoot an arrow there, or come before it with a shield or cast up a mound against it. By the way that he came, by the same he shall return, and he shall not come into this city.' Sennacherib did in fact fail to capture Jerusalem. The Assyrian scribes gloss over this setback with fine words; but the Bible regards the retreat of the armies as a miracle: 'And that night the angel of the Lord went forth, and slew a hundred and eighty-five thousand in the camp of the Assyrians.'

The greatly reduced territory of Judah remained tributary to Assyria in the time of Hezekiah and during the long reign of his son Manasseh, whose tribute is recorded in the Annals of Esarhaddon (680–669 B.C.) and Ashurbanipal (668–

259

259, 260 / *The Mighty Babylon of Nebuchadnezzar II*. Reconstruction of Eckhard Unger. 259: In the foreground is the Euphrates, spanned by the massive bridge. Behind the double wall of the city are the enormous ziggurat on the left, and the temple of Marduk on the right. 260: The famous gate of Ishtar; a solemn procession is passing through. The processional way stretches to the horizon of this vast capital. In the distance, at the right, is the ziggurat behind the trees of the 'Hanging Gardens'.

260

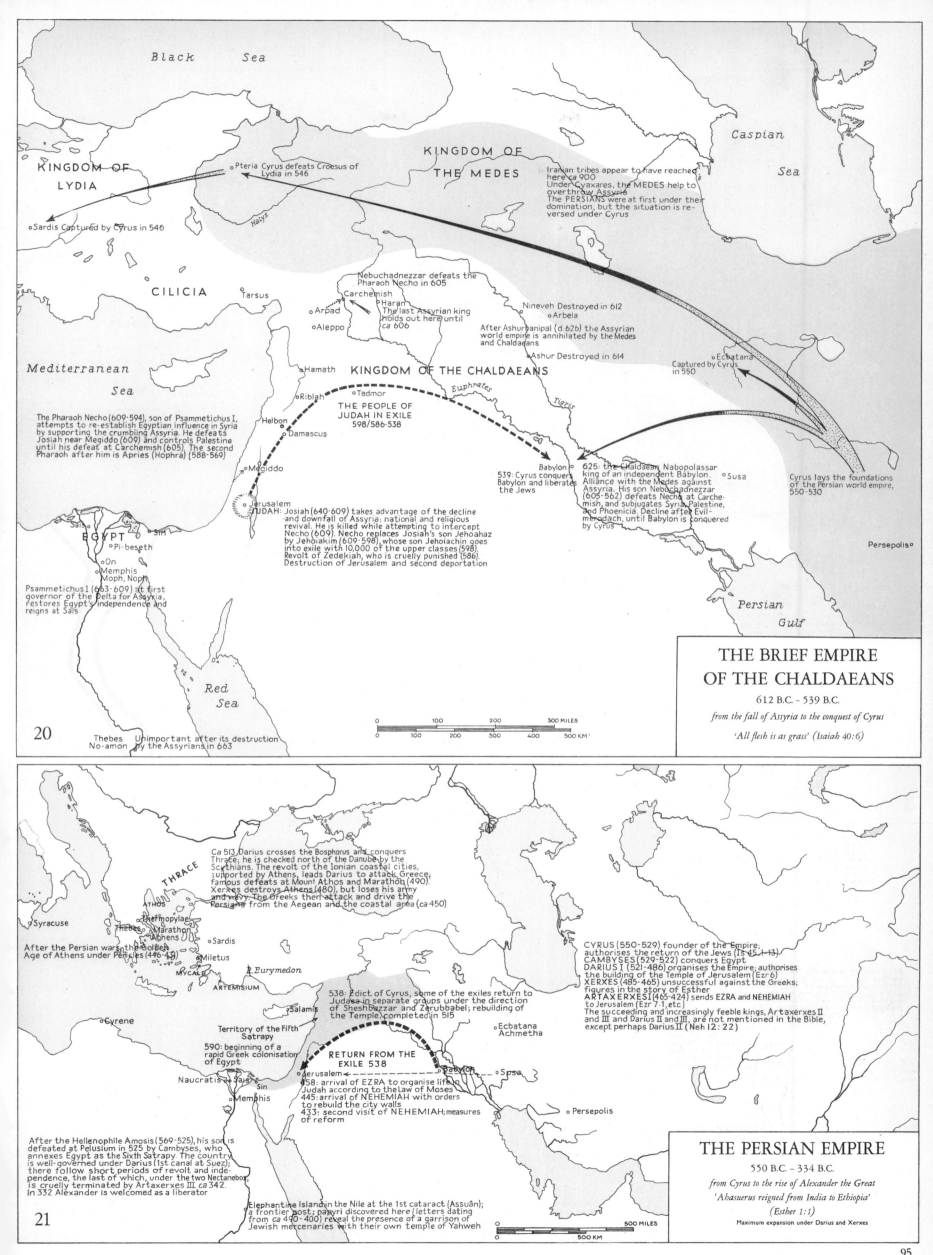

Map 20: THE BRIEF EMPIRE OF THE CHALDAEANS

Black Sea

Caspian Sea

KINGDOM OF THE MEDES

KINGDOM OF LYDIA

Pteria Cyrus defeats Croesus of Lydia in 546

Iranian tribes appear to have reached here ca 900
Under Cyaxares, the MEDES help to overthrow Assyria
The PERSIANS were at first under their domination, but the situation is reversed under Cyrus

Sardis Captured by Cyrus in 546

CILICIA

Tarsus

Halys

Nebuchadnezzar defeats the Pharaoh Necho in 605

Carchemish

Haran
The last Assyrian king holds out here until ca 606

Arpad

Aleppo

Nineveh Destroyed in 612
Arbela

After Ashurbanipal (d.626) the Assyrian world empire is annihilated by the Medes and Chaldaeans

Ashur Destroyed in 614

Ecbatana Captured by Cyrus in 550

Mediterranean Sea

Hamath

KINGDOM OF THE CHALDAEANS

Euphrates

Riblah

Tadmor

Tigris

The Pharaoh Necho (609-594), son of Psammetichus I, attempts to re-establish Egyptian influence in Syria by supporting the crumbling Assyria. He defeats Josiah near Megiddo (609) and controls Palestine until his defeat at Carchemish (605). The second Pharaoh after him is Apries (Hophra) (588-569)

Helbon

Damascus

THE PEOPLE OF JUDAH IN EXILE 598/586-538

Babylon

625: the Chaldaean Nabopolassar king of an independent Babylon. Alliance with the Medes against Assyria. His son Nebuchadnezzar (605-562) defeats Necho at Carchemish, and subjugates Syria, Palestine, and Phoenicia. Decline after Evil-merodach, until Babylon is conquered by Cyrus

539: Cyrus conquers Babylon and liberates the Jews

Susa

Cyrus lays the foundations of the Persian world empire, 550-530

Megiddo

Jerusalem

JUDAH: Josiah (640-609) takes advantage of the decline and downfall of Assyria; national and religious revival. He is killed while attempting to intercept Necho (609). Necho replaces Josiah's son Jehoahaz by Jehoiakim (609-598), whose son Jehoiachin goes into exile with 10,000 of the upper classes (598). Revolt of Zedekiah, who is cruelly punished (586). Destruction of Jerusalem and second deportation

Sais

EGYPT

Pi-beseth

On

Memphis Moph, Noph

Psammetichus I (663-609) at first governor of the Delta for Assyria, restores Egypt's independence and reigns at Sais

Persepolis

Persian Gulf

Red Sea

20

Thebes   Unimportant after its destruction
No-amon   by the Assyrians in 663

100   200   300 MILES
100   200   300   400   500 KM

THE BRIEF EMPIRE OF THE CHALDAEANS

612 B.C. – 539 B.C.

from the fall of Assyria to the conquest of Cyrus

'All flesh is as grass' (Isaiah 40:6)

Map 21: THE PERSIAN EMPIRE

THRACE

Ca 513 Darius crosses the Bosphorus and conquers Thrace; he is checked north of the Danube by the Scythians. The revolt of the Ionian coastal cities, supported by Athens, leads Darius to attack Greece; famous defeats at Mount Athos and Marathon (490). Xerxes destroys Athens (480), but loses his army and navy. The Greeks then attack and drive the Persians from the Aegean and the coastal area (ca 450)

ATHOS

Syracuse

Thebes

Thermopylae

Athens

Marathon

MYCALE

ARTEMISIUM

Sardis

Miletus

R. Eurymedon

After the Persian wars the Golden Age of Athens under Pericles (446-431)

CYRUS (550-529) founder of the Empire; authorises the return of the Jews (Is 45.1-13)
CAMBYSES (529-522) conquers Egypt
DARIUS I (521-486) organises the Empire; authorises the building of the Temple of Jerusalem (Ezr 6)
XERXES (485-465) unsuccessful against the Greeks; figures in the story of Esther
ARTAXERXES I (465-424) sends EZRA and NEHEMIAH to Jerusalem (Ezr 7.1, etc)
The succeeding and increasingly feeble kings, Artaxerxes II and III and Darius II and III, are not mentioned in the Bible, except perhaps Darius II (Neh 12: 22)

Salamis

Cyrene

Territory of the Fifth Satrapy

590: beginning of a rapid Greek colonisation of Egypt

538: Edict of Cyrus, some of the exiles return to Judaea in separate groups under the direction of Sheshbazzar and Zerubbabel; rebuilding of the Temple completed in 515

Ecbatana Achmetha

Naucratis

Sais

Sin

Jerusalem

RETURN FROM THE EXILE 538

Babylon

Susa

458: arrival of EZRA to organise life in Judah according to the Law of Moses
445: arrival of NEHEMIAH with orders to rebuild the city walls
433: second visit of NEHEMIAH; measures of reform

Memphis

After the Hellenophile Amosis (569-525), his son is defeated at Pelusium in 525 by Cambyses, who annexes Egypt as the Sixth Satrapy. The country is well-governed under Darius (1st canal at Suez); there follow short periods of revolt and independence, the last of which, under the two Nectanebos, is cruelly terminated by Artaxerxes III ca 342. In 332 Alexander is welcomed as a liberator.

Persepolis

21

Elephantine Island in the Nile at the 1st cataract (Assuân); a frontier post; papyri discovered here (letters dating from ca 490-400) reveal the presence of a garrison of Jewish mercenaries with their own temple of Yahweh

500 MILES
500 KM

THE PERSIAN EMPIRE

550 B.C. – 334 B.C.

from Cyrus to the rise of Alexander the Great

'Ahasuerus reigned from India to Ethiopia'
(Esther 1:1)

Maximum expansion under Darius and Xerxes

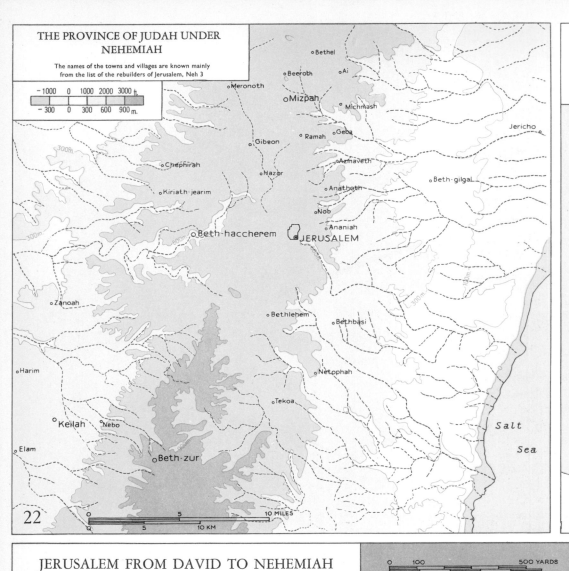

THE PROVINCE OF JUDAH UNDER NEHEMIAH

The names of the towns and villages are known mainly from the list of the rebuilders of Jerusalem, Neh 3

1000   0   1000   2000   3000 ft
300   0   300   600   900 m.

Bethel
Beeroth   Ai
Meronoth
Mizpah   Michmash
Gibeon   Ramah   Geba   Jericho
Chephirah   Nazor   Azmaveth
Kiriath-jearim   Anathoth   Beth-gilgal
Nob
Ananiah
Beth-haccherem   JERUSALEM

Zanoah
Bethlehem   Bethbasi
Netophah
Harim   Tekoa

Keilah   Nebo
Elam   Beth-zur

Salt Sea

22

5   10 MILES
5   10 KM

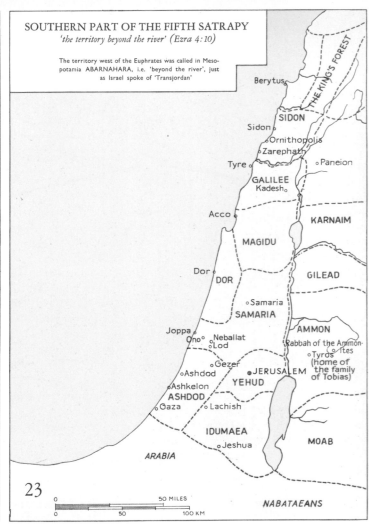

SOUTHERN PART OF THE FIFTH SATRAPY
'the territory beyond the river' (Ezra 4:10)

The territory west of the Euphrates was called in Mesopotamia ABARNAHARA, i.e. 'beyond the river', just as Israel spoke of 'Transjordan'

THE KING'S FOREST
Berytus
SIDON
Sidon   Ornithopolis
Zarephath   Paneion
Tyre
GALILEE   Kadesh
Acco   KARNAIM
MAGIDU
Dor   DOR   GILEAD
Samaria
SAMARIA   AMMON
Joppa   Ono   Neballat   Rabbah of the Ammon-
Lod   ites
Gezer   Tyros
Ashdod   JERUSALEM   (home of
Ashkelon   YEHUD   the family
ASHDOD   of Tobias)
Gaza   Lachish
Jeshua
IDUMAEA
ARABIA   MOAB

23

50 MILES
50   100 KM

NABATAEANS

JERUSALEM FROM DAVID TO NEHEMIAH

A. The Jebusite city conquered by David.

B. The Jerusalem of Solomon and its extension to the west (disputed by some scholars) under the succeeding kings.

C. The ramparts and gates inspected (Neh 2:13–15), repaired (Neh 3), and solemnly dedicated (Neh 12:27 ff.) by Nehemiah. These are the ramparts of the latest royal period, destroyed in 586 B.C. by the Chaldaeans. The doubt mentioned above (B) holds equally here. The reconstruction opposite (following H. Vincent) is uncertain, owing to the problems of composition posed by the book of Nehemiah, the defective transmission of the text, and the lack of incontestable archaeological data. The dotted red line shows the position of the western rampart according to the minimal hypothesis. All the references are to the book of Nehemiah.

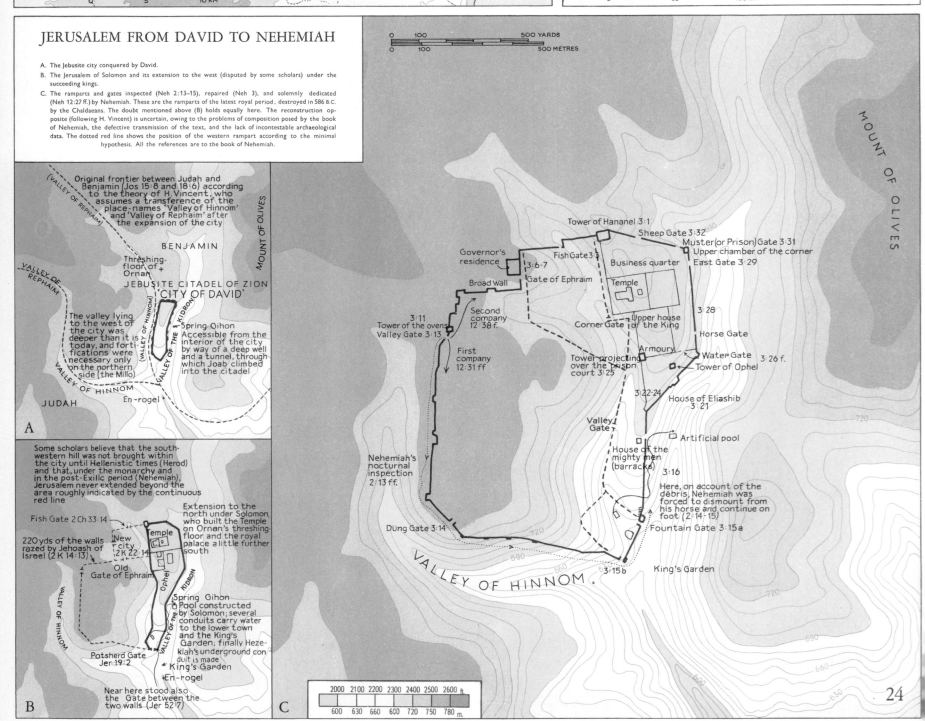

100   500 YARDS
100   500 METRES

A

Original frontier between Judah and Benjamin (Jos 15:8 and 18:6) according to the theory of H. Vincent, who assumes a transference of the place-names 'Valley of Hinnom' and 'Valley of Rephaim' after the expansion of the city

(VALLEY OF REPHAIM)
VALLEY OF REPHAIM
BENJAMIN
Threshing-floor of Ornan
JEBUSITE CITADEL OF ZION 'CITY OF DAVID'
MOUNT OF OLIVES

The valley lying to the west of the city was deeper than it is today, and fortifications were necessary only on the northern side (the Millo)

Spring Gihon Accessible from the interior of the city by way of a deep well and a tunnel, through which Joab climbed into the citadel

VALLEY OF THE KIDRON
VALLEY OF HINNOM
JUDAH
En-rogel

B

Some scholars believe that the southwestern hill was not brought within the city until Hellenistic times (Herod) and that, under the monarchy and in the post-Exilic period (Nehemiah), Jerusalem never extended beyond the area roughly indicated by the continuous red line

Fish Gate 2 Ch 33:14
220 yds of the walls razed by Jehoash of Israel (2 K 14:13)
New city 2 K 22:14
Temple
Old Gate of Ephraim
Ophel
VALLEY OF THE KIDRON
Spring Gihon
Pool constructed by Solomon; several conduits carry water to the lower town and the King's Garden, finally Hezekiah's underground conduit is made
VALLEY OF HINNOM
Potsherd Gate Jer 19:2
King's Garden
En-rogel
Near here stood also the Gate between the two walls (Jer 52:7)

C

MOUNT OF OLIVES

Tower of Hananel 3:1
Sheep Gate 3:32
Muster (or Prison) Gate 3:31
Upper chamber of the corner
East Gate 3:29
Governor's residence
Fish Gate 3:3
3:6-7
Business quarter
Broad Wall
Gate of Ephraim
Temple
Upper house of the King
3:11
Tower of the ovens
Valley Gate 3:13
Second company 12:38 f.
Corner Gate 3:25
3:28
Horse Gate
First company 12:31 ff
Tower projecting over the prison court 3:25
Water Gate 3:26 f.
Armoury
Tower of Ophel
3:22-24
House of Eliashib 3:21
Valley Gate
Artificial pool
Nehemiah's nocturnal inspection 2:13 ff.
House of the mighty men (barracks) 3:16
Here, on account of the debris, Nehemiah was forced to dismount from his horse and continue on foot (2:14-15)
Dung Gate 3:14
Fountain Gate 3:15a
3:15b
King's Garden
VALLEY OF HINNOM

2000 2100 2200 2300 2400 2500 2600 ft
600 630 660 690 720 750 780 m.

24

626 B.C.). The foreign elements in the cult, whose influence is denounced in the Bible, doubtless resulted from this subservience to Assyria, where Manasseh may even have spent some time in exile. His son Amon was assassinated after a very brief reign (ca 642–640 B.C.) as the result of a conspiracy among high officers of state; but the people of Judah remained loyal to the house of David. They lynched the assassins and placed Amon's son Josiah on the throne. He was to be the last great king of Judah (ca 640–609 B.C.), and his name is associated with a national revival. The Bible describes little more than its religious aspects, and it is once again the discovery of Assyrian records which has clarified the background for us.

The conquest of Egypt, begun under Esarhaddon in 673 B.C. and completed by Ashurbanipal with the destruction of Thebes in 660 B.C., had given Assyria an empire far vaster than any hitherto known to man. Fortunately for us, the highly-gifted Ashurbanipal, who may originally have been intended for the priesthood, was deeply versed in all the arts and sciences of his time. His interest in literature and history led him to build the great library at Nineveh, discovered during excavations in the middle of last century; it contained more than 20,000 documents. To this discovery we owe not only detailed information about his own reign, but also the bulk of our documentation on Assyro-Babylonian culture and even on the Sumerian culture from which it evolved. His love of art also inspired the bas-reliefs which are now the pride of the British Museum. By comparing them with a hunting-scene of the time of Ashurnasirpal, more than a century earlier, we can appreciate the perfect flowering of this art under Ashurbanipal (see pp. 85–86). But the vast areas of wall-space devoted to lion-hunting scenes do not only testify to Ashurbanipal's enthusiasm for the chase. The king appears to have intended the visitor to his palaces to carry away something more than an idea of his favourite pastime. Like his god, who fought the dark monsters of chaos to bring order to the universe, the king of Assyria brought order to his own world. He was constantly engaged in the struggle against untamed forces, whether in pursuit of the lion or in military campaigns against rebellious vassals.

After the destruction of Babylon (647 B.C.), where his brother was installed as priest-king, and the devastation of Elam and of Susa, its splendid capital (640 B.C.), Ashurbanipal's reign was outwardly peaceful, and he was able to patronise the arts and sciences until his death in 626 B.C. Under him, the Assyria of the Sargonids reached its highest point of power and prosperity. The many public works of his predecessors - temples, palaces, roads, systems of irrigation and drainage - were continued and expanded, and Nineveh, the wonder of its age, attained the dazzling apogee of its splendour. The wealthy classes wore rich and gaily embroidered garments, and indulged their love of elaborate jewellery and costly perfumes; their houses were decorated with rare works of art, carved and inlaid furniture, and all the exotic products which the subject territories could be made to yield. Trade, art, and literature flourished. But in spite of the seemingly invincible power and unlimited material wealth of this great civilisation, in spite of the military victories and skilful diplomacy of the brilliant Ashurbanipal, the vast empire was about to founder. Powerful Indo-European tribes were massed on the northern and eastern frontiers, ready to invade Mesopotamia. In the south were the Aramaean tribes of Chaldaeans; led by Merodach-baladan, they had already attacked the empire in Babylon, and their prince, Nabopolassar, was ready to seize that ancient centre of inexhaustible spiritual strength as soon as Ashurbanipal was dead.

Less than fifteen years after the death of Ashurbanipal, Assyria had completely disappeared from the map of the world. Nineveh fell in 612 B.C. before the onslaughts of the Medes and Chaldaeans. Since the discovery in 1923 of a chronicle covering these final years, we have known of the tragic fate and heroic courage of Ashur-uballit II, the last of the Sargonids. After the destruction of Nineveh, he had himself proclaimed king in the old city of Haran and, even after the Medes and Chaldaeans had captured his capital, he succeeded in holding out for a few more years with the help of Egypt and the support of a number of small Aramaean states.

With the first signs of Assyria's approaching dissolution, Josiah made it plain that his chief ambition was to purge the cult of Yahweh of all foreign elements. Through the years, a succession of measures was enacted, culminating in the promulgation of the Code discovered during a restoration of the Temple and identified by most exegetes with the legislative section of Deuteronomy. There are many signs that this religious reform was accompanied by wise economic measures and a reorganisation of the army. Some scholars also date from the time of Josiah the long lists of cities in the territory of Judah found in the book of Joshua (see pp. 58–61). Whatever our view of this, there was at the time every indication that Judah was entering upon a period of well-being and prosperity. But in reality the end was near.

With the fall of Nineveh (612 B.C.), the Chaldaean Nabopolassar, who had wielded limited power in Babylon since 626 B.C., gained possession of the world empire. Besides the territories in the south, around Babylon and on the edge of the Persian Gulf, and in addition to Assyria proper, he gained control of Elam, of territories to the east of the Tigris, and of the region to the west of the Euphrates which gave access to Syria and Palestine. The Medes contented themselves with the mountainous regions in the north, although they had been responsible for the destruction of the last vestiges of Assyrian power at Haran. Only the extreme south, Syria and Palestine, was lost to Babylon and was to fall into the hands of the Pharaoh Necho, who in the year 609 B.C. led his troops to the north to support the crumbling power of Assyria (Map 20, p. 95).

Josiah attempted to block his path. With his reorganised army, he confidently took his stand at the pass of Megiddo, the classic place to intercept an army coming from the south. But his troops were defeated and he himself was killed. Judah consequently fell under the domination of Egypt and was quickly made aware of her situation. Perhaps because they suspected his eldest son of Egyptian sympathies, the people had placed Josiah's second son upon the throne of David. When the Pharaoh returned three months later from his campaign at Haran, he replaced this Jehoahaz, also known as Shallum, by his elder brother Eliakim, whose name he changed to Jehoiakim. It was of little account to the Egyptian whether a Judaean name contained the universal Semitic word El, 'god', or the specific Jo (Yo), 'Yahweh'. What interested him was that, in imposing the change of name, he demonstrated that the king of Judah had fallen into his power. Jehoahaz had gone unsuspectingly to the army headquarters of the Egyptian king. When he left Jerusalem the period of mourning for his father Josiah had not yet ended. We can imagine that among the men who accompanied him to the city gate was the prophet Jeremiah, who urged in moving tones that they should lament no longer for the dead Josiah, but for the departing king:

> Weep not for him who is dead
> nor bemoan him;
> but weep bitterly for him who goes away,
> for he shall return no more
> to see his native land.

Jer 22:10

Jehoahaz did indeed die far from home, an exile in the land of the Nile. But the Egyptians' hold on Palestine was soon to be loosed. In 605 B.C. they were defeated near Carchemish by a Chaldaean army led by the young Nebuchadnezzar. He could not at once take possession of Syria and Palestine, because his father Nabopolassar had just died in Babylon. Without upheaval, Nebuchadnezzar ascended the throne of this holy city and began upon a reign which was to last for forty-two years and stamp him as in many respects the equal of his distant predecessor Hammurabi. In 604 B.C. he marched into Palestine and captured Ashkelon, but in 601 he suffered a severe set-back in a great battle with Egypt. Two years later Jehoiakim rebelled against him; Nebuchadnezzar could not return immediately, but he caused Judah to be devastated by neighbouring peoples who had remained loyal to him and by Chaldaean garrisons from the north. In 598 B.C. he sent an army to Jerusalem and himself followed in its train with reinforcements. Jehoiakim had died three months earlier and had been succeeded by his son Jehoiachin. To avert total devastation, the new king went into voluntary exile in Babylon with all the royal household, a number of notables, men of military age, and skilled craftsmen. Jehoiachin was freed thirty-seven years later, when Nebuchadnezzar's successor ascended the throne. But he had not been harshly treated. A number of tablets inscribed with his name and his rank as king of Judah have been found in the palace at Babylon. They concern the supplies of oil to be provided for him and his five sons by the royal stewards.

2 K 25:27

Nebuchadnezzar wished, however, to preserve the little kingdom of Judah, which lay so close to the Egyptian frontier. He accordingly installed on the throne of David a third son of Josiah, Mattaniah, changing his name to Zedekiah. One can form an idea of this weak personality from the biographical chapters in the book of Jeremiah. He was for ever wavering between the wise counsels of Jeremiah, who enjoined loyal submission to Nebuchadnezzar as being the manifest will of Yahweh, and the pressure of a group who found the existing situation intolerable and urged him to conspire with Egypt and the neighbouring states against the authority of Babylon. This faction finally prevailed upon the king to rebel. Thereupon, in 588 B.C., the armies of Babylon reappeared in Palestine. We have no detailed information about this campaign, for the many texts we possess of the time of Nebuchadnezzar tell us more of his erection of temples and other public works than they do of his military operations. But the Lachish ostraca give a good idea of the confused situation, and the concluding words of ostracon no. 4 (see p. 92) may be connected with the conquest of Azekah, mentioned in the book of Jeremiah.

Jer 34:7

What is certain is that in 586 B.C., after a siege which he interrupted to rout reinforcements sent by Egypt, Nebuchadnezzar razed the city of Jerusalem and deported the flower of her people to Babylon. Zedekiah was captured in flight. At the Babylonian headquarters in Riblah, near the ancient city of Kadesh on the Orontes, he suffered the punishment of a rebellious vassal: he was first obliged to witness the murder of his sons, and then his eyes were put out. With this dreadful picture in his memory, Zedekiah followed his people into exile. All that Jeremiah had prophesied to him was thus fulfilled:

Jer 34:2-3

> Thus says the Lord: Behold, I am giving this city into the hand of the king of Babylon, and he shall burn it with fire. You shall not escape from his hand, but shall surely be captured and delivered into his hand; you shall see the king of Babylon eye to eye and speak with him face to face; and you shall go to Babylon.

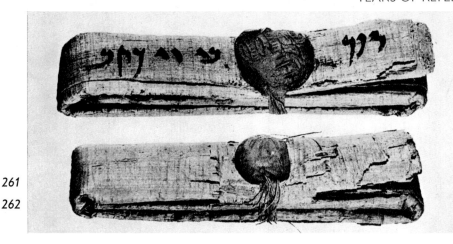

261
262

YEARS OF REFLECTION AND HOPE

hat most surprises the modern reader in the history of the preceding period is the failure of the prophets. Many passages in Isaiah make a deep impression upon us, even in translation, where they inevitably lose part of their force. Moreover, we know that our present books of Hosea and Amos, of Isaiah and Micah, and of Jeremiah and Zephaniah are no more than anthologies in the modern sense of the word, which means a selection of the best or most characteristic passages from an author. The prophetic books are, in fact, collections of prophecies which have been preserved owing to circumstances of which we know nothing. There were other prophets, not only in the early period of Elijah and Elisha but also in Judah's closing years, whose teaching has not survived in written form. We are told, for example, of a certain 'Uriah the son of Shemaiah from Kiriath-jearim. He prophesied against this city and against this land in words like those of Jeremiah'; he was put to death by Jehoiakim on this account. We are astonished to find that the prophets' teaching, constantly repeated in new forms, concerning the nature of Yahweh, the meaning of Israel's election, and the requirements of the Covenant, fell on deaf ears and that the voice of Israel's conscience was raised in vain.

But this deduction is not entirely justified. As sometimes happens in the life of a man, the voice of conscience went unheeded until after the catastrophe which removed all possibility of action on the material plane. The downfall of Israel as a political force led her to reflect upon the significance of her election as God's people. The destruction of Jerusalem and the Temple and the sojourn in a pagan land made a living issue of the meaning of Yahweh's presence in the Temple and of the worship offered to Him there. And then the words of the prophets, repeated or recorded by faithful disciples, suddenly took on meaning for Israel.

This is not an idle speculation. Admittedly we know very little about the circumstances of the Exile in Babylon. From the Biblical figures for the various deportations, it has been estimated that about 50,000 Judaeans, including women and children, were subjected to the cruel march of more than 600 miles to their

new land. We cannot be sure in exactly which part of Babylonia the people were settled. Of the places mentioned in the Bible, only the 'river Chebar' can be identified; it was the great canal near the ancient city of Nippur. Our picture of the exiles' manner of life is equally vague. They must at first have been held in concentration camps. But very soon they appear to have enjoyed some measure of freedom. Jeremiah advises them to build houses and plant gardens, and Ezekiel possessed a home in which he received the elders of Israel. Some Judaeans engaged in commerce and a few became comparatively wealthy, as can be deduced from the composition of the caravans at the Return and from the creation, in these years, of a substantial national fund. Apart from tablets bearing the name of the king Jehoiachin (see p. 97), archaeology has yielded no documents dating from before the Return. On the other hand, meticulous excavation has given us a fantastic picture of the Babylon of the Chaldaeans, whose glittering splendour surpassed that of all the capitals of the ancient world, including Athens and Rome. We can imagine the fascination which this city, the holiest in the Ancient East, must have held for the Judaeans, what a severe test it must have been for their faith in Yahweh, what a challenge to their belief that He, whose domain had so recently been razed by the Chaldaeans, was nevertheless more powerful than Marduk of Babylon and held even this vast empire in the hollow of His hand.

Although we know little of the material conditions of the exiles, we are better informed about their spiritual development during their ordeal. The book of Ezekiel is an important source of information on this subject, and its author – for in this case we can use the word author – appears to have been one of the moving spirits in this development. Chapters 40–55 of Isaiah also bear witness to a great deepening of spiritual consciousness. Their historical background is formed by a revolution which changed the face of the Near East and made it possible for the Judaeans to return to the land of their fathers. The great processional way (Pl. 260) was soon to re-echo to the tramp of a conqueror's army.

Jer
26:20

263
264

261–264 / *Elephantine and its Papyri.* On the Nile, at the first cataract, lies the small town of *Assuân*, the *Sewêne* of the Hebrew Bible (the classical form *Syene* is used in the translations). At this point the desert closes in on both sides of the river, which has to carve its way through solid granite. 263: View looking south; at the left, the beautiful 'Island of Lord Kitchener'; behind it stretches the island of Elephantine, nearly a mile long (in the photograph it is difficult to distinguish the island from *Assuân*, on the right bank of the river). 264: View from Elephantine, looking south. 261: Two of the papyri found in 1893 at Elephantine, folded and sealed. On the upper papyrus we see the first words of the endorsement: *spr bî zî ktb*, 'letter concerning a house, written by . . .' 262: First lines of an unfolded letter.

[Map 21, p. 95]

265
266

267
268

269
270

265, 266 / *The Ruins of Persepolis.* From every part of the conquered eastern world, the young Persian people borrowed elements which they fused to form an art of their own. Here we see remains of the palace of Darius at Persepolis, which rivalled the greatest buildings in Egypt. 265: We can detect an Assyrian influence in the colossal figures of bulls flanking the entrance to a hall of columns (on the Egyptian model), while some of the motifs on the only visible column are Ionian. 266: Like those of Babylon, the palace stood on a terrace approached by monumental stairways; the gates in the background again suggest Egypt. **267, 268** / *Bas-reliefs from Susa,* in glazed brick, whose vivid colours may be admired in the Louvre. **269, 270** / *Ambassadors from Subject Peoples Bearing New Year Gifts. Left:* A deputation from Bactria; *right:* A group of Syrians.

RETURN AND RESURGENCE

The Chaldaean Empire was engulfed with incredible speed. Map 20 (p. 95) outlines the course of its ephemeral existence. It shows a number of Assyrian towns with the date of their destruction. Nineveh was so completely annihilated that, shortly afterwards, even the site of this proud metropolis had already been forgotten. With the overthrow of Assyria, Nabopolassar had, at one stroke, gained control of the whole empire of the Sargonids. And yet, in the upper half of the map, the red arrows heralding the end of Chaldaean power, which had deported the flower of Judah to Babylon, are already in evidence. In the 7th century B.C. Phraortes had subjected the Persians to Median suzerainty; and his son, Cyaxares, had combined with Nabopolassar to destroy the power of Assyria (see p. 97). The domination of the Medes in the north and of the Chaldaeans in the south was, however, short-lived. Cyaxares' successor, Astyages, found himself facing a rebellion of the Persians; and during 550 B.C. and the following years, the political leaders of Babylon must have trembled to hear the news that came from the east and the north. The revolt of Cyrus, a petty king of Anshan, against the high authority of the Medes had at first seemed no more than a purely local disturbance. But when, after a forced march, Cyrus occupied Ecbatana and soon afterwards gained control of the vast empire of the Medes, the situation grew more serious. And once the Persian and his powerful army had managed to penetrate into Lydia, and even occupied the Greek colonies in Asia Minor, Babylon realised that her days were numbered.

Among the deported Jews (after 586 B.C. the word Jew may be used, since, of all the tribes of Israel, only part of Judah remained) there arose a prophet who, by the fervour of his preaching, was to re-kindle the smouldering fire of hope. We hear the echo of his voice in Chapters 40–55 of Isaiah. As has been said, these chapters reveal the deepening of spiritual consciousness which Israel experienced during those painful years after the fall of Jerusalem and the deportation. Her idea of God is here more clearly defined than ever before. The people appear to have reflected upon all the past deeds of Yahweh and to have read and re-read the surviving traditions of Moses and the great prophets. While Assyria had been for Isaiah a rod in the hand of God, and Nebuchadnezzar, for Jeremiah, the instrument of His purpose, Cyrus is here hailed as Yahweh's anointed who is Is 44:28, 45:1 to authorise the return of the Jews and the rebuilding of the Temple. The Exodus from Egypt had been a mighty deed wrought by the strong arm of Yahweh, but this new Exodus will be greater still. Moreover, the awareness of Israel's universal mission is here more vivid than in earlier years. The people has been chosen to make Yahweh known to all other peoples, even to the ends of the earth. The tribulations of Israel also appear to be considered in relation to this mission, in the light both of faith in a just and merciful God and of the lessons of the past concerning the fate of the greatest of His prophets. In the celebrated Is 42:1ff. 49:1ff. 50:4ff. 52:13– 53:12 'Songs of the Servant of Yahweh', regarded since the end of last century as a separate series of literary compositions, the visionary power of the Old Testament touches heights which come near to the heart of the Gospels.

In the year of his accession as king of Babylon, Cyrus promulgated an edict authorising the Jews to return to their own land. The text of the edict, together Ezr 1, 6 with an order to the royal treasurer, has been preserved in the book of Ezra. In this document the king orders the return of the Jews at the behest of Yahweh, the God of Heaven, whom he seems to accept as his own God. He gives detailed instructions about the rebuilding of the Temple, which is to be paid for by his treasury, and also directs that the sacred vessels which had been carried off to Babylon should be placed in the new Temple. Many scholars regarded these texts as spurious, until other inscriptions of Cyrus were found in several local temples in Mesopotamia; they show that he treated all the subject peoples in this manner, returning their idols from Babylon to their original homes and paying for the rebuilding of the sanctuaries. One wonders whether the way in which the Jews spoke of their universal and wholly spiritual God and of His ethical demands did not make a particularly deep impression upon this Persian prince.

Some 50,000 Jews responded to the call of Cyrus and returned to Jerusalem, where they immediately began work on the construction of a temple. This was the beginning of a new period, upon which the Bible sheds no light, apart from the meagre information in Ezra and Nehemiah and a few details in the Minor Prophets Haggai and Zechariah. The two former books were originally included with the books of Chronicles in a single work. This whole work was put together only towards the end of the fourth century B.C., in an attempt to review, from one specific religious angle, the whole course of history from the Creation down to the time of the compiler. For the period of the return from Babylon and the succeeding years, the compiler had a certain number of original documents at his disposal: lists of people, official letters, and, above all, the personal memoirs of Ezra and Nehemiah. From these we are able to deduce that the Jews returned home in separate groups. The building of the Temple, which was hindered by the activities of the hostile Samaritans, was encouraged by the prophets Haggai and Zechariah and completed in 515 B.C., twenty-three years after the return of the first group of exiles. Of the next fifty years we are told nothing, except that the Samaritans lodged a complaint against the Jews with King Xerxes.

Ezra and Nehemiah date their activities by the years of the reign of King Artaxerxes. Since there are three rulers of this name in the list of the Persian kings, scholars disagree upon the chronology, and consequently upon the way in which the compiler of the books of Chronicles arranged and worked over his documents. If we assume that both Ezra and Nehemiah lived in the reign of the first Artaxerxes (465–424 B.C.), Ezra must have gone to Jerusalem in 458 B.C. at the command of the Persian king, in whose service he was; he was charged with the task of organising the life of the Jewish community in accordance with the Law of Moses. By the same reckoning, Nehemiah's first visit was in 445 B.C., when he supplemented the religious reorganisation by more material measures, including the rebuilding of the walls (shown on Map 24, p. 96). His second visit, during which he stamped out various abuses, must have been in 433 B.C. The Bible is then completely silent about the history of the Jewish people until the Maccabaean rising in 168 B.C. There is thus a period of more than two and a half centuries for which the Scriptures provide no information. It would seem that during this time no event occurred which could be interpreted as an intervention of Yahweh in the life of His people. Judaea was incorporated into the huge Persian Empire as a district of the Fifth Satrapy, or Abarnahara, 'over the river' (Euphrates) (Map 23, p. 96). The Persian kings recognised this little territory, with Jerusalem at its centre, as a sacral region administered by priests in accordance with the Law of Moses.

The holy city of Jerusalem also held a place in the hearts of the ever-increasing number of Jews who were settling in all parts of the empire. The Diaspora or Dispersion dates from these centuries, especially in Lower Egypt, where, in the tracks of the early emigrants, many Jews had fled after the catastrophe of 586 B.C., and in Babylonia, where they had spread out from the original centres of deportation. The famous Elephantine papyri have shed some light upon the life of the Jewish colonists on the southern frontier of Egypt; they had their own temple of Yahweh, but were still in touch with the High Priest of Jerusalem, and, like Ezra, they received precise instructions on the subject of the cult from the king of Persia in his distant capital.

During the centuries which elapsed between the completion of the Temple and the Maccabaean rising, the Jewish people remained grouped with its priests around the altar of Yahweh, more than ever 'the people of God', isolated from the pagan world and outside the great political arena. It was during this silent withdrawal that the Old Testament was given its present form. With contrite hearts, men reflected upon the past and completed the epic story of God's bounties on the one hand, and of the persistent unfaithfulness of His people on the other. The Pentateuch took on the form which we know today; the works of the 'Former Prophets' received final revision and the utterances of the 'Latter Prophets' were systematically arranged. Much of the 'Writings' (see p. 27) dates from this period. They may be said to express Israel's response to the revelation of God. We see the people praying in the Psalms, weeping in the Lamentations, struggling in Job, and loving in the Song of Songs. The prophets were now succeeded by the Sages, who infused the heritage of Israel with the wisdom of the Ancient East. For the heathen were also, unconsciously, seeking God, as is shown by the story of Jonah, which denounces a narrow parochialism, and also by the story of Job who, like his friends, was a heathen. There are many points of contact between the Wisdom literature in the Bible and the old proverbs and songs of Mesopotamia and Egypt. We have included a picture of the harper of Leiden (Pl. 271, opposite), not only because this masterpiece is too little known, but also because the words of his song, inscribed above his head, always come to mind when we read the book of Ecclesiastes:

Those who build houses, their dwelling-place is no more. What has befallen them? I have heard the words of the sages Imhotep and Hordehef, whose sayings are on all men's lips. Where are their tombs? The walls lie in ruins as if they had never existed. No man returns from beyond to tell us what one has need of and to comfort us before in our turn we go where they have gone. Fulfil thy dreams whilst thou livest, pour myrrh upon thy head, and deck thyself in fine linen. Add to thy possessions and do not give way to despair. Do what is needful in this earthly life and trouble not thy heart before the day of weeping is upon thee. The peaceful god [of the dead, i.e. Osiris] does not hear the entreaties of men, and lamentations save no man from the tomb.

Opposite, **271** / *The Blind Harper of Leiden.* In the Museum of Antiquities at Leiden is the mortuary chapel, built of limestone, of the courtier Patenemheb; it dates from the Amarna period. On one of the sides of the tomb, 'a very pure example of the art of the New Empire, which is remarkable less for strength and simplicity than for delicacy and distinction' *(Museum Guide),* is a representation of the solemn funeral sacrifice. Four musicians, a harper, a lute-player, and two flute-players appear as secondary figures. The harper (see opposite; $1\frac{1}{4}$ times actual size) is the finest example we possess of this recurrent motif (cf. Pl. 204). *[Map 7, p. 43]*

272
|
278

THE TIDE OF HELLENISM

In stunned silence, the peoples of the East witnessed the meteoric rise of Alexander the Great. He appeared superhuman, this twenty-year-old Macedonian who marched in victorious progress across the domains of the most venerable civilisations of the ancient world, and in whom a supreme mastery of the art of war was coupled with a mystic's vision of world unity.

It was not until a hundred and fifty years after his death that the small Jewish community, shut away in the mountains of Judah and far from the great coast road, felt the brutal impact of Alexander's great dream: 'All men must become one people'. Antiochus IV took up this cry and called upon the tiny community of Jews to abandon the heritage of their fathers. It was then that the Maccabees proved by their example that a living core of the old spirit of Judah still survived.

It is in the account of these troubled times that the name of Alexander is first mentioned in the Bible. When the author of the first book of Maccabees records the courageous and successful resistance of the orthodox Jews to Hellenisation, he first briefly outlines its historical background. His style bears the imprint of the prophetic books. Alexander 'went through to the ends of the earth . . . And the earth was quiet before him'. Essentially Biblical in its outlook and choice of words, the book points the contrast between the transience of Alexander's triumphs and his claim to divine origin. 'And he [Alexander] was exalted, and his heart was lifted up, and he gathered together an exceeding strong host, and ruled over countries and nations and principalities, and they became tributary unto him. And after these things he fell sick, and perceived that he should die.' Out of the chaos which follows his death there finally comes forth 'a sinful root' which assails the property of God Himself by attacking the Jewish people in and around Jerusalem.

In the book of Daniel the emergence of Alexander is set in a broader framework. The author sees the history of the preceding centuries as a succession of empires. The fourth empire has the audacity to make a direct attack upon the God of Israel. It is therefore the last such empire; it will be destroyed and succeeded by the reign of God. Among the various and somewhat strange symbols which are used for the empires, that of the ram and the he-goat is particularly striking. Should we see in this an allusion to the constellations of Persia and Greece? 'Behold, a he-goat came from the west across the face of the whole earth, without touching the ground.' This goat is the power of Greece incarnate in the person of Alexander, who is represented by the great horn between its eyes. The ram with two horns, standing on the bank of the river, symbolises the Medes and the Persians, who have overstepped their natural

1 Mac 1:41

1 Mac 1:3

1 Mac 1:3-5

Dn 8:5

frontier, the Euphrates. The goat charges the ram, breaks its two horns, throws it to the ground and tramples upon it. 'But when he [the goat] was strong, the great horn was broken, and instead of it there came up four conspicuous horns toward the four winds of heaven.' These horns symbolise the Diadochi, and when there emerges from one of them a little horn which finally assails 'the glorious land', the writer has reached the grim realities of his own times, for which his book has a message.

The successive phases of this prelude to the epic of the Maccabees are indicated on the maps opposite. A little imagination is needed to grasp the full implications of Map 25. The small scale of the map should not be overlooked; and one should also bear in mind the youth and education of Alexander himself. Did not Philip, his shrewd father, have his coins struck with a head of Hercules because he regarded this hero as his ancestor? And when we realise that, on his mother's side, Alexander believed himself to be descended from Achilles, his visit to Troy is more easily understood, and the later episodes at Ammon–Zeus and Babylon seem less strange. At the age of thirteen he was the pupil of Aristotle, to whom he owed not only the breadth of his scientific interests, which partly inspired his expedition to India, but also his fondness for Homeric songs and his steadfast faith in the absolute superiority of Greek civilisation.

After Issus, the defeated Darius offered him a favourable peace. Alexander refused, for he was determined to deprive the powerful Persian fleet of all its bases and to defeat the Great King at the heart of his empire. The Phoenician ports of Arvad, Byblos, Berytus *(Beirut)*, and Sidon capitulated and placed their fleets at the disposal of the conqueror. After a bitter struggle lasting for seven months, he also captured Tyre and destroyed its proud isolation for ever by linking it to the mainland (Map 28, p. 103). In two months he broke the heroic resistance of the defenders of Gaza, and the road to Egypt lay open before him. Overjoyed to shake off the heavy Persian yoke, the Egyptians hailed him as a liberator, and it was as the successor of the Pharaohs that he sacrificed, according to the ancient rites, to the gods of the land.

Drawn by some mystical impulse to the oasis of Ammon–Zeus, he sailed down the Canopic arm of the Nile and stood in meditation on the spot of which Homer sang (Odyssey IV, 354):

In the surge that breaks across the mouth of the river of Egypt there lies a certain island which men call Pharos . . . In it is a harbour with good landing beaches and clean deep wells of fresh water, from which, after drawing their fill, men run down the trim hulls into the sea. *(trans. T. E. Shaw)*

279
|
280

272, 273 / *Stater of Tarsus*, under Datames (378–372 B.C.). *Reverse* (272): Datames before Ana; *obverse* (273): the seated Baal of Tarsus, with the letter b'ltrs, 'Baal of Tarsus', in Phoenician script. 274, 276 / *Double Shekel of Sidon*, under Evagoras ca 345–342 B.C. *Obverse* (274): a galley; *reverse* (276): th Persian king in a war chariot. 275 / *Alexander the Great*, on a tetradrachm of Lysimachus ca 295 B.C. He is shown deified, with the horns of the ram c Zeus-Ammon. 277, 278 / *Tetradrachm of Alexander the Great*, from Amphipolis ca 324–323 B.C. *Obverse* (278): Heracles-Melkart; *reverse* (277): Zeus Baal. 279 / *Aerial Photograph of Alexandria;* the white lines indicate the plan of the ancient city. Observe the accumulation of sand on both sides of the cause way. 280 / *Aerial Photograph of Tyre* (see Pl. 17). [*Map opposite*

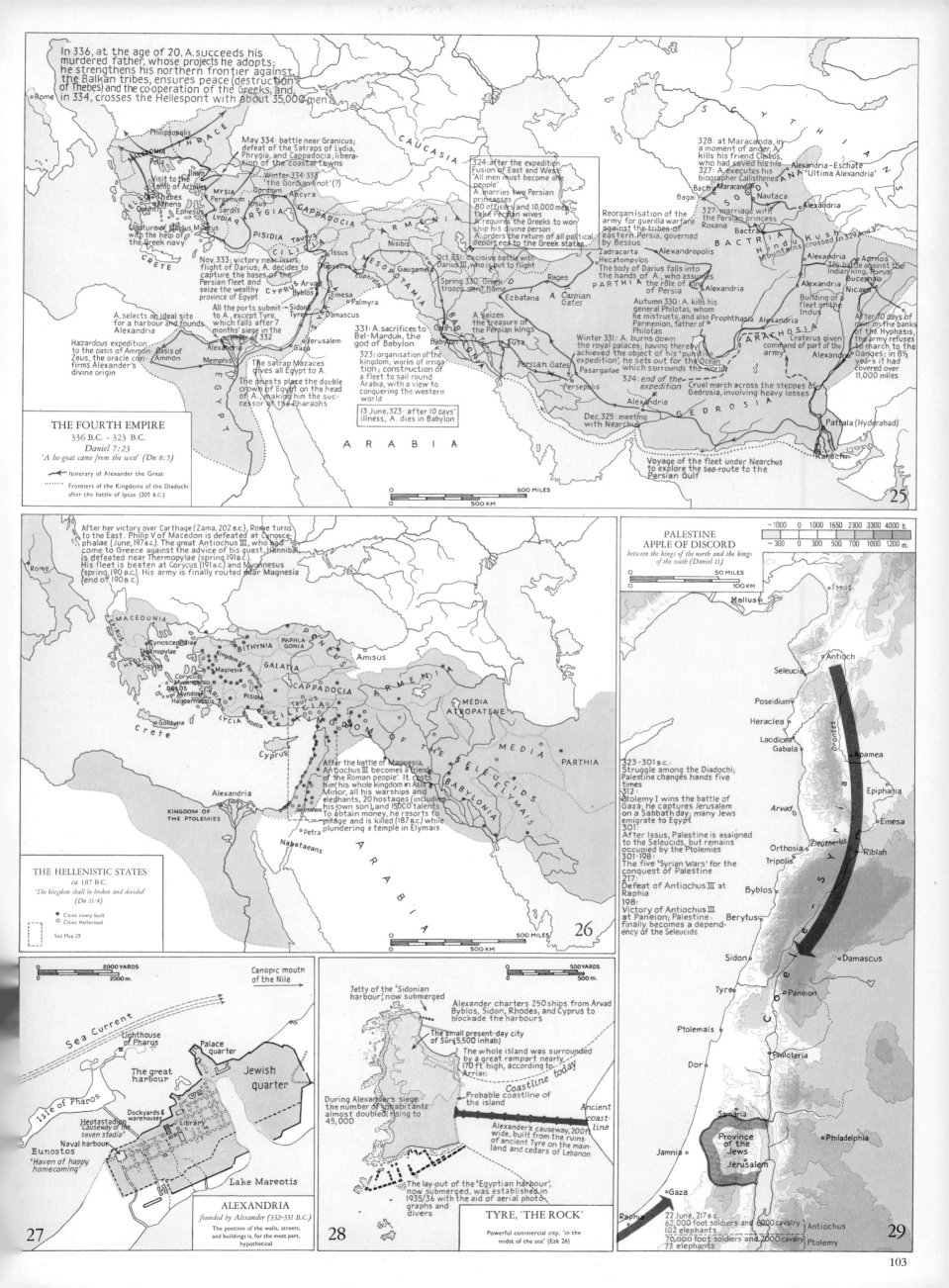

Map 25 — THE FOURTH EMPIRE

In 336, at the age of 20, A. succeeds his murdered father, whose projects he adopts; he strengthens his northern frontier against the Balkan tribes, ensures peace (destruction of Thebes) and the co-operation of the Greeks, and in 334, crosses the Hellespont with about 35,000 men.

May 334: battle near Granicus; defeat of the Satraps of Lydia, Phrygia, and Cappadocia; liberation of the coastal towns

Winter 334-333 'the Gordian knot'(?)

Capture of Miletus with the help of the Greek navy

Nov. 333: victory near Issus; flight of Darius; A. decides to capture the bases of the Persian fleet and seize the wealthy province of Egypt

All the ports submit to A., except Tyre, which falls after 7 months' siege in the summer of 332

A. selects an ideal site for a harbour and founds Alexandria

Hazardous expedition to the oasis of Ammon. Basis of Zeus, the oracle confirms Alexander's divine origin

The satrap Mazaces gives all Egypt to A.

The priests place the double crown of Egypt on the head of A., making him the successor of the Pharaohs

331: A. sacrifices to Bel-Marduk, the god of Babylon

323: organisation of the kingdom; works of irrigation; construction of a fleet to sail round Arabia, with a view to conquering the western world

13 June, 323: after 10 days' illness, A. dies in Babylon

324: after the expedition Fusion of East and West 'All men must become one people'
A. marries two Persian princesses
80 officers and 10,000 men take Persian wives
A. requires the Greeks to worship his divine person
A. orders the return of all political deportees to the Greek states.

Oct. 331: decisive battle with Darius III, who is put to flight

Spring 330: Greek troops sent home

A. seizes the treasure of the Persian kings

Reorganisation of the army for guerilla warfare against the tribes of eastern Persia, governed by Bessus

Autumn 330: A. kills his general Philotas, whom he mistrusts, and also Parmenion, father of Philotas

Winter 331: A. burns down the royal palaces; having thereby achieved the object of his 'punitive expedition', he sets out for the Ocean which surrounds the world

324: end of the expedition

328: at Maracanda, in a moment of anger, A. kills his friend Cleitus, who had saved his life

327: A. executes his biographer Callisthenes

327: marriage with the Persian princess Roxana

326: battle against the Indian king, Porus

Building of a fleet on the Indus

After 10 days of rain on the banks of the Hyphasis, the army refuses to march on; in 8½ years it had covered over 11,000 miles

Craterus given command of part of the army

Cruel march across the steppes of Gedrosia, involving heavy losses

Dec. 325: meeting with Nearchus

Voyage of the fleet under Nearchus to explore the sea-route to the Persian Gulf

THE FOURTH EMPIRE
336 B.C. – 323 B.C.
Daniel 7:23
'A he-goat came from the west' (Dn 8:5)
→ Itinerary of Alexander the Great
····· Frontiers of the Kingdoms of the Diadochi after the battle of Ipsus (301 B.C.)
500 MILES / 500 KM

Map 26 — THE HELLENISTIC STATES

After her victory over Carthage (Zama, 202 B.C.), Rome turns to the East. Philip V of Macedon is defeated at Cynoscephalae (June, 197 B.C.). The great Antiochus III, who had come to Greece against the advice of his guest, Hannibal, is defeated near Thermopylae (spring, 191 B.C.). His fleet is beaten at Corycus (191 B.C.) and Myonnesus (spring, 190 B.C.). His army is finally routed near Magnesia (end of 190 B.C.)

After the battle of Magnesia, Antiochus III becomes a 'friend of the Roman people'. It costs him his whole kingdom in Asia Minor, all his warships and elephants, 20 hostages (including his own son), and 15,000 talents. To obtain money, he resorts to pillage and is killed (187 B.C.) while plundering a temple in Elymais.

THE HELLENISTIC STATES
ca 187 B.C.
'The kingdom shall be broken and divided' (Dn 11:4)
• Cities newly built
○ Cities Hellenised
⌐ ⌐ See Map 29

Map 29 — PALESTINE APPLE OF DISCORD
between the kings of the north and the kings of the south (Daniel 11)

-1000 0 1000 1650 2300 3300 4000 ft.
-300 0 300 500 700 1000 1200 m.
50 MILES / 100 KM

323-301 B.C.: Struggle among the Diadochi; Palestine changes hands five times
312: Ptolemy I wins the battle of Gaza; he captures Jerusalem on a Sabbath day; many Jews emigrate to Egypt
301: After Issus, Palestine is assigned to the Seleucids, but remains occupied by the Ptolemies
301-198: The five 'Syrian Wars' for the conquest of Palestine
217: Defeat of Antiochus III at Raphia
198: Victory of Antiochus III at Paneion; Palestine finally becomes a dependency of the Seleucids

22 June, 217: 62,000 foot soldiers and 6000 cavalry 102 elephants (Antiochus)
70,000 foot soldiers and 7000 cavalry 73 elephants (Ptolemy)

Map 27 — ALEXANDRIA

2000 YARDS / 2000 m.
Canopic mouth of the Nile
Sea Current
Lighthouse of Pharos
Isle of Pharos
Palace quarter
The great harbour
Jewish quarter
Heptastadion 'Causeway of the seven stadia'
Dockyards & warehouses
Library
Naval harbour
Eunostos 'Haven of happy homecoming'
Lake Mareotis

ALEXANDRIA
founded by Alexander (332-331 B.C.)
The position of the walls, streets, and buildings is, for the most part, hypothetical

Map 28 — TYRE, 'THE ROCK'

Jetty of the 'Sidonian harbour', now submerged
Alexander charters 250 ships from Arvad, Byblos, Sidon, Rhodes, and Cyprus to blockade the harbours
The small present-day city of Sûr (5,500 inhab.)
The whole island was surrounded by a great rampart nearly 170 ft. high, according to Arrian
Probable coastline of the island
Coastline today
Ancient coast-line
During Alexander's siege the number of inhabitants almost doubled, rising to 45,000
Alexander's causeway, 200 ft. wide, built from the ruins of ancient Tyre on the mainland and cedars of Lebanon
The lay-out of the 'Egyptian harbour', now submerged, was established in 1935/36 with the aid of aerial photographs and divers

TYRE, 'THE ROCK'
Powerful commercial city, 'in the midst of the sea' (Ezk 26)

103

GEOGRAPHY OF THE BOOKS OF MACCABEES

This map shows all the identifiable sites and districts of
Palestine named in 1 and 2 Maccabees

➤ Advances of the Seleucid armies

➤ Operations of Judas Maccabaeus

⇢ Operations after the death of Judas

GREAT SEA

GALILEE

SAMARIA

IDUMAEA

PHILISTINES

AKRABATTINE

SALT SEA

Tyre
Kedesh
Plain of Hazor
JONATHAN defeats an army led by Demetrius (1 Mac 11)
Bascama Assassination of JONATHAN (1 Mac 13:23)
JONATHAN treacherously captured by Tryphon and carried across the country as a hostage (1 Mac 12-13)
The commanders Bacchides and Alcimus (1 Mac 9:2)
Lake of Gennesaret
Arbela 1 Mac 9:2
Ptolemais

The Great Plain

ARBATTA

Dor
Ephron
Beth-shan Scythopolis
In Galilee, SIMON defeats the Gentiles who are persecuting the Israelites and brings the liberated families back to Judaea. JUDAS takes similar action in the land of Gilead cf. Map 31 (1 Mac 5:21-54)

Samaria

Pharathon

Tephon

JUDAS defeats the commander Seron (1 Mac 3)

Joppa
Ramathaim
Timnath
JUDAS killed in the battle against Bacchides (1 Mac 9)
Jazer
Expedition of JUDAS against the children of Ammon (1 Mac 5:6-8)
Adida
Birzaith
Ephraim
Lydda
Modin Original home of the Maccabees
Bethel
Berea
SIMON treacherously assassinated (1 Mac 16)
Unsuccessful attack by the incompetent leaders Joseph and Azarias (1 Mac 5:55)
Beth-horon
Mizpah
Dok
Jamnia
Ekron
Capharsalama
Michmash
Jericho
Gezer
Adasa
JUDAS defeats Nicanor (1 Mac 7)
JONATHAN defeats Bacchides (1 Mac 9:43-60)
Kedron
Emmaus
JUDAS defeats a Syrian army led by Gorgias (1 Mac 4)
Jerusalem MOUNT ZION
JONATHAN defeats Apollonius and captures Azotus (1 Mac 10)
Azotus
Medaba
Nadabath
Bethbasi
JONATHAN and SIMON avenge the murder of JOHN (1 Mac 9:37-42)
Ashkelon
Beth-zechariah JUDAS fails to check the army of Lysias, heroic death of ELEAZAR crushed beneath an elephant; siege of Jerusalem (1 Mac 6)
Tekoa
Bezeth (Beth-zaitha)
Marisa
Beth-zur JUDAS defeats an army led by Lysias (1 Mac 4:26-61); purification of the Temple of Jerusalem (165 B.C.); feast of the Dedication (Jn 10:22)
Gaza
Adora
Hebron
JUDAS fights against the children of Esau (1 Mac 5:3)

-1000 0 1000 2000 3000 4000 ft.
-300 0 300 600 900 1200 m.

0 10 20 MILES
0 10 20 30 KM

Inset map (upper left):

Hamath
Aradus
Orthosia
Tripolis
COELE-SYRIA
Sidon
Damascus
Tyre
Maked
Ptolemais
Raphon
Casphor
Bosor
Dathema
GALILEE
Carnaim
Ephron
GILEAD
Bosora
Dora
Beth-shan
SAMARIA
EXPEDITION OF JUDAS, 1 Mac 5
Modin
Jamnia
Emmaus
JUDAEA
Jerusalem
Gaza
Beth-zur
Hebron

0 25 50 MILES
0 50 100 KM

31

30

With characteristic speed of thought and action, he drew in the sand the boundaries and principal buildings of a new town which was to bear his name. The island of Pharos, which acted as a breakwater, was to be attached by a causeway to the narrow tongue of land between the sea and Lake Mareotis. Besides a river harbour, the town was thus to have a sea harbour, which the strong eastward currents would keep clear of the silt brought down by the Nile (Map 27, p. 103). Shortly after the premature death of its founder, Alexandria was already the cultural and commercial metropolis of the Hellenistic world. While in Palestine Judaism set its face against Hellenism, this city was to give birth to the Greek Bible, that indispensable vehicle for the diffusion of the Gospel.

With a deepened conviction of his divine origin, Alexander resumed his campaign against the Persians, and not until he had burnt down the palaces of Persepolis, thus avenging the sack of Athens by Xerxes, did he feel that his chief task was accomplished. But his ambitions grew ever greater; he dreamed of a world empire, stretching from India to Gibraltar and from the Danube to the sources of the Nile, united by the Greek language and culture and by the worship of his divine person.

The many Alexandrias which appear on Map 25 (p. 103) and the frontiers indicated by dotted lines (the kingdoms of the Diadochi) across the territories under his domination already foreshadow the shape of things to come; the succeeding period was to see the progressive dismemberment of his empire, but also the triumph of Greek civilisation (Map 26, p. 103). Everywhere there were new towns, spaciously laid out with straight, colonnaded thoroughfares, and called after the founders they commemorated: Antiochs, Seleucias, Apameas, Lysimachias. Age-old cities were transformed or enlarged according to new ideas, and Semitic place-names gave way to Greek; in Palestine the former Rabbah of the Ammonites became Philadelphia, Beth-shan became Scythopolis, and Acco was renamed Ptolemais. By reason of its situation, Palestine was overwhelmed on two sides by the wave of Hellenism; Map 29 (p. 103) illustrates the rivalry between North and South which preceded the emergence of the Maccabees and which is described with increasing precision in the vision of Chapter 11 of Daniel.

The brilliant Ptolemy, son of Lagus and Alexander's comrade-in-arms, laid the foundations of Hellenistic Egypt by blending the new Greek elements with the old indigenous culture. The administration of the country, to which the great Pharaohs of old had already devoted so much of their attention, now became superlatively efficient. But the traditional policy was renewed; wood for building and for the navy must still come from the Lebanon, and the Phoenician ports were still indispensable to the economy and military security of Egypt.

Coele-Syria, corresponding to the valley of the Beqa' and formed by the 'hollow' (κοῖλος) between the Lebanon and Mount Hermon, later embraced all the mountain area as far as Judaea, and once more became Egypt's first line of defence. After many vicissitudes during the quarrels among the Diadochi, Palestine remained in the power of the Ptolemies during the third century B.C. But the Seleucids, to whom it had been officially assigned in 301 B.C., made several attempts to reconquer it.

Though very firm in their administration of Egypt, the Ptolemies were indulgent in their treatment of Coele-Syria. Very little is known about the history of the Jews in this century, but we are able to form some idea of it by studying the situation in neighbouring lands. The Ptolemies undoubtedly respected the theocratic constitution which had been proclaimed by Ezra with the consent of the Persians. Under the watchful eye of a garrison, Jewish life could therefore follow its normal course, always provided that the levies imposed by Alexandria were promptly paid. Discoveries at Beth-zur have revealed that in these years the Jews even enjoyed the right to mint money.

But the Law, which protected the small Jewish community like a great sea wall, could not hold back the rising tide. There was continuous contact with the emigrés of the Diaspora, who, although they lived in their own quarters, were inevitably exposed to alien influences. Even those who had settled in Babylonia were almost as Hellenised as the Jews of Alexandria, the cultural and commercial metropolis. A remarkable picture of the colourful life which flourished in the lands around Judaea is provided by the papyri of a certain Zeno, a trading agent in the service of a minister of Ptolemy II Philadelphus. In his correspondence are several letters from an important Jew in Transjordan, the governor of a 'fortress' in a crown domain which had automatically fallen to the Ptolemies. This Tobias ('Yahweh is good'), who came from the same family as the High Priest, was in continuous trading relations with Jerusalem and with merchants supplying the Egyptian court. His letters are written in impeccable Hellenistic Greek and he does not scruple to include occasional invocations to the gods. We must realise that directly a Jew left the territory of Judaea he passed at once into Hellenistic centres, where Greek was spoken, where there were Greek statues, and buildings in the Greek style, theatres, gymnasia, sacred groves of the nymphs, temples, and endless colonnades, and where a sound general education required that he should engage in sports and pastimes as well as in reading literature and philosophy.

At the end of the third century B.C., there emerged from the feeble Seleucid dynasty a man who fully deserved the epithet 'Great' given him by the ancients:

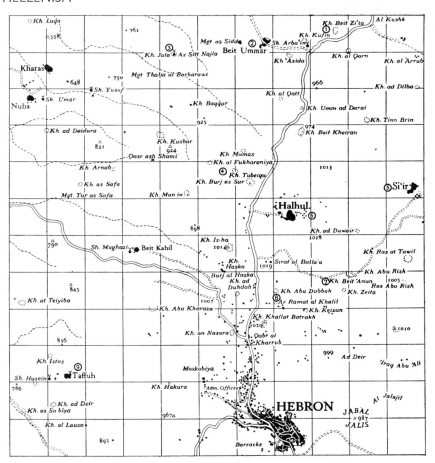

THE REGION NORTH OF HEBRON, SCENE OF SOME OF THE battles between the Maccabees and the armies of Syria. The above map covers an area of 11 by 12 km (about 7 by 7½ miles), on a scale of 1 in 100,000 (1 cm to 1 km). It may also serve to illustrate our earlier remarks on the problems of Biblical geography (pp. 19ff.). The most important remains are indicated as on the map of Palestine on the same scale published under the Mandate. The Arabic names – spelt as on the aforementioned map – are those in current use by the population. Not all the ruined sites are marked on this map, still less all the place-names; it must be remembered that the Palestinian Arabs have a special name for nearly every valley, conspicuous hill, or geological feature. It is these names which sometimes give the archaeologist a clue to ancient sites. We list below (numbered from north to south) the names of those ruined sites and places still inhabited which are marked on the maps or mentioned in the text of this Atlas.

1) Khirbet Beit Zi'ta, probable site of the Bezeth of 1 Mac 7:19; this name is variously spelt in the manuscripts: Bezet, Bethzeth, Bethzaith.

2) The village of Beit Ummar may be the Maarath mentioned only in the portion of Judah (Jos 15:59). There is only a faint resemblance between the two names (the element 'mar'), but the location fits in well with the context in which Maarath is listed.

3) Khirbet Jala, believed, mainly because of its name, to be the Biblical Giloh, the native village of Ahithophel (the g is softened to the sound of the English j; vowels are easily changed).

4) Khirbet Tubeiqa is the ruined site of the ancient Beth-zur, whose name has been transferred to the remains of a fortress of the Crusaders a little further south, Burj as Sur ('burj' comes from Greek 'purgos', 'fortified tower'). The very able American excavation of Khirbet Tubeiqa has shed light on the history of Beth-zur from the time of the Hyksos until its emergence as an important fortified town in the Maccabaean wars. Apart from the more modest investigations carried out at Mamre (No. 8), Beth-zur is the only place on this map to have been systematically excavated.

5) The village of Si'ir still preserves the name of the little place called Zior, listed in the portion of Judah immediately after Hebron (Jos 15:54); it may be the Zair of 2 K 8:21.

6) Halhul still bears the same name as in the portion of Judah (Jos 15:58); it is not mentioned elsewhere in the Bible.

7) Khirbet Beit 'Anun probably covers the ruins of Beth-anoth (Jos 15:59). This location is suggested both by the name (spelt Baithanoon in the Greek translation) and by the list of Eusebius, which situates it four miles from Hebron. The Idumaean Christians built a church dedicated to John the Baptist in this place, which they identified, without sufficient proof, with the Aenon of Jn 3:23.

8) Ramat al-Khalil, the 'height of the friend', venerated since early Christian times as the site of Mamre (see p. 28).

9) The village of Taffuh is no doubt the modern representative of Beth-tappuah which, according to the list of towns and villages apportioned to Judah, lay 'in the hill country' in the vicinity of Hebron (Jos 15:48, 53). It does not appear elsewhere in the Bible.

281

282

Antiochus III. His dream of a world empire like that envisaged by Alexander would have been realised, had he not encountered the might of Rome, which he continually under-estimated. In a war with the Ptolemies for Coele-Syria, he finally won a decisive victory after suffering initial reverses. During the winter of 199–198 B.C. he marched through Apamea, where he collected reinforcements, to the southern slopes of Mount Hermon, at whose foot the Egyptian army was encamped, near the source of the Jordan not far from Paneion, the famous sanctuary of the god Pan. There his elephants broke through the enemy lines. The remnants of the army of the Ptolemies fled to the fortress of Sidon, where they capitulated after a lengthy siege. In the course of the year 198 B.C., Antiochus gained control of all Coele-Syria; the Jews submitted and helped him to drive the Egyptian garrison from the citadel of Jerusalem.

The first benefit conferred by a Hellenistic ruler upon a conquered city was always the restoration of those rights and institutions lost by reason of the conquest itself. Antiochus was prepared to be generous to Jerusalem. Josephus has preserved for us the text of the edict in which the new sovereign recognised the Jewish community as a theocratic state and provided money for the upkeep and embellishment of the Temple and for the daily offerings. He also granted exemption from tribute to all members of the priesthood and even, for a period of three years, to all the inhabitants of Jerusalem. Recognising the importance of the Law of Moses to the Jewish community, the king guaranteed the maintenance of certain customs, such as the observance of the Sabbath, abstinence from unclean foods, circumcision, and the freedom to administer justice in accordance with traditional principles.

Antiochus the Great, however, came badly out of his war with the Romans. When his treasury ran dry and he could not pay the heavy indemnity imposed by Rome, he went to Mesopotamia to plunder an old temple famed for its rich treasure. But the irate inhabitants assassinated him and killed all his troops. His son Seleucus IV Philopator (187–175 B.C.) continued the same policy, but he had trouble in Judaea with a group which adhered to the Ptolemies and was apparently very active. He, too, attempted to obtain money by plundering a temple, and in succeeding years these hoards of unproductive treasure which lay hidden in well-nigh inaccessible places were to prove a continual temptation to more than one impoverished Hellenistic prince. It was the Temple of the Jews which attracted Seleucus, and his chief minister, Heliodorus, was sent to Jerusalem to seize its treasure. We know of this incident only from the second book of Maccabees, where it is made to appear as the primary cause of the revolt. In accordance with his usual practice (see p. 109), the author presents this episode in a highly dramatic form, but the nucleus of his story is undoubtedly historical, and is corroborated by an allusion in the book of Daniel. In spite of the protest of the High Priest, Heliodorus tried to enter the sanctuary in person, but his attempt to seize the treasure failed.

After murdering his master, Heliodorus seized power, but was soon deposed by the brother of Seleucus, Antiochus IV. This ruler had been among the twenty hostages whom the Romans exacted from his father, Antiochus the Great, after the latter's defeat at Magnesia (Map 26, p. 103), and was the only one who was not released after three years. He thus spent nearly fourteen years in Rome, where he was virtually a free man, able to live in luxury and to make friends in high places. He was released in 176 B.C., at the request of his brother, Seleucus, who was then in power and who sent his own son to replace him. Since Seleucus was securely installed on the throne in Antioch, Antiochus was in no hurry to return to the East and, from love of Greek culture, he took the opportunity to spend some time in the heart of the Hellenic world, at the foot of the Acropolis. There he played the Maecenas, contributing vast sums of money towards the construction of the Olympieum (the foundation of this temple of Zeus Olympius had been laid in the sixth century B.C. under Pisistratus on a scale which was to make it one of the largest buildings in the ancient world). In 175 B.C. he learned in Athens that his brother had been assassinated by his friend and minister Heliodorus. He at once set out to claim the inheritance of the Seleucids, with the help of troops lent to him by the powerful king of Pergamum. His express desire was to unite by the common bond of Hellenism the peoples of widely different cultures who made up his great kingdom.

His own person was to assume increasing importance over the years. Most of the coins from the early years of his reign bear a life-like head – the star which sometimes appears above it symbolises his reception among the gods – with the inscription 'King Antiochus'. After his victory over the king of Egypt in 169 B.C. he adds 'Theos Epiphanes'; he is himself the god incarnate. And in his closing years he makes the further addition 'Nikephoros', an epithet of Zeus, whose features and traditional beard replace his own. In this belief, he laid claim to absolute power over all existing religions and over all temples and their treasures. The Temple of Jerusalem was to be no exception: in it the gods of Olympus were to usurp the Holy of Holies, presided over by Zeus, identified with Antiochus himself. In 167 B.C., following an order by the king to convert the Temple to a shrine of Zeus, a Greek altar was placed over the Jewish altar of burnt offering. This attack upon the God of Israel marks the beginning of a new period in the history of the Jewish people. In the following year a priest, Mattathias, provided the spark which led to a general explosion by slaying a renegade Jew who came to worship at a heathen altar. By the time that Antiochus IV died in 163 B.C. a full-scale war was being fought between his forces and the men who had flocked to join Mattathias and his sons.

283
I
288

281 / *The Lighthouse of Alexandria*, built of white limestone in the time of Ptolemy II, under the direction of the architect Sostratus of Cnidus; the work was completed in 279 B.C. This huge construction, about 460 feet high and one of the seven wonders of the ancient world, remained standing until the earthquakes of A.D. 1303 and 1326. 282 / *Cleopatra*, a bas-relief in the temple of Denderah. 283 / *Antiochus IV Epiphanes*. 284 / *Antiochus IV Epiphanes as Zeus*. 285 / *Coin from Alexandria*, of the time of Commodus, bearing the lighthouse and a sailing-ship. 286 / *Ptolemy III Euergetes* (246–221 B.C.). Posthumous head on a gold octadrachm; he is shown with the rayed crown of the sun-god, the trident of Poseidon, and the divine aegis. 287, 288 / *Gold Octadrachm of Ptolemy III Euergetes. Obverse* (288): Ptolemy I Soter deified, with his wife; *reverse* (287): Ptolemy II Philadelphus, with his wife who was also his sister.

[Map 26, p. 103]

289
290

291
292
293

294
295

289–293 / *The Temple of Horus at Edfu.* One of the best-preserved buildings of the ancient world. The work was begun in 237 B.C. at the command of Ptolemy III, who placed in the inner sanctuary a niche 13 feet high, hollowed out of a single block of grey granite, which came from the earlier temple (292). In 122 B.C. Ptolemy VI added its magnificent peristyle. Both the six exterior columns, which form a harmonious façade (290), and the twelve interior columns have capitals delicately carved with flowers (293). Under Ptolemy VIII and Ptolemy IX an enormous forecourt was added, closed by a colossal pylon (258 by 115 feet) decorated with bas-reliefs in the traditional style, which show the king slaying his enemies before his gods (289; see also Pls. 182 and 41). Two statues of the god Horus in the likeness of a falcon guard the entrance (291). **294, 295** / *Small Temple of Ptolemy VI and Ptolemy VII.* In 295 a market can be seen outside Edfu; in the distance are the mountains which flank the Nile valley. [Map 10, p. 44]

107

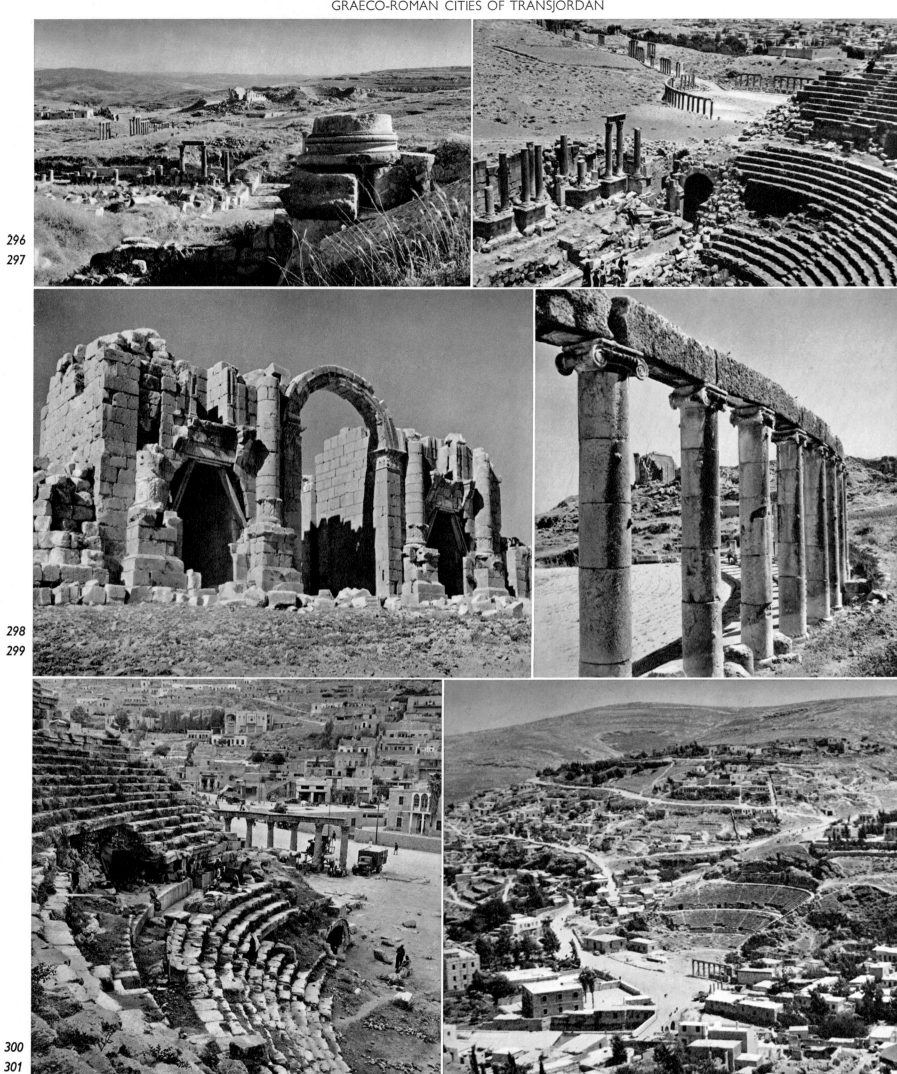

296
297
298
299
300
301

296–299 / *The Ruins of Gerasa*, a Hellenistic city in Transjordan, founded by, or slightly after, Alexander the Great. After being conquered by the Jew Alexander Jannaeus, Gerasa was liberated by Pompey, who incorporated it in the Decapolis. It is not certain that Gerasa is mentioned in the N.T., but from its ruins we are able to form an idea of the appearance of a Graeco-Roman city in the early Christian period. 296, *top centre:* Ruins of the temple of Zeus, also seen in 299 between the Ionic columns of the oval forum. 297: A view of this forum from the southern theatre. 298: The great triumphal gate. **300, 301** / *Philadelphia.* The ancient Rabbah of the Ammonites, Hellenised by Ptolemy II Philadelphus. The new name did not take root and today the town is once more called 'Ammân. From his palace, the king of Jordan can survey the remains of a skilfully-constructed theatre. [Map 34, p. 116]

THE MACCABEES

Today, when a book makes a lasting appeal to the tastes and needs of a wide circle of readers, it runs into several editions and large numbers of copies are issued. In ancient times, a successful work was recopied by hand, either on rolls or sheets of the perishable papyrus (the sheets being gathered into a 'codex', which resembled our books), or on leather or parchment, again in the form of rolls or books. If the work was not of wide interest only a few copies would be in circulation and, since these were not written on a durable (and more costly) material, the book was likely to be lost. These circumstances are partly responsible for the fact that certain ancient Jewish writings have not survived in the original Hebrew or Aramaic, but only in Greek translations.

Towards the end of the second century B.C., a devout and learned Jew compiled a book on the revolt of the Maccabees against the attempted Hellenisation of the Jewish community by the Seleucids. This author, who lived in Jerusalem, wrote in Hebrew, which in his day had ceased to be the spoken language and was used only for religious purposes. He deliberately adopted the idiom of the past and made constant efforts to imitate the style of the old historical books of Israel; for he saw in the persecution by Antiochus IV and his successors an attack upon Israel as the people of God. In this crisis, the Maccabees had upheld the ancestral heritage, and their house had therefore earned the right to the high priesthood and the royal crown. This is how the recent past appeared to the writer of the work we now call the first book of the Maccabees, who had himself witnessed some of these events.

This work, quickly translated into Greek, circulated among the Jews of the Diaspora, especially those in Alexandria. Now when the Early Christian Church adopted the sacred books of the Jews, it did so in the form in which they were current among the Jews of the Diaspora, who spoke and read Greek. Among these books, the translation of the history of the Maccabees rapidly became very popular with the Christians. Continually persecuted and martyred for their religious beliefs, they were heartened by the example of the Maccabees, who stood so steadfastly by their principles and were manifestly sustained by God. In the early days this work was also undoubtedly very popular with many Palestinian Jews. But, as we shall see, the later Maccabaean princes eventually aroused the hatred of a section of the people led by the Pharisees. Their glorious deeds ceased to be commemorated, and it is no accident that in all the great outpouring of rabbinical literature there is no mention of the name of Judas Maccabaeus. The feast of Hanukkah, instituted by Judas in 165 B.C. on the occasion of the purification of the Temple, was indeed still observed, but in Jewish tradition all trace of its Maccabaean origin was eliminated. Since the reading of the book about the Maccabees was not recommended by the rabbis, those who possessed it in Hebrew would not have a new copy made when their own became tattered. The learned St Jerome was still able to obtain a Hebrew copy, but by the time printing was invented, none survived; and it is entirely owing to the interest of the Christians that the modern historian has at his disposal at least the Greek translation of this work.

We can now understand why the first book of the Maccabees is included in the Catholic but not in the Protestant Bible. As we have said, the Early Church adopted the Old Testament in the form current among the Greek-speaking Jews of the Diaspora. At about the same period, the rabbis of Palestine fixed the number of the sacred books, limiting it to those which we now find in the printed Hebrew Bible. This limitation did not affect the Law, which had for centuries past been a clearly-defined whole of which no jot or tittle could be changed. Nor did it affect the Prophets, as, well before the time of Jesus, the prophetic books were already a definitive collection (see p. 27) which could not be modified in any way. It concerned only the Writings, which, both in Palestine and Alexandria (the most important centre of the Diaspora), had remained open to additions over a longer period than the Law or the Prophets. Scholars are unable to ascertain exactly when (a synod held at Jamnia in 100 A.D. has been suggested) or on what principles the rabbis made their choice. But it is an estab-

lished fact that the Early Church, following the Jews of the Diaspora, regarded as Holy Writ a number of works (some translated from Hebrew or Aramaic, others written directly in Greek) which had been excluded by the rabbis from the list of sacred books. The Catholic Church adhered to the view of the first generation of Christians, while the Reformation adopted the list of the rabbis. Certain Protestant editions of the Bible do, however, include the missing books in an appendix as Apocrypha (Tobit, Judith, The Wisdom of Solomon, Ecclesiasticus, Baruch, 1 and 2 Maccabees, and a few additions to the books of Esther and Daniel).

There never was a Hebrew text of the second book of the Maccabees. It is not a continuation of the first book, as 2 Kings is of 1 Kings, since it covers part of the same ground. In his preface, the writer explains that his work is an abridgement of a history in five books by a certain Jason of Cyrene. Nothing is known of this Jason. All that can be deduced from the résumé of his work is that he was a Jew of Hellenistic upbringing from the large community established in and around Cyrene, on the coast of North Africa, and that he had numerous contacts in Jerusalem, as well as a good knowledge of the Seleucid administration. His chief aim, however, was to edify his co-religionists, not to write accurate, objective history, and he chose for this purpose the literary genre which has been called *historiographie pathétique*. As abridged in 2 Maccabees, the work has more often the tone of the preacher than of the historian. Certain dogmas of the Judaism of his day which the author stresses were among those also accepted by the early Christians; and this fact, together with his glorification of the Maccabaean martyrs, doubtless contributed to the popularity of his book in the early centuries of the Church. Jason was well-informed about the course of contemporary events, and the modern historian of the Maccabaean revolt gratefully makes use of the concrete details to be gleaned from the résumé of his voluminous writings.

Besides these two sacred books, we possess many other sources of information on this period. After the Greeks came into contact with the Persian Empire, and especially after the expansion of Roman power in the East, many historians in the cultural centres of the Roman and Hellenic worlds had considerably enlarged their horizons. Herodotus personally visited the lands in the Near East, and other historiographers followed his example. Their surviving works sometimes provide us with important supplementary details concerning the history of the Jews. In Jewish tradition, for example, Antiochus IV became a monster, a cruel and wicked tyrant, the incarnation, indeed, of all the forces opposed to God. But the writings of the historian Polybius enable us to reach a better understanding of this ruler. Like Antiochus, Polybius was taken as a hostage to Rome (he arrived shortly after Antiochus left) and for sixteen years (166–150 B.C.) he moved in the same circles as Antiochus had done. Trained for a diplomatic career, he had previously been in Egypt as an ambassador of the Achaean League. While a hostage, he was allowed to travel freely in Italy and even to join Roman diplomats in their journeys through Gaul and Spain. Later he also accompanied Scipio to Mauretania and all along the coast of North Africa. What he tells us about the behaviour of Antiochus IV at Rome is therefore at first hand, and we may be sure that he followed with some interest the news he received of the later activities of this remarkable figure. The important historians of the following century, such as Diodorus Siculus and Livy, base their accounts of Antiochus and his successors partly upon Polybius. Josephus drew upon the first book of the Maccabees for his *Jewish Antiquities*, while in his *History of the Jewish War* he summarised the Maccabaean period with the help of the résumé by Nicolaus of Damascus, counsellor and historiographer at the court of Herod the Great. All these literary sources are illustrated by papyri, by official inscriptions in temples and public buildings, and by numerous coins which throw light on the titles and dates of the rulers and their connections with this or that town.

When Antiochus IV ascended the throne in 175 B.C., the Jewish community

302
I
307

302–305 / *Two Jewish Coins* of the type until recently ascribed to Simon Maccabaeus (142–135 B.C.), but now more plausibly attributed to the Jewish nationalists who rebelled against the Romans in the spring of A.D. 66. 302, *obverse*: The letter *aleph* above the chalice indicates the first year; the inscription, written in archaising characters, reads: sh-q-l y-s-r-'-l, 'shekel of Israel'. 303, 304, *reverse*: A spray bearing three pomegranates, and the words: y-r-sh-l-m q-d-sh-h, 'Jerusalem (the) holy'. The obverse of the second coin (305) bears the letter *beth* above the chalice, indicating the second year. 306, 307 / *Coin of Alexander Jannaeus* (103–76 B.C.). 306, *reverse*: Two cornucopias are visible. 307, *obverse*: the inscription, in archaic characters: y-n-t-n k-h-n g-d-l v-h-b-r h-y-h-d, 'Jonathan high priest and the community of the Jews'.

was already deeply divided. There was a strong group of intelligent and influential men who believed that Judaism should adapt itself to the Hellenistic culture which was sweeping the world. This universal civilisation was everywhere gaining ground, and if Judaism was to have a place in the new world it must abandon all those things which set the Jew apart: the weekly day of rest, circumcision, abstinence from certain foods. These 'progressives' were opposed by the 'traditionalists', who held that the law of segregation was of divine origin and vitally related to the religious vocation of Israel. We are given a vivid picture of life in the various circles and classes in Jewish society about 190 B.C. in the book of the Sage whose Hebrew name was, presumably, Jesus, son of Eleazar, son of Sira. Like the first book of the Maccabees, this work was not widely read by later generations of Jews, and it was only by chance that fragments in Hebrew were found fifty years ago in Cairo. But in the Early Church the Greek translation of this book was so popular that it was given the name Ecclesiasticus, the book of the Church *par excellence*. In the early liturgy it is quoted oftener than any other book of the Bible, with the obvious exception of the Psalms. Its wealth of practical advice and especially of observations on the nature of Wisdom reveals an obvious preference for the native tradition of Israel as against foreign influences. Wisdom, personified as a woman, seeks a home among all the peoples of the earth; in the end, God Himself gives her a dwelling-place on Mount Zion in Jerusalem, and Ben Sira identifies her with 'the book of the covenant of the Most High God, even the law which Moses commanded us for a heritage unto the assemblies of Jacob'.

Sir 24:23

Fidelity to the Law of Moses finally led to the outbreak of violent opposition to the drastic Hellenisation which Antiochus IV was attempting to impose. The books of the Maccabees give a detailed description of this dramatic episode. But the objective account in the first book shows how what were at first purely religious aims gradually took on a political colour; if they were to be completely free to practise their religion, the Jews must achieve independence from Seleucid domination. At the same time, one notices that, in their struggle against Hellenism, Judas and his successors themselves often acted in a Hellenistic spirit. After his first great success, for example, Judas instituted a new feast. Up to this time the Jews had observed only those feasts prescribed by the Law of Moses; the institution of new ceremonies to commemorate important events was a Hellenistic custom. Again, when Jonathan succeeded in becoming High Priest and King of the Jewish people, he sent an embassy not only to Rome, the mistress of the world, but also to Sparta. The Spartans received a letter which, in truly Hellenistic fashion, traced the fraternal bond between themselves and the Jews back to the remote past. Whereas the Romans, conscious of the superiority of Greece, claimed that Romulus was descended from a Greek hero, the Jews made it appear that the Spartans were descended from Abraham: 'It hath been found in writing, concerning the Spartans and the Jews, that they are brethren, and that they are of the stock of Abraham.'

1 Mac 4:59

1 Mac 12:21

The holy war against Hellenism was proclaimed in 166 B.C. by the priest Mattathias: 'And he saw the blasphemies that were committed in Judah and in Jerusalem, and he said, Woe is me! wherefore was I born to see the destruction of my people, and the destruction of the holy city, and to dwell there, when it was given into the hand of the enemy, the sanctuary into the hand of aliens?' Very quickly, bands of valiant men rallied round him to form an army. From the start, Judas, surnamed Maccabaeus, the third of his five sons, took strategical command. After six years of fighting, Judas was killed in 161 B.C. at the battle of

1 Mac 2:6f.

Birzaith (Elasa), about 12 miles north of Jerusalem. After describing the battle and its tragic end, the sacred author concludes in a style very reminiscent of the books of Samuel or Kings: 'And all Israel made great lamentation for him, and mourned many days, and said, How is the mighty fallen, the saviour of Israel! And the rest of the acts of Judas, and his wars, and the valiant deeds which he did, and his greatness, they are not written; for they were exceeding many.'

1 Mac 20—

Under Jonathan (161–142 B.C.) and Simon (142–135 B.C.), brothers of Judas, the territory of the Jews was recognised as independent and was greatly extended, at first by regions of the Mountain of Samaria and later by the fertile coastal plain, so that at this time Jerusalem possessed a port in Joppa. When the first book of the Maccabees closes, with the violent death of Simon in the stronghold of Dok, which dominated Jericho, the dynasty is firmly established. It is often called the house of the Hasmonaeans, a name which may derive from that of an ancestor. During the reign of the only surviving son of Simon, John Hyrcanus (135–104 B.C.), Antiochus VII led an army against Jerusalem; he imposed a tribute on Judaea and took John away with him to campaign against the Parthians. John managed to escape before the defeat in which Antiochus was killed and, taking advantage of the ensuing upheaval in Syria, he succeeded in restoring the independence of his country and even considerably enlarged its territories.

These years saw the definite emergence of the two parties of whom we hear so much in the New Testament, the Pharisees and the Sadducees. The Pharisees developed from a group of the 'pious', who had at first supported the Maccabees in their struggle. The foundations of the Sadducees were laid when Jonathan assumed the office of High Priest and the old priestly families, from whose ranks the High Priests had formerly been drawn, joined forces against him in a bid to regain their ancient position.

Aristobulus, John's son, reigned for only a year (104–103 B.C.). His widow married his brother Alexander Jannaeus (103–76 B.C.) who, with the title of king, governed a territory which he enlarged by continual warfare. He occupied all the coastal plain from Carmel to the Egyptian frontier (only Ashkelon retained its independence); he conquered the whole of Galilee in the north, Idumaea in the south, and a wide belt of land stretching from north to south in Transjordan. At the same time he had also to quell violent revolts at home, provoked by the Pharisees who were dissatisfied with their bellicose priest-king. The scion of the Maccabees was thus attacked by the descendants of the 'pious' who had supported his ancestor. It was this hostility between the Pharisees and the later Hasmonaean kings which led the Pharisees to remove the name of Judas Maccabaeus from Jewish records, and to dissociate his name and those of his brothers from the traditional feasts instituted in the time of the Maccabaean victories over the Seleucid kings (see p. 109). In an attempt to rid themselves of Alexander Jannaeus, the Pharisees even appealed for help to Demetrius III of Syria, the descendant of the impious Antiochus IV. Demetrius defeated Alexander, but the people then rallied to his side. With appalling brutality, Alexander thereupon put to death a number of rebels in Jerusalem. He was succeeded by his widow Alexandra (76–67 B.C.), who gave the Pharisees a position of great influence in the government which they were never completely to lose. When she died, her eldest son Hyrcanus was already High Priest, but he was forced to relinquish the throne to his brother Aristobulus, who was supported by the Sadducees. A fratricidal struggle ensued, which gave the Romans an opportunity to intervene in Jewish affairs.

308–310 / *Jericho.* By comparing Pls. 38, 160, and 172, the reader can see the situation of *Tell es-Sultân*, the ruins of the Jericho captured by Joshua. The magnificent city of Herod the Great, with its palaces, hippodrome, amphitheatres, villas, and baths, lay further to the south. Nothing remains of this Jericho, the city known to Jesus. The flourishing Byzantine city, destroyed by Persian and Arab invaders, has also vanished. But, thanks to the water of the *Wâdi el-Qelt* (Pl. 354) and the spring of Elisha, the palm trees of the modern town still recall its ancient name, 'city of palm trees', while the sycamores remind us of Zacchaeus (Lk 19:4). On one of the summits of the mountain stands the stronghold of Dok, where Simon Maccabaeus was assassinated (309) and, a closer view, 310). Half-way up the steep rock wall nestles a monastery which commemorates Christ's forty days in the wilderness.

[Maps 30, p. 104; 34, p. 116]

311–317 / *Petra*. East of the Arabah, in a broad zone of rose-red sandstone (Pl. 151), lie the faery ruins of Petra ('the rock' in Greek). In the time of the kings of Judah it was a city of the Edomites (Jer 49:16). It later became the capital of the Nabataeans, accessible only by way of a narrow ravine, nearly a mile long, running between vertical walls of rock over 260 feet high in some places (316). At the other end of the plain, on which the Nabataeans built temples, market-places, palaces, and baths in the Hellenistic style, towers an enormous rock (311). There the Edomites withdrew, as to an eagle's nest, and, according to 2 Ch 25:12, it was from this height that King Amaziah hurled down 10,000 prisoners. The lower rock alongside served as the acropolis of the Nabataeans (311, *right;* more clearly visible in 314). Countless tombs are cut in the rock (317 shows a detail of 312).   [Maps 3, p. 10; 26, p. 103]

UNDER THE ROMAN YOKE

The Passover celebrations of 64 B.C. were the most remarkable that Jerusalem had ever seen: in the Temple of God, as in a fortress, were Aristobulus, king and High Priest of the Jews, with his soldiers and the priests of the Sadducees; outside the city were fanatical besiegers, the leaders of the Pharisees, who were inciting a large army of uncircumcised Nabataeans, led by their king, Aretas, to storm the defences. In the week before the Passover, envoys were sent out from the Temple to the besiegers; it was the greatest feast of the year, and there were no animals left for the sacrifice! Negotiations took place and prices were stipulated, very high prices. But when the priests lowered the great sacks containing the agreed sum of money over the walls, the besiegers, zealots of the Law though they were, refused to supply the promised beasts.

The Pharisees were supporting the eldest son of Alexandra, Hyrcanus, who in 67 B.C. had been obliged to make way for his younger brother Aristobulus. Hyrcanus would have acquiesced, had not one of his partisans, the very shrewd Idumaean, Antipater, drawn a third party, Aretas, king of the Nabataeans, into the affair. But the Nabataean troops, who came from Petra, had no experience of attacking a walled city, and the siege dragged on. In the meantime word came that the Romans were on the march.

After receiving from a distracted people such powers as had never before been granted to a general, the brilliant Pompey had first of all, in a lightning operation, cleared the eastern Mediterranean of the pirates who were paralysing trade and communications; he had then restored order in Asia Minor and now intended to complete this task by annexing Syria to the Roman Empire, thereby destroying the last vestiges of the Seleucid kingdom. To this end, M. Aemilius Scaurus was sent on ahead to Damascus, where he learned of the siege of Jerusalem. Whenever a nation was rent by civil war, Rome delighted in acting as peacemaker. Soon the two brothers Hyrcanus and Aristobulus were bargaining with the Roman legate and, as Aristobulus made the more favourable offer, the Nabataeans received orders to raise the siege.

When Pompey arrived, the play was on again, with new actors; the wily Idumaean, Antipater, championed Hyrcanus, while a delegation from the Jews, who wanted to be rid of the Hasmonaeans, petitioned the Romans to restore the theocratic régime which had obtained under the Persians and Alexander. Bewildered by the cross-fire of pleas and counter-pleas, Pompey shelved the affair and decided to deal first with the Nabataeans. Aristobulus chose to accompany him on his march against Petra, but, half way there, he stubbornly elected to withdraw into his fortress of Alexandrium. From this eyrie he attempted to re-open negotiations with Pompey, who was naturally more than a match for him. Smarting under this diplomatic defeat, Aristobulus set out for the capital with the intention of holding it against the Romans. Pompey followed him; at Jericho he received news from Asia of the tragic death of Mithridates, his most powerful enemy, and his legions marched in jubilation along the old highway from Jericho up to Jerusalem. The terrified Aristobulus came out to meet the Romans and offered them money to abandon the siege. But he could not pay them, for his fanatical followers closed the city and Temple gates behind him against the legions. From his camp high on the southwestern hill, near the Bethlehem road, Pompey surveyed the walled city, surrounded on three sides by deep valleys, with its sanctuary which resembled a citadel. It would be a long siege. He would first have liked to bring the Nabataeans and their world-wide trade under Roman control and to consolidate his victories in Pontus.

But Jerusalem was weaker than she appeared. The city was divided. The partisans of the two brothers were locked in a bitter struggle. Soon the supporters of Aristobulus withdrew into the Temple and destroyed the viaduct leading from there to the upper city. Meanwhile, Hyrcanus and his men welcomed the Romans with open arms and Pompey prepared to besiege the Temple. The attack could only be made from the north, and even at this point a deep ditch had first to be filled in under the missiles of the beleaguered garrison. Only on the Sabbath, when there was no shooting from the Temple, could this work make real headway. For the Sabbath was still as punctiliously observed as the ritual of the sacrifices; every day the ceremonies took place, often under showers of arrows and stones. After three months the ditch was filled and powerful battering-rams breached the walls. The assault was followed by an appalling massacre. Most of the 12,000 Jews who perished were killed by their fanatical compatriots, who marched in through the breach in the train of the Roman army. Pompey went with his officers into the sanctuary and even into the Holy of Holies. He installed Hyrcanus as High Priest and ethnarch ('leader of the people'), but not as king. Aristobulus, in heavy chains, with his family and adherents, was to add lustre to his coming triumph at Rome.

318 / Antiochus III. 319 / Pompey. 320 / Julius Caesar. 321 / Tiberius.
322 / Ptolemy I. 323 / Augustus. 324 / Claudius. 325 / Nero.

The victor quickly reorganised the conquered territory. The Jewish state was once more reduced to the rural areas of Judaea, Samaria, Galilee, and Peraea, and shorn of all the towns which John Hyrcanus and Alexander Jannaeus had annexed by force, such as Pella and Gaza, and even of towns which had been in Jewish hands for much longer and were by this time Judaised, like Joppa, Jamnia, Adora, Mareshah, Samaria, and Scythopolis. All these liberated towns were to form part of the new province of Syria, to be governed by Scaurus, who was also to supervise the ethnarchy of Hyrcanus. For long years the Holy Land was to be at the mercy of insatiable tax-gatherers.

But Rome had not heard the last of the Hasmonaeans. The governor of Syria was more than once obliged to take action against the sons of Aristobulus, who eventually made common cause against the Romans with the descendants of Hyrcanus. The cunning Antipater then assumed the rôle of a Quisling. When civil war broke out between Pompey and Caesar he sided with the latter and had himself appointed procurator of the Jewish state as it had been before its dismemberment by Pompey. He allowed the weak Hyrcanus to remain titular ethnarch and High Priest, but installed his own son Phasael as military commander in Jerusalem, and gave his second son, Herod, similar powers in Galilee. But once again there emerged a descendant of the Hasmonaeans, Antigonus, the last son of Aristobulus, who reigned from 40–37 B.C. Herod, who at first fled to the Nabataeans, eventually made his way to Rome, where the Senate proclaimed him king of Judaea. With the help of Roman troops, he occupied the country, though Jerusalem held out until the arrival of the two legions which had been placed at his disposal. After another siege, lasting for two months, and further massacres, he finally established himself as king (37 B.C.) and successfully retained the throne till his death in 4 B.C.

If Herod, the son of an Idumaean father and a Nabataean mother, was deserving of his epithet 'the Great', it was primarily on account of his political ability. But he used this gift only for his personal gain and showed himself to be incredibly jealous, proud, vain, and cruel. No less cunning than his father, he contrived to profit by the disturbances which marked the last years of the Roman Republic. At first on the side of Antony, he went over at the right time to Octavian, regained the territories he had been forced to cede to Cleopatra and also appropriated her superb Gaulish bodyguard. He weeded out from his own family all the probable, or even possible, pretenders to the throne. He embarked on this policy, shortly after his capture of Jerusalem, with the execution of the adherents of Antigonus; he next put to death Hyrcanus and had one of his brothers-in-law drowned in a swimming-bath; there followed the deaths of his uncle Josephus, of the guardian of his favourite wife Mariamne, of Mariamne herself, and of her mother. Little wonder that he was not troubled by rival claimants!

The most brilliant period of Herod's reign was from 25 to 14 B.C. Relieved of all anxiety in the political field, the 'friend and ally of Rome', exempt from tribute, autonomous in his civil and judicial administration, and in command of a strong army of Gaulish, German, and Thracian mercenaries, he devoted himself, like a true Hellenistic ruler, to the erection of magnificent buildings in a great many towns of his kingdom. He also built temples to Augustus, his deified benefactor. By his efforts he changed the face of Jerusalem, beautifying the city with new buildings in the current Hellenistic style: theatres, amphitheatres, and a hippodrome. In honour of his friend the emperor, he also instituted quinquennial games, with athletes, gladiators, and wild animals. About the year 24 B.C. he erected his imposing royal palace, as celebrated for the luxury of its appointments as for the strength of the three impregnable towers which flanked it. The site is seen on Plate 378.

But all true Jews were deeply shocked by the ruinous condition of the Temple, whose miserable inadequacy was only made more painfully obvious by the fine new buildings. It was therefore a real stroke of genius on the part of Herod, who was not himself a Jew, to put the resources of his sovereign power at the service of the deep-seated longings of the chosen people. Not only did he democratically explain his impressive plan for the replacement of the modest post-Exilic sanctuary by a temple larger and more beautiful than even the Temple of Solomon itself; he also gave clear proof of his intention to respect all the prescriptions of the Law in the process of its construction. Ten thousand workmen prepared the stones in advance and one thousand priests were trained as masons at his expense. In those parts of the Temple where only a priest could set foot, they were to demolish the old building stone by stone and gradually rebuild it with the prepared materials, without interrupting the ceremonies for a single day. Work proceeded for eighteen months on the sanctuary itself, and for eight years on the courtyards and porticoes. We learn from the Gospel of St John that Jn 2:20 forty years later the work was still in progress. It was completed only under the procurator Albinus (A.D. 62–64).

Today nothing remains but the vast terrace, whose fine situation can be seen 192 from our aerial photographs. The present outer walls of this terrace are in part the 327 work of Herod. They may be identified by the large size and distinctive working of the stones, where these have not been weathered by time, as at the

326

326 / The Mount of Olives, seen from the southeastern corner of the Temple terrace (the aerial photograph, 192, was taken from almost the same direction). At the extreme left is the Church of Gethsemane, built on the foundations of a 4th century basilica. Between the walls across the centre of the photograph runs the modern road to Jericho. A steep path, flanked by walls, runs down from Gethsemane towards the bed of the Kidron and the funerary monuments (Pls. 375–377 and 382). The innumerable white stones at the right are tombstones. After the valley of the Kidron had been given the symbolic name of 'valley of Jehoshaphat' (meaning 'Yahweh judges'; Jl 3:2, 12), Jews and Moslems were brought from far and wide to be buried there. The left-hand tower of the three at top right stands on the spot which, since the 4th century, has been identified as the scene of the Ascension. The small sanctuary 'Dominus flevit' (Lk 19:41) lies halfway between this minaret and Gethsemane. [Map 33, p. 115]

327

THIS PHOTOGRAPH IS INTENDED TO SERVE AS A COMPLEMENT *and an illustration to Map 33 (p. 115, opposite). It is an aerial view, looking NNW, and was taken at sunset when the light is at its best. The relief stands out with remarkable clarity. In order to understand the following comments, the reader should refer both to Map 33 and to Plates 191 and 192 and their caption.*

At the right of the photograph, in full light, are the slopes of the Mount of Olives and the Mount of Offence. At the foot of the latter are ranged the little white cubes of the houses of the village of Silwân, whose name recalls the conduit of Shiloah, and the 'pool of Siloam'. On the other side of the valley of the Kidron (lying in shadow), to the south of the Temple terrace, we can clearly distinguish the rocky spur of Ophel, along which the city of David formerly stood (cf. Plates 192 and 380). To the left of Ophel runs the Tyropoeon valley, whose course may be traced to the north along the line of a shadow which cuts the city in half near the middle of the photograph. The hill to the west of the valley rises to well over 2,600 feet; on the lower hill to the east stands the Temple terrace at a height of some 2,450 feet.

At the left of the photograph, towards the bottom, is the valley of Hinnom, which runs at first to the west and then bends northwards. It thus curves around the south-western hill ('Mount Zion'; see pp. 68–70), which is sunlit here and appears in bolder relief than on Plate 191.

Apart from the northwestern sector, almost the whole of the present city wall can be seen; it may be identified with the help of the indications on Map 33. It is easy to observe how, in the course of centuries, Jerusalem has gradually shifted towards the northwest. The early stages of this process are indicated on Map 24 A, B, and C (p. 96). This development is a direct consequence of geographical factors: flanked to the east and south by the deep gorges of Kidron and Hinnom, the Holy City can extend only to the northwest, where there is no valley to check its expansion.

Until the beginning of the present century all the inhabitants of Jerusalem could be accommodated within the walls built in the sixteenth century by the Sultan Sulaiman II the Magnificent (i.e. within the 'old city'). This is no longer the case. The modern city (outside the walls, to the northwest), capital of the state of Israel with some 150,000 inhabitants, covers a much larger area than the old city, which is now in the territory of Jordan and has about 70,000 inhabitants in the crowded warren of streets which fill the 250 acres within its walls.

It is difficult to visualise, upon the great terrace to the east of the old city, the Temple erected at the command of Herod the Great. The foundations of this magnificent sanctuary were laid in the eighteenth year of his reign (19 B.C.), but it was not completed until long after his death (A.D. 64), and was razed to the ground by the Romans in

A.D. 70. In its place there now stands the Mosque of Omar, or, more precisely, the 'Dome of the Rock' (Qubbet es-Sakhra). This Moslem monument, built at the end of the seventh century A.D. and subsequently restored on several occasions, serves essentially to enshrine the rock upon which stood the Temple of the Jews, and which is as sacred to the Moslems as the Black Stone of Mecca (cf. Plate 201). The fact that this is a holy place has so far precluded all archaeological investigation. In order to form even an approximate idea of the size and arrangement of the buildings, scholars are therefore obliged to resort to the meagre information to be obtained from literary sources. This is far from adequate, and the reconstructions displayed in various museums are all highly conjectural. For this reason we have refrained from including in this Atlas any illustrations of these reconstructions.

We are told that 'As he [Jesus] came out of the temple, one of his disciples said to him, "Look, Teacher, what wonderful stones and what wonderful buildings!" And Jesus said to him, "Do you see these great buildings? There will not be left here one stone upon another, that will not be thrown down."' (Mk 13:1f.)

But, as we study this photograph, let us also recall the words of the Psalmist:

I was glad when they said to me,
"Let us go to the house of the LORD!"
Our feet have been standing
within your gates, O Jerusalem!
Jerusalem, built as a city
which is bound firmly together,
to which the tribes go up,
the tribes of the LORD,
as was decreed for Israel,
to give thanks to the name of the LORD.
There thrones for judgment were set,
the thrones of the house of David.
Pray for the peace of Jerusalem!
"May they prosper who love you!
Peace be within your walls,
and security within your towers!"

(Ps 122:1-7)

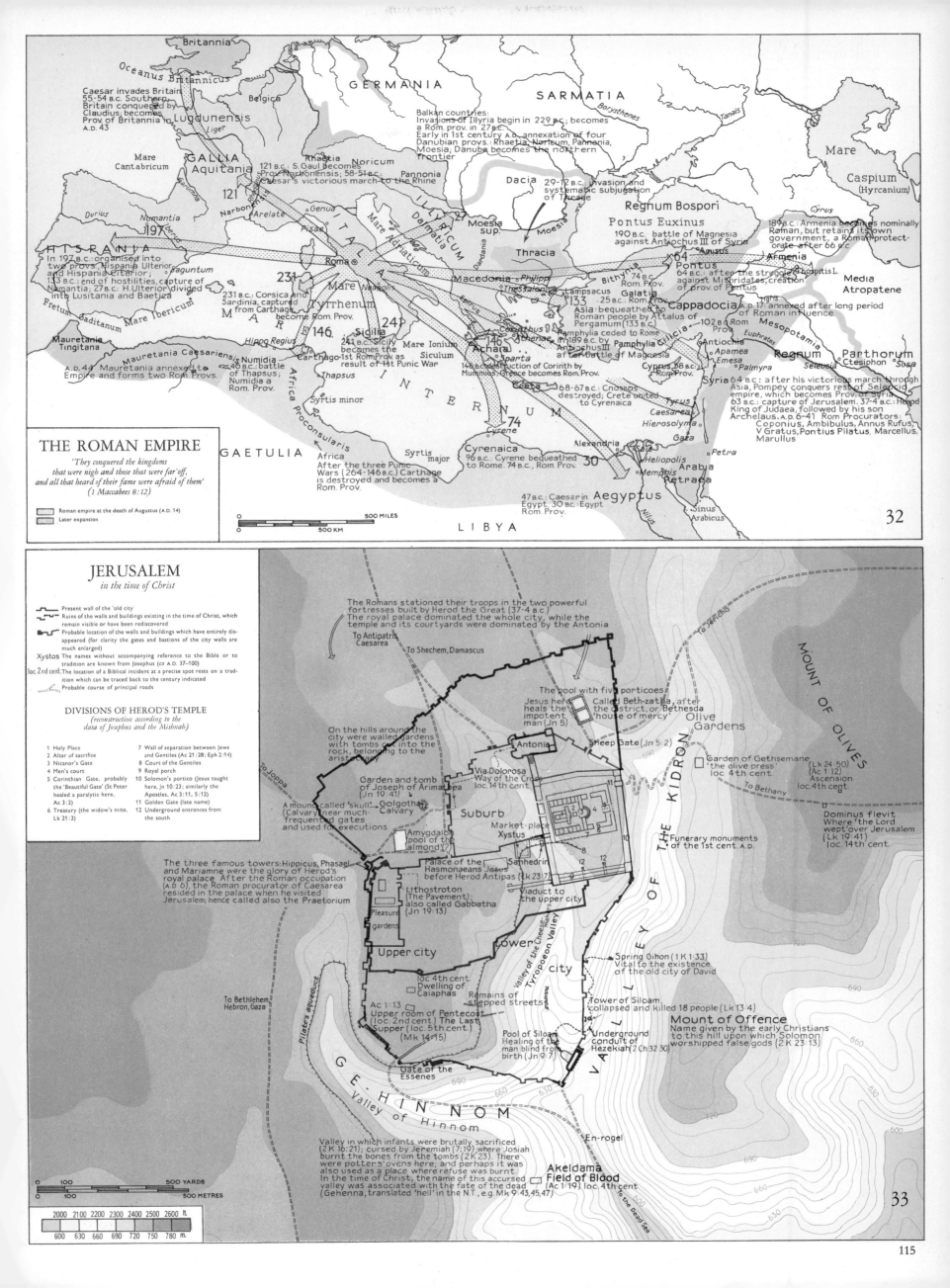

THE ROMAN EMPIRE

*'They conquered the kingdoms
that were nigh and those that were far off,
and all that heard of their fame were afraid of them'*
(1 Maccabees 8:12)

| | Roman empire at the death of Augustus (A.D. 14) |
| | Later expansion |

GERMANIA

SARMATIA

Oceanus Britannicus

Caesar invades Britain
55-54 B.C. Southern
Britain conquered by
Claudius, becomes
Prov. of Britannia in
A.D. 43

Britannia

Belgica

GALLIA Lugdunensis

Aquitania

Balkan countries:
Invasions of Illyria begin in 229 B.C., becomes
a Rom. prov. in 27 B.C.
Early in 1st century A.D. annexation of four
Danubian provs.: Rhaetia, Noricum, Pannonia,
Moesia; Danube becomes the northern
frontier

Mare
Caspium
(Hyrcanium)

Mare
Cantabricum

Rhaetia Noricum

121 B.C.: S. Gaul becomes
Prov. Narbonensis; 58-51 B.C.
Caesar's victorious march to the Rhine

Pannonia

Dacia

29-12 B.C. invasion and
systematic subjugation
of Thrace

Regnum Bospori

189 B.C.: Armenia becomes nominally
Roman, but retains its own
government, a Roman protect-
orate after 66 B.C.

HISPANIA

In 197 B.C. organised into
two provs. Hispania Ulterior
and Hispania Citerior;
133 B.C.: end of hostilities, capture of
Numantia; 27 B.C.: H. Ulterior divided
into Lusitania and Baetica

ILLYRICUM
Dalmatia

Pontus Euxinus

190 B.C. battle of Magnesia
against Antiochus III of Syria

Armenia

Pontus

64 B.C. after the struggle
against Mithridates, creation
of prov. of Pontus

Media
Atropatene

Numantia

Thracia

Macedonia

Philippi

Bithynia 74 B.C.
Rom. Prov.

Galatia
25 B.C. Rom. Prov.

Cappadocia

A.D. 17 annexed after long period
of Roman influence

Mesopotamia

231

ITALIA

Roma

Thessalonica

Lampsacus

Asia bequeathed to
Roman people by Attalus of
Pergamum (133 B.C.)

Regnum
Parthorum

Corsica and
Sardinia, captured
from Carthage,
become Rom. Prov.

Mare
Tyrrhenum

Mare
Adriaticum

Epirus

Corinthus

Achaia

Athenae

Pamphylia ceded to Rome
in 189 B.C. by
Antiochus III

102 B.C. Rom.
Prov.

Cilicia

Apamea

Ctesiphon

Susa

146

Sicilia

Sparta

146 destruction of Corinth by
Mummius; Greece becomes Rom. Prov.

Pamphylia

Cyprus 58 B.C.
Rom. Prov.

Syria 64 B.C.: after his victorious march through
Asia, Pompey conquers rest of Seleucid
empire, which becomes Prov. of Syria.
63 B.C.: capture of Jerusalem. 37-4 B.C.: Herod
King of Judaea, followed by his son
Archelaus. A.D. 6-41 Rom. Procurators:
Coponius, Ambibulus, Annus Rufus,
V. Gratus, Pontius Pilatus, Marcellus,
Marullus

241 B.C.: Sicily
becomes the
Carthago-1st Rom Prov. as
result of 1st Punic War

Mare
Ionium
Siculum

Seleucia

Palmyra

Emesa

241

Hippo Regius

Mauretania
Tingitana

Mauretania Caesariensis

A.D. 44 Mauretania annexed to
Empire and forms two Rom. Provs.

Thapsus

Numidia

46 B.C.: battle
of Thapsus;
Numidia a
Rom. Prov.

68-67 B.C.: Cnossos
destroyed; Crete united
to Cyrenaica

Creta

Tyrus

Caesarea

Hierosolyma

Gaza

Petra

Fretum Gaditanum

Mare Ibericum

Saguntum

Africa Proconsularis

Syrtis minor

74

Cyrene

Cyrenaica

THE ROMAN EMPIRE

GAETULIA

Africa
After the three Punic
Wars (264-146 B.C.) Carthage
is destroyed and becomes a
Rom. Prov.

Syrtis
major

96 B.C.: Cyrene bequeathed
to Rome. 74 B.C., Rom. Prov.

30

Alexandria

Heliopolis

Memphis

Arabia
Petraea

LIBYA

47 B.C.: Caesar in
Egypt. 30 B.C.: Egypt
Rom. Prov.

Aegyptus

Nilus

Sinus
Arabicus

32

JERUSALEM
in the time of Christ

	Present wall of the 'old city'
	Ruins of the walls and buildings existing in the time of Christ, which remain visible or have been rediscovered
	Probable location of the walls and buildings which have entirely disappeared (for clarity the gates and bastions of the city walls are much enlarged)

Xystos The names without accompanying reference to the Bible or to tradition are known from Josephus (ca A.D. 37–100)

loc. 2nd cent. The location of a Biblical incident at a precise spot rests on a tradition which can be traced back to the century indicated

Probable course of principal roads

DIVISIONS OF HEROD'S TEMPLE
(reconstruction according to the data of Josephus and the Mishnah)

1 Holy Place
2 Altar of sacrifice
3 Nicanor's Gate
4 Men's court
5 Corinthian Gate, probably the 'Beautiful Gate' (St Peter healed a paralytic here. Ac 3:2)
6 Treasury (the widow's mite. Lk 21:2)
7 Wall of separation between Jews and Gentiles (Ac 21:28; Eph 2:14)
8 Court of the Gentiles
9 Royal porch
10 Solomon's portico (Jesus taught here, Jn 10:23; similarly the Apostles, Ac 3:11, 5:12)
11 Golden Gate (late name)
12 Underground entrances from the south

The Romans stationed their troops in the two powerful
fortresses built by Herod the Great (37-4 B.C.)
The royal palace dominated the whole city, while the
temple and its courtyards were dominated by the Antonia

To Antipatris
Caesarea

To Shechem, Damascus

To Jericho

MOUNT OF OLIVES

The pool with five porticoes
Jesus here
heals the
impotent
man (Jn 5)

Called Beth-zatha, after
the district, or Bethesda
'house of mercy'

Olive
Gardens

Sheep Gate (Jn 5:2)

Garden of Gethsemane
'the olive press'
loc. 4th cent.

(Lk 24:50)
Ascension
loc. 4th cent.
(Ac 1:12)

On the hills around the
city were walled gardens
with tombs cut into the
rock, belonging to the
aristocracy

Antonia

To Bethany

Garden and tomb
of Joseph of Arimathea
(Jn 19:41)

Via Dolorosa
Way of the Cross
loc. 14th cent.

Dominus flevit
Where 'the Lord
wept' over Jerusalem
(Lk 19:41)
loc. 14th cent.

A mound called 'skull'
(Calvary) near much-
frequented gates
and used for executions

Golgotha
Calvary

Suburb

Market-place
Xystus

Funerary monuments
of the 1st cent. A.D.

To Joppa

Amygdalon
pool of the
almond (?)

Sanhedrin

The three famous towers: Hippicus, Phasael
and Mariamne were the glory of Herod's
royal palace. After the Roman occupation
(A.D. 6), the Roman procurator of Caesarea
resided in the palace when he visited
Jerusalem; hence called also the Praetorium

Palace of the
Hasmonaeans Jesus
before Herod Antipas (Lk 23:7)

Viaduct to
the upper city

Lithostroton
(The Pavement);
also called Gabbatha
(Jn 19:13)

Pleasure
gardens

Lower

Spring Gihon (1 K 1:33)
Vital to the existence
of the old city of David

Upper city

city

Mount of Offence
Name given by the early Christians
to this hill upon which Solomon
worshipped false gods (2 K 23:13)

To Bethlehem
Hebron, Gaza

loc. 4th cent.
Dwelling of
Caiaphas

Remains of
stepped streets

Tower of Siloam,
collapsed and killed 18 people (Lk 13:4)

Ac 1:13
Upper room of Pentecost
(loc. 2nd cent.) The Last
Supper (loc. 5th cent.)
(Mk 14:15)

Pilate's aqueduct

Underground
conduit of
Hezekiah (2 Ch 32:30)

Pool of Siloam
Healing of the
man blind from
birth (Jn 9:7)

VALLEY OF THE KIDRON

Gate of the
Essenes

GE-HINNOM Valley of Hinnom

En-rogel

Akeldama
Field of Blood
(Ac 1:19) loc. 4th cent.

Valley in which infants were brutally sacrificed
(2 K 16:21); cursed by Jeremiah (7:19) where Josiah
burnt the bones from the tombs (2 K 23). There
were potter's ovens here; and perhaps it was
also used as a place where refuse was burnt.
In the time of Christ, the name of this accursed
valley was associated with the fate of the dead
(Gehenna, translated 'hell' in the N.T., e.g. Mk 9:43,45,47)

| 100 | | | 500 YARDS |
| 100 | | | 500 METRES |

| 2000 | 2100 | 2200 | 2300 | 2400 | 2500 | 2600 ft. |
| 600 | 630 | 660 | 690 | 720 | 750 | 780 m. |

33

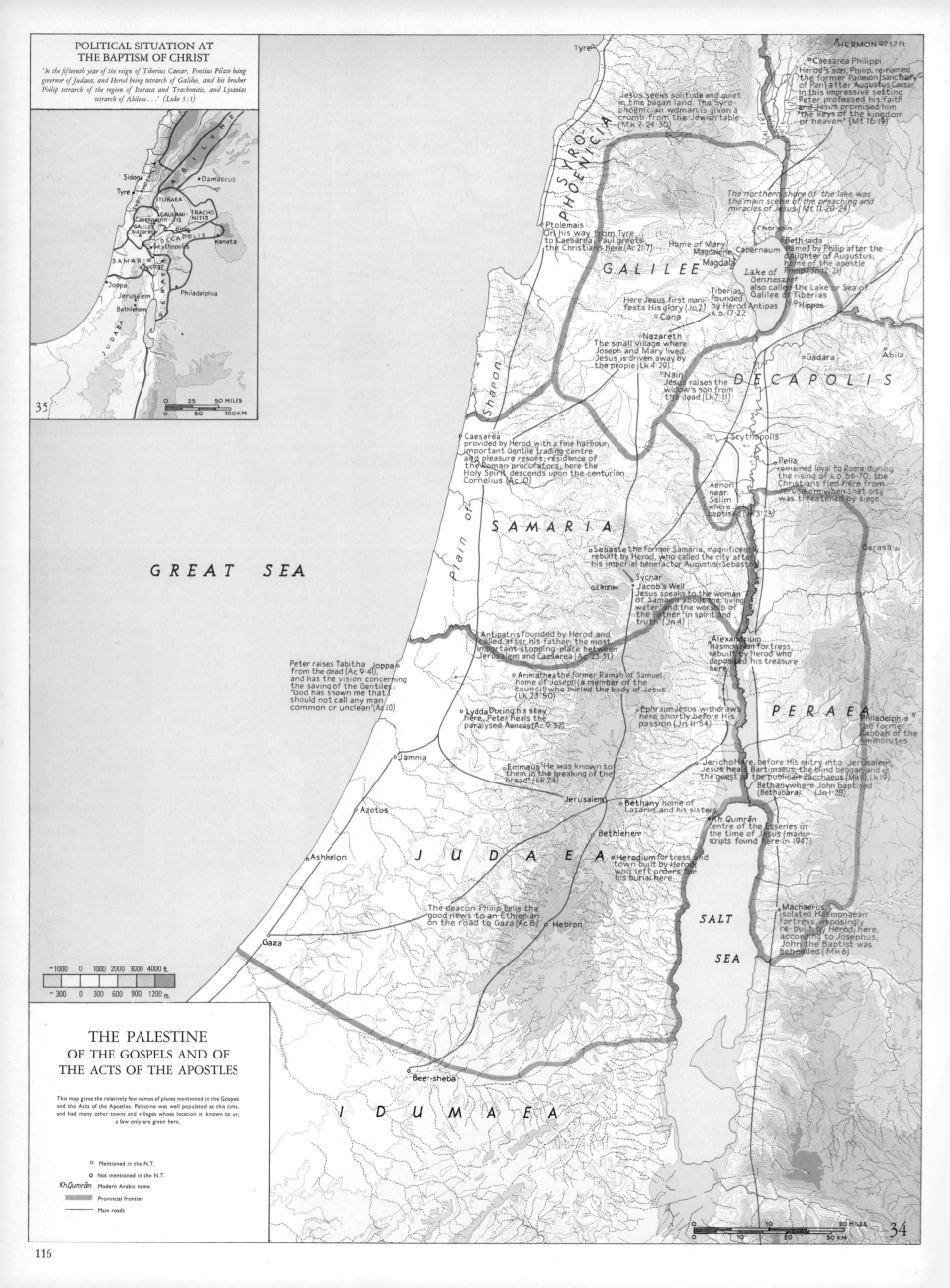

HERMON 9232ft

Caesarea Philippi
Herod's son, Philip, re-named
the former Paneion (sanctuary
of Pan) after Augustus Caesar.
In this impressive setting
Peter professed his faith
and Jesus promised him
'the keys of the kingdom
of heaven' (Mt 16:19)

Tyre

Jesus seeks solitude and quiet
in this pagan land. The Syro-
phoenician woman is given a
crumb from the Jewish table
(Mk 7:24-30)

PHOENICIA

The northern shore of the lake was
the main scene of the preaching and
miracles of Jesus (Mt 11:20-24)

Ptolemais
On his way from Tyre
to Caesarea Paul greets
the Christians here (Ac 21:7)

Chorazin

GALILEE

Home of Mary
Magdalene   Capernaum

Beth-saida
named by Philip after the
daughter of Augustus;
home of the apostle
Philip (Jn 12:21)

Magdala

Lake of
Gennesaret
also called the Lake or Sea of
Galilee or Tiberias

Here Jesus first mani-
fests His glory (Jn 2)
Cana

Tiberias
founded
by Herod Antipas
A.D. 17-22

Hippos

Nazareth
The small village where
Joseph and Mary lived.
Jesus is driven away by
the people (Lk 4:29)

Gadara   Abila

Nain
Jesus raises the
widow's son from
the dead (Lk 7:11)

DECAPOLIS

Sharon

Scythopolis

Caesarea
provided by Herod with a fine harbour;
important Gentile trading centre
and pleasure resort; residence of
the Roman procurators; here the
Holy Spirit descends upon the centurion
Cornelius (Ac 10)

Pella
remained loyal to Rome during
the rising of A.D. 66-70; the
Christians fled here from
Jerusalem when that city
was threatened by siege

Aenon
near
Salim
where John
baptised
(Jn 3:23)

SAMARIA

Plain of

Gerasa

Sebaste the former Samaria, magnificently
rebuilt by Herod, who called the city after
his imperial benefactor Augustus (=Sebastos)

GREAT SEA

GERIZIM

Sychar
Jacob's Well
Jesus speaks to the woman
of Samaria about the 'living
water' and the worship of
the Father 'in spirit and
truth' (Jn 4)

Antipatris founded by Herod and
called after his father; the most
important stopping-place between
Jerusalem and Caesarea (Ac 23:31)

Alexandrium
Hasmonaean fortress
rebuilt by Herod who
deposited his treasure
here

Peter raises Tabitha
from the dead (Ac 9:41),
and has the vision concerning
the saving of the Gentiles:
'God has shown me that I
should not call any man
common or unclean' (Ac 10)

Joppa

Arimathea the former Ramah of Samuel,
home of Joseph (a member of the
council) who buried the body of Jesus
(Lk 23:50)

PERAEA

Ephraim Jesus withdraws
here shortly before His
passion (Jn 11:54)

Philadelphia
the former
Rabbah of the
Ammonites

Lydda During his stay
here, Peter heals the
paralysed Aeneas (Ac 9:32)

Jamnia

Jericho Here, before His entry into Jerusalem,
Jesus heals Bartimaeus the blind beggar, and is
the guest of the publican Zacchaeus (Mk 10, Lk 19)

Emmaus 'He was known to
them in the breaking of the
bread' (Lk 24)

Bethany where John baptised
(Bethabara) (Jn 1:28)

Jerusalem

Bethany home of
Lazarus and his sisters

Azotus

Kh. Qumrân
centre of the Essenes in
the time of Jesus (manu-
scripts found here in 1947)

Bethlehem

Ashkelon

Herodium fortress and
town built by Herod,
who left orders for
his burial here

JUDAEA

The deacon Philip tells the
good news to an Ethiopian
on the road to Gaza (Ac 8)

Hebron

SALT

Machaerus
isolated Hasmonaean
fortress, imposingly
re-built by Herod; here,
according to Josephus,
John the Baptist was
beheaded (Mk 6)

Gaza

SEA

- 1000 0 1000 2000 3000 4000 ft.
- 300 0 300 600 900 1200 m.

Beer-sheba

IDUMAEA

THE PALESTINE
OF THE GOSPELS AND OF
THE ACTS OF THE APOSTLES

This map gives the relatively few names of places mentioned in the Gospels
and the Acts of the Apostles. Palestine was well populated at this time,
and had many other towns and villages whose location is known to us;
a few only are given here.

○ Mentioned in the N.T.

◦ Not mentioned in the N.T.

Kh.Qumrân   Modern Arabic name

　　　　　Provincial frontier

　　　　　Main roads

10   20 MILES
10 20 30 KM

34

329
330

southeastern corner and the 'Wailing Wall'. It is impossible to ascertain exactly what the sanctuary, the adjoining buildings, and the porticoes looked like at this period. We could certainly learn a great deal, at least about the ground-plan of Herod's Temple, from an archaeological investigation of the terrace. But this holy place is in the hands of the Moslems, and there is at present no prospect of obtaining permission to excavate.

The reconstructions on paper and the models which can be seen in various places are based on literary data. Josephus included a description of the Temple in his *Jewish Antiquities*, and in the course of his account of the siege and capture of the city by the Romans he occasionally refers to the position of a wall or a building. One of the sixty-three tractates of the Mishnah (a collection of the oral teachings of the rabbis, compiled in the second and third centuries A.D.) is also devoted to the Temple. Unfortunately its description of the details is very often inadequate and leaves too much to the imagination of those who attempt reconstructions. What is certain is that Herod intended to provide the Jews with a building which in magnificence and beauty would rival, if not surpass, the many Hellenistic temples in Palestine. There is, indeed, a ring of truth in what we are told of the white or coloured marble used to face the outer walls and of the gold which covered some of the roofs. Even today when, apart from the elegant Mosque of Omar in the centre and the Mosque El-Aksa at its southern end, the great terrace is quite empty, it makes an unforgettable impression on the visitor who climbs the Mount of Olives and gazes down at the city. He can well understand how the simple Galileans who accompanied Jesus must have marvelled when, from the hilltop, they looked down upon these magnificent buildings and how shocked they must have been by His confident prophecy of the imminent destruction of the Temple.

A complete list of all Herod's constructions outside Jerusalem obviously cannot be given here. We need mention only his palaces in and around Jericho, a few remains of which were brought to light in 1950; his restoration of ancient Samaria, which lent itself admirably to development as a Hellenistic city, and where the imposing temple of Augustus must have splendidly crowned the sum- 228 mit of the natural acropolis; and Caesarea on the coast, which in the space of a few years he enlarged into a veritable metropolis, whose vanished glory is faintly 330 reflected in the colonnades pictured above. All the Hellenistic cities of Palestine were endowed with new buildings, embellishments, and statues. And outside Palestine itself, Tyre, Sidon, Byblos, Berytus, Tripolis, Damascus, and even Athens counted him among their benefactors. At Antioch he lined the principal street with columns; and on the island of Rhodes he restored the temple of Apollo, which had been burned.

Herod's glittering reign closed with a further outburst of family quarrels. As a result of his good relations with the imperial house, he had sent the two sons of his favourite wife Mariamne to be educated in Rome. They returned home about 14 B.C., when there began a series of complicated intrigues owing to the jealousy of Herod's sister, Salome, and his brother, Pheroras. At this period Herod himself was in no mood to be trifled with, for he was in danger of losing the favour of Augustus; by embarking upon a war against the Nabataeans without the permission of the emperor he had exceeded the powers delegated to him as a king allied to Rome. He promptly recalled his eldest son Antipater from exile to intrigue against the two sons of Mariamne and, in 12 B.C., he sought the emperor's permission to execute them.

This favour was at first denied him, but he was eventually granted the necessary authority on condition that the execution took place outside Judaea. In 7 B.C. the two young men were strangled in Samaria, the city in which Herod had married Mariamne, their mother. After further intrigues, Antipater left for

331
332
333

329, 330 / *Caesarea.* In the massive Roman style, Herod constructed two moles, forming a narrow entrance channel facing NNW. He thus created the only safe harbour on this straight coast, which has no bays, and where the unloading of ships is always dangerous on account of the southwest winds. Opposite this harbour, there rose, like a vast amphitheatre, the magnificent city of Caesarea, soon to become the 'caput Judaeae' (Tacitus), the real capital of Judaea; little evidence now remains of its former glory. **331, 332** / *The Wall encircling Abraham's Tomb at Hebron.* An impressive rectangle measuring 194 feet by 112 (see aerial photograph, Pl. 89); all the stones are the same height and some are 23 feet long. Its general appearance is partly disfigured by a white coping of Arab construction. **333** / *The 'Wailing Wall' at Jerusalem*, part of the western wall of the Temple terrace. We can recognise the work of the same skilful masons (see also Pl. 383). [Map 34, p. 116]

Rome to seek confirmation of his right to the succession. Before he returned, Herod petitioned the emperor for permission to have him assassinated. At this point he fell gravely ill. Rumours of his death spread among the people, and the Pharisees ventured to remove the golden eagle which had been set up in the Temple. Those responsible were burnt alive. The warm springs on the north-east coast of the Dead Sea (in this Atlas they appear only on the mosaic map of Madaba, p. 61, *Therma Kallirhoes*) brought no relief to the sick king, who returned to Jericho weaker than before. He now ordered the imprisonment of a number of Judaean nobles, who were to be killed after his death: the country would thus have good cause to mourn him! Meanwhile, he received imperial authority to execute Antipater, whom he caused to be assassinated five days before his own death.

During this time another King was born in Judaea, in fulfilment of the words of the prophets: 'Behold, a virgin shall conceive and bear a son, and his name shall be called Emmanuel'... 'But you, O Bethlehem Ephrathah, who are little to be among the clans of Judah, from you shall come forth for me one who is to be ruler in Israel.'

Mt 1:23

Mic 5:2

Mt 2:16

The only Biblical reference to Herod the Great is the story of his massacre of the innocents, an act wholly in keeping with the foregoing portrait, for which we have drawn upon contemporary writers. In his will, he left instructions that he was to be buried in the powerful fortress which he had built high upon a hill in the desert near Bethlehem. His funeral took place with great ceremony; arrayed in purple, with the golden crown upon its head and the sceptre in its hand, his body was laid upon a bier of solid gold encrusted with precious stones. In the procession walked the few members of his family whom he had not previously assassinated and detachments of his mercenaries. Five hundred slaves bore perfumes and swung censers all along the winding track which leads across the desert from Jericho to Bethlehem. The solitary ruins of the fortress in which he was buried still dominate the distant view from Bethlehem, where thousands of pilgrims come every year to honour the birthplace of the lowliest subject of Herod the Great.

358

It is not surprising that terrible upheavals should have followed the death of Herod. The discontent of the people everywhere came to a head, and was aggravated by the ill-advised rapacity of a certain Sabinus, who was sent to inspect taxes in the name of the emperor. The legate of Syria, Publius Quinctilius Varus, finally restored order, but only after some 2,000 Jews had been crucified. The emperor appointed Archelaus, the eldest son of Malthace, one of Herod's wives, as ethnarch of Judaea, together with Samaria and Idumaea; her second son, Herod Antipas, was made tetrarch of Galilee and Peraea, while the northern territories were assigned to Philip, the son of Herod and Cleopatra, a woman of Jerusalem.

We know very little about the ten years' reign of Archelaus (4 B.C.–A.D. 6) apart from its ending. A delegation of Judaeans and Samaritans went to Rome to complain of his misgovernment. He was summoned to give an account of himself and then exiled to Vienne in Gaul. The emperor appointed a procurator over his territory. This official was to live in the great port of Caesarea and to come to Jerusalem only to maintain order during the feasts; he was then to reside in the western quarter of the city in the magnificent palace of Herod, called the praetorium on this account. The procurator of Judaea was in some respects the subordinate of the legate of Syria; the latter had Roman legions at his disposal, whereas the procurator had to be content with mercenaries. The Jews retained the right to administer the law, but could not pass sentence of death. The procurator also had a hand in the appointment and dismissal of the High Priests. The Jews could practise their religion freely, and their feelings were as far as possible respected; for example, Roman soldiers were forbidden to carry their standards bearing the portrait of the emperor into Jerusalem, nor did his head appear on the coins struck in Judaea. Finally, the Jews were not required to worship the deified emperor. We even learn that Augustus gave orders for an ox and two lambs to be sacrificed daily in the Temple at his expense, on behalf of himself and the Roman people.

The list of the seven officials who governed Judaea from A.D. 6 to 41 would be of no greater interest to us than similar lists for other regions of the great empire, did it not contain the name of Pontius Pilate, procurator from A.D. 26 to 36. Of unknown origin, he was a mixture of arrogance and weakness. Once he ordered the Roman standards to be carried into Jerusalem, but provoked such a storm of opposition that he was forced to yield. On another occasion he quelled opposition to his seizure of Temple money by the use of disguised soldiers to scatter the people with their clubs. The Gospels record that once he mingled the blood of Galileans with their sacrifices. His part in the trial of Jesus is familiar to all readers of the New Testament. Here he shows a willingness to do what he knows to be right, but reveals the essential weakness of his character in yielding to the popular cry and releasing Barabbas, while delivering Jesus to be crucified.

334

334 / Palmyra, in the heart of the Syrian desert and at the foot of a chain of chalky hills; one of the finest fields of ruins in Syria. Tadmor is mentioned in documents as early as the 2nd millennium B.C., but it was not until the beginning of the Christian era that this oasis became increasingly important as a stopping-place on the route of the caravans which carried the treasures of Asia to the Phoenician ports, and, through them, to the Roman world. The Greek merchants corrupted the ancient name into the form *Palmyra*, which suggests an oasis rich in palm-trees. The culture of this commercial centre, whose ruins again bear the old name of *Tudmur*, is a typical mixture of Romano-Hellenistic and Oriental elements. Above is an aerial photograph taken from the east. In the foreground is the temple of Bel (Baal), built in the Hellenistic style, but surrounded by courts and an outer wall in the Semitic manner.

[Map 25, p. 103]

335

336
337

338
339

35 / *General View of Palmyra*, looking east (taken from the opposite direction to Pl. 334; the black arrow on Pl. 334 shows the position from which 335 was photographed). *Top left:* The long colonnaded street (1,236 yards) leading to the buildings of the temple of Bel. To the left, and especially to the right, of he temple are the gardens of the oasis. Behind stretch the endless Syrian steppes. **336** / *Part of the Colonnade*, with the temple in the background. **337**/ *Northwest Corner of the Temple Court.* The holes in the walls and columns are the work of plunderers bent on recovering the metal bonds by which the tone blocks were ingeniously held together. On the left are the remains of a 16th century Arab stronghold. **338** / *Monumental Gate in the Colonnaded Street.* also seen in Pls. 334 and 336. **339**/*Sanctuary (Naos) in the Centre of the Temple;* golden sandstone against a deep blue sky. [Map 4, p. 29]

340–345 / *Ba'albek.* Here the Phoenicians worshipped a local deity (the Baal of the Beqa', i.e. of the valley; see Pl. 18). Later, in the flourishing city of Heliopolis, the Romans worshipped Jupiter Heliopolitanus. The great emperors of the 2nd century A.D. built a vast complex of temples, whose ruins are still very impressive. A great court, surrounded by covered arcades with round and angular exedrae in alternation, leads to the steps of the principal temple, raised on a substructure 43 feet high. Of the fifty-four columns which surrounded the sanctuary six are still standing. 340: A general view of this court, showing, *centre:* a pool; *left:* two altars; *background:* the steps (seen from a different angle in 345). 342: The small piece that is missing from the frieze above the six columns in 341. 344: The temple of Bacchus, in a better state of preservation. [Map 3, p. 10

346 / *A Roll of Isaiah of the time of Christ*, found in 1947 in a cave near the Dead Sea. Pieces of parchment 10¼ inches wide are sewn together to form a roll just over 24 feet long. On the second line of the column which is entirely visible are the words: 'A voice cries: "In the wilderness prepare the way of the Lord" ' (Is 40:3; cf. Mk 1:3).

THE FULLNESS OF TIME

In A.D. 71 Rome celebrated with great splendour the triumph of Vespasian, the new emperor who had been raised to the throne by the Eastern legions, and of his sons Titus and Domitian. Titus had just dealt a final crushing blow to Judaea, and in the procession the admiring crowds could see some of the treasures he had removed from the Temple of Jerusalem before razing it to the ground: a remarkable golden candlestick with seven branches, a sacrificial table, also of solid gold, and trumpets of silver.

One can imagine the thoughts of some old Roman diplomat as he watched this spectacle. Rome, he would reflect, had not always been fortunate in the procurators she had sent to Judaea. Pontius Pilate, the second procurator appointed by Tiberius, had never properly understood how to treat this strange people, so fanatically wedded to its many curious religious practices. He had even fallen out with the son of the great Herod, Herod Antipas, whom Augustus had appointed tetrarch of the northern part of his father's kingdom. And this quarrel was said to have been made up at the time of the execution of a Galilean in Jerusalem.

After Pontius Pilate, Herod Agrippa I, of Hasmonaean descent, had taken advantage of the madness of Caligula and the weakness of Claudius to have himself proclaimed king over a Judaea which embraced all the territories formerly held by Herod the Great. He had governed reasonably well (A.D. 37–44). Unlike the procurators, he had realised that to collect the taxes without friction he must respect the religious opinions of the people and enlist the support of the powerful party of the Pharisees. After the sudden death of Agrippa, Claudius had once more resorted to placing the greater part of Judaea under a procurator. But there had been a series of very bad appointments. Cuspius Fadus (A.D. 44–46), Tiberius Alexander (A.D. 46–48), and Ventidius Cumanus (A.D. 48–52) were men of limited vision, who thought of nothing but money; they were not educated enough to know from history of the explosive power latent in the Jewish people, whom their every action was calculated to provoke. The freedman Antonius Felix (A.D. 52–60) was a typical parvenu who had married no fewer than three queens and who, in his insatiable greed, scarcely noticed the growing unrest among the people. All kinds of zealots were fomenting opposition to the hated authority of Rome, while fanatics were claiming to have been sent by God to free the people for ever from this yoke. When it was too late, Felix had acted with incredible cruelty against the agitators, particularly an Egyptian Jew who had mustered a body of men on the Mount of Olives, and was preparing to march on the capital. Nero had recalled Felix and appointed Porcius Festus (A.D. 60–62) in his place. This wise and noble Roman had the qualities needed to restore order, but unfortunately he died after two years in office. There had followed first Albinus (A.D. 62–64) and then the unspeakable Gessius Florus, who seemed to have done everything in his power to unleash general rebellion against the authority of Rome. Nero had then been away carousing in Greece, and had sent his general Vespasian with orders to quell the disturbances. But the 60,000 Roman soldiers had not found it easy to deal with the fanatical rebels. When Vespasian was proclaimed emperor and set out for Rome, he had left his son Titus to complete the operations. It had taken him five months to starve out and finally storm Jerusalem, and unparalleled atrocities had been committed. The Roman officers had made excuses: the relentless fanaticism of the rebel leaders had exasperated them beyond endurance – or so our old diplomat believed, as he watched the Jewish treasures carried by.

And now his reflections on the political problems of Judaea would lead him to ponder over the strange phenomenon of the colonies of Jews scattered all over the empire; resisting Hellenistic culture, they lived a life apart, established in their own quarters of the great cities and preferring their humble places of prayer to the magnificent temples of the gods.

The Romans did not realise that the suppression of the Jewish nation was more than a purely political episode. There was only a handful of men in the great empire for whom the destruction of the Temple was a profoundly significant event: it confirmed their belief that the world had reached the last and crucial turning-point in its history. These men, who were called Christians, were still regarded as a Jewish sect and were of no account in world affairs. When, 'in the fifteenth year of the reign of Tiberius Caesar, Pontius Pilate being governor of Judaea', a prophet began to go abroad in the region of the Jordan, proclaiming that the Kingdom of God was at hand, his message did not spread beyond Palestine. And shortly afterwards, it was only the inhabitants of Nazareth who heard Jesus, a humble workman of the village, read in the synagogue the prophecy of Isaiah and announce its fulfilment: *(Lk 3:1)* *(Lk 4:16)*

> The Spirit of the Lord God is upon me, *(Is 61: 1f.)*
> because the Lord has anointed me
> to bring good tidings to the afflicted;
> he has sent me to bind up the brokenhearted,
> to proclaim liberty to the captives,
> and the opening of the prison to those who are bound;
> to proclaim the year of the Lord's favour . . .

It may be that in the course of his duties Pontius Pilate formally reported the crucifixion of this Jesus of Nazareth to the emperor. But no-one in Rome was likely to be interested in this event. Had not thousands of Jews been crucified by the procurators? And the politicians could not see the witnesses of the Risen Lord who were journeying along the imperial highways joyfully proclaiming the dawn of a new era. Nor did they notice that, in response to this call, increasing numbers of men were forsaking the old gods to turn to the God of Abraham, Isaac, and Jacob.

The New Testament had its origins among the small groups of fervent Christians, who were in many respects cut off from the world around them. They proclaimed and reflected upon the great events in the history of salvation, cul-

347
348

minating in the death and resurrection of Jesus of Nazareth. Disciples who had known Him in His earthly life recalled His words and deeds and, in the light of the resurrection, understood their full significance. Other believers transmitted to new converts the stories told of Him, together with His sayings and parables. From all this teaching there emerged a clear impression of His personality and His message concerning God and man. This oral tradition was gradually crystallised in written Gospels.

A careful reading of the four Gospels preserved in the New Testament reveals a number of discrepancies between them, which are all the more striking because of their fundamental similarity. It is clear that the writers were primarily interested in Jesus Himself as revealed in His words and deeds, and paid comparatively little attention to the chronological sequence and localisation of events. That is why it is impossible to produce a detailed map showing the movements of Jesus. For this we should require clear indications both of the places He visited and of the time at which each visit was made, and in neither respect do the Gospels provide sufficient data. For instance, from a reading of the first three Gospels (the Synoptic Gospels) we might conclude that the public ministry of Jesus lasted only a few months, whereas in the Gospel of St John we learn that it certainly extended over two or three years. This Gospel also refers to journeys between Galilee and Jerusalem which are not mentioned in the Synoptic Gospels.

There is a similar lack of detail about places. A good example of this is the very important scene of the Transfiguration. The three Gospels which describe it refer only to a 'mountain' or a 'high mountain', without giving its name. The traditional site is Mount Tabor, between Nazareth, the town of Jesus, and the Sea of Galilee, on whose shores He so often preached. Admittedly, historians object that in the time of Jesus there was probably a village on the summit, which hardly agrees with the New Testament story. There are several possible ways of resolving this difficulty. And such problems are forgotten when one is privileged to spend a few hours in the celestial calm of this mountain-top and to look down over a great part of the Holy Land.

Other sites are mentioned by name in the Gospels, but cannot be identified with certainty. This applies to 'Aenon near Salim', where 'John also was baptizing', whose exact situation is still in dispute. On Map 34 (p. 116) we have shown the most probable site, near Scythopolis. But this is by no means certain. In the sixth century A.D. the Idumaean Christians built a church dedicated to St John the Baptist much farther south, in the vicinity of Hebron (cf. Map on p. 105, no. 7); here there was a village whose name in its Greek form, *Ainun*, resembled the Aenon of the fourth Gospel. Though this place had not the abundant water mentioned in the text of St John, this difficulty did not deter the Idumaeans. It may at least be inferred that there was at this time no other

349
350

347–350 / *Khirbet Qumrân*, which has become famous in recent years. The search for the place where the rolls found in 1947 had been stored led to cave in the cliffs along the northwest coast of the Dead Sea. On a plateau at the foot of the rock-face is a rectangular ruin (99 by 121 feet), long believed to be the remains of a small Roman fort. Excavation of this site was begun in 1949, and it is now almost certain that the ruins are those of the headquarters of the Essenes, a sect which flourished in the time of Christ. Pliny mentions that Essenes lived 'to the west of the Asphalt Lake'. 347: An aerial photograph taken from the south; the dark patch at the top is Jericho. 348: A view from the cliff, looking northeast. (In these two views the main building of the Essenes is indicated by an arrow.) 349: The plateau, seen from the shore of the Dead Sea. 350: A view from the plateau, looking south. [*Map 34, p. 116*]

351

352

351 / *The Highlands to the East of Jerusalem*, looking NNW. The thin black line in the valley is one of the few straight sections of the asphalt road from Jerusalem to Jericho. While the average altitude of old Jerusalem is about 2,450 feet, the hills at the left of the photograph are well under 2,000 feet high. The land falls away steeply towards Jericho, only 14 miles further east as the crow flies, but lying 820 feet below the level of the Mediterranean. In this lonely waste, where rain is infrequent, are many ruins of 4th to 6th century monasteries, for men came here from all Christendom to lead a life of penitence and meditation. **352** / *The Jordan Valley South of Jericho*, *near the Dead Sea*, looking west. This photograph shows the deeply-eroded strata of marl and limestone. On the horizon are the rugged hills on the eastern edge of the desert of Judah. [*Map 2, p. 10*]

353 / *Remains of the Fortress of Machaerus, where John the Baptist was beheaded.* They rise like a natural hill on the slopes to the east of the Dead Sea. The massive walls enclosed a palace, an arsenal, and huge cisterns. The photograph conveys something of the wild desolation of this place. Unfortunately the colours are missing – the deep blue of the Dead Sea and the red, grey, and violet of the rocks, which make this landscape one of the most impressive and beautiful in the world. **354** / *The Wâdi el-Qelt near Jericho.* The building is a dependent house of the monastery of St George of Koziba. **355** / *The Valley of the Kidron and the Monastery of Mar Saba*, founded in A.D. 486 by Sabas of Cappadocia. **356, 357** / *The Jordan near Jericho*, close to the place where, according to ancient tradition, Jesus was baptised by John the Baptist.

[Maps 2, p. 10; 34, p. 116]

358

359

358 / *The Sanctuary of the Nativity and the Forgotten Tomb of Herod*. In the centre, between the two bell-towers, is the famous basilica built *ca* A.D. 325 by the Emperor Constantine over the grotto which had long been venerated. Old Bethlehem lies to the right, partly concealed by the trees. Behind the basilica, we see in the distance the site of the fortress which Herod built on a hill-top three miles southeast of Bethlehem and where, in accordance with his wishes, he was buried with great pomp and ceremony. **359** / *Bethlehem from the South*. In the time of Herod, Bethlehem was no more than a tiny cluster of small houses (on the left half of the photograph). In the hill at the right, outside the village, there were many natural caves where shepherds and nomads could shelter.

[*Map 34, p. 116*]

360 / *Mount Hermon in the Evening Sun*, seen from the SW. With better light, the photograph would have revealed, at the foot of Mt Hermon and at the far side of the plain (well-watered and provided with fish-ponds), *Tell el-Qâdi*, the Biblical Dan and, to its right, *Bâniyas*, the ancient Caesarea Philippi. **361** / *A Glimpse of Mt Hermon from the Slopes of the Lebanon.* **362** / *'Whited Sepulchre'* of a rabbi at Tiberias. **363** / *Kafr Kenna*, since the 4th century A.D. regarded by pilgrims as the Cana of the wedding feast (Jn 2). **364** / *Mount Tabor from Megiddo.* In the foreground are some of the remains of Solomon's stables (Pl. 210); behind them stretches the great plain of Jezreel; in the background is the majestic Mt Tabor. At the left are the hills of Galilee where Nazareth lies hidden. **365–367** / *Capernaum.* The town of Jesus has completely disappeared; the ruins seen here are those of a synagogue of the 2nd or 3rd century A.D. [Map 34, p. 116]

368

369

368, 369 / *Mount Tabor*. A lonely height, Mount Tabor rises over 1,300 feet above the plain of Jezreel. Its 'marvellous roundness' (St Jerome) is clearly seen in Pls. 364 and 368 (an aerial photograph taken from the west at a low altitude; Nazareth lies in the centre, half-way to Mt Tabor). It was at this unique observation-post, where the territories of the three northern tribes met, that Barak mustered his troops before descending upon the army of Sisera on the plain (Jg 4:14). The Israelites were moved to worship their God on this height, which drew a protest from Hosea (Hos 5:1). Christian tradition regards Mount Tabor as the scene of the transfiguration of Jesus (Mt 17); this event is now commemorated by a Greek Orthodox church and monastery (at the left in 369: see Pl. 22) and by a beautiful Latin basilica in the old Syrian style on the very top of the mountain. [*Map 34, p. 116*]

127

370

371

370 / *The Sea of Galilee*, looking east. In the foreground is the little town of Tiberias (cf. Pl. 27). On the opposite shore, 5½ miles away, the Transjordanian plateau rises nearly 2,000 feet above the lake. **371** /*Fishing-boats at the Edge of the Lake*, north of Tiberias. The majesty of snow-clad Hermon dominates the northern shores of the lake, where Jesus confirmed His message of reconciliation and peace with countless miracles of healing. The traveller who seeks out the remains of Chorazin, Beth-saida, and Capernaum on the distant slopes near the lake is vividly aware, in this profoundly peaceful setting, of the terrifying nature of the warnings uttered by Jesus in Mt 11:20–24. *Opposite*, **372** / *Alley in Old Nazareth*. The present small town bears little resemblance to the hamlet Jesus knew; only a single narrow street still evokes something of the earlier atmosphere. [*Map 34, p. 116*]

373 / *The Damascus Gate.* The present gate dates only from the 16th century A.D. But it stands on the site of a gate in the wall by which Herod Agrippa (A.D. 41–44) extended Jerusalem to the northwest, bringing Calvary and the Holy Sepulchre (under the large dome at top right) within the city walls. **374**/ *The so-called 'Herod's Gate'.* Another section of the present very fine wall, erected by the Sultan Sulaiman II between 1537 and 1540. This gate lies in the same direction from the Temple as the Sheep Gate of the time of Jesus, and a sheep market is still held here. **375–377** / *Tombs in the Valley of the Kidron;* attributed for some centuries past to Absalom (375), St James, and Zechariah (376, 377); for their situation, see Pls. 326 and 382. **378**/ *The West Wall of the City* already followed this line in the time of Jesus. The minaret shows the site of Herod's palace. [*Map 33, p. 115*]

379 / *The Temple Terrace*. In the centre is the famous Mosque of Omar, built by Byzantine architects in the service of the Moslems, over the sacred rock which once bore the sacrificial altar or, according to some scholars, the Holy of Holies. The porticoes at the north and west sides are only a feeble reminder of the great colonnades around the terrace in the time of Jesus. 380 / *Site of the Fortress of Antonia*, at the northwest corner. Nothing now remains but a few traces of the foundations in the rock behind the trees. 381 / *The Temple Seen from the Valley of the Kidron*. The village of *Silwân*, at the right, recalls Siloam; at the left are the gardens below the old city of David. 382 / *Southeast Corner of the Temple Wall*, seen from Gethsemane. 383 / *Detail of the Southeast Corner*. 82 feet of this wall lie buried in the accumulated débris. Was this the 'pinnacle of the temple' (Mt 4:5)? 384 / *The Golden Gate*. [Map 33, p. 115]

131

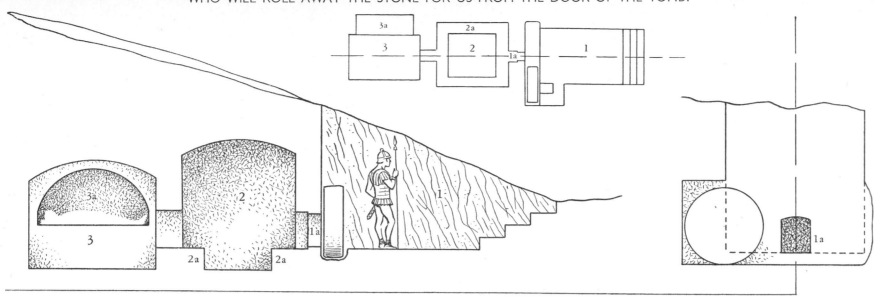

place in Palestine which could seriously claim to be the village near Salim where John baptised.

Lk 24:13 A similar difficulty arises over Emmaus. Exactly where, on the evening of Easter Day, did the meeting of the risen Christ with His two disciples and the breaking of the bread take place? Some writers situate the scene of these events near the modern *Amwâs*, on the eastern edge of the great plain of Lydda, 19 miles from Jerusalem (the Emmaus of Maccabees). Others suggest villages or sites very much nearer Jerusalem (within seven or eight miles). These divergences arise from the earliest manuscripts of St Luke which disagree about the distance between Emmaus and Jerusalem; some refer to 160 stadia and others to 60 stadia.

Fortunately such problems do not arise over all the places mentioned in the New Testament. The situation of such important towns and villages as Jericho, Bethlehem, and Nazareth has never been in doubt. But the visitor should always bear in mind that the outward appearance of these settlements has been completely transformed by the building of churches, convents, and accommodation for pilgrims, and by the increase in the population.

A separate map of New Testament Jerusalem has been included in this Atlas (Map 33, p. 115). Two observations are necessary: in the first place, very little remains of the buildings in existence in the time of Christ; in the second place, the identification of the holy places is based upon traditions of varying antiquity and reliability. There is, however, no doubt about the principal sites: the Temple, the fortress of Antonia, the upper city with Herod's palace, the valley of the Kidron, and the Mount of Olives. The Garden of Gethsemane undoubtedly lay on or very near the site of the present basilica. The position of Calvary and the Holy Sepulchre is equally well established. But the present basilica has had a very chequered history. The emperor Constantine cut away the rock around the burial chamber where the body of Christ had lain and erected a rotunda over this holy place. This building was flanked by an atrium, which took in the rock of Calvary at one corner. The whole was extended by a basilica with five naves,

whose façade gave on to the principal street of Jerusalem (cf. Map of Madaba, p. 61). Over the centuries all manner of disasters befell the buildings of Constantine: earthquakes, fires, pillage, systematic demolition. The Sepulchre itself was almost completely destroyed by the Arabs in 1009. Reconstructions followed upon the demolitions, so that the present church is a patchwork of elements dating from all periods, and the visitor can no longer detect the original plan. For this reason, no picture of the present Church of the Holy Sepulchre is included in this Atlas (though its dome appears on some of the photographs). We have chosen instead to help the modern reader to form an idea of the tomb of Jesus by means of a sketch and pictures of graves closed by a rolling stone.

Today the labours of literary criticism on the one hand, and historical and archaeological research on the other, enable us to form a general picture of the composition of the Gospels, which proves to be substantially the same as for the various historical books of the Old Testament. The Gospels are not verbatim reports of a series of events, nor are they intended to be a work of history in the modern sense of the word. They are the written record of a body of preaching concerning the human and divine person of Jesus of Nazareth, the Messiah of the Jews and the Saviour of all mankind.

On the other hand, many circumstances or details which are incidentally mentioned by the Evangelists entirely agree with what we know of the motley Palestinian scene in the first century of our era, with its changes of administration and variety of languages. Roman governors and Herodian kings ruled concurrently or successively. While Latin was the official language, a kind of 'basic Greek' was used by all the travellers and merchants of the vast Hellenistic world; the people of Palestine spoke Aramaic, but in the Temple and the synagogues they heard Hebrew chanted and read. What the Gospels tell us of certain persons or groups corresponds closely with the descriptions in extra-Biblical sources. This is true, for example, of the various Herods, of Pontius Pilate, of the High Priest Annas, and of the Pharisees and Sadducees.

385
386

385, 386 / *Tombs Cut in the Rock.* The above photographs and drawing give us some idea of the tomb in which the body of Jesus was laid. First an open trench was dug in the soft limestone hillside (1), very often stepped, in order to reach the required depth more quickly. After a low opening had been made (1a), a first chamber was excavated (2), a ledge being left all round it as a seat (2a); then a second chamber was cut (3), with one or more niches in its walls. The body was laid in one of these niches (3a). When the niche was required for a second body, the bones of the first were placed in a hole in the floor of the tomb. The Gospels state that the tomb of Jesus was 'new' (*kainos*, Mt 27:60; and even more explicitly, Jn 19:41) and not merely 'emptied' (*kenos*) as in some manuscripts.

387
388
389
390

391

387–390 / *'The Street called Straight'*. Like all Hellenised cities, Damascus had its *cardo maximus*, a straight main thoroughfare, flanked by a double line of columns, with archways at the cross-roads and huge gates at each end. Successive demolitions and reconstructions have swept away all but the original line of the 'street called Straight' (387) and fragments of columns and arches hemmed in by houses of a later date (389), or discovered amid the débris of centuries (388). Of the east gate of Paul's day there remains a small lateral arch, which still gives access to the 'street called Straight'; part of the old main entrance gate is also standing (390, *left*). **391** / *Antioch on the Orontes*. The modern *Antakya*, at the foot of Mt Silpius on which the citadel once stood, preserves only the name and a few miserable remains of the magnificent capital of the Seleucids. [Map II, End-paper]

392, 393 / *Roman Roads in Transjordan.* Every emperor who built or repaired an important road set up milestones bearing his own inscriptions. This is why we sometimes find several milestones side by side, as on the south side of the Arnon valley (393; see Pl. 155). Farther north is the road which runs across a fertile plateau towards *Madaba* (392: the town, which can be seen in the distance, stands on the tell of the Biblical Medeba). **394** / *Great Roman Road between Aleppo and Antioch.* Nearly 20 feet wide, this road is paved with carefully cut blocks of hard limestone. **395** / *The Via Egnatia near Philippi.* Paul and his companions travelled along it on several occasions. **396** / *The Road from Damascus to Beirut.* The Roman engineers cut their road through the rock and carved an inscription in honour of their emperor. **397** / *The Via Appia*, by which Paul reached Rome. [*Map II, End-paper*]

398

399

400

401

402

403

398 / *The Taurus*, separating Anatolia from the fertile plain of Cilicia, on which lies Tarsus. **399** / *One of the Cilician Gates*, deep clefts in the Taurus mountains. Paul and his companions passed through here several times. Perhaps he was thinking of these journeys when he listed 'danger from robbers' among the perils he had encountered (2 Co 11:26). **400**/*Ephesus*. Once an important harbour and a meeting-place of East and West; now a field of ruins about three-quarters of a mile from the sea. In the course of several visits, Paul founded a flourishing Christian community here. **401**/*Seleucia*, the port of Antioch; now also some distance from the bay. Here Paul embarked for his first apostolic voyage. **402** / *Corinth*. **403** / *Miletus*. Part of the theatre can be seen. In the background is the former harbour, now a marsh.

[Map II, End-paper]

404

404 / *The Acropolis at Athens.* Originally an almost entirely isolated limestone height on the principal plain of Attica, in the second half of the 5th century B.C. it was adorned with famous buildings which are among the greatest creations of Greek culture. Paul found these marvels much less ravaged than they are today. To the left of the Parthenon are the Erechtheum and the Propylaea. *Opposite,* **405** / *Portico of the Erechtheum.*

The gaps in our knowledge of the background of the New Testament are constantly being filled in by archaeology. To give one illustration among many: we had long been puzzled by a detail of the solemn formula by which St Luke, alone among the Evangelists, situates the ministry of John the Baptist in world history. He refers to a certain Lysanias, tetrarch of Abilene. Now non-Biblical documents do mention a Lysanias, but he was king of the Ituraeans and reigned about 40 B.C. St Luke's statement stood alone until the discovery of an inscription on a steep rock-face in a valley west of Damascus, near a tell which perpetuates the name of Abila; it named Lysanias as governor of this region, and at the time mentioned by St Luke.

Archaeological discoveries have also shed important light on the fourth Gospel. The writings of St John had long been regarded as the fruit of profound speculation in Hellenistic circles upon a more or less mythical figure having its remote historical origins in Jesus of Nazareth. It was thought that the Gospel was not composed until the end of the second century A.D., and that its apparently historical details were purely symbolical. We were assured, for instance, that 'a pool . . . which has five porticoes' was unthinkable in the architecture of the period; this must be a pentagon symbolising the five books of the Law of Moses. But then, at the northern end of the Temple terrace, well below the present level of the soil, the remains of the pool in question came to light; there were in fact 'five porticoes', but it was not a pentagon (cf. Map 33, p. 115).

In 1935, there was published a fragment of papyrus containing a short passage from the Gospel of St John; it came from Egypt. Papyrologists and palaeographers agreed in dating it earlier than A.D. 150. Its discovery proved that the fourth Gospel, probably written in Asia Minor, was already circulating in Egypt during the first half of the second century A.D. This did not allow sufficient time for the long mythological speculations postulated by certain scholars. Greater confidence could now be felt in the authenticity of the recollections which form the basis of St John's message concerning Jesus.

We cannot fail to mention here a recent discovery which will certainly throw fresh light on the background of the New Testament: the now famous Dead Sea Scrolls, the first group of which was found in 1947. The largest and best-preserved of these scrolls, containing the book of Isaiah, is reproduced at the

Lk 3:1

Jn 5:2

346

beginning of this chapter (p. 121). Another proved to contain part of a document believed to be a *Manual of Discipline* of the religious sect to whose 'library' these scrolls may have belonged. Later came the discovery of the cache from which the texts had been taken, a cave in the cliff-face on the northwestern shore of the Dead Sea. Since then, many more fragments of all kinds of Biblical and non-Biblical texts have been found in this and other neighbouring caves, which have been thoroughly searched by archaeologists. There are fragments of almost every book of the Old Testament, and some fragments of commentaries, in which the history of the sect is reflected in cryptic terms whose interpretation is difficult and disputed.

Greatly excited by these discoveries, the archaeologists next turned their attention to a ruin which lay on a small plateau at the foot of the steep cliff (*Khirbet Qumrân*). Until this time, these remains were believed to be those of a small Roman fort, like the many others in Palestine. The site was systematically excavated, and we now know that the ruin was not a guard-post, but in all probability the headquarters of a sect who lived in the cliff caves and had stored their 'library' there.

One of the rooms was used as a scriptorium, and we even have a vessel with the dried remains of the ink which was used for writing. The headquarters of the sect appear to have been destroyed not long before the Fall of Jerusalem in A.D. 70, for a large number of coins of the period between the latter part of the second century B.C. and A.D. 66 have been found, while there is evidence that after its destruction the place was rebuilt on a different ground plan and occupied for a short time. This part of the building contained coins from after the Fall of Jerusalem. It is therefore probable that all the manuscripts of the Qumrân find were written before A.D. 70, and that they give us knowledge of a Jewish sect which was in existence before the time of Christ. This sect was - at least at one period of its history - strongly nationalistic, and looked forward to a war which should carry Jewish arms in victory throughout the world. The scroll in which this war is described is known as *The War of the Sons of Light against the Sons of Darkness*. At the same time the sect was deeply religious and sought to guard the faith by its careful organisation.

Now there existed, in the time of Jesus, a Jewish sect known as the Essenes; Josephus and Philo of Alexandria provide some information about them, while

406

407
408

406–408 / *The Forum Romanum and the Triumphal Arch of Titus.* 406: View of the Forum Romanum, looking southwest. At the left, in the foreground, is the triumphal arch of Septimius Severus. In the distance, at the other end of the Forum, is the triumphal arch of Titus, erected by the Senate under Domitian (or possibly Trajan) to commemorate the war against the Jews, which Titus brought to an end in A.D. 70 with the destruction of Jerusalem. Later, when badly dilapidated, the arch was built into a medieval fortress as a gateway. Pope Sixtus IV (1471–1484) extricated it, and in 1823, under Pius VII, its restoration was completed (408). One of the bas-reliefs under the arch is of great historical interest (407); it shows Romans crowned with laurels carrying precious objects from the Temple in triumphal procession: the golden table of the showbread, the silver trumpets, and the candlestick of pure gold with seven branches.

[*Map II, End-paper*]

Pliny mentions that they lived not far from the west coast of the Dead Sea. We are now almost certain that the building and the scrolls were the property of this community. Shortly after the publication of the *Manual* mentioned above, a somewhat hasty French scholar made the sensational statement that it contained a reference to a dead Messiah and concluded that the message of Jesus was not original. This judgment is reminiscent of that passed on the book of Genesis in the nineteenth century after the discovery of a Babylonian version of the Flood, when scholars wrongly concluded that the Bible was merely copying contemporary non-Biblical texts. On the contrary, a closer and more complete study of the important body of documents discovered since 1947 will greatly enrich New Testament scholarship by providing the sacred writings with a better historical and cultural background.

John the Baptist, for example, whose work began in this very region of the Dead Sea and the Jordan, has until now been an isolated figure for us. The newly found manuscripts will probably enable us to situate him in a movement and a setting in which his thought and ministry will take on fresh significance. No doubt these writings will also provide a missing link in the literary history of Judaism, and shed light on the question of possible Persian influences. They appear also to illumine certain features of the unique character of the message in the Gospel of St John. But it is still too early to draw final conclusions from these very important discoveries. We must wait until the scholars concerned have been able to complete publication of all the texts. But it is already quite clear that they will give a new stimulus to Biblical scholarship.

Of all the writings of the New Testament, the Acts of the Apostles most closely resembles a work of history in the modern sense of the word, and is therefore particularly suitable for those who are beginning upon a reading of the Scriptures. The greater part of this work deals with the journeys of St Paul, and the story is provided with numerous indications of time and place (a detailed map of these journeys appears on the end-paper at the back of this Atlas). Like the Gospel of St Luke, of which it is the continuation, Acts, though very Greek in spirit and style, clearly reveals certain characteristics of Biblical historiography. Drawing upon all kinds of information, possibly including written sources, and upon his own experience, the writer describes how the Gospel spread from Jerusalem all over the empire and finally reached Rome itself. The bearers of this message are endowed with a mysterious power from on high, the Holy Spirit, which St Luke shows us constantly at work. He also gives a masterly summary of the preaching of the first missionaries and excels in drawing vivid character-sketches of these men.

Comparison with the Letters of St Paul shows that the account contained in the Acts of the Apostles is far from complete. A complete account would indeed have been impossible. If, for example, St Luke had had to deal with every episode of Paul's sojourn of three years at Ephesus as fully as he deals with the rising of the silversmiths, his book would have become unduly enlarged and would have lost much of its persuasive force. He was better informed on some events than on others, and chose to describe those scenes which he had himself witnessed or taken part in. To this we owe the most enthralling story of a sea voyage which has come down to us from antiquity, a story which presents the figure of St Paul in bold relief.

Today the pilgrim who follows in the steps of the Apostle through Turkey and Greece finds hardly a trace of the towns where he preached. The ancient Hellenistic centres have been reduced to vast fields of ruins, strewn with the remains of temples, forums, and theatres. Traces of the former harbours lie on bays now engulfed by sand, often far from the present coast-line. But though the cities are no more, the traveller does at least realise the enormous distances covered by St Paul and the dangers he must have faced. One cannot look unmoved upon the remains of a Roman road which was certainly trodden by the Apostle, such as that near ancient Philippi. It is easy to visualise Paul and his disciples among the cosmopolitan travellers who constantly thronged the great imperial highways: officials, messengers, merchants, doctors, invalids, pilgrims, athletes, circus performers, soothsayers, and all sorts of wandering philosophers. Paul himself was often regarded as one of the last-named fraternity, and he sometimes used the current philosophy of the Hellenistic world as the quickest means of approaching the sphere of the Truth of which he was the witness.

The exposition of that Truth does not fall within the purview of this book. But perhaps, on this last page, we may draw attention to certain aspects of the preaching of Christ's disciples, in the belief that they provide an answer to various general questions which may have occurred to the reader. If he has had the patience to read thus far, the reader has perhaps a clearer picture than before of the multiplicity and diversity of the traditions and documents on which the Bible is based. He must also have realised the enormous amount of work which has been devoted each year for centuries past to the study of the numerous textual, literary, and historical problems raised by the Scriptures. Two questions may now occur to him. What influence impelled men to assemble this multitude of widely different writings into one volume? And, above all, wherein lies the mysterious power and fascination of this Book, that thousands of scholars should have devoted their lives to it and countless millions of men should have held it to be the Book of books?

In the preaching of the Apostles the story of Jesus of Nazareth is presented as the culmination of a series of divine interventions and as the beginning of a new and final era in world history. 'In many and various ways God spoke of old to our fathers by the prophets; but in these last days he has spoken to us by a Son, whom he appointed the heir of all things, through whom also he created the world.' He 1: 1-2

The people of Israel had been chosen by God and guided by Him through all their long history. The prophets and sages had constantly reminded their compatriots of the duties which flowed from the election; they had explained the significance of political and military events in the light of the Covenant and shown men the term and consummation to which God wished to lead the history of the world. Their testimony was assembled by the Jews into a collection of sacred books which embodied the expression of God's will and purpose.

In His teaching Jesus of Nazareth continually returns to these sacred writings. This He does not only like any devout rabbi with a respect for the tradition, but also in order to demonstrate that with His Coming the great day has dawned, the day for which the prophets had yearned, the 'day of Yahweh', the final intervention of God in the world of men. After His death and resurrection, His first disciples explained the meaning of these events by reference to the old texts. The young Church regarded these writings as her own property, in the belief that they had after all been composed with this final period in view and had been misinterpreted by the Jews who refused to accept Christ. Soon the Church was to place alongside this collection, and on the same footing, certain writings of those men who had preached with authority, as authentic witnesses of the life, death, and resurrection of Jesus. Jewish texts and Christian texts were thus brought together in one Book, which has a character in some ways as absolute and final as Christ Himself.

We see on the opposite page the monument commemorating the triumph of Titus. For the Romans, the capture of Jerusalem and the destruction of the Temple was merely one of the many victories of the Empire. But for the Christians it was the material confirmation of a spiritual certainty. For them, the glory of Yahweh no longer dwelt in the Temple of Jerusalem, but in the glorified body of Jesus. Jesus had said that He would destroy the Temple and build another in three days, and for this statement He was condemned by the Sanhedrin as a blasphemer. But His disciples later realised that 'he spoke of the temple of his body'. The building destroyed by the Roman legions had already lost all meaning and purpose with the glorification of Jesus. Sacred History, as the story of a single people dwelling in one particular part of the world, was at an end. There was now a new Israel whose spiritual centre was in the new temple of God, the man Jesus sitting at the right hand of the Father. In Him the new creation had begun, from which sin and death were banished for ever. The time had now come for all mankind to hear the good tidings and to learn how, made one with Christ through faith and baptism, they escaped the corruption of this world, became worshippers of the Father in spirit and in truth and partook of the holy indestructibility of the new creation, of which Jesus Christ was at once the first-born and the culmination. 408

Mk 14:58

Jn 2:21

The Christian of today shares the views of the Early Church. He knows that he is living in the latter days, in the closing phase of world history. Whether this period be long or short, all that now matters to each man is to find God in Christ.

Henceforward, it is impossible to propose any other way of salvation in the name of God. In Jesus He has said all and given all. Even God cannot give more than Himself. For all Christians the Bible shares the definitive character of the historic revelation of God in Jesus Christ. Like that revelation, it can never be replaced or surpassed.

INDEX
OF PLACES AND PERSONS

THE principal purpose of this Index is to catalogue and describe all the *geographical indications* provided by the Bible. It therefore contains the name of every town and village, every mountain and valley, and every region, river, country, and people which occurs in the Bible. Proper names of *persons* mentioned in the Bible are included only if they played an important part in Biblical history, or if their inclusion seemed desirable on other grounds. *Non-Biblical* place-names and personal names are included only when their mention on the Maps or in the text appeared to require further elucidation.

For Biblical names the head entry is normally given under the spelling adopted in the Revised Standard Version of the Bible, save that some hyphens, as in Mach-pelah and Mel-chizedek, are omitted. Cross-references are supplied for the spellings of the Authorized (King James) Version and of the Douay and Knox Versions. Names found in the Apocryphal books are normally given under the spelling found in the Revised Version, with the appropriate cross-references. Where this rule is occasionally departed from, the cross-references will ensure the easy finding of the head entry.

The greatest difficulty in the preparation of the Index has been created by the innumerable cases where some versions retain the Hebrew form of a name, while others translate it into English (e.g. *Sitnah*, Douay: 'Enmity', Knox: 'Feud'; *Ascent of Akrabbim*, A.V.: 'Maaleh-acrabbim', Douay: 'Ascent of the Scorpion', Knox: 'Scorpion Pass'). Here many of the translations are given as cross-references, but it has sometimes seemed inadvisable to multiply entries by

giving them all. In addition, a single name frequently has a great variety of forms in a single version of the Bible, and it may well be found that occasionally a variant which stands in an uncited text is not given. Where one or other version follows a reading which differs from the Hebrew text, this is indicated, either under the head entry or by the cross-reference.

Many names are accompanied by a suggested translation, for a personal name often expresses the religious feelings of a child's parents, while the meaning of a place-name may explain its repeated occurrence. Some of these translations are conjectural, and, in any case, it must not be assumed that the Israelite users were always conscious of such a meaning, any more than the modern John Bennett of Sutton is necessarily aware that Bennett means 'blessed' and Sutton means 'south town'.

To avoid overloading the Maps of Palestine, we have not usually shown on them the modern Arabic names of Biblical places. They are given in this Index, printed in italics, preceded, where necessary, by the word *possible* or *probable* to indicate the degree of certainty of the identification. Any attempt to list possible alternative localisations of the same site falls outside the scope of this Atlas; it could serve no useful purpose unless accompanied by much more detailed maps of present-day Palestine than even the section on p. 105. Places which cannot be located with any degree of probability are not marked on the Maps. They appear in this Index with the comment *situation unknown* and, in some cases, an indication of the district where they are to be sought.

ABBREVIATIONS

abb.	= abbreviation	inc.	= including, included	prob.	= probable, probably
Ass.	= Assyrian	*J.*	= *Jebel* (mount)	q.v.	= which see
Bab.	= Babylonian	*Kh.*	= *Khirbet* (ruin)	Rom.	= Roman
beg.	= beginning	Lat.	= Latin	R.S.V.	= Revised Standard Version
ca	= *circa*	loc.	= locality	sit.	= situation, situated
cent.	= century	LXX	= Septuagint	unk.	= unknown
cf.	= compare	ment.	= mentioned	*var.*	= variant
Class.	= Classical	mod.	= modern	Vulg.	= Vulgate
conj.	= conjecture	MS(S)	= manuscript(s)	*W.*	= *Wâdi* (torrent)
Eg.	= Egyptian	Mt	= Mount or mountain	□	This sign at the end of an entry indicates
e.p.	= maps on end papers	n.	= name		that all the Biblical passages in which the
EVV	= English Versions	N.T.	= New Testament		word occurs are cited.
foll.	= following	O.T.	= Old Testament	=	This sign between two Biblical references
Gk.	= Greek	p.	= page of text		indicates that the two texts are similar in
G&L	= Greek and Latin	Pers.	= Persian		content.
Heb.	= Hebrew	Pl.	= Plate		
Hel.	= Hellenistic	poss.	= possible, possibly		*For Biblical abbreviations see page 8*

A

Aaron, Heb. *'Aharon*, meaning unk.; son of Amram and Jochebed, brother of Moses, of the tribe of Levi. As mouthpiece (prophet) to Moses he helped in the liberation of the Hebrews from Egypt. Because he lacked faith in God, he, like Moses, was not permitted to enter the Promised Land. With his sons he was consecrated to the priesthood. He died on Mt Hor, q.v.

Abaddon, Heb. word = 'destruction', Job 26:6, 28:22, 31:12, which came to be applied to the kingdom of the dead as a place of destruction, Ps 88:11 (Heb. 12), Pr 15:11; and later to the king of that kingdom, 'the angel of the bottomless pit', Rev 9:11.

Abana, river of Damascus, 2 K 5:12; prob. mod. *Nahr Baradâ*, which rises 19 m. NW of Damascus and flows through the city. See PHARPAR and AMANA. □

Abarim, 'passes'; name given to summits (inc. Mt Nebo) and slopes W of the plateau of Moab; ment. in Jer 22:20 with the Lebanon and Bashan as heights from which the land of Israel could be surveyed. Moses climbed them to see the Promised Land, Nu 27:12, Dt 32:49; cf. Nu 33:47. See also IYIM; Map 9. □

Abdemelech, see EBED-MELECH.

Abdenago, see ABEDNEGO.

Abdias, see OBADIAH.

Abdon, 1. city listed in portion of Asher, Jos 19:28 (where Heb. text wrongly has Ebron); Levitical city, Jos 21:30,

1 Ch 6:74 (Heb. 59); mod. *Kh. 'Abde;* Map 11; p. 58. □
2. 'minor servant'; n. of 4 persons, inc. one of the Judges, Jg 12:13; Map 14.

Abednego, 'servant of (the god) Nebo'; Bab. name given to Azariah, one of the 3 friends of Daniel in Babylon, Dn 1:7.

Abel-, in many place-names, prob. = 'irrigated meadow', 'field'.

Abel, G&L form of Heb. *hebel*, 'fragility'; n. of 2nd son of Adam and Eve, whose offering pleased God; murdered by his jealous brother, Cain, Gn 4:1–16, cf. Mt 23:35.

Abel-beth-maacah, city in the N of Palestine where Sheba the rebel was killed, 2 S 20:14f; captured with Ijon, Dan etc. by Ben-hadad of Damascus, 1 K 15:20 = 2 Ch 16:4 (where it is called Abel-maim); later captured by Tiglath-pileser, 2 K 15:29; mod. *Tell Abil*; top of Maps 2, 15, 17; Pls. 33, 34. Cf. ARAM (3). □

Abel beth-maacha(h), see ABEL-BETH-MAACAH.

Abel-keramim, 'field of vineyards'; city ment. with Minnith in Jephthah's pursuit of the Ammonites, Jg 11:33; poss. mod. *Na'ûr*, in Transjordan, NE of Nebo; Map 14. □

Abel-maim, 'water meadow'; 2 Ch 16:4; *var.* of ABEL-BETH-MAACAH, q.v.; Map 17.

Abel-meholah, 'field of dancing'; city ment. in the flight of the Midianites before Gideon, Jg 7:22; on the boundary of Solomon's 5th district, 1 K 4:12; birthplace of Elisha, 1 K 19:16; poss. mod. *Tell Abû S'fri*, W of the Jordan, about halfway between the Sea of Galilee and the Dead Sea; Maps 14, 15, 17. □

Abelmehula, see ABEL-MEHOLAH.

Abel-mizraim, 'field of Egypt'; other name of 'the threshing floor of Atad', Gn 50:11; used in a play on words with *'ebel*, 'mourning'. Cf. ATAD. □

Abel of Beth-maacah, see ABEL-BETH-MAACAH.

Abelsatim, see ABEL-SHITTIM.

Abel-shittim, 'field of acacias'; loc. ment. with Beth-jeshimoth as outer limit of Israelite camp before Jericho, Nu 33:49; called Shittim in Nu 25:1, Jos 2:1, 3:1, cf. Mic 6:5; poss. mod. *Tell Kefrein*, E of Jericho; Map 14. □

Abes, see EBEZ.

Abesalom, see ABSALOM.

Abesan, see IBZAN.

Abez, see EBEZ.

Abiam, see ABIJAM.

Abiathar, faithful servant of David and High Priest, 2 S 15: 24ff.

Abib, 'ears of ripe corn'; name of a month and a city. Cf. TEL-ABIB.

Abiel, 'God is father'; n. of Saul's grandfather, 1 S 9:1.

Abiezer, 'father is help'; n. of 2 persons, one a comrade-in-arms of David, 2 S 23:27.

Abigail, 'father is joyful'; n. of the wife of Nabal, later the wife of David, 1 S 25:3, 42; Map 15.

Abihu, n. of 2nd son of Aaron and Elisheba, consecrated priest with his 3 brothers, Ex 28:1.

Abijah, G&L *Abias*, 'Yah(weh) is father'; n. of 7 persons, inc. a son of Jeroboam I, who died in infancy, p. 77; cf. ABIJAM.

Abijam, *var.* Abijah, 2nd king of Judah (*ca* 913–911 B.C.), who fought against Jeroboam, 1 K 15:1ff; Map 17.

Abila, see DECAPOLIS (10).

Maps: 1 p. 9 / 2, 3 p. 10 / 4 p. 29 / 5, 6 p. 30 / 7, 8 p. 43 / 9, 10 p. 44 / 11, 12 p. 59 / 13 p. 60 / 14 p. 65 / 15, 16 p. 66 / 17 p. 81 / 18, 19 p. 82 / 20, 21 p. 95 / 22–24 p. 96 / 25–29 p. 103 / 30, 31 p. 104 / 32, 33 p. 115 / 34 35 p. 116 / I, II end-papers.

140

Abilena, see ABILENE.
Abilene, 'territory of Abila'; NW of Damascus (therefore not the preceding Abila), Lk 3:1; Map 35; p. 136.
Abimelech, 'father is king'; n. of several persons, inc. kings of Gerar, Gn 20, 26, Map 4; and a son of Gideon who became king at Shechem, Jg 9, Map 14.
Abiram, 'father is exalted'; n. of a Hebrew who rebelled against Moses, Nu 16.
Abiron, see ABIRAM.
Abisag, see ABISHAG.
Abisai, see ABISHAI.
Abishag, n. of a wife and nurse of David, a Shunammite, 1 K 1:3.
Abishai, 'father is a gift'; n. of a warrior and nephew of David, 1 S 26; p. 38.
Abishalom, see ABSALOM.
Abiu, see ABIHU.
Ablesatim, see ABEL-SHITTIM.
Abner, *var.* Abiner, 'father is light'; army commander under Saul, then under David, killed by Joab; David's lament, 2 S 3:33f; pp. 67, 68.
Abraham, Abram, two forms of the name of the progenitor of Israel, found also in Mesopotamia (beg. 2nd millennium B.C.). In W Semitic the meaning seems to be 'he is exalted as regards his father' (i.e. of noble lineage). Gn 17:5 prob. gives a popular etymology: *'ab hamôn*, 'father of a multitude'. Pp. 28ff.
Abran, see ABDON (1).
Abronah, stopping-place on the journey through the wilderness, Nu 33:34f.; poss. mod. *'Ain ed-Defiyeh*, in the Arabah to the N of Ezion-geber; Map 9. □
Absalom, *var.* Abishalom (1 K 15:2, 10), 'father is peace'; rebellious son of David, 2 S 13–19, etc.; p. 71.
Abû Simbel, loc. in Upper Egypt; Map 10; Pl. 154 A.
Accad, city in northern Babylonia, Gn 10:10; residence of Sargon (*ca* 2600 B.C.); poss. mod. *Tell ed-Dêr*; in non-Biblical documents the region around the city is also called Accad; Maps 1, 5, 6. □
Accadian, see SEMITIC LANGUAGES.
Accain, see KAIN.
Accaron, see EKRON.
Accho, see ACCO.
Acco, city of Asher, Jg 1:31; ment. on the prism of Sennacherib, p. 89; later called PTOLEMAIS, q.v.; the ancient site, *Tell el-Fukhkhâr*, lies E of the mod. town called *'Akkâ*; Maps 2, 4, 7, 11, 14, 23; p. 105. Cf. UMMAH. □
Aceldama, see AKELDAMA.
Achab, see AHAB.
Achad, see ACCAD.
Achaia, Rom. province in Greece from 146 B.C., ment. in the N.T. principally in connection with the preaching of the Gospel in its capital, Corinth, Ac 18:27, 1 Co 16:15, 2 Co 1:1, etc.; Maps 32, II (e.p.).
Achaicus, n. of a Christian, 1 Co 16:17.
Achan, n. of a Judahite who 'broke faith in the matter of the devoted things' after the capture of Jericho, 'and wrath fell upon... Israel' (*'âchar*); he was stoned in the Valley of Achor, Jos 7:1, 18ff., 22:20. In 1 Ch 2:7 he is called Achar in allusion to his action. Cf. ACHOR.
Achaz, see AHAZ.
Achiacharus, see ACHIOR (2).
Achimaas, see AHIMAAZ.
Achimelech, see AHIMELECH.
Achinoam, see AHINOAM.
Achior, 'brother is a light'; n. of 1. an Ammonite commander in the book of Judith who pleads for the Jews and finally becomes a proselyte.
2. a nephew of Tobit, To 11:20 (so Vulgate; Greek text (11:18) has Achiacharus), evidently a person representing the famous sage Achiqar, chancellor of Sennacherib, to whom many wise sayings were attributed.
Achiqar, see ACHIOR (2).
Achis, see ACHISH.
Achish, king of Gath, whose service David entered, 1 S 21:10 (Heb. 11), 27:2; cf. 1 K 2:39.
Achitophel, see AHITHOPHEL.
Achmetha, Aramaic name of ECBATANA, q.v.
Achor, a valley in the wild region between Jericho and the Dead Sea which gives access to the mountains of Judah (cf. Pl. 352). The name evoked the idea of 'misfortune, destruction'. Achan was stoned there, Jos 7:24, 26. Later the valley is named in the description of the N boundary of Judah, Jos 15:7. In the time of salvation this desolate region is to be a 'door of hope' for God's people returning purified in spirit from the wilderness, Hos 2:15 (Heb. 17), and to become wonderfully fruitful, Is 65:10. We cannot be certain which of the many valleys S of Jericho was the Valley of Achor. □
Achsah, n. of 2 women, inc. a daughter of Caleb, Jos 15:16.
Achshaph, city of Asher, listed Jos 19:25; Canaanite royal city, Jos 11:1, 12:20; poss. mod. *et-Tell*; Maps 11, 14. □
Achzib, n. of two cities, 1. city of Asher, listed Jos 19:29, cf. Jg 1:31; mod. *ez-Zîb*; Map 11. □
2. city of Judah, in the lowland, listed Jos 15:44, cf. Mic 1:14; poss. mod. *Tell el-Beida*; Maps 13, 19. Cf. CHEZIB. □
Achziba, see ACHZIB (1).
Acrabathane, see AKRABATTINE.
Acron, see EKRON.
Adad, see HADAD.
Adada(h), see ARARAH.
Adadremmon, see HADAD-RIMMON.
Adam, 1. 'man'; associated in Gn 2:7 (cf. 3:19, 23) with *'adamah*, 'earth', 'ground', and afterwards used as n. of the first man, Gn 4:25, 5:1, 3.
2. city on the Jordan, where the waters were held back for the miraculous crossing, Jos 3:16; mod. *Tell ed-Dâmiyeh*; Map 14; cf. Pl. 158. □
Adamah, n. of city of Naphtali, listed Jos 19:36; sit. unk. □
Adami-nekeb, loc. of Naphtali, listed Jos 19:33; mod. *Kh. ed-Dâmiyeh*; Map 11. □
Adanah, see ARARAH.
Adar, see ADDAR and HADAD.
Adarezer, see HADADEZER.
Adarsa, see ADASA.
Adasa, on the road to Beth-horon, 1 Mac 7:40, 45; poss. mod. *Kh. 'Addâseh*, N of Jerusalem; Map 30. □
Addan, loc. in Babylonia, Ezr 2:59, Neh 7:61 (Addon); sit. unk. □
Addar, loc. on S boundary of Judah, W of Kadesh-barnea, listed Jos 15:3, called Hazar-addar in Nu 34:4; exact sit. unk. □
Addo, see IDDO.
Addon, see ADDAN.
Addus, see ADIDA and HADID.
Adeodatus, 2 S 21:19 (Vulg.), for ELHANAN, q.v.
Adiada, see ADIDA and HADID.
Adida, city to the NE of Lydda, 1 Mac 12:38, 13:13; Map 30; prob. identical with HADID, q.v.
Adithaim, city of Judah, in the lowland, listed Jos 15:36; poss. mod. *Kh. el-Hadatha* (*Hadîtheh*) N of Aijalon; Maps 13, 19. □
Admah, name of city in the PENTAPOLIS (1), q.v.
Adom, see ADAM (2).
Adommim, see ADUMMIM.
Adon, see ADDAN.
Adonai, 'my Lords'; originally a form of address (royal plural), later n. of God alone. Cf. JEHOVAH, YAHWEH.
Adonias, see ADONIJAH.
Adonibezec, see ADONI-BEZEK.
Adoni-bezek, 'lord of Bezek'; Canaanite king defeated and mutilated at Bezek, Jg 1:5–7.
Adonijah, 'Yah(weh) is Lord'; n. of 3 persons, inc. the son of David and pretender to the throne, assassinated by Solomon, 1 K 1, 2; p. 72.
Adoniram, '(my) Lord is exalted'; official in charge of forced labour under David and Solomon, 1 K 4:6, 5:14 (Heb. 28). A shortened form, Adoram, occurs in 2 S 20:24, 1 K 12:18 and, with the spelling Hadoram, in 2 Ch 10:18.
Adonisedec, see ADONI-ZEDEK.
Adoni-zedec, see ADONI-ZEDEK.
Adoni-zedek, 'the Lord is just'; Canaanite king of Jerusalem, Jos 10:1; Map 14.
Ador, see ADORA.
Adora, city in S of Judaea, 1 Mac 13:20; prob. identical with the ancient ADORAIM, q.v.; Map 30; p. 113. □
Adoraim, city of Judah, fortified by Rehoboam, 2 Ch 11:9; mod. *Dûra*; Map 17. □
Adoram, see ADONIRAM.
Adramyttium, port in NW Asia Minor, Ac 27:2; mod. *Edremit*; Map II (e.p.). □
Adremutum, see ADRAMYTTIUM.
Adria (Sea of), n. used in Ac 27:27 for the sea to the S of Italy. □
Adullam, city of Judah, in the lowland, listed Jos 15:35; Canaanite royal city, Jos 12:15; fortified by Rehoboam, 2 Ch 11:7; cf. Mic 1:15; re-settled after the Exile, Neh 11:30; mod. *Tell esh-Sheikh-Madhkûr*, near *'Id el-Mâ*; Maps 4, 13, 14, 15, 17, 19. □
Adullam (Cave of), 1 S 22:1, 2 S 23:13, 1 Ch 11:15, one of the caves, difficult of access, in the vicinity of Adullam, where David took refuge. □
Adummim (Ascent of), 'redness' (signifying red limestone rock); a pass on the boundary between Judah and Benjamin, Jos 15:7, 18:17; mod. *Talat ed-Damm*, on the mod. road from Jerusalem to Jericho, near the traditional site of the inn of the good Samaritan (Lk 10:30–37); Maps 13, 19. □
Aduram, see ADONIRAM and ADORAIM.
Aen, see AIN.
Aeneas, n. of a paralysed man healed by St Peter at Lydda, Ac 9:32ff.; Map 34.
Aenon, near Salim, where John the Baptist baptised, S of Beth-shan; Jn 3:23. Cf. SALIM; Map 34; pp. 105, 122.
Africa, see PUT, and PUL (2).
Agabus, n. of a Christian prophet of Jerusalem, Ac 11:28, 21:10.
Agag, n. or title of 2 Amalekite kings, 1. in a prophecy of Balaam, Nu 24:7.
2. spared by Saul and killed by Samuel, 1 S 15; cf. also Est 3:1 (Haman the Agagite).
Agagite, cognomen of Haman, Est 3:1.
Agar, see HAGAR.
Agarenes, Agarites, see HAGRITES.
Aggaeus, see HAGGAI.
Agrippa, see HEROD (3) and (4).
Agur, author of sayings of Arabia, Pr 30:1.
Ahab, 'brother of father'; n. of 7th king of Israel (*ca* 874–853 B.C.), son of Omri, 1 K 16ff.; Maps 17, 18; Pls. 211, 217, 227, 228, 229; pp. 80, 84, 87, 90, 92.
Ahalab, see MAHALAB.
Ahasuerus, Lat. form of *Ahashveros*, Biblical n. of a king of the Medes and Persians, son of Darius I Hystaspis, called XERXES (q.v.) by the Greeks (485–465 B.C.); ment. Ezr 4:6 and often in Est; Map 21. The Ahasuerus of Dn 9:1, father of Darius the Mede, cannot be the same person.
Ahava, city and river (or canal) in Babylonia, where Ezra mustered the Israelites for the return from exile, Ezr 8:15, 21; doubtless near Babylon (cf. Ezr 7:9 and 8:31). □
Ahaz, '(Yahweh) has taken possession'; n. of 12th king of Judah (*ca* 736–716 B.C., but cf. p. 93), 2 K 15:38, 16:1ff.; Map 17; pp. 92ff.
Ahaziah, 'Yahweh has seized'; n. of 2 kings, 1. 8th king of Israel (853–852 B.C.), 1 K 22 ff.; Map 17.
2. 6th king of Judah (841 B.C.), 2 K 8:24ff.; also called Jehoahaz; p. 87.
Ahiah, see AHIJAH.
Ahialon, see ELON (1).
Ahicam, see AHIKAM.
Ahijah, 'Yah(weh) is brother'; n. of 8 persons, inc. a priest of Shiloh under Saul and a prophet of Shiloh under Jeroboam I; Map 17; p. 76.
Ahikam, 'brother rises'; n. of an official at the court of Josiah, king of Judah, 2 K 22:12.
Ahimaaz, n. of 3 persons, inc. 1. an ally of David at the time of Absalom's revolt, son of the priest Zadok, 2 S 15:27, 36; 17.
2. a son-in-law of Solomon, 1 K 4:15.
Ahiman, n. of 2 persons, inc. one of the giants defeated by Joshua and Caleb, Jos 15:14.
Ahimelech, 'brother is king'; n. of a priest under Saul, a supporter of David, 1 S 21; the name occurs on a seal from Lachish, Pl. 221, no. 1; p. 67.
Ahinoam, 'brother is charming'; n. of 2 persons, inc. a wife of David, mother of Amnon, David's first-born child, 1 S 25:43, 2 S 3:2.
Ahio, 'Yah(weh) is brother'; n. of 2 persons, inc. a son of Abinadab who 'went before the Ark' with Uzzah when it was carried to Jerusalem, 2 S 6:3ff.
Ahion, see IJON.
Ahithophel, n. of a counseller and betrayer of David, 2 S 15:12; p. 105.
Ahlab, see MAHALAB.
Ai, 'ruin'; name of 2 cities, 1. near Bethel; Abraham pitched his tent in the vicinity, Gn 12:8, 13:3; a Canaanite royal city destroyed by Joshua, Jos 7, 8; ment. with Bethel in the lists of Ezra (2:28) and Nehemiah (7:32); prob. mod. *Kh. et-Tell*, some 10 miles N of the old city of Jerusalem (though excavation has produced results which conflict with the story in Joshua); Maps 4, 13, 14, 22; pp. 28, 57. Cf. AIATH, AVVIM. □
2. city in Moab, Jer 49:3; sit. unk. □
Aialon, see AIJALON.
Aiath, loc. ment. in description of the Ass. invasion, Is 10:28; repopulated after the Exile, Neh 11:31 (Aija); cf. 1 Ch 7:28 (Ayyah; some Heb. MSS Gaza); prob. identical with Ai (1), although archaeological findings also suggest *Kh. Hayyân*, just under a mile SSE of Ai (1). □
Aija, see AIATH.
Aijalon, 'place of deer'; 1. city of Dan, listed Jos 19:42; Jg 1:35; Levitical city, Jos 21:24; 1 Ch 6:69 (Heb. 54); inhabited by Benjamites according to 1 Ch 8:13; near the Philistine frontier, 1 S 14:31; later in Solomon's 2nd district, 1 K 4:9 (cf. ELON (3)); fortified by Rehoboam, 2 Ch 11:10; captured by the Philistines, 2 Ch 28:18; mod. *Yâlo*; Maps 2, 11, 13, 14, 15, 17, 19. The valley of Aijalon, Jos 10:12, is an important means of access to the mountains of Judah; cf. Pl. 180. □
2. loc. in Zebulun, Jg 12:12, where the reading should doubtless be Elon; sit. unk. □
Aila, see ELATH.
Ailath, see ELATH.
Ain, 'spring'; in compounds En-, 1. only in appearance a distinct town in Jos 15:32, 1 Ch 4:32; the word should rather be joined to Rimmon which follows it. Cf. EN-RIMMON. □
2. city on the NW frontier of Canaan, Nu 34:11; sit. unk. □
3. Levitical city, Jos 21:16, where it is better to read Ashan with the parallel list of 1 Ch 6:59 (Heb. 44); cf. ASHAN. □
Aion, see IJON.
Ajalon, see AIJALON.
Akeldama, 'field of blood'; Ac 1:19; where Judas killed himself, Mt 27:3–10; localised since the 4th century A.D. in the valley of Hinnom, S of Jerusalem; Map 33.
Akhenaton, other n. of the Pharaoh Amenophis IV; pp. 41, 68.
Akhetaton, for a short time capital of Egypt under Akhenaton; Map 7. Cf. AMARNA.
Akkad, see ACCAD.
Akrabattine, 1 Mac 5:3, region in S of Judaea, on the frontier with Idumaea, in the vicinity of 'the ascent of Akrabbim', SW of the Dead Sea; Map 30.
Akrabbim (Ascent of), 'ascent of the scorpions'; between the Arabah and the hill country of Judah, on the S frontiers of Canaan, Nu 34:4, and of Judah, Jos 15:3; cf. Jg 1:36; prob. mod. *Naqb es-Safa*; Map 12; cf. AKRABATTINE. □
Alalakh, ancient city in N Syria, on the Orontes; mod. *Tell 'Atshâneh*; Maps 4, 5, 6.
Alammelech, see ALLAMMELECH.
Alcimus, 'the strong'; Hellenised form of Eliakim; n. of a Hellenised Jew, appointed High Priest by Demetrius I and opposed by Judas Maccabaeus, 1 Mac 7, 9.
Alema, city in Transjordan, 1 Mac 5:26; poss. identical with HELAM, q.v.
Alemeth, see ALMON.
Aleppo, city in Syria, one of the oldest cities still in existence; appears under the name of Khalab in Hittite texts of the 2nd millennium B.C., called BEROEA (q.v.) under the Seleucids; Maps 4–8, 20, I (e.p.).
Alexander, n. of 7 persons, inc. 1. Alexander the Great (357–

Maps: 1 p. 9 / 2, 3 p. 10 / 4 p. 29 / 5, 6 p. 30 / 7, 8 p. 43 / 9, 10 p. 44 / 11, 12 p. 59 / 13 p. 60 / 14 p. 65 / 15, 16 p. 66 / 17 p. 81 / 18, 19 p. 82 / 20, 21 p. 95 / 22–24 p. 96 / 25–29 p. 103 / 30, 31 p. 104 / 32, 33 p. 115 / 34, 35 p. 116 / I, II end-papers

141

323 B.C.), king of Macedon; Map 25; Pls. 275, 277, 278; p. 102, 105.
2. Alexander Balas, king of Syria (150-145 B.C.), 1 Mac 10.
3. Alexander Jannaeus, a Hasmonaean (103-76 B.C.); Pls. 296, 306, 307; pp. 110 ff.
Alexandria, name of many cities built by (or in honour of) Alexander the Great (Gk. *Alexandreia*, Lat. *Alexandria*). The most important stands at the Canopic mouth of the Nile; Maps 25, 26, 27, 32, I and II (e.p.); Pls. 279, 281; pp. 105 ff.
Alexandrium, fortress of the Hasmonaeans and of Herod; mod. *Qarn Sartabeh*, N of Jericho; Map 34; p. 112; cf. ZARETHAN.
Alicarnassus, see HALICARNASSUS.
Alima, see ALEMA.
Allammelech, loc. of Asher, listed Jos 19:26; sit. unk. □
Almon, Levitical city of Benjamin, listed Jos 21:18; Alemeth in the parallel list in 1 Ch 6:60 (Heb. 45); mod. *Kh. 'Almît;* Maps 11, 13, 19. □
Almon-diblathaim, stopping-place on the Exodus, Nu 33:46f.; N of Dibon, in Transjordan; exact sit. unk. □
Aloth, loc. in Solomon's 9th district, 1 K 4:16 (R.S.V. Bealoth); poss. we should read, with one Gk. translation, 'on the slopes', which may refer to the mountainous coast between Acco and Tyre. □
Alphaeus, Hellenised form of *Chalphai*, 'God gives a substitute'; n. of 2 persons, 1. father of Levi-Matthew, Mk 2:14. 2. father of St James, Mt 10:3.
Alpheus, see ALPHAEUS.
Alus, see ALUSH.
Alush, stopping-place on the route of the Exodus, Nu 33:13, 14; poss. mod. *W. el-'Eshsh*; Map 9. □
Amaad, see AMAD.
Amad, loc. of Asher, listed Jos 19:26; sit. unk. □
Amalecites, see AMALEK, AMALEKITES.
Amalek, Amalekites, a nomadic people who wandered between the Negeb and the Sinai peninsula, often ment. as enemies of Israel down to the time of David; Map 16; p. 67.
Amam, city of Judah, listed Jos 15:26; sit. unk. □
Aman, see AMAM.
Amana, one of the peaks of the Anti-Lebanon, W of Damascus, Ca 4:8; according to a *var.* of the Heb. text of 2 K 5:12, an alternative spelling of ABANA, q.v. □
Amanus, G&L n. of the mountain on the E side of the plain of Cilicia; Map 4.
Amarna, village near the ruins of Akhetaton, for a short time capital under Akhenaton, where very important royal archives were discovered; Map 7; Pl. 271; p. 68.
Amasa, '(Yahweh) has taken the burden'; n. of 2 persons, inc. an army commander appointed by the rebellious Absalom, later in the service of David, 2 S 17:25.
Amasias, see AMAZIAH.
Amath, Amathis, see HAMATH.
Amaziah, 'Yahweh is strong'; 9th king of Judah (796-781 B.C.), son of Joash, 2 K 14; Map 17; Pl. 311; p. 90.
Amisus, see SAMPSAMES.
Amma, see UMMAH.
Ammah, n. of a hill near Gibeon, 2 S 2:24; exact sit. unk. □
'Ammân, see AMMON.
Ammon, Ammonites, n. of a region, and of a people which adopted a settled life at about the same date as the Israelite tribes, who regarded them as kinsmen (Gn 19:38). They occupied the country around the mod. city of *'Ammân*, the capital of Jordan; cf. RABBAH (1), PHILADELPHIA; Maps 2, 16, 18, 23, I (e.p.); pp. 28, 64, 67, 71.
Ammonites (Town of), see CHEPHAR-AMMONI.
Ammon-Zeus, Eg. oasis; Map 25; p. 102.
Amnon, 'worthy of trust'; n. of 2 persons, inc. the first-born son of David, killed by Absalom, 2 S 13.
Amon, n. of 3 persons, inc. 1. the 15th king of Judah (642-640 B.C.), 2 K 21; p. 97.
2. the god of Thebes, whose sacred animal was the ram; Pls. 123, 131, 135, 136, 183; pp. 46, 64.
Amon of Thebes, see NO-AMON, THEBES.
Amorites, Semitic clan in Palestine before and during the Israelite occupation, belonging to the horde of nomads who in the 2nd millennium B.C. overran Mesopotamia and the Syrian coastal region; Maps 5, 6; p. 58.
Amorrhites, see AMORITES.
Amos, '(God) has taken charge (of him)'; n. of a prophet under Jeroboam II; Map 17; name of the book which contains his utterances, the 3rd of the 12 Minor Prophets; p. 98.
Amosa, see MOZAH.
Amphipolis, city in Thrace, visited by St Paul, Ac. 17:1; mod. *Neochori;* Map II (e.p.); Pls. 277, 278. □
Amplias, see AMPLIATUS.
Ampliatus, a Roman Christian, Ro 16:8.
Amram, n. of 2 persons, inc. the father of Moses, Aaron, and Miriam, Ex 6:20.
Amraphel, king of Shinar, one of the 4 allies of Gn 14 (Map 4), formerly often identified with Hammurabi.
Amri, see OMRI.
Ana, see ANAH, HENA.
Anab, 'place of grapes'; city in the hill country of Judah, listed Jos 15:50; cf. Jos 11:21; mod. *Kh. 'Anab;* Maps 13, 14. □
Anah, 'prince'; son of Seir, in the genealogy of Esau, Gn 36.
Anaharath, city of Issachar, listed Jos 19:19; sit. unk. □
Anak (Descendants of), Anakim, Canaanite tribe of the region of Hebron, exterminated by Caleb, Nu 13:22, Jos 15:13f.; Jos 21:11; represented as giants, Nu 13:33, Dt 2:10; after the extermination, 'only in Gaza, in Gath, and in Ashdod, did some remain', Jos 11:22.
Anamim, tribe engendered by Egypt (Mizraim) in the genealogy of Ham, Gn 10:13 = 1 Ch 1:11.
Anania, see ANANIAH.
Ananiah, city of Benjamin, Neh 11:32; prob. mod. *el-'Azarîyeh* (Bethany); Map 22. □
Ananias, Gk. form of Hananiah, 'Yahweh is merciful'; n. of 4 persons, 1. To 5:12 (Gk. 13; Vulg. 18).
2. a Christian of Jerusalem punished with sudden death, Ac 5.
3. a Christian of Damascus who restored St Paul's sight, Ac 9:17.
4. Jewish High Priest, adversary of St Paul, Ac 23, 24. See also HANANIAH (1).
Anathoth, Levitical city of Benjamin, listed Jos 21:18; N of Jerusalem, Is 10:30; home of Jeremiah, Jer 1:1, etc.; mod. *Râs el-Kharrûbeh*, near the village of *'Anâta;* Maps 2, 11, 13, 19, 22; Pl. 250 (cf. Pl. 192, no. 12).
Andrew, n., of Gk. origin, of one of the first disciples; he came from Capernaum and was a brother of Simon (called Peter), Mk 1:16.
Andronicus, n. of 3 persons, inc. 1. the heathen governor who assassinated the High Priest Onias, 2 Mac 4:31 ff.
2. a Roman Christian, Ro 16:7.
Anem, Levitical city of Issachar, 1 Ch 6:73 (Heb. 58), where the corresponding list in Jos 21:29 has EN-GANNIM, q.v.; exact sit. unk. □
Aner, Levitical city of Manasseh, 1 Ch 6:70 (Heb. 55); sit. unk. □
Anim, city of Judah, in the hill country, listed Jos 15:50; poss. mod. *Kh. Ghuwein et-Tahta;* Map 13. □
Anna, Gk. form of Hannah, 'favoured'; n. of 3 women, inc. 1. in the O.T., the wife of Tobit, To 1:9.
2. in the N.T., a prophetess who witnessed the presentation of Jesus in the Temple, Lk 2.
Annas, abb. of *Ananos*, Gk. form of Hananiah, 'Yahweh is merciful'; High Priest A.D. 6-15. Because of his great authority, he interrogated Jesus under the high priesthood of his son-in-law Caiaphas, Jn 18:13; p. 136.
Anti-Lebanon, non-Biblical name of a mountain chain parallel to the Lebanon, having Mt Hermon at its S end; Map 4; p. 15; cf. AMANA.
Antioch, n. of 2 cities, 1. in Syria, on the Orontes; Seleucid capital (as such often ment. in 1 and 2 Mac), later an important Christian centre from which the faith was disseminated, Ac 11:19f., etc., Gal 2:11; mod. *Antakya*; Maps 29, I and II (e.p.); Pl. 391; pp. 106, 117.
2. in Pisidia; St Paul preached there on his 1st and 2nd journeys, Ac 13:14, 14:19, 21, 2 Ti 3:11; mod. *Yalovatch*; Map II (e.p.). □
Antiochus, 'adversary'; n. of 10 Syrian kings of the Seleucid dynasty. 4 are ment. in the Bible, inc. 1. Antiochus III; see SELEUCIDS.
2. Antiochus IV Epiphanes (175-164 B.C.), who, in his efforts to suppress the Jewish faith, provoked the rising of the Maccabees; pp. 102, 106, 109, 110. Like Nebuchadnezzar, he typifies the forces opposed to God, 1 Mac 1:10 ff. Alluded to in Dn 7-9. Pls 283, 284.
3. Antiochus V Eupator (164-162 B.C.), son of the above, who made peace with Judas Maccabaeus, 1 Mac 6, 7.
4. Antiochus VII Sidetes, defeated Tryphon with the help of Simon Maccabaeus and then turned against Simon, 1 Mac 15 f.; p. 110.
Antipas, see HEROD (2).
Antipater, n. of several persons, inc. 1. son of Jason, Jonathan's ambassador to Rome and Sparta, 1 Mac 12.
2. father of Herod the Great and governor of Judaea (*ca* 55-43 B.C.); pp. 112 f., 117 f.
Antipatris, Gk. name (from Antipater, father of Herod) of the ancient city of Aphek (1), Ac 23:31; Map 34.
Antonia, fortress at the NW corner of the Temple of Jerusalem built by Herod; cf. Ac 21:34 (R.S.V. 'the barracks'); Map 33; Pl. 380; p. 132.
Antonius Felix, see FELIX.
Aod, see EHUD.
Apamea, n. of several cities, inc. an important Hel. city founded by the Seleucids, S of Hamath; mod. *Qala'at el- Mudîq;* Map 29; pp. 105, 106.
Apelles, n. of a Christian, Ro 16:10.
Aphara, see PARAH.
Apharsaeans, see APHARSITES.
Aphaerema, Gk. form (1 Mac 11:34) of EPHRAIM (4), q.v.
Apharsites, ment. Ezr 4:9 (R.S.V. Persians); prob. a class of officials, and not from a place-name, Apharsa. □
Aphec, see APHEK (1), (2), (3).
Apheca, see APHEK (4), (5).
Aphek, 'bed of a torrent' (or 'fortress'?); name of 4 cities, 1. Canaanite royal city, Jos, 12:18; rallying-point of the Philistine forces, 1 S 4:1, 29:1; later G&L ANTIPATRIS, q.v.; prob. mod. *Râs el-'Ain;* Maps 14, 15, 34; pp. 57, 64. □
2. city of Asher, listed Jos 19:30; cf. Jg 1:31 (Aphik); prob. mod. *Tell Kurdâneh;* Map 11. □
3. loc. where Ahab was defeated by Ben-hadad of Damascus, 1 K 20:26, 30; cf. 2 K 13:17; poss. mod. *Fîq*, E of the Sea of Galilee; Map 17; p. 84. □
4. loc. on the frontier between Canaanites and Amorites, Jos 13:4; poss. mod. *Afqa*, in the Lebanon; Map 12. □
Aphekah, loc. of Judah, in the hill country, listed Jos 15:53; poss. mod. *Kh. Kana'an*, SW of Hebron; Maps 13, 19. □
Apherema, see APHAEREMA.
Aphik, see APHEK (2).
Aphrah, see BETH-LE-APHRAH.
Apocalypse, name of Gk. origin ('revelation') of the last book of the Bible.
Apocrypha, Jewish or Christian books which are not recognised as Holy Writ. Certain books of the O.T. (Tobit, Judith, 1 and 2 Maccabees, Baruch, Wisdom of Solomon, Ecclesiasticus) and the Gk. parts of Daniel and Esther, regarded as Holy Writ by the Roman Catholic Church, are placed among the Apocrypha by most of the Protestant Churches; cf. p. 109.
Apollo, see APOLLOS.
Apollonia, loc. in Macedonia, between Amphipolis and Thessalonica, Ac 17:1; mod. *Pollina;* Map II (e.p.). □
Apollonius, n. of 4 officials under the Seleucids, all persecutors of the Jews in their different ways. Apollonius of Tarsus instigated the attempted confiscation of the Temple treasure by Heliodorus, 2 Mac 3:5.
Apollos, abb. form of *Apollonios;* n. of a converted Jew of Alexandria, who disseminated the teaching of Jesus with great rhetorical skill. One of the consequences of his success was a schism in the Church of Corinth, 1 Co 1. Regarded by some scholars as the author of the Letter to the Hebrews.
Apollyon, Rev 9:11, Gk. for ABADDON, q.v.
Apphia, a Christian woman of Colossae, Philem 2.
Appia, see APPHIA.
Appii forum, see APPIUS (Forum of).
Appius (Forum of), market town on the Via Appia, S of Rome, Ac 28:15; near mod. *Foro Appio;* Map II (e.p.). □
Apries, n. of a Pharaoh, called Hophra in the Bible, 2nd successor of Necho; Map 20.
'Aqaba, mod. name of a small town at the head of the gulf to the E of the Sinai Peninsula (Gulf of 'Aqaba); p. 56; cf. ELATH, SEA OF REEDS.
Aqueduct (Hill of the), see AMMAH.
Aquila, a Jew of Pontus. Expelled from Rome with his wife Priscilla by the Emperor Claudius, he settled in Corinth where, like St Paul, he was a tent-maker. He converted Apollos; Ac 18.
Ar, another name for the territory of Moab, Dt 2:9, 18, 29; cf. Nu 21:15; this territory is called Ar of Moab in Nu 21:28, cf. Is 15:1. These last two texts may refer to a city (the capital?): in Heb. the consonants of *'Ar* are the same as those of *'ir*, 'city'; Map 9. Cf. KIR-HARESETH. □
Ara, see HARA.
Arab, 'place of wild asses'; city of Judah, in the hill country, listed Jos 15:52; poss. mod. *Kh. er-Râbiyeh*, SSW of Hebron; Map 13. □
Arab, Arabia, Arabia is ment. in ancient texts after Dedan and Tema, Jer 25:24; in trading relations with Tyre, Ezk 27:21, and with Solomon, 2 Ch 9:14, cf. 1 K 10:15. Is 13:20 and Jer 3:2 refer to nomadic Arabs. In 2 Ch they appear as enemies of the Kingdom of Judah to the S: 17:11, 21:16, 22:1, 26:7; similarly in the time of Nehemiah: Neh 2:19, 4:7, 6:1. In the N.T. the name Arabia is applied to the kingdom of the Nabataeans, which extends to the SE and E of Palestine as far as Damascus, Gal 1:17, 4:25; Arabians were present at the Pentecost, Ac 2:11. □
Arabah, Heb. *'Arabah*, 'steppe, desert'; n. frequently applied in the Bible to the Jordan valley, Dt 1:7, 3:17, Jos 11:2, 2 S 2:29, 4:7, 2 K 25:4; other versions translate 'plain, plains, desert, valley, wilderness'. The Dead Sea is sometimes called the Sea of the Arabah, Dt 3:17, Jos 12:3. In mod. usage this term is restricted to the southern continuation of the depression, extending for over 100 miles from the Dead Sea to the Gulf of 'Aqaba. Maps 1, 3, 9; Pls. 31, 151, 311; pp. 56, 74, 90. Cf. PLAIN, PLAINS, VALLEY (The).
Arabah (Brook of the), ment. Am 6:14; doubtless the Zered. Cf. ZERED (Brook, Valley of).
Arabah (Sea of), see SEA OF THE ARABAH.
Arabattine, see AKRABATTINE.
Arabia, see ARAB and SHEBA (1).
Arach, see ERECH.
Aracites, see ARKITES.
Arad, in the Negeb, Canaanite royal city, Nu 21:1, 33:40, Jos 12:14, cf. Jg 1:16; poss. identical with the Eder of Jos 15:21; mod. *Tell 'Arad*, S of Hebron; Maps 9, 13, 14; p. 56. See also ARVAD.
Arada, see HARADAH.
Aradites, see ARVAD.
Arados, Gk. name of the island of ARVAD, q.v.; 1 Mac 15:23 (Aradus); Maps 25, 29.
Aradus, see ARADOS.
Arah, city ment. in Jos 13:4, assuming that Mearah = 'from Arah'; mod. *Kh. 'Ara;* Map 12. □
Aram, generic name in Biblical Heb. of all the peoples dwelling to the N of Palestine as far as the Euphrates; formerly translated as 'Syrians' (so in R.S.V.), now usually as 'Aramaeans'. Successive waves of these peoples issued from the Syro-Arabian desert in the 12th century B.C. (Map 8), but much earlier there had been nomadic groups along the Euphrates. In Gn 22 : 21ff. 12 Aramaean tribes are listed as sons of Nahor. In the time of David and Solomon, there were to the N of Palestine and in Transjordan several small Aramaean kingdoms: 1. Aram of Damascus, 2 S 8:5f. = 1 Ch 18:5f. Because it was continually at war with Israel (cf. Map 17, top), this little kingdom is better known than the others and is often called simply Aram: 1 K 19:15, 20:1, 20 ff., 22:3, Is 7:2. Map 18; pp. 28, 80.
2. Aram of Zobah, or Zobah, defeated by David, 2 S 8:3ff., 10:6ff.; the cities of Betah and Berothai must have been situated in the Beqa', with its supplies of copper; Aram-zobah in Ps 60: Heading (Heb. 2). Map 16. □
3. Aram-maacah, defeated by David, 1 Ch 19:6 (the sole reference to this kingdom; the Maacah of the following

Maps: 1 p. 9 / 2, 3 p. 10 / 4 p. 29 / 5, 6 p. 30 / 7, 8 p. 43 / 9, 10 p. 44 / 11, 12 p. 59 / 13 p. 60 / 14 p. 65 / 15, 16 p. 66 / 17 p. 81 / 18, 19 p. 82 / 20, 21 p. 95 / 22-24 p. 96 / 25-29 p. 103 / 30, 31 p. 104 / 32, 33 p. 115 / 34, 35 p. 116 / I, II end-papers.

142

verse and of 2 S 10:6ff. prob. indicates the town of Abel-beth-maacah). Cf. MAACAH. □
4. Aram of Beth-rehob, defeated by David, 2 S 10:6; cf. BETH-REHOB. □
5. Aram-naharaim, 'Aram of the rivers' (usually rendered Mesopotamia in R.S.V.), on the upper course of the Euphrates between the *Balîkh* and the *Khâbûr* (Maps 4, 5, 6), Gn 24:10, Dt 23:4 (Heb. 5), Jg 3:10, 1 Ch 19:6, Ps 60: Heading (Heb. 2); cf. PADDAN-ARAM. □
N.B. Owing to the resemblance between the written forms of Edom and Aram, some texts have Aram instead of an original Edom: 2 S 8:12, 1 K 11:25, Ezk 16:57, 2 K 16:6 (R.S.V. reads Edom, save in 1 K 11:25).
Arama, see HORMAH and RAMAH (3).
Aramaic, the language of some passages of the Bible: Ezr 4:8–6:18, 7:12–26, Dn 2:4b–7:28. It was the language of the Aramaean tribes who overran the Near East in the 12th century B.C. (cf. ARAM); cf. 2 K 18:26 = Is 36:11; under the Persians, the language of commerce and administration (cf. Ezr 4:7); the language of the Elephantine papyri (cf. Pls. 261–264). This language became differentiated into dialects, and in the time of Jesus the dialect of Galilee was distinct from that of Judaea (Mt 26:73).
Aram-maacah, see ARAM (3), MAACAH.
Aram-naharaim, see ARAM (5) and PADDAN-ARAM.
Aram of Beth-rehob, see ARAM (4), BETH-REHOB.
Aran, see HARAN (1).
Ararah, city of Judah, in the Negeb, listed Jos 15:22 (which has the erroneous form Adadah); identical with AROER (3); mod. *Kh. 'Ar'arah*, S of Hormah; Maps 11, 13. □
Ararat, name of a region (Urartu) in Armenia, 2 K 19:37; cf. Is 37:38, Jer 51:27; owing to a misunderstanding of Gn 8:4, applied to the highest group of mountains in Armenia; Maps 1, 18, 25, 26, I (e.p.). □
Araunah, n. of a Jebusite from whom David purchased a threshing-floor upon which to build an altar, 2 S 24:16ff. In the parallel passage of 1 Ch 21:15ff., he is called Ornan. According to 2 Ch 3:1 this was the site of Solomon's Temple; p. 71.
Arbata, see ARBATTA.
Arbatta, region S of Mt Carmel, 1 Mac 5:23, poss. connected with Arubboth, 1 K 4:10; Map 30. □
Arbattis, see ARBATTA.
Arbela, 1. loc. W of the Sea of Galilee, 1 Mac 9:2; prob. mod. *Kh. Irbid;* Map 30. □
2. city near Nineveh; Map 20.
3. see RIBLAH.
Arbella, see ARBELA.
Archelaus, 'chief of the people'; son of Herod the Great, ethnarch of Judaea, Samaria, and Idumaea 4 B.C.–A.D. 6. While he was in power the Holy Family returned to Israel from Egypt, Mt 2:22; p. 118.
Archippus, fellow-soldier of St Paul, no doubt the son of Philemon, Philem 2.
Arebba, see RABBAH (2).
Arecon, see RAKKON.
Areopagus, 'hill of Ares'; in Athens; scene of the famous discourse of St Paul, Ac 17.
Aretas, n. of 4 Nabataean kings; the best-known is Aretas IV, 9 B.C.–A.D. 40, father-in-law of Herod Antipas. During his reign St Paul fled from Damascus, 2 Co 11:32 f.; p. 112.
Areuna, see ARAUNAH.
Argob, a region of Bashan, to the E of the Sea of Galilee, Dt 3:4, 13f.; in Solomon's 6th district, 1 K 4:13; in 2 K 15:25 (text uncertain), some scholars interpret Argob as a person. Cf. ARIEH. □
Arie, see ARIEH.
Arieh, near Argob in 2 K 15:25 (R.S.V. omits). Some scholars suggest reading 'Argob and Havvoth-jair'. Cf. ARGOB.
Arimathea, home of Joseph, a member of the Sanhedrin; in the O.T., RAMAH (2) or RAMATHAIM, qq.v.; mod. *Rentis;* Map 34.
Arioch, n. of 3 persons, inc. one of the 4 allied kings of Gn 14; Map 4.
Aristarchus, companion of St Paul on several of his journeys, Ac 19:29; also shared his imprisonment in Rome, Col 4:10.
Aristobulus, n. of several Biblical persons (2 Mac 1:10, Ro 16:10); also of 1. a son of John Hyrcanus, who reigned for 1 year (104–103 B.C.), p. 110.
2. a son of Alexander Jannaeus, who supplanted his elder brother in 67 B.C. and was deposed by Pompey, pp. 110–113.
Arius, n. of 2 kings of Sparta; Arius I, 309–265 B.C., offered a treaty of friendship to the High Priest Onias, 1 Mac 12:7ff.
Arkites, a people of Canaan, Gn 10:17 = 1 Ch 1:15, who lived in the city of Arqa, mod. *Tell 'Arqa,* on the Syrian coast, S of Arvad; Map 4.
Armageddon, Rev 16:16, = in Heb. 'the mountain of Megiddo'; this city, where Josiah was defeated and killed, is a symbol of disaster for armies which assemble there, cf. Zec 12:11.
Armagedon, see ARMAGEDDON.
Armenia, see ARARAT.
Armon, see HARMON.
Armourers' Gate, see GUARD (Gate of the).
Arnon, torrent on the E bank of the Dead Sea, crossed by the Israelites, Dt 2:24; cf. Nu 21:13ff.; N boundary of Moab, Jg 11:18; S boundary of Transjordan, Jos 12:1f., Dt 3:8, 4:48; ment. on the Moabite Stone, p. 80; mod. *W. el-Mûjib;* Maps 2, 9, 14, 17; Pls. 155–157, 393; pp. 16, 56. □
Aroer, 'junipers'; name of 4 cities, 1. N of the Arnon, ment. in the description of tribal boundaries, Jos 13:9; allotted to Reuben, Jos 13:16; cf. 2 K 10:33; built by the Gadites, Nu 32:34; starting-point of David's census, 2 S 24:5; mod. *'Arâ'ir;* Maps 11, 14, 15, 17.
2. city of Gad, E of Rabbah, listed Jos 13:25; ment. also in Jg 11:33; exact sit. unk. □
3. city in the S of Judah, 1 S 30:28, identical with ARARAH, q.v.; Map 15. □
4. city in the territory of Damascus, Is 17:2; sit. unk. (Instead of 'the cities of Aroer' (Heb.), the Gk. has 'her cities for ever' (R.S.V.).)
Arpad, according to the Bible, captured with Hamath by the Assyrians, Is 10:9; cf. 2 K 18:34, 19:13 = Is 36:19, 37:13; mod. *Tell Erfâd,* N of Aleppo; Maps 18, 20. □
Arphad, see ARPAD.
Arqa, see ARKITES.
Arslân-Tash, ruins W of Haran, where a palace of Tiglath-pileser has been found, with ivory objects prob. from Damascus; Pls. 211, 219; Map 1.
Artaxerxes, n. of 3 Persian kings. The Bible mentions only one, frequently named in Ezr and Neh, making it difficult to date the events in these books, cf. p. 100; Map 21.
Artemas, fellow-worker of St Paul, Tit 3:12.
Artemis or Diana, goddess of fertility; famous temple at Ephesus, Ac 19:24–35.
Arubboth, loc. in Solomon's 3rd district, 1 K 4:10; poss. mod. *Kh. er-Râbiyeh (Pardes Hanna);* Map 17. Cf. also ARBATTA. □
Aruboth, see ARUBBOTH.
Arumah, city ment. in the story of Abimelech, Jg 9:31 (Heb. differently), 41; prob. mod. *Kh. el-'Orma;* Map 14. □
Arvad, Vulg. *Aradium,* an island near the Phoenician coast; ment. with Sidon in Ezk 27:8 (cf. 11); ment. by Sennacherib, p. 89; in the list of Gn 10:18 = 1 Ch 1:16, the Arvadites were neighbours of the Zemarites. The name became *Arados* in Gk., 1 Mac 15:23 (Aradus); mod. *Ruâd;* Maps 1, 3, 4, 25, 29, 31; Pls. 15, 16; pp. 15, 89. □
Arvadites, see ARVAD.
Asa, n. of 2 persons, inc. the 3rd king of Judah (911–870 B.C.), 1 K 15ff.; Map 17; p. 80.
Asael, see ASAHEL.
Asahel, 'God has wrought'; n. of 4 persons, inc. one of David's valiant warriors, slain by Abner, 2 S 2:18–32.
Asan, see ASHAN.
Asaph, 'He has been merciful'; n. of leader of the Levites under David, 1 Ch 25:1–2; he gave his name to a company of singers in the Temple; ment. in the headings of Ps 50, 73–83.
Asarhaddon, see ESARHADDON.
Asarmoth, see HAZARMAVETH.
Asasonthamar, see HAZAZON-TAMAR.
Ascalon, see ASHKELON.
Ascenez, see ASHKENAZ.
Ascent of Adummim, see ADUMMIM (Ascent of).
Ascent of Akrabbim, see AKRABBIM (Ascent of).
Ascent of Ziz, see ZIZ (Ascent of).
Asedoth, see ASHDOTH-PISGAH.
Asem, see EZEM.
Asemona, see AZMON.
Asena, see ASHNAH (2).
Asenath, Heb. form of Eg. *nsy-Njt,* 'she belongs to (the goddess) Neit'; n. of the daughter of Potiphera, priest of On, given in marriage to Joseph; mother of Ephraim and Manasseh; Gn 41:45ff.
Aseneth, see ASENATH.
Aser, see ASHER and HAZOR (1).
Asergadda, see HAZAR-GADDAH.
Ashan, city of Judah, in the lowland, listed Jos 15:42; doubtless a different place from the Ashan of Simeon, listed Jos 19:7; 1 Ch 4:32 (cf. 1 Ch 6:59 (Heb. 44) and Jos 21:16 (where Heb. has Ain)); identical with Borashan, 1 S 30:30; prob. mod. *Kh. 'Asan,* NW of Beer-sheba. □
Ashdod, one of the 5 Philistine cities, cf. PENTAPOLIS (2); inhabited by the Anakim, Jos 11:22; city of Judah, in the lowland, listed Jos 15:46f.; cf. 2 Ch 26:6; the Philistines carried the Ark here, 1 S 5:1ff.; captured by the Assyrians, Is 20:1; ment. on Sennacherib's prism, p. 89; capital of a district under the Persians (cf. Map 23); its inhabitants intermarried with the Judaeans, Neh 13:23; called Azotus in the Hel. period, 1 Mac 10:77ff.; ment. in the account of the journeys of Philip, Ac 8:40; mod. *Esdûd;* Maps 11, 14, 15, 17, 18, 23, 30, 34; p. 94. (In Am 3:9 read Assyria with the Gk. (so R.S.V.), instead of the Heb. Ashdod.) □
Ashdoth-pisgah, 'slopes of Pisgah', see PISGAH.
Asher, 1. one of the 12 tribes of Israel, settled in the N of Palestine on the Mediterranean coast, Jg 5:17; its territory is indicated in Jos 19:24–31 (cf. Map 11). In Gn 30:12–13, the tribal ancestor is given as the son of Jacob and Zilpah. The Asher of Jos 17:7 is not a loc.; the text here means that the territory of Manasseh borders on that of Asher; pp. 57 f.
2. see HAZOR (1).
Ashkelon, one of the 5 Philistine cities, cf. PENTAPOLIS (2); occupied by Judah according to Jg 1:18, but in Philistine hands according to Jg 14:19 and 2 S 1:20; cf. Jer 47:5, 7; part of the region conquered by the Maccabees, 1 Mac 10:86, 11:60, 12:33; its ruins are near *'Askalân;* Maps 2, 7, 9, 11, 14, 15, 23, 30, 34; Pls. 29, 154B; pp. 45, 46, 89, 110.
Ashkenaz, a people of Asia Minor, listed among the sons of Gomer in Gn 10:3 = 1 Ch 1:6; ment. together with Ararat and Minni (therefore presumably in the region of Armenia) in Jer 51:27. □
Ashnah, 2 cities of Judah, in the lowland, 1. listed Jos 15:43; poss. mod. *Idhna,* E of Lachish; Maps 13, 19. □
2. listed Jos. 15:33, near Zorah; sit. unk. □
Ashtaroth, 'place of Ashtoreth'; city of Og, king of Bashan, Jos 9:10, 12:4, 13:12, 31, Dt 1:4; Levitical city, 1 Ch 6:71 (Heb. 56); mod. *Tell 'Ashtara,* E of the Sea of Galilee; Map 12; Pl. 258. Cf. BEESHTERAH. □
Ashtarte, see ASHTORETH.
Ashteroth-karnaim, loc. of a battle, Gn 14:5, prob. very near Ashtaroth; under the Persians, capital of a district of the Fifth Satrapy; cf. CARNAIM; Map 4.
Ashtoreth, Bab. *Ishtar,* goddess of fertility; in Canaan, female counterpart of Baal; sometimes worshipped by the Israelites, and even by Solomon, 1 K 11:5; cf. Pls. 162–166, 218.
Ashur, 1. city on the Tigris, Gn 2:14 (R.S.V. Assyria), the oldest and southernmost of the Ass. empire; ruins near mod. *Qala'ah Sherqât;* also n. of the region later called Assyria: Maps 1, 5–8, 18, 20; pp. 84, 88f., 94, 97. For Ass. art cf. Pls. 234–249.
2. a tribe living in the S of Palestine, Gn 25:3 (R.S.V. Asshurim), 18 (R.S.V. Assyria), Nu 24:24 (R.S.V. Asshur), Ps 83:8 (Heb. 9; R.S.V. Assyria).
Ashur-uballit I, an Ass. king (*ca* 1380–1347 B.C.); Map 7; p. 97.
Asia, in the Maccabaean period, n. for the Kingdom of the Seleucids (1 Mac 8:6, 2 Mac 3:3), and, after the battle of Magnesia (Map 26), the territory in Asia Minor ceded to the Romans. Cf. 1 Mac 11:13, 12:39, 13:32, 2 Mac 10:24. In N.T. times the province of Asia comprised the territory between Bithynia to the N, Lycia to the S, Galatia to the E, and the sea to the W. In the Acts, the name is often applied in a more restricted sense to the region of Ephesus and Smyrna, as on Map II (e.p.).
Asiongaber, see EZION-GEBER.
Askelon, see ASHKELON.
Asmodaeus, G&L form of Pers. *Eshma-dewa,* n. of the evil spirit who slew the 7 husbands of Sarah, To 3:8.
Asmodeus, see ASMODAEUS.
Asom, see EZEM.
Asor, see HAZOR.
Asphalt Lake, see DEAD SEA.
Assedim, see ZIDDIM.
Asshur, see ASHUR (2).
Asshurim, see ASHUR (2).
Assidaeans, see HASIDAEANS.
Assos, sea-port in Asia Minor, where St Paul embarked for his last journey to Jerusalem, Ac 20:13, 14; mod. *Behram Keui;* Map II (e.p.). □
Assuerus, see AHASUERUS.
Assur, see ASHUR (2).
Assyria, see ASHUR.
Astaroth, see ASHTAROTH.
Astaroth-Carnaim, see ASHTEROTH-KARNAIM.
Astarthe, see ASHTORETH.
Astharoth, see ASHTAROTH.
Astyages, n. of the last king of the empire of the Medes (*ca* 580–550 B.C.), overthrown and succeeded by Cyrus the Persian, Bel 1 (Dn 13:65); Map 21.
Asyncritus, n. of a Roman Christian, Ro 16:14.
Atad (threshing-floor of), Heb. *Goren ha-'Atad,* 'threshing-floor of thorns'; loc. on the route from Egypt to Hebron, the point to which the Egyptians followed in Jacob's funeral procession, Gn 50:10f.; sit. unk. Cf. ABEL-MIZRAIM. If we attempt to situate it SW of Canaan, the last words of Gn 50:11 must be regarded as a faulty gloss. □
Ataroth, n. of 3 cities, 1. in Transjordan, built by the Gadites, Nu 32:3, 34; ment. on the Moabite Stone, cf. p. 80; prob. mod. *Kh. Attarûs,* NW of Dibon; Map 17. □
2. on the NE boundary of Ephraim, Jos 16:7; poss. mod. *Tell Sheikh edh-Dhiâb;* Map 11. □
3. on the S boundary of Ephraim, Jos 16:2; called Ataroth-addar in Jos 16:5, 18:13; sit. unk. □
Ataroth-adar, see ATAROTH-ADDAR.
Ataroth-addar, see ATAROTH (3).
Athach, loc. ment. 1 S 30:30, poss. identical with ETHER (2), q.v. □
Athalia, see ATHALIAH.
Athaliah, 'Yahweh has shown His greatness'; n. of 3 persons; the most important is the queen of Judah, daughter of Jezebel, who systematically encouraged the worship of Baal and attempted to wipe out the house of David, 2 K 11; Map 17; pp. 87, 90.
Athar, see ETHER (2).
Atharim, Israel seeks to enter Canaan 'by the way of Atharim', Nu 21:1; sit. unk., unless the reading should be *('ir) hatte-marîm,* '(the city) of palms', Jg 1:16, identical with TAMAR (2) and so prob. with HAZAZON-TAMAR, qq.v. □
Athens, 2 Mac 9:15, Ac 17, cf. 1 Th 3:1; Maps I and II (e.p.), 21, 25, 32; Pls. 404, 405; pp. 98, 105f., 117. □
Athmatha, see HUMTAH.
Atroth-Shophan, city of Gad, Nu 32:35; sit. unk. □
Attalia, sea-port of Pamphylia, founded by Attalus II of Pergamum; mod. *Adalia;* visited by St Paul on his first journey; Maps I and II (e.p.).
Augustus, Gk. *Sebastos,* Roman emperor (31 B.C.–A.D. 14). Jesus was born in his reign, Lk 2:1; Pl. 323; pp. 113, 117f., 121.
Auran, see HAURAN.
Ausitis, see UZ.
Ava(h), see AVVA and IVVAH.
Avaris, later Gk. *Tanis,* capital of the Hyksos, residence of the Ramessides; identical with ZOAN, q.v.; Maps 6, 9; pp. 40, 45.
Aven, see ON.
Avim, Avims, Avites, see AVVITES, AVVIM.
Avith, loc. in the list of cities in Edom, Gn 36:35 = 1 Ch 1:46; sit. unk. □

Maps: 1 p. 9 / 2, 3 p. 10 / 4 p. 29 / 5, 6 p. 30 / 7, 8 p. 43 / 9, 10 p. 44 / 11, 12 p. 59 / 13 p. 60 / 14 p. 65 / 15, 16 p. 66 / 17 p. 81 / 18, 19 p. 82 / 20, 21 p. 95 / 22–24 p. 96 / 25–29 p. 103 / 30, 31 p. 104 / 32, 33 p. 115 / 34, 35 p. 116 / I, II end-papers.

Avva, loc. ment. 2 K 17:24. Cf. IVVAH.
Avvim, city of Benjamin, listed Jos 18:23; poss. identical with AI (1), q.v.; thus on Map 13. See also AVVITES, AVVIM.
Avvites, Avvim, 1. first inhabitants of the land of the Philistines near Gaza, Dt 2:23, Jos 13:3; Map 12.
2. inhabitants of Avva, also called Ivvah, transplanted by the Assyrians to replace the deportees from the Northern Kingdom, 2 K 17:24, 31, 18:34, 19:13; the site of the town is unknown.
Axa, see ACHSAH.
Axaph, see ACHSHAPH.
Ayyah, see AIATH.
Aza, 1 Ch 7:28, see AIATH.
Azanoth-Thabor, see AZNOTH-TABOR.
Azariah, 'Yahweh helps'; very common n., especially of 1. 10th king of Judah, also called Uzziah (781–740 B.C.), 2 K 14:21ff.; Map 17; p. 90.
2. one of the 3 friends of Daniel, deported by Nebuchadnezzar to Babylon where he was given the name ABEDNEGO, q.v.
Azarias, Gk. form of AZARIAH.
Azazel, evil spirit of the wilderness, the adversary of Yahweh, to whom the scapegoat was given as prey on the great day of Atonement, Lv 16.
Azeca, Azecha, see AZEKAH.
Azekah, city of Judah, in the lowland, listed Jos 15:35; Canaanite royal city, Jos 10:10; cf. 1 S 17:1; fortified by Rehoboam, 2 Ch 11:9; besieged by Nebuchadnezzar, Jer 34:7 (cf. 4th Lachish letter, p. 92); repopulated after the Exile, Neh 11:30; mod. *Tell Zakariyeh;* Maps 2, 11, 13, 14, 15, 17, 19; Pl. 179; p. 97. □
Azem, see EZEM.
Azmaveth, loc. ment. Ezr 2:24, Neh 7:28 (Beth-azmaveth), 12:29; prob. mod. *Hizmeh,* N of Anathoth; Map 22. □
Azmon, loc. on the S boundary of Judah, listed Jos 15:4; prob. mod. *Quseime;* Map 12. □
Aznoth-tabor, loc. ment. in the indication of the boundaries of Naphtali, Jos 19:34; near Mt Tabor, cf. TABOR (1); exact sit. unk. □
Azor, loc. of Dan, listed Jos 19:45 (LXX; Heb. Jehud); captured by Sennacherib, cf. p. 89 (Azuru); mod. *Yazûr;* Map 11. □
Azotus, Gk. n. for ASHDOD, q.v.
Azuru, see AZOR.
Azzah, see GAZA.

B

Baal, 'lord'; name originally applied to each of the local deities of Canaan; later restricted to a god of fertility and of the sun, in whom all the other deities had been merged; Pls. 167–171; pp. 77, 80, 92. Baal is an element in many place-names.
Baala, see BAALAH.
Baalah, name of 2 cities, 1. on the boundary of Judah, Jos 15:9f., 1 Ch 13:6; identical with KIRIATH-JEARIM, q.v. Cf. also BAALE-JUDAH. □
2. city of Judah, in the Negeb, listed Jos 15:29, and of Simeon, listed Jos 19:3 (Heb. Balah); exact sit. unk., doubtless E of Beer-sheba. Cf. BILHAH (2). □
Baalah (Mount), loc. ment. in the indication of the boundaries of Judah, Jos 15:11; sit. unk. □
Baalam, see IBLEAM.
Baalath, loc. of Dan, listed Jos 19:44; sit. unk. □
Baalath-beer, loc. of Simeon, listed Jos 19:8; sit. unk.; poss. identical with BEALOTH (1), q.v., Jos 15:24. □
Baalath-Beer-Ramath, see BAALATH-BEER, and RAMAH OF THE NEGEB.
Ba'albek, Gk. *Heliopolis,* a city in the Beqa', now famous for its temple ruins; Map 3; Pls. 18, 340–345; p. 15.
Baale-judah, loc. ment. 2 S 6:2. See BAALAH (1) and KIRIATH-JEARIM. □
Baale of Judah, see BAALE-JUDAH.
Baal-gad, 'Baal of good fortune'; loc. at the foot of Mt Hermon, Jos 11:17, 12:7, 13:5; poss. mod. *Hasbeiyah;* Map 12. □
Baal-hamon, loc. ment. Ca 8:11; sit. unk. □
Baal-Hasor, see BAAL-HAZOR.
Baal-hazor, loc. ment. 2 S 13:23, a holy place where Absalom's servant skilled Amnon; mod. *J. el-'Asûr;* Maps 2, 15; Pl. 250.
Baal-hermon, loc. ment. 1 Ch 5:23, Jg 3:3; on the slopes of Mt Hermon; exact sit. unk. □
Baal-hermon (Mount), see BAAL-HERMON.
Baalmaon, Baal-meon, see BETH-BAAL-MEON.
Baal-peor, Dt 4:3, Hos 9:10, (cf. Baal of Peor Nu 25:3, 5, Ps 106:28), see BETH-PEOR.
Baal-perazim, loc. near Jerusalem where David defeated the Philistines, 2 S 5:20 = 1 Ch 14:11; cf. Is 28:21; prob. mod. *Râs en-Nâdir,* NW of the old city of Jerusalem; Map 15. □
Baal-Pharasim, see BAAL-PERAZIM.
Baal-Salisa, Baal-shalisha, see BAAL-SHALISHAH.
Baal-shalishah, city to the SW of Samaria, 2 K 4:42; mod. *Kefr Thilth,* SW of Shechem; Map 17. Cf. SHALISHA. □
Baal-tamar, loc. ment. Jg 20:33, N of Jerusalem; sit. unk. □
Baal-Thamar, see BAAL-TAMAR.
Baal-zebub, 'Lord of flies'; 2 K 1:2, a derogatory corruption of BAAL-ZEBUL, q.v.
Baal-zebul, 'Baal the prince'; a Canaanite deity, the god of Ekron, 2 K 1:2 (where Heb. has Baal-zebub); in monotheistic orthodoxy he became the prince of demons, Mt 12:24 (where Gk. has Beelzebul).
Baal-zephon, a stopping-place on the Exodus, Ex 14: 2,9, Nu 33:7; poss. mod. *J. Murr;* Map 9; p. 48. □
Baasa, see BAASHA.
Baasha, n. of the 3rd king of Israel (909–886 B.C.), a usurper who exterminated the family of Jeroboam, 1 K 15, 16; Map 17; p. 80.
Babel, Heb. name of BABYLON; cf. Gn 11:9.
Babylon, from *Bab-ili,* 'gate of the gods'; capital of Babylonia, in the S of Mesopotamia; Maps 1, 5, 6, 7, 8, 18, 21, 25; Pls. 259, 260; pp. 64, 97f., 100, 102.
Bacchides, n. of a general of Antiochus IV Epiphanes and Demetrius I; he fought 3 campaigns in Judah, 1 Mac 7, 9; Map 30.
Badan, see BEDAN.
Bagoas, n. of the eunuch of Holofernes, Jth 12:11.
Bahurim, village NE of the Mt of Olives, 2 S 3:16; David passed through it in flight, 2 S 16:5; ment. also 17:18, 19:16, 1 K 2:8; mod. *Râs et-Tmin;* Map 15; Pl. 192 (no. 11). □
Bala, see BAALAH, BELA (1), and BILHAH.
Balaam, 1. n. of a prophet summoned by the Moabite king to curse Israel who blessed her instead, Nu 22–24.
2. see BILEAM.
Balac, see BALAK.
Balah, loc. of Simeon, listed Jos 19:3, identical with BAALAH (2), q.v.; prob. identical with Bilhah (2), 1 Ch 4:29; sit. unk. □
Balak, n. of the king of Moab who summoned Balaam, Nu 22–24, Jos 24:9.
Balîkh, a tributary of the upper Euphrates; Maps 5, 6.
Baloth, see BEALOTH.
Baltassar, see BELSHAZZAR and BELTESHAZZAR.
Bamoth, see BAMOTH-BAAL.
Bamoth-baal, 'heights of Baal'; loc. of Reuben, listed Jos 13:17; on the W edge of the Transjordan plateau, Nu 22:41; ment. earlier in the final stage of the Exodus, Nu 21:19 (Bamoth); Beth-bamoth on the Moabite Stone (p. 80); poss. the ancient holy places S of Mt Nebo near mod. *Kh. el-Quweiqiyeh;* Maps 9, 11. □
Banaias, see BENAIAH.
Banai-barqa, BENE-BERAK.
Bane, see BENE-BERAK.
Barabbas, 'son of Abba'; n. of a murderer released by Pilate instead of Jesus, Mt 27:16ff.
Barac, see BARAK.
Barach, see BENE-BERAK.
Barachiah, Barachias, see BERECHIAH.
Barad, see BERED.
Barak, 'lightning'; n. of a Judge, Jg 4, 5; Map 14; p. 57.
Barasa, see BOSORA.
Barbarians, Barbarous People, word of Sanscrit origin, 'stammerer'; a derogatory term for all foreigners ignorant of Gk. culture; in the Bible sometimes applied to a non-Jew or Gentile, e.g. Ac 28:2, 4 (natives), Ro 1:14.
Bar-Jesus, a magician at the court of the Roman pro-consul of Cyprus, Ac 13; Map II (e.p.). Cf. ELYMAS.
Barnabas, 'son of encouragement' (Ac 4:36); n. of a Jewish Christian; plays an important part as the companion of St Paul in the events in Ac 13–15; Map II (e.p.).
Barsabas, see BARSABBAS.
Barsabbas, cognomen of 2 persons, 1. Joseph, a candidate with Matthias for the apostleship of Judas Iscariot, Ac 1:23.
2. Judas, a Christian prophet of Jerusalem, Ac 15:22, 32.
Bartholomew, n. of one of the 12 apostles (the same person as Nathanael?), Mt 10:3 and parallels, Ac 1:13.
Bartimaeus, n. of the blind beggar of Jericho, healed by Jesus, Mk 10:46ff; Map 34.
Baruch, 'blessed'; n. of 4 persons; the most important is the friend and secretary of Jeremiah, Jer 36:4. He gave his name to a book of the APOCRYPHA, q.v.; p. 92.
Barzillai, 'man of iron'; n. of 3 persons, inc. a faithful follower of David, 2 S 17, 19.
Basan, see BASHAN.
Bascama, loc. where Jonathan was murdered, 1 Mac 13:23; poss. mod. *el-Jummeizeh,* NE of the Sea of Galilee; Map 30. □
Bascath, see BOZKATH.
Basemath, 'balm-scented'; n. of 2 persons, 1. wife of Esau, Gn 26:34.
2. daughter of Solomon, and wife of Ahimaaz, 1 K 4:15.
Bashan, a region in Transjordan, N of Gilead. Ment. in geographical texts: kingdom of Og (Nu 21:33, Dt 3:1, Jos 12:5, 13:11); attributed to the half-tribe of Manasseh (Jos 13:30, 17:1, 5, 21:6, 22:7, 1 Ch 5:23); sometimes also to Gad (1 Ch 5:11, 16); region in which lay Golan, a Levitical city and city of refuge (Dt 4:43, Jos 20:8, 1 Ch 6:71 (Heb. 56)); in Solomon's 6th district (1 K 4:13). Ment. also in poetic texts: the 'many-peaked mountain' (Ps 68:15 (Heb. 16)); region overlooking Palestine (Jer 22:20, cf. ABARIM); renowned for its great oak-trees (Is 2:13, Zec 11:2) used by the Phoenicians (Ezk 27:6); very fruitful area, like Carmel (Is 33:9, Jer 50:19, Nah 1:4); famous for its pasture lands, like Gilead (Mic 7:14); rich and fertile (Dt 32:14, Ezk 39:18, Am 4:1, Ps 22:12 (Heb. 13)). Cf. Dt 33:22; Map 12; p. 15.
Bashan-havoth-jair, see HAVVOTH-JAIR.
Bashemath, see BASEMATH (1).
Basmath, see BASEMATH (2).
Bathsheba, 'daughter of plenitude'; wife of Uriah and mother of Solomon, 2 S 11, 12; pp. 71f.
Bathuel, see BETHUEL.
Bathzacharias, see BETH-ZECHARIAH.
Bealoth, 'goddesses'; 1. loc. of Judah, in the Negeb, listed Jos 15:24; poss. identical with BAALATH-BEER, q.v., Jos 19:8.
2. loc. ment. 1 K 4:16. See ALOTH.
Beautiful (Gate that is called), a gate of the Temple of Jerusalem, Ac 3:2; Map 33 no. 5.
Bedan, n. of a Judge in Heb. text of 1 S 12:11; prob. for Barak, or may be an abb. of Abdon (2).
Beelmeon, see BETH-BAAL-MEON.
Beelphegor, see BAAL-PEOR.
Beelsephon, see BAAL-ZEPHON.
Beelzebub, see BAAL-ZEBUB.
Beer, 1. city ment. Jg 9:21; sit. unk. □
2. stopping-place of the Israelites in Moab, Nu 21:16; exact sit. unk. □
Beer-elim, city ment. Is 15:8; poss. identical with Beer (2); sit. unk. □
Beer-lahai-roi, poss. 'well of the living One who seeth me'; a well 'on the way to Shur', Gn 16:7, 14; cf. 21:19; later visited by Isaac, Gn 24:62, 25:11; sit. unk. □
Beeroth, city of Benjamin, listed Jos 18:25; cf. 2 S 4:2f; part of the Gibeonite confederation, Jos 9:17; repopulated after the Exile, Ezr 2:25, Neh 7:29; prob. identical with BEREA (1), q.v., 1 Mac 9:4; poss. mod. *el-Bîre,* N of Jerusalem; Maps 13, 14, 15, 22, 30; cf. BENE-JAAKAN. □
Beer-sheba, 'the well of the oath', or 'the well of the seven'; city of Judah, in the Negeb, listed Jos 15:28; also of Simeon, listed Jos 19:2, 1 Ch 4:28; situated in the S of the Israelite territory, cf. the expression 'from Dan to Beer-sheba': Jg 20:1, 1 S 3:20, 2 S 17:11, or 'from Beer-sheba to Dan': 1 Ch 21:2; ment. as early as Gn 21:14 and passim; mod. *Tell es-Seba',* near *Bîr es-Seba';* Maps 2, 4, 9, 11, 13, 14, 15, 17, 34; pp. 28, 80.
Beeshterah, Levitical city, Jos 21:27; identical with ASHTAROTH, q.v., 1 Ch 6:71 (Heb. 56).
Behemoth, poss. intensive plural of a Heb. word meaning 'beast', or an adaptation of the Eg. word for 'hippopotamus', Job 40:15ff.
Beirut, see BERYTUS.
Bel, 'lord', cf. BAAL; title of the principal deity in the Bab. pantheon, borne by the god Marduk, Is 46:1, Jer 50:2, 51:44, Bar 6:41, Bel 3 (Dn 14:3).
Bela, 1. city ment. Gn 14:2, 8 and there identified with Zoar, a town of the Pentapolis; cf. PENTAPOLIS (1). □
2. n. of an Edomite king, Gn 36:32f.
Belial, n. of Satan in Jewish literature, cf. 2 Co 6:15; in O.T. the expression 'son of Belial' signifies 'scoundrel', cf. 1 S 10:27 ('worthless fellows').
Beliar, Gk. form of BELIAL, q.v.
Belshazzar, n. of the last king of the Chaldaeans, Dn 5:1.
Belteshazzar, Bab. n. of Daniel, Dn 1:7, 2:26, etc.
Benadad, see BEN-HADAD.
Benaiah, 'Yahweh has given progeny'; n. of 7 persons, of whom the best-known is the son of Jehoiada, one of David's valiant warriors, 2 S 23:20ff.
Bene-berak, loc. of Dan, listed Jos 19:45; ment. by Sennacherib, p. 89; mod. *el-Kheirîyeh (Ibn-Ibrâq);* Map 11. □
Benejaacan, see BENE-JAAKAN.
Bene-jaakan, a stopping-place on the Exodus, Nu 33:31f.; Dt 10:6 has Beeroth Bene-jaakan (A.V. Beeroth of the children of Jaakan) instead of Bene-jaakan; poss. mod. *Birein;* Map 9. □
Benennom, see HINNOM (Valley of).
Ben-hadad, 'son of Hadad'; n. of 3 kings of Aram (Damascus), 1. Ben-hadad I (d. *ca* 875 B.C.), twice invaded Israel.
2. Ben-hadad II, son of the above (?), also made war on Israel, as did
3. Ben-hadad III, son of Hazael, three times defeated by Joash of Israel (*ca* 790 B.C.); Map 17.
Ben-hinnom (Valley of), see HINNOM (Valley of).
Beni-hasan, village on the Nile, near which have been found tombs of the Middle Empire with well-preserved mural paintings; Map 5; Pl. 121.
Benjamin, 'son of the right hand' (i.e. 'of good omen'), according to Gn 35:18; poss. originally 'son of the South'; n. of the youngest son of Jacob, ancestor of one of the 12 tribes, whose territory lies NE of Jerusalem and is indicated in Jos 18:11-28 (Maps 11, 13); for the rôle of this tribe, see Gn 49:27, Dt 33:12, Jg 5:14; 19-21, Ro 11:1, Ph 3:5.
Benjamin Gate, in Jerusalem, ment. Jer 37:13, 38:7, Zec 14:10; prob. one of the N gates of Nehemiah; Map 24 C.
Beon, see BETH-BAAL-MEON.
Beqa', vast valley, altitude about 3300 ft., between the Lebanon and the Anti-Lebanon; cf. Map 4; Pls. 18, 361; pp. 15, 105.
Bera, see BEER (1).
Beracah (Valley of), 'valley of blessing'; ment. 2 Ch 20:26; prob. in the Negeb between Tekoa and En-gedi, where there is still a *W. Berekût.* □
Berachah (Valley of), see BERACAH (Valley of).
Berea, 1. town ment. 1 Mac 9:4; prob. identical with BEEROTH, q.v.; Map 30. □
2. see BEROEA (1).
3. see BEROEA (2).
Berechiah, 'Yahweh has blessed'; n. of several persons, inc. the father of the Minor Prophet Zechariah, Zec 1:1; according to Mt 23:35 (Barachiah), father of the prophet Zechariah, murdered by order of Joash (text uncertain).
Bered, loc. in the S of Canaan, ment. with Kadesh in Gn 16:14 in the locating of the well BEER-LAHAI-ROI, q.v.; sit. unk. □
Berenice, n. of 1. incestuous daughter of Herod Agrippa I; St Paul defended himself before her and her brother Herod Agrippa II, Ac 25, 26.
2. daughter of Ptolemy II of Egypt, wife of Antiochus II; alluded to in Dn 11:6.
Bernice, see BERENICE.
Beroea, 1. Macedonian city, ment. Ac 17:10, 13, 20:4; mod. *Verria;* Map II (e.p.). □

Maps: 1 p. 9 / 2, 3 p. 10 / 4 p. 29 / 5, 6 p. 30 / 7, 8 p. 43 / 9, 10 p. 44 / 11, 12 p. 59 / 13 p. 60 / 14 p. 65 / 15, 16 p. 66 / 17 p. 81 / 18, 19 p. 82 / 20, 21 p. 95 / 22–24 p. 96 / 25–29 p. 103 / 30, 31 p. 104 / 32, 33 p. 115 / 34, 35 p. 116 / I II end-papers.

144

2. Hellenistic name of Aleppo, 2 Mac 13:4; cf. ALEPPO. □
Beroth, see BEEROTH and BEROTHAI.
Berotha, see BEROTHAH.
Berothah, loc. ment. Ezk 47:16; cf. BEROTHAI.
Berothai, city from which 'David took very much bronze', 2 S 8:8; poss. mod. *Bereitân,* in the Beqa', N of Damascus; Map 16; poss. identical with Berothah (ideal N frontier of the Promised Land), Ezk 47:15f. □
Bersabee, see BEER-SHEBA.
Berytus, ancient city on the Phoenician coast; one of the main centres of the Gebalites; mod. *Beirut;* Maps I (e.p.), 7, 29; pp. 102, 117.
Berzellai, see BARZILLAI.
Besecath, see BOZKATH.
Beseleel, see BEZALEL.
Besor (Brook), a stream S of Ziklag, 1 S 30:9f., 21; sit. unk. □
Bessur, see BETH-ZUR.
Betah, city ment. 2 S 8:8; so Heb. but perhaps read Tebah; cf. TIBHATH.
Bete, see BETAH.
Beten, 'green almond'; loc. of Asher, listed Jos 19:25; prob. mod. *Abtûn*; Map 11. □
Bethabara, in several MSS of Jn 1:28, in place of an unknown Bethany; on the left bank of the Jordan; cf. BETHANY (2). Map 34.
Bethacarem, Bethacharam, see BETH-HACCHEREM.
Bethanan, see ELON-BETH-HANAN.
Beth-anath, loc. of Naphtali, listed Jos 19:38; Jg 1:33; poss. mod. *Ba'neh (Bi'na)*; Maps 11, 14. □
Bethania, see BETHANY.
Beth-anoth, loc. of Judah, in the hill country, listed Jos 15:59; poss. mod. *Beit 'Anun,* N of Hebron; Maps 13, 19, p. 105 no. 7. □
Bethany, 'house of the poor', or 'house of Ananiah'; 1. village near Jerusalem, on the E slopes of the Mt of Olives, near Bethphage, Mk 11:1 = Lk 19:29; about 2 miles (15 stadia) from Jerusalem, Jn 11:18; home of Simon the leper, Mt 26:6 = Mk 14:3, and of Mary, Martha, and Lazarus, Jn 11:1, 12:1; Jesus spent a night there, Mt 21:17, Mk 11:11f.; near the scene of the Ascension, Lk 24:50; mod. *el-'Azarîyeh,* preserving the name of Lazarus; Map 34; cf. ANANIAH. □
2. loc. on the left bank of the Jordan where John the Baptist baptised, Jn 1:28 (BETHABARA, q.v., in some MSS); exact sit. unk. (the position marked on Map 34 is conjectural). □
Beth-aphra, see BETH-LE-APHRAH.
Betharaba, see BETH-ARABAH.
Beth-arabah, loc. on the boundary between Judah and Benjamin, Jos 15:6, 18:18; listed for Judah, in the wilderness, Jos. 15:61; also listed for Benjamin, Jos 18:22; prob. mod. *'Ain Gharba,* SW of Jericho; Map 11. □
Beth-aram, Betharan, see BETH-HARAM.
Beth-arbel, site of a battle, Hos 10:14; prob. in Transjordan; poss. mod. *Irbid*; Map 17. □
Beth-aven, 'house of vanity'; derogatory corruption of Bethel, 'house of God', Hos 4:15, 5:8, 10:5; cf. Am 5:5. Jos. 7:2 distinguishes between Beth-aven and Bethel, and in such texts as 1 S 13:5, 14:23, Beth-aven does not appear to be a corruption of Bethel; it may refer to a loc. near Bethel.
Beth-azmaveth, see AZMAVETH.
Bethazmoth, see BETH-AZMAVETH.
Beth-baal-meon, loc. of Reuben, listed Jos 13:17; cf. Nu 32:3 (Heb. Beon), 32:38 and 1 Ch 5:8 (Baal-meon), later Moabite according to Jer 48:23 (Beth-meon); Ezk 25:9 (Baal-meon); ment. on the Moabite Stone, cf. Pl. 229; mod. *Ma'in,* SW Medeba; Maps 11, 17; p. 80. □
Beth-bamoth, see BAMOTH-BAAL.
Beth-barah, loc. in the Jordan valley, ment. Jg 7:24; exact sit. unk. □
Bethbasi, village SE of Bethlehem, ment. 1 Mac 9:62, 64; mod. *Beit Bassa;* Maps 22, 30. □
Bethbera, see BETH-BARAH.
Bethberai, see BETH-BIRI.
Bethbessen, see BETHBASI.
Beth-birei, see BETH-BIRI.
Beth-biri, loc. of Simeon, ment. 1 Ch 4:31, replacing the Beth-lebaoth in the corresponding list of Jos 19:6; sit. unk. Cf. LEBAOTH. □
Beth-car, loc. ment. with Mizpah in the struggle against the Philistines, 1 S 7:11; sit. unk. □
Bethchar, see BETH-CAR.
Beth-dagon, 'house of Dagon'; 1. loc. of Judah, in the lowland, listed Jos 15:41; sit. unk. □
2. loc. of Asher, listed Jos 19:27; sit. unk. □
Beth-diblathaim, 'house of the fig cakes'; Moabite city, ment. Jer 48:22; in the vicinity of Medeba; ment. on the Moabite Stone, p. 80; Pl. 229.
Beth-eden, loc. in the region of Damascus, ment. Am 1:5; sit. unk., unless identical with EDEN (2), q.v. □
Beth-eked (of the Shepherds), loc. on the road from Jezreel (1) to Samaria, 2 K 10:12 ff.; exact sit. unk. □
Bethel, 1. city N of Jerusalem, best known for its connection with the story of the patriarchs and as the site of the schismatic sanctuary of Jeroboam I; mod. *Beitin;* Maps 4, 13, 14, 15, 17, 22, 30; pp. 72, 76f., 80, 90. Cf. LUZ (1).
2. in 1 S 30:27 an error for BETHUEL (2), q.v.
Bethemec, see BETH-EMEK.
Beth-emek, 'house of the plain'; loc. of Asher, listed Jos 19:27; poss. mod. *Tell Mimâs*; Map 11. □
Bether, loc. of Judah, in the hill country, listed Jos 15:59 (LXX); mod. *Bittîr,* SW of Jerusalem; Maps 11, 13, 19.
Bethesda, prob. Gk. form of Aramaic *Beth Chesda,* 'house of mercy'; name used in some MSS for the pool near the Sheep Gate in Jerusalem, Jn 5:2; Map 33; cf. BETH-ZATHA. □
Beth-ezel, loc. ment. Mic 1:11; poss. mod. *Deir el-'Asal,* SW of Hebron; Map 17. □
Beth-gader, loc. in Judah ment. 1 Ch 2:51; sit. unk. □
Beth-gamul, loc. in Moab, ment. Jer 48:23; mod. *Kh. Jumaiyil (Jumeil),* E of Dibon; Map 17. □
Beth-gilgal, village ment. Neh 12:29; poss. identical with the Gilgal of Jos 15:7; poss. near mod. *Khan es-Sahel;* Map 22. □
Beth-haccherem, city in Judah, ment. with Tekoa in Jer 6:1; later capital of a district, Neh 3:14; identical with KAREM, q.v.; mod. *'Ain Karim,* W of Jerusalem; Map 22. □
Beth-haggan, city N of Samaria, ment. 2 K 9:27; prob. identical with En-gannim; prob. mod. *Jenîn;* Map 17. □
Beth-hagla, see BETH-HOGLAH.
Beth-hanan, see ELON-BETH-HANAN.
Beth-haram, loc. of Gad, in the Jordan valley, listed Jos 13:27; called Beth-haran in the list of Nu 32:36; poss. mod. *Tell Iqtanû,* E of *Tell er-Râmeh,* which appears to preserve the ancient name. Map 11. □
Beth-haran, loc. ment. Nu 32:36, *var.* of BETH-HARAM, q.v., Jos 13:27.
Beth-haraphid, loc. ment. in the 4th Lachish letter, p. 92; sit. unk.
Beth-hogla, see BETH-HOGLAH.
Beth-hoglah, loc. of Benjamin, listed Jos 18:21; on the boundary of Benjamin, Jos 18:19, and of Judah, Jos 15:6; mod. *'Ain Hajlah,* SE of Jericho; Map 11. □
Beth-horon, city on the boundary between Ephraim and Benjamin, Jos 18:13; Levitical city, Jos 21:22; later divided into Lower Beth-horon and Upper Beth-horon; mod. *Beit 'Ûr et-Tahta* (altitude over 1300 ft.) and *Beit 'Ûr el-Fôqa* (altitude over 2000 ft.); Maps 11, 13, 14, 15, 17, 19.
Bethiesimoth, see BETH-JESHIMOTH.
Beth-jeshimoth, 'house of the steppes'; loc. on the final stage of the Exodus, Nu 33:49; in the S of the Jordan Valley, Jos 12:3, 13:20; later Moabite, Ezk 25:9; prob. mod. *Tell el-'Azeimeh,* about 12 miles SE of Jericho; Maps 11, 14. □
Beth-le-aphrah, loc. ment. in Mic 1:10, in the SW of Judah, exact sit. unk. □
Beth-lebaoth, loc. of Simeon, listed Jos 19:6; sit. unk.; prob. identical with BETH-BIRI and LEBAOTH, qq.v.
Bethlehem, 'house of bread'; name of 2 cities, 1. S of Jerusalem, city of David and of Jesus; mod. *Beit Lahm;* shown on nearly all the Maps of Palestine; Pls. 358, 359.
2. city of Zebulun, listed Jos 19:15; cf. Jg 12:8; mod. *Beit Lahm,* W of Nazareth; Maps 11, 14; pp. 112, 118, 132. □
Beth-maacah, see ARAM (3).
Bethmaon, see BETH-BAAL-MEON.
Beth-marcaboth, loc. of Simeon, listed Jos 19:5; poss. identical with the Beth-marcaboth of Simeon in 1 Ch 4:31; sit. unk., unless it is the Madmannah in the corresponding list of Jos 15:31. □
Bethmarchaboth, see BETH-MARCABOTH.
Beth-meon, see BETH-BAAL-MEON.
Beth-millo, 1. fortress near Shechem, ment. Jg 9:6, 20; exact sit. unk. Cf. MILLO (The). □
2. another loc. ment. 2 K 12:21; sit. unk. □
Bethnemra, see BETH-NIMRAH.
Beth-nimrah, 'house of leopards'; loc. of Gad, listed Jos 13:27; cf. Nu 32:36; identical with the Nimrah in Nu 32:3; poss. mod. *Tell Bileibil,* near *Tell Nimrin;* Map 11. □
Beth-palet, see BETH-PELET.
Beth-pazzez, loc. of Issachar, listed Jos 19:21; sit. unk. □
Beth-pelet, loc. of Judah, in the Negeb, listed Jos 15:27; cf. 2 S 23:26, Neh 11:26; sit. unk. □
Beth-peor, loc. of Reuben, listed Jos 13:20; near the mountain where the Baal of Peor was worshipped, cf. Nu 23:28, 25:3, 5, 18, 31:16, Jos 22:17, Hos 9:10 (Baal-peor), Ps 106:28; cf. 'the valley opposite Beth-peor', Dt 3:29, 4:46, 34:6; poss. mod. *Kh. esh-Sheikh-Jâyil,* N of Mt Nebo; Map 11. □
Bethphage, village near Jerusalem, on the slopes of the Mt of Olives, from which Jesus set out for his triumphal entry into Jerusalem, Mt 21:1, Mk 11:1, Lk 19:29; traditional site is shown on Pl. 192, no. 8. □
Bethphaleth, Beth-phelet, see BETH-PELET.
Bethpheses, see BETH-PAZZEZ.
Bethphogor, see BETH-PEOR.
Beth-rehob, Aramaean principality where the Ammonites recruited auxiliary troops to fight against David, 2 S 10:6; N limit of Canaan, Nu 13:21 (Rehob); near the source of the Jordan, Jg 18:28; prob. sit. in the S of the Beqa'; Map 16. Cf. ARAM (4).
Bethsabee, see BATHSHEBA.
Beth-saida, 1. city of Andrew, Peter, and Philip, Jn 1:44, 12:21; ment. after the miracle of the loaves and fishes, Mk 6:45, cf. Lk 9:10; a blind man is healed there, Mk 8:22; cursed by Jesus with Chorazin, Mt 11:21, Lk 10:13; according to Josephus, Beth-saida was a fishing village, which the tetrarch Philip developed into a town and named Julias, in honour of the daughter of Augustus; mod. *et-Tell* and *Kh. el 'Araj,* N of the Sea of Galilee, E of the mouth of the Jordan; Map 34; Pl. 371. □
2. name used in some MSS for the pool near the Sheep Gate in Jerusalem, Jn 5:2; cf. BETH-ZATHA.
Bethsames, Bethsemes, see BETH-SHEMESH.
Bethsan, see BETH-SHAN.
Bethsetta, see BETH-SHITTAH.
Beth-shan, powerful Canaanite city in the plain of Jezreel, Jos 17:16; in the territory of Issachar, though attributed to Manasseh, Jos 17:11, 1 Ch 7:29, but not immediately conquered, Jg 1:27, Saul's body was fastened to the wall by the Philistines, 1 S 31:10ff., 2 S 21:12; later in Solomon's 5th district, 1 K 4:12; called Scythopolis in the Hellenistic period, 2 Mac 12:29f.; in the Decapolis; mod. *Tell el-Hosn,* near the village of *Beisân* which preserves the ancient name; Maps 2, 5, 7, 11, 14, 15, 17, 30, 31, 34; Pls. 37, 193, 197; pp. 19, 20, 24, 46, 71, 105.
Beth-shean, see BETH-SHAN.
Beth-shemesh, 'house of the sun'; name of 4 cities, 1. on the N boundary of Judah, Jos 15:10; Levitical city of Judah, Jos 21:16, 1 Ch 6:59 (Heb. 44); prob. identical with Ir-shemesh, 'city of the sun', of Dan, listed Jos 19:41; first place to receive the Ark after its return by the Philistines, 1 S 6:9ff.; later in Solomon's 2nd district, 1 K 4:9; scene of the battle between Amaziah and Jehoash, 2 K 14:11ff. = 2 Ch 25:21ff.; under Ahaz, captured by the Philistines, 2 Ch 28:18; mod. *Tell er-Rumeileh;* Maps 11, 13, 15, 17, 19; p. 68. Cf. HAR-HERES. □
2. city of Naphtali, listed Jos 19:38; not immediately conquered, Jg 1:33; sit. unk., poss. identical with (3).
3. city on the boundary of Issachar, Jos 19:22; poss. mod. *el 'Ubeidiyeh,* S of the Sea of Galilee and E of *Kh. Shamsâwi,* which preserves the ancient name; Map 11. □
4. city ment. Jer 43:13 (R.S.V. HELIOPOLIS, q.v.).
Beth-shittah, loc. ment. Jg 7:22; poss. mod. *Tell Slihat;* Map 14. □
Bethsimoth, see BETH-JESHIMOTH.
Bethsur(a), see BETH-ZUR.
Beth-tappuah, 'house of the apple-tree'; loc. of Judah, in the hill country, listed Jos 15:53; mod. *Taffuh,* W of Hebron; Maps 11, 13, 19, p. 105, no. 9.
Beththaphua, see BETH-TAPPUAH.
Beth-togarmah, city or region which sold horses and mules to Tyre, Ezk 27:14; according to Ezk 38:6, sit. in the N; associated with Gomer, as in Gn 10:3 = 1 Ch 1:6 (Togarmah); ment. in Hittite texts. □
Bethuel, 1. n. of the son of Nahor, brother of Abraham; father of Rebekah and Laban, Gn 22:22, 24:15.
2. city ment. 1 Ch 4:30, identical with the Bethul of Simeon, listed Jos 19:4, and with the Chesil of Jos 15:30; prob. also identical with the Bethel of 1 S 30:27; poss. mod. *Kh. el-Qaryatein,* S of Hebron; Maps 11, 13. □
Bethul, city of Simeon, listed Jos 19:4; identical with BETHUEL (2), q.v.
Bethzacharam, Bethzacharias, see BETH-ZECHARIAH.
Beth-zatha, seems to be the original form of the name of the pool near the Sheep Gate in Jerusalem, Jn 5:2; cf. BETHESDA; Map 33. □
Bethzecha, see BEZETH.
Beth-zechariah, site of a battle, 1 Mac 6:32f.; mod. *Kh. Beit Sakaria,* SW of Jerusalem; Map 30. □
Beth-zur, city of Judah, in the hill country, listed Jos 15:58; cf. 1 Ch 2:45; rebuilt by Rehoboam, 2 Ch 11:7; centre of a district of Judah after the Exile, Neh 3:16; strategic point often ment. in 1 and 2 Mac; mod. *Kh. et-Tubeiqeh,* near *Burj es-Sûr* which preserves the ancient name; Maps 13, 17, 19, 22, 30, 31, p. 105 no. 4.
Betonim, 'green almonds'; loc. of Gad, listed Jos 13:26; mod. *Kh. Batneh;* Map 11. □
Bezaleel, see BEZALEL.
Bezalel, 'in the shadow of God'; n. of 2 persons, inc. one of the craftsmen who built the tabernacle, Ex 31:2ff.
Bezec, see BEZEK.
Bezek, city ment. 1 S 11:8; poss. identical with the Bezek in Jg 1:4f.; prob. mod. *Kh. Ibziq,* S of the mountains of Gilboa; Map 15; p. 67. □
Bezer, Levitical city of Reuben, Jos 21:36, 1 Ch 6:78 (Heb. 63); city of refuge, Dt 4:43, Jos 20:8; according to the Moabite Stone (p. 80), in the territory of Moab; poss. identical with Bozrah (2), Jer 48:24; poss. mod. *Umm el-'Amad,* NE of Medeba; Map 11. □
Bezeth, city ment. 1 Mac 7:19; mod. *Beit Zi'ta,* N of Beth-zur; Maps 30, p. 105 no. 1.
Bileam, city ment. 1 Ch 6:70 (Heb. 55), identical with IBLEAM, q.v. □
Bilhah, 1. n. of a maid of Rachel; concubine of Jacob and mother of Dan and Naphtali, Gn 30.
2. loc. in the territory of Simeon, ment. 1 Ch 4:29; prob. an error for Balah (Jos 19:3); prob. identical with BAALAH (2), q.v. □
Birzaith, according to Josephus the village where Judas pitched his last camp; mod. *Bir-Zeit,* 13 miles N of Jerusalem; Map 30; p. 110. But see ELASA.
Bithynia, region in the N of Asia Minor, Ac 16:7; Maps 26, 32, II (e.p.).
Bitter Lakes, lakes in Lower Egypt; Map 9; pp. 41, 46, 48.
Blessing (Valley of), see BERACAH (Valley of).
Boanerges, 'son of thunder'; name given by Jesus to John and James when He called them to be His disciples, Mk 3:17.
Boaz, 1. n. of the great-grandfather of David, according to the book of Ruth and the genealogy of Christ in Mt 1:5.
2. pillar at the entrance to the Temple of Solomon, 1 K 7:21. □
Bochim, 'the weepers'; loc. where the Angel of the Lord announced misfortunes for Israel, Jg 2:1, 5. In v.1 the Gk. has Bethel in place of Bochim; poss. Bochim was an occasional name for Bethel. Cf. Allon-bacuth, the 'oak of weeping' which, according to Gn 35:8, stood near Bethel. Some editors read Bochim in Mic 1:10 (conj.). □
Boen (Stone of), see BOHAN (Stone of).
Boghaz-keui, see HATTUSHASH.
Bohan (Stone of), on the boundary between Judah and Benja-

Maps: 1 p. 9 / 2, 3 p. 10 / 4 p. 29 / 5, 6 p. 30 / 7, 8 p. 43 / 9, 10 p. 44 / 11, 12 p. 59 / 13 p. 60 / 14 p. 65 / 15, 16 p. 66 / 17 p. 81 / 18, 19 p. 82 / 20, 21 p. 95 / 22–24 p. 96 / 25–29 p. 103 / 30, 31 p. 104 / 32, 33 p. 115 / 34, 35 p. 116 / I, II end-papers.

145

min, in the wilderness to the SW of Jericho, Jos 15:6, 18:17; poss. mod. *Hajar el-Asbah*; Map 13. □
Booz, see Boaz.
Borashan, 1 S 30:30. Cf. Ashan.
Boscath, see Bozkath.
Boses, see Bozez.
Bosor, city E of the Sea of Galilee, ment. 1 Mac. 5:26; mod. *Busr el-Harîri;* Map 31. □ See also Bezer.
Bosora, city E of the Sea of Galilee, ment. 1 Mac 5:26; called Bostra in the Graeco-Roman period; mod. *Busra Eski-Shâm*; Map 31. □
Bosra, see Bozrah.
Bosra(m), Jos 21:27. See Beeshterah.
Bozez, 'rocky crag' in the gorge between Geba and Michmash, 1 S 14:4; sit. in mod. *W. Suweinit*; Pls. 189, 190. □
Bozkath, city of Judah, in the lowland, listed Jos 15:39; home of the mother of Josiah, 2 K 22:1; prob. in the vicinity of Lachish, exact sit. unk. □
Bozrah, 1. important Edomite city ment. Gn 36:33 = 1 Ch 1:44; cf. Am 1:12, Jer 49:13, 22, Is 34:6, 63:1; prob. mod. *Buseira*, 25 miles SE of the Dead Sea; Map 18.
2. city in Moab ment. Jer 48:24; poss. identical with Bezer.□
Breach of Oza, see Perez-uzzah.
Brick Walls (City of), see Kir-hareseth.
Brook Besor, see Besor (Brook).
Brook of Egypt, see Egypt (Brook of).
Brook of the Arabah, see Arabah (Brook of the).
Brook of the Willows, see Willows (Brook of the).
Brook Zered, see Zered (Brook, Valley of).
Bubastis, see Pi-beseth.
Burning (Place of), see Taberah.
Buz, region ment. with Dedan and Tema, Jer 25:23; in Gn 22:21, n. of the second son of Nahor and Milcah; sit. in the Syro-Arabian desert; cf. Job 32:2. □
Byblos, Gk. name of the city of Gebal, whose inhabitants are called Gebalites in the Bible; mod. *Jebeil*; Maps 1, 3, 5, 7, 8, 25, 29; Pls. 205–208; pp. 15, 24, 64, 102, 117.

C

Cabbon, loc. of Judah, in the lowland, listed Jos 15:40; poss. mod. *Kh. Habra*, E of Lachish; Maps 13, 19. □
Cabseel, see Kabzeel.
Cabul, see Kabul.
Cademoth, see Kedemoth.
Cades, see Kadesh (1) and Kedesh (1).
Cadesbarne, see Kadesh-barnea.
Caesarea, n. of 2 cities, 1. seaport, formerly Strato's tower, S of Mt Carmel, built by Herod; an important centre of early Christianity; mod. *Keisâriyeh*; Maps 2, 32, 34, II (e.p.); Pls. 329, 330; pp. 117f.
2. Caesarea Philippi, city near the source of the Jordan; built by the tetrarch Philip, near a sanctuary of the god Pan (Paneas or Paneion); scene of St Peter's confession of faith, Mt 16:13, Mk 8:27; mod. *Bâniyas*; Maps 2, 34; Pl. 360. □
Caiaphas, n. of the High Priest in the account of Christ's Passion; son-in-law of Annas. Since the 4th cent. the 'dwelling of Caiaphas' has been traditionally situated on the hill SW of Jerusalem; Map 33.
Cain, 1. n. of the son of Adam and Eve, who murdered his brother Abel, Gn 4.
2. city of Judah; cf. Kain.
Caiphas, see Caiaphas.
Calah, city S of Nineveh, Gn 10:11f.; residence of the Assyrian kings for *ca* 150 years; the black obelisk of Shalmaneser was found here; mod. *Nimrûd*; Map 1; cf. Pl. 247.
Calano, see Calno.
Caleb, 'dog'; one of the 12 spies, Nu 13; his clan lived around Hebron and was incorporated in the tribe of Judah; p. 57.
Calneh, 1. city ment. Am 6:2, identical with Calno, q.v.
2. city ment. Gn 10:10, text prob. faulty.
Calno, city in N Syria, Is 10:9, Am 6:2 (Calneh); mod. *Kullan-Keui*, NE of Aleppo; Map 18.
Calumny, see Esek.
Calvary, from Lat. *calva*, 'skull'; Lat. name of Golgotha, q.v.
Cambyses, n. of the son and successor of Cyrus; Map 21.
Camon, see Kamon.
Cana, loc. in Galilee, not ment. in the O.T., where Jesus performed His first miracle, Jn 2:1, 11, 4:46; home of Nathanael, Jn 21:2; according to ancient tradition, the mod. *Kafr Kenna*, Pl. 363, thus shown on Maps 2, 34; more prob. *Kh. Qâna*, 9 miles N of Nazareth. □
Canaan, prob. '(land of) purple' (one of the principal exports of Canaan and Phoenicia); n. of the coastal territory of Palestine and Phoenicia. In the Bible the word sometimes designates: the Promised Land, Gn 17:8; the region W of the Jordan, Gn 13:12; Phoenicia proper, Is 23:11; the Philistine coast, Zeph 2:5. Canaan appears in Gn 10:6 as a 'son' of Ham (cf. table of the peoples), and in Gn 10:15–20 as 'father' both of the cities in the N as far as Arvad and of the territory W of the Jordan between Sidon and Gaza. Its inhabitants are the Canaanites who frequently figure as merchants (originally in purple): Zeph 1:11 (traders), Zec 14:21 (trader), Pr 31:24 (merchant), Job 41:6 (Heb. 40:30) (traders, merchants). The Bible contains various lists of the pre-Israelite peoples of Canaan: (a) list of 7 peoples, Hittites, Girgashites, Amorites, Canaanites, Perizzites, Hivites, Jebusites, Dt 7:1, Jos 3:10, 24:11. (b) list of 6 peoples, omitting Girgashites, Ex 3:8, 17, 23:23, 33:2, 34:11, Dt 20:17, Jos 9:1, 11:3, 12:8, Jg 3:5, Neh 9:8 (inc. Girgashites, but omitting Hivites). (c) list of 5 peoples, omitting Perizzites, Ex 13:5; omitting Canaanites, 1 K 9:20, 2 Ch 8:7. (d) list of 10 peoples (Gn 10:15ff.), 5 from (a) (omitting Perizzites, Canaanites) with the addition of Arkites, Sinites, Arvadites, Zemarites, Hamathites. (e) list of 10 peoples (Gn 15:19ff.), 6 from (a) (omitting Hivites) with the addition of Kenites, Kenizzites, Kadmonites, Rephaim.
Canath, see Kenath.
Candace, title of the queens of Ethiopia, used as a n., Ac 8:27.
Canneh, loc. ment. between Haran and Eden as trading with Tyre, Ezk 27:23; sit. unk. □
Canon, 'rule'; n. given to the list of books recognised as Holy Writ.
Capernaum, city on the NW shore of the Sea of Galilee, where Jesus performed many of His miracles; cf. Mt 4:13, 8:5, 11:23, Mk 2:1, Lk 4:31; mod. *Tell Hum*; Maps 2, 34, 35; Pls. 365–367; cf. caption to Pl. 371.
Caphara, see Chephirah.
Capharnaum, see Capernaum.
Capharsalama, loc. ment. 1 Mac 7:31; mod. *Kh. Selma*, NW of Jerusalem; Map 30. □
Caphira, see Chephirah.
Caphthorim, see Caphtorim.
Caphtor, island ment. Jer 47:4, Am 9:7; original home of the Philistines, Gn 10:14 = 1 Ch 1:12 (Caphtorim), Dt 2:23 (Caphtorim, Caphtor); poss. Crete.
Caphtorim, inhabitants of Caphtor, q.v.
Cappadocia, region in the centre of Asia Minor, Ac 2:9, 1 P 1:1; Maps 25, 26, 32. □
Carcaa, see Karka.
Carchemish, city in N Syria, capital of a Hittite kingdom; captured by the Assyrians, Is 10:9; cf. Jer 46:2, 2 Ch 35:20; mod. *Jerablus (Jerâbish)*; Maps 1, 4, 5, 6, 7, 8, 18, 20; p 94. □
Caria, region in the SW of Asia Minor, ment. in the list of countries and cities which received the letter of Lucius, 1 Mac 15:23; Maps 26, II (e.p.). □
Cariath, see Kiriath-jearim.
Cariathaim, see Kiriathaim.
Cariath-arbe, see Kiriath-arba.
Cariathbaal, see Kiriath-jearim.
Cariath-hesron, see Kerioth-hezron.
Cariathiarim, see Kiriath-jearim.
Cariath-senna, see Kiriath-sannah.
Cariath-sepher, see Kiriath-sepher.
Carioth, see Kerioth.
Carith, see Cherith (Brook).
Carmel, 1. loc. of Judah, in the hill country, listed Jos 15:55; cf. 1 S 15:12, 25:2ff.; ment. in the list of cities in the S of Judah, 1 S 30:29 (LXX); mod. *el-Kirmil*, S of Hebron; Maps 13, 15. □
2. mountain on the boundary of Asher, Jos 19:26; cf. Jos 12:22, Jer 46:18, 1 K 18:19f., 42, 2 K 2:25, 4:25, Is 33:9, 35:2, Jer 50:19, Am 1:2, 9:3, Nah 1:4, Ca 7:5; Maps 2, 4, 11, 14, 17; Pl. 251; pp. 16, 71.
Carnaim, city in Transjordan, 1 Mac 5:26, 43f.; called Carnion (Gk. form of the n.) in 2 Mac 12:21; mod. *Sheikh-Sa'ad*; Map 31; poss. identical with Ashteroth-karnaim, q.v. □
Carnion, see Carnaim.
Cartha, see Kartah.
Carthage, see Tarshish.
Carthan, see Kartan.
Casaloth, see Chesulloth.
Casiphia, loc. in Babylonia where the Exiles dwelt, Ezr 8:17; sit. unk. □
Casis (Vale of), see Emek-keziz.
Casphia, see Casiphia.
Casphin, see Casphor.
Casphor, loc. ment. 1 Mac 5:26, 36; poss. identical with the Caspin of 2 Mac 12:13; prob. mod. *Khisfîn*, 9 miles E of the Sea of Galilee; Map 31. □
Caspin, Caspis, see Casphor.
Cateth, see Kattath.
Cauda, small island S of Crete, ment. Ac 27:16; mod. *Gaudos* or *Gozzo*; Map II (e.p.).
Cedar, see Kedar.
Cedars of Lebanon, the Bible frequently refers to these majestic trees; Pls. 19–21.
Cedes, see Kedesh.
Cedron, see Kedron and Kidron.
Ceelatha, see Kehelathah.
Ceila, see Keilah.
Cele-Syria, Celosyria, see Coele-Syria.
Cenacle, scene of the Last Supper; identified since the 5th century A.D. with the 'upper room' of the Apostles (Ac 1:13), on the hill SW of Jerusalem; Map 33.
Cenchra, Cenchrae, Cenchre, Cenchrea, see Cenchreae.
Cenchreae, E port of Corinth, ment. Ac 18:18, cf. Ro 16:1; Map II (e.p.).
Cenereth, Ceneroth, see Chinnereth, Chinneroth.
Cenez, see Kenaz.
Cenezites, see Kenaz.
Cenneroth, see Chinnereth, Chinneroth.
Cephas, 'rock'; Aramaic n. with a Gk. termination corresponding to Petros; n. given by Jesus to Peter, Jn 1:42; cf. Mt 16:18.
Cephira, see Chephirah.
Cerethi, Cerethites, see Cherethites and Pelethites.
Cesarea, see Caesarea.
Ceseleth-Thabor, see Chisloth-tabor.
Cesil, see Chesil.
Cesion, see Kishion.
Ceteans, Cethim, see Kittim.
Cethites, see Hittites.
Cethlis, see Chitlish.
Cetron, see Kitron.
Cetthim, see Kittim.
Chabul, see Kabul.
Chalane, see Calneh (1).
Chalanne, see Calneh (2).
Chaldaeans, Aramaean tribe who settled in S Babylonia and founded an empire under Nabopolassar; Maps 18, 20; p. 97.
Chaldeans, see Chaldaeans.
Chale, see Calah.
Chali, see Hali.
Cham, see Ham.
Chamaam, see Geruth Chimham.
Chamaan, see Geruth Chimham.
Chamos, see Chemosh.
Chanaan, see Canaan.
Chanaanites, see Canaanites.
Characa, see Charax.
Charax, apparently a place-name in 2 Mac 12:17; a common term for a fortified place (Gk. = 'entrenched camp'). □
Charcamis, Charchemish, see Carchemish.
Chasidim, see Hasidaeans.
Chasphia, see Casiphia.
Chebar (River of), river of Babylonia near which the exiles lived, Ezk 3:15; scene of Ezekiel's vision, Ezk 1:1, 3, 3:23, 10:15ff., 43:3. Probably the great canal near the town of Nippur, called *Naru Kabari* in the ancient texts; p. 98.
Chebbon, see Cabbon.
Chedor-laomer, 'servant of (the goddess) Lagamar'; n. of a king of Elam pursued by Abraham, Gn 14.
Cheesemakers (Valley of the), see Tyropoeon Valley.
Cheleab, see Chileab.
Chelmad, see Chilmad.
Chemosh, n. of the principal god of the Moabites, 1 K 11:7, Nu 21:29, Jer 48:46; cf. the Moabite Stone, p. 80.
Chene, see Canneh.
Chephar-ammoni, loc. of Benjamin, listed Jos 18:24; sit, unk. □
Chephar-haammonai, see Chephar-ammoni.
Chephirah, loc. of Benjamin, listed Jos 18:26; one of the cities in the Gibeonite alliance, Jos 9:17; repopulated after the Exile, Ezr 2:25, Neh 7:29; mod. *Tell Kefîreh*, WNW of Jerusalem; Maps 13, 14, 19, 22. □
Chephirim, loc. near Ono, ment. Neh 6:2 (R.S.V. 'one of the villages'); sit. unk. □
Cherethims, see Cherethites and Pelethites.
Cherethites and Pelethites, troops of David's bodyguard, 2 S 8:18 = 1 Ch 18:17, 2 S 15:18, 20:7, 1 K 1:38, 44; the Cherethites were prob. Philistines, cf. 1 S 30:14, Zeph 2:5, Ezk 25:16. We have no equivalent for Pelethites, poss. a primitive n. which was modified to obtain the assonance; p. 71. □
Cherith (Brook), torrent flowing into the Jordan from the E, 1 K 17:3ff., near which Elijah was fed by ravens; poss. the mod. *W. Yâbis*; Map 17. □
Cherub, loc. in Babylonia, Ezr 2:59, Neh 7:61; sit. unk. □
Chesalon, loc. on the N boundary of Judah, W of Jerusalem, ment. Jos 15:10, where it is identified with Mt Jearim; mod. *Kesla*; Maps 13, 19. □
Chesil, loc. of Judah, in the lowland, listed Jos 15:30 (LXX Bethel); the corresponding n. in the territory of Simeon is Bethul in Jos 19:4, and Bethuel in 1 Ch 4:30; poss. mod. *Kh. el-Qaryatein*, S of Hebron; Map 13. Cf. Bethuel (2). □
Cheslon, see Chesalon.
Chesulloth, loc. of Issachar, listed Jos 19:18; identical with Chisloth-tabor; poss. the ruins N of *Iksâl*, which preserves the ancient name; Map 11. □
Chezib, loc. in Judah, Gn 38:5; poss. identical with Achzib (2), q.v.; Map 4. □
Chileab, n. of a son of David and Abigail, 2 S 3:3.
Chilmad, loc. ment. as trading with Tyre, Ezk 27:23; sit. unk. □
Chimham (Habitation of), see Geruth Chimham.
Chinnereth, Chinneroth, loc. of Naphtali, listed Jos 19:35; cf. Dt 3:17, Jos 11:2; centre of a region, 1 K 15:20; n. of the lake (Sea of Chinnereth), Nu 34:11, Jos 12:3, 13:27; mod. *Tell el-'Oreimeh;* Maps 11, 14, 17. Cf. Galilee (Sea of), Gennesaret. □
Chios, island W of Smyrna, ment. Ac 20:15; Map II (e.p.).
Chisloth-tabor, 'flank of Tabor'; loc. on the boundary between Zebulun and Issachar, Jos 19:12; identical with Chesulloth, q.v.; Map 11. Cf. Tabor (1). □
Chitlish, loc. of Judah, in the lowland, listed Jos 15:40; poss. mod. *Kh. el-Maqhaz*, SW of Lachish; Maps 13, 19. □
Chittim, see Kittim.
Chloe, n. of a woman of Corinth, 1 Co 1:11.
Chobar (River of), see Chebar (River of).
Chodorlahomor, see Chedor-laomer.
Chorashan, see Borashan.
Chorazin, city NW of the Sea of Galilee, cursed by Jesus, Mt 11:21 = LK 10:13; mod. *Kh. Kerâzeh*, 2 miles N of Capernaum; Map 34. □
Chorreans, see Horites.
Chun, see Cun.
Chusai, see Hushai.
Cibsaim, see Kibzaim.
Cidimoth, see Kedemoth.
Cilicia, highly fertile coastal plain in the S of Asia Minor, flanked on the N and W by the Taurus Mts (cf. Jth 2:21), and separated from Syria by the Amanus Mts; Maps 1, 4. In the O.T. called Que or Qewê (R.S.V. Kue, Vulg. Coa), the region from which Solomon purchased horses, 1 K 10:28, 2 Ch 1:16; later part of the Seleucid kingdom, 1 Mac 11:14,

Maps: 1 p. 9 / 2, 3 p. 10 / 4 p. 29 /5, 6 p. 30 / 7, 8 p. 43 / 9, 10 p. 44 / 11, 12 p. 59 / 13 p. 60 / 14 p. 65 / 15, 16 p. 66 / 17 p. 81 / 18, 19 p. 82 / 20, 21 p. 95 / 22–24 p. 96 / 25–29 p. 103 / 30, 31 p. 104 / 32, 33 p. 115 / 34, 35 p. 116 / I, II end-papers.

2 Mac 4:36, cf. Jth 1:7. The Jews of Cilicia had a synagogue in Jerusalem, Ac 6:9; some were converted to Christianity and visited by St Paul, Gal 1:21, Ac 15:23, 41; native land of St Paul, Ac 21:39, 22:3, 23:34; Maps 18, 20, 25, 26, II (e.p.); Pls. 398, 399; pp. 74, 84. □

Cilician Gates, deep gorges in the Taurus Mts; Pl. 399.

Cina, see KINAH.

Cineans, see KENITES.

Cinites, see KENITES.

Cinneroth, see CHINNERETH, CHINNEROTH.

Cis, see KISH.

Cison, Cisson, see KISHON.

City of David, that part of Jerusalem inhabited in the time of David, 2 S 5:7, 9; cf. JERUSALEM, ZION. 'Stairs of the city of David', Neh 12:37; Map 24; Pls. 191, 192.

City of Palm Trees, Palms, see PALM TREES, PALMS (City of).

City of Refuge, see REFUGE (City of).

City of Salt, Heb. *'Ir-hammelach*; loc. of Judah, in the wilderness, listed Jos 15:62; near the Dead Sea, exact sit. unk. □

Clauda, see CAUDA.

Claudia, n. of a Christian woman of Rome, 2 Ti 4:21.

Claudius, n. of a Roman emperor (A.D. 41–54), ment. Ac 11:28, 18:2; Pl. 324; p. 121.

Claudius Lysias, n. of the Roman tribune who arrested St Paul and sent him to Caesarea, Ac 21–24.

Clement, n. of a Christian of Philippi, formerly identified with Clement I, the 4th Pope, Ph 4:3.

Cleopas, n. of one of the disciples of Emmaus, Lk 24:18.

Cleopatra, n. of a daughter of Ptolemy VI Philometor; successively the wife of Alexander Balas, 1 Mac 10:57ff., Demetrius II Nicator, 1 Mac 11:12, and Antiochus VII Sidetes.

Cleophas, see CLEOPAS and CLOPAS.

Clopas, n. of the husband of one of the Marys who stood by the Cross of Jesus, Jn 19:25.

Cnidus, loc. on the SW coast of Asia Minor, ment. in the list of countries and cities which received the letter of Lucius, 1 Mac 15:23; ment. in the account of St Paul's journey to Rome, Ac 27:7; mod. *Cap Krio*; Map II (e.p.).

Coa, see QEWÊ.

Coast(s), Coastland(s), translation of a Heb. term which is also used for 'island'; rendered 'isle(s), island(s)' or 'land(s)' in some versions; applied particularly to the coast of Palestine and Phoenicia, Is 20:6, 23:2, 6; Elishah and Caphtor, Ezk 7:7, Jer 47:4; the Mediterranean islands, Is 11:11, 24:15, Jer 25:22; the coastal towns of Asia Minor, Dn 11:18; Greece and the Aegean islands, Is 40:15 and often in the foll. chapters, Ps 72:10, Ps 97:1; cf. Gn 10:5, Zeph 2:11.

Coele-Syria, originally the n. of a valley between the Lebanon and the Anti-Lebanon, later applied to all Palestine and Phoenicia; Maps 29, 31; pp. 105f.

Colossa, see COLOSSAE.

Colossae, city on the banks of the Lycus in Phrygia; the Christians there received an epistle from St Paul, written during his captivity in Rome; the ruins lie near *Khonai*; Map II (e.p.).

Colosse, see COLOSSAE.

Coos, see COS.

Corinth, Gk. city with two harbours, ment. Ac 18:1ff., 19:1, 1 and 2 Co, 2 Ti 4:20; Maps 32, II (e.p.); Pl. 402. □

Corinthian Gate, gate of Jerusalem, prob. identical with the Beautiful Gate; Map 33 no. 5.

Cornelius, n. of a Roman centurion of the Italian Cohort at Caesarea; the first Gentile to be converted to Christianity, Ac 10; Map 34.

Corner Gate, gate of Jerusalem, 2 K 14:13 = 2 Ch 25:23, 2 Ch 26:9, cf. Jer 31:38, Zec 14:10; prob. identical with the VALLEY GATE, q.v.; Map 24c. □

Corozain, see CHORAZIN.

Corruption (Mount of), see OFFENCE (Mount of).

Cos, island SW of Caria, ment. 1 Mac 15:23, Ac 21:1; Map II (e.p.). □

Court of the Gentiles, court of the Temple of Jerusalem; Map 33 no. 8.

Crescens, n. of a fellow-worker of St Paul, ment. 2 Ti 4:10.

Crete, island in the Mediterranean, prob. the CAPHTOR (q.v.) in the story of Demetrius, 1 Mac 10:67; ment. in the journeys of St Paul, Ac 27:7, 12f., 21; later the residence of Titus, Tit 1:5; Map II (e.p.). □

Crispus, n. of the ruler of the synagogue at Corinth who was converted with all his household, Ac 18:8.

Crusaders, those who took part in the Crusades, expeditions which sought to stem the Moslem advance towards the W, and to safeguard the Christian communities living at or near the Holy Places. Seven Crusades were undertaken between A.D. 1095 and 1270; a short-lived Christian kingdom was founded in Jerusalem; Pls. 43–51.

Cun, city from which David obtained copper, 1 Ch 18:8; mod. *Râs Ba'albek*; Map 16. □

Cush, Biblical n. of ETHIOPIA, q.v.

Cuth(a), see CUTHAH.

Cuthah, city in Mesopotamia whose inhabitants were sent to repopulate Samaria, 2 K 17:24, 30 (Cuth); poss. mod. *Tell Ibrahîm*, N of Babylon; Map 1. □

Cyprus, island in the Mediterranean (R.S.V. Is 23:1, 12, Ezk 27:6, Jer 2:10; see KITTIM); doubtless the O.T. ELISHAH (q.v.); apple of discord between the Ptolemies and the Seleucids, 2 Mac 10:13; cf. 1 Mac 15:23, 2 Mac 4:29, 12:2. In the N.T. ment. only in Acts: 4:36, 11:20, 13:4ff. (cf. 11:19), 15:39, 21:3, 16, 27:4; Maps 1, 5, 6, 7, 18, 25, 26, 32, I and II (e.p.). □

Cyrene, Gk. colony in N Africa, ment. 1 Mac 15:23, 2 Mac 2:23, Ac 2:10, 6:9, 11:20, 13:1, Mt 27:32 and parallel passages; the small mod. town of *Cirene* stands near the huge necropolis of the ancient city; Maps 21, 32. See also KIR (1). □

Cyrenius, Cyrinus, see QUIRINIUS.

Cyrus, n. of the founder of the Persian empire; he allowed the Jews to return to Palestine from their Exile in Babylon, Is 44, 45, cf. 2 Ch 36:22f., Ezr 1:1ff., 4:3ff., Dn 1:21, 10:1; cf. DARIUS (2); Map 21; p. 100.

D

Dabareh, see DABERATH.

Dabbasheth, see DABBESHETH.

Dabbesheth, 'hump'; loc. of Zebulun, listed Jos 19:11; poss. mod. *Tell esh-Shammâm*, E of Jokneam; Map 11. □

Daberath, loc. on the boundary of Zebulun, Jos 19:13; Levitical city of Issachar, Jos 21:28, 1 Ch 6:72 (Heb. 57); prob. the ruins near the mod. village of *Dabûriyeh*, at the foot of Mt Tabor; Map 11. Cf. RABBITH. □

Dabereth, see DABERATH.

Dabir, see DEBIR (1), (3).

Dadan, see DEDAN.

Dagon, Mesopotamian god of the weather, also worshipped by the Philistines. Cf. BETH-DAGON.

Dalmanutha (District of), region to which Jesus went after the second miracle of the loaves and fishes, Mk 8:10; called the 'region of Magadan' in the parallel passage of Mt 15:39, and 'Magdala' in the Textus Receptus. □

Dalmatia, district on the W Balkan coast where Titus preached, 2 Ti 4:10; Maps 32, II (e.p.). □

Damaris, n. of an Athenian woman converted by St Paul, Ac 17:34.

Damascus, ancient settlement at the foot of Mt Hermon and the Anti-Lebanon, on the edge of the Syro-Arabian desert; important centre of trade in the Hyksos period; became capital of an Aramaean state *ca* 1200 B.C. (cf. ARAM (1)); frequently ment. in 1 and 2 Kings and by the prophets; city of the Decapolis; ment. in Ac 9 in connection with St Paul's conversion; mod. *esh-Shâm*; Maps 1, 4, 7, 8, 17, 18, 20, 29, 35, I and II (e.p.); Pls. 387-390; p. 117.

Damna, see DIMNAH.

Dan, 1. son of Jacob and Bilhah, Gn 30:6; ancestor of a tribe whose territory is indicated in Jos 19:40ff.; cf. Maps 11, 13. This tribe migrated from the S to the N of Palestine and captured Laish, near the source of the Jordan, Jg 18; these events are apparently alluded to in Gn 49:17 and Dt 33:22.
2. the city formerly called LAISH (q.v.), renamed Dan by the Danites; the most northerly city of Israel, cf. the expression 'from Dan to Beer-sheba', Jg 20:1, etc.; cf. BEER-SHEBA; mod. *Tell el-Qâdi;* Maps 2, 4, 14, 15, 17; Pl. 360; pp. 76f., 80. Cf. VEDAN.

Dan (Camp of), see MAHANEH-DAN.

Daniel, 'God is judge'; n. of several persons, in particular 1. an ancient sage, Ezk 28:3; ment. with Noah and Job, Ezk 14:14, 20; prob. the Danel ment. in the texts from Râs Shamra.
2. the principal figure in the Biblical book which bears his name; cf. p. 102.

Danna, see DANNAH.

Dannah, loc. of Judah, in the hill country, listed Jos 15:49; sit. unk. □

Daphca, see DOPHKAH.

Daphne, loc. near Antioch (1), 2 Mac 4:33, famous for its holy grove and temple of Apollo, and for its pleasure gardens; mod. *Beit el-Mâ*, 5 miles SSW of *Antakya*. □

Darius, 1. n. of 3 Persian kings; the most important was Darius I Hystaspis (521–486 B.C.) who organised his kingdom into 20 Satrapies, cf. Map 23, Pls. 265–266; he authorised the reconstruction of the Temple of Jerusalem, Ezr 4–6, cf. Hag 1:1, 2:10, Zec 1:1, 7:1. Darius the Persian, ment. Neh 12:22, is poss. Darius II (423–405 B.C.).
2. Darius the Mede, whom the author of Daniel places between Belshazzar and Cyrus the Persian (Dn 5:31 (Heb. 6:1), 9:1, 11:1), bears some resemblance to Darius I.

Dathan, n. of a son of Eliab, a Reubenite; with his brother Abiram he aspired to the priesthood and was punished, Nu 16.

Dathema, fortress in Gilead where the Jews took refuge, 1 Mac 5:9; poss. mod. *Tell Hamad*; Map 31. □

Datheman, see DATHEMA.

David, 2nd king of Israel (*ca* 1010–970 B.C.) and real founder of the kingdom. The Messiah is the 'Son of David'. Maps 17, 18; pp. 64ff.

David (City of), see CITY OF DAVID.

Dead Sea, also called Salt Sea, Sea of the Arabah, Sea of the Plain, Eastern Sea, Asphalt Lake; 53 miles long, 10 miles across at the widest point, reaches a depth of 1311 ft; 1290 ft below the level of the Mediterranean; mod. *Bahr Lût* (Sea of Lot); shown on nearly all the Maps; Pls. 28, 160, 347f.; p. 16.

Debara, see DEBIR (2).

Debbaseth, see DABBESHETH.

Debbora, see DEBORAH.

Debir, 1. Canaanite royal city, ment. Jos 10:38f., 12:13; inhabited by the Anakim, Jos 11:21; called Kiriath-sepher in Jos 15:15f., Jg 1:11f., and listed as Kiriath-sannah in the territory of Judah, in the hill country, Jos 15:49; Levitical city, Jos 21:15, 1 Ch 6:58 (Heb. 43); poss. mod. *Tell Beit Mirsim*, 12½ miles WSW of Hebron; Maps 13, 14, 19; p. 57. □
2. loc. on the N boundary of Judah, SW of Jericho, Jos 15:7; exact sit. unk. □
3. see LIDEBIR.
4. n. of a king of Eglon defeated by Joshua, Jos 10:3.
5. n. of the Holy of Holies in the Temple, 1 K 6 (R.S.V. 'the inner sanctuary'); Pls. 199, 200.

Deblatha, see RIBLAH.

Deblathaim, see BETH-DIBLATHAIM.

Deborah, 1. n. of a nurse of Rebekah, Gn 35:8.
2. n. of a prophetess who incited Barak to fight against Jabin. The famous 'Song of Deborah', Jg 5, is attributed to her and Barak. Map 14; p. 57.

Decalogue, Gk. n. for the 10 Commandments (Words), Ex 20; Heb. *'aseret haddebarim*, Ex 34:28; cf. Dt 5:6–21.

Decapolis, federation of 10 Hel. cities, all except Scythopolis in Transjordan, arising from Pompey's reorganisations; cf. p. 113. Inhabitants of these cities came to hear Jesus, Mt 4:25, cf. Mk 5:20, 7:31. Maps 34, 35.
1. Scythopolis, see BETH-SHAN.
2. PELLA, q.v.
3. GADARA, q.v.
4. Dion, prob. mod. *Tell el-Ash'ari*; Map 35.
5. Hippos, mod. *Qala'at el-Hosn*, on the slopes above the E shore of the Sea of Galilee; Map 34; Pl. 370.
6. Philadelphia, see RABBAH.
7. GERASA, q.v.
8. Kanata, see KENATH.
9. DAMASCUS, q.v.
10. Abila, mod. *Tell Abil*, S of the Yarmuk valley; Map 34.

Dedan, district or boundary of Edom, Jer 49:8, Ezk 25:13; ment. as trading with Tyre, Ezk 27:15, 20, cf. 38:13; listed before Tema and Buz, Jer 25:23; listed with Sheba among the regions and peoples of Arabia, Gn 10:7, 25:3 = 1 Ch 1:9, 32; prob. the oasis of *el-'Ula ('Ela)*, in N Arabia, SE of the Sinai peninsula; Map 18. □

Delean, see DILEAN.

Delos, island in the Aegean; ment. among the countries and cities which received the letter of Lucius, 1 Mac 15:23; Map 26. □

Delus, see DELOS.

Demas, n. of a Roman Christian and fellow-worker of St Paul, Philem 24.

Demetrius, n. of 4 persons, 1. Demetrius I Soter, king of Syria (162–150 B.C.); appointed Alcimus High Priest, 1 Mac 7:5ff.
2. Demetrius II Nicator, king of Syria (145–138 B.C. and 129–125 B.C.), son of (1); under his government Judah was almost independent, 1 Mac 10–14; Map 30.
3. a silversmith of Ephesus, Ac 19:24ff.
4. a Christian, 3 Jn 12.

Derbe, city of Lycaonia in Asia Minor, Ac 14:6, 20, 16:1, 20:4; prob. the ruins near mod. *Zosta*; Map II (e.p.). □

Desert Sea, see DEAD SEA.

Desert (Sea of the), see DEAD SEA.

Desert (Torrent of the), see ARABAH (Brook of the).

Dessau, see LESSAU.

Deutero-canonical, term designating those books of the Scriptures whose canonicity has been questioned. In the O.T.: Tobit, Judith, The Wisdom of Solomon, Ecclesiasticus, 1 and 2 Maccabees, Baruch and a few passages from Esther and Daniel. In the N.T.: Hebrews, James, 2 Peter, 2 and 3 John, Jude, Revelation, and a few short passages from other books.

Deutero-Isaiah, 'the second Isaiah'; n. used for the unknown author of the 'book of the consolation of Israel' (Is 40–55); he lived at the time of the Exile; p. 100.

Deuteronomy, 'the second law'; 5th book of the Pentateuch.

Diana, see ARTEMIS.

Diaspora, 'dispersion'; n. used for the Jewish communities who settled outside Palestine from the time of the Exile onwards.

Diblah, Diblath, see RIBLAH.

Dibon, 1. loc. in Transjordan; rebuilt by Gad, Nu 32:34, whence the form Dibon-gad, Nu 33:45f.; allotted to Reuben, listed Jos 13:17; later reconquered by Moab, Jer 48:18, 22; ment. on the Moabite Stone which was found at *Dibân*, cf. p. 80; mod. *Dibân;* Maps 9, 11, 17.
2. loc. ment. Neh 11:25, an error for DIMONAH, Jos 15:22. □
3. see DIMON.

Dibon-gad, see DIBON (1).

Didymus, 'twin'; cognomen of the Apostle Thomas, Jn 11:16.

Dilean, loc. of Judah, in the lowland, listed Jos 15:38; poss. mod. *Tell en-Najileh;* Map 13. □

Dimnah, see RIMMON (2).

Dimon, loc. in Moab, ment. Is 15:9 (R.S.V. Dibon); poss. identical with Madmen, Jer 48:2. See MADMEN. □

Dimonah, loc. of Judah, in the Negeb, listed Jos 15:22; sit. unk. Cf. DIBON (2). □

Dina, see DINAH.

Dinah, n. of the daughter of Jacob, Gn 30:21.

Dion, see DECAPOLIS.

Diotrephes, n. of a church leader censured in 3 Jn 9f.

Di-zahab, loc. in Moab, Dt 1:1; sit. unk. □

Doch, see DOK.

Doeg, n. of an Edomite who was 'chief of Saul's herdsmen' (bodyguard), 1 S 21, 22.

Dok, fortress near Jericho, 1 Mac 16:15; the spring at the foot of the hill is still called *'Ain Duq;* Map 30; Pls. 309, 310; p. 110.

Dominus flevit, 'the Lord wept'; loc. on the Mt of Olives, since the 14th century the traditional scene of Lk 19:41. Cf. Map 33, Pls. 191, 192 no 7, 326.

Dommim (Borders of, Region of), see EPHES-DAMMIM.

Dophkah, stopping-place on the Exodus, before Sinai, Nu 33:12f.; poss. mod. *Serâbit el-Khâdim*, a mining centre in the Sinai peninsula; Map 9. □

Maps: 1 p. 9 / 2, 3 p. 10 / 4 p. 29 / 5, 6 p. 30 / 7, 8 p. 43 / 9, 10 p. 44 / 11, 12 p. 59 / 13 p. 60 / 14 p. 65 / 15, 16 p. 66 / 17 p. 81 / 18, 19 p. 82 / 20, 21 p. 95 / 22 24 p. 96 / 25–29 p. 103 / 30, 31 p. 104 / 32, 33 p. 115 / 34, 35 p. 116 / I, II end-papers.

147

Dor, city on the Mediterranean coast; Canaanite royal city which gave its name to the surrounding region, Jos 11:2 (Naphoth-dor), 12:23 (Naphath-dor); in the territory of Asher, but attributed to Manasseh, Jos 17:11, Jg 1:27, 1 Ch 7:29; later in Solomon's 4th district, 1 K 4:11 (Naphath-dor); called Dora in the Gk. period, 1 Mac 15:11, 13, 25; mod. *el-Burj*, N of *Tantûrah;* Maps 11, 14, 17, 23, 29, 30, 31. □

Dora, see DOR.

Dorcas, Gk. form of TABITHA, q.v.

Dothain, see DOTHAN.

Dothan, city N of Samaria, ment. Gn 37:17, 2 K 6:13; mod. *Tell Dotan;* Maps 4, 17. □

Double Cave, see MACHPELAH.

Dragon Fountain, Dragon Well, see JACKAL'S WELL.

Drusilla, n. of the youngest daughter of Herod Agrippa I; wife of the king of Emesa and later of the Roman governor Felix, Ac 24:24.

Dumah, loc. of Judah, in the hill country, listed Jos 15:52; mod. *ed-Dômeh*, SW of Hebron; Map 13. □

Dung Gate, gate of Jerusalem, Neh 2:13, 3:13f., 12:31; localised by H. Vincent on the SW side of the city; Map 24C. See ESSENES (Gate of the). □

Dunghill (Gate of the), Dung Port, see DUNG GATE.

Dura, plain in the province of Babylon, Dn 3:1. □

Dura-Europos, city on the Euphrates; founded in the Seleucid period; mod. *Nahiye es-Salihye;* Map 1; Pl. 4.

Dur Sharrukîn, 'fortress of the true king' (Sargon); built during the years 713–707 B.C. by Sargon II; mod. *Khorsabad*, NE of Nineveh; well-known on account of the excavations of Botta in 1843; Maps 1, 18; Pl. 249.

E

Earthen Gate, see POTSHERD GATE.

Eastern Sea, ment. Ezk 47:18, Jl 2:20, Zec 14:8. Cf. DEAD SEA.

East Gate, gate on the E side of Jerusalem, Neh 3:29, cf. Ezk 40:6; poss. corresponded to the present Golden Gate; Map 24C.

East Sea, see EASTERN SEA.

Ebal, 1. n. of an Edomite, Gn 36:23, 1 Ch 1:40.
2. n. of a tribe of S Arabia according to 1 Ch 1:22; called Obal in the list of Gn 10:28.
3. n. of a mountain facing Mt Gerizim, Dt 11:29, 27:4 (where the Samaritan Pentateuch has Gerizim instead of Ebal), 13, Jos 8:30, 33; mod. *J. Eslâmiyeh* (2950 ft.), N of Shechem; Maps 2, 14; Pls. 95, 96, 100, 101; p. 51. □

Ebed-melech, n. of an Ethiopian eunuch in the service of Zedekiah; he saved Jeremiah's life, Jer 38, 39.

Ebenezer, 1. 'stone of help'; loc. ment. 1 S 4:1, 5:1; sit. unk., but near Aphek (1); prob. to be distinguished from
2. a stone set up by Samuel and called Ebenezer, 1 S 7:12; sit. unk. □

Eber, n. of the 3rd patriarch after Shem, Gn 11:14ff., cf. 10:21 where Shem is described as the father of all the children of Eber; in Gn 10:25ff. Eber is linked with the tribes of Arabia. Later Eber recurs as a n., Neh 12:20.

Ebez, loc. of Issachar, listed Jos 19:20; sit. unk. □

Ebron, loc. of Asher, listed Jos 19:28 in error for ABDON, q.v.

Ebronah, see ABRONAH.

Ecbatana, 'the capital which is in the province of Media', Ezr 6:2, 2 Mac 9:3, Jth 1:1, To 3:7, etc.; capital from *ca* 700 B.C.; name derives from Pers. *Hagmatan* which became in Gk. *Agbatana* and *Ecbatana* and is preserved in the mod. *Hamadân;* Maps 18, 20, 21, 25, I (e.p.); p. 100. Cf. ACHMETHA.

Edar (Tower of), see EDER (Tower of).

Edema, see ADAMAH.

Eden, 1. n. of the region of the earthly paradise, Gn 2:8, 10, 4:16; usually called 'the garden of Eden', Gn 2:15, 3:23f., or 'Eden', Is 51:3, cf. Ezk 28:13, 31:9, 16, 18, 36:35, Jl 2:3. The geographical indications in Gn 2:10ff. do not permit of identification. □
2. n. of a region conquered by the Assyrians together with Gozan, Haran and Rezeph, 2 K 19:12 = Is 37:12; ment. as trading with Tyre, Ezk 27:23; called *Bit-Adini* in the Ass. texts; to be sought somewhere along the middle course of the Euphrates; Map 18. Cf. BETH-EDEN and TEL-ASSAR.

Eder, 'irrigated place'; loc. of Judah, in the Negeb, listed Jos 15:21; poss. identical with Arad, Nu 21:1; poss. mod. *Tell 'Arad;* Map 13. □

Eder (Tower of), 'tower of the flock'; loc. ment. Gn 35:21; sit. unk. In Mic 4:8 'tower of the flock' means Jerusalem. □

Edfu, Eg. town famous for its temple of the Ptolemaic period; Pls. 289–295.

Edissa, see HADASSAH.

Edom, Edomites, n. of a people who settled S of the Dead Sea *ca* 1300 B.C.; regarded by Israel as kinsfolk (Esau, the ancestor of the Edomites, was the brother of Jacob, Gn 25:25ff., 36:1); from the time of David and Solomon frequently at war with Israel for possession of the Arabah, which gave access to the gulf of Elath and the neighbouring mines; after 586 B.C., prob. under pressure from the Nabataeans, Edom occupied a great part of Judah, Ezk 25:12ff., Ps 137:7, La 4:21; this region of S Judah was later called Idumaea; cf. N.B. under ARAM; Maps 7, 17, 18, 23, 30, 34; pp. 64, 71, 74, 87.

Edrai, see EDREI (1), (2).

Edrei, n. of 2 cities, 1. residence of Og, king of Bashan, Jos 12:4, 13:12, 31 (with Ashtaroth) and scene of Israel's battles against him, Nu 21:33, Dt 1:4, 3:1; ment. with Salecah as a frontier of Bashan, Dt 3:10; mod. *Der'a;* Map 12. □
2. loc. of Naphtali, listed Jos 19:37; poss. mod. *Tell Khureibeh*, S of Kedesh (1); Map 11. □

Eglaim, loc. ment. Is 15:8; in Moab, exact sit. unk. □

Eglon, 1. Canaanite royal city, Jos 10:3ff., 12:12; later in the territory of Judah, in the lowland, listed Jos 15:39; sit. unk. □
2. n. of a Moabite king in the story of the Judge Ehud, Jg 3:12ff.

Egypt, Heb. *Mizraim*, mod. *Misr;* for a description of this land on the Nile, see p. 11; for the division of Eg. history into 30 dynasties, see p. 40. The Middle Kingdom (11th–12th dynasties, *ca* 2050–1780 B.C.) was followed by the intermediate period, which includes the period of the Hyksos. Under the New Kingdom (17th–24th dynasties, *ca* 1610–715 B.C.) Egypt at times controlled the coastal territory of Canaan as far as the Euphrates, but the first Pharaoh ment. by name in the Bible, Shishak (cf. SHESHONQ) (22nd dynasty) already belongs to the period of Egypt's decline. The other Pharaohs named in the Bible belong to the so-called final period (25th–30th dynasties, 715–332 B.C.). See also HAM.

Egypt (Brook of), torrent forming the ideal SW frontier of Israel, Nu 34:5, Jos 15:4, 47, 1 K 8:65 = 2 Ch 7:8, 2 K 24:7, Is 27:12, Ezk 47:19, 48:28; prob. the mod. *W. el-'Arîsh*, S of Gaza; Maps 9, 12. □

Egypt (River, Stream, Torrent of), see EGYPT (Brook of).

Ehud, n. of a Judge; he liberated Israel from Eglon, king of Moab, Jg 3.

Ekron, loc. of Judah, in the lowland, listed Jos 15:45, cf. Jg 1:18; ment. in the indication of the N boundary of Judah, Jos 15:11; on the boundary of Dan, Jos 19:43; Philistine city, 1 S 5:10, 17:52; city of Baal-zebub, 2 K 1:2 ff.; city of the PENTAPOLIS (2), q.v.; given to Jonathan by Alexander Balas, 1 Mac 10:89; ment. on the prism of Sennacherib, p. 89; prob. mod. *'Âqir;* Maps 13, 14, 15, 17, 19, 30.

Ela, see ELAH.

Elah, n. of 6 persons, in particular of the 4th king of the kingdom of Israel (886–885 B.C.), assassinated with all his family by Zimri, 1 K 16.

Elah (Valley of), 'valley of the terebinth'; valley SW of Jerusalem where David fought Goliath, 1 S 17:2, 21:9 (Heb. 10); the mod. *W. es-Sant;* Pl. 179.

Elam, 1. city W of Beth-zur, ment. Neh 7:34, Ezr 2:31; prob. mod. *Kh. Beit-'Alam;* Map 22. □
2. n. of the hill country E of Babylon, with Susa as its capital; in the table of the peoples the name appears among the descendants of Shem, Gn 10:22 = 1 Ch 1:17; kingdom of Chedor-laomer, Gn 14:1ff.; often ment. by the prophets, Is 21:2, 22:6, Jer 25:25, 49:34–39, Ezk 32:24; called Elymais in the Hel. period; there were Jewish inhabitants, Is 11:11, To 2:10; cf. also 1 Mac 6:1, Ac 2:9; Maps 1, 5, 8, 18, 26; p. 97. □

El-Amarna, see AMARNA.

Elasa, according to 1 Mac 9:5 the place of Judas' last camp; identification uncertain, but see BIRZAITH.

Elath, Eloth, loc. ment. with Ezion-geber (cf. Dt 2:8) as the starting-point of Solomon's expedition to Ophir, 1 K 9:26ff. (Eloth), 2 Ch 8:17f. (Eloth); lost under Joram, but recaptured by Azariah, 2 K 14:22, 2 Ch 26:2 (Eloth); again conquered by the Edomites in the reign of Ahaz, 2 K 16:6; called Aila in the Roman period; prob. the ruins WNW of *'Aqaba;* Maps 9, 18, I (e.p.). Cf. 'AQABA, EZION-GEBER, EL-PARAN.

Elcana, see ELKANAH.

Eldad, 'God has loved'; n. of one of the 70 elders chosen by Moses, Nu 11:26.

Eleale, see ELEALEH.

Elealeh, city in Transjordan built by the Reubenites, Nu 32:3, 37; later Moabite, Is 15:4, 16:9, Jer 48:34; always ment. with Heshbon; mod. *el-'Âl*, N of Heshbon; Map 17. □

Eleasa, see ELASA.

Eleazar, 'God helps'; n. of 11 persons, inc. 1. 3rd son of Aaron, Lv 10:16.
2. brother of Judas Maccabaeus, 1 Mac 2:4f.; killed near Beth-zechariah, 1 Mac 6:43ff.; Map 30.
3. a fearless martyr in the time of Antiochus IV Epiphanes, 2 Mac 6.

Elehanan, see ELHANAN.

Eleph, see HA-ELEPH.

Elephantine, island in the Nile near *Assuân;* famous for the papyri found there; Pls. 261–264; p. 100.

Eleutherus, river in Syria, ment. 1 Mac 11:7, 12:30; prob. mod. *Nahr el-Kebir*, 19 miles N of Tripolis; Map 29.

El-Faiyûm, n. of the large oasis SW of the Nile Delta, famous for the papyri discovered there; Map 5.

Elhanan, 'God is merciful'; n. of two brave warriors, 2 S 21:19, 23:24.

Eli, n. of 2 persons, in particular of a priest of Shiloh, the teacher of Samuel and last of the Judges, 1 S 1–4.

Eliab, 'God is father'; n. of 6 persons, inc. the eldest brother of David, 1 S 16:6.

Eliachim, see ELIAKIM (3).

Eliacim, see ELIAKIM (1), (2) and JEHOIAKIM.

Eliakim, 'God will lift up'; n. of 5 persons, inc. 1. master of the royal household under Hezekiah of Judah, 2 K 18:18.
2. son of Josiah, placed on the throne of Judah by the Pharaoh Necho and re-named JEHOIAKIM, q.v., 2 K 23:34; p. 97.
3. priest ment. Neh 12:41.

Elias, see ELIJAH.

Eliashib, 'may God cause to return'; n. of several persons, inc. a High Priest in the time of Nehemiah, Ezr 10:6; his house is ment. in Neh 3:20; Map 24C.

Eliasib, see ELIASHIB.

Eliezer, 'God is support'; n. of 10 persons, inc. 1. servant of Abraham, Gn 15:2.
2. son of Moses and Zipporah, Ex 18:4.
3. prophet in the reign of Jehoshaphat of Judah, 2 Ch 20:37.

Elihu, n. of 5 persons, in particular of the young man who acted as an arbiter between Job and his 3 friends, Job 32–37.

Elijah, 'God is Yahweh'; n. of 2 persons, in particular the prophet of the time of Ahab of Israel, 1 K 17ff.; carried up into Heaven, according to 2 K 2:11; to return again before the coming of the Messiah, Mal 4:5 (Heb. 3:23); cf. Mt 11:10; Map 17; Pls. 153, 251; pp. 31, 77, 80, 92, 98.

Elim, stopping-place on the Exodus, Ex 15:27, 16:1, Nu 33:9f.; poss. mod. *W. Gharandel;* Map 9. □

Elimelech, 'God is king'; n. of the father-in-law of Ruth, Ru 1:2ff.

Eliphaz, n. of 2 persons, 1. eldest son of Esau, Gn 36:15.
2. one of the 3 friends of Job; a native of Teman in Edom, Job 2:11, etc.

Elisa, see ELISHAH.

Elisabeth, see ELISHEBA and ELIZABETH.

Eliseus, G&L form of ELISHA, q.v.

Elisha, 'God is salvation'; n. of a prophet of the N Kingdom; he was a disciple of Elijah and wrought many miracles, 1 K 19:16–2 K 13:20; cf. Lk 4:27; Map 17; pp. 80, 87, 90, 92, 98.

Elisha (Spring of), see 2 K 2:19ff.; mod. *'Ain es-Sultân*, at the foot of the ancient site of Jericho; Pl. 38.

Elishah, region trading with Tyre, Ezk 27:7; inc. among the sons of Javan in the table of the peoples, Gn 10:4 = 1 Ch 1:7; usually identified as the island of CYPRUS, q.v. □

Elisheba, 'God is perfection'; n. of the wife of Aaron, Ex 6:23.

Eliu, see ELIHU.

Elizabeth, Gk. form of Elisheba; n. of the mother of John the Baptist, a kinswoman of the Virgin Mary, Lk 1:36ff.

Elkanah, 'God has created'; n. of 10 persons, inc. the father of Samuel, 1 S 1.

Elkosh, city where the prophet Nahum was born, Nah 1:1; sit. unk., prob. in Judah. □

Ellasar, city (or kingdom) of Arioch, one of the 4 kings of Gn 14 (14:1, 9; Vulg. *Pontus*); often identified as the ancient city of Larsa in S Mesopotamia, but more probably the city of *Ilanzura*, between Carchemish and Haran, ment. in the texts from Mari.

Elmelech, see ALLAMMELECH.

Elon, 'oak'; 1. n. of 2 persons, in particular one of the minor Judges, Jg 12:11f.
2. loc. of Dan, listed Jos 19:43; sit. unk. □
3. loc. ment. 1 K 4:9 in error for AIJALON (1), q.v. (R.S.V. combines with following name, Elon-beth-hanan). □

Elon-beth-hanan, city in Solomon's 2nd district, 1 K 4:9; poss. mod. *Beit 'Anan*, 12 miles NW of Jerusalem; Map 17. Cf. ELON (3). □

Eloth, see ELATH.

El-paran, loc. 'on the border of the wilderness', according to Gn 14:6; prob. the ancient n. of ELATH, q.v. □

Eltecon, see ELTEKON.

Elteke, see ELTEKEH.

Eltekeh, 'meeting-place'; loc. of Dan, listed Jos 19:44; Levitical city, Jos 21:23 (Elteke); ment. with Timnah on the prism of Sennacherib, p. 89; poss. mod. *Kh. el-Muqanna';* Maps 11, 13, 19. □

Eltekon, loc. of Judah, in the hill country, listed Jos 15:59; poss. mod. *Kh. ed-Deir*, W of Bethlehem; Maps 13, 19. □

Elthece, Eltheco, see ELTEKEH.

Eltholad, see ELTOLAD.

Eltolad, loc. of Judah, in the Negeb, listed Jos 15:30; inc. among the cities of Simeon, Jos 19:4; called Tolad in the parallel list of 1 Ch 4:29; sit. uncertain; Map 11. □

Elymais, n. of the region of Elam in the Hel. period; Map 26. Cf. ELAM (2).

Elymas, meaning uncertain; cognomen of the magician of Cyprus, BAR-JESUS, q.v.

Emath, 1. see HAMATH.
2. see HAMMATH.

Emath (Approaches of, Entering into), see LEBO-HAMATH.

Emath Suba, see HAMATH-ZOBAH.

Emek-keziz, loc. of Benjamin, listed Jos 18:21; sit. unk. □

Emer, see IMMER.

Emesa, Hel. city on the Orontes; mod. *Homs;* Maps 29, 32.

Emim, Emims, n. of inhabitants of Moab, Dt 2:10, cf. Gn 14:5; Map 4.

Emmanuel, see IMMANUEL.

Emmaus, loc. on the W edge of the hill country of Judah; ment. several times in Maccabees, 1 Mac 3:40, 57, 4:3, 9:50; mod. *Amwâs*, 19 miles WNW of Jerusalem; Maps 30, 31. The Emmaus of Lk 24 may have been nearer Jerusalem, see p. 132. □

Emmer, see IMMER.

Emona, see CHEPHAR-AMMONI.

En- as an element in place-names is a contracted form of Ain, 'fountain, spring'.

Enac, see ANAK.

Enaim, loc. ment. Gn 38:14, 21; prob. identical with ENAM, q.v. □

Enam, loc. of Judah, in the lowland, listed Jos 15:34 (Vulg. Enaim); near Adullam, exact sit. unk. □

Enan (Village of, Court of), see HAZAR-ENAN.

En-dor, city of Manasseh in the territory of Issachar, Jos 17:11; home of the witch consulted by Saul, 1 S 28:7; cf. Ps 83:10 (Heb. 11); prob. in the vicinity of mod. *Endôr (Indûr)*, S of Mt Tabor; Maps 11, 15; Pl. 188; p. 67. □

Eneas, see AENEAS.

Maps: 1 p. 9 / 2, 3 p. 10 / 4 p. 29 / 5, 6 p. 30 / 7, 8 p. 43 / 9, 10 p. 44 / 11, 12 p. 59 / 13 p. 60 / 14 p. 65 / 15, 16 p. 66 / 17 p. 81 / 18, 19 p. 82 / 20, 21 p. 95 / 22–24 p. 96 / 25–29 p. 103 / 30, 31 p. 104 / 32, 33 p. 115 / 34, 35 p. 116 / I, II end-papers.

148

En-eglaim, 'spring of calves'; loc. on the shores of the Dead Sea, Ezk 47:10; exact sit. unk. □
Engaddi, see EN-GEDI.
Engallim, see EN-EGLAIM.
En-gannim, 'spring of gardens'; n. of 2 loc., 1. loc. of Judah, in the lowland, listed Jos 15:34; sit. unk. □
2. loc. of Issachar, listed Jos 19:21; Levitical city, Jos 21:29; prob. mod. *Jenîn;* Map 11. Cf. BETH-HAGGAN. □
En-gedi, 'spring of the kid'; loc. of Judah, in the wilderness, listed Jos 15:62; David took refuge there, 1 S 24:1f.; ment. in the vision of Ezk 47:10 (cf. p. 16); cf. Ca 1:14, Sir 24:14 (Vulg. 18, where Vulg. has Kadesh, and some Gk. MSS have 'sea shore'), 2 Ch 20:2 (where it is wrongly identified with HAZAZON-TAMAR, q.v.); mod. *Tell ej-Jurn,* on the W shore of the Dead Sea, near the spring of *'Ain Jidi* which preserves the name; Maps 2, 11, 13, 15, 17, 19; Pl. 32. □
Enhadda, see EN-HADDAH.
En-haddah, loc. of Issachar, listed Jos 19:21; sit unk. □
Enhasor, see EN-HAZOR.
En-hazor, loc. of Naphtali, listed Jos 19:37; sit. unk. □
En-mishpat, 'spring of judgment'; loc. identified as KADESH (1), q.v., in Gn 14:7.
Enmity, see SITNAH.
Ennom, see HINNOM.
Ennon, see AENON.
Enoch, n. of 4 persons, in particular 1. an antediluvian patriarch who lived for '365 years' and was carried up into Heaven, Gn 5:21ff.
2. eldest son of Cain who gave his name to the first city, Gn 4:17f.
Enos, see ENOSH.
Enosh, 'man'; n. of the son of Seth, Gn 4:26.
En-rimmon, 'spring near the pomegranate-tree'; loc. of Judah, in the Negeb, listed Jos 15:32 (Ain and Rimmon, cf. AIN (1)); inc. among the cities of Simeon, Jos 19:7, 1 Ch 4:32 (Ain, Rimmon, cf. AIN (1)); repopulated after the Exile, Neh 11:29; mod. *Kh. Umm er-Ramamîn,* NNE of Beer-sheba; Maps 11, 13. Cf. RIMMON (1).
En-rogel, 'spring of the fuller'; loc. on the boundary of Judah and Benjamin, S of the fortress of the Jebusites, Jos 15:7, 18:16; ment. in the account of David's flight, 2 S 17:17; also ment. in connection with Adonijah, 1 K 1:9; now called Job's Well, *Bîr Ayyûb;* Maps 13, 19, 24, 33. □
Ensemes, see EN-SHEMESH.
En-shemesh, 'spring of the sun'; loc. E of Jerusalem, ment. in the boundaries of Judah, Jos 15:7, 18:17; mod. *'Ain el-Hôd;* Maps 13, 19. □
En-tappuah, spring N of Tappuah, on the boundary between Ephraim and Manasseh, Jos 17:7; Map 11. Cf. TAPPUAH (1).
Epaenetus, n. of 'the first convert in Asia for Christ', Ro 16:5.
Epaphras, 'the attractive'; n. of a companion of St Paul; founder of the Christian community at Colossae, Col 1:7, 4:12f.
Epaphroditus, 'the attractive'; n. of a fellow-worker of St Paul, Ph 2:25.
Epenetus, see EPAENETUS.
Ephah, n. of a Midianite tribe, ment. among the descendants of Abraham, Gn 25:4, 1 Ch 1:33; cf. Is 60:6; unk. □
Epher, see HEPHER.
Ephes-dammim, loc. between Socoh and Azekah (see Map 15) where the Philistines encamped with their champion Goliath, 1 S 17:1; called Pas-dammim in 1 Ch 11:13 and prob. also in the original text of the parallel passage in 2 S 23:9. □
Ephesus, sea-port in Asia Minor, ment. Ac 18:21ff.; 19; 20:17; 1 Co 15:32; 16:8; Eph 1:1; 1 Ti 1:3; 2 Ti 1:18; 4:12; Rev 1:11; 2:1–7; Maps 25, II (e.p.); Pl. 400; p. 139. □
Ephra, see OPHRAH.
Ephraim, 'the fruitful'; 1. Israelite tribe, descended from a son of Joseph, Gn 41:52, cf. 49:22, Dt 33:13–17.
2. hill country (Mt Ephraim) in the centre of Canaan, later the heart of the N Kingdom; Maps 11, 15; Pls. 30, 177.
3. forest of Ephraim, ment. 2 S 18:6; near Mahanaim; Map 15.
4. city N of Jerusalem, ment. 2 S 13:23, Jn 11:54; mod. *et-Taiyibeh;* Maps 15, 30, 34. Cf. APHAEREMA, EPHRON (2), OPHRAH (1).
5. Gate of Ephraim at Jerusalem, 2 K 14:13 = 2 Ch 25:23, Neh 8:16, 12:39; Map 24 C. Cf. OLD GATE. □
Ephrain, see EPHRON (2).
Ephrata(h), see EPHRATH.
Ephrath, 'fruitful land'; city N of Jerusalem, where Rachel died, Gn 35:16ff., near Ramah, in the territory of Benjamin, 1 S 10:2, Jer 31:15; in Judah according to Jos 15:59 (LXX, Ephrathah); a late and erroneous gloss on Gn 35:19 identifies this city with Bethlehem because the latter was later inhabited by a group of Ephrathites, 1 Ch 2:19, 50f.; Ru 1:2, 4:11; Mi 5:2.
Ephrathah, see EPHRATH.
Ephree, see HOPHRA.
Ephrem, see EPHRAIM (4).
Ephron, 1. city in Transjordan captured by Judas Maccabaeus, 1 Mac 5:46, 2 Mac 12:27; prob. mod. *et-Taiyibeh,* SE of the Sea of Galilee; Maps 30, 31. □
2. city N of Jerusalem; identical with Ephraim (4) and Ophrah (1), 2 Ch 13:19; Map 17.
3. Mt Ephron, near Kiriath-jearim, Jos 15:9.
4. n. of a wealthy Hittite from whom Abraham bought the cave of Machpelah, Gn 23:8ff.
Epiphania, Hel. n. of HAMATH, q.v.; Map 29.
Erastus, n. which occurs 3 times in the N.T., Ac 19:22, Ro 16:23, 2 Ti 4:20; it is not clear whether these all refer to the same person.
Erech, one of the most ancient cities in Mesopotamia, ment. Gn 10:10, Ezr 4:9; called *Uruk* in Ass. and Bab. texts; mod. *Warka,* S of Babylon; Map 1. □
Esaan, see ESHAN.
Esarhaddon, 'Ashur has given a brother'; n. of an Ass. king (681–668 B.C.), successor of Sennacherib, 2 K 19:37 = Is 37:38; one of the kings who sent colonists to Samaria, Ezr 4:2; Map 18; Pl. 257.
Esau, twin brother of Jacob, Gn 25; ancestor of the Edomites; his name remains a mystery, for 'red' and 'hairy mantle' (Gn 25:25) are a play on words on Edom and Seir (his territory) respectively.
Esbaal, see ISH-BOSHETH.
Escol, Gn 14:13, 24, see ESHCOL.
Esdraelon, Gk. form of JEZREEL, q.v.
Esdras, Gk. form of EZRA, q.v.
Esdrelon, see JEZREEL.
Esek, 'dispute'; n. of a spring near Gerar, Gn 26:20; sit. unk. □
Esem, see EZEM.
Eshan, loc. of Judah, in the hill country, listed Jos 15:52; W of Dumah, exact sit. unk. □
Esh-baal, see ISH-BOSHETH.
Eshcol, 'cluster of grapes'; valley near Hebron, so called because of the cluster of grapes cut down there, Nu 13:23f., 32:9, Dt 1:24; cf. Gn 14:13, 24, where Eshcol and Mamre are persons. □
Eshean, see ESHAN.
Eshtaol, loc. of Judah, in the lowland, listed Jos 15:33; also inc. among the cities of Dan, Jos 19:41 (ment. with Zorah in both lists); figures in the stories of Samson, Jg 13:25, 16:31; starting-point of the expedition of the Danites, Jg 18:2, 8, 11; poss. mod. *Eshwa';* Maps 13, 14, 19. □
Eshtemoa, 'listening-post'; loc. of Judah, in the hill-country, listed Jos 15:50 (Eshtemoh); cf. 1 Ch 4:17, 19; Levitical city, Jos 21:14, 1 Ch 6:57 (Heb. 42); among the cities to which David sent spoil, 1 S 30:28; mod. *es-Semû',* S of Hebron; Maps 13, 15. □
Eshtemoh, see ESHTEMOA.
Esna, see ASHNAH (1).
Esron, see HEZRON (1).
Essenes, n. of a Jewish sect which grew up in the centuries immediately before the Christian era; known to Josephus, Philo and Pliny, and now known to us through the Dead Sea Scrolls; pp. 136ff.; Pls. 347–350.
Essenes (Gate of the), gate of Jerusalem ment. by Josephus; prob. the DUNG GATE (Neh 2:13, etc.), q.v.; Maps 24C, 33.
Estaol, see ESHTAOL.
Estemo, Esthamo, Esthemo, see ESHTEMOA.
Esthaol, see ESHTAOL.
Esther, n. of a Jewess whose story is related in the book of that name; the scene is laid in Susa; Map 21.
Etam, 1. loc. of Judah, in the hill-country, listed Jos 15:59 (LXX); cf. 1 Ch 4:3; fortified by Rehoboam, 2 Ch 11:6; mod. *Kh. el-Khôkh,* SW of Bethlehem, near *'Ain 'Atan* which preserves the ancient name; Maps 13, 14, 17, 19. □
2. loc. inc. among the cities of Simeon, 1 Ch 4:32; not in the parallel list of Jos 19; sit. unk. □
3. 'the rock of Etam', the cave where Samson took refuge, Jg 15:8, 11; sit. unk. □
Ethai, see ITTAI.
Etham, 1st stopping-place after Succoth on the Exodus, 'on the edge of the wilderness', Ex 13:20, Nu 33:6f.; poss. the ruins of an Eg. fortress N of the Bitter Lakes; Map 9; p. 48. The 'wilderness of Etham' stretches to the E of this fortress, Nu 33:8; Map 9; p. 48. □
Etham (Wilderness of), see ETHAM.
Ethan, n. of 2 persons, in particular a psalmist ment. 1 Ch 6:44; Ps 89 is attributed to him.
Ethbaal, king of Sidon and father of Jezebel, the wife of Ahab, 1 K 16:31.
Ether, 1. loc. of Judah, in the lowland, listed Jos 15:42; poss. mod. *Kh. el-'Ater,* NE of Lachish; Maps 13, 15, 19. Should doubtless be distinguished from (2).
2. loc. inc. among the cities of Simeon, Jos 19:7; a little further S than (1), and poss. identical with the Athach of 1 S 30:30; sit. unk. □
Ethiopia, 'land of the black faces'; Biblical Cush; region S of Egypt, described in Is 18; cf. Ac 8:27; Map 10.
Eth-kazin, loc. of Zebulun, listed Jos 19:13; sit. unk. □
Etroth, see ATROTH-SHOPHAN.
Eubulus, n. of a Roman Christian, 2 Ti 4:21.
Eumenes II, 'the benevolent'; n. of a king of Pergamum (197–150 B.C.), ment. 1 Mac 8:8.
Eunice, n. of the mother of Timothy; St Paul praised her faith, Ac 16:1, 2 Ti 1:5.
Euodia, n. of a Christian woman of Philippi, Ph 4:2.
Euodias, see EUODIA.
Euphrates, Heb. *Perath;* largest river in western Asia, *ca* 1,700 miles long; one of the 4 rivers of Paradise in Gn 2:14; mod. *Shatt el-Furât;* Maps 1, 5, 6, 7, 8, 20, 25, 32; Pls. 2, 4, 5, 259. Cf. PERATH. For the Egyptians the Euphrates was 'the river which flows backwards' (i.e. in the opposite direction from the Nile), cf. Map 6.
Eutychus, n. of the young man of Troas who was brought to life by St Paul, Ac 20:9ff.; Map II (e.p.).
Eve, G&L form of Heb. *Hawwah;* 'mother of all living', Gn 3:20.
Evil-merodach, Heb. form of *Awil Marduk;* n. of the king of Babylon who freed Jehoiachin after he had been 37 years in captivity, 2 K 25:27, Jer 52:31.
Evodia, see EUODIA.
Exile (Babylonian), deportation of the Jews to Babylonia after the capture of Jerusalem by Nebuchadnezzar; the Exile lasted from 586 to 536 B.C.; Maps 20, 21; pp. 93f.
Ezechias, see HEZEKIAH.
Ezechiel, see EZEKIEL.
Ezekiel, 'God is strong'; n. of the prophet of the time of the Exile; a book of the Bible bears his name; pp. 53, 98.
Ezem, 'bone'; loc. of Judah, in the Negeb, listed Jos 15:29; also listed for Simeon, Jos 19:3, 1 Ch 4:29; poss. mod. *Umm el-'Azam,* SE of Beer-sheba; Map 11. □
Ezion-gaber, see EZION-GEBER.
Ezion-geber, stopping-place on the Exodus, Nu 33:35f.; ment. with Elath (Eloth), Dt 2:8, 1 K 9:26, 2 Ch 8:17; ment. alone, 1 K 22:48 (Heb. 49), 2 Ch 20:36; mod. *Tell el-Kheleifeh,* on the gulf of Elath ('Aqaba); Maps 9, 17, I (e.p.); p. 74. Cf. 'AQABA, ELATH. □
Ezra, 'God is support'; n. of the leader of a group of repatriated Israelites; he reorganised the life of the Jewish community, cf. p. 100; a book of the Bible, based partly on his memoirs, bears his name; Map 21.

F

Fair Havens, bay on the S coast of Crete, Ac 27:8; mod. *Kali Limenes;* Map II (e.p.). □
Faiyûm (El-), see EL-FAIYÛM.
False claim, see ESEK.
Felix, n. of the Roman procurator of Judaea (A.D. 52–59); St Paul appeared before him, Ac 24; Map II (e.p.); p. 121.
Festus, see PORCIUS FESTUS.
Feud, see SITNAH.
Field of Blood, see AKELDAMA.
Fish Gate, gate on the N side of Jerusalem, 2 Ch 33:14 (cf. Zeph 1:10), Neh 3:3, 12:39; Map 24 C. □
Fishmongers' Gate, see FISH GATE.
Flock Gate, see SHEEP GATE.
Flock tower, Flock (Tower of), see EDER (Tower of).
Forest of Haret(h), Forest of Hereth, see HERETH (Forest of).
Forests (Valley of the), n. replacing the Valley of Siddim in some versions of Gn 14:3. Cf. PLAIN, PLAINS.
Former Sea, see EASTERN SEA.
Fortunatus, n. of a Christian of Corinth, 1 Co 16:17f.
Forum Appii, Forum of Appius, see APPIUS (Forum of).
Foundation (Gate of the), gate of Jerusalem, between the Temple and the royal palace, 2 Ch 23:5; prob. mistakenly called 'the gate Sur' in the parallel passage of 2 K 11:6; poss. identical with 'the gate of the guards', 2 K 11:19. □
Fountain Gate, gate on the SE side of Jerusalem, Neh 2:14, 3:15, 12:37; Map 24 C. □
Freedom, see REHOBOTH (1).
Furthermost Sea, see WESTERN SEA.

G

Gaal, 'scarab'; n. of the man who stirred up the men of Shechem against Abimelech, who defeated him, Jg 9:26–41.
Gaas (Mount, Torrent, Valley of), see GAASH (Mountain of, Brooks of).
Gaash (Mountain of, Brooks of), mountainous region S of Timnath-serah where Joshua was buried, Jos 24:30 = Jg 2:9 (Mt Gaash); birthplace of one of David's warriors, 2 S 23:30 = 1 Ch 11:32 (brooks of Gaash); cf. TIMNATH-SERAH. □
Gaba, see GEBA.
Gabaa, see GEBA, GIBEAH (1), (2), and GIBEON.
Gabaath, see GIBEAH (2).
Gabae, see GEBA.
Gabaon, see GIBEON.
Gabathon, see GIBBETHON.
Gabbatha, 'eminence'; Heb. n. of the place where Pontius Pilate judged Jesus, Jn 19:13; Gk. *Lithostroton,* 'THE PAVEMENT', q.v.
Gabee, see GEBA.
Gabim, see GEBIM.
Gabriel, 'God has shown Himself strong'; n. of an archangel, the bearer of the good tidings of the coming of the Messiah (Dn 8–9), and the birth of John the Baptist and Jesus (Lk 1).
Gad, 1. god of good fortune; see explanation in Gn 30:11; alluded to in Is 65:11 (Fortune).
2. a son of Jacob, Gn 30:11; ancestor of a tribe whose territory lay in Transjordan; Maps 11, 14, 17.
3. a prophet in the time of David, 2 S 24:11–14.
Gadara, city of the Decapolis, SE of the Sea of Galilee; according to Mt 8:28, its territory extended as far as the lake; mod. *Muqeis,* or *Umm Qeis;* Map 34. Cf. DECAPOLIS.
Gader, see GEDER.
Gaderoth, see GEDEROTH.
Gadgad, see HOR-HAGGIDGAD.
Gador, see GEDOR (3).
Gaius, n. of 4 persons, 1. a companion of St Paul at Ephesus, Ac 19:29.
2. another companion of St Paul; a native of Derbe, Ac 20:4.
3. a Corinthian, baptised by St Paul, 1 Co 1:14.
4. person to whom the 3rd Letter of John was addressed, 3 Jn 1:1.
Galaad, see GILEAD.
Galatia, region of Asia Minor; Maps 26, 32, II (e.p.). Cf. GALATIANS.
Galatians, n. of an Indo-European people who settled in the centre of Asia Minor *ca* 300 B.C. They gave their name to an

Maps: 1 p. 9 / 2, 3 p. 10 / 4 p. 29 / 5, 6 p. 30 / 7, 8 p. 43 / 9, 10 p. 44 / 11, 12 p. 59 / 13 p. 60 / 14 p. 65 / 15, 16 p. 66 / 17 p. 81 / 18, 19 p. 82 / 20, 21 p. 95 / 22–24 p. 96 / 25–29 p. 103 / 30, 31 p. 104 / 32, 33 p. 115 / 34, 35 p. 116 / I, II end-papers.

149

area between Pontus, Bithynia, and Lycaonia, Maps 26, II (e.p.). This territory was later extended, and the Roman Province of Galatia (created in 25 B.C.) also included the cities of Antioch (2), Lystra, and Derbe, Map 32 (S Galatia). The Letter of St Paul was prob. addressed to N Galatia, which he visited on his 2nd and 3rd journeys: Ac 16:6, 18:23, cf. 1 Co 16:1, Gal 1:2, 3:1, 2 Ti 4:10, 1 P 1:1 (cf. 1 Mac 8:2, 2 Mac 8:20). □

Galgal, see GILGAL (1), (2), (4) and (5).

Galgala, see GILGAL (3).

Galilee, Heb. *galîl*; n. quickly restricted in application to the hill country N of the plain of Jezreel; here the Israelites were mingled with the pagan inhabitants, and the region was referred to as GALILEE OF THE NATIONS *(Gelîl-hag-goyîm)*, q.v., Is 9:1 (Heb. 8:23); scene of the campaigns of Simon Maccabaeus, 1 Mac 5:14ff.; conquered by Alexander Jannaeus, p. 110; at the time of Jesus Galilee was part of the tetrarchy of Herod Antipas, Lk 23:6f., cf. Jn 7:41, etc.; Maps 23, 30, 31, 34, 35; Pls. 22, 252, 362, 364, 368.

Galilee of the Gentiles, see GALILEE OF THE NATIONS.

Galilee of the nations, Heb. *Gelîl-hag-goyîm;* n. given to Galilee on account of the strong pagan element in its population, Is 9:1 (Heb. 8:23), cf. 1 Mac 5:15. Cf. GALILEE; Map 23.

Galilee (Sea of), lake in the N of the Jordan valley; 13 miles long by 7½ miles wide, 700 ft. below sea level, 165-230 ft. deep; mod. *Bahr Tabarîyeh;* Maps 2, 30, 34; Pls. 27, 370, 371.

Gallim, 1. loc. N of Jerusalem, ment. Is 10:30; prob. the home of Palti, husband of Michal, 1 S 25:44; poss. mod. *Kh. Ka'kûl;* Map 19. □
2. loc. of Judah, in the hill country, listed Jos 15:59 (LXX); poss. mod. *Beit Jâla*, WNW of Bethlehem; Maps 13, 19. □
3. see EGLAIM.

Gallio, n. of the proconsul of Achaia in the time of St Paul, Ac 18.

Gamaliel, 'God has repaid'; n. of the teacher of St Paul, Ac 5, 22:3.

Gamarias, see GEMARIAH.

Gamzo, see GIMZO.

Gareb, 1. n. of one of David's warriors, 2 S 23:38.
2. n. of a hill near Jerusalem, Jer 31:39. □

Garizim (Mount), see GERIZIM (Mount).

Gate between the two walls, gate on the S side of Jerusalem, Jer 39:4, 52:7 = 2 K 25:4; Map 24 B. □

Gate of Ephraim, see EPHRAIM (5).

Gate of the Corner, see CORNER GATE.

Gate of the Dunghill, see DUNG GATE.

Gate of the Essenes, see ESSENES (Gate of the).

Gate of the Foundation, see FOUNDATION (Gate of the).

Gate of the Fountain, see FOUNTAIN GATE.

Gate of the Guard, see GUARD (Gate of the).

Gate of the guards, see FOUNDATION (Gate of the).

Gate of the New Quarter, see NEW QUARTER (Gate of the).

Gate of the Shieldbearers, see GUARD (Gate of the).

Gate of the Valley, see VALLEY GATE.

Gate of the Well, see FOUNTAIN GATE.

Gate Sur, see SUR (The gate), FOUNDATION (Gate of the).

Gath, 'wine-press'; one of the 5 Philistine cities, cf. PENTAPOLIS (2); home of giants (Goliath), Jos 11:22, 1 S 17:4, 2 S 21:20ff.; the Ark was sent there, 1 S 5:8; royal city of Achish, 1 S 21:10ff. (Heb. 11 ff.), 27:2 ff., 1 K 2:39 ff., Ps 56: Heading; fortified by Rehoboam, 2 Ch 11:8; captured by Hazael of Damascus, 2 K 12:17; captured from the Philistines by Uzziah, 2 Ch 26:6; poss. mod. *'Arâq el-Menshîyeh;* Maps 11, 13, 15, 17, 19.

Gath-hepher, 'wine-press near the well'; loc. of Zebulun, listed Jos 19:13; birthplace of Jonah, 2 K 14:25; prob. mod. *Kh. ez-Zurra';* Maps 11, 17. □

Gath-rimmon, 'wine-press by the pomegranate'; n. of two cities, 1. loc. of Dan, Jos 19:45; Levitical city, Jos 21:24f., 1 Ch 6:69 (Heb. 54); sit. unk. □
2. Levitical city of W Manasseh according to Jos 21:25; sit. unk. □

Gaulanitis, region of Transjordan which took its name from the city of Golan (cf. Map 11, Jos 20:8); Maps 34, 35.

Gaulon, see GOLAN.

Gaver, see GUR.

Gaza, most southerly of the 5 Philistine cities, cf. PENTAPOLIS (2); ment. as S frontier of Canaan, Gn 10:19, 1 K 4:24; originally inhabited by the Avvim, Dt 2:23, Jos 10:41; allotted to Judah, Jos 15:47, Jg 1:18, but still occupied by the Philistines, Jg 16:1, 21, 2 K 18:8; captured by the Egyptians, Jer 47:1ff.; the Hel. city was taken and sacked by Jonathan, 1 Mac 11:61 ff.; ment. once in the N.T., Ac 8:26; mod. *Ghazzeh;* Maps 7, 9, 11, 12, 14, 15, 17, 23, 29, 30, 31, 34. See also AIATH.

Gazara, see GEZER.

Gazer, see GEZER and JAZER.

Gazera, see GEZER.

Geba, 'height'; loc. of Benjamin, listed Jos 18:24; Levitical city, Jos 21:17, 1 Ch 6:60 (Heb. 45); cf. 1 Ch 8:6; ment. in the battle between Benjamin and Israel, Jg 20:33, and in Saul's battles with the Philistines, 1 S 13:3,16, 14:5; ment. under David, 2 S 5:25 (Heb. Geba; Gk. and parallel passage of 1 Ch 14:16 have Gibeon, cf. Is 28:21); after the Disruption, on the N boundary of Judah, 1 K 15:22 = 2 Ch 16:6, whence the expressions 'from Geba to Beer-sheba', 2 K 23:8, 'from Geba to Rimmon', Zec 14:10, to indicate the whole extent of the territory of Judah; repopulated after the Exile, Ezr 2:26, Neh 7:30, 11:31, 12:29; mod. *Jeba'*, 6 miles NNW of the Temple terrace in Jerusalem; Maps 2, 13, 14, 15, 17, 19, 22; Pls. 189, 190, 250. □

Gebal, 1. Phoenician city, ment. Ezk 27:9; inhabited by the Gebalites, Jos 13:5, 1 K 5:18 (Heb. 32); identical with the Gubla of the Accadian texts; called BYBLOS, q.v., by the Greeks; Maps 4, 12. □
2. n. of a region in the vicinity of Petra, ment. Ps 83:7 (Heb. 8). □

Gebalites, inhabitants of Gebal, Jos 13:5; cf. GEBAL.

Gebbethon, see GIBBETHON.

Gebim, 'the cisterns'; loc. just N of Jerusalem, ment. Is 10:31; prob. the ruins SW of *Shu'fat;* Map 19. □

Gedaliah, 'Yahweh has shown Himself mighty'; n. of the protector of Jeremiah; appointed governor of Judah after the deportation and later assassinated, 2 K 25.

Gedeon, see GIDEON.

Geder, Canaanite royal city, Jos 12:13, 1 Ch 27:28; sit. unk.

Gedera, see GEDERAH.

Gederah, loc. of Judah, in the lowland, listed Jos 15:36, cf. 1 Ch 4:23; poss. mod. *Kh. esh-Sheikh 'Ali Jadir;* Maps 13, 19. □

Gederoth, loc. of Judah, in the lowland, listed Jos 15:41; captured by the Philistines in the time of Ahaz, 2 Ch 28:18; poss. mod. *Qatra;* Maps 13, 19. □

Gederothaim, 'the two walls'; loc. of Judah, in the lowland, listed Jos 15:36; near Gederah; sit. unk. □

Gedor, 'wall'; 1. loc. of Judah, in the hill country, listed Jos 15:58; poss. mod. *Kh. Judûr*, SW of Bethlehem; Maps 13, 19. □
2. loc. in Judah, near Socoh and Zanoah, ment. 1 Ch 4:18; exact sit. unk.
3. loc. of Benjamin, ment. 1 Ch 12:7; sit. unk. □
4. loc. inc. in the territory of Simeon, 1 Ch 4:39 (Heb.; Gk. has GERAR, q.v.); sit. unk. □

Geennom, see HINNOM.

Gehazi, n. of the servant of Elisha, 2 K 4ff.

Gehenna, see HINNOM.

Gehon, see GIHON (1).

Gelboe, see GILBOA.

Geliloth, loc. ment. Jos 18:17; cf. GILGAL (5).

Gemariah, 'Yahweh has accomplished'; n. of 1. a scribe in the service of Jehoiakim, Jer 36.
2. an envoy sent by Zedekiah to Nebuchadnezzar, Jer 29:3.

Genesar, Genesareth, see GENNESARET.

Gennesaret, loc. on the NW shore of the Sea of Galilee where Jesus landed, Mt 14:34, Mk 6:53; also applied to the fertile and densely-populated plain W of the Sea of Galilee and S of Capernaum, mod. *el-Ghuweir;* finally a n. for the Sea of Galilee itself, Lk 5:1, cf. 1 Mac 11:67; Map 34. See also CHINNERETH, CHINNEROTH.

Geon, Sir 24:27, see GIHON.

Gerar, loc. in the S of Canaan, Gn 10:19; visited by the patriarchs, Gn 20:1f., 26:1ff.; inc. in the territory of Simeon, 1 Ch 4:39 (Gk.; Heb. has GEDOR, q.v.); figures in the campaigns of Asa, 2 Ch 14:13 (Heb. 12) f.; poss. mod. *Tell Jemmeh*, S of Gaza; Maps 4, 17. □

Gerara, see GERAR.

Gerasa, city of the Decapolis; impressive ruins; mod. *Jerash;* Maps 2, 34; Pls. 296–299. Cf. DECAPOLIS.

Gerasenes, inhabitants of Gerasa and its territory which, according to Mk 5:1 and Lk 8:26, extended to the Sea of Galilee; the parallel passage of Mt 8:28 has Gadarenes, the inhabitants of GADARA, q.v.; the reading Gergesenes derives from a conj. of Origen, who may have been thinking of the GIRGASHITES (q.v.) of the O.T.

Gergesenes, see GERASENES.

Gergesites, see GIRGASHITES.

Gerizim (Mount), n. of a mt near Shechem, S of Mt Ebal, Dt 11:29, 27:12, Jos 8:33, Jg 9:7; site chosen by the Samaritans for their schismatic temple (cf. 2 Mac 5:23, 6:2), built in the 4th cent. B.C. and destroyed by John Hyrcanus in 128 B.C.; the name does not occur in the N.T., but the mountain is referred to in Jn 4:20; mod. *J. et-Tôr* (2900 ft.); Maps 2, 14, 34; Pls. 95, 96. Cf. EBAL (3). □

Gersam, see GERSHOM.

Gershom, n. of the eldest son of Moses, Ex 2:22.

Gershon, n. of the eldest son of Levi; a group of the Levites was called after him, Gn 46:11.

Geruth Chimham, loc. near Bethlehem where a halt was made on Johanan's flight to Egypt, Jer 41:17; probable translation 'inn of Chimham' (for the n. cf. 2 S 19:37 ff. (Heb. 38 ff.)). □

Gerzi, see GIRZITES.

Geshur, territory E of the upper course of the Jordan, inhabited by an Aramaean tribe; ment. with Maacath, Jos 13:13, cf. Dt 3:14, Jos 12:5, 13:11, 13, 1 Ch 2:23; home of Absalom's mother, 2 S 3:3 = 1 Ch 3:2; Absalom took refuge there, 2 S 13:37f., 14:23, 32, 15:8; Maps 15, 16. □

Geshuri, see GESHURITES.

Geshurites, Geshuri, 1. n. of the inhabitants of GESHUR, q.v.
2. n. of a people living S of the Philistine territory, Jos 13:2, 1 S 27:8; Map 12.

Gessen, see GOSHEN (1).

Gessur, see GESHUR.

Gessuri, see GESHUR and GESHURITES, GESHURI.

Geth, see GATH.

Gethaim, see GITTAIM.

Gethhepher, see GATH-HEPHER.

Gethites, see GITTITES.

Geth-Opher, see GATH-HEPHER.

Gethremmon, see GATH-RIMMON.

Gethsemane, 'olive-press'; garden on the E side of the valley of the Kidron, at the foot of the Mt of Olives, Mt 26:36, Mk 14:32, not named in Lk 22:39f.; scene of the agony and arrest of Jesus; Map 33; Pls. 191, 192 no. 4, 326; p. 132.

Gethsemani, see GETHSEMANE.

Gezer, Canaanite royal city, Jos 10:33, 12:12; ment. in the indication of the boundaries of Ephraim, Jos 16:3, cf. 1 Ch 7:28; the Canaanites were not driven out, Jos 16:10 = Jg 1:29; Levitical city, Jos 21:21 = 1 Ch 6:67 (Heb. 52); figures in David's battles against the Philistines, 1 Ch 14:16, ('from Gibeon to Gezer' = 2 S 5:25; see GEBA), 1 Ch 20:4; captured by Pharaoh and given by him to his daughter, the wife of Solomon, who rebuilt it, 1 K 9:15ff.; cf. also 1 Mac 4:15, 7:45 (Gazara); mod. *Tell Jezer*, W of Jerusalem, where very important excavations have been carried out; Maps 7, 13, 14, 15, 17, 19, 23, 30.

Gezrites, see GIRZITES.

Giah, loc. ment. 2 S 2:24; the text is probably corrupt. □

Giants (Valley of the), see REPHAIM (Valley of).

Gibbethon, 'undulation'; loc. of Dan, listed Jos 19:44; Levitical city, Jos 21:23; the kings of the N Kingdom fought the Philistines for its possession, 1 K 15:27, 16:15; prob. mod. *Tell el-Melât*, W of Gezer; Maps 11, 13, 17, 19.

Gibea, see GIBEAH (1).

Gibeah, 1. loc. of Judah, in the hill country, listed Jos 15:57; cf. 1 Ch 2:49; poss. mod. *el-Jeba'*, WSW of Bethlehem; Maps 13, 19. □
2. loc. of Benjamin, listed Jos 18:28; N of Jerusalem, Is 10:29, Hos 5:8; scene of a crime, Jg 19–20, which sullied Israel, Hos 9:9, 10:9; later the residence of Saul, 1 S 10:26, 11:4, 15:34 (Gibeah of Saul), 22:6, 23:19, 26:1; also called Gibeath-elohim = 'Gibeah of God', 1 S 10:5, 10; mod. *Tell el-Fûl*, 3 miles N of the Temple terrace in Jerusalem; Maps 13, 14, 15, 19; p. 67. Often confused with the nearby GEBA, q.v. □

Gibeath, Gibeath-elohim, see GIBEAH (2).

Gibeon, 'height'; loc. of Benjamin, listed Jos 18:25; cf. 1 Ch 8:29, 9:35; Levitical city, Jos 21:17; negotiations of its inhabitants, the Hivites, with Joshua, Jos 9–10, 11:19; later the scene of the struggle between Abner and Joab, 2 S 2:12ff. (cf. HELKATH-HAZZURIM and Jer 41:12, 16), 2 S 3:30; cf. 2 S 20:8; the 7 sons of Saul were hanged on a neighbouring hill, 2 S 21:6; where Yahweh appeared to Solomon, 1 K 3:4ff., 9:2; according to 1 Ch 16:39, 21:29, 2 Ch 1:3, 13, the tabernacle and altar of burnt offering were for a time 'in the high place at Gibeon'; ment. Neh 7:25, cf. 3:7; prob. mod. *el-Jîb*, 6 miles NNW of the Temple of Jerusalem; the 'high place' is just over a mile further S at *Nebi Samwîl;* Maps 2, 13, 14, 15, 17, 19, 22; Pls. 174, 176. Cf. GEBA, GIBEAH (2). □

Giblites, see GEBALITES.

Gideon, n. of one of the great Judges, surnamed Jerubbaal, 'may Baal show himself mighty'; famous for his struggle against the Midianites, Jg 6–8; Map 14; p. 57.

Gideroth, see GEDEROTH.

Giezi, see GEHAZI.

Gihon, 1. one of the 4 rivers of Eden, Gn 2:13, cf. Sir 24:27 (Vulg. 37).
2. spring E of Jerusalem, 2 Ch 32:30; Solomon was anointed king there, 1 K 1:33, 38, 45; Hezekiah's conduit, 2 Ch 32:30 (cf. 2 K 20:20); ment. in the description of Manasseh's wall, 2 Ch 33:14; mod. *'Ain Sitti-Mariam;* Maps 24, 33; Pl. 191 no. 3. □

Gilboa, chain of mts in the territory of Issachar; where Saul and Jonathan died, 1 S 28:4, 31:1 (Mt Gilboa), 8 (Mt Gilboa) = 1 Ch 10:1, 8, cf. 2 S 1:6, 21, 21:12; mod. *J. Faqqu'a* (1650 ft.), W of Beth-shan; the ancient name is preserved in that of the village of *Jelbûn* on the S slopes; Maps 2, 15; Pls. 23, 188; p. 67. □

Gilead, 1. originally the n. of a small area S of the Jabbok in Transjordan, then of all Transjordan from the Arnon to the Yarmuk, and finally also of the part N of the Jabbok; Maps 15, 23, 31.
2. n. of a people, Nu 36:1.
3. n. of the son of Machir, Nu 26:29.

Gilgal, 'circle of stones'; n. of several loc., 1. E of Jericho Jos 4:19, Mic 6:5; on entering the Promised Land, the Israelites set up 12 stones there, Jos 4:20, 5:9f.; Joshua's military headquarters, Jos 9:6, 10:6ff., 14:6, cf. Jg 2:1, 3:19; religious centre, 1 S 7:16, 10:8, 11:14f., 13:4ff., 15:12ff.; prob. mod. *Kh. el-Etheleh;* Maps 14, 15; Pl. 160; p. 67. □
2. loc. in the stories of Elijah and Elisha, 2 K 2:1, 4:38; some scholars identify it with (1), others situate it at *Jiljiliyeh*, 7 miles N of Bethel, Map 17; similar doubts arise over the Gilgal condemned with Bethel as a place of unlawful worship, Am 4:4, 5:5, Hos 4:15 (cf. 9:15, 12:11 (Heb. 12)). □
3. loc. near Shechem, E of Mt Ebal and Mt Gerizim, Dt 11:30; identified by some scholars with the Gilgal of Amos and Hosea, cf. (2).
4. loc. ment. in the list of defeated Canaanite kings, Jos 12:23 (Heb.), where we should doubtless read 'king of the Goim of Galilee' with the Gk. (cf. R.S.V.), and possibly identify the place with HAROSHETH-HA-GOIIM, q.v.
5. loc. on the N boundary of Judah, near the ascent of Adummim, Jos 15:7, and on the S boundary of Benjamin, Jos 18:17 (Geliloth); prob. identical with BETH-GILGAL, q.v.

Gilo, see GILOH.

Giloh, loc. of Judah, in the hill country, listed Jos 15:51; city of David's counsellor, Ahithophel, 2 S 15:12, 23:34 (Gilo); poss. mod. *Kh. Jâla*, NNW of Hebron; Maps 13, 15, 19, p. 105 no. 3. □

Gimzo, city ment. 2 Ch 28:18; N of Gezer; mod. *Jimzu;* Map 17. □

Maps: 1 p. 9 / 2, 3 p. 10 / 4 p. 29 / 5, 6 p. 30 / 7, 8 p. 43 / 9, 10 p. 44 / 11, 12 p. 59 / 13 p. 60 / 14 p. 65 / 15, 16 p. 66 / 17 p. 81 / 18, 19 p. 82 / 20, 21 p. 95 / 22–24 p. 96 / 25–29 p. 103 / 30, 31 p. 104 / 32, 33 p. 115 / 34, 35 p. 116 / I, II end-papers.

150

Girgashites, n. of a Canaanite tribe, Gn 15:21, Dt 7:1, Jos 3:10; cf. CANAAN, (a), (d), (e).
Girzites, n. of a people living in the S of Palestine who were raided by David, 1 S 27:8. □
Gittah-hepher, see GATH-HEPHER.
Gittaim, 'the two wine-presses'; loc. to which the Beerothites fled, 2 S 4:3; repopulated after the Exile, Neh 11:33; sit. unk. □
Gittites, inhabitants of Gath, Jos 13:3, 2 S 6:10, 15:18ff.
Gnidus, see CNIDUS.
Goah, loc. near Jerusalem, Jer 31:39.
Goath, Goatha, see GOAH.
Gob, city ment. 2 S 21:18; unk., unless we should read Gezer, with the parallel passage of 1 Ch 20:4. □
Godolias, see GEDALIAH.
Gog, apocalyptic figure in Ezekiel, representing the king of the Scythians who symbolises all the forces opposed to God, Ezk 38, 39, Rev 20:8. Cf. MAGOG.
Golan, Levitical city and city of refuge in Bashan (in the territory of Manasseh), Dt 4:43, Jos 20:8, 21:27 = 1 Ch 6:71 (Heb. 56); prob. mod. *Sahem el-Jolân;* Map 11. Golan later gave its name to GAULANITIS, q.v. □
Golden Gate, gate of Jerusalem, E of the Temple terrace; Byzantine erection of the 5th century A.D.; poss. corresponds to the East Gate of Neh 3:29; Map 33, no. 11; Pl. 384.
Golgotha, from Aramaic *gulgulta* or *gogalta,* 'skull'; n. of a hill near Jerusalem, shaped like a skull and used for executions, 'the place of a skull', Mt 27:33, Mk 15:22, Jn 19:17; today the Church of the Holy Sepulchre stands on the site; Map 33; cf. CALVARY.
Goliath, Philistine giant defeated by David, 1 S 17.
Gomer, 1. eldest son of Japheth, Gn 10:2.
2. wife of Hosea, Hos 1:3.
Gomorrah, 'small drinking-cup'; city of the PENTAPOLIS (1), q.v.
Gomorrha, see GOMORRAH.
Goren ha-Atad, see ATAD (Threshing-floor of).
Gorgias, n. of a general of Antiochus IV Epiphanes; defeated by Judas Maccabaeus, 1 Mac 3:38, 4:1–25.
Gortyna, city in Crete, ment. in the list of countries and cities which received the letter of Lucius, 1 Mac 15:23; mod. *Haghia Dheka;* Map 26. □
Gosen, see GOSHEN (2).
Goshen, 1. region of Egypt where the Hebrews settled, Gn 45:10, 46:28ff., 47:1ff., 50:8, Ex 8:22 (Heb. 18), 9:26; prob. the region N of *W. Tumilât;* Map 9; p. 41. □
2. loc. of Judah, in the hill country, listed Jos 15:51; identical with the Goshen of Jos 10:41 which, according to Jos 11:16, gave its name to the surrounding region; poss. mod. *edh-Dhahiriyeh,* SW of Hebron; Map 13. □
Gozam, see GOZAN.
Gozan, region devastated by the Assyrians, 2 K 19:12 = Is 37:12; sit. on the banks of the Habor ('the river of Gozan'), one of the places to which the people of the N Kingdom were deported, 2 K 17:6, 18:11, 1 Ch 5:26 (river Gozan); prob. mod. *Tell Halâf* and the surrounding region, E of Haran; Maps 1, 7, 18. □
Graves of greed, Graves of lust, see KIBROTH-HATTAAVAH.
Great Sea, n. for the Mediterranean Sea, Nu 34:6f., Jos 1:4, 15:12, 47, 23:4, Ezk 47:10, 48:28; called the 'sea of the Philistines' in Ex 23:31; cf. the 'sea of Joppa' in some versions of Ezr 3:7 (R.S.V. 'to the sea, to Joppa'); 'sea' often signifies 'the west'.
Grecia, Grecians, see JAVAN.
Greece, O.T., see JAVAN; N.T., see ACHAIA.
Guard (Gate of the), gate of Jerusalem, Neh 12:39. Cf. MUSTER GATE.
Guards (Gate of the), see FOUNDATION (Gate of the).
Gur (Ascent of), loc. near Ibleam, ment. 2 K 9:27; exact sit. unk. □
Gurbaal, city in the Negeb, where the Arabs lived, according to 2 Ch 26:7; sit. unk. □

H

Habacuc, see HABAKKUK.
Habakkuk, n. of a prophet who lived at the end of the 7th century B.C.; he gave his name to the 8th of the 12 books of the Minor Prophets; poss. the Habakkuk ment. in Bel 33ff. (Dn 14:33ff.).
Habor, 'the river of Gozan', whither Israel was deported, 2 K 17:6, 18:11, 1 Ch 5:26; still called the *Khâbûr;* Maps 5, 6; Pls. 6, 7. Cf. GOZAN, HARA. □
Haceldama, see AKELDAMA.
Hachila, see HACHILAH.
Hachilah, n. of a hill where David took refuge, 1 S 23:19, 26:1, 3; poss. at *Dahret el-Kôlâ,* between Ziph and En-gedi; Map 15. □
Hadad, 1. n. of the Semitic god of the storm; Pl. 219; this n. does not occur in the O.T. except as an element in proper names.
2. n. of an Edomite king listed in Gn 36:35f.; the parallel list of 1 Ch 1:43ff. contains two kings of this name, the second of whom is called Hadar in Gn 36:39.
3. n. of an Edomite prince who fled to Egypt in the time of David and later fought against Solomon, 1 K 11; p. 74.
Hadadezer, n. of a king of Zobah defeated by David, 2 S 8.
Hadad-rimmon, ment. Zec 12:11; long believed to be a place-name (city in the plain of Megiddo?), now usually regarded as a combination of the names of 2 gods; the Aramaean Hadad and the Accadian Rammân.
Hadar, see HADAD (2).
Hadarezer, see HADADEZER.
Hadashah, loc. of Judah, in the lowland, listed Jos 15:37; poss. between Lachish and Gath; exact sit. unk. □
Hadassa, see HADASHAH.
Hadassah, Heb. n. of Esther, Est 2:7.
Hadattah, see HAZOR-HADATHAH.
Hadid, city near Lod and Ono, ment. Ezr 2:33, Neh 7:37, 11:34; prob. the Adida of 1 Mac 12:38, 13:13; prob. mod. *el-Hadîtheh;* Map 30.
Hadoram, see ADONIRAM.
Hadrach, district in N Syria, Zec 9:1, between Arpad and Hamath (see Map 18); known in Ass. texts as *Hatarikka.* □
Ha-eleph, loc. of Benjamin listed Jos 18:28; sit. unk. Poss. this n. should be joined to that which precedes, i.e. ZELA, q.v.
Hagar, n. of the Eg. servant of Sarah; mother of Ishmael, Gn 16; later cast out by Abraham, Gn 21.
Hagarenes, Hagarites, Hagerites, see HAGRITES.
Haggai, 'feaster'; a prophet who, *ca* 520 B.C., encouraged the re-building of the Temple; his utterances are found in the 10th book of the Minor Prophets.
Haggith, n. of a concubine of David; mother of Adonijah, 2 S 3:4.
Hagrites, n. of a people defeated by the Israelite tribes of Transjordan in the time of Saul, 1 Ch 5:10, 19f.; cf. 1 Ch 27:30 (Heb. 31), Ps 83:6 (Heb. 7). It is not certain whether this people should be connected with Hagar, the mother of Ishmael.
Hai, see AI and AIATH (Neh 11:31).
Haifa, mod. port on the Mediterranean coast at the foot of Mt Carmel; Maps I (e.p.), 2; Pl. 251.
Hala, see HALAH.
Halah, region of Assyria to which the Israelites were deported, 2 K 17:6, 18:11, 1 Ch 5:26; poss. Ob 20 (conj.); sit. unk.
Halak (Mount), 'the bald mountain'; ment. Jos 11:17, 12:7, as southern limit of Joshua's conquest; sit. unk. □
Halcath, see HELKATH.
Halhul, loc. of Judah, in the hill country, listed Jos 15:58; mod. *Halhul,* N of Hebron; Maps 13, 19, p. 105 no. 6. □
Hali, loc. of Asher, listed Jos 19:25; sit. unk. □
Halicarnassus, city in Caria, ment. in the list of countries and cities which received the letter of Lucius, 1 Mac 15:23; mod. *Bodrum;* Map 26. □
Ham, 1. n. of the youngest son of Noah, cursed for his misconduct, Gn 9; in the table of the nations (Gn 10) he appears as the ancestor of the peoples of Egypt, Ethiopia, Arabia, and Canaan. In Ps 78, 105 and 106, Ham means Egypt.
2. city NE of the mts of Gilboa, Gn 14:5; mod. *Ham;* Map 4. □
Hamath, city in Syria, on the Orontes; ment. in the description of the ideal N frontier of the Promised Land, Nu 34:8; in the time of David and Solomon, 2 S 8:9, 2 Ch 8:4; the reference in 2 K 14:28, in the time of Jeroboam, is uncertain; captured by Assyria, Is 10:9; its inhabitants were settled in Samaria, 2 K 17:24; renamed Epiphania by Antiochus IV, but the ancient n. occurs in 1 Mac 12:25 and survives in the mod. *Hama;* Maps 1, 8, 12, 16, 18, 20, 29, 31, I (e.p.); Pls. 35, 36; p. 19.
Hamath (Entrance of), see LEBO-HAMATH.
Hamath-zobah, loc. captured by Solomon, according to 2 Ch 8:3. The puzzling association of these two names suggests that Hamath was in Zobah, which is impossible (cf. Map 16) unless the reference is to a different Hamath further S. It is more likely that the compiler is here combining the campaigns of David and Solomon (cf. 1 Ch 18:3). Cf. HAMATH, ZOBAH.
Hammath, loc. of Naphtali, listed Jos 19:35; prob. identical with the Levitical cities Hammoth-dor (Jos 21:32) and Hammon (1 Ch 6:76 (Heb. 61)); mod. *Hammâm Tabarîyeh,* on the W shore of the Sea of Galilee; Map 11. □
Hammon, 1. Levitical city ment. 1 Ch 6:76 (Heb. 61); prob. identical with HAMMATH, q.v.
2. loc. of Asher, listed Jos 19:28; poss. mod. *Umm el-Awamîd,* near the coast SW of Tyre; Map 11. □
Hammoth-dor, see HAMMATH.
Hammurabi, 6th king of the 1st dynasty of Babylon; famous for his codification of contemporary law; Maps 5, 6; Pls. 5, 79–81; p. 35.
Hamon, see HAMMON.
Hamor, n. of a Hurrian king of Shechem, Gn 33:19; 34.
Hananeel (Tower of), see HANANEL (Tower of).
Hananel (Tower of), n. of one of the towers in the wall of Jerusalem, Jer 31:38, Zec 14:10, Neh 3:1, 12:39; Map 24 C. □
Hanani, 'Yahweh has shown mercy'; n. of several persons, in particular of a prophet under Asa and Jehoshaphat, 2 Ch 16:7.
Hananiah, very common n., in particular of 1. one of the 3 friends of Daniel, Dn 1.
2. a false prophet who opposed Jeremiah, Jer 28. Cf. ANNAS.
Hananias, see HANANIAH (2).
Hanathon, see HANNATHON.
Hanes, city in Egypt ment. with Zoan, Is 30:4; poss. Heracleopolis (S of Memphis); mod. *Ihnâsiyeh el-Medineh* which suggests the ancient n.; Map 9. □
Hannathon, loc. of Zebulun, listed Jos 19:14; poss. mod. *Tell el-Bedeiwîyeh;* Map 11. □
Hanon, see HANUN.
Hanun, n. of 3 persons, inc. the son of Nahash, king of Ammon, 2 S 10.
Hapharaim, loc. of Issachar, listed Jos 19:19; sit. unk. □
Haphraim, see HAPHARAIM.
Haphsiba, see HEPHZIBAH.
Hara, region to which the Assyrians deported the Transjordanian tribes, according to 1 Ch 5:26; the text may be corrupt.
Harad, see HAROD.
Haradah, stopping-place on the Exodus, S of Kadesh, Nu 33:24f.; poss. in the mod. *W. Lussân;* Map 9. □
Haram, see HARAN (2).
Haran, 1. n. of several persons, in particular a brother of Abraham, Gn 11:26ff.
2. trading centre in N Mesopotamia, Gn 11:31f., 12:4f., 27:43, 28:10, 29:4, 2 K 19:12, Is 37:12, Ezk 27:23; the ruins lie near the mod. village of *Harrân;* Maps 1, 4, 5, 6, 8, 18, 20; Pls. 83–85; pp. 28ff., 97.
Harem, see HARIM.
Hares, see HAR-HERES.
Haret(h) (Forest of), see HERETH (Forest of).
Har-heres, loc. ment. Jg 1:35; prob. identical with Beth-shemesh (1). □
Harim, city of Judah, Neh 7:35; mod. *Kh. Horân,* W of Bethlehem; Map 22. □
Harma, see HORMAH.
Harmon, region into which the inhabitants of Samaria were to be cast, Am 4:3; unk. unless the meaning is '(in the direction of) Hermon', i.e. to the NE where Assyria lay. □
Harod, spring ment. Jg 7:1; prob. also referred to in 1 S 29:1 (fountain); mod. *'Ain Jalûd,* on the NW spur of the mts of Gilboa; Map 14. The home of David's warrior Shammah, 2 S 23:25, prob. lay E of Bethlehem, where *Kh. Khareidân* (*Kharazân*) recalls the ancient n.; Map 15.
Harodi, see HAROD.
Haroseth of the Gentiles, see HAROSHETH-HA-GOIIM.
Harosheth-ha-goiim, home of Sisera and scene of his defeat by Barak, Jg 4; mod. *Tell 'Amr,* at the foot of Mt Carmel, near *el-Haritiyeh* which preserves the ancient name; Map 14. □
Harosheth of the Gentiles, see HAROSHETH-HA-GOIIM.
Harrân, mod. n. of HARAN, q.v.
Hasarsuhal, see HAZAR-SHUAL.
Hasarsusim, see HAZAR-SUSAH.
Haseroth, see HAZEROTH.
Hasersual, see HAZAR-SHUAL.
Hasersusa, see HAZAR-SUSAH.
Hashmonah, stopping-place on the Exodus, Nu 33:29f.; prob. mod. *W. Hashim,* near Kadesh; Map 9. □
Hasidaeans, Heb. *Chasidim,* 'pious'; a Jewish sect which supported Judas Maccabaeus in his struggle against Antiochus IV Epiphanes, 1 Mac 2:42.
Hasmonaeans, non-Biblical n. of the family and dynasty of the Maccabees; pp. 110, 112f.
Hasor, see HAZOR.
Hassemon, see HESHMON.
Hassenaah, see SENAAH.
Hattushash, capital of the Hittite Empire; the ruins lie near the mod. village of *Boghaz-keui,* E of Ankara; Maps 1, 5–8; Pls. 102–105.
Hauran, region E of the Sea of Galilee whose limits are not precisely defined, Ezk 47:16, 18; the same n. is used today.
Havilah, region which traded in its gold, Gn 2:11; ment. with other regions of Arabia, Gn 10:29 = 1 Ch 1:23; 'son' of Egypt (Cush), Gn 10:7 = 1 Ch 1:9; the expression 'from Havilah to Shur', Gn 25:18, appears to indicate that the territory of the Ishmaelites was in NW Arabia and the Sinai peninsula, cf. 1 S 15:7. □
Havoth-jair, see HAVVOTH-JAIR.
Havvoth-jair, a group of villages of Manasseh in Gilead, Nu 32:41, 1 Ch 2:23, Dt 3:14; according to 1 K 4:13, in Solomon's 6th district; linked with the minor Judge Jair in Jg 10:4; sit. S of the Yarmuk; Maps 11, 14, 17. See also ARIEH. □
Hazael, 'God has seen'; n. of the assassin and successor of King Ben-hadad II of Damascus, 2 K 8:7ff.; he fought against Judah and Israel, 2 K 10ff.
Hazar-, Heb. word = 'a place enclosed by a wall', where shepherds and their flocks could shelter; an element in many place-names.
Hazar-addar, loc. ment. Nu 34:4; doubtless identical with the ADDAR (q.v.) of Judah, listed Jos 15:3. □
Hazar-enan, terminal point of the ideal N frontier of the Promised Land, Nu 34:9f., Ezk 47:17 (Hazar-enon), 48:1 (Hazar-enon); doubtless near Damascus, exact sit. unk. □
Hazar-enon, see HAZAR-ENAN.
Hazar-gaddah, loc. of Judah, in the Negeb, listed Jos 15:27; sit. unk. □
Hazar-hatticon, see HAZER-HATTICON.
Hazar-maveth, region of S Arabia, Gn 10:26 = 1 Ch 1:20; the same n. as mod. *Hadhramaut.* □
Hazar-shual, 'homestead of foxes'; loc. of Judah, in the Negeb, listed Jos 15:28; inc. among the cities of Simeon, Jos 19:3, 1 Ch 4:28; repopulated after the Exile, Neh 11:27; poss. mod. *Kh. el-Watan,* E of Beer-sheba; Map 13. □
Hazar-susah, loc. of Simeon, listed Jos 19:5; cf. 1 Ch 4:31 (Hazar-susim); S of Hebron, exact sit. unk. □
Hazar-susim, see HAZAR-SUSAH.
Hazar Tichon, see HAZER-HATTICON.
Hazazon-tamar, Amorite city, according to Gn 14:7; prob. near mod. *'Ain el-'Arûs,* S of the Dead Sea; Map 4. There is no record of the site after the Exile; the reference to En-gedi in 2 Ch 20:2 gives an approximate indication of its position relative to Jerusalem. Cf. ATHARIM, TAMAR. □
Hazer-hatticon, 'the middle Hazer'; ment. Ezk 47:16 as on the ideal N frontier of the Promised Land; poss. identical with HAZAR-ENAN, q.v. □
Hazeroth, stopping-place on the Exodus, Nu 11:35, 12:16,

Maps: 1 p. 9 / 2, 3 p. 10 / 4 p. 29 / 5 6 p. 30 / 7, 8 p. 43 / 9, 10 p. 44 / 11, 12 p. 59 / 13 p. 60 / 14 p. 65 / 15, 16 p. 66 / 17 p. 81 / 18, 19 p. 82 / 20, 21 p. 95 / 22–24 p. 96 / 25–29 p. 103 / 30, 31 p. 104 / 32, 33 p. 115 / 34, 35 p. 116 / I, II end-papers.

151

33:17f., Dt 1:1; poss. mod. *'Ain Khudra;* Map 9. □

Hazezon-tamar, see HAZAZON-TAMAR.

Hazor, 'court'; 1. loc. of Naphtali, listed Jos 19:36; Canaanite royal city, Jos 11:1, 10ff., 12:19; residence of Jabin, Jg 4:2, 17, 1 S 12:9; rebuilt by Solomon, 1 K 9:15; captured by Tiglath-pileser, 2 K 15:29; cf. To 1:2 (where LXX has Asser and Vulg. (1:1) has Naasson); 'the plain of Hazor', 1 Mac 11:67; mod. *Tell el-Qedah;* Maps 4, 5, 7, 11, 14, 17, 30.
2. loc. in the territory of Benjamin, ment. Neh 11:33; mod. *Kh. Hazzur*; Map 22. □
3. loc. of Judah, in the Negeb, listed Jos 15:23; sit. unk. □
4. loc. of Judah, in the Negeb, listed Jos 15:25, where it is identified with Kerioth-hezron; cf. HEZRON (2), KERIOTH-HEZRON. □
5. collective n. used in Jer 49:28ff. for the semi-nomadic Arabs.

Hazor-hadattah, loc. of Judah, in the Negeb, listed Jos 15:25; S of Hebron; exact sit. unk.

Hazor-ithnan, see ITHNAN.

Hebal, see EBAL (2), (3).

Hebel, see MAHALAB.

Heber, see EBER.

Hebrews, n. of the ancient Israelites; used in the stories of Joseph and Moses, particularly when an Egyptian refers to the Israelites or an Israelite addresses an Egyptian; used in dealings with the Philistines in 1 S; occurs in the expressions 'Hebrew slave' (Ex 21:2), 'Hebrew man, . . . Hebrew woman' (Dt 15:12), 'Hebrew slaves' (Jer 34:9), 'fellow Hebrew' (Jer 34:14), 'Abraham the Hebrew' (Gn 14:13); also found in the archaic language of Jon 1:9. In short, a n. used contemptuously by non-Israelites and reluctantly by the Israelites themselves. The exact meaning of the word is unk.; it may be connected with the *Khabiru* (or *Khapiru*) of the cuneiform texts and the *'Apiru* of the Eg. texts.

Hebron, also called Kiriath-arba, cf. Jos 15:54; Canaanite royal city, Nu 13:22, Jos 10:3ff., 12:10; visited by Abraham, Gn 13:18 (cf. MAMRE), who bought a family grave there, Gn 23:2ff.; given to Caleb by Joshua, Jos 14:13; city of Judah, in the hill country, listed Jos 15:54; city of refuge and Levitical city, Jos 20:7, 21:11 = 1 Ch 6:55 (Heb. 40), 57 (Heb. 42); David's first capital, 2 S 2:1ff.; fortified by Rehoboam, 2 Ch 11:10; repopulated after the Exile, Neh 11:25; later Edomite, 1 Mac 5:65; mod. *el-Khalîl;* Maps 1, 4, 9, 11, 13, 14, 15, 17, 19, 30, 31, 34; Pls. 88–90, 331f.; pp. 28ff., 67ff., 105. Cf. also ABDON (1), EBRON.

Hebrona, see ABRONAH.

Helam, city in Transjordan, 2 S 10:16f.; poss. identical with the ALEMA (q.v.) of 1 Mac 5:26; prob. mod. *'Alma;* Map 16. □

Helba, see MAHALAB.

Helbon, city which traded wine to Tyre, Ezk 27:18; mod. *Halbun*, about 16 miles N of Damascus; Map 20. □

Helcath, see HELKATH.

Helcias, see HILKIAH.

Heleph, loc. of Naphtali, listed Jos 19:33; sit. unk. □

Heliodorus, chief minister of Seleucus IV, 2 Mac 3; p. 106.

Heliopolis, Gk. n. of On and Ba'albek, cf. Jer 43:13. Cf. ON, BA'ALBEK.

Helkath, loc. of Asher, listed Jos 19:25; Levitical city, Jos 21:31; poss. mod. *Tell el-Harbaj;* Map 11. □

Helkath ha-ziddim, see HELKATH-HAZZURIM.

Helkath-hazzurim, 'field of rocks'; n. of a field near Gibeon, 2 S 2:16 (so R.S.V.; perhaps read Helkath ha-ziddim, 'field of sides').

Hellene, term which originally meant 'Greek', and later 'civilised'; in the Bible it means 'pagan'.

Helmondeblathaim, see ALMON-DIBLATHAIM.

Helon, see HOLON (1) and (2).

Heman, n. of 1. a sage in the time of Solomon, 1 K 4:31.
2. a singer in the Temple, 1 Ch 6:33 (Heb. 18).

Hemath, see HAMATH-ZOBAH.

Hemath (Entering in of), see LEBO-HAMATH.

Hemor, see HAMOR.

Hena, town on the upper Euphrates, in the list of territories conquered by the Assyrians, 2 K 18:34; 19:13 = Is 37:13; sit. unk. □

Henoch, see ENOCH.

Hepher, Canaanite royal city, Jos 12:17; in Solomon's 3rd district, 1 K 4:10; poss. mod. *Tell Ibshâr;* Maps 14, 17. □

Hephzibah, n. of the mother of Manasseh, 2 K 21:1.

Heres, see HAR-HERES.

Hereth (Forest of), ment. 1 S 22:5; between Adullam and Giloh; Map 15. □

Herma, see HORMAH.

Hermas, n. of a Roman Christian, Ro 16:14.

Hermes, n. of 1. a Roman Christian, Ro 16:14.
2. the Gk. god (Mercurius, Mercury), cf. Ac 14:12.

Hermogenes, n. of a Christian of Asia, 2 Ti 1:15.

Hermon (Mount), S part of the Anti-Lebanon (9,232 ft.), 25 m. long; always snow-covered, hence its mod. n. *J. esh-Sheikh*, 'mountain of the old man'; N frontier of Transjordan, Dt 3:8, 9 (which mentions 2 other names, SIRION and SENIR, (qq.v.), 4:48; frontier of the territory of Og, Jos 12:5, 13:11, 1 Ch 5:23; ment. in the indication of the territories of the tribes, Jos 11:3, 17; Maps 2, 34; Pls. 360, 361, 371; pp. 15f.

Herod, n. of various princes, 1. Herod the Great, king of Judaea at the time of the Nativity (37–4 B.C.), Lk 1:5, Mt 2; pp. 113, 117f.
2. Herod Antipas, son of (1), tetrarch of Galilee; he beheaded John the Baptist, Mt 14, and later mocked Jesus, Lk 23; p. 118.
3. Herod Agrippa I, grandson of (1), king of Judaea; he persecuted the Early Christian community, Ac 12; p. 121.
4. Herod Agrippa II, son of (3); he questioned St Paul at Caesarea, Ac 25.
5. Herod Philip, son of (1), see PHILIP (5).

Herod (Palace of), built by Herod the Great on a site to the W of Jerusalem; cf. PRAETORIUM, HIPPICUS, MARIAMNE, PHASAEL; Map 33; Pls. 191, 192, 378.

Herodias, n. of the wife of Herod Philip (son of Herod the Great); mistress of his brother, Herod Antipas, and both mother and aunt of Salome, Mt 14:3ff.

Herodium, fortress built by Herod the Great on a hill 3 miles SE of Bethlehem; site of his tomb; mod. *J. Fureidis;* Map 34; Pl. 358; p. 118.

Hesebon, see HESHBON.

Heser, see HAZOR.

Heshbon, capital of the Amorite king Sihon, Nu 21:25ff., Jos 13:21; loc. of Gad, listed Jos 13:26, and of Reuben, listed Jos 13:17; Levitical city of Gad, Jos 21:39; later Moabite, Is 15:4, Jer 48:2; famous for its fishponds, Ca 7:4; mod. *Hesbân;* Maps 11, 14, 17.

Heshmon, loc. of Judah, in the Negeb, listed Jos 15:27; in the vicinity of Beer-sheba, exact sit. unk. □

Hesmona, see HASHMONAH.

Hesron, see HEZRON (2).

Heth (Sons, Children of), Hethites, see HITTITES.

Hethalon, see HETHLON.

Hethlon, loc. on the ideal NW frontier of the Promised Land, Ezk 47:15, 48:1; sit. unk. □

Hevila, Hevilath, see HAVILAH.

Hevites, see AVVITES and HIVITES.

Hezekiah, 'strength of Yahweh'; n. of 4 persons, in particular the 13th king of Judah (716–687 B.C.), 2 K 18–20; cf. Is 36–39; pp. 93f.; Pl. 231.

Hezron, 1. loc. on the S boundary of Judah, Jos 15:3; sit. unk. □
2. loc. of Judah, in the Negeb, linked with Kerioth (R.S.V. Kerioth-hezron) and identified with Hazor, Jos 15:25; cf. HAZOR (4). □

Hiddekel, Heb. n. of the TIGRIS, q.v.

Hiel, n. of the rebuilder of Jericho, 1 K 16:34.

Hierapolis, city in Asia Minor, near Colossae, Col 4:13; mod. *Pambuk Kalesi;* Map II (e.p.).

Hierosolyma, Hellenised form of the n. JERUSALEM, q.v.; the aspirated pronunciation of the first syllable resembled the word *hiero-*, 'holy'; frequently used by some writers of the N.T. in imitation of Tobit, 2 Maccabees, etc.

Hilaz, Hilen, see HOLON (1).

Hilkiah, 'God is my heritage'; n. of several persons, inc. the High Priest who, in the reign of Josiah, found the book of the Law in the Temple, 2 K 22.

Hill of Shame, see OFFENCE (Mount of).

Hinder Sea, see WESTERN SEA.

Hinnom (Valley of, Valley of the son(s) of), flanking Jerusalem on the S; through it passed N boundary of Judah (Jos 15:8, cf. Neh 11:30) and S boundary of Benjamin (Jos 18:16); later the scene of the sacrifice of children to Moloch (2 K 23:10, 2 Ch 28:3, 33:6); Jeremiah called down the wrath of God upon it (Jer 7:31ff., 19:2, 6, 32:35, cf. 2:23). This valley came to symbolise Hell and gave its name to the Gehenna of the Gk. N.T., 'hell' in EVV (Mt 5:22, 29f., 10:28, 18:9, 23:15, 33, Mk 9:43 ff., Lk 12:5, Ja 3:6). Mod. n. of the valley is *W. er-Rabâbi;* Maps 24, 33. □

Hippicus, n. of one of the 3 famous towers of the Palace of Herod at Jerusalem; Map 33.

Hippos, see DECAPOLIS.

Hira, see IRA (1).

Hiram, 'father is exalted'; n. of 1. a king of Tyre, 1 K 9:10ff.
2. a half-Jewish bronze-worker who helped to build the Temple, 1 K 7:13ff.

Hir-semes, see IR-SHEMESH.

Hittites, one of the pre-Israelite peoples of CANAAN (q.v.), Ex 23:28, Nu 13:29, Ezr 9:1. In the time of Abraham they lived near Hebron, Gn 23:3ff.; cf. the origins of Jerusalem, Ezk 16:3, 45; Hittites ment. in the Bible include Ahimelech (1 S 26:6), Uriah (2 S 11:3), and wives of Solomon (1 K 11:1). The excavations at *Boghaz-keui* have brought to light the history and civilisation of a people of this name who, after 1450 B.C., challenged Assyria and Egypt for possession of the world empire; cf. Maps 5, 6, 7; Pls. 102–111, 139, 184; pp. 45f., 64, 74, 88. After 1200 B.C. (cf. Map 8) there remained only a few independent Hittite cities in N Syria; cf. 1 K 10:29 = 2 Ch 1:17, 2 K 7:6. The question of the connection between the Hittites of Asia Minor and N Syria and the Hittites who, according to the Bible, inhabited the hill country of Palestine before the Israelites is highly controversial.

Hivites, n. of a pre-Israelite people of Canaan, ment. in the lists (cf. CANAAN (a)-(d)), usually in a penultimate position, (a)-(c). There were Hivites at Shechem and Gibeon, Gn 34:2, Jos 9:7, 11:19 (LXX Horites); ment. in connection with Tyre, 2 S 24:7, with Sidon, Jg 3:3, with Mt Hermon, Jos 11:3; cf. Gn 36:2, Ex 23:28, Is 17:9 (LXX). □

Hoba, see HOBAH.

Hobab, n. of a relation of Moses, Nu 10:29.

Hobah, region N of Damascus, Gn 14:15; Map 4.

Holda, see HULDAH.

Holofernes, n. of the general of Nebuchadnezzar who figures in the book of Judith.

Holon, n. of 2 cities, 1. loc. of Judah, in the hill country, listed Jos 15:51; Levitical city, Jos 21:15; called Hilen (or Hilaz) in 1 Ch 6:58 (Heb. 43); sit. unk. □
2. city in Moab, Jer 48:21; sit. unk. □

Hophni, Eg. n. meaning 'tadpole', borne by a son of Eli, 1 S 1:3, 2:34.

Hophra, Biblical n. of the Pharaoh Apries, Jer 44:30. Cf. APRIES.

Hor (Mount), 1. mt on the confines of Edom; stopping-place on the Exodus and scene of Aaron's death, Nu 20:22ff., 21:4, 33:37ff., Dt 32:50; poss. the mt range NE of Kadesh; Map 9. □
2. mt forming the N frontier of Canaan, Nu 34:7f., exact sit. unk. □

Horeb (Mount), another n. for Mt Sinai, Ex 3:1, 17:6, 33:6, 9 passages in Dt, 1 K 8:9 = 2 Ch 5:10, Mal 4:4 (Heb. 3:22), Ps 106:19, Sir 48:7; apart from these passages, the n. occurs only in 1 K 19:8, to designate the terminus of Elijah's journey; Map 9.

Horem, loc. of Naphtali, listed Jos 19:38; sit. unk. □

Horesh, city of Judah where David took refuge, 1 S 23:15ff.; mod. *Kh. Khureisa,* 6 miles S of Hebron; Map 15. □

Hor-haggidgad, stopping-place on the Exodus, Nu 33:32f.; called Gudgodah in Dt 10:7; poss. a spring of the mod. *W. Khadakhid;* Map 9. □

Hor-hagidgad, see HOR-HAGGIDGAD.

Horims, see HORITES.

Horites, a people who lived in the mts of Seir, Gn 14:6; driven out by the Edomites, Dt 2:12, 22 (cf. list of Gn 36:20f. = 36:29f.); the n. stood perhaps in the original text of Gn 36:2, instead of the Hivites (cf. 36:20), and according to the Gk. text of Gn 34:2, Jos 9:7, there were Horites in Shechem and Gibeon; cf. p. 68. These Horites are doubtless the Hurrians who, as archaeological research has revealed, inhabited Mesopotamia and Syro-Palestine in the first half of the 2nd millennium B.C.; Maps 5, 6, 7. □

Horma, see HORMAH and RAMAH (4).

Hormah, Canaanite royal city, Jos 12:14; loc. of Judah, in the Negeb, listed Jos 15:30; inc. among the cities of Simeon, Jos 19:4, 1 Ch 4:30; cf. Nu 14:45, Dt 1:44, Nu 21:3; originally called Zephath, according to Jg 1:17; city to which David sent spoil, 1 S 30:30; poss. mod. *Tell el-Mishâsh*, ESE of Beer-sheba; Maps 9, 11, 13, 14, 15. □

Horonaim, city of Moab, ment. Is 15:5, Jer 48:3ff., and on the Moabite Stone (cf. p. 80); sit. unk. □

Horrhites, Horrites, see HORITES.

Horse Gate, gate on the E side of Jerusalem, Jer 31:40; near the royal palace, 2 K 11:16, 2 Ch 23:15, Neh 3:28; Map 24 C. □

Hosa, see HOSAH.

Hosah, loc. of Asher, listed Jos 19:29; sit. unk. □

Hosea, abb. of Heb. *Hosha'yah*, 'Yahweh saves'; identical in Heb. with HOSHEA, q.v.; n. of prophet of the 8th century B.C.; first of the Minor Prophets.

Hoshea, abb. of Heb. *Hosha'yah*, 'Yahweh saves'; identical in Heb. with HOSEA, q.v.; n. of several persons, in particular 1. son of Nun, later renamed Joshua by Moses, Nu 13:8, 16.
2. last king of Israel (732–724 B.C.), 2 K 17.

House of the sun, see HELIOPOLIS.

Hucac, see HUKOK.

Hucuca, see HUKKOK.

Hukkok, loc. of Naphtali, listed Jos 19:34; mod. *Yakuk*; Map 11. □

Hukok, Levitical city of Asher, 1 Ch 6:75 (Heb. 60); prob. a scribal error for HELKATH, q.v. □

Huldah, prophetess of Jerusalem consulted when, in the reign of Josiah, the book of the Law was found in the Temple, 2 K 22.

Huleh (Lake), non-Biblical n. of the lake near the source of the Jordan; mod. *Bahret el-Hûleh;* Map 2. Cf. MEROM (Waters of).

Humtah, loc. of Judah, in the hill country, listed Jos 15:54; sit. unk. □

Hurrians, see HORITES.

Hus, see UZ.

Husah, see HUSHAH.

Husathite, see HUSHAH.

Hushah, (whence Hushathite), home of Sibbecai (2 S 21:18, 1 Ch 11:29, 20:4, 27:11), and Mebunnai (2 S 23:27), 2 of David's warriors; mod. *Husan*, W of Bethlehem; Map 15. □

Hushai, n. of 2 persons, in particular a friend of David, 2 S 15, 16.

Hushathite, see HUSHAH.

Huzal, see UZAL.

Hyenas (Valley of), see ZEBOIM (2).

Hyksos, n. of a group of peoples who controlled Egypt in the 17th century B.C., at the period when Joseph and his brothers were living there; Map 6; pp. 40ff.

Hymenaeus, n. of a renegade Christian, 1 Ti 1:20, 2 Ti 2:17.

Hymeneus, see HYMENAEUS.

Hyrcanus, n. of 1. John Hyrcanus, son of Simon Maccabaeus; p. 110.
2. Hyrcanus II, eldest son of Alexandra; pp. 110, 112.

I

Ibleam, loc. of Manasseh in the territory of Asher, listed Jos 17:11, cf. Jg 1:27; Levitical city, 1 Ch 6:70 (Heb. 55) (Bileam); ment. 2 K 9:27; mod. *Tell Bel'ameh*, N of Shechem; Maps 11, 17. □

Ibzan, n. of the 9th Judge of Israel, Jg 12:8ff.; Map 14.

Ichabod, 'where is the glory?'; n. of the son of Phinehas, 1 S 4:19ff.

Iconium, city in Asia Minor, Ac 13:51, 14:1, 19, 21; cf. 16:2, 2 Ti 3:11; mod. *Konya;* Maps I and II (e.p.). □

Idalah, loc. of Zebulun, listed Jos 19:15; sit. unk. □

Iddo, n. of 4 persons, inc. a prophet and chronicler under Jeroboam I, 2 Ch 12:15.

Maps: 1 p. 9 / 2, 3 p. 10 / 4 p. 29 / 5, 6 p. 30 / 7, 8 p. 43 / 9, 10 p. 44 / 11, 12 p. 59 / 13 p. 60 / 14 p. 65 / 15, 16 p. 66 / 17 p. 81 / 18, 19 p. 82 / 20, 21 p. 95 / 22–24 p. 96 / 25–29 p. 103/ 30, 31 p. 104/ 32, 33 p. 115 / 34 35 p. 116 / I, II end-papers.

152

Idumaea, G&L n. of Edom; Idumaea extended further to the NW than the former Edom and thus included the Negeb and the Shephelah. Herod the Great came from this region. Maps 23, 30, 34.

Iim, 'heaps of ruins'; loc. of Judah, in the Negeb, listed Jos 15:29; poss. mod. *Deir er-Ghawi*, between Beer-sheba and Hebron; Map 13. Cf. also IYIM. □

Ije-abarim, see IYE-ABARIM, IYIM.

Ijon, loc. in the extreme N of Palestine; captured by Ben-hadad together with Dan and Abel-beth-maacah, 1 K 15:20, 2 Ch 16:4; later captured by Tiglath-pileser, 2 K 15:29; prob. mod. *Tell Dibbîn*, near *Merjayûn* which preserves the ancient name; Map 17. □

Illyria, region W of Macedonia, Ro 15:19; Maps 32, II (e.p.). □

Immanuel, 'God with us'; n. of the miraculous child of Isaiah's prophecy, Is 7:14ff., cf. 8:8; identified as Christ in Mt 1:22f. (Emmanuel).

Immer, loc. in Babylonia, Ezr 2:59, Neh 7:61; sit. unk. □

India, Heb. *Hoddu*; the territory around the Indus, added to the Persian empire by Darius I; used in the expression 'from India to Ethiopia' in Est 1:1, 8:9, 13:1 (LXX), 16:1 (LXX); also in 1 Mac 8:8.

Indiana, see INDIA.

Iphtah, loc. of Judah, in the lowland, listed Jos 15:43; poss. mod. *Tarqûmiya*, E of Lachish; Maps 13, 19. □

Iphtahel (Valley of), ment. as a boundary of Zebulun, Jos 19:14, 27; poss. mod. *Sahl el-Battôf;* Map 11. □

Ira, n. of 1. one of David's warriors, 2 S 23:26.
2. one of David's priests, 2 S 20:26.

Iralah, so some Heb. MSS and ancient versions in Jos 19:15 for IDALAH, q.v.

Ir-hammelach, see CITY OF SALT.

Iron, see YIRON.

Irpeel, loc. of Benjamin, listed Jos 18:27; poss. mod. *Rafat*, NW of Jerusalem; Maps 13, 19. □

Ir-shemesh, loc. of Dan, listed Jos 19:41; prob. identical with BETH-SHEMESH (1), q.v. □

Isaac, G&L form of a Heb. n. which is an abb. of *Yishaq-El*, 'may God be benevolent'; n. of the son of Abraham and Sarah, Gn 21; husband of Rebekah and father of Esau and Jacob, Gn 25.

Isai, see JESSE.

Isaiah, 'Yahweh is salvation'; n. of the greatest prophet of Israel, who lived towards the end of the 8th century B.C.; his preaching is preserved in Is 1–39, see pp. 93ff.; for a discussion of Is 40–55, see p. 100.

Isaias, see ISAIAH.

Isboseth, Ish-baal, see ISH-BOSHETH.

Ish-bosheth, n. of the son of Saul, 2 S 2–4; also called Ish-baal or Esh-baal, 1 Ch 8:33; p. 67.

Ishmael, 'God hears'; n. of several persons, inc. 1. the son of Abraham and Hagar, Gn 16, cast out with his mother by Abraham so that he should not share Isaac's inheritance, Gn 21, cf. Gal 4; ancestor of 12 tribes (Gn 25:12ff.) which are localised in N Arabia, cf. Gn 21:21.
2. the murderer of Gedaliah, Jer 40.

Ish-tob, see TOB.

Isin, ancient city of Mesopotamia, SE of Babylon; the rival of Larsa from *ca* 2000 B.C.; subjugated by Hammurabi; mod. *Ishân Bahriyât;* Maps 5, 6.

Isle(s), Island(s), see COAST(S), COASTLAND(S).

Ismael, see ISHMAEL (1).

Ismahel, see ISHMAEL (2).

Israel, cognomen of Jacob, prob. = 'may God show Himself strong', Gn 32:29; in popular etymology explained as 'he has proved strong against God'; cf. Hos 12:4 (Heb. 5).

Issachar, n. of the 5th son of Jacob and Leah, Gn 30:17f.; ancestor of an Israelite tribe whose territory is described in Jos 19:17–23; Maps 11, 14, 15, 17.

Istemo, see ESHTEMOA.

Istob, see TOB.

Italy, ment. Ac 18:2, 27:1,6, cf. 10:1, He 13:24; Map II (e.p.). See also KITTIM and TUBAL. □

Ithamar, n. of a son of Aaron, Ex 28:1.

Ithlah, loc. of Dan, listed Jos 19:42; sit unk. □

Ithnan, loc. of Judah, in the Negeb, listed Jos 15:23; perhaps to be read Hazor-ithnan, and identified with HAZOR (3), q.v.; sit. unk. □

Ittah-kazin, see ETH-KAZIN.

Ittai, n. of a faithful supporter of David at the time of Absalom's rebellion, 2 S 18.

Ituraea, kingdom to the N of Palestine, Lk 3:1; Map 35. □

Iturea, see ITURAEA.

Ivah, see IVVAH.

Ivvah, one of the cities whose inhabitants colonised Samaria after the deportation, 2 K 18:34 and 19:13 = Is 37:13; called Avva in 2 K 17:24; sit. unk. See AVVITES, AVVIM (2). □

Iye-abarim, see IYIM.

Iyim, stopping-place on the Exodus, S of Moab, Nu 33:45; a fuller n., Iye-abarim, occurs in Nu 21:11, 33:44; poss. mod. *Mahay;* Map 9. See also IIM. □

J

Jaar (Fields of), poetic n. in Ps 132:6 for KIRIATH-JEARIM, q.v.

Jaazaniah, 'may Yahweh listen'; n. of 4 persons, inc. 1. leader of the Rechabites, Jer 35:3.
2. army commander under Gedaliah, Jer 40:8 (Jezaniah); cf. Pl. 221 no. 2.

Jaazer, see JAZER.

Jabal, n. of a son of Lamech, ancestor of the wandering shepherds, Gn 4:20. The n. suggests the verb *ybl*, 'to lead'. Cf. TUBAL-CAIN.

Jaban, see JABIN.

Jabbok, n. of a tributary flowing into the Jordan from the E; ment. in the story of Jacob, Gn 32:22 (Heb. 23), where the n. has suggested the use of the verb *ye'abeq* in Gn 32:24 (Heb. 25) ('a man wrestled with him'); apart from this passage, the Jabbok is not ment. in the Bible except as a boundary, Nu 21:24, Jg 11:13, 22, Dt 2:37, 3:16, Jos 12:2; mod. *Nahr ez-Zerqa*; Map 2; Pl. 91; p. 15. □

Jabel, see JABAL.

Jabes Galaad, Jabesh, see JABESH-GILEAD.

Jabesh-gilead, city in Transjordan, Jg 21:8–14; city delivered by Saul, 1 S 11:1–11; the inhabitants took charge of Saul's body, 1 S 31:11ff. (Heb. 12ff.), 1 Ch 10:11ff., for which service David thanked them, 2 S 2:4ff., cf. 21:12; poss. the ruins near mod. *Halâwa*, on the edge of the *W. Yâbis*, SE of Beth-shan; Maps 14, 15. □

Jabin, n. of a king of Hazor defeated by Joshua, Jos 11:1; poss. the Jabin whose commander, Sisera, was defeated by Barak, Jg 4:2ff., Ps 83:9 (Heb. 10).

Jabneel, 1. loc. of Naphtali, listed Jos 19:33; poss. mod. *Kh. Yamma;* Map 11. □
2. loc. on the boundary of Judah, Jos 15:11; captured by Uzziah, 2 Ch 26:6 (Jabneh); later called Jamnia, 1 Mac 4:15, 5:58, 10:69, 15:40, 2 Mac 12:8, 40; mod. *Yebna*; Maps 11, 13, 17, 19, 29, 30, 31, 34. □

Jabneh, Jabnia, see JABNEEL (2).

Jaboc, see JABBOK.

Jacan, see BENE-JAAKAN.

Jachanan, see JOKNEAM.

Jachin, n. of 1. a son of Simeon, Gn 46:10.
2. a pillar at the entrance to the Temple of Solomon, 1 K 7:21.

Jackal's Well, near the Valley Gate of Jerusalem, Neh 2:13; prob. the spring N of the Valley of Hinnom; Map 24 C. □

Jacob, abb. form of Heb. *Ya'aqob-El*, 'may Yahweh protect!'; n. of a son of Isaac; ancestor of the Israelites.

Jacob's Well, well near Shechem, ment. only in Jn 4:6, but cf. Gn 33:18f., Jos 24:32; mod. *Bir Ja'qûb;* Map 34; Pls. 95, 96, 101. □

Jael, 'wild goat'; n. of the murderess of Sisera, Jg 4:17ff.

Jaffa, mod. n. of JOPPA, q.v.; Map 2.

Jagur, loc. of Judah, in the Negeb, listed Jos 15:21; exact sit. unk. □

Jahaz, loc. of Reuben, listed Jos 13:18; site of Sihon's battle against Israel, Nu 21:23, Dt 2:32, Jg 11:20; Levitical city, Jos 21:36, 1 Ch. 6:78 (Heb. 63) (Jahzah); later Moabite, Is 15:4, Jer 48:21 (Jahzah), 34; ment. on the Moabite Stone, cf. p. 80; poss. mod. *Kh. Umm el-Idhâm;* Maps 11, 14. □

Jahaza(h), see JAHAZ.

Jahaziel, n. of several persons, inc. one of David's warriors, 1 Ch 12:4.

Jahel, see JAEL.

Jahzah, see JAHAZ.

Jair, n. of several persons, inc. one of the minor Judges, Jg 10:3ff.; Map 14.

Jair (Towns, Villages of), see HAVVOTH-JAIR.

Jairus, G&L form of Heb. *Jair;* n. of a ruler of the synagogue, Mk 5:22.

Jambres, see JANNES AND JAMBRES.

James, G&L form of Jacob; n. of several persons, in particular 1. St James (the Greater), son of Zebedee and brother of St John, Mt 4:21; martyred by Herod Agrippa I, Ac 12:2.
2. son of Alphaeus, Mt 10:3; also an Apostle; poss. identical with (3).
3. son of Mary, Mt 27:56; called the Less, Mk 15:40; brother of Our Lord, Gal 1:19; head of the Church in Jerusalem; often identified with (2).
4. father or brother of the Apostle Judas (Jude), Lk 6:16, Ac 1:13.

Jamnia, G&L form of JABNEEL (2), q.v.; Maps 29, 30, 31, 34; p. 109.

Janim, loc. of Judah, in the hill country, listed Jos 15:53; poss. mod. *Beni Na'im*, E of Hebron; Maps 13, 19. □

Jannes and Jambres, nn. of the Eg. magicians who opposed Moses, according to 2 Ti 3:8.

Janoah, 1. loc. on the E boundary of Ephraim, listed Jos 16:6f.; mod. *Kh. Yanûn;* Map 11. □
2. loc. in N Palestine captured by Tiglath-pileser, 2 K 15:29; sit. unk. □

Janoe, see JANOAH (1) and (2).

Janohah, see JANOAH (1).

Janum, see JANIM.

Japheth, n. of a son of Noah, Gn 6:10; ancestor of 7 peoples in Asia Minor and the Mediterranean islands, Gn 10:1ff.

Japhia, loc. of Zebulun, listed Jos 19:13; mod. *Yafa;* Map 11. □

Japhie, see JAPHIA.

Japho, see JOPPA.

Jaramoth, see JARMUTH (2).

Jarephel, see IRPEEL.

Jarim (Mount), see JEARIM (Mount).

Jarmuth, 1. loc. of Judah, in the lowland, listed Jos 15:35; Canaanite royal city, Jos 10:3, 5, 23, 12:11; repopulated after the Exile, Neh 11:29; mod. *Kh. Yarmûq*, E of Azekah; Maps 13, 14, 19. □
2. Levitical city of Issachar, Jos 21:29; poss. identical with Ramoth, 1 Ch 6:73 (Heb58),. and Remeth, Jos 19:21; sit. unk. □

Jasa, see JAHAZ.

Jaser, see JAZER.

Jashub, loc. conjecturally found by some scholars in Jos 17:7, by reading Jashub instead of 'inhabitants of' before En-tappuah; prob. mod. *Yasuf*, three-quarters of a mile NE of *Tell Sheikh Abû Zarad* which is the site of Tappuah (1); cf. Map 11.

Jason, n. of several persons, inc. 1. Jason of Cyrene, author of a history of the Maccabaean revolt which was used as a source for 2 Mac; p. 109.
2. a brother of the High Priest Onias III who bought the office of High Priest and attempted to Hellenise the Jews, 2 Mac 4.
3. a Christian of Thessalonica, Ac 17:5ff.

Jassa, see JAHAZ.

Jattir, loc. of Judah, in the hill country, listed Jos 15:48; Levitical city, Jos 21:14, 1 Ch 6:57 (Heb. 42); city to which David sent spoil, 1 S 30:27; mod. *Kh. 'Attir*, SSE of Hebron; Maps 13, 15. □

Javan, Heb. equivalent of 'Ionian'; n. applied to the Greek-speaking regions in Asia Minor and the Mediterranean islands, cf. Gn 10:2–4 = 1 Ch 1:5–7; ment. with Tubal in Is 66:19, Ezk 27:13; cf. Ezk 27:19(?), Jl 3 (Heb. 4):6 (Greeks). Rendered Greece, designating Greece proper, in Dn 8:21, 10:20, 11:2; prob. also in Zec 9:13. □

Jazar, see JAZER.

Jazer, loc. of Gad, listed Jos 13:25; Levitical city, Jos 21:39, 1 Ch 6:81 (Heb. 66); captured and occupied by the tribes of Reuben and Gad, Nu 21:32, 32:1ff.; on the route of the census-takers sent out by David, 2 S 24:5; later Moabite, Is 16:8f., Jer 48:32; captured by Judas Maccabaeus, 1 Mac 5:8; prob. *Kh. Jazzir*, near mod. *es-Salt*; Maps 11, 15, 30. □

Jeabarim, see IYE-ABARIM.

Jearim (Mount), mt on the boundary of Judah, Jos 15:10; identical with Seir (2) ment. in the same verse.

Jeblaam, see IBLEAM.

Jebnael, see JABNEEL (1).

Jebneel, see JABNEEL (2).

Jeboc, see JABBOK.

Jebus, another n. for Jerusalem, Jg 19:10f., 1 Ch 11:4f. This n. is apparently derived from that of the inhabitants, the Jebusites. □

Jebusi, see JEBUSITES.

Jebusites, early inhabitants of Jerusalem, Jos 15:8, 63, 18:16; ment. among the peoples of CANAAN (q.v.), Nu 13:29, Jg 1:21, Ezr 9:1, Zec 9:7. □

Jecmaan, Jecnam, Jeconam, see JOKNEAM.

Jectehel, see JOKTHEEL (2).

Jecthel, see JOKTHEEL (1).

Jedala, see IDALAH.

Jegbaa, see JOGBEHAH.

Jeheziel, see JAHAZIEL.

Jehoahaz, 'Yahweh has seized'; n. of 3 kings, 1. 17th king of Judah (609 B.C.); also called Shallum; deported to Egypt by the Pharaoh Necho after a reign of three months, 2 K 23; Map 20; p. 97.
2. 11th king of Israel (814–798 B.C.), 2 K 13.
3. other n. of Ahaziah, 6th king of Judah; cf. AHAZIAH (2).

Jehoash, see JOASH, JEHOASH.

Jehoiachin, n. of the 19th king of Judah (598–597 B.C.); deported to Babylon by Nebuchadnezzar, 2 K 24; Map 20; pp. 97f.

Jehoiakim, n. of 3 persons, in particular the 18th king of Judah (609–598 B.C.); also called Eliakim; son of Josiah, 2 K 23–24; Map 20; pp. 97f.

Jehoram, see JORAM, JEHORAM.

Jehoshaphat, 'Yahweh judges'; n. of several persons, in particular the 4th king of Judah (870–848 B.C.), 1 K 22; p. 87.

Jehoshaphat (Valley of), valley of the last judgment, Jl 3:2, 12 (Heb. 4:2, 12); cf. Pl. 326.

Jehoshua, see JOSHUA.

Jehovah, meaningless spelling of the n. of the God of Israel. When the Jews of the first centuries of our era encountered the 4 consonants of this n., *Yhwh*, they pronounced with reverent awe the common noun *Adonai*, 'the Lord', (of which the first *a* sounded almost like a weak *e*). When, towards the 9th century, the text of the Bible was pointed with vowels, the n. of God was therefore provided with the vowels of the word *Adonai* which was to be pronounced. Later this fact was no longer understood in the West, and the 4 letters *Yhwh* were read with the vowels of *A(e)donai*, hence *Jehovah*.

Jehu, 'Yahweh is God'; n. of 2 persons, 1. prophet who condemned Baasha and Jehoshaphat, 1 K 16:1ff., 2 Ch 19:2f.
2. 10th king of Israel (841–814 B.C.); he exterminated the house of Ahab and took action against the cult of Baal, 2 K 9–10; Map 17; pp. 87, 90.

Jehud, loc. of Dan, listed Jos 19:4–5; mod. *el-Yahûdîyeh*, E of Jaffa; Map 11. See also AZOR. □

Jekabzeel, loc. ment. Neh 11:25; identical with KABZEEL, q.v.

Jephtahel, see IPHTAHEL (Valley of).

Jephte, see JEPHTHAH.

Jephtha, see IPHTAH.

Jephthael, see IPHTAHEL (Valley of).

Jephthah, n. of one of the great Judges; he liberated Israel from the Ammonites, and sacrificed his daughter as the result of a vow, Jg 11:1–12:7; Map 14.

Jercaam, see JOKDEAM.

Jeremiah, n. of one of the great prophets of Israel; he prophesied in the S Kingdom at the period of the Fall of Jerusalem (586 B.C.); p. 97. His utterances are contained in the book of the Bible which bears his name.

Jeremias, see JEREMIAH.

Jericho, important city in the Jordan valley; also called the CITY OF PALM TREES, q.v.; ment. frequently in Nu, Dt, and Jos; rebuilt under Ahab, 1 K 16:34; visited by Elijah and Elisha; ment. in the N.T. in the parable of the Good Sama-

Maps: 1 p. 9 / 2, 3 p. 10 / 4 p. 29 / 5, 6 p. 30 / 7, 8 p. 43 / 9, 10 p. 44 / 11, 12 p. 59 / 13 p. 60 / 14 p. 65 / 15, 16 p. 66 / 17 p. 81 / 18, 19 p. 82 / 20, 21 p. 95 / 22–24 p. 96 / 25–29 p. 103 / 30, 31 p. 104 / 32, 33 p. 115 / 34, 35 p. 116 / I, II end-papers.

153

ritan, Lk 10:30; in the story of the healing of a blind man (or 2 blind men), Mt 20:29 and parallel passages; in the story of Zacchaeus, Lk 19; mod. *Tell es-Sultân*, 1 mile NW of the mod. small town of *Rîha*, is the site of O.T. Jericho; the ruins of the Herodian Jericho lie a little further S; Maps 2, 3, 11, 14, 15, 17, 22, 30, 34; Pls. 38, 160, 172, 308–310; p. 19.

Jerimoth, Jerimuth, see JARMUTH (1).

Jeroboam, n. of 2 kings of the N Kingdom, 1. Jeroboam I (931–910 B.C.), 1st king of Israel; Map 17; pp. 76ff.
2. Jeroboam II (783–743 B.C.); p. 90.

Jeron, see YIRON.

Jeruel (Wilderness of), scene of the encounter between Jehoshaphat's army and the Ammonites, 2 Ch 20:16; SE of Tekoa; Map 17. □

Jerusalem, capital of the kingdom from the time of David, who captured it, pp. 68ff.; mod. *el-Qudds*, 'the holy'; marked on nearly all the Maps; Pls. 191, 192, 327, 373–384. Cf. JEBUS.

Jesana, see JESHANAH.

Jeshanah, loc. captured by Abijah, 2 Ch 13:19; perhaps ment. with Mizpah in 1 S 7:12 (Heb. SHEN, q.v.); prob. mod. *Burj el-Isâneh*, N of Jerusalem; Map 17. □

Jeshua, 1. n. of the 1st High Priest after the return from the Exile, Ezr 3ff.
2. loc. ment. Neh 11:26; poss. mod. *Tell es-Sa'wi*, E of Beer-sheba; Map 23. □

Jesse, n. of the father of David, 1 S 16, etc.

Jesue, see JESHUA.

Jesus Ben Sira, n. of the author of the book of Ecclesiasticus; pp. 27, 110.

Jesus, Joshua, 'Yahweh is salvation'; n. applied in the N.T. to 4 persons, 1. Joshua, the successor of Moses, Ac 7:45, He 4:8.
2. an ancestor of the Messiah, Jesus Christ, Lk 3:29.
3. Jesus Christ (cf. the explanation of the n. in Mt 1:21).
4. Jesus, surnamed Justus, a Christian of Colossae, Col 4:11.
For this n. in the O.T., cf. JESHUA, and JOSHUA.

Jeta, see JUTTAH.

Jeteba, see JOTBAH.

Jetebatha, see JOTBATHAH.

Jethela, see ITHLAH.

Jether, see JATTIR.

Jethlah, see ITHLAH.

Jethnam, see ITHNAN.

Jethro, n. of the father-in-law of Moses, Ex 3:1, 4:18; also called REUEL, q.v.

Jezabel, see JEZEBEL.

Jezaniah, see JAAZANIAH.

Jezebel, n. of the Tyrian wife of Ahab; she encouraged the cult of Baal and was killed on the order of Jehu, 2 K 9:30ff.

Jezonias, see JAAZANIAH.

Jezrael, Jezrahel, see JEZREEL.

Jezreel, 'God sows'; n. of 1. loc. of Issachar, listed Jos 19:18; after the Disruption, frequently ment. as the country residence of the kings of Israel; mod. *Zer'în*. Sometimes the n. is applied to the whole fertile plain, e.g. 2 S 2:9, Jos 17:16 (Valley of Jezreel), Jg 6:33 (Valley of Jezreel). The Gk. form of the n. is Esdraelon, Jth 1:8, 4:6; also applied to the plain, Jth 1:8 ('the great plain of Esdraelon'), Jth 4:6, 1 Mac 12:49; Maps 2, 11, 14, 15, 17; Pls. 23, 188, 364; pp. 16, 20, 67.
2. loc. of Judah, in the hill country, listed Jos 15:56; home of David's wife, Ahinoam, 1 S 25:43; poss. mod. *Kh. Tarrâma*, SW of Hebron; Maps 13, 15, 19. □

Jezreel (Plain, Valley of), see JEZREEL (1).

Jim, see IIM.

Jiphtah, see IPHTAH.

Jiphthah-el (Valley of), see IPHTAHEL (Valley of).

Joab, 'Yahweh is father'; n. of several persons, inc. David's best general, ment. more than 110 times between 2 S 2:13 and 1 K 11:21; pp. 70f.

Joachaz, see JEHOAHAZ.

Joachin, see JEHOIACHIN.

Joahaz, see JEHOAHAZ.

Joakim, see JEHOIAKIM.

Joas, see JOASH, JEHOASH.

Joash, Jehoash, n. of 4 persons, inc. 1. 8th king of Judah (835–796 B.C.); son of Ahaziah who escaped death at the hands of Athaliah, 2 K 11, 12.
2. 12th king of Israel (798–783 B.C.); son of Jehoahaz (2); fought against Amaziah and seized Jerusalem, 2 K 13.

Joatham, see JOTHAM.

Job, n. of the principal figure in the book of Job.

Joel, 'Yahweh is God'; n. of several persons, in particular a post-Exilic prophet; a book of the Bible bears his name.

Jogbehah, loc. in the territory of Gad, Nu 32:35; ment. in connection with Gideon, Jg 8:11; mod. *Jubeihât*, NW of *'Ammân*; Map 14. □

John, G&L form of Heb. *Jehohanan*, 'God is merciful'; n. of 16 persons in the O.T.; n. of several persons in the N.T., inc. 1. John the Baptist, forerunner of the Messiah, Mt 11:11.
2. the Apostle, son of Zebedee, brother of James the Greater; the disciple 'whom Jesus loved', Jn 13:23; the authorship of the 4th Gospel, the 3 Epistles of John and the Revelation is very often attributed to him.
3. John 'whose other name was Mark'; cf. MARK.

Jokdeam, loc. of Judah, in the hill country, listed Jos 15:56; called Jorkeam in 1 Ch 2:44 and Jos 15:56 (LXX); poss. mod. *Kh. Raqa'*, S of Hebron; Maps 13, 19. □

Jokmeam, see JOKNEAM.

Jokneam, loc. of Zebulun, listed Jos 19:11; Levitical city, Jos 21:34 (and 1 Ch 6:68 (Heb. 53), where it appears as Jokmeam in error for the Kibzaim of Jos 21:22); Canaanite royal city, Jos 12:22; in Solomon's 5th district, 1 K 4:12 (Jokmeam); mod. *Tell Qeimûn*, SE of Mt Carmel; Maps 11, 14, 17.

Joktheel, 1. loc. of Judah, in the lowland, listed Jos 15:38; sit. unk. □
2. n. given by Amaziah to Sela ('the rock'), 2 K 14:7. □

Jonah, n. of a prophet in the reign of Jeroboam II, 2 K 14:25; he figures in the book of Jonah; Map 17.

Jonas, see JONAH.

Jonathan, 'Yahweh has given'; n. of several persons, in particular 1. son of Saul and friend of David, 1 S 14ff.; killed on Mt Gilboa, 1 S 31, 2 S 1; p. 67.
2. Jonathan Maccabaeus, who succeeded his brother Judas as leader of the Jews in their war of independence, 1 Mac 9–13; Map 30; p. 110.

Joppa, G&L form of Heb. *Yapho;* in the O.T.: loc. on the boundary of Dan, Jos 19:46; cf. 2 Ch 2:16 (Heb. 15), Ezr 3:7, Jon 1:3; cf. also 1 Mac 10:75f., 11:6, 12:33, 2 Mac 4:21; in the N.T.: Ac 9–11; mod. *Yâfa (Jaffa)*, on the outskirts of *Tel-Aviv;* Maps 2, 11, 17, 23, 30, 34, 35.

Joppa (Sea of), see GREAT SEA.

Joppe, see JOPPA.

Joppe (Sea of), see GREAT SEA.

Joram, Jehoram, n. of 4 persons, inc. 1. 5th king of Judah (848–841 B.C.); under the influence of his wife, Athaliah, he killed all his brothers and encouraged the cult of Baal, 2 K 8; p. 87.
2. 9th king of Israel (852–841 B.C.); took action against the cult of Baal, 2 K 3; assassinated by Jehu, 2 K 9; Map 17; p. 87.

Jordan, n. of the largest river in Palestine; rises at the foot of Mt Hermon, flows through Lake Huleh and the Sea of Galilee, and finally enters the Dead Sea; mod. *Sheri'at el-Kebireh;* shown on nearly all the Maps; Pls. 26, 158, 160, 356, 357.

Jorkeam, Jorkoam, see JOKDEAM.

Josaphat, see JEHOSHAPHAT.

Jose, see JESUS, JOSHUA (2).

Joseph, n. of several persons, inc. 1. the Heb. patriarch, Gn 37–50; p. 40.
2. the husband of Mary and supposed father of Jesus, Lk 3:23.
3. Joseph of Arimathea; member of the Sanhedrin, Lk 23:50, and secret disciple of Jesus, Jn 19:38; he buried the body of Jesus in his own tomb, Mt 27:57ff.

Joses, see JOSEPH.

Joshua, n. of several persons in the O.T., in particular the successor of Moses, Nu 13:16; pp. 56f. This n. is also found in the N.T.; cf. JESUS, JOSHUA.

Joshua (Tomb of), see TIMNATH-SERAH.

Josiah, n. of the 16th king of Judah (640–609 B.C.); he was among the most devout of the kings and destroyed the high places; during his reign the book of the Law was found in the Temple, 2 K 22; killed in the battle of Megiddo, 2 K 23; Map 20; p. 97.

Josias, see JOSIAH.

Josue, see JOSHUA.

Jota, see JUTTAH.

Jotapata, see JOTBAH.

Jotbah, home of the mother of Amon, 2 K 21:19; some scholars identify it with the mod. *Kh. Jefât* in Galilee (Jotapata in the Roman period); others read JUTTAH, q.v.

Jotbath, see JOTBATHAH.

Jotbathah, stopping-place on the Exodus, Nu 33:33f., Dt 10:7; poss. mod. *Bir Taba*, N of Ezion-geber; Map 9. □

Jotham, 'Yahweh has shown Himself just'; n. of 2 persons, 1. the youngest son of Gideon, known for the fable he related to the Shechemites, Jg 9.
2. 11th king of Judah (740–736 B.C.), 2 K 15:32ff.

Jubal, n. of a son of Lamech and ancestor of the musicians, Gn 4:21; his n. suggests *yôbel*, 'trumpet'. Cf. TUBAL-CAIN.

Jucadam, see JOKDEAM.

Jud, see AZOR and JEHUD.

Juda, see JUDAH.

Judaea, G&L form of Heb. Judah; n. of the territory around Jerusalem; it varied in size in different periods. The 'hill country' of Judaea (or Judah) is the highland region between Samaria and the Negeb, flanked on the W by the Shephelah ('lowland'). The wilderness of Judaea (or Judah) lies between the 'hill country' and the Dead Sea. Map 2; Pls. 24, 25.

Judah, n. of 1. several persons, inc. the son of Jacob and Leah, Gn 29:35; ancestor of a tribe whose territory formed the core of the kingdom of Judah (S Kingdom); Maps 14, 15, 17, 20. Cf. JUDAEA.
2. loc. of Naphtali, listed Jos 19:34; sit. unk.; text uncertain.

Judas, G&L form of Heb. Judah, n. of several persons, 1. Judas Maccabaeus, great leader of Jewish resistance to Hellenisation by the Seleucids, 1 Mac 5–9; p. 110.
2. Judas Iscariot, one of the twelve disciples; he betrayed Jesus.
3. Judas, Jude; another Apostle; son or brother of James, Lk 6:16, Ac 1:13; also called Thaddaeus, Mt 10:3, Mk 3:18. Cf. JAMES (4).
4. see JUDE (2).

Jude, 1. see JUDAS (3).
2. author of the Letter of Jude; prob. to be identified with one of the brothers of Jesus, Mt 13:55, Mk 6:3 (Judas).

Judgment Gate, see MUSTER GATE.

Judith, n. of the heroine of the book of the Apocrypha which bears her name.

Julia, n. of a Christian woman of Rome, Ro 16:15.

Julias, see BETH-SAIDA.

Julius, n. of the Roman centurion who accompanied St Paul to Rome, Ac 27:1.

Junia, see JUNIAS.

Junias, n. of a kinswoman of St Paul, Ro 16:7.

Justus, cognomen of 3 persons in the N.T., 1. Joseph called Barsabbas, Ac 1:23.
2. Titius (or Titus), a Corinthian, Ac 18:7.
3. Jesus, a fellow-worker of St Paul, Col 4:11.

Juttah, loc. of Judah, in the hill country, listed Jos 15:55; Levitical city, Jos 21:16; mod. *Yatta*, S of Hebron; Maps 11, 13. □

K

Kabul, loc. of Asher, listed Jos 19:27, 1 K 9:13 (Cabul); mod. *Kabûl*; Maps 11, 17. □

Kabzeel, loc. of Judah, in the Negeb, listed Jos 15:21; 2 S 23:20 = 1 Ch 11:22; spelt Jekabzeel in Neh 11:25; poss. mod. *Kh. Hora*, NE of Beer-sheba; Map 13. □

Kadesh, 1. city of Judah, in the Negeb in the extreme S of Palestine, Gn 14:7, Nu 13:26; listed Jos 15:23 (Kedesh); also called Kadesh-barnea, where the Hebrews spent a long period during the Exodus, Nu 34:4, Dt 1:2; cf. Jos 15:3; mod. *'Ain Qedeis;* Maps 4, 9, 12; Pls. 152, 153; p. 56.
2. city in Syria, on the Orontes; site of the battle between Rameses II and the Hittites; mod. *Tell Nebi-Mend;* Maps 4, 7; Pls. 61, 137, 139; p. 45; cf. 2 S 24:6 (conj.; see TAHTIM-HODSHI).

Kadesh-barnea, see KADESH (1).

Kain, city of Judah, in the hill country, listed Jos 15:57; prob. mod. *Kh. Yaqîn*, SE of Hebron; Maps 13, 19. □

Kamon, loc. ment. Jg 10:5; poss. mod. *Qamm*, SE of the Sea of Galilee; Map 14. □

Kanah, 'reed'; 1. loc. of Asher, listed Jos 19:28; prob. mod. *Qâna*, 6 miles SE of Tyre; Map 11. □
2. a torrent forming the boundary between Manasseh and Ephraim, Jos 16:8, 17:9; mod. *W. Qâna;* Map 11. □

Kanata, see KENATH.

Kanish, ancient and wealthy Hittite city in W Asia Minor, revealed by excavation; mod. *Kültepe;* Maps 5, 6.

Karem, city of Judah, in the hill country, listed Jos 15:59 (LXX); mod. *'Ain Kârim;* Maps 13, 19; cf. BETH-HACCHEREM. □

Karka, loc. on the S boundary of Judah, Jos 15:3; sit. unk. □

Karkaa, see KARKA.

Karkar, see QARQAR.

Karkor, loc. ment. Jg 8:10; no doubt a small plain on the lower course of the Jabbok. □

Karnaim, region E of the Sea of Galilee; a subdivision of the Fifth Satrapy; Map 23.

Karnak, see LUXOR.

Kartah, Levitical city in the territory of Zebulun, Jos 21:34; sit. unk. □

Kartan, Levitical city of Naphtali, listed Jos 21:32; doubtless identical with the Kiriathaim in the parallel list of 1 Ch 6:76 (Heb. 61); sit. unk., unless it is the Rakkath of Jos 19:35. Cf. RAKKATH. □

Kassites, n. of the Indo-European tribes from the Zagros mountains who overran Babylonia *ca* 1600 B.C.; Maps 1, 6, 7; p. 64.

Kattath, loc. of Zebulun, listed Jos 19:15; sit. unk., doubtless identical with Kitron, Jg 1:30. □

Kedar, n. of a nomadic tribe of the Syro-Arabian desert, often ment. in the prophetic books, Is 21:16, 60:7, Jer 2:10, 49:28, Ezk 27:21; listed among the sons of Ishmael in Gn 25:13 = 1 Ch 1:29.

Kedemoth, loc. of Reuben, listed Jos 13:18; Levitical city, Jos 21:37, 1 Ch 6:79 (Heb. 64); this city gave its n. to the 'wilderness of Kedemoth', Dt 2:26; poss. mod. *Qasr ez-Za'farân;* Map 11. □

Kedesh, 1. city of Naphtali, listed Jos 19:37; Canaanite royal city, Jos 12:22; Levitical city, Jos 21:32, and city of refuge, Jos 20:7; mod. *Tell Qades*, NW of Lake Huleh; Maps 11, 14, 17, 23, 30; Pl. 154 C.
2. Levitical city of Issachar, 1 Ch 6:72 (Heb. 57); cf. Jg 4:11; (Kishion in the list of Jos 21:28); poss. mod. *Tell Abû Qedeis;* Map 14.
3. see KADESH (1).

Kedron, city S of Jamnia, ment. 1 Mac 15:39, 41, 16:9; poss. mod. *Qâtra;* Map 30. □

Kehelathah, stopping-place on the Exodus, Nu 33:22f.; poss. a doublet of MAKHELOTH (q.v.), Nu 33:25f.; Map 9.

Keilah, loc. of Judah, in the lowland, listed Jos 15:44; 1 S 23:1–13; n. of a district, Neh 3:17f.; mod. *Kh. Qîla;* Maps 13, 15, 19, 22. □

Kenath, city in N Transjordan, ment. 1 Ch 2:23; captured and renamed by Nobah, Nu 32:42; later the Kanata of the Decapolis; poss. mod. *Qanawât;* Map 35. □

Kenaz, n. of a descendant of Esau, Gn 36:11; ancestor of the Kenizzites who lived in S Judah, Gn 15:19.

Kenites, Midianite tribe of the Sinai peninsula, 1 S 15:6, 27:10; later partially incorporated in the tribes of Israel, 1 Ch 2:55.

Kenizzites, see KENAZ.

Kephirim, loc. near Ono, Neh 6:2 (R.S.V. 'villages'); sit. unk. □

Kerioth, 1. loc. in Moab, ment. Jer 48:24, Am 2:2, and on the Moabite Stone, cf. p. 80; sit. unk. □
2. see KERIOTH-HEZRON.

Kerioth-hezron, loc. of Judah, in the Negeb, listed Jos 15:25, where it is identified with Hazor; sit. unk. Cf. HEZRON (2).

Kerith, see CHERITH (Brook).

Keziz (Valley of), see EMEK-KEZIZ.

Khâbûr, mod. n. of a tributary of the Euphrates; Biblical HABOR, q.v.

Khalab, see ALEPPO.

Maps: 1 p. 9 / 2, 3 p. 10 / 4 p. 29 / 5, 6 p. 30 / 7, 8 p. 43 / 9, 10 p. 44 / 11, 12 p. 59 / 13 p. 60 / 14 p. 65 / 15, 16 p. 66 / 17 p. 81 / 18, 19 p. 82 / 20, 21 p. 95 / 22–24 p. 96 / 25–29 p. 103 / 30, 31 p. 104 / 32, 33 p. 115 / 34, 35 p. 116 / I, II end-papers.

154

Khirbet Qumrân, see QUMRÂN.
Khorsabad, mod. n. of the capital of Sargon II, DUR SHARRU-KÎN, q.v. Here, in 1843, Botta began work upon the first Ass. excavations. Maps 1, 18; Pl. 249.
Kibroth-hattaavah, 'graves of craving'; stopping-place on the Exodus, Nu 11:34f., 33:16f., Dt 9:22; prob. mod. *Ruweis el-Ebeirig*, NE of Mt Sinai; Map 9. □
Kibzaim, Levitical city in the territory of Ephraim, Jos 21:22; exact sit. unk. □
Kidron, torrent-bed (nearly always dry) between Jerusalem and the Mt of Olives; mod. *W. el-Nahr;* Maps 24, 33; Pls. 191, 192, 326, 327, 355, 375–377, 381.
Kinah, loc. of Judah, in the Negeb, listed Jos 15:22; sit. unk. □
King's dale, see SHAVEH (Valley of).
King's Forest, ment. Neh 2:8; a sub-division of the Fifth Satrapy, on the slopes of the Lebanon; Map 23. Cf. PARADISE.
King's Garden, in Jerusalem, near the 'gate between the two walls', SE of Ophel, in the Valley of the Kidron, 2 K 25:4 = Jer 52:7; Maps 24B and C; Pl. 381.
King's Vale, King's Valley, see SHAVEH (Valley of).
Kings (Valley of the), valley across the Nile from Thebes, where the Pharaohs of the New Empire were buried; Pls. 9, 11.
Kir, 1. land to which the Aramaeans of Damascus were deported by the Assyrians, 2 K 16:9, Am 1:5, 9:7; Kir is ment. with Elam in Is 22:6, and poss. lay in the same region.
2. loc. ment. Is 15:1. Cf. KIR-HARESETH.
Kir-haraseth, see KIR-HARESETH.
Kir-hareseth, loc. ment. 2 K 3:25, where it appears to be the capital city of Moab; also ment. Is 16:7, and, under the n. Kir-heres, Is 16:11, Jer 48:31, 36. In Is 15:1 the city is called Kir; poss. its Moabite n. was Kir-hadesheth, 'new town', which the Israelites corrupted into Kir-hareseth, 'wall of the potsherds'; mod. *el-Kerak;* Map 17.
Kir-haresh, Kir-heres, see KIR-HARESETH.
Kiriath, see KIRIATH-JEARIM.
Kiriathaim, 1. loc. of Reuben, listed Jos 13:19, cf. Nu 32:37; later a Moabite city, Jer 48:1, 23, Ezk 25:9; ment. on the Moabite Stone, cf. p. 80; poss. mod. *Kh. el-Qureiyât*, NW of Dibon; Map 11. □
2. the plain of Kiriathaim, see SHAVEH-KIRIATHAIM.
3. Levitical city of Naphtali, listed 1 Ch 6:76 (Heb. 61), doubtless identical with the Kartan in the parallel list of Jos 21:32.
Kiriath-arba, ancient n. of Hebron which is used in the list of Jos 15:54 and elsewhere; cf. HEBRON.
Kiriatharim, Ezr 2:25, *var.* of KIRIATH-JEARIM, q.v.
Kiriath-baal, see KIRIATH-JEARIM.
Kiriath-huzoth, loc. ment. Nu 22:39; in Moab, exact sit. unk. □
Kiriath-jearim, 'city of forests'; city of the Gibeonite tetrapolis, Jos 9:17; on the boundary between Judah and Benjamin, Jos 18:15; called Kiriath-baal in Jos 18:14 and Baalah in the parallel passage of Jos 15:9 (cf. Jos 15:60, Kiriath-baal, and poss. 18:28, where Heb. has Kiriath); cf. Jg 18:12; known from the story of the Ark, 1 S 6:21, 7:1f., 1 Ch 13:5f., 2 Ch 1:4; called Baale-judah in 2 S 6:2, and 'the fields of Jaar' in Ps 132:6; also ment. as the home of Uriah, Jer 26:20; in the list of repatriated Israelites, Neh 7:29, Ezr 2:25 (Kiriath-arim); mod. *Tell el-Azhar*, W of Jerusalem; Maps 13, 14, 15, 17, 19, 22; p. 70.
Kiriath-sannah, loc. of Judah, in the hill country; identical with Debir (1) according to Jos 15:49; cf. DEBIR (1).
Kiriath-sepher, loc. identified as Debir (1) in Jos 15:15f., Jg 1:11f.; cf. DEBIR (1).
Kirjath, see KIRIATH-JEARIM.
Kirjathaim, see KIRIATHAIM.
Kirjath-arba, see KIRIATH-ARBA, HEBRON.
Kirjath-arim, Kirjath-baal, see KIRIATH-JEARIM.
Kirjath-huzoth, see KIRIATH-HUZOTH.
Kirjath-jearim, see KIRIATH-JEARIM.
Kirjath-sannah, see KIRIATH-SANNAH.
Kirjath-sepher, see KIRIATH-SEPHER.
Kish, n. of several persons, inc. the father of Saul, 1 S 9:1.
Kishion, loc. of Issachar, listed Jos 19:20; Levitical city, Jos 21:28, doubtless identical with the Kedesh in the parallel list of 1 Ch 6:72 (Heb. 57); cf. KEDESH (2).
Kishon, 1. n. of a torrent in the plain of Jezreel which flows into the Mediterranean near Haifa; ment. in the stories of Barak and Sisera, Jg 4:7, 13, 5:21, Ps 83:9 (Heb. 10), etc.; where Elijah put to death the prophets of Baal, 1 K 18:40; mod. *Nahr el-Muqatta';* Maps 14, 17.
2. see KISHION.
Kison, see KISHON.
Kithlish, see CHITLISH.
Kitron, loc. ment. Jg 1:30; cf. KATTATH. □
Kittim, n. originally used for the inhabitants of the Phoenician colony of Kition (Citium) in Cyprus (hence rendered by Cyprus in the following passages in some versions); later extended to all the inhabitants of Cyprus, cf. Is 23:1, 12, 13 (conj. for Chaldaeans), Ezk 27:6 (Vulg. Italy); finally applied to all the peoples N of the basin of the Mediterranean, Nu 24:24 (Vulg. Italy), Jer 2:10; listed as a son of Javan, Gn 10:4 = 1 Ch 1:7; in 1 Mac 1:1, 8:5 = Macedonians; in Dn 11:30 = Romans. □
Koa, n. of a Chaldaean tribe, Ezk 23:23. □
Konya, mod. n. of ICONIUM, q.v.
Koulon, loc. of Judah, in the hill country, listed Jos 15:59 (LXX); sit. unk.
Krak des Chevaliers, n. of a fortress of the Knights Hospitallers, captured by the Sultan Baibars in A.D. 1271; mod. *Qala'at el-Hosn;* Map 3; Pls. 43–50.
Kue, see QEWÊ.

L

Laban, 'white'; 1. n. of the brother of Rebekah and father of Leah and Rachel; ment. over 50 times in Gn.
2. stopping-place on the Exodus, Dt 1:1; sit. unk. □
Labana, see LIBNAH.
Labanath, see SHIHOR-LIBNATH.
Lachis, see LACHISH.
Lachish, city of Judah, in the lowland, listed Jos 15:39; Canaanite royal city, Jos 10:3ff., 12:11; fortified by Rehoboam, 2 Ch 11:9; scene of Amaziah's assassination, 2 K 14:19 = 2 Ch 25:27; cf. Mic 1:13 (alliteration between Lachish and *rekesh*, 'steed'); military headquarters of Sennacherib, 2 K 18:14, 17, 19:8, 2 Ch 32:9, Is 36:2, 37:8; withstood Nebuchadnezzar, Jer 34:7, cf. 4th Lachish Letter, p. 92; repopulated after the Exile, Neh 11:30; mod. *Tell ed-Duweir;* Maps 7, 11, 13, 14, 17, 19, 23; Pls. 196, 233. □
Lahela, see HALAH.
Lahmam, loc. of Judah, in the lowland, listed Jos 15:40; poss. mod. *Kh. el-Lahm;* Maps 13, 19. □
Lahmas, see LAHMAM.
Lais, see LAISH (1).
Laisa, see ELASA and LAISHAH.
Laish, 1. city in the extreme N of Palestine; captured by the Danites who renamed it Dan, Jg 18:7, 14, 27, 29; listed as Leshem of Dan, Jos 19:47. Cf. DAN (2), LASHA. □
2. see LAISHAH.
Laishah, city N of Jerusalem, Is 10:30; poss. mod. *el-'Isawiyeh;* Map 19. □
Lake Huleh, see HULEH (Lake).
Lake Mareotis, see MAREOTIS (Lake).
Lake Timsâh, see TIMSÂH (Lake).
Lakkum, loc. of Naphtali, listed Jos 19:33; poss. mod. *Kh. el-Mansûrah;* Map 11. □
Lakum, see LAKKUM.
Lamech, n. of 2 persons, in particular one of the antediluvian patriarchs; son of Methuselah and father of Noah, Gn 5:25ff.
Lampsacus, city of Mysia in Asia Minor; poss. ment. in the list of countries and cities which received the letter of Lucius, 1 Mac 15:23, but cf. SAMPSAMES; Map 32. □
Lamuel, see LEMUEL.
Land of Zuph, see ZUPH.
Laodicea, 1. city in Asia Minor, near Colossae, Col 2:1, 4:13, 15f. Eph 1:1 (in some MSS instead of Ephesus); one of the letters, in the Revelation to John is addressed to 'the church in Laodicea', Rev 3:14ff.; mod. *es-Eskihisar;* Map II (e.p.).
2. Hellenised city on the Phoenician coast; mod. *Latakia;* Maps 29, I (e.p.).
Larsa, very ancient city of S Mesopotamia; from *ca* 2000 B.C. engaged in a struggle with Isin (city further N) for control of Sumer and Accad; subjugated by Hammurabi; mod. *Senkereh;* Maps 1, 5, 6.
Lasea, city in Crete, Ac 27:8; Map II (e.p.). □
Lasha, loc. ment. in the indication of the frontiers of Canaan, Gn 10:19; according to an old Jewish tradition it lay near Callirhoë on the E shore of the Dead Sea (cf. ZERETH-SHAHAR); a more satisfactory localisation would be in the NE of Canaan, identical with Laish (1).
Lasharon, see SHARON.
Last Sea, see WESTERN SEA.
Latitude, see REHOBOTH (1).
Lazarus, G&L form of Heb. *Lazar*, an abb. of Eleazar, 'God helps'; n. of 2 persons, 1. the brother of Martha and Mary of Bethany, and friend of Jesus, who raised him from the dead, Jn 11.
2. the beggar in the parable of the wicked rich man, Lk 16.
Leah, 'cow'; n. of the elder daughter of Laban and first wife of Jacob, Gn 29, 30.
Lebanon, 'white mountains'; n. of a chain of mts, 106 miles long, running parallel to the coast N of Palestine; its peaks rise to about 10,000 ft and are always snow-clad; Maps 4, 12; Pls. 13, 18–21; p. 15.
Lebaoth, 'haunt of lionesses'; loc. of Judah, in the Negeb, listed Jos 15:32; sit. unk.; prob. identical with the Beth-lebaoth of Simeon, listed Jos 19:6. □
Lebbaeus, see THADDAEUS.
Lebna, see LIBNAH.
Lebo-hamath, Nu 34:8, Jos 13:5, Jg 3:3, 1 K 8:65, 2 K 14:25, Am 6:14; rendered in R.S.V. 'entrance of Hamath'; ment. almost always as N extremity of Israel (sometimes with the 'brook of Egypt' as the other extremity); poss. Lebo conceals n. of a city, 'Labo which belongs to (the territory of) Hamath', preserved in the n. of mod. *Lebweh* in the Beqa' (so on Maps 4, 12).
Lebona, see LEBONAH.
Lebonah, city ment. Jg 21:19; mod. *Lubbân*, N of Shiloh; Map 14. □
Lechi, see LEHI.
Lecum, see LAKKUM.
Leheman, see LAHMAM.
Lehi, 'jaw-bone'; city which figures in the story of Samson, Jg 15:9, 14, 17 (Ramath-lehi, 'hill of the jaw-bone'), 19; cf. 2 S 23:11; sit. unk. □
Lemuel, n. of an Ishmaelite king, Pr 31:2–9.
Lesa, see LASHA.
Lesem, Leshem, see LAISH (1).
Lessau, village N of Jerusalem, 2 Mac 14:16; sit. uncertain. □
Levi, n. of several persons in the O.T., in particular the 3rd son of Jacob and Leah, Gn 29:34. In the N.T., another n. for Matthew, Mk 2:14, Lk 5:27, 29.
Leviathan, n. of a mythological monster, Is 27:1, Ps 74:14, 104:26, symbolising the Chaos which Yahweh vanquished in the Creation, and which man must beware of arousing, Job 3:8; incarnate in the crocodile of Egypt, Job 40, 41; cf. Am 9:3, Ezk 29:3, 32:2.
Lia, see LEAH.
Libnah, 'white (city)'; 1. loc. of Judah, in the lowland, listed Jos 15:42; Levitical city, Jos 21:13, 1 Ch 6:57 (Heb. 42); Canaanite royal city, Jos 10:29, 31f., 12:15; strategically important city, 2 K 8:22, 2 Ch 21:10, 2 K 19:8 = Is 37:8, 2 K 23:31, 24:18 = Jer 52:1; poss. mod. *Tell es-Sâfi;* Maps 13, 14, 17, 19. □
2. stopping-place on the Exodus between Mt Sinai and Kadesh, Nu 33:20f.; sit. unk. □
Libya, Libyans, region W of the Nile Delta, Nah 3:9, Dn 11:43, 2 Ch 12:3, 16:8, Ac 2:10. Cf. PUT. □
Lidebir, loc. ment. Jos 13:26 (R.S.V. Debir); prob. identical with LO-DEBAR, q.v.
Linus, n. of a Roman Christian, 2 Ti 4:21.
Lithostroton, see PAVEMENT (The).
Lithostrotos, better read as a noun, Lithostroton, 'pavement', than as an adjective; see PAVEMENT (The).
Lo-ammi, 'not my people'; symbolic n. of the 3rd child of the prophet Hosea, Hos 1:9.
Lobna, see LIBNAH.
Lod, G&L *Lydda;* city SE of Jaffa, in the plain of Sharon, Ezr 2:33, Neh 7:37, 11:35, 1 Ch 8:12; annexed by the Jews in the Maccabaean period, 1 Mac 11:34 (Lydda), Ac 9 (Lydda); mod. *Ludd;* Maps 23, 30, 34. □
Lodabar, see LO-DEBAR.
Lo-debar, loc. in Transjordan, 2 S 9:4f., 17:27, Am 6:13; near Mahanaim, N of the Jabbok; exact sit. unk.; prob. identical with LIDEBIR (q.v.) of Jos 13:26.
Lois, n. of the grandmother of Timothy, 2 Ti 1:5.
Lo-ruhamah, 'not pitied'; symbolic n. of the 2nd child of the prophet Hosea, Hos 1:6.
Lot, n. of the son of Haran and nephew of Abraham, Gn 11–13, 19.
Lot (Sea of), see SEA OF LOT.
Lowland, see SHEPHELAH.
Lubim, Lubims, see LIBYA, LIBYANS.
Lucius, n. of 2 persons, 1. Lucius of Cyrene, a prophet and teacher of Antioch, Ac 13:1.
2. a Christian Jew of Rome, Ro 16:21.
Lud, Ludim, n. of a people sometimes ment. with Egypt, Gn 10:13, 1 Ch 1:11, Ezk 30:5, Jer 46:9; and sometimes with Semitic peoples, Gn 10:22, 1 Ch 1:17; ment. with Tarshish and Put in Is 66:19. The n. suggests the Lydians of Asia Minor, but this identification does not accord with the majority of the contexts.
Luhith (Ascent of), loc. in Moab ment. Is 15:5, Jer 48:5; sit. unk. □
Luith, see LUHITH.
Luke, n. of a companion of St Paul on his journeys; author of the 3rd Gospel and the Acts of the Apostles.
Luxor, small town in Upper Egypt; sit. with the neighbouring Karnak on the site of the famous city of Thebes; Map 1; Pls. 9, 39.
Luz, 'almond'; 1. ancient n. of Bethel, Gn 28:19, 35:6, 48:3, Jos 18:13, Jg 1:23; loc. of Ephraim, listed Jos 16:2; ment. in the indication of the boundary of Benjamin, Jos 18:13. Cf. BETHEL (1). □
2. loc. in the territory of the Hittites, Jg 1:26; sit. unk. □
Luza, see LUZ.
Lycaonia, region of Asia Minor, Ac 14:6, cf. 11; Map II (e.p.).
Lycia, region of Asia Minor; ment. among the countries and cities which received the letter of Lucius, 1 Mac 15:23; also ment. in the account of St Paul's voyage to Italy, Ac 27:5; Maps 26, II (e.p.).
Lydda, G&L form of LOD, q.v.
Lydia, n. of 1. a region of Asia Minor, 1 Mac 8:8; Maps 20, 25, II (e.p.). Some versions read Lydia (Lydians) for Lud in Ezk 30:5, Jer 46:9, Is 66:19; cf. LUD, LUDIM.
2. a Christian woman of Philippi, Ac 16.
Lysanias, n. of the tetrarch of Abilene in the time of Jesus, Lk 3:1; p. 136.
Lysias, n. of 2 persons, 1. a commander of Antiochus Epiphanes; defeated by Judas Maccabaeus, 1 Mac 4, 2 Mac 11; Map 30.
2. see CLAUDIUS LYSIAS.
Lysimachus, n. of the brother of the High Priest Menelaus; he was massacred by the people, 2 Mac 4:39ff.
Lystra, loc. in Asia Minor; home of Timothy, Ac 14:6ff., 16:1f., cf. 2 Ti 3:11; mod. *Zoldera;* Map II (e.p.). □

M

Maacah, 1. n. of several persons.
2. n. of territory S of Mt Hermon; the king of this state fought against David as an ally of the Ammonites, 2 S 10:6ff., 1 Ch 19:6f. (Aram-maacah); its people were not driven out by the Israelites, according to Jos 13:13 (Maacath); Map 16. Cf. ARAM (3).
Maacath, Maacha(h), see MAACAH.
Maaleh-acrabbim, see AKRABBIM.
Maara, see ARAH and MEARAH.
Maarath, loc. of Judah, in the hill country, listed Jos 15:59; poss. identical with the Maroth of Mic 1:12; poss. mod. *Beit Ummar*, N of Beth-zur; Maps 13, 19, p. 105 no. 2. □
Maccabees, n. of a Jewish family, derived from the cognomen of Judas Maccabaeus, 1 Mac 2:4. Their fight for freedom is described in 1 and 2 Maccabees; Maps 30, 31; pp. 109f.
Macces, see MAKAZ.
Maceda, see MAKKEDAH.

Maps: 1 p. 9 / 2, 3 p. 10 / 4 p. 29 / 5, 6 p. 30 / 7, 8 p. 43 / 9, 10 p. 44 / 11, 12 p. 59 / 13 p. 60 / 14 p. 65 / 15, 16 p. 66 / 17 p. 81 / 18, 19 p. 82 / 20, 21 p. 95 / 22–24 p. 96 / 25–29 p. 103 / 30, 31 p. 104 / 32, 33 p. 115 / 34, 35 p. 116 / I, II end-papers.

155

Macedonia, region N of Greece, ment. several times in the Bible; kingdom of Philip and Alexander, 1 Mac 1:1, 6:2, cf. 2 Mac 8:20, Est 16:14 (Gk.); in the N.T. period Macedonia was a Roman province with Thessalonica as its capital; St Paul founded flourishing churches there, Ac 16, 19:21f., 20:1ff., 1 Co 16:5, 2 Co 8:1; Maps 25, 26, 32, II (e.p.); Pl. 395.

Maceloth, see MAKHELOTH.

Machaerus, Hasmonaean fortress rebuilt by Herod; on the E shore of the Dead Sea; mod. *Mukâwer;* Map 34; Pl. 353.

Machati, see MAACAH (2).

Machbena(h), see MECONAH.

Machir, n. of 1. a faithful supporter of David, 2 S 9:4f., 17:27f.
2. a clan of Manasseh, Gn 50:23; established in Gilead, Nu 32:39, Dt 3:15, Jos 13:31; in Jg 5:14 the n. refers to the W territory of Manasseh.

Machmas, see MICHMASH.

Machmethath see MICHMETHATH.

Machpelah, n. of the field, containing a cave, which Abraham bought as a burying-place for Sarah, Gn 23:9ff.; Abraham was also buried there, Gn 25:9, and after him, Rebekah, Isaac, Leah, and Jacob, Gn 49:30, 50:13. The Mosque of Hebron (*Haram el-Khalîl*) now stands on the site of this cave; Pls. 88–90, 331f.; p. 35.

Madaba, see MEDEBA.

Madai, see MEDES, MEDIA.

Madian (Day of), see MIDIAN (Day of).

Madian, Madianites, see MIDIAN, MIDIANITES.

Madmannah, loc. of Judah, in the Negeb, listed Jos 15:31, cf. 1 Ch 2:49; mod. *Umm Deimneh;* Map 13. Cf. BETH-MARCABOTH. □

Madmen, loc. in Moab, ment. Jer 48:2; poss. identical with the Dimon (Heb.) of Is 15:9 (Vulg. and R.S.V. Dibon); Dimon and Madmen seem unlikely to be variants of Dibon; sit. unk. □

Madmena, see MADMANNAH.

Madmenah, loc. N of Jerusalem, Is 10:31; poss. mod. *Shuʿfat;* Map 19. □

Madon, Canaanite royal city, Jos 11:1, 12:19; prob. mod. *Qarn Hattîn,* W of the Sea of Galilee; Map 14. Cf. ZER. □

Magadan (Region of), see DALMANUTHA.

Magbish, loc. in Judah; repopulated after the Exile, Ezr 2:30; sit. unk. □

Magdal, see MIGDOL.

Magdala (Coasts of), region from which Mary Magdalene came; mod. *Kh. Mejdel,* on the W shore of the Sea of Galilee; Map 34. Cf. DALMANUTHA.

Magdalel, see MIGDAL-EL.

Magdalgad, see MIGDAL-GAD.

Magdalum, Magdalus, see MIGDOL (1).

Magedan, see DALMANUTHA.

Mageddo, see MEGIDDO.

Mageth, see MAKED.

Magidu, n. of a subdivision of the Fifth Satrapy (region of Megiddo); Map 23.

Magog, n. of a people (and country) listed among the sons of Japheth with other peoples of Asia Minor, Gn 10:2 = 1 Ch 1:5, cf. Ezk 38f.; sometimes identified with the Scythians; Gog and Magog in Rev 20:8 personify the heathen peoples rallied by Satan to attack the Church. □

Magron, see MIGRON.

Mahalab, loc. of Asher, listed Jos 19:29 (Heb. Mehebel, perhaps = 'from Hebel'); an error for Ahlab, Jg 1:31 (where Helbah is a doublet); called Mahalliba on the prism of Sennacherib, cf. p. 89; mod. *Kh. el-Mahalib,* 4 miles NE of Tyre; Map 11. □

Mahalliba, see MAHALAB.

Mahanaim, 'double camp'; loc. on the boundary of Gad, Jos 13:26, and Manasseh, Jos 13:30; Levitical city, Jos 21:38, 1 Ch 6:80 (Heb. 65); the n. is explained in Gn 32:2 (Heb. 3), where it means 'two armies'; figures in the story of David as the city where Ish-bosheth was proclaimed king, 2 S 2:8, and where David took refuge, 2 S 17ff.; in Solomon's 7th district, 1 K 4:14; prob. mod. *Tell el-Hajjâj,* S of the Jabbok; Maps 4, 11, 15, 17; pp. 67, 68.

Mahaneh-dan, 'camp of Dan'; temporary encampment of the Danites; sit. W of Kiriath-jearim, according to Jg 18:12; Jg 13:25 gives a less prob. sit. between Zorah and Eshtaol. □

Makaz, loc. in Solomon's 2nd district, 1 K 4:9; prob. mod. *Kh. el-Mukheizin,* S of Ekron; Map 17. □

Maked, loc. in the region of Gilead, 1 Mac 5:26; mod. *Tell Miqdâd;* Map 31. □

Makheloth, stopping-place on the Exodus, between Mt Sinai and Kadesh, Nu 33:25f.; poss. a doublet of Kehelathah, Nu 33:22f.; poss. mod. *Kuntillet Jerâya;* Map 9. □

Makkedah, loc. of Judah, in the lowland, listed Jos 15:41; Canaanite royal city, Jos 10:10, 16ff., 12:16; poss. mod. *Kh. el-Kheishûm,* $14\frac{1}{2}$ miles W of Bethlehem; Maps 13, 14,19. □

Malachi, n. of the last of the Minor Prophets.

Malachias, see MALACHI.

Malchus, n. of the High Priest's slave whose ear was cut off by St Peter, Jn 18:10.

Mallos, see MALLUS.

Mallus, loc. in Cilicia, whose inhabitants are mentioned with those of Tarsus, 2 Mac 4:30; near mod. *Kara Tash;* Map 29. □

Malta, n. of an island in the Mediterranean, Ac 28:1ff.; Map II (e.p.).

Mambre, see MAMRE.

Mambres, see JANNES AND JAMBRES.

Mamre, *Mambre* in the G&L translations; according to Gn 13:18 and 18:1, Abraham pitched his tent beneath the oaks (or terebinths) of Mamre; the ancient translations refer to one tree only, cf. Gn 18:4, 8; the rabbis doubtless replaced the earlier singular by a plural in order to remove the suggestion of tree worship; in Gn 23:17, 19, 25:9, 49:30, 50:13, the cave of Machpelah is localised 'to the east of Mamre', which is thus identified with Hebron (explicit identification in Gn 23:19, 35:27); these texts reflect a more recent tradition, and originally Mamre was certainly distinct from Hebron; Mamre is localised at mod. *Ramet el-Khalil,* cf. p. 28; Maps 4, p. 105 no. 8; Pls. 97–99. In Gn 14:13, 24, Mamre is the n. of a person: perhaps the owner of the oak?

Manaen, n. of a prophet and teacher of the Church at Antioch and member of the court of Herod Antipas, Ac 13:1.

Manahath, Manahathites, see MANOCHO.

Manahem, see MENAHEM.

Manahen, see MANAEN.

Manahethites, see MANOCHO.

Manaim, see MAHANAIM.

Manasseh, 'making to forget' (cf. Gn 41:51); n. of several persons, inc. 1. eldest son of Joseph, Gn 41:51; ancestor of a tribe; tribal territory shown on Map 11.
2. 12th king of Judah (687–642 B.C.), 2 K 21; Map 18; pp. 94f.

Manasses, see MANASSEH.

Manoah, n. of the father of Samson, Jg 13.

Manocho, loc. of Judah, in the hill country, listed Jos 15:59 (LXX); prob. identical with the Manahath of 1 Ch 8:6; cf. 1 Ch 2:52, 54; prob. mod. *Malha (Malîha),* SW of Jerusalem; Maps 13, 19. □

Manue, see MANOAH.

Maon, loc. of Judah, in the hill country, listed Jos 15:55, cf. 1 S 25:2, 23:24 ('wilderness of Maon'); listed as a descendant of Caleb, 1 Ch 2:45; for Maonites in Jg 10:12, read Midianites (LXX); mod. *Tell Maʿîn,* S of Hebron; Maps 13, 15. □

Mara, see MARAH.

Marah, 'bitter'; stopping-place on the Exodus, Ex 15:23, Nu 33:8f.; poss. mod. *ʿAin Hawâra;* Map 9. □

Maralah, see MAREAL.

Marcus, see MARK.

Mardochai, see MORDECAI.

Marduk, Bab. n. vocalised in Heb. as MERODACH, q.v.

Mareal, loc. of Zebulun, listed Jos 19:11; poss. mod. *Tell Ghalta;* Map 11. □

Mareotis (Lake), sit. S of Alexandria; Map 27.

Maresa, see MARESHAH.

Mareshah, loc. of Judah, in the lowland, listed Jos 15:44; presented as a person, 1 Ch 4:21; fortified by Rehoboam, 2 Ch 11:8; site of a battle fought by Asa, 2 Ch 14:9f.; home of the prophet Eliezer, 2 Ch 20:37; used in a play on words with 'conqueror', *yorêsh-marêshah,* Mic 1:15; called Marisa in the period of the Maccabees, 2 Mac 12:35, also perhaps in 1 Mac 5:66, in place of the reading Samaria; mod. *Tell Sandahanna* (from St Anna!); Maps 13, 17, 19, 30. □

Mareth, see MAARATH.

Mari, city on the middle course of the Euphrates; not. ment. in the Bible; the site has been excavated from 1933 and has provided most important information on the history of the Near East before 1700 B.C.; Maps 1, 5; Pls. 5, 112–120; p. 27.

Mariamne, n. of several women in the family of Herod, in particular the favourite wife of Herod the Great, mother of Alexander and Aristobulus; one of the towers of the Palace of Herod at Jerusalem was called after her; Map 33; pp. 113, 117.

Marisa, see MARESHAH.

Mark, n. of the cousin of Barnabas, Col 4:10; fellow-worker of St Paul who also shared his imprisonment, Philem 24, 2 Ti 4:11; certainly the 'John whose other name was Mark' of Ac 12:12, 25, 13:5, 13, 15:37, 39; doubtless also 'my son Mark' ment. 1 P 5:13, a disciple of St Peter to whom the 2nd Gospel is traditionally attributed.

Maroth, loc. ment. Mic 1:12; poss. identical with MAARATH, q.v.; Map 17. □

Martha, n. of the sister of Mary and Lazarus, Lk 10:38, Jn 11.

Mary, G&L *Maria* from Heb. MIRIAM, q.v., meaning uncertain; n. of several persons, inc. 1. Mary the Mother of Jesus.
2. Mary Magdalene (i.e. of Magdala), Lk 8:2, Mt 27:56, 61, 28:1.
3. Mary of Bethany, sister of Martha and Lazarus, Lk 10:39, 42, Jn 11.
4. Mary the mother of James and Joseph, Mt 27:56, 61, 28:1, cf. Mk 16:1, Lk 24:10.
5. Mary the mother of John (Mark), Ac 12:12.

Masal, see MASHAL.

Masaloth, see MESALOTH.

Masepha, see MIZPAH, MIZPEH (2).

Maserephoth, see MISREPHOTH-MAIM.

Mash, n. in the table of the peoples, Gn 10:23; an Aramaean region. □

Mashal, see MISHAL.

Maspha, see MIZPAH, MIZPEH (1), (3), (4), (5).

Masphath, see MIZPAH, MIZPEH (1).

Masreca, see MASREKAH.

Masrekah, loc. in Edom, Gn 36:36, 1 Ch 1:47; sit. unk. □

Massa, n. of a tribe of N Arabia, cf. Gn 25:14 = 1 Ch 1:30, Pr 30:1, 31:1.

Massah, 'trial'; symbolic n. of a rock near Horeb where the Israelites tested God; in some passages (Dt 33:8, Ps 95:8, cf. Ex 17:7) ment. with the equally symbolic n. Meribah, 'contention', given to the spring at Kadesh, Nu 27:14, Dt 32:51 (Meribath-kadesh).

Mathana, see MATTANAH.

Mathathias, see MATTATHIAS.

Matthana, see MATTANAH.

Mattanah, stopping-place on the Exodus, N of Moab, Nu 21:18f.; sit. unk. □

Mattathias, G&L form of Heb. *Mattithyah,* 'gift of Yahweh'; n. of the priest of Modin, the father of the Maccabees, who gave the signal for the rising against Antiochus Epiphanes, 1 Mac 2; p. 110.

Matthew, n. of an Apostle ment. in the lists of Mk 3:18, Lk 6:15, Ac 1:13; called 'Matthew the tax collector' in Mt 10:3; called Matthew in Mt 9:9, but Levi in the parallel passages of Mk 2:14 and Lk 5:27ff. The 1st Gospel is traditionally attributed to this Apostle.

Matthias, abb. of *Mattathias;* n. of the Apostle who replaced the traitor Judas Iscariot, Ac 1:26.

Mearah, loc. ment. Jos 13:4; the reading should prob. be Arah with the prefix *me-,* 'from'; mod. *Kh. ʿAra;* Map 12. Cf. ARAH. □

Mechmas, see MICHMASH.

Meconah, loc. ment. after Ziklag in the list of repopulated cities, Neh 11:28; poss. identical with Machbenah which was near Madmannah, according to 1 Ch 2:49; sit. unk. □

Medaba, see MEDEBA.

Meddin, see MIDDIN.

Medeba, loc. of Reuben in Transjordan, listed Jos 13:16, cf. 13:9, 1 Ch 19:7, Nu 21:30; Moabite, according to Is 15:2; called Medaba in 1 Mac 9:36; ment. on the Moabite Stone, cf. p. 80; mod. *Madeba* or *Madaba;* Maps 2, 11, 17, 30. Famous for the mosaic map discovered in a church there, Pl. 173, cf. Pl. 392.

Medemena, see MADMANNAH and MADMENAH.

Medes, Media, Media was situated NE of Babylonia; the Medes became known to the Israelites at the time of the Ass. conquest; in Gn 10:2 and 1 Ch 1:5 they are included among the sons of Japheth; according to 2 K 17:6 and 18:11, the Israelites of the N Kingdom were deported to 'the cities of the Medes'; their struggle with Assyria, and later with Babylon, is reflected in Is 13:17, 21:2, Jer 51:11, 28; Media later became part of the Pers. Empire, cf. Ezr 6:2; the books of Daniel and Esther refer to the laws of the Medes and the Persians, and the events in the book of Tobit take place in Media; cf. also 1 Mac 6:56, 8:8, 14:1f., Ac 2:9; Maps 20, 25, 26.

Megbis, see MAGBISH.

Megiddo, city of Manasseh in the territory of Issachar, Jos 17:11, 1 Ch 7:29; Canaanite royal city, Jos 12:21, Jg 1:27; in Solomon's 5th district, 1 K 4:12; fortified by Solomon, 1 K 9:15; Ahaziah died there, 2 K 9:27; Josiah was killed there in the battle of Megiddo against the Pharaoh Necho, 2 K 23:29f., 2 Ch 35:22, cf. Zec 12:11 and ARMAGEDDON; 'the waters of Megiddo', Jg 5:19; mod. *Tell el-Mutesellim;* Maps 2, 4, 7, 11, 14, 17, 20; Pls. 195, 209f., 364; p. 20.

Mehebel, see MAHALAB.

Mehunim(s), see MEUNIM, MEUNITES.

Mejarcon, see ME-JARKON.

Me-jarkon, loc. of Dan, listed Jos 19:46; near Joppa, exact sit. unk. □

Mekonah, see MECONAH.

Melchisedech, see MELCHIZEDEK.

Melchizedek, n. of the priest-king of Salem (= Jerusalem?); 'priest of God Most High' to whom Abraham gave a tithe, Gn 14:18ff.; presented as a Messianic figure in Ps 110:4; his resemblance to Christ is developed in Heb 7.

Melchom, see MOLECH.

Melita, see MALTA.

Mello, see MILLO (The).

Mello (City of), see BETH-MILLO.

Memphis, Eg. *mn-nfr;* capital of Lower Egypt, ment. Hos 9:6 (Heb. Moph), Is 19:13, Jer 2:16, 44:1, 46:14,19, Ezk 30:13, 16 (Heb. Noph in all these passages); its ruins lie near *Mit Rahîneh* and the necropolis of *Sakkârah;* Maps 5, 6, 7, 8, 9, 18, 20, 21, I (e.p.); Pls. 9–11, 126–128.

Menahem, n. of the 16th king of Israel (743–737 B.C.), 2 K 15:14ff.; pp. 90, 92.

Menni, see MINNI.

Mennith, see MINNITH.

Men's Court, court of the Temple of Jerusalem; Map 33 no. 4.

Menuhoth, see MANOCHO.

Mephaath, loc. of Reuben, listed Jos 13:18; Levitical city, Jos 21:37, 1 Ch 6:79 (Heb. 64); later Moabite, Jer 48:21; mod. *Tell Jâwah,* near *Kh. Nefaʿa* which preserves the ancient n.; Maps 11, 17. □

Mephibosheth, deliberate corruption of Meri(b)-baal, 1 Ch 8:34, 9:40; n. of 2 persons, 1. son of Saul, 2 S 21:8 only.
2. son of Jonathan, 2 S 4:4, 21:7.

Merala, see MAREAL.

Merathaim, n. for Babylon in Jer 50:21, strictly the region around the mouth of the Tigris-Euphrates (*nâr marrâtu*), used in a play on the Heb. word for a revolt against God (*marah*). □

Mercurius, Mercury, see HERMES (2).

Meribah, Meribah-Kadesh, Meribath-kadesh, see MASSAH.

Merneptah, n. of a Pharaoh; son and successor of Rameses II; Pl. 131; p. 46.

Merodach, Heb. vocalisation of Bab. *Marduk,* n. of a Bab. god, Jer 50:2; also found as an element in the names Merodach-baladan, Is 39:1, and Evil-merodach, 2 K 25:27.

Merodach-baladan, Heb. form of Bab. *Marduk-apal-iddina,* 'Marduk has given a son'; n. of a king of Babylon who sent envoys to Hezekiah, Is 39; p. 94.

Merom (Waters of), site of a battle between Joshua and Jabin, king of Hazor, Jos 11:5ff.; often identified with Lake Huleh (Map 2), but more likely to designate a spring and a wâdi near the mod. village of *Meirôn,* SW of Lake Huleh; Map 14. □

Meron, see SHIMRON.

Maps: 1 p. 9 / 2, 3 p. 10 / 4 p. 29 / 5, 6 p. 30 / 7, 8 p. 43 / 9, 10 p. 44 / 11, 12 p. 59 / 13 p. 60 / 14 p. 65 / 15, 16 p. 66 / 17 p. 81 / 18, 19 p. 82 / 20, 21 p. 95 / 22–24 p. 96 / 25–29 p. 103 / 30, 31 p. 104 / 32, 33 p. 115 / 34, 35 p. 116 / I, II end-papers.

156

Meronoth, loc. ment. Neh 3:7 (Jadon the Meronothite), cf. 1 Ch 27:30; poss. mod. *Beitûniyah*, NW of Gibeon; Map 22. □
Meroz, loc. ment. Jg 5:23; poss. mod. *Kh. Marûs*, SW of Lake Huleh; Map 14. □
Mesa, see MESHA (1).
Mesaloth, near Arbela (Map 30); place where the insurgents took refuge, 1 Mac 9:2; prob. caves in the steep sides of the *W. Hamâm* (the n. can be translated 'steps, ascents'), W of the Sea of Galilee.
Mesech, see MESHECH.
Mesha, 1. n. of a king of Moab; defeated by Joram of Israel and Jehoshaphat of Judah, 2 K 3; the stele (Moabite Stone) found at Dibon sheds light on his reign, cf. p. 80.
2. loc. ment. Gn 10:30 as a limit of the territory of the sons of Joktan; poss. identical with Massa.
Meshach, Bab. n. given to Mishael, Dn 1:7.
Meshech, n. of a people and region of Asia Minor; listed among the sons of Japheth, Gn 10:2 = 1 Ch 1:5, cf. 1:17; ment. with Tubal, Ezk 27:13, 32:26; ment. with Gog, Ezk 38:2f., 39:1; cf. Ps 120:5, Is 66:19 (LXX); prob. identical with the Mushku of the Ass. texts and the Moschoi of Herodotus. □
Mesopotamia, region of the 2 rivers, Tigris and Euphrates; Maps 6, 8, 25, 32, I (e.p.). Cf. ARAM (5) and PADDAN-ARAM.
Mesphe, see MIZPAH, MIZPEH (1), (3).
Mesraim, see MIZRAIM.
Mess, see MASH.
Messa, see MESHA (2).
Messal, see MISHAL.
Methca, see MITHKAH.
Meunim, Meunites, n. of a tribe, 1 Ch 4:41, 2 Ch 20:1 (so R.S.V. with LXX; Heb. Ammonites), 26:7, 8 (LXX; Heb. Ammonites); usually linked with the village of *Ma'ân*, SE of Petra, cf. Ezr 2:50, Neh 7:52. □
Micah, n. of several persons, in particular a prophet who was a contemporary of Isaiah; his utterances form the 6th book of the Minor Prophets.
Michael, 'who is like God'; n. of an archangel, Dn 10:13, 21, Rev 12:7; the protector of God's people.
Michal, n. of the daughter of Saul and wife of David, 2 S 6
Micheas, see MICAH.
Michmas, see MICHMASH.
Michmash, loc. N of Jerusalem which played an important part in the story of Jonathan, 1 S 13, 14, Is 10:28, Ezr 2:27 (Michmas), Neh 7:31 (Michmas), 11:31; where Jonathan, the brother of Judas Maccabaeus, judged, 1 Mac 9:73; mod. *Mukhmâs*; Maps 2, 15, 19, 22, 30; Pls. 189 f., 250. □
Michmethah, see MICHMETHATH.
Michmethath, loc. of Ephraim, listed Jos 16:6; on the boundary of Manasseh, Jos 17:7; mod. *Kh. Juleijil*, E of Shechem; Map 11. □
Michol, see MICHAL.
Middin, loc. of Judah, in the wilderness, listed Jos 15:61; sit. unk. □
Midian (Day of), an expression used in Is 9:4 (Heb. 3), cf. 10:26; it refers to Gideon's defeat of the Midianites (Jg 7:16ff.).
Midian, Midianites, nomadic clans who came into frequent contact with the Israelites; they wandered in the region of the Gulf of Elath, from Mt Sinai in the S to Moab in the N; they raided Canaan in the time of the Judges; their ancestor is ment. among the sons of Abraham, Gn 25:2; Moses took refuge with the Midianites, Ex 2:15ff. (Jethro, his father-in-law, was a Midianite); war between the Hebrews and the Midianites, Nu 31; defeat of the Midianites by Gideon, Jg 6–8; Map 9; Pls. 143f. Cf. MAON.
Migdal-, Migdol-, 'watch-tower, fortress'; an element in many place-names.
Migdal-el, loc. of Naphtali, listed Jos 19:38; sit. unk. □
Migdal-gad, loc. of Judah, in the lowland, listed Jos 15:37; poss. mod. *Kh. el-Majdala*, ESE of Lachish; Maps 13, 19. □
Migdol, 1. Eg. fort on *J. Abû Hassa*, Ex 14:2, Nu 33:7; Map 9; p. 48.
2. city E of the Nile Delta, Jer 44:1, 46:14, Ezk 29:10, 30:6; prob. mod. *Tell el-Hêr*; Map 9. □
Migron, loc. ment. in the march of the Ass. army, Is 10:28; mod. *Tell Miryam*, near Michmash; Map 19. Poss. identical with the Migron of 1 S 14:2, unless the latter should be read 'near the threshing-floor' instead of 'at Migron'.
Milcom, see MOLECH.
Miletum, see MILETUS.
Miletus, sea-port of Asia Minor, Ac 20:15ff., 2 Ti 4:20; its ruins lie near mod. *Palatia;* Maps 21, 25, II (e.p.); Pl. 403. □
Millo (House of), see BETH-MILLO.
Millo (The), fortification, on the N side of the city of David, 2 S 5:9, 1 K 9:15, 24, 11:27, 1 Ch 11:8, 2 Ch 32:5; there was a similar fortification, called BETH-MILLO, q.v., at Shechem, Jg 9:6, 20; p. 70. Cf. also 2 K 12:20. □
Minni, region ment. with Ararat and Ashkenaz in Jer 51:27; prob. identical with the Manna of Ass. texts of the 7th century B.C. and doubtless in Armenia. □
Minnith, loc. ment. Jg 11:33, Ezk 27:17 (Heb.); poss. mod. *Kh. Hamzeh*, 4 miles NE of Heshbon; Map 14. □
Miphiboseth, see MEPHIBOSHETH.
Miriam, n. of the daughter of Amram and Jochebed and sister of Moses and Aaron, Nu 26:59; cf. Ex 2:4.
Misach, see MESHACH.
Misael, see MISHAEL.
Mishael, n. of one of the companions of Daniel, Dn 1:7.
Mishal, loc. of Asher, listed Jos 19:26; Levitical city, Jos 21:30; called Mashal in 1 Ch 6:74 (Heb. 59); near Mt Carmel, exact sit. unk. □
Misheal, see MISHAL.
Misphat (Spring of), see EN-MISHPAT.
Misrephoth-maim, loc. ment. only as a point on the NW frontier of Palestine, Jos 11:8, 13:6; mod. *Kh. el-Musheirefeh;* Maps 12, 14. □
Mithcah, see MITHKAH.
Mithkah, stopping-place on the Exodus, near Hashmonah, Nu 33:28f.; exact sit. unk. □
Mitylene, sea-port on the island of Lesbos off the coast of Asia Minor, Ac 20:14; Map II (e.p.). □
Mizpah, Mizpeh, 'guard-post'; 1. loc. of Benjamin, listed Jos 18:26; religious centre with a sanctuary in the time of the Judges, Jg 20, 1 S 7, 10, 1 Mac 3:46; on the boundary between Israel and Judah, 1 K 15:22, 2 Ch 16:6; residence of Gedaliah, 2 K 25:23, Jer 40, 41; capital of a district, Neh 3:19; prob. mod. *Tell en-Nasbeh*, 8 miles N of Jerusalem; Maps 13, 14, 15, 17, 19, 22, 30; Pl. 221 no. 2; p. 80.
2. loc. of Judah, in the lowland, listed Jos 15:38; sit. unk. □
3. loc. in Gilead, on the frontier between Israel and Aram, where Laban and Jacob made a covenant, Gn 31:49 (Samaritan text); identical with the Ramath-mizpeh of Gad, listed Jos 13:26, and Mizpah of Gilead, Jg 10:17, 11:29; prob. mod. *Kh. Jel'ad*, S of the Jabbok; Maps 11, 14.
4. loc. in Moab, 1 S 22:3 (Mizpeh of Moab); sit. unk. □
5. region in the N of Palestine, towards Mt Hermon, Jos 11:3 (land of Mizpah), 8 (valley of Mizpeh). □
Mizpeh, see MIZPAH, MIZPEH.
Mizraim, Heb. n. for Egypt; in some versions replaces Egypt as n. of a son of Ham, Gn 10:6, 13; ment. in some passages with reference to horses, 1 K 10:28 = 2 Ch 1:16, 2 K 7:6, and therefore identified by some scholars with the Musur or Musri of the Ass. texts, a region in Asia Minor, to the N of Nineveh, and famous for horse-breeding.
Mnason, n. of a Cypriot Christian at whose house St Paul stayed, Ac 21:16.
Moab, Moabites, popular etymology, *me'abi*, 'of my father', cf. Gn 19:36f.; region E of the Dead Sea whose inhabitants were related to the Hebrews, cf. Gn 19:31–37; plays an important part in the history of Israel, cf. Nu 22, Jg 3:12ff., 2 K 3; threatened, like Israel, by Assyria, Is 15f., Jer 48; later occupied by the Nabataeans; Maps 7, 9, 14, 15, 17, 18, 23; Pl. 28. The 'plains of Moab' = the SE part of the Jordan valley, Nu 22:1, etc.; Pl. 160; pp. 52, 71, 94.
Moab (Plains, Field, Steppes of), see MOAB, MOABITES.
Moabite Stone, see MESHA (1).
Mochona, see MECONAH.
Modin, loc. NW of Jerusalem; home of the Maccabees, 1 Mac 2:15, 23, 70, 9:19; mod. *el-'Arba'în*, near *el-Midyah;* Maps 30, 31.
Molada, see MOLADAH.
Moladah, loc. of Judah, in the Negeb, listed Jos 15:26, and of Simeon, listed Jos 19:2, 1 Ch 4:28; repopulated after the Exile, Neh 11:26; poss. mod. *Tell el-Milh*, E of Beer-sheba; Map 13.
Molech, 'king'; n. of a god venerated by the Ammonites under the n. of Milcom, cf. 1 K 11:5, 33, 2 K 23:13; the Israelites venerated him under the n. of Melek, 'king', changed in the text of the Bible to Molech (G&L Moloch, cf. Ac 7:43), by reading Melek with the vowels of *bosheth*, 'shame'; children were sacrificed to this god, 2 K 23:10, Jer 32:35.
Moloch, see MOLECH.
Moph, see MEMPHIS.
Morasthi, see MORESHETH-GATH.
Morasthite, epithet of Micah, meaning 'of MORESHETH-GATH', q.v.
Mordecai, n. of the adoptive father of Esther, Est 2:15; derived from the n. of the god Marduk.
Moreh, 'teacher', or poss. 'diviner'; n. of 1. a tree near Shechem, Gn 12:6; the Heb. text of Dt 11:30 refers to several trees (singular only in all the translations), prob. a tendentious emendation made by the rabbis (cf. MAMRE); cf. Gn 35:4, Jg 9:37.
2. hill ment. Jg 7:1; mod. *J. Dahi*, S of Mt Tabor; Map 14; Pl. 188. □
Moreseth-gath, see MORESHETH-GATH.
Moresheth, Moresheth-gath, home of the prophet Micah, Mic 1:1, 14 (Moresheth-gath), Jer 26:18; mod. *Tell el-Judeideh*, E of Gath; Map 17. □
Moria (Mount), see MORIAH (Land of).
Moriah (Land of), region in which was the mountain upon which Isaac was to be sacrificed, Gn 22:2; identified with the hill of the Temple in 2 Ch 3:1 (Mount Moriah), a localisation which has been preserved in tradition.
Mosel, see UZAL.
Mosera(h), see MOSEROTH.
Moseroth, stopping-place on the Exodus, Nu 33:30f.; scene of Aaron's death, Dt 10:6 (Moserah); prob. the mt range S of mod. *'Abde*, N of Kadesh; Map 9. □
Moses, popular etymology, Heb. *Mosheh* from *mashah*, 'drawn out (of the water)', Ex 2:10, but the scientific derivation is uncertain; life and work of Moses, pp. 46ff.
Mosoch, see MESHECH.
Mount Carmel, see CARMEL (2).
Mount Ebal, see EBAL (3).
Mount Ephraim, see EPHRAIM (2).
Mount Gaash, see GAASH.
Mount Gadgad, see HOR-HAGGIDGAD.
Mount Gelboe, see GILBOA.
Mount Gerizim, see GERIZIM (Mount).
Mount Gilboa, see GILBOA.
Mount Halak, see HALAK (Mount).
Mount Hermon, see HERMON (Mount).
Mount Hor, see HOR (Mount).
Mount Horeb, see HOREB (Mount).
Mount Jearim, see JEARIM (Mount).
Mount Moriah, see MORIAH (Land of).
Mount Nebo, see NEBO (1).
Mount of Corruption, see OFFENCE (Mount of).
Mount of Offence, see OFFENCE (Mount of).
Mount of Olives, see OLIVES (Mount of).
Mount Paran, see PARAN (Mount).
Mount Scopus, see SCOPUS (Mount).
Mount Seir, see SEIR (2).
Mount Shepher, see SHEPHER (Mount).
Mount Sinai, see SINAI (Mount).
Mount Tabor, Mount Thabor, see TABOR (1).
Mount Zalmon, see ZALMON (Mount).
Mount Zemaraim, see ZEMARAIM.
Mount Zion, see ZION.
Mozah, loc. of Benjamin, listed Jos 18:26; sit. unk. □
Muster Gate, gate on the NE side of Jerusalem, Neh 3:31; identified by H. Vincent with the Gate of the Guard, Neh 12:39; Map 24C. □
Myndos, city of Caria in Asia Minor; ment. in the list of countries and cities which received the letter of Lucius, 1 Mac 15:23; Map 26. □
Myndus, see MYNDOS.
Myra, sea-port of Lycia in Asia Minor, Ac 27:5; mod. *Dembre;* Map II (e.p.). □
Mysia, region of Asia Minor, Ac 16:7f.; Maps 25, II (e.p.). □

N

Naalol, see NAHALAL.
Naama, see NAAMAH (1), (3).
Naamah, 1. loc. of Judah, in the lowland, listed Jos 15:41; prob. mod. *Kh. Farad*, near *Beit en-Nu'man*, W of Beth-shemesh; Maps 13, 19. □
2. daughter of Lamech and sister of Tubal-cain, Gn 4:22.
3. mother of Rehoboam, 1 K 14:21.
4. home of Zophar the Naamathite, one of the 3 friends of Job, Job 2:11; prob. situated to the E of Palestine, on the edge of the Arabian desert.
Naaman, n. of several persons, inc. one of Ben-hadad's commanders who was healed by Elisha, 2 K 5.
Naamath, see NAAMAH (4).
Naarah, loc. of Ephraim, listed Jos 16:7; called Naaran in 1 Ch 7:28; sit. unk. □
Naaran, Naarath, Naaratha, see NAARAH.
Naas, see NAHASH.
Naasson, To 1:1, see HAZOR.
Nabaioth, Nabajoth, see NEBAIOTH.
Nabal, 'stupid'; n. of the husband of Abigail, a rich landowner of Maon, 1 S 25.
Nabataeans, nomadic tribe of Arab origin; they controlled the caravan-routes of the Persian Gulf, Arabia, and the Red Sea, and thus became the most important merchants in N Arabia; they drove out the Edomites from the region around Petra, which became their capital; unless the n. NEBAIOTH (q.v.) was applied to them, they do not figure in Biblical history until the time of the Maccabees, 1 Mac 5:25, 9:35 (Nabathaeans); several of their kings were called ARETAS, q.v.; pp. 112 f.
Nabathaeans, Nabathites, see NABATAEANS.
Nabo, see NEBO (2), (4).
Nabopolassar, n. of the father of Nebuchadnezzar; p. 97.
Naboth, n. of the owner of a vineyard which he refused to sell to Ahab; stoned to death as a result of Jezebel's intrigue, 1 K 21.
Nabuchodonosor, see NEBUCHADNEZZAR.
Nabutheans, see NABATAEANS.
Nabuzardan, see NEBUZARADAN.
Nachor, see NAHOR.
Nachor (City of), see NAHOR (City of).
Nadab, n. of 2 persons, 1. son of Aaron, Ex 28:1.
2. 2nd king of Israel (910–909 B.C.); son of Jeroboam; assassinated by Baasha, 1 K 15:25ff.
Nadabath, loc. in Transjordan, ment. 1 Mac. 9:37; poss. mod. *Kh. et-Teim*, S of Medaba; Map 30. □
Nahalal, loc. of Zebulun, listed Jos 19:15, cf. Jg 1:30 (Nahalol); Levitical city, Jos 21:35; sit. unk. □
Nahaliel, one of the last stopping-places on the Exodus, in Moab, Nu 21:19. □
Nahallal, Nahalol, see NAHALAL.
Nahash, 'serpent'; n. of 2 persons, 1. 1st husband of David's mother, 2 S 17:25.
2. Ammonite prince whose siege of Jabesh-gilead provoked the intervention of Saul, 1 S 11.
Nahor, n. of 2 persons, 1. grandfather of Abraham, Gn 11:22ff.
2. brother of Abraham, Gn 11:26 ff.
Nahor (City of), loc. ment. Gn 24:10; also known from texts of the 19th century B.C. (Nahur), and the 7th century B.C. (Til-Nahiri); it must have lain in the region of Haran, but the site has not yet been discovered.
Nahr el-Kelb, 'river of the dog'; S of Byblos; Map 7; Pl. 14; p. 45.
Nahum, abb. of Heb. *Nehamyah*, 'Yahweh consoles'; n. of a Minor Prophet of the 7th century B.C.
Naim, see NAIN.
Nain, city where Jesus brought to life the widow's son, Lk 7:11; mod. *Nein*, S of Nazareth; Map 34; Pl. 188. □
Naioth (Navith), n. of a dwelling-place of the prophets, in or near Ramah, 1 S 19:18 - 20:1; exact meaning of the n. is uncertain. □

Maps: 1 p. 9 / 2, 3 p. 10 / 4 p. 29 / 5, 6 p. 30 / 7, 8 p. 43 / 9, 10 p. 44 / 11, 12 p. 59 / 13 p. 60 / 14 p. 65 / 15, 16 p. 66 / 17 p. 81 / 18, 19 p. 82 / 20, 21 p. 95 / 22–24 p. 96 / 25–29 p. 103 / 30, 31 p. 104 / 32, 33 p. 115 / 34, 35 p. 116 / I, II end-papers.

157

Najoth, see NAIOTH.
Naphath-dor, Naphoth-dor, see DOR.
Naphtali, popular etymology, 'I have wrestled with my sister', according to Gn 30:8; n. of the son of Jacob and Bilhah; ancestor of one of the 12 tribes; the tribal territory was in N Palestine, Jos 19:32-39; Maps 11, 14, 15, 17.
Nasor, 1 Mac 11:67, see HAZOR.
Nathan, 'He has given'; n. of several persons, inc. a prophet of the time of David, 2 S 12.
Nathanael, 'God has given'; n. of many persons in the O.T. In the N.T., n. of one of the 12 Apostles, Jn 1:45ff., 21:2; prob. identical with the Bartholomew of the Synoptic Gospels, Mt 10:3 and parallel passages.
Naucratis, loc. in Lower Egypt, on the Canopic arm of the Nile; mod. *Tell en-Nabireh*; Map 21.
Nazareth, small city in Galilee where Joseph and Mary lived; insignificant, Jn 1:45f.; where the Angel visited Mary, Lk 1:26, and to which Joseph and Mary returned with Jesus after His birth at Bethlehem, Lk 2:4, 39, Mt 2:23; here Jesus was brought up by His parents and was 'obedient to them', Lk 2:51, 4:16; later He went from here to be baptised, Mk 1:9, and to live in Capernaum, Mt 4:13. The term 'Jesus of Nazareth' occurs twice in the Gk. text of the N.T., Mt 21:11, Ac 10:38, and Jesus is 6 times described as a Nazarene and 13 times as a Nazorite (with unexplained 'o') in the Gk. text (R.S.V. 'of Nazareth', or 'Nazarene'). Maps 2, 34, 35; Pls. 22, 368, 372. □
Neah, loc. of Zebulun, listed Jos 19:13; poss. mod. *Tell el-Wâwiyât;* Map 11. □
Neapolis, sea-port of Greece, Ac 16:11; mod. *Kavalla*; Map II (e.p.). □
Nebahaz, see NIBHAZ.
Nebaioth, n. of an Arab tribe ment. with Kedar, Is 60:7; listed among the sons of Ishmael, Gn 25:13, 1 Ch 1:29, cf. Gn 28:9, 36:3; identified with the Nabataeans by many scholars. □
Nebajoth, see NEBAIOTH.
Neballat, loc. ment. in Neh 11:34; prob. mod. *Beit Nabala*, NE of Lod (v. 35); Map 23. □
Nebo, n. of 1. Mt Nebo, 2,740 ft high, 12 miles E of the mouth of the Jordan; scene of the death of Moses; ment. only Dt 32:49, 34:1; mod. *J. en-Neba*; Maps 2, 9, 14; Pls. 159 f.; p. 56. □
2. city of Reuben in Transjordan, Nu 32:3, 38, 33:47, 1 Ch 5:8; later Moabite, Is 15:2, Jer 48:1, 22; ment. on the Moabite Stone, cf. p. 80; exact sit. unk., prob. one of the tells near Mt Nebo. □
3. loc. in Judah, ment. in the lists of repatriated Israelites, Ezr 2:29, 10:43, Neh 7:33; poss. mod. *Nuba*, NW of Beth-zur; Map 22. □
4. Heb. transcription of the n. of the Bab. god *Nabu*; found in Is 46:1, and as an element in some proper names (e.g. Nebuchadnezzar, Nebuzaradan, etc.).
Nebsan, see NIBSHAN.
Nebuchadnezzar, Nebuchadrezzar, Heb. form of Bab. *Nabu-kudurri-usur*, 'Nabu protect the son'; spelled Nebuchadrezzar in the books of Jeremiah and Ezekiel; n. of the son and successor of Nabopolassar, who reigned from 605 to 562 B.C. and built the neo-Babylonian Empire upon the foundations laid by his father; he three times captured Jerusalem, and on the 3rd occasion (586 B.C.) deported its inhabitants to Babylon; Map 20; p. 97.
Nebuchadrezzar, see NEBUCHADNEZZAR.
Nebuzaradan, Heb. form of Bab. *Nabu-zer-iddina*, 'Nabu has given offspring'; n. of the captain of Nebuchadnezzar's bodyguard, 2 K 25:8ff.
Neceb, see ADAMI-NEKEB.
Nechao, see NECHO.
Necho, n. of a Pharaoh (609–594 B.C.); he defeated Josiah at Megiddo, 2 K 23 (R.S.V. Neco), and was himself defeated by Nebuchadnezzar at Carchemish, 2 K 24:7; Map 20.
Neco, see NECHO.
Negeb, n. which originally meant 'the dry land' and designated the region between Hebron and Kadesh, in S Judah; Maps 2, 14; Pls. 31, 151; later extended to designate the South in general; pp. 16, 28.
Nehemiah, 'Yahweh consoles'; n. of one of the leaders of the Jews after the Exile, cf. Sir 49:13; Map 21; p. 100.
Nehemias, see NEHEMIAH.
Nehiel, see NEIEL.
Neiel, loc. of Asher, listed Jos 19:27; poss. mod. *Kh. Ya'nîn;* Map 11. □
Nekeb, see ADAMI-NEKEB.
Nemra, see NIMRAH.
Nemrim (Waters of), see NIMRIM (Waters of).
Nephath-Dor, see NAPHATH-DOR.
Nephtali, see NAPHTALI.
Nephtoa (Waters of), see NEPHTOAH (Waters of).
Nephtoah (Waters of), spring ment. in the indication of the boundaries of Judah, Jos 15:9; on the S boundary of Benjamin, Jos 18:15; the n. may derive from that of the Pharaoh Merneptah; mod. *Lifta*, W of Jerusalem; Maps 13, 19.
Neregal, see NERGAL-SHAREZER.
Nereus, n. of a Roman Christian, Ro 16:15.
Nergal, n. of a Bab. god of the underworld, ment. only 2 K 17:30.
Nergal-sharezer, Heb. form of Bab. *Nergal-shar-usur*, 'Nergal protect the king'; n. of one of Nebuchadnezzar's officers, Jer 39:3, 13.
Nergel, see NERGAL.
Nero, Roman emperor (A.D. 54–68) who persecuted the Christians; prob. the 'Caesar' to whom St Paul appealed, Ac 25:11f., and in whose reign he was martyred; Pl. 325; p. 121.
Nesib, see NEZIB.
Nesroch, see NISROCH.
Nethanel, see NATHANAEL.
Nethuphati, see NETOPHAH.
Netophah, loc. SE of Bethlehem, Ezr 2:22, cf. Neh 7:26; home of several persons living in the period of the monarchy, 2 S 23:28f., 2 K 25:23, Jer 40:8; 1 Ch 2:54, 9:16, 11:30, 27:13ff., Neh 12:28; poss. mod. *Kh. Badd Falûh*, in the vicinity of *'Ain en-Natûf*, which preserves the ancient n.; Maps 15, 22. □
Netophathi, Netophathite, Netophati, Netupha, see NETOPHAH.
New Asor, see HAZOR-HADATTAH.
New Quarter (Gate of the), gate of Jerusalem, Neh 3:6 (conj.), 12:39 (conj.). Cf. OLD GATE.
Nezib, loc. of Judah, in the lowland, listed Jos 15:43; mod. *Kh. Beit Nasib*, E of Lachish; Maps 13, 19. □
Nibhaz, n. of a deity of the Avvites, 2 K 17:31, of whom nothing further is known.
Nibshan, loc. of Judah, in the wilderness, listed Jos 15:62; sit. unk. □
Nicanor, n. of 1. a commander chosen by Lysias who was defeated by Judas Maccabaeus near Emmaus, 1 Mac 3f.
2. one of the 'Seven', Ac 6:5.
Nicanor's Gate, gate of the Temple of Jerusalem; Map 33 no. 3.
Nicodemus, n. of a member of the Sanhedrin who was sympathetic to the teaching of Jesus, Jn 3, 7:50, 19:39.
Nicolaitanes, see NICOLAITANS.
Nicolaitans, n. of a Christian sect which embraced strange beliefs and practices akin to the errors denounced in the Letter to the Colossians, Rev 2:6, 15.
Nicolaites, see NICOLAITANS.
Nicolas, see NICOLAUS.
Nicolaus, n. of one of the 'Seven', Ac 6:5.
Nicopolis, 'city of victory'; 1. city in Greece, Tit 3:12; prob. mod. *Paleoprevesa* in N Epirus (WNW of Corinth); Map II (e.p.). □
2. n. by which Emmaus (mod. *Amwâs*) was known from the 3rd century A.D.
Nile, one of the longest (over 4,000 miles) rivers in the world; the Heb. n. *Ye'ôr* applied to it in the Bible sometimes means only 'river' in general, as in Dn 12:5-7 (= the Tigris?); Maps 5, 6, 9, I (e.p.); Pls. 9, 10, 263f.; p. 11. See also SHIHOR (The).
Nimrah, loc. ment. Nu 32:3. Cf. BETH-NIMRAH. □
Nimrim (Waters of), n. of an oasis in Moab, near the Dead Sea, Is 15:6, Jer 48:34; poss. in the mod. *W. Numeira* (*Hudeira*), which flows into the Dead Sea S of the peninsula; Map 17. □
Nineve, see NINEVEH.
Nineveh, city on the E bank of the Tigris; residence of the Ass. kings from 1100 B.C.; became the capital city under Sennacherib, 2 K 19:36 = Is 37:37; founded by Nimrod, according to Gn 10:11; also ment. Nah (3 times), Zeph 2:13, Jon (frequently), cf. Mt 12:41 = Lk 11:32; mod. *Tell Quyunjiq* and *Tell Nebi Yûnus* (Jonah); Maps 1, 5, 6, 7, 8, 18, 20, I (e.p.); p. 97.
Ninive, see NINEVEH.
Nippur, Sumerian city in S Babylonia; not ment. in the Bible; mod. *Nuffar*, where important excavations have been carried out; Map 1.
Nisroch, n. of an Ass. deity, ment. 2 K 19:37 = Is 37:38, of whom nothing further is known; poss. a corruption of Marduk.
No, see NO-AMON, THEBES.
Noa, see NEAH.
Noah, n. of the hero of the story of the Flood, Gn 5ff.
No-amon, Heb. spelling of Eg. *nw. t-imn*, 'town of Amon'; n. of the capital city of Upper Egypt, cf. Nah 3:8 (Heb.); called *Thebai* by the Greeks, and rendered Thebes in Jer 46:25 (Amon of Thebes), Ezk 30:14ff., Nah 3:8; some versions read No, No-amon, or even Alexandria in these passages; the ruins lie at Luxor and Karnak in Upper Egypt; Maps 1, 5, 6, 8, 10, 20, I (e.p.); Pls. 9f. Cf. THEBES. □
Nob, loc. near Jerusalem, 1 S 21:1 (Heb. 2), 22:9, 11, 19; on the route of the Ass. army, Is 10:32; repopulated after the Exile, Neh 11:32; prob. mod. *Râs Umm et-Tala'*, on the E slopes of Mt Scopus, NE of Jerusalem; Maps 15, 19, 22; Pl. 192 no. 10. □
Nobah, n. of 2 cities, 1. in Transjordan, in the neighbourhood of JOGBEHAH, q.v., Jg 8:11; exact sit. uncertain. □
2. see KENATH.
Nobe, see NOB.
Noe, see NOAH.
Noema, see NAAMAH (2).
Noph, see MEMPHIS.
Nophah, loc. in Transjordan, N of Dibon, Nu 21:30; sit. uncertain; the text is doubtful (R.S.V. 'fire spread'). □
Nophe, see NOPHAH.
Noran, see NAARAH.
Nuzu (Nuzi), city in Mesopotamia; mod. *Yorghan Tepe*, near *Kirkuk*, where important archaeological discoveries have been made; Map 1; p. 35.

O

Obadiah, 'servant of Yahweh'; n. of 11 persons, inc. the 4th of the 12 Minor Prophets; his book contains a prophecy against Edom.
Obal, n. listed Gn 10:28. Cf. EBAL (2).
Obed, n. of David's grandfather, Ru 4:17ff.; ment. in the genealogy of Jesus Christ, Mt 1:5.
Oboth, stopping-place on the Exodus, Nu 21:10f., 33:43f.; poss. mod. *'Ain el-Weiba*, S of the Dead Sea; Map 9. □
Ochozias, see AHAZIAH.
Odollam, see ADULLAM (Cave of).
Offence (Mount of), n. given by the Early Christians to the hill SE of Jerusalem and S of the Mt of Olives, on which Solomon worshipped false gods, 1 K 11:7, cf. 2 K 23:13 (mount of corruption); Map 33.
Og, n. of a king of Bashan; defeated by the Hebrews in a victory which became a legend, Dt 3:1ff., Nu 21:33ff., cf. Neh 9:22, Ps 135:11, 136:20; Og's 'bedstead of iron', Dt 3:11.
Old Gate, gate of Jerusalem, Neh 3:6, 12:39; by reading 'gate of the new quarter' we are able to localise it W of the Temple.
Olives (Mount of), hill E of Jerusalem, separated from the city by the deep valley of the Kidron, 2 S 15:23, 30, 32, Ezk 11:23, Zec 14:4; frequently ment. in the Gospels, Mt 21:1, Mk 13:3, Lk 22:39, etc.; scene of the Ascension, according to Ac 1:12 ('mount called Olivet'); the summit is about 250 ft higher than the Temple terrace; Maps 24, 33; Pls. 192, 326.
Olivet (Mount), see OLIVES (Mount of).
Olon, see HOLON (1).
Olympas, n. of a Christian to whom St Paul sent greetings, Ro 16:15.
Olympias, see OLYMPAS.
Omri, n. of several persons, in particular the 6th king of Israel (885–874 B.C.); founder of Samaria, 1 K 16:16ff.; Map 17; pp. 80ff.
On, city in Lower Egypt; centre of the sun cult; identical with Heliopolis; ment. Gn 41:45, Ezk 30:17; cf. Jer. 43:13 (LXX); mod. *Matarîyeh*, 5 miles NE of Cairo; Maps 10, 20.
Onesimus, n. of the Christian slave of Philemon, Philem 10; ment. also Col 4:9.
Onesiphorus, n. of a Christian, ment. 2 Ti 1:16ff., 4:19.
Onias, G&L form of Heb. *Honyah;* n. of several High Priests in the time of the Seleucids, in particular Onias III who resisted HELIODORUS (q.v.); later supplanted by his brother JASON (q.v.), and assassinated at Daphne, near Antioch, 2 Mac 3f. Poss. the 'anointed one' alluded to in Dn 9:26.
Ono, loc. ment. Ezr 2:33; repopulated by Benjamites after the Exile, Neh 6:2 (plain of Ono), 7:37, 11:35, cf. 1 Ch 8:12; mod. *Kafr 'Ana*, E of Joppa; Map 23.
Ophaz, see UPHAZ.
Ophel, 'swelling'; technical term apparently applied to a fortified height within a city; ment. in connection with Samaria, 2 K 5:24 ('the hill'), and especially with Jerusalem, 2 Ch 27:3, 33:14, Neh 3:26f., 11:21, Is 32:14 ('the hill'), Mic 4:8 ('hill'); Pls. 192, 381. □
Opher, see HEPHER.
Ophera, see OPHRAH (1).
Ophir, ment. 12 times in the Bible, chiefly as a distant land from which gold could be obtained; Solomon sent a fleet to Ophir from Ezion-geber, 1 K 9:26ff.; listed among the regions of S Arabia, Gn 10:29; prob. the SW coast of Arabia, and poss. also the Somali coast, which has always had close links with Arabia.
Ophni, 1. loc. of Benjamin, listed Jos 18:24; sit. unk. □
2. see HOPHNI.
Ophrah, 1. loc. of Benjamin, listed Jos 18:23, cf. 1 S 13:17; identical with the Ephron of 2 Ch 13:19, and the Ephraim of 2 S 13:23 and Jn 11:54; mod. *et-Taiyibeh*, N of Jerusalem; Maps 11, 15, 17. Cf. EPHRON (2), EPHRAIM (4). □
2. city of Gideon, Jg 6:11, 24, 8:27, 32, 9:5; poss. mod. *et-Taiyibeh*, NW of Beth-shan; Map 14. □
Oreb, 'raven'; n. of a Midianite leader defeated by Gideon, Jg 7:25, 8:3, cf. Ps 83:11 (Heb. 12); also the n. of the rock where he was killed, Jg 7:25, Is 10:26.
Ornan, see ARAUNAH.
Ornithopolis, city on the coast S of Sidon; poss. mod. *Tell el-Buraq*; Map 23.
Oronaim, see HORONAIM.
Orontes, principal river of Syria; 398 miles long, rises in the Anti-Lebanon at a height of 3,740 ft, flows into the Mediterranean W of Antioch; mod. *Nahr el-'Asi*; Kadesh (2), Hamath and Antioch stand on its banks; Maps 1, 7, 29; Pls. 35, 391.
Orthosia, sea-port N of Tripolis, 1 Mac 15:37; mod. *Ard Artûsi;* Maps 29, 31. □
Orthosias, see ORTHOSIA.
Osee, see HOSEA and HOSHEA.
Oshea, see HOSHEA (1).
Othniel, n. of the 1st Judge; he delivered Israel from an Edomite king, Jg 3:9ff.; Map 14; p. 57.
Othoniel, see OTHNIEL.
Oza's Ruin, see PEREZ-UZZAH.
Ozensara, see UZZEN-SHEERAH.
Ozias, see AZARIAH (1).

P

Padan-aram, see PADDAN-ARAM.
Paddan-aram, n. applied to Upper Mesopotamia, Gn 25:20, 28:2; identical with Aram-naharaim, 'Aram of the rivers', of Gn 24:10 (R.S.V. Mesopotamia); Maps 1, 4.
Pai, see PAU.
Palace (The), Am 4:3, see HARMON.
Palestine, n. not found in the Bible; originally a Gk. adjective, 'the Philistine (region)'; from the time of Herodotus, and in Latin authors, applied to the whole land of Israel.
Palmira, see TAMAR (2) and PALMYRA.
Palm Trees, Palms (City of), 1. n. often used for Jericho, Dt

Maps: 1 p. 9 / 2, 3 p. 10 / 4 p. 29 / 5, 6 p. 30 / 7, 8 p. 43 / 9, 10 p. 44 / 11, 12 p. 59 / 13 p. 60 / 14 p. 65 / 15, 16 p. 66 / 17 p. 81 / 18, 19 p. 82 / 20, 21 p. 95 / 22–24 p. 96 / 25–29 p. 103 / 30, 31 p. 104 / 32, 33 p. 115 / 34, 35 p. 116 / I, II end-papers.

158

34:3, Jg 3:13 ('city of palms'), 2 Ch 28:15. Cf. JERICHO.
2. loc. S of the Dead Sea, Jg 1:16 (R.S.V. 'city of palms'); poss. identical with Tamar (2) and Hazazon-tamar. Cf. TAMAR (2), HAZAZON-TAMAR, ATHARIM.

Palmyra, G&L form of TADMOR, q.v.; n. of an oasis in the Syrian desert; mod. *Tudmur;* Maps 1, 4, 20, 25, 32, I (e.p.); Pls. 334–339. The restoration of this famous city has been attributed to Solomon by the writer of 2 Ch 8:4, who has substituted Tadmor for the Tamar (cf. TAMAR (2)) of 1 K 9:18. □

Pamphylia, region of Asia Minor, ment. in the list of countries and cities which received the letter of Lucius, 1 Mac 15:23, and in Ac 13:13, 14:24, 15:38, 27:5, cf. 2:10; Maps 32, II (e.p.). □

Paneas, see PANEION.

Paneion, n. of the sanctuary of the god Pan and the adjoining city, later renamed Caesarea Philippi (cf. CAESAREA (2)) by Herod Philip; situated at the foot of Mt Hermon, near the source of the Jordan; mod. *Bâniyas;* Maps 2, 23, 29, 34; Pl. 360.

Paphlagonia, region of Asia Minor; Map 26.

Paphos, city on the island of Cyprus, Ac 13:6, 13; Map II (e.p.). □

Paradise, Heb. *pardes,* from ancient Indian through Accadian *pardîsu* (cf. Gk. *paradeisos*) = 'orchard', 'garden'; is found only in Ec 2:5 (gardens), Ca 4:13 (orchard), and Neh 2:8 (see KING'S FOREST). Cf. EDEN (1).

Parah, loc. of Benjamin, listed Jos 18:23; sit. NE of Jerusalem, mod. *Tell Fâra,* near the spring of the same name; Maps 13, 19; Pls. 190, 253, 254. Cf. PERATH. □

Paran (Mount), ment. Dt 33:2, Hab 3:3; in the wilderness of PARAN, q.v.

Paran (Wilderness of), region S and SE of Kadesh (1); home of Ishmael, Gn 21:21; crossed by the Israelites, Nu 10:12, 12:16, 13:3, 26, and by Hadad the Edomite, 1 K 11:18. For 'wilderness of Paran', 1 S 25:1, it is preferable to read 'wilderness of Maon' with the Gk.; Map 9; p. 56. Cf. EL-PARAN.

Parmenas, n. of one of the 'Seven', Ac 6:5.

Parthians, n. of an Iranian tribe established SE of the Caspian Sea; their territory was extended by Mithridates I (Arsaces VI) at the expense of Syria, 1 Mac 14:1ff.; the Parthians present at Pentecost, Ac 2:9, were Jews of the Diaspora; Map 26.

Parvaim, unk. region, ment. 2 Ch 3:6; poss. in N Arabia. □

Pas-dammim, loc. between Socoh and Azekah where the Philistines were encamped when David fought Goliath, 1 Ch 11:13; identical with the Ephes-dammim of 1 S 17:1, and prob. also in the original text of 2 S 23:9. □

Pashur, n. of several persons, inc. a priest who persecuted Jeremiah, Jer 20:1ff.

Patara, sea-port of Lycia, Ac 21:1; mod. *Gelemish;* Map II (e.p.). □

Pathros, Eg. *pa-ta-rsh,* 'land of the south'; n. applied to Upper Egypt, Is 11:11, Jer 44:1, 15, Ezk 29:14, 30:14, and read by some scholars in Ps 68:30 (Heb. 31). □

Patmos, island off the W coast of Asia Minor, Rev 1:9; Map II (e.p.). □

Patriarchs, pp. 28–38; Pls. 97–99, 141, 142; Map 4.

Patrobas, n. of a Roman Christian, Ro 16:14.

Pau, city of Edom, Gn 36:39; called Pai in 1 Ch 1:50; sit. unk. □

Paul, Roman n. of the Apostle; first used in Ac 13:9, after which it replaces his Heb. n. Saul; Paul's journeys are charted on Map II (e.p.).

Pavement (The), Gk. *lithostroton;* also called Gabbatha, 'eminence'; where Jesus was brought before Pontius Pilate, Jn 19:13. If we situate this incident in the former Palace of Herod (cf. PRAETORIUM), The Pavement must be the public square in front of the Palace; in that case Gabbatha may have been first applied to the hill SW of Jerusalem and the upper city, and may later have been restricted to the buildings forming the Palace which dominated the upper city; Map 33. If we situate the Praetorium in the fortress of Antonia, The Pavement must be identified with the impressive paved courtyard discovered in 1932, and Gabbatha must be otherwise explained. □

Pekah, n. of the 18th king of Israel (737–732 B.C.), 2 K 15:25ff.; Map 17.

Pekahiah, n. of the 17th king of Israel (738–737 B.C.), 2 K 15:22ff.; Map 17.

Pekod, n. of a Chaldaean tribe, Ezk 23:23; used for all Babylonia in Jer 50:21 in a play on the Heb. imperative form *peqod,* 'punish'. □

Pelethites, see CHERETHITES AND PELETHITES.

Pella, n. of 2 cities, neither of which is ment. in the Bible, 1. according to tradition, city of the Decapolis to which the Christians fled when Jerusalem was destroyed in A.D. 70; mod. *Kh. Fahil,* in Transjordan, SE of Scythopolis; Map 34. Cf. DECAPOLIS.
2. city in Macedonia, in the time of Philip and Alexander; Map 25.

Pelusium, see SIN (2).

Peniel, see PENUEL.

Pentapolis, '(territory of) the five cities'; 1. n. applied in Wis 10:6 to the 5 cities of Sodom, Gomorrah, Admah, Zeboiim and Bela (Zoar), ment. Gn 14:2, 8 (the following verses mention only Sodom and Gomorrah). Lot lived at Sodom, a depraved city, Gn 13:12f., which plays the major rôle in Gn 18f. (destruction of Sodom and Gomorrah). Lot fled to Zoar, Gn 19:22f. The destruction of the cities (excluding Zoar, cf. Gn 10:19) is ment. in Dt 29:23 (Heb. 22). Hos 11:8 refers only to Admah and Zeboiim. In the prophetic tradition Sodom and Gomorrah symbolise the depths of depravity, Dt 32:32, Is 1:10, Jer 23:14; their fate is an example, Is 1:9 = Ro 9:29, Zeph 2:9, cf. Is 13:19, Jer 49:18, 50:40, Am 4:11. Sodom only is ment. in Is 3:9, Ezk 16:46ff., La 4:6. Zoar only is ment. in indications of the territory, Gn 13:10, Dt 34:3, Is 15:5, Jer 48:34, and poss. 48:4. The tradition is alluded to several times in the N.T., sometimes mentioning both cities, Mt 10:15, 2 P 2:6, Jude 7, sometimes Sodom alone, Mt 11:23f., Lk 10:12, 17:29, cf. Rev 11:8. From the earliest times the territory of this Pentapolis has been localised in the shallow S part of the Dead Sea; *J. Usdum,* on the W shore, suggests the n. of Sodom. Zoar may in that case be identified with the ruins near *Bâb ed-Drâ'*. But some scholars, basing themselves on the descriptions of the territory (especially Gn 13:10), place Zoar, and consequently the whole Pentapolis, N of the Dead Sea. Map 4. □
2. non-Biblical n. applied to the 5 Philistine cities of GAZA, ASHDOD, ASHKELON, GATH, and EKRON, qq.v., ment. Jos 13:3, 1 S 6:16, and (excluding Gath, which belonged to Judah) Jer 25:20, Am 1:6ff., Zeph 2:4, Zec 9:5f.

Pentateuch, Gk. n. applied to the 5 books of Moses (Heb. *Torah*): Genesis, Exodus, Leviticus, Numbers, and Deuteronomy.

Penuel, 'face of God'; place near a ford of the Jabbok where Jacob wrestled with God, Gn 32:20 (Peniel), 31; later a city, Jg 8:8f, 17; capital city of Jeroboam, 1 K 12:25; prob. mod. *Tulûl edh-Dhahab;* Maps 4, 14, 17; p. 76. □

Peoples of the Sea, n. applied to the Indo-European tribes who invaded the Near East *ca* 1200 B.C., overthrew the Hittite Empire, and settled along the Mediterranean coast; Map 8; p. 46.

Peoples (Table of the), see TABLE OF THE PEOPLES.

Peor, 1. loc. of Judah, listed Jos 15:59 (LXX); mod. *Kh. Faghûr,* SW of Bethlehem; Maps 13, 19. □
2. mt in Transjordan where the Baal of Peor was venerated. Cf. BAAL-PEOR, BETH-PEOR.

Peraea, non-Biblical n. applied to Transjordan, from Pella to Machaerus; corresponds to the term πέραν τοῦ Ἰορδάνου, 'beyond the Jordan', used in the N.T., Mt 4:25, Mk 3:8, Jn 1:28; Maps 34, 35.

Perath, n. of a river ment. Jer 13:4ff. (Heb.); the Heb. spelling is the same as for the n. of the Euphrates which is poss. referred to; or it may be the spring and wâdi of Parah, N of Anathoth. Cf. PARAH.

Perez-uzza, see PEREZ-UZZAH.

Perez-uzzah, n. given to the loc., ment. 2 S 6:8 = 1 Ch 13:11 (Perez-uzza), where Yahweh struck down Uzzah because he touched the Ark of the Covenant; W of Jerusalem, exact sit. unk.

Perga, city of Pamphylia, Ac 13:13f., 14:25; mod. *Murtana;* Map II (e.p.). □

Pergamos, see PERGAMUM.

Pergamum, city of Mysia, Rev 1:11, 2:12; mod. *Bergama;* Maps 25, II (e.p.).

Pergamus, see PERGAMUM.

Perge, see PERGA.

Perizzites, n. of a people of Canaan, ment. in connection with Bethel, Gn 13:7, and with Shechem, Gn 34:30; defeated at Bezek, Jg 1:4f.; according to Jos 17:15, they lived with the Rephaim in the wooded region of Ephraim; cf. also Ezr 9:1; not ment. elsewhere, except in lists and summaries. Cf. CANAAN, (a), (b), (e).

Persepolis, Pers. city, ment. 2 Mac 9:2; mod. *Takht-i-Jamshîd;* Maps 1, 20, 21; Pls. 265f., 269 f. □

Persians, n. of an Indo-European people established SE of Elam; played an important part in the Near East from 550 to 450 B.C.; Map 21; Pls. 265–270. See also APHARSITES.

Peter, n. given by Jesus to Simon, the 1st of the 12 Apostles, Mt 16:18; it appears that this n. had not previously been used, either in Gk. *(Petros)* or in Aramaic *(Kepha).* Cf. CEPHAS.

Pethor, city S of Carchemish, ment. as the home of Baalam, Nu 22:5; in Aram, Nu 23:7, Dt 23:4 (Heb. 5); poss. mod. *Tell Ahmar;* Map 4. □

Petra, 'rock'; capital city of the Nabataeans whose impressive ruins lie in the mod. *W. Mûsa,* E of the Arabah; prob. identical with SELA (q.v.) of the Edomites, 2 K 14:7; Maps 3, 26, 32; Pls. 151, 311–317; p. 112.

Phacee, see PEKAH.

Phaceia, see PEKAHIAH.

Phanuel, see PENUEL.

Phara, see PHARATHON.

Pharan, see EL-PARAN.

Pharan (Desert of), see PARAN (Wilderness of).

Pharan (Mount), see PARAN (Mount).

Pharan (Plains of), see EL-PARAN.

Pharaoh, Heb. spelling of Eg. *pr-'a,* 'the great house'; this word originally designated the palace, then the court, and, from the 18th dynasty, the person of the king.

Pharaoh-hophra, see HOPHRA, APRIES.

Pharaoh-nechoh, see NECHO.

Pharathon, city in Samaria, 1 Mac 9:50; prob. identical with PIRATHON, q.v.; Map 30. □

Pharathoni, see PHARATHON.

Pharisees, Gk. *Pharisaioi,* Heb. *Perûshim,* 'the separate ones'; n. of a Jewish sect which held to the strict letter of the Law and resisted all foreign influences. They sometimes regarded their own oral commentaries on the Law as more authoritative than the Law itself; in contrast to the Sadducees, they believed in the resurrection of the dead; p. 110.

Pharos, island W of the Canopic mouth of the Nile; linked to the mainland by Alexander, who thus formed the 2 harbours of the future metropolis of Alexandria; Map 27; pp. 102f. The n. was later applied to the lighthouse built on the island; Pl. 281.

Pharpar, one of the 2 rivers of Damascus, 2 K 5:12. Cf. ABANA. □

Pharphar, see PHARPAR.

Phasael, n. of several persons, inc. a brother of Herod the Great; one of the 3 towers of the Palace of Herod at Jerusalem was called after him; Map 33.

Phaselis, sea-port of Lycia, on the boundary of Pamphylia, ment. in the list of countries and cities which received the letter of Lucius, 1 Mac 15:23; mod. *Tekirova;* Map 26. □

Phasga, see PISGAH.

Phassur, see PASHUR.

Phatures, see PATHROS.

Phau, see PAU.

Phebe, see PHOEBE.

Phelethi(tes), see CHERETHITES AND PELETHITES.

Phenice, see PHOENICIA and PHOENIX.

Phenicia, see PHOENICIA.

Phesdomim, see EPHES-DAMMIM.

Phetros, see PATHROS.

Phigellus, see PHYGELUS.

Phihahiroth, see PI-HAHIROTH.

Philadelphia, 1. Gk. n. of Rabbah of the Ammonites, see RABBAH (1); mod. *'Ammân;* Maps 29, 34, 35; Pls. 300f.
2. city of Lydia, Rev 1:11, 3:7; mod. *Alashehir;* Map II (e.p.). □

Philemon, n. of a Christian of Colossae to whom St Paul addressed one of his Letters.

Philetus, n. of a Christian criticised by St Paul for having 'swerved from the truth', 2 Ti 2:17.

Philip, n. of several persons, in particular 1. king of Macedon and father of Alexander the Great, 1 Mac 1:1, 8:5.
2. one of the Friends of Antiochus Epiphanes, 1 Mac 6:14.
3. one of the 12 Apostles, Mt 10:3.
4. tetrarch of Ituraea, Lk 3:1.
5. Herod Philip, husband of Herodias and father of Salome.
6. one of the 'Seven', Ac 6:5.

Philippi, city of Macedonia, Ac 16:12–40, 20:6, 1 Th 2:2; St Paul addressed a Letter to the faithful Christians there, Ph 1:1, 4:15; mod. *Filibedjik;* Maps 32, II (e.p.). □

Philistines, n. of a non-Semitic people from the island of Caphtor who apparently settled in the S of the coastal plain of Palestine after 1200 B.C., following Rameses III's campaigns against the 'Peoples of the Sea'. They were the principal enemy of the Israelites during the period of the Judges. Their incursions were finally checked by David and their importance declined in the succeeding centuries. Very little is known of their language, script, or culture. Map 8; Pls. 183f., 187; pp. 64ff. Cf. CAPHTOR, PALESTINE, PENTAPOLIS (2).

Philistines (Sea of the), see GREAT SEA.

Philologus, n. of a Roman Christian, Ro 16:15.

Phinees, see PHINEHAS.

Phinehas, n. of Eg. origin borne by several persons, inc. one of the sons of Eli, 1 S 1:3, 2:34.

Phinon, see PINON.

Phison, see PISHON.

Phlegon, n. of a Roman Christian, Ro 16:14.

Phoebe, n. of a deaconess of the church at Cenchreae, Ro 16:1.

Phoenicia, Gk. n. of the narrow coastal plain between the Lebanon and the Mediterranean; well provided with natural harbours; principal cities: TYRE, SIDON, BYBLOS, and ARVAD, qq.v.; cf. 2 Mac 3:5, 8, 4:4, Ac 11:19, 15:3, 21:2; Maps 1, 5, 17; Pls. 51, 205–208.

Phoenix, sea-port of Crete, Ac 27:12; poss. mod. *Porto Lutro;* Map II (e.p.). □

Phogor, see PEOR.

Phrygia, region of Asia Minor, Ac 16:6, 18:23, cf. 2:10; Maps 25, II (e.p.). □

Phul, see PUL.

Phunon, see PUNON.

Phut, Phuth, see PUT.

Phygellus, see PHYGELUS.

Phygelus, n. of a Christian of Asia who 'turned away' from St Paul, 2 Ti 1:15.

Pi-beseth, city in Egypt, Ezk 30:17; doubtless the city of the goddess Bastet; later called Bubastis by the Greeks; mod. *Tell Basta,* in the S part of the Nile Delta; Maps 9, 20. □

Pi-hahiroth, 'house of the marshes (?)'; one of the first stopping-places on the Exodus, Ex 14:2, 9, Nu 33:7, 8 (Hahiroth); poss. W of the largest of the Bitter Lakes; Map 9; p. 48.

Pilate, see PONTIUS PILATE.

Pinon, loc. in Edom, ment. Gn 36:41 = 1 Ch 1:52; prob. identical with PUNON, q.v.

Pirathon, city in Ephraim; home of Abdon, one of the Judges, Jg 12:15, and of Benaiah, one of David's warriors, 2 S 23:30 = 1 Ch 11:31, 27:14; prob. identical with PHARATHON (q.v.), 1 Mac 9:50; mod. *Far'ata;* Maps 14, 15. □

Pisgah, n. of a height W of the plains of Moab with an extensive view over Palestine, Nu 21:20, 23:14, Dt 3:27, 34:1; the 'slopes of Pisgah' are ment. in the indications of territories, Dt 3:17, 4:49, Jos 12:3, 13:20; prob. mod. *Râs es-Siâgha,* separated only by a depression from *J. Neba* which preserves the n. of Mt Nebo. □

Pisgah (Springs of), see ASHDOTH-PISGAH.

Pishon, one of the 4 rivers of the Garden of Eden, Gn 2:11, cf. Sir 24:25; sit. unk. □

Pisidia, region of Asia Minor, Ac 13:14, 14:24; Maps 25, 26, II (e.p.). □

Maps: 1 p. 9 / 2, 3 p. 10 / 4 p. 29 / 5, 6 p. 30 /7, 8 p. 43 / 9, 10 p. 44 / 11, 12 p. 59 / 13 p. 60 / 14 p. 65 / 15, 16 p. 66 / 17 p. 81 / 18, 19 p. 82 / 20, 21 p. 95 / 22–24 p. 96 / 25–29 p. 103 / 30, 31 p. 104 / 32, 33 p. 115 / 34, 35 p. 116 / I, II end-papers.

Pison, see Pishon.

Pithom, prob. Heb. form of Eg. *pr-Itm*, 'house of Atum'; one of the Eg. store-cities built by the forced labour of the Hebrews, Ex 1:11; poss. mod. *Tell el-Maskhûta*, in the E part of the Nile Delta; Map 9; p. 46. □

Plain, Plains, in some versions the Heb. term '*Arabah*, applied to the Jordan valley, is rendered 'plain', 'plains', instead of Arabah, cf. Dt 1:7, 3:17, Jos 11:2, 2 S 2:29, 4:7, 2 K 25:4. A different Heb. term, meaning 'circle', 'circumscribed area', or 'district', and applied to the Jordan valley below Succoth, is also often rendered 'plain', cf. 2 Ch 4:17, Dt 34:3, 2 S 18:23. In Gn 13, where it is called 'the valley' ('plain, hollow, country', in other versions), this area appears to extend to the S end of the Dead Sea, assumed to have been dry land at this period (cf. Gn 14:3 (Valley of Siddim), 19:17, 25, 28f.); but cf. Pentapolis (1). In some versions the Dead Sea is called the Sea of the Plain, cf. Dt 3:17, Jos 12:3. Cf. Arabah, Valley (The), Dead Sea.

Plain (Sea of the), see Dead Sea and Sea of the Arabah.

Pontius Pilate, n. of the procurator of Judaea (A.D. 26–36) who passed sentence on Jesus; Map 32; pp. 118, 121.

Pontus, region in the N of Asia Minor, Ac 2:9, 1 P 1:1; Maps 26, 32, II (e.p.). □

Porch (Royal), see Royal Porch.

Porcius Festus, n. of the Roman procurator of Judaea, (A.D. 60–62); successor of Antonius Felix; he sent St Paul to Rome, Ac 24:27, 25; Map II (e.p.); p. 121.

Portico of Solomon, see Solomon (Portico of).

Portius Festus, see Porcius Festus.

Potiphar, Eg. 'gift of Re'; n. of the officer of the Pharaoh, to whom Joseph was sold, Gn 37:36, Gn 39.

Potiphera, n. of the priest of On to whose daughter Joseph was married, Gn 41:45ff.; the same n. as Potiphar.

Potipherah, see Potiphera.

Potsherd Gate, gate of Jerusalem leading into the Valley of Hinnom, Jer 19:2; not ment. in Nehemiah; Map 24 B. □

Pozzuoli, see Puteoli.

Praetorium, originally the n. of the praetor's tent, and later of his official residence; hence the n. used in the Gospels for the building where Pontius Pilate tried Jesus (the fortress Antonia or the Palace of Herod), Mt 27:27, Mk 15:16, Jn 18:28, 33, 19:9; Map 33; 'Herod's praetorium' at Caesarea, ment. Ac 23:35, certainly refers to Herod's palace. Cf. Ph 1:13 where it is used of Caesar's guard in Rome. □

Prisca, Priscilla, n. of the wife of the Jew Aquila, q.v.; called Prisca in Ro 16:3, 1 Co 16:19, 2 Ti 4:19, and Priscilla in Ac 18:1ff.

Prison Gate, see Guard (Gate of the).

Prochorus, n. of one of the 'Seven', Ac 6:5.

Pteria, city of Asia Minor; Cyrus defeated Croesus of Lydia near here in 546 B.C.; Map 20.

Ptolemais, n. given to the city of Acco by Ptolemy Philadelphus, 2 Mac 13:24f., Ac 21:7; Maps 29, 30, 31, 34, II (e.p.).

Ptolemee, see Ptolemy.

Ptolemy, n. of various Eg. kings of the time of the Maccabees, inc. 1. Ptolemy Philometor, 1 Mac 10f.
2. Ptolemy Euergetes, 1 Mac 15:16ff.; Pls. 286–288.

Publius, n. of the 'chief man of the island' of Malta who received St Paul, Ac 28:7f.

Pul, n. of 1. an Ass. king, 2 K 15:19, 1 Ch 5:26; prob. identical with Tiglath-pileser III.
2. a people or region, Is 66:19 (Heb.). □

Punon, stopping-place on the Exodus, Nu 33:42f.; from a comparison of Nu 33:43 with 21:10, we deduce that the episode of the bronze serpent (21:4–9) took place at Punon; poss. mod. *Feinân*, 25 miles S of the Dead Sea; copper was mined there in ancient times; Map 9. Cf. Pinon. □

Put, n. of a people or a region, Jer 46:9 and Ezk 30:5 (between Ethiopia and Lud(?)), Ezk 27:10 (after Persia and Lud (?)), cf. Ezk 38:5 (after Persia and Cush), Nah 3:9 (after Ethiopia and Egypt, and before the Libyans), Is 66:19 (with Lud(?); so R.S.V. following some ancient versions; Heb. Pul, q.v.); Gn 10:6, cf. 1 Ch 1:8, suggests that Put was a region of Egypt; poss. a part of Libya, or the Libyans. □

Puteoli, important port in the bay of Naples, Ac 28:13; mod. *Pozzuoli;* Map II (e.p.). □

Putiphar, see Potiphar.

Putiphare, see Potiphera.

Pyrrhus, n. of the father of St Paul's companion Sopater, Ac 20:4.

Q

Qarqar, city on the Orontes, NW of Hamath; site of a battle between Shalmaneser III and the allied kings of Syro-Palestine (854 B.C.); Map 18; p. 84.

Qatna, very ancient Accadian settlement in Syria; during the 2nd millennium B.C. came first under Hittite and then under Hurrian and Amorite influence; mod. *Tell el-Mishrifeh*, S of *Hama;* not ment. in the Bible, but its large-scale excavation has proved important for Biblical history; Maps 4, 5, 6.

Qewê, ancient n. of Cilicia, q.v.; p. 74.

Que, see Qewê.

Quicksands (The), see Syrtis (The).

Quirinius, n. of a Roman governor of Syria, Lk 2:2.

Qumrân, loc. on the NW shore of the Dead Sea where the famous Dead Sea Scrolls were discovered; Maps 2, 34; Pls. 28, 347–350; p. 136.

R

Raama, see Raamah.

Raamah, n. of a region and people of S Arabia, Gn 10:7 = 1 Ch 1:9 (Raama); ment. with Sheba as trading with Tyre, Ezk 27:22; otherwise unk. □

Raamses, see Rameses (2).

Rabba, see Rabbah (1).

Rabbah, n. of 2 cities, 1. capital of the Ammonites, called Rabbah of the Ammonites, Rabbath of the children of Ammon (Heb. Rabbath-Ammon, Rabbath bene-Ammon); King Og's iron bedstead was at Rabbah, Dt 3:11; besieged by Joab, 2 S 11:1, 1 Ch 20:1; citadel captured by David, 2 S 12:26–29; home of Shobi, 2 S 17:27; ment. in order to situate Aroer (2), Jos 13:25; ment. in the prophetic texts, Jer 49:2f., Ezk 25:5, 21:20 (Heb. 25), Am 1:14; renamed Philadelphia in the Hel. period and included by Pompey in the Decapolis; mod. '*Ammân*, capital of Jordan; Maps 1, 15, 23, I (e.p.); Pls. 300, 301. Cf. Decapolis.
2. loc. of Judah, in the hill country, listed Jos 15:60; exact sit. unk., prob. near Kiriath-jearim. □

Rabbath-Ammon, Rabbath bene-Ammon, Rabbath of the children of Ammon, see Rabbah (1).

Rabbith, loc. of Issachar, listed Jos 19:20; poss. identical with Daberath of Zebulun, listed Jos 19:13. □

Rabboth, see Rabbith.

Racal, in the list of cities of S Judah to which David sent booty, 1 S 30:29; the LXX reading Carmel is preferable. See Carmel (1). □

Rachal, see Racal.

Rachel, n. of the wife of Jacob and mother of Joseph and Benjamin, Gn 30:22ff., 35:16ff.

Rages, Median city frequently ment. in To (1:14, 5:5, 6:10, 12, etc.); prob. mod. *Rai*, about 6 miles SE of Teheran; Map 25.

Raguel, see Reuel.

Rahab, n. of 1. a harlot of Jericho, Jos 2.
2. a mythological sea monster, Ps 89:10 (Heb. 11), symbolising the Chaos vanquished by God at the Creation; cf. Job 9:13, 26:12; sometimes symbolises Egypt, Is 30:7, Ps 87:4, vanquished by God at the Exodus, Is 51:9. □

Rakkath, loc. of Naphtali, listed Jos 19:35; mod. *Tell Eqlâtîyeh;* Map 11. Cf. Kartan, Kiriathaim (3). □

Rakkon, loc. of Dan, listed Jos 19:46; sit. unk. □

Rama, see Ramah (1).

Ramah, 'height'; very common place-name; 1. loc. of Benjamin, listed Jos 18:25, near Bethel and Gibeah, Jg 4:5, 19:13, Hos 5:8; on the boundary between the Kingdoms of Israel and Judah, 1 K 15:17; on the route of the Ass. army to Jerusalem, Is 10:29; where Rachel lamented, Jer 31:15, cf. Mt 2:18; repopulated after the Exile, Neh 7:30, 11:33, Ezr 2:26; mod. *er-Râm*, 5 miles N of Jerusalem; Maps 13, 14, 15, 17, 19, 22.
2. loc. in Ephraim, ment. 14 times in 1 S (1 S 1:19, etc.) as the city of Samuel; identical with Ramathaim-zophim and Ramathaim, q.v.
3. loc. of Naphtali, listed Jos 19:36; sit. unk. □
4. loc. of Asher, listed Jos 19:29; sit. unk. □
5. Ramah of the Negeb, q.v.

Ramah of the Negeb, loc. of Simeon, listed Jos 19:8; poss. the Ramoth of the Negeb of 1 S 30:27; sit. unk. □

Ramatha, see Ramah (2) and Ramathaim.

Ramathaim, later form of Ramah (2), ment. 1 S 1:1 (Ramathaim-zophim); capital of a district in the time of the Maccabees, 1 Mac 11:34; G&L Arimathaea, Mt 27:57, Jn 19:38; doubtless mod. *Rentis*, on the W edge of the hill country of Ephraim; Maps 15, 30, 34. □

Ramathaim-sophim, Ramathaim-zophim, see Ramathaim.

Ramathan, Ramathem, see Ramathaim.

Ramath-lehi, see Lehi.

Ramath-mizpeh, loc. of Gad, listed Jos 13:26; identical with Mizpah (3), q.v.

Rameses, 1. n. of several Pharaohs of the 19th and 20th dynasties, in particular Rameses II (*ca* 1301–1234 B.C.) who fought the Hittites at Kadesh, and Rameses III (*ca* 1197–1165 B.C.) who campaigned against the 'Peoples of the Sea'; Maps 7, 8; Pls. 39–42, 130, 133, 137–139, 154, 181–185, 187; pp. 40ff., 64.
2. Eg. city where the Hebrews did forced labour, Ex 1:11 (Raamses), 12:37, Nu 33:3, 5; prob. mod. *Qantir*, or *Sân el-Hagar* (cf. p. 45); Map 9. The term 'land of Rameses', Gn 47:11, is an anachronism; it designates either Egypt or the region of Goshen only. □

Rameses (Land of), ment. Gn 47:11. Cf. Rameses (2).

Ramesses, see Rameses (2).

Rameth, see Remeth.

Ramoth, Levitical city of Issachar, 1 Ch 6:73 (Heb. 58); poss. identical with Remeth and Jarmuth (2), qq.v. □ See also Ramoth-gilead and Ramoth of the Negeb.

Ramoth-Galaad, Ramoth in Galaad, see Ramoth-gilead.

Ramoth-gilead, city in Transjordan; Levitical city of Gad, Jos 21:38; city of refuge, Jos 20:8, Dt 4:43; capital of Solomon's 6th district, 1 K 4:13; apple of discord between Aram and Israel, 1 K 22; the tell lies near mod. *el-Hosn;* Maps 11, 17; p. 87.

Ramoth in Gilead, see Ramoth-gilead.

Ramoth in (or to) the south, see Ramah of the Negeb.

Ramoth of the Negeb, loc. ment. 1 S 30:27; poss. identical with Ramah of the Negeb, q.v.

Raphaim, see Rephaim.

Raphaim (Valley of), see Rephaim (Valley of).

Raphia, city S of Gaza; not ment. in the Bible, but certainly in existence at the time of the Exodus; on the military highway from Egypt to Asia and site of many battles; important in the struggle between the Ptolemies and the Seleucids; Maps 9, 29.

Raphidim, see Rephidim.

Raphon, city in the region of the Yarmuk, 1 Mac 5:37; prob. mod. *er-Râfeh;* Map 31. □

Rasin, see Rezin.

Râs Shamra, 'hill of fennel'; tell on the coast of Syria, accidentally discovered in 1927 and since excavated; it proved to be the Ugarit of the Amarna letters and others texts, which was inhabited by Semites from 2000 B.C.; flourished especially after the 16th century B.C., and was destroyed *ca* 1200 B.C. The principal source of our knowledge of the ancient Canaanite civilisation, and, since it was a cosmopolitan city, of various other cultural phenomena of the 2nd millennium B.C. Is being further excavated in annual campaigns. Maps 1, 4, 5, 6, 7, 8; p. 15.

Ravine of Besor, see Besor (Brook).

Razon, see Rezon.

Rebecca, see Rebekah.

Rebekah, n. of the wife of Isaac and mother of Esau and Jacob, Gn 24f.

Rebla, Reblatha, see Riblah.

Reccath, see Rakkath.

Recem, see Rekem.

Red Sea, see Suph, Suphah.

Reeds (Sea of), see Sea of Reeds.

Reema, see Raamah.

Refuge (City of), loc. where any man who had committed a murder unwittingly and without malice aforethought might seek refuge, Jos 20:1–6. There were 3 such cities in Transjordan: Bezer, Ramoth in Gilead, and Golan, Dt 4:43, Jos 20:8; and 3 in Cisjordan: Kedesh (Kedesh (1)), Shechem, and Kiriath-arba (Hebron), Jos 20:7.

Regma, see Raamah.

Rehob, 'free space, market'; 1. loc. of Asher, listed Jos 19:28, 30; Levitical city, Jos 21:31, 1 Ch 6:75 (Heb. 60); cf. Jg 1:31; poss. mod. *Tell el-Bîr el-Gharbi;* Maps 11, 14. □
2. See Beth-rehob.

Rehoboam, 'the people has spread'; n. of the son of Solomon; 1st king of Judah after the Disruption (*ca* 931–913 B.C.), 1 K 14:21ff.; pp. 76f.

Rehoboth, 1. n. of a well SW of Beer-sheba, Gn 26:22; poss. in the vicinity of mod. *Ruheibeh*, which appears to preserve the n.; Map 4. □
2. loc. in Edom, near the Dead Sea, Gn 36:37 = 1 Ch 1:48 (Rehoboth on the Euphrates); sit. unk. □
3. see Rehoboth-ir.

Rehoboth-ir, 'fore-courts of the city'; city in Assyria, ment. Gn 10:11; sit. unk. □

Rekem, loc. of Benjamin, listed Jos 18:27; sit. unk. □

Remeth, loc. on the boundary of Issachar, Jos 19:21; poss. identical with the Ramoth of 1 Ch 6:73 (Heb. 58) and Jarmuth (2), qq.v. □

Remmon, see En-rimmon, Rimmon (1).

Remmon-methoar, Remmono, see Rimmon (2).

Remmonphares, see Rimmon-perez.

Rephaim, n. of a pre-Israelite people of Canaan, Gn 14:5, 15:20; identified with the Emim (q.v.) and described as 'tall as the Anakim' (cf. Anak (Descendants of)), Dt 2:10f.; cf. Nu 13:33; identified with the Zamzummim, Dt 2:20.

Rephaims, see Rephaim.

Rephaim (Valley of), plain NW of Jerusalem, Jos 15:8, 18:16; scene of battles between David and the Philistines, 2 S 5:18, 22 = 1 Ch 14:9, 2 S 23:13 = 1 Ch 11:15, cf. Is 17:5; Map 24A.

Rephidim, last stopping-place on the Exodus before Mt Sinai, Ex 17:1, 8, 19:2, Nu 33:14f.; poss. mod. *W. Refâyid*; Map 9. □

Resen, city in Assyria, Gn 10:12; sit. unk. □

Reseph, see Rezeph.

Respha, see Rizpah.

Ressa, see Rissah.

Rethma, see Rithmah.

Reuben, n. of the eldest son of Jacob and Leah, Gn 29:32; ancestor of a tribe of Israel whose territory was in Transjordan, N of the Arnon, listed Jos 13:15–23, cf. Nu 32:33–38; Maps 11, 14.

Reuel, n. of the father-in-law of Moses, Ex 2:18; also called Jethro, q.v.

Rezeph, loc. or region conquered by the Assyrians, 2 K 19:12 = Is 37:12; poss. mod. *Ressâfeh*, E of *Hama;* Map 18. □

Rezin, Heb. form of Razon (LXX and Ass. texts); n. of 2 persons, in particular the last king of Damascus; defeated by Tiglath-pileser III, 2 K 15:37, 16:5, 6, 9, Is 7:1, 4, 8, 8:6, 9:11 (Heb. 10).

Rezon, n. of the founder of the kingdom of Damascus and enemy of Solomon, ment. only 1 K 11:23–25.

Rhegium, sea-port of S Italy, Ac 28:13; mod. *Reggio;* Map II (e.p.). □

Rhoda, n. of the servant of the mother of John called Mark, Ac 12:13.

Rhode, see Rhoda.

Rhodes, island in the Aegean Sea, ment. among the countries and cities which received the letter of Lucius, 1 Mac 15:23; also ment. Ac 21:1; Maps 1, II (e.p.). □

Riblah, city on the Orontes; military headquarters of the Pharaoh Necho, 2 K 23:33, and later of Nebuchadnezzar who caused Zedekiah to be blinded there, 2 K 25:6f., 20f., cf. Jer 39:5f., 52:9f., 26f.; Ezk 6:14 (where Heb. has Diblah); the n. is preserved in the mod. village of *Ribleh* (*Rableh*), S of *Hama;* the ruins of the ancient city lie on the banks of the Orontes; Maps 20, 29. Ha-riblah in Nu 34:11 (Heb.; R.S.V.

Maps: 1 p. 9 / 2, 3 p. 10 / 4 p. 29 / 5, 6 p. 30 / 7, 8 p. 43 / 9, 10 p. 44 / 11, 12 p. 59 / 13 p. 60 / 14 p. 65 / 15, 16 p. 66 / 17 p. 81 / 18, 19 p. 82 / 20, 21 p. 95 / 22–24 p. 96 / 25–29 p. 103 / 30, 31 p. 104 / 32, 33 p. 115 / 34, 35 p. 116 / I, II end-papers.

160

Riblah) should be read as Harbela (Arbela) and identified with mod. *Hermel* at the source of the Orontes, in the Beqa'. □

Rimmon, n. of a god of Damascus, 2 K 5:18; identical with Hadad, the god of the storm.

Rimmon, 'pomegranate'; n. of several places, 1. loc. of Judah, listed Jos 15:32, and of Simeon, listed Jos 19:7 (En-rimmon), 1 Ch 4:32; the Rimmon of Jos 15:32 and 1 Ch 4:32 should be linked with the n. Ain which precedes to form the single n., EN-RIMMON, q.v.; cf. also Zec 14:10 (Rimmon). □
2. loc. of Zebulun, listed Jos 19:13; Levitical city, Jos 21:35, where it is called Dimnah, while it appears as Rimmono in the list of 1 Ch 6:77 (Heb. 62); mod. *Rummâneh*; Map 11. □
3. a rock on which the Benjamites took refuge, Jg 20:45, 47, 21:13; prob. mod. *Rammûn*, nearly 4 miles E of Bethel; Map 14. □

Rimmono, see RIMMON (2).

Rimmon-parez, see RIMMON-PEREZ.

Rimmon-perez, stopping-place on the Exodus between Mt Sinai and Kadesh, Nu 33:19f.; poss. mod. *Naqb el-Biyâr*; Map 9. □

Rissah, stopping-place on the Exodus, Nu 33:21f.; poss. mod. *el-Kuntilla;* Map 9. □

Rithmah, 'broom-bush'; stopping-place on the Exodus, Nu 33:18f.; one of the wâdis N of mod. *'Ain Khudra;* Map 9. □

Rizpah, n. of Saul's concubine, 2 S 3:7, 21:8.

Roboam, see REHOBOAM.

Rock of the plain, poetic n. for OPHEL (q.v.), Jer 21:13. □

Rock (The), see SELA.

Rocks of the wild goats, see WILD-GOATS' ROCKS.

Rogel (Fountain, or **Spring of),** see EN-ROGEL.

Rogelim, city in Transjordan, and home of Barzillai, ment. only 2 S 17:27, 19:31 (Heb. 32); poss. mod. *Bersîniyah*, near the *W. er-Rujeili*, which appears to preserve the ancient n., E of Beth-shan; Map 15. □

Rohob, see BETH-REHOB and REHOB.

Rohoboth, see REHOBOTH.

Rosh, land perhaps ment. after Meshech in Is 66:19 (where 'Meshech and Rosh' may have stood instead of 'who draw the bow'); poss. also referred to in Ezk 38:2f., 39:1 (where we should perhaps read 'prince of Rosh' instead of 'chief prince'); sit. unk. □

Royal Porch, porch of the Temple of Jerusalem; Map 33 no. 9.

Royal Valley, see SHAVEH (Valley of).

Ruben, see REUBEN.

Rufus, n. of a son of Simon of Cyrene, Mk 15:21; poss. identical with the Rufus of Ro 16:13.

Rulers (Land of the), see MERATHAIM.

Ruma, see ARUMAH, DUMAH, and RUMAH.

Rumah, birthplace of the mother of Jehoiakim, 2 K 23:36; poss. mod. *Kh. er-Rûmeh*, in Galilee, Map 17; or poss. an error for DUMAH (q.v.), SW of Hebron; Map 13.

Ruth, n. of the principal character in the book of Ruth, a masterpiece of Jewish narrative art.

S

Saanan, see ZAANAN.

Saananim, see ZAANANNIM (1).

Saaraim, see SHAARAIM (1).

Saarim, see SHAARAIM (2).

Saba, see SEBA and SHEBA (1).

Saba (Queen of), see SHEBA (Queen of).

Sabaim, see SEBA.

Sabama, see SIBMAH.

Saban, see SEBAM.

Sabarim, see SIBRAIM.

Sabatha, see SABTAH.

Sabathaca, see SABTECA.

Sabeans, see SEBA.

Sabee, see SHEBA (2) and SHEMA.

Sabta, see SABTAH.

Sabtah, n. of a people listed among the sons of Cush with tribes of S Arabia, Gn 10:7, 1 Ch 1:9 (Sabta).

Sabteca, n. of a people listed among the sons of Cush with tribes of S Arabia, Gn 10:7, 1 Ch 1:9.

Sabtecha, see SABTECA.

Sachacha, see SECACAH.

Sadducees, n. (prob. derived from Zadok, High Priest under Solomon) of a Jewish sect whose members were drawn from the priestly aristocracy; in contrast to the Pharisees, they rejected oral traditions and did not believe in the resurrection of the dead, Mk 12:18, Ac 23:6ff.; pp. 110, 112.

Sadoc, see ZADOK.

Saïs, city in the Nile Delta; residence of the Pharaohs of the 26th dynasty (633–525 B.C.), inc. 2 of the Pharaohs ment. by n. in the Bible, Necho and Hophra; mod. *Sân el-Hagar;* Maps 9, 18, 20, 21.

Salamina, see SALAMIS.

Salamis, important sea-port on the E coast of Cyprus, Ac 13:5; its ruins lie N of mod. *Famagusta;* Maps 21, II (e.p.). □

Salcah, Salchah, see SALECAH.

Salebim, see SHAALABBIN.

Salecah, loc. in Transjordan on the boundary of Bashan, Jos 12:5, 13:11, Dt 3:10, 1 Ch 5:11; poss. mod. *Salkhad;* Map 12. □

Salem, city of the priest-king Melchizedek, Gn 14:18; identified with Jerusalem in tradition as old as Ps 76:2 (Heb. 3); Map 4.

Salim, loc. ment. Jn 3:23, where John the Baptist is said to be 'baptizing at Aenon near Salim, because there was much water there'. Aenon (from *'ain*, 'spring') suggests a group of springs. Such a group exists in the Jordan valley nearly 8 miles S of Beth-shan (Scythopolis). Mod. *Tell Ridgha*, slightly to the N, poss. contains the ruins of Salim. Map 34; pp. 122, 132.

Salim (Land of), see SHAALIM (Land of).

Salisa (Land of), see SHALISHA (Land of).

Salmana, see ZALMUNNA.

Salmanasar, see SHALMANESER.

Salmon, see ZALMON (Mount).

Salmona, see ZALMONAH.

Salmone, cape at the NE extremity of Crete, Ac 27:7; mod. *Cape Sidero;* Map II (e.p.). □

Salome, n. of 2 persons, 1. one of the women present at the Crucifixion, Mk 15:40, cf. 16:1.
2. the daughter of Herodias, Mt 14 (the n. Salome is supplied by Josephus).

Salt (City of), see CITY OF SALT.

Salt Sea, ment. Gn 14:3, Dt 3:17, Jos 12:3, etc. Cf. DEAD SEA.

Salt (Valley of), scene of battles against the Edomites, in the time of David, 2 S 8:13, 1 Ch 18:12, Ps 60: Heading (Heb. 2), and in the time of Amaziah, 2 K 14:7 = 2 Ch 25:11; prob. the *W. 'Araba*, the S continuation of the Dead Sea, also called the Salt Sea.

Sama, see SHEMA.

Samaraim, see ZEMARAIM.

Samaria, G&L form of Heb. *Shomrôn;* n. of the capital city of the N Kingdom, built by Omri, 1 K 16:24; later the n. of the whole region, cf. 2 K 17:26 which refers to 'the cities of Samaria'. Also the n. of the region in Neh 4:2 (Heb. 3:34), Ezr 4:17, and particularly of the district of the Fifth Satrapy called Samerina whose inhabitants, the Samaritans, obstructed the re-building of the Temple of Jerusalem and built their own temple on Mt Gerizim. In 1 and 2 Mac the n. is applied both to the city and to the region. The city was magnificently rebuilt by Herod the Great and renamed Sebaste in honour of Augustus (Gk. *Sebastos*). Jesus excluded 'the towns of the Samaritans' from the preaching of salvation, Mt 10:5, but cf. Jn 4, and the parables of Lk 10:30ff., 17:11ff. Samaria received the Gospel after the Resurrection, Ac 1:8, 8:5. The localisation of the city is not in doubt, and has been confirmed by excavation. The Gk.n. is preserved in the mod. *Sebastiyeh*. Maps 2, 17, 18, 23, 29, 30, 31, 34, 35; Pls. 224–228.

Samgar, see SHAMGAR.

Samir, see SHAMIR.

Samos, island off the coast SW of Ephesus; listed among the places which received the letter of Lucius, 1 Mac 15:23; also ment. Ac 20:15; Map II (e.p.). □

Samothrace, small island in the Aegean Sea between Troas and Neapolis, Ac 16:11; Map II (e.p.).

Samothracia, see SAMOTHRACE.

Sampsames, ment. in the list of countries and cities which received the letter of Lucius, 1 Mac 15:23 (some MSS have Sampsaces); prob. another n. for the port of Amisus on the Black Sea (Maps 26, 32), and preserved in the mod. n. *Samsûn* (Map I (e.p.)). The Latin translators wrongly identified this town with Lampsacus on the Hellespont, which was better known to them. □

Samson, n. of the last of the Judges, Jg 13–16; Map 14.

Samuel, Heb. *Shemû-el*, 'name of God'; popular etymology, 'I have asked him of the Lord', 1 S 1:20; n. of the Judge and prophet who is the central figure of 1 S and is ranked with Moses in Jer 15:1, cf. Ps 99:6; 2 books of the O.T. bear his n., cf. p. 64; Map 15.

Sanaballat, see SANBALLAT.

Sanan, see ZENAN.

Sanballat, Heb. form of Ass. *Sin-uballit*, '(the god) Sin grants life'; n. of the Pers. governor of Samaria who was hostile to Nehemiah, Neh 2ff.

Sanhedrin, Aramaic transcription of Gk. *synedrion*, 'assembly'; n. of the supreme Council, the highest authority of the Jewish people at the time of Jesus; the meeting-place of this assembly is indicated on Map 33.

Sanir, see SENIR.

Sansannah, 'a bunch of dates'; loc. of Judah, in the Negeb, listed Jos 15:31; mod. *Kh. es-Shamsâniyât;* Map 13. □

Saphir, see SHAPHIR.

Saphon, see ZAPHON.

Sapphira, n. of the wife of Ananias; both were punished with sudden death, Ac 5.

Sara, see SARAH (1) and (2).

Saraa, see ZORAH.

Sarah, n. of 2 persons, 1. the wife of Abraham, also called Sarai, Gn 11ff.
2. the daughter of Raguel of Ecbatana, To 3:7.

Sarai, see SARAH (1).

Saraias, see SERAIAH.

Sarathasar, see ZERETH-SHAHAR.

Sardis, city in Asia Minor, 50 miles E of Smyrna, and one of the 'seven churches', Rev 1:11, 3:1, 4; mod. *Sart;* Maps 20, 21, 25, II (e.p.). Cf. SEPHARAD. □

Sarea, see ZORAH.

Sareda, see ZEREDAH (1).

Saredatha, see ZEREDAH (2).

Sarephta, Sarephtha, see ZAREPHATH.

Sarepta, G&L form of ZAREPHATH, q.v.

Sargon, n. of several Ass. kings; Sargon II (721–705 B.C.) finally conquered Samaria; ment. Is 20:1; Map 18; Pls. 248f., p. 94.

Sarid, loc. on the boundary of Zebulun, Jos 19:10, 12; prob. mod. *Tell Shadûd*, N of Megiddo; Map 11. Poss. we should read Shadud with the ancient versions. □

Sarion, see SIRION.

Sarohen, see SHARUHEN.

Saron, see SHARON.

Sarthan, Sarthana, see ZARETHAN.

Sassabasar, see SHESHBAZZAR.

Saul, 'asked for'; 1. n. of the 1st king of the 12 tribes (*ca* 1040–1010 B.C.); p. 67.
2. Heb. n. of St Paul, not used after Ac 13:9. Cf. PAUL.

Save of Cariathaim, see SHAVEH-KIRIATHAIM.

Save (Valley of), see SHAVEH (Valley of).

Scavengers' Gate, see DUNG GATE.

Scopus (Mount), n. of the ridge which is the continuation of the Mt of Olives to the N of Jerusalem.

Scorpion Pass, see AKRABBIM (Ascent of).

Scythians, n. of a people from the steppes of S Russia who, according to Herodotus, plundered Syria-Palestine *ca* 625 B.C. and even penetrated into Egypt; this invasion is poss. alluded to in Jer 4:5ff., 5:15ff., 6:1ff.; regarded by the Gks. as the most backward and ruthless of the barbarians, cf. 2 Mac 4:47, Col 3:11; Map 21.

Scythopolis, Hel. n. of BETH-SHAN, q.v.; 2 Mac 12:29; Maps 30, 34, 35; p. 105.

Sea of Chinnereth, Chinneroth, see CHINNERETH, CHINNEROTH.

Sea of Galilee, see GALILEE (Sea of).

Sea of Joppa, Sea of Joppe, see GREAT SEA.

Sea of Lot, translation of mod. Arabic n. of the DEAD SEA, q.v.

Sea of Reeds, Heb. *Yam Sûph*; n. of the 2 arms of the Red Sea which encompass the Sinai peninsula, Ex 10:19, 13:18, etc. (R.S.V. Red Sea); Maps 1, 9; p. 48.

Sea of the Arabah, ment. Dt 3:17, Jos 12:3; called Sea of the Plain in some versions. Cf. DEAD SEA.

Sea of the desert, see SEA OF THE ARABAH, DEAD SEA.

Sea of the Philistines, see GREAT SEA.

Sea of the Plain, see SEA OF THE ARABAH, DEAD SEA.

Seba, n. of a people and region ment. after Egypt and Ethiopia in Is 43:3 (cf. 45:14 (Sabeans)), and with Sheba in Ps 72:10; listed among the sons of Cush (Ethiopia), Gn 10:7 = 1 Ch 1:9, and therefore identified since the time of Josephus with Meroë, a province of Ethiopia; some mod. scholars place it in S Arabia. □

Sebam, loc. in Transjordan, ment. Nu 32:3; doubtless identical with SIBMAH, q.v. □

Sebaste, Gk. n. given by Herod the Great to the city of SAMARIA, q.v.

Seboim, see ZEBOIIM and ZEBOIM.

Secacah, loc. of Judah, in the wilderness, listed Jos 15:61; sit. unk. □

Sechrona, see SHIKKERON.

Sechu, see SECU.

Secu, loc. ment. 1 S 19:22; near Ramah (2), exact sit. unk. According to some G&L MSS the word refers to a threshing-floor on a bare hill-top and is not a place-name.

Sedada, see ZEDAD.

Sedecias, see ZEDEKIAH.

Sedi, see SUD.

Segor, see ZOAR.

Sehesima, see SHAHAZUMAH.

Sehon, see SIHON.

Seir, 1. mountainous region SW of the Dead Sea, extending as far N as Hormah and the hill country of the Amorites, Dt 1:44; inhabited by the Horites, Gn 36:20, cf. 14:6; the n. was later transferred to the hill country E of the Arabah. Cf. ESAU.
2. Mt Seir, a peak W of Kiriath-jearim, ment. in the indication of the boundary of Judah, Jos 15:10. □

Seira, see ZAIR.

Seirah, loc. to which Ehud escaped, Jg 3:26; sit. unk., poss. in the desert W of Jericho. □

Seirath, see SEIRAH.

Sela, 'the rock'; 1. scene of Amaziah's victory over the Edomites, 2 K 14:7; prob. 'the rock' ment. 2 Ch 25:12 from which he cast down 10,000 Edomite captives; also ment. Is 16:1, 42:11, and alluded to in Jer 49:16 = Ob 3 ('the rock'); prob. later the site of Petra, capital of the Nabataeans (the high rock in Pl. 311). Cf. PETRA. The Sela in Jg 1:36 seems to be another rock, perhaps that at Kadesh, Nu 20:8ff. □
2. see ZELA.

Selacha, see SALECAH.

Selah, see SELA (1).

Selcha, see SALECAH.

Selebin, see SHAALABBIN.

Seleucia, Gk. *Seleukeia;* sea-port of the city of Antioch on the Orontes, 1 Mac 11:8 ('Seleucia which is by the sea'), Ac 13:4; Maps 29, II (e.p.); Pl. 401.

Seleucids, n. of the Syrian dynasty founded by Seleucus I (312–280 B.C.); the best-known Seleucid kings were, 1. Antiochus III, called the Great, (223–187 B.C.), who greatly extended his kingdom, but was defeated by the Romans in 190 B.C. at the battle of Magnesia; Map 26; p. 105f.
2. Antiochus IV Epiphanes (175–164 B.C.), against whom the Maccabees rebelled.

Selim, see SHILHIM.

Sella, see SILLA.

Sellum, see SHALLUM.

Selmon, see ZALMON (Mount).

Sem, see SHEM.

Semei, see SHIMEI.

Semeias, see SHEMAIAH.

Semeron, see SHIMRON and ZEMARAIM.

Semites, mod. n. applied to the 'sons of Shem'; according to the table of the peoples, they represented a third of mankind, the third to which the tribes of Israel belonged, Gn 10:22ff., 11:10ff., 9:26. The compiler also includes among the 'sons of Shem' the tribes which were related or allied to Israel. For the racial type, see Pls. 42, 126–128, 132, 184.

Semitic languages, an important family of languages, divided into an eastern group comprising Accadian and, later, Babylonian and Assyrian; and a western group, comprising, in the N, Canaanite (inc. Hebrew) and Aramaic, and, in the S, Arabic', etc. Cf. ARAMAIC.

Sen, see SHEN.

Senaa, see SENAAH.

Senaah, loc. to which the exiles returned, Ezr 2:35, Neh 7:38; supplied builders of the walls of Jerusalem, Neh 3:3 (Hassenaah); sit. unk. □

Sene, see SENEH.

Seneh, n. of a 'rocky crag' in the gorge between Geba and Michmash, 1 S 14:4; Pls. 189f. □

Senir, Amorite n. of Mt Hermon, according to Dt 3:8f., Ezk 27:5; but to be distinguished from Mt Hermon, according to 1 Ch 5:23, Ca 4:8. □

Senna, see ZIN (Wilderness of).

Sennaar (Land of), see SHINAR (Land of).

Sennacherib, Heb. form of Ass. *Sin-achê-eriba*, 'may (the god) Sin increase my brothers'; n. of the son of Sargon; king of Assyria (705–681 B.C.), 2 K 18f.; Map 18; Pl. 248; pp. 88f.

Sennesar, see SHESHBAZZAR.

Sennim, see ZAANANNIM (2).

Sensenna, see SANSANNAH.

Seon, see SHION and SIHON.

Sephaath, see ZEPHATH.

Sephama, see SHEPHAM.

Sephamoth, see SIPHMOTH.

Sephar, in the indication of the boundary of the territory of the sons of Joktan, Gn 10:30; sit. unk. □

Sepharad, loc. where there was a settlement of Jews of the Diaspora, Ob 20; the Vulgate renders it Bosphorus, while Syriac and Targums read Spain; poss. a region of Media, or the region of SARDIS, q.v.

Sepharvaim, loc. conquered by the Assyrians, whose inhabitants were sent to colonise Samaria after the deportation, 2 K 17:24 (cf. 17:31, 18:34, 19:13 = Is 36:19, 37:13); sit. unk.; poss. identical with the Sibraim of Ezk 47:16, in the region of Hamath. □

Sephata, see ZEPHATHAH.

Sepher (Mount), see SHEPHER (Mount).

Septuagint (LXX), n. applied to the Gk. translation of the O.T. made in Alexandria in the 3rd century B.C. for the Hellenised Jews.

Sepulchre (Church of the Holy), basilica in Jerusalem which stands on the site of Calvary and the tomb where the body of Jesus was laid; originally built by Constantine in the 4th century A.D. and several times destroyed and restored during the succeeding centuries; Map 33; Pls. 191, 373, 379, 385f.; p. 132.

Ser, see ZER.

Seraiah, n. of several persons in the O.T., in particular a 'secretary' under David, 2 S 8:17; called Shisha in 1 K 4:3, Shavsha in 1 Ch 18:16, and Sheva in 2 S 20:25; p. 71.

Sereser, see NERGAL-SHAREZER.

Sergius Paulus, n. of the proconsul of Cyprus, Ac 13:6–12; Map II (e.p.).

Serpent's Stone, stone in the valley below Jerusalem, near En-rogel, 1 K 1:9; Maps 24A, B, 33.

Sesac, see SHESHONQ.

Sesach, see SHESHACH.

Settim, see ABEL-SHITTIM.

Sewêne, Heb. form of SYENE, q.v.

Shaalabbin, 'place of foxes'; loc. of Dan, listed Jos 19:42; inhabited by Amorites, according to Jg 1:35 (Shaalbim); later in Solomon's 2nd district, 1 K 4:9 (Shaalbim); poss. mod. *Selbit*; Maps 13, 14, 17, 19. □

Shaalbim, see SHAALABBIN.

Shaalim (Land of), region in the hill country of Ephraim, 1 S 9:4; poss. between Aijalon and Ramah (2). □

Shaaraim, 'double gate'; 1. loc. of Judah, in the lowland, listed Jos 15:36; also ment. 1 S 17:52; sit. unk. □
2. loc. of Simeon, 1 Ch 4:31; called Sharuhen in the parallel list of Jos 19:6, and Shilhim in Jos 15:32. Cf. SHARUHEN, SHILHIM. □

Shadrach, Bab. n. given to Daniel's friend Hananiah, Dn 1:7.

Shadud, see SARID.

Shahazimah, see SHAHAZUMAH.

Shahazumah, loc. of Issachar, listed Jos 19:22; between Mt Tabor and the Jordan, exact sit. unk. □

Shalim (Land of), see SHAALIM (Land of).

Shalisha (Land of), region in which the city of BAAL-SHALISHAH (q.v.) was situated, 1 S 9:4; in the hill country of Ephraim; Map 15.

Shallum, n. of several persons, in particular 1. 15th king of Israel (743 B.C.), the assassin and successor of Zechariah, 2 K 15.
2. other n. of JEHOAHAZ (1), q.v., who succeeded his father, Josiah, as king of Judah, Jer 22:11.

Shalmaneser, n. of several Ass. kings, of whom only Shalmaneser V, who deported the Israelites to Assyria, is ment. in the Bible, 2 K 17:3; p. 94.

Shame (Hill of), see OFFENCE (Mount of).

Shamgar, n. of the 3rd of the Judges, Jg 3:31; Map 14.

Shamir, 'place of thistles'; 1. loc. of Judah, in the hill country, listed Jos 15:48; prob. mod. *Kh. el-Bireh*, near *Kh. Sumara* which preserves the ancient n.; Map 13. □
2. loc. ment. Jg 10:1; poss. later the site of Samaria; Map 14. □

Shapher (Mount), see SHEPHER (Mount).

Shaphir, loc. ment. Mic 1:11; poss. mod. *Kh. el-Kôm*, W of Hebron; Map 17. □

Sharaim, see SHAARAIM (1).

Sharon, 'plain'; coastal plain from Jaffa to Caesarea; ment. in the poetic texts with the Lebanon, Mt Carmel, and Bashan on account of its fertility, Is 33:9, 35:2, Ca 2:1; rich pastures, 1 Ch 27:29, Is 65:10; in the N.T. ment. only with Lydda, Ac 9:35. In 1 Ch 5:16 it is preferable to read SIRION, q.v.; in Jos 12:18 Lasharon prob. stands for 'of Sharon', indicating that the preceding Aphek is Aphek (1). Maps 2, 34. □

Sharuhen, loc. of Simeon, listed Jos 19:6; erroneously called Shaaraim (cf. SHAARAIM (2)) in 1 Ch 4:31, and replaced by SHILHIM (q.v.) in Jos 15:32; prob. mod. *Tell el-Fâr'ah*, S of Gaza; Maps 5, 6, 11; p. 41. □

Shaveh (Valley of), scene of the meeting between Abraham and the king of Sodom, Gn 14:17; place where Absalom set up a pillar for himself ('Absalom's monument'), 2 S 18:18 (King's Valley); the site has not been identified, but, according to Josephus, the valley lay within 440 yds of the old city of Jerusalem.

Shaveh-kiriathaim, 'the plain of Kiriathaim'; loc. ment. Gn 14:5; should be sought S of the Arnon, where *el-Qaryatein* is situated; Map 4. □

Shavsha, see SERAIAH.

Sheba, 1. n. of a region and a people famous for trading in spices, frankincense, gold, and precious stones, 1 K 10:1f., Is 60:6, Jer 6:20, Ezk 27:22, Ps 72:15; the queen of Sheba visited Solomon, 1 K 10:1ff.; listed among the sons of Cush in Gn 10:7 = 1 Ch 1:9, and among the sons of Joktan in Gn 10:28; prob. in SW Arabia.
2. loc. of Simeon, listed Jos 19:2; prob. an error for SHEMA (LXX and other versions), q.v.

Sheba (Queen of), queen who visited Solomon, 1 K 10:1ff.; called 'the queen of the South' in Mt 12:42 = Lk 11:31; p. 74; for her kingdom, see SHEBA (1).

Shebam, see SEBAM.

Shebna, n. of the master of the royal household, or secretary, under Hezekiah, Is 22:15, 36:3, 11, 22, cf. 2 K 18:18ff. (Shebnah).

Shebnah, see SHEBNA.

Shechem, 'shoulder, back of a neck' (between Mt Ebal and Mt Gerizim); important city in the centre of Palestine, ment. in the story of the patriarchs, Gn 12:6, 33:18, 34:2–26 (represented as a person), 37:12ff., 48:22 (Heb.); also in the time of the Judges, Jg 9; after the Disruption Jeroboam was made king in Shechem and fortified it as his capital, 1 K 12; ment. incidentally in the indication of the boundaries of Manasseh, Jos 17:2, 7, and explicitly as a city of refuge, Jos 20:7, and as a Levitical city, Jos 21:21; after the Exile, capital city of the Samaritans, Sir 50:26 (Heb. 28); destroyed by John Hyrcanus in 128 B.C.; rebuilt by the Romans farther to the W as Flavia Neapolis, a n. which the Arabs have corrupted to *Nâblus;* the ancient site is the partly-excavated *Tell Balâta; Maps* 2, 4–6, 8, 11, 14, 17; Pls. 95f., 100f.; p. 19.

Sheep Gate, gate of Jerusalem, Neh 3:1, 32, 12:39, Jn 5:2; prob. N of the Temple; Maps 24 C, 33. □

Sheep Market, see SHEEP GATE.

Shelah (Pool of), see SHILOAH, SILOAM.

Shem, n. of the eldest son of Noah, Gn 6:10, etc.

Shema, 'hyena'; loc. of Judah, in the Negeb, listed Jos 15:26; prob. erroneously called Sheba in Jos 19:2; poss. mod. *Kh. el-Far*, SE of Gaza; Map 11. □

Shemaiah, n. of several persons, in particular a prophet of the time of Rehoboam, 1 K 12:22.

Shen, loc. ment. with Mizpah in 1 S 7:12 (in R.S.V. emended to JESHANAH, q.v.); sit. unk. □

Shenazzar, see SHESHBAZZAR.

Shenir, see SENIR, HERMON (Mount).

Sheol, n. used 65 times in the O.T. to designate the place where all men are brought together after death to lead a ghostly existence, cf. Is 14:9, Job 7:9, Ec 9:10; hence the kingdom of the dead, which was believed to lie under the earth, cf. Nu 16:30, Am 9:2. Cf. ABADDON.

Shepham, loc. on the NE frontier of Canaan, Nu 34:10f.; exact sit. unk. □

Shephat, loc. in N Palestine, To 1:1; mod. *Safad*, NW of the Sea of Galilee.

Shephelah, region called the 'lowland' in the Bible; it lies between the mountains (the 'hill country') of Judah and the Mediterranean coastal plain, cf. p. 16; Maps 2, 13, 14; p. 16.

Shepher (Mount), stopping-place on the Exodus, Nu 33:23f.; poss. mod. *J. 'Araif en-Nâja*, S of Kadesh; Map 9. □

Shepherds' Gate, see SHEEP GATE.

Sheshach, n. designating Babylon in Jer 25:26, cf. 51:41 (R.S.V. Babylon); by substituting the last letter of the Heb. alphabet for the first, the last but one for the second, and so on, this form is obtained for Babel, or Babylon.

Sheshbazzar, n. of the 'prince of Judah' (poss. identical with the Shenazzar ment. 1 Ch 3:18) installed by Cyrus as governor of the repatriated Jews, Ezr 1:8, 11, 5:14ff.; Map 21.

Sheshonq, n. of the Pharaoh called Shishak in the Bible, 1 K 11:40, 14:25, 2 Ch 12:2, 9; 1st Pharaoh of the 22nd dynasty; reigned *ca* 945–924 B.C.; Map 17; pp. 20, 80.

Sheva, see SERAIAH.

Shibmah, see SIBMAH.

Shicron, see SHIKKERON.

Shieldbearers (Gate of the), see GUARD (Gate of the).

Shihon, see SHION.

Shihor (The), 'water of Horus'; applied to an E arm of the Nile, Jos 13:3, 1 Ch 13:5, cf. Is 23:3, Jer 2:18 ('the Nile'); Map 12.

Shihor-libnath, 'stream of the poplars'; stream forming the S boundary of Asher, Jos 19:26; prob. mod. *Nahr ez-Zerqa*, S of Carmel; Map 11. □

Shikkeron, loc. on the N boundary of Judah, Jos 15:11; sit. unk. □

Shilhim, loc. of Judah, in the Negeb, listed Jos 15:32; replaced by Sharuhen in the list of the cities of Simeon, Jos 19:6; sit. unk. Cf. SHARUHEN, SHAARAIM (2). □

Shiloah, Siloam, 1. n. of the conduit on the SE side of Jerusalem which carried water from the spring Gihon to a pool within the city, Is 8:6 (Shiloah), cf. pp. 93f.; scene of one of the miracles of Jesus, Jn 9:7 ('pool of Siloam'), cf. Map 33; the small mod. village of *Silwân* preserves the ancient n.; Pls. 327, 381.
2. Siloam inscription, cf. Pls. 231f.; p. 93.
3. 'tower in Siloam', ment. Lk 13:4; Map 33.

Shiloh, city where the tribal territories were apportioned, Jos 18:1, 8ff., 19:51, 21:2, 22:9, 12; religious centre in the time of the Judges, Jg 18:31, 21:12, 1 S 1:3, 2:14, 3:21, 4:3f., 12; laid in ruins by the Philistines, Jer 26:6, cf. p. 67; home of the prophet Ahijah, according to 1 K 14:2ff.; mod. *Kh. Seilûn;* Maps 2, 11, 14, 15, 17; Pl. 175; p. 67.

Shimei, n. of several persons, in particular a man who belonged to the same tribe as Saul, 2 S 16, 19.

Shimron, loc. of Zebulun, listed Jos 19:15; Canaanite royal city, Jos 11:1, 12:20 (Shimron-meron, where Shimron should prob. be separated from Meron; LXX has Symoôn); poss. mod. *Kh. Sammuniyeh*, 5 miles W of Nazareth; Maps 11, 14. □

Shimron-meron, see SHIMRON.

Shinar (Land of), Heb. form of the Accadian n. of a region in N Mesopotamia; apparently used by the Israelites to designate the whole of Mesopotamia, Gn 10:10, 11:2; kingdom of Amraphel, Gn 14:1, 9; Jos 7:21 mentions 'a beautiful mantle from Shinar'; among the lands of the Diaspora listed in Is 11:11; apparently identified with Babylonia in Zec 5:11, Dn 1:2. □

Shion, loc. of Issachar, listed Jos 19:19; sit. unk. □

Shisha, see SERAIAH.

Shishak, see SHESHONQ.

Shittim, see ABEL-SHITTIM.

Shoa, n. of a Chaldaean tribe, Ezk 23:23. □

Shocho, Shochoh, Shoco, see SOCOH (2).

Shophan, see ATROTH-SHOPHAN.

Shual (Land of), ment. 1 S 13:17; near Michmash, exact sit. unk. □

Shunem, loc. of Issachar, listed Jos 19:18; ment. 1 S 28:4, 2 K 4:8; birthplace of Abishag, 1 K 1:3, 15, 2:17; mod. *Sôlem;* Maps 11, 15, 17; Pl. 188. □

Shur, 'wall'; region E of the Nile Delta; cf. ETHAM; indicates the edge of the steppes in the N of the Sinai peninsula, Gn 16:7, 20:1, 25:18, 1 S 15:7, 27:8; called the 'wilderness of Shur' in Ex 15:22; Map 9; p. 48. □

Shushan, see SUSA.

Sibmah, loc. of Reuben, listed Jos 13:19, cf. Nu 32:38; called Sebam in Nu 32:3; later Moabite, Is 16:8f., Jer 48:32; sit. uncertain; Map 11. □

Sibraim, loc. ment. Ezk 47:16; in the region of Hamath; poss. identical with SEPHARVAIM, q.v. □

Siceleg, see ZIKLAG.

Sichar, see SYCHAR.

Sichem, see SHECHEM.

Sicyon, loc. on the gulf of Corinth, ment. in the list of countries and cities which received the letter of Lucius, 1 Mac 15:23; mod. *Vasilika;* Map 26. □

Siddim (Valley of), valley where the kings of the Pentapolis (1) fought against the 4 kings of Mesopotamia, Gn 14:3, 8ff.; explicitly identified with the Salt Sea (i.e. Dead Sea) in Gn 14:3; prob. situated in what is now the shallow part of the Dead Sea, S of the peninsula of *el-Lisân*, 'the tongue'; also rendered 'valley of the forests', 'woodland vale'. Cf. PLAIN, PLAINS. □

Side, sea-port of Pamphylia, ment. in the list of countries and cities which received the letter of Lucius, 1 Mac 15:23; mod. *Eski Adalia;* Map 26. □

Sidon, ancient sea-port of Phoenicia, ment. Gn 10:15, Jg 1:31, Is 23:2, Ezk 27:8, Ac 27:3, etc.; mod. *Saida;* Maps 1, 3, 4, 7, 8, 23, 29, 31, 35; Pls. 12, 274, 276.

Sidrach, see SHADRACH.

Sihon, n. of the Amorite king of Heshbon whose defeat by the Israelites is frequently ment. in the O.T., Dt 2:26ff., Nu 21:21ff., Jos 2:10, 12:2, Jg 11:19ff., Neh 9:22, Ps 135:11, 136:19; cf. 1 K 4:19, where 'the country of Sihon' is localised in Gilead, and Jer 48:45, where 'the house of Sihon' means Heshbon.

Sihor, see SHIHOR and SHIHOR-LIBNATH.

Sihor-Labanath, see SHIHOR-LIBNATH.

Silas, n. of a Christian who accompanied St Paul on his journeys, Ac 15:22–18:5; identical with the Silvanus of 1 Th 1:1, 2 Th 1:1, 2 Co 1:19, 1 P 5:12.

Silla, loc. ment. in the corrupt text of 2 K 12:20; sit. unk. □

Silo, see SHILOH.

Siloah (Pool of), Siloam (Pool, Inscription, Tower of), Siloe (Pool, Tower of), see SHILOAH, SILOAM.

Silvanus, see SILAS.

Simeon, n. of 1. one of the patriarchs, son of Jacob and Leah and ancestor of a tribe, Gn 29:33, 34:25ff.; the tribal territory was located in the S part of the territory of Judah, Jos 19:9; the cities of Simeon, listed in Jos 19:1–9 (and, with some

Maps: 1 p. 9 / 2, 3 p. 10 / 4 p. 29 / 5, 6 p. 30 / 7, 8 p. 43 / 9, 10 p. 44 / 11, 12 p. 59 / 13 p. 60 / 14 p. 65 / 15, 16 p. 66 / 17 p. 81 / 18, 19 p. 82 / 20, 21 p. 95 / 22–24 p. 96 /25–29 p. 103 / 30, 31 p. 104 / 32, 33 p. 115 / 34, 35 p. 116 / I, II end-papers.

162

variants, in 1 Ch 4:28–33), consequently reappear among the cities of Judah, listed in Jos 15:21–32; Maps 11, 13.
2. an old man of Jerusalem, Lk 2:25.

Simon, Gk. n. corresponding to the Heb. n. *Shim'ôn* (Simeon) as pronounced by Greeks; borne by several persons in the O.T. and N.T., inc. 1. Simon Maccabaeus; Map 30; p. 110.
2. Simon Peter. Cf. Cephas, Peter.
3. Simon the Cananaean (Canaanite), or the Zealot (Zelotes), Mk 3:18, Mt 10:4, Lk 6:15, Ac 1:13.
4. Simon the leper, host of Jesus at Bethany, Mt 26:6, Mk 14:3.
5. Simon the Pharisee, host of Jesus, Lk 7:40.
6. Simon of Cyrene, the father of Alexander and Rufus, Mk 15:21, Mt 27:32, Lk 23:26.
7. Simon, a magician from Samaria, Ac 8.

Sin, 1. desert region between Elim and Mt Sinai, Ex 16:1, 17:1, Nu 33:11f. ('wilderness of Sin'); mod. *Debbet er-Ramleh;* Map 9 (not be to confused with the 'wilderness of Zin', W of the mts of Seir on the same Map). □
2. loc. ment. in prophecy against Egypt in Ezk 30:15ff. (R.S.V. Pelusium), and described as 'the strength of Egypt'; poss. mod. *Tell Farama*, identical with the Pelusium of the classical period; Maps 9, 20, 21. Some scholars read Syene (q.v.) instead of Sin. □
3. city of the Sinites (1), q.v.

Sin (Desert of), Sina, see Zin (Wilderness of).

Sinai (Mount), mt of the theophany, Ex 19, 34; this n. does not occur outside the Pentateuch, except in the poetic texts of the 'Song of Deborah', Jg 5:5, of Ps 68:8, 17 (Heb. 9, 18), in the prayer of Ezra, Neh 9:13, and in Sir 48:7; prob., according to tradition, the mt range of which *J. Mûsa* is the highest peak; Map 9; Pls. 145–150; p. 48. Cf. Horeb (Mount).

Sinites, 1. n. of one of the pre-Israelite peoples of Canaan, listed between the Arkites and the Arvadites, Gn 10:17 = 1 Ch 1:15; they lived in the city of Sin, poss. mod. *Shein*, N of the Lebanon; Map 4. □
2. the 'land of the Sinites' (Sinim), Is 49:12 (Heb.), is unk., but perhaps we should read 'the land of Syene' (Sewêne); so R.S.V. Cf. Syene. □

Sion, see Zion.

Sion (Mount), see Sirion, Hermon (Mount).

Sior, see Zior.

Siphmoth, loc. ment. in the list of the cities of S Judah to which David sent spoil, 1 S 30:28; sit. unk. □

Sippar, ancient city of Mesopotamia, N of Babylon; mod. *Abû Habbah;* Maps 1, 5, 6.

Sira (Pool of), see Sirah (Cistern of).

Sirah (Cistern of), ment. 2 S 3:26; N of Hebron, exact sit. unk. □

Sirion, Sidonian n. of Mt Hermon, according to Dt 3:8f. (cf. 4:48); cf. Ps 29:6, 1 Ch 5:16 (conj.; Heb. Sharon).

Sis, see Ziz.

Sisa, see Seraiah.

Sisara, see Sisera.

Sisera, n. of Hittite origin borne by the commander of Jabin's army, Jg 4:2; he was defeated by Deborah and Barak, Jg 4:12ff., and murdered by Jael, Jg 4:21; Map 14.

Sitnah, 'accusation'; n. of a well between Gerar and Beer-sheba, Gn 26:21.

Siva, see Seraiah.

Slaughter (Valley of), derogatory n. applied to the Valley of Hinnom (q.v.), Jer 7:32. □

Smyrna, sea-port N of Ephesus in Asia Minor; one of the 'seven churches', Rev 1:11, 2:8; mod. *Izmir;* Maps I and II (e.p.). □

Soba, see Zobah.

Soba of the land of Hemath, see Hamath-zobah.

Sobna, see Shebna.

Soccoth, see Succoth.

Socho, see Secu and Socoh (2), (3).

Sochoh, see Socoh (3).

Sochot, see Succoth.

Soco, see Socoh (2).

Socoh, 'thorn-hedge'; 1. loc. of Judah, in the hill country, listed Jos 15:48; mod. *Kh. Shuweikeh*, SSW of Hebron, which preserves the consonants of the Heb. name (*swkh*); Map 13. □
2. loc. of Judah, in the lowland, listed Jos 15:35; important in the war with the Philistines, 1 S 17:1, 2 Ch 28:18 (Soco); fortified by Rehoboam, 2 Ch 11:7 (Soco); mod. *Kh. 'Abbâd;* Maps 13, 15, 17, 19. □
3. loc. in Solomon's 3rd district, 1 K 4:10; mod. *Tell er-Râs*, WNW of Samaria; Map 17. □

Socoth, see Socoh (1) and Succoth.

Sodi, see Sud.

Sodom, see Pentapolis (1).

Solomon, n. of the son of David and Bathsheba; one of the greatest kings of Israel (*ca* 960–931 b.c.), 1 K 1–11; pp. 71ff.

Solomon (Portico of), Solomon's Portico, colonnade along the E side of the Temple terrace, flanking the valley of the Kidron; frequented by Jesus and the first Christians, Jn 10:23, Ac 3:11, 5:12; Map 33 no. 10.

Solomon's Porch, see Solomon (Portico of).

Soph (Valley of), loc. ment. in some versions of 2 Ch 20:16; sit. unk., but near the ascent of Ziz and the wilderness of Jeruel; instead of 'in the valley of Soph', we may read 'at the end of the valley' (so R.S.V.).

Sophonias, see Zephaniah.

Sorec (Valley of), see Sorek (Valley of).

Sorek (Valley of), home of Delilah, Jg 16:4; prob. the mod. *W. es-Sarâr*, in the lowland of Judah, between Zorah and Timnah; Map 14.

Sores, loc. of Judah, in the hill-country, listed Jos 15:59 (LXX); mod. *Sâris*, SW of Kiriath-jearim; Maps 13, 19.

Sosthenes, n. of 1. the ruler of the synagogue at Corinth, Ac 18:17.
2. a fellow-worker of St Paul, 1 Co 1:1.

South Country, see Negeb.

South Ramoth, see Ramoth of the Negeb.

Spain, ment. in 1 Mac 8:3 as conquered by the Romans; according to Ro 15:24, 28, St Paul planned to visit Spain. It is not certain whether he did so.

Spartans, n. of the people of Sparta (Map 32), ment. several times in 1 and 2 Mac (1 Mac 14:19f., etc.); listed among the countries and cities which received the letter of Lucius, 1 Mac 15:23; 2 Mac 5:9 has Lacedaemonians instead of Spartans.

Spring of Harod, see Harod (Spring of).

Springs of Pisgah, see Ashdoth-pisgah.

Stephen, n. of one of the 'seven men of good repute', Ac 6:5; cf. Ac 6:8 – 7:60.

Stone of Bohan, see Bohan (Stone of).

Stone of help, see Ebenezer.

Straight (Street called), street in Damascus where Saul (St Paul) lodged, Ac 9:11; Pls. 387–390. □

Sual (Land of), see Shual (Land of).

Succoth, 'tabernacles', for an explanation of the n., cf. Gn 33:17; 1. loc. of Gad, listed Jos 13:27; ment. Gn 33:17; on the route of Gideon's army, Jg 8:5ff.; ment. in order to localise the foundry which cast bronze for the Temple, 1 K 7:46 = 2 Ch 4:17; cf. Ps 60:6 (Heb. 8) = 108:8 (Vale of Succoth); prob. mod. *Tell Deir 'Alla*, in the Jordan valley E of Shechem; Maps 2, 4, 11, 14, 17; Pl. 60. □
2. 1st stopping-place on the Exodus, Ex 12:37, 13:20, Nu 33:5f.; situated somewhere between Rameses and Etham; Map 9; p. 48. □

Sud, a river or canal at Babylon, Bar 1:4; otherwise unk. □

Sukkiim, ment. in 2 Ch 12:3 as mercenary troops of the Pharaoh Shishak; otherwise unk. □

Sukkiims, see Sukkiim.

Sumer, in ancient times the n. of the S part of Mesopotamia, then very fertile; the old Sumerian culture greatly influenced the Semites who, after 2000 b.c., occupied this region; Maps 1, 5, 6.

Sunam, Sunem, see Shunem.

Suph, 'reed'; n. which chiefly occurs as an element in *Yam-Sûph*, 'Sea of Reeds' or Red Sea; occurs alone as a place-name only in Dt 1:1; sit. unk. See also Zuph.

Suphah, region or valley in Moab, Nu 21:14; sit. unk. □

Sur, see Shur.

Sur (The gate), gate of the Temple of Jerusalem. Cf. Foundation (Gate of the).

Susa, 1. ancient capital of Elam; later the winter residence of the Pers. kings; ment. in Neh 1:1, and Est 1:2, 5, 3:15, etc., Dn 8:2; mod. *Shush;* Maps 1, 5, 6, 8, 18, 20, 21, 25, 32, I (e.p.); Pls. 267f.; p. 38.
2. see Seraiah.

Susan, see Susa (1).

Sychar, loc. in Samaria, near Jacob's well, Jn 4:5; sit. unk.; Maps 34, 35. □

Syene, Heb. *Sewêne;* ment. in Ezk 29:10, 30:6, as a city on the S frontier of Egypt; mod. *Assuân*, at the 1st cataract of the Nile; Map 10; Pl. 263; p. 11. Cf. Sin (2), Sinites (2).

Sylvanus, see Silas.

Symoôn, see Shimron.

Syntyche, n. of a Christian woman of Philippi, Ph 4:2.

Syracusa, see Syracuse.

Syracuse, sea-port of Sicily, Ac 28:12; Maps 21, II (e.p.). □

Syria, Gk. n., poss. from an abb. of *Assur(ia)*, applied since the time of Herodotus to the territory of the Aramaeans, hence in some versions of the Bible the usual translation of Aram. Modern Syria and Lebanon combined (Map I (e.p.)) do not exactly correspond to the ancient Syria (often taken to include the whole of Palestine), which, moreover, had only vague frontiers and never constituted a definite political unit. In the period of the Kings, it consisted of a number of small independent states; cf. Aram. The commercial activity of the Phoenicians on its coast, and the fact that it was disputed territory between Mesopotamia and Egypt and was repeatedly overrun by Hittites, Hurrians, and Aramaeans, combined to produce a cosmopolitan culture which deeply influenced Palestine. In the N.T. period Syria was a Roman province with Antioch as its capital.

Syria (Desert of), region of steppes between Mesopotamia and Syria-Palestine.

Syria Maacha, Syria-maachah, see Maacah (2).

Syrians, see Aram.

Syro-Phoenicia, n. applied in Mk 7:26 to Phoenicia, in order to distinguish it from the Libyan Phoenicia on the coast of N Africa; Maps 34, 35.

Syrtis (The), shallow bay with sandbanks on the coast of Tripolitania, Ac 27:17; Map II (e.p.). □

T

Taanach, loc. of Manasseh, in the territory of Issachar, which long remained Canaanite, Jos 17:11ff., cf. 1 Ch 7:29, Jg 1:27f.; Levitical city, Jos 21:25; ment. with Megiddo, Jg 5:19, Jos 12:21; in Solomon's 5th district, 1 K 4:12; mod. *Tell Ta'annak;* Maps 4, 11, 14, 17. □

Taanath-shiloh, loc. on the N boundary of Ephraim, Jos 16:6; prob. mod. *Kh. Ta'nah el-Fôqa;* Map 11. □

Tabbath, loc. in the Jordan valley, Jg 7:22; sit. unk. □

Taberah, 'burning'; stopping-place on the Exodus shortly after the departure from Mt Sinai, Nu 11:3, Dt 9:22; shown on Map 9 near Kibroth-hattaavah, in the SE of the Sinai peninsula. □

Tabitha, Gk. *Dorcas;* n. of a Christian woman of Joppa, Ac 9:36ff.

Table of the peoples, n. applied to the list of the 71 peoples descended from Shem, Ham, and Japheth, Gn 10. The compiler's grouping is based not so much on racial affinities as on commercial, political, and cultural ties; thus Canaan is listed not among the descendants of Shem, but among those of Ham, because of its political links with Egypt. The compiler wishes to emphasise the unity of all the peoples in the world as he knew it, extending from the Black Sea to Ethiopia and from Persia to Greece.

Tabor, 1. mt on the boundary between Zebulun and Naphtali, Jos 19:12 (Chisloth-tabor, q.v.), 22, 34 (Aznoth-tabor, q.v.); where Barak mustered his troops, Jg 4:6, 12, 14; perhaps also ment. in Jg 8:18; place of worship, according to Hos 5:1; ment. with Mt Carmel as an important mt, Jer 46:18; ment. with Hermon, Ps 89:12 (Heb. 13); not ment. in the N.T., but cf. p. 122; mod. *J. et-Tôr;* Maps 2, 11, 14; Pls. 364, 368, 369; p. 16. □
2. Levitical city of Zebulun, 1 Ch 6:77 (Heb. 62); prob. on the slopes of Tabor (1). □
3. an oak or terebinth in the vicinity of Bethel, 1 S 10:3 ('the oak of Tabor'); poss. the reading should be Deborah, cf. Gn 35:8. □

Tadmor, G&L Palmyra, q.v.; n. of an oasis in the Syrian desert; mod. *Tudmur;* Maps 4, 20, I (e.p.); Pls. 334–339. Tadmor in 2 Ch 8:4 and some versions of 1 K 9:18 is an error for Tamar (2), q.v.

Tahapanes, see Tahpanhes.

Tahath, stopping-place on the Exodus, Nu 33:26f.; in the vicinity of Makheloth, exact sit. unk. □

Tahpanhes, city in the Nile Delta, Jer 2:16, 43:7ff., 44:1, 46:14, Ezk 30:18 (Tehaphnehes); poss. mod. *Tell Dafna (Deffeneh);* the n. may even have been applied to the whole region between *Sân el-Hagar* and *Qantir;* Map 9.

Tahtim-hodshi, loc. ment. 2 S 24:6 (Heb.), through which David's census-takers passed on their journey from Aroer (1) to the north; sit. unk.; R.S.V. reads with Gk. 'Kadesh in the land of the Hittites'. Cf. Kadesh (2). □

Tamar, 'palm-tree'; 1. n. of several women in the O.T.
2. city in the S of Judah, 1 K 9:18 (where Heb. marg., followed by some versions, has Tadmor (q.v.)), Ezk 47:19, 48:28; prob. identical with Hazazon-tamar, q.v. □

Tanach, see Taanach.

Tanis, G&L n. of the city also called Zoan and Avaris, qq.v.; residence of the Ramessides, Ps 78:12 (R.S.V. Zoan); its ruins are near *Sân el-Hagar;* Maps 7, 8, 9; pp. 45, 64.

Taphne, Taphnes, Taphnis, see Tahpanhes, Tappuah.

Taphon, see Tephon, Tappuah (1).

Taphua, see Tappuah.

Taphua (Fountain, Springs of), see En-tappuah.

Tappuah, 'apple-tree'; 1. loc. on the boundary between Manasseh and Ephraim, Jos 16:8, 17:8, cf. 17:7 (En-Tappuah); prob. identical with the Canaanite royal city ment. Jos 12:17; prob. we should also read Tappuah instead of Tiphsah (Heb.) in 2 K 15:16, cf. Tiphsah; later called Tephon, 1 Mac 9:50; prob. mod. *Tell Sheikh Abû Zarad*, S of Shechem; Maps 11, 14, 17, 30. □
2. loc. of Judah, in the lowland, listed Jos 15:34; poss. mod. *Beit Nettîf*, E of Azekah; Maps 13, 19. □

Taracha, see Tirhakah.

Tarah, see Terah (2).

Taralah, loc. of Benjamin, listed Jos 18:27; sit. unk. □

Tarshish, region or city to which ships sailed from Joppa and Tyre, Jon 1:3, 4:2, Is 23:6; ment. with the 'isles' (or 'coastland(s)', cf. Coast(s), Coastland(s)) in Ps 72:10, and with other distant regions in Is 66:19, Ezk 38:13; listed among the sons of Javan, Gn 10:4 = 1 Ch 1:7; exported all kinds of metals, Jer 10:9, Ezk 27:12, apparently carried in special 'ships of Tarshish', Is 2:16, cf. 23:1, 14, Ps 48:7 (Heb. 8), built by Tyrian craftsmen for Solomon and Jehoshaphat, 1 K 10:22, 22:48f., 2 Ch 9:21, 20:36. The identification with Tartessus at the mouth of the Guadalquivir in S Spain, which flourished down to *ca* 500 b.c. especially as a centre of the metal trade, is far from certain. Other cities and regions in the E Mediterranean area have been proposed. Since the Phoenician word *tarshîsh* seems to have meant 'metal refinery', it has also been suggested that the n. was used for various metal-manufacturing centres on the Mediterranean coasts. A 'ship of Tarshish' may then have denoted originally a cargo-ship serving such centres, and, by a later extension, any heavy freighter. □

Tarsus, important city in Cilicia, ment. on the black obelisk of Shalmaneser (Pl. 247); ment. 2 Mac 4:30; home of St Paul, Ac 9:11, 21:39, 22:3, cf. 9:30, 11:25; Maps 1, 4, 20, I and II (e.p.); Pls. 272f. □

Tatam, loc. of Judah, in the hill country, listed Jos 15:59 (LXX); sit. unk. □

Taurus, chain of mts in N Cilicia; Maps 1, 4, 26; Pls. 398f.

Tebah, see Tibhath.

Tebbath, see Tabbath.

Tehaphnehes, see Tahpanhes.

Tekoa, loc. of Judah, in the hill country, listed Jos 15:59 (LXX); city of the prophet Amos, Am 1:1, and of the 'wise woman' of 2 S 14:2; fortified by Rehoboam, 2 Ch 11:6; also ment. Jer 6:1; 2 Ch 20:20 and 1 Mac 9:33 refer to the 'wilderness of Tekoa(h)'; mod. *Tequ'a;* Maps 11, 13, 15, 17, 19, 22, 30. □

Maps: 1 p. 9 / 2, 3 p. 10 / 4 p. 29 / 5, 6 p. 30 / 7, 8 p. 43 / 9, 10 p. 44 / 11, 12 p. 59 / 13 p. 60 / 14 p. 65 / 15, 16 p. 66 / 17 p. 81 / 18, 19 p. 82 / 20, 21 p. 95 / 22–24 p. 96 / 25–29 p. 103 / 30, 31 p. 104 / 32, 33 p. 115 / 34, 35 p. 116 / I, II end-papers.

163

Tekoah, see TEKOA.
Tel-abib, hill near the river Chebar in the land of the Chaldaeans; Ezekiel visited the exiles there, Ezk 3:15, cf. 1:3; exact sit. unk. □
Telaim, loc. ment. 1 S 15:4; doubtless identical with TELEM, q.v.
Tel-assar, region of Assyria, ment. 2 K 19:12 = Is 37:12; sometimes emended to Tel Bassar, which corresponds with the mod. n. of *Tell Basher*, in the land of Eden (2). □
Tel Bassar, conj. reading for Tel-assar in 2 K 19:12 = Is 37:12. Cf. TEL-ASSAR.
Telem, loc. of Judah, in the Negeb, listed Jos 15:24; poss. mod. *Tell Umm es-Salafeh;* Map 11. See TELAIM. □
Tel-harsa, see TEL-HARSHA.
Tel-harsha, loc. in Babylonia, Ezr 2:59, Neh 7:61; sit. unk. □
Tell el-Fâr'ah, prob. covers the ruins of Tirzah; Map 2; Pls. 62–69; pp. 24, 26. Not to be confused with the tell of the same n. S of Gaza (cf. SHARUHEN), or with the *Tell Fâra* N of Anathoth (cf. PARAH).
Tell-haresha, see TEL-HARSHA.
Telmela, see TEL-MELAH.
Tel-melah, loc. in Babylonia, Ezr 2:59, Neh 7:61; sit. unk. □
Tema, region of N Arabia, Is 21:14, Jer 25:23, Job 6:19; its inhabitants are listed as descendants of Ishmael, Gn 25:15 = 1 Ch 1:30; mod. oasis of *Teima;* Map 18.
Teman, region of Edom, Jer 49:7, 20, Ezk 25:13, Am 1:12, Ob 9, cf. Hab 3:3; listed as a grandson of Esau, Gn 36:11, 15, 42, 1 Ch 1:36, 53; sit. unk., poss. N of Petra. □
Tephon, see TAPPUAH (1).
Terah, 1. n. of the father of Abraham, Gn 11:24ff.
2. stopping-place on the Exodus, Nu 33:27f.; exact sit. unk. □
Terebinth (Valley of the), see ELAH (Valley of).
Tertius, n. of the letter-writer employed by St Paul, Ro 16:22.
Tertullus, n. of the spokesman for Ananias and the elders who accused St Paul before Felix, Ac 24:1.
Thabor, see TABOR.
Thacasin, see ETH-KAZIN.
Thadal, see TIDAL.
Thaddaeus, n. of one of the 12 Apostles, Mk 3:18, Mt 10:3 (some MSS read Lebbaeus, or 'Lebbaeus whose surname was Thaddaeus' in these passages); corresponds to Judas (Jude), brother or son of James, in Lk 6:16, Ac 1:13.
Thaddeus, see THADDAEUS.
Thahath, see TAHATH.
Thalassa, see LASEA.
Thalassar, see TEL-ASSAR.
Thamar, see TAMAR.
Thamna, see TIMNAH.
Thamnan, Thamnas, see TIMNAH (1).
Thamnatha, see TIMNAH (1) and TIMNATH-SERAH.
Thamnath-Saraa, Thamnath-Sare, see TIMNATH-SERAH.
Thanac(h), see TAANACH.
Thanath-selo, see TAANATH-SHILOH.
Thaphsa, see TIPHSAH.
Tharaca, see TIRHAKAH.
Thare, see TERAH (2).
Tharela, see TARALAH.
Tharshish, Tharsis, see TARSHISH.
Tharsus, see TARSUS.
Thebath, see TIBHATH.
Thebes, Gk. *Thebai;* n. of the capital city of Upper Egypt, ment. Jer 46:25 (Amon of Thebes), Ezk 30:14ff., Nah 3:8; the ruins lie at Luxor and Karnak; Maps 1, 5, 6, 8, 10, 20, I (e.p.); Pls. 9f.; p. 64. Cf. NO-AMON. □
Thebez, loc. NE of Shechem, Jg 9:50, 2 S 11:21; mod. *Tûbas;* Maps 2, 14, 15; Pl. 178. □
Thecoe, Thecua, Thecue, see TEKOA.
Theglath-Phalasar, Theglath-Phalnasar, see TIGLATH-PILESER.
Thelasar, Thelassar, see TEL-ASSAR.
Thelharsa, see TEL-HARSHA.
Thelmala, Thelmela, see TEL-MELAH.
Thema, see TEMA.
Theman, see TEMAN.
Themna, see TIMNAH (1).
Thenac, see TAANACH.
Theodas, see THEUDAS.
Theophilus, n. of a Christian to whom St Luke dedicated his Gospel and the Acts of the Apostles, Lk 1:3, Ac 1:1.
Theraca, see TIRHAKAH.
Thersa, see TIRZAH.
Thessalonica, city in Macedonia, Ac 17:1, 11, 13, Ph 4:16, cf. Ac 20:4 (Thessalonians), 27:2, 2 Ti 4:10; Paul wrote two letters to the Church here; mod. *Saloniki* (Salonica); Maps 32, I and II (e.p.). □
Theudas, n. of a false Jewish prophet of the Early Christian period, Ac 5:36.
Thimnathah, see TIMNAH (1).
Thochen, see TOCHEN.
Thogorma, see BETH-TOGARMAH.
Thola, see TOLA.
Tholad, see TOLAD.
Thomas, n. of one of the 12 Apostles, Mt 10:3 and parallel passages; also called Thomas the Twin (Gk. *Didymos*), cf. Jn 20:24.
Thophel, see TOPHEL.
Thopo, see TEPHON, TAPPUAH (1).
Thou, see TOU.
Three Taverns, loc. on the Appian Way, about 30 miles SE of Rome, Ac 28:15; Map II (e.p.). □
Thubal, see TUBAL.
Thyatira, city of Lydia and one of the 'seven churches', Rev 1:11, 2:18, 24; home of Lydia, Ac 16:14; mod. *Akhisar;* Map II (e.p.). □
Tiberias, city on the SW shore of the Lake of Gennesaret, Jn 6:23; it was founded by Herod Antipas during the youth of Jesus, and gave its n. to the lake, cf. Jn 6:1; Maps 2, 34; Pl. 27.
Tiberias (Sea of), ment. Jn 6:1. Cf. GALILEE (Sea of).
Tiberius Caesar, n. of a Rom. emperor (A.D. 14–37), Lk 3:1; Pl. 321.
Tibhath, city in Syria, ment. 1 Ch 18:8, also called Betah, 2 S 8:8, where Tebah should prob. be read; sit. in the Beqa', somewhere near Berothai; Map 16. □
Tichon (The house of), see HAZER-HATTICON.
Tidal, n. of the king of Goiim, one of the 4 allied kings ment. in Gn 14 (named in 14:1, 9); this word is no doubt the Heb. form of Tudhalia(s), a n. borne by several Hittite princes and, as early as the 19th cent. B.C., by other persons in Asia Minor. The compiler describes him as king of Goiim (rendered 'of nations' in some versions), which means king of a distant and unk. people.
Tiglath-pileser, n. of several Ass. kings, of whom the best-known is Tiglath-pileser III (745-726 B.C.), also called PUL (q.v.) in the Bible; cf. 2 K 15:19, 29, 1 Ch 5:26 (Tiglath-pilneser); Map 18; pp. 90, 92.
Tiglath-pilneser, see TIGLATH-PILESER.
Tigris, one of the 2 great rivers of Mesopotamia; called by its Heb. n. Hiddekel and ment. as one of the 4 rivers of the Garden of Eden in Gen 2:14; also Dn 10:4 (R.S.V. Tigris); in LXX Tigris, Sir 24:25, Jth 1:6, To 6:1; Maps 1, 5, 6, 7, 8, 20, 32, I (e.p.); Pl. 3. □
Timnah, 1. loc. on the N boundary of Judah, W of Beth-shemesh, Jos 15:10; loc. of Dan, listed Jos 19:43; where Samson killed a lion, Jg 14:1ff.; later captured by the Philistines, 2 Ch 28:18; mod. *Kh. Tibneh;* Maps 11, 13, 14, 19. □
2. loc. of Judah, in the hill country, listed Jos 15:57; identical with the Timnah of Gn 38:12ff.; poss. mod. *Kh. Tibneh (Thabbana)*, W of Bethlehem; Maps 13, 19. □
Timnath, see TIMNAH (1), (2), and TIMNATH-SERAH.
Timnath-heres, see TIMNATH-SERAH.
Timnath-serah, city given to Joshua as an inheritance, Jos 19:50; he was buried there, Jos 24:30; called Timnath-heres in Jg 2:9, and Timnath in 1 Mac 9:50; prob. mod. *Kh. Tibneh*, SSW of Shechem; Maps 11, 14, 30. □
Timotheus, see TIMOTHY.
Timothy, n. of the companion and fellow-worker of St Paul, Ac 16:1ff.; 17–20, Col 1:1, He 13:23.
Timsâh (Lake), lake in Lower Egypt, N of the Bitter Lakes; Map 9.
Tiphsah, loc. ment. as the N limit of Solomon's territory, 1 K 4:24 (Heb. 5:4); prob. the city on the Euphrates later called Thapsakos (Thapsacus); mod. *Dibseh;* Map 25. The city of Tiphsah ment. in 2 K 15:16 must have lain somewhere in the kingdom of Israel; poss. we should read Tappuah (1) with a Gk. version (so R.S.V.). □
Tirhakah, Heb. transcription of *Taharka;* n. of the 3rd Pharaoh of the 25th dynasty, 2 K 19:9 = Is 37:9.
Tirzah, Canaanite royal city, Jos 12:24; later the capital of the kings of the N Kingdom, from Jeroboam I to Omri, 1 K 14:17, 15:21, 33, 16:6–23, cf. 2 K 15:14, 16; a beautiful city, cf. Ca 6:4; prob. mod. TELL EL-FÂR'AH, q.v.; Maps 14, 17. □
Tishbe, loc. in Gilead, and home of Elijah the Tishbite, 1 K 17:1 (LXX, foll. by R.S.V.); poss. mod. *Kh. Lisdib;* Map 17. □
Titus, n. of 1. Rom. emperor. Cf. pp. 121, 139.
2. companion and fellow-worker of St Paul, Gal 2:1ff., 2 Co 2:13, 7:6f., Tit 1:4, 2 Ti 4:10.
Tob, region in N Transjordan where Jephthah took refuge, Jg 11:3, 5, and where the Ammonites hired mercenary troops, 2 S 10:6, 8; Map 16. □
Tochen, loc. listed among the cities of Simeon, 1 Ch 4:32; no corresponding place is ment. in the Heb. text of Jos 19:7; sit. unk. □
Togarmah, see BETH-TOGARMAH.
Toi, see TOU.
Tola, n. of one of the minor Judges, Jg 10:1f.; Map 14.
Tolad, loc. ment. 1 Ch 4:29; cf. ELTOLAD.
Tophel, loc. ment. Dt 1:1; poss. mod. *et-Tafîleh*, SE of the Dead Sea; Map 9. □
Tophet, see TOPHETH.
Topheth, 'place of burning'; place in the Valley of Hinnom where infants were sacrificed by fire, 2 K 23:10, Jer 7:31f., 19:6, 11ff., cf. Is 30:33 ('a burning place').
Torrent Besor, see BESOR (Brook).
Tou, n. of the king of Hamath, 1 Ch 18:9f.; called Toi in 2 S 8:9f.
Tower of the Furnaces, see TOWER OF THE OVENS.
Tower of the Ovens, tower of the ramparts of Jerusalem, near the Valley Gate, Neh 3:11, 12:38 (Tower of the Furnaces); Map 24C. □
Trachonitis, region NE of the Sea of Galilee, forming part of the tetrarchy of Philip, Lk 3:1; Map 35. □
Tripolis, city on the coast of Phoenicia, 2 Mac 14:1; mod. *Tarâbulus;* Maps 3, 29, 31, I (e.p.); Pl. 13.
Troas, city in Asia Minor, Ac 16:8, 11, 20:5f., 2 Co 2:12, 2 Ti 4:13; mod. *Eskistanbul;* Map II (e.p.). □
Troglodites, see SUKKIIM.
Trogyllium, promontory and town SW of Ephesus, ment. according to some ancient authorities in Ac 20:15 (R.S.V. omits). □
Trophimus, n. of an Asian Christian from Ephesus, Ac 20:4, 21:29, 2 Ti 4:20.
Tryphon, cognomen of Diodotus, a military commander under Alexander Balas; he was responsible for the assassination of Jonathan, 1 Mac 11:39, 12:39–49, 13:12ff.
Tubal, n. of a people and of a region near the Black Sea where copper was mined; listed among the sons of Japheth, Gn 10:2 = 1 Ch 1:5; ment. with Javan and Meshech as trading with Tyre, Ezk 27:13; ment. with Meshech, Ezk 32:26, 38:2f., 39:1, and with Javan, Is 66:19.
Tubal-cain, n. of the son of Lamech, the ancestor of workers in metal, Gn 4:22. The 3 groups of the shepherds, the musicians, and the workers in metal are linked in Genesis with 3 ancestors whose names evoke the callings of their descendants: Jabal, the ancestor of shepherds, suggests the verb *ybl*, 'to lead'; Jubal, the ancestor of musicians, resembles the word *yôbel*, 'trumpet'; and TUBAL (q.v.) is the n. of a people and of a region near the Black Sea where copper was mined, to which has been added the n. Cain, meaning 'worker in metal' in other Semitic languages.
Tychicus, n. of an Asian Christian, Ac 20:4, Eph 6:21, Col 4:7, 2 Ti 4:12, Tit 3:12.
Tyranny (Land of), see MERATHAIM.
Tyre, commercial city of the Phoenicians (Ezk 27), built on an island; David and Solomon traded with her, 2 S 5:11, 1 K 5:1ff., etc.; often threatened with disaster by the prophets, Is 23, Ezk 26ff.; joined to the mainland by Alexander the Great, p. 102; quinquennial games were held there, according to 2 Mac 4:18. Always ment. with Sidon in the Gospels. St Paul found a Christian community there, according to Ac 21:3ff. Mod. *Sûr;* shown on nearly all the Maps, in particular Map 28; Pls. 17, 280.
Tyropoeon Valley, '(valley of) the cheesemakers'; Gk. n. of the valley separating the city of David and the Temple from the upper city; Map 33; Pls. 191, 192 no. 2; p. 114.
Tyros, city in Transjordan; Map 23.
Tyrus, see TYRE.

U

Ugarit, see RÂS SHAMRA.
Ulai, river flowing to the E of Susa, Dn 8:2, 16. □
Ummah, loc. of Asher, listed Jos 19:30; an error for ACCO, q.v. □
Uphaz, region ment. only in the expression 'gold of Uphaz', Jer 10:9, Dn 10:5; sit. unk. Some scholars read OPHIR (q.v.) with certain ancient versions; others regard Uphaz as the past participle of a verb, and render 'purified' (i.e. the finest gold). □
Upper Room, see CENACLE.
Ur of the Chaldeans, city from which Terah and Abraham set out for Canaan, Gn 11:28, 31, 15:7, Neh 9:7 (Ur of the Chaldees); discovered in the ruins at mod. *el-Muqaiyar;* Maps 1, 5, 6, 18, I (e.p.); Pls. 86f.; p. 28.
Urartu, Ass. n. of ARARAT, q.v.
Uruk, Accadian n. of ERECH, q.v.
Us, see UZ.
Usal, see UZAL.
Utmost Sea, see WESTERN SEA.
Uttermost Sea, see WESTERN SEA.
Uz, land of Job, Job 1:1; linked with Edom, Gn 36:28 = 1 Ch 1:42, La 4:21; linked with Aram, Gn 10:23 = 1 Ch 1:17, cf. Gn 22:21, Jer 25:20. Taking into account the countries of origin of Job's 3 friends, Uz prob. lay in the E of the land of the Edomites, in N Arabia, in any case outside the territory of Yahweh's people. □
Uzal, land ment. as trading with Tyre, Ezk 27:19; listed among the regions of S Arabia, Gn 10:27 = 1 Ch 1:21. □
Uzzen-sheerah, loc. ment. 1 Ch 7:24; sit. unk. □
Uzzen-sherah, see UZZEN-SHEERAH.
Uzziah, other n. of Azariah, 10th king of Judah (781–740 B.C.), 2 K 15:13, Is 6:1, Mt 1:8f.; Map 17. Cf. AZARIAH (1).

V

Vagoa, see BAGOAS.
Valley Gate, gate of Jerusalem, 2 Ch 26:9, Neh 2:13, 15, 3:13; located at the N end of the Valley of Hinnom, according to H. Vincent; Map 24C. □
Valley of Beracah, Valley of Blessing, see BERACAH (Valley of).
Valley of Elah, see ELAH (Valley of).
Valley of Hinnom, see HINNOM (Valley of, Valley of the son(s) of).
Valley of Hyenas, see ZEBOIM (2).
Valley of Iphtahel, see IPHTAHEL (Valley of).
Valley of Jehoshaphat, see JEHOSHAPHAT (Valley of).
Valley of Rephaim, see REPHAIM (Valley of).
Valley of Salt, see SALT (Valley of).
Valley of Shaveh, see SHAVEH (Valley of).
Valley of Siddim, see PLAIN, PLAINS, and SIDDIM (Valley of).
Valley of Slaughter, see SLAUGHTER (Valley of).
Valley of Sorek, see SOREK (Valley of).
Valley of the cluster of grapes, see ESHCOL.
Valley of the Forests, see SIDDIM (Valley of).
Valley of the Kings, see KINGS (Valley of the).
Valley of the Salt Pits, see SALT (Valley of).
Valley of the Terebinth, see ELAH (Valley of).
Valley of Zeboim, 'valley of hyenas'; cf. ZEBOIM (2).
Valley of Zered, ment. Nu 21:12. Cf. ZERED (Brook, Valley of).
Valley (The), term applied to the Jordan valley below Succoth, Gn 13:12 (cf. 13:10f.), 19:17, 25, 28f. Variously rendered

Maps: 1 p. 9 / 2, 3 p. 10 / 4 p. 29 / 5, 6 p. 30 / 7, 8 p. 43 / 9, 10 p. 44 / 11, 12 p. 59 / 13 p. 60 / 14 p. 65 / 15, 16 p. 66 / 17 p. 81 18, 19 p. 82 / 20, 21 p. 95 / 22–24 p. 96 / 25–29 p. 103 / 30, 31 p. 104 / 32, 33 p. 115 / 34, 35 p. / 116 I, II end-papers.

164

'plain, country, hollow' in some versions. Cf. PLAIN, PLAINS, ARABAH.

Vedan, according to a doubtful reading in Ezk 27:19 (some versions have Dan; R.S.V.'and wine' for Heb. 'Vedan and Javan') loc. with which Tyre traded. □

Via Dolorosa, expression used to designate the itinerary Jesus is believed to have followed from the Praetorium (assuming that it was in the fortress of Antonia) to Calvary; it winds through a network of streets in mod. Jerusalem; the traditional positions of the stations of the Cross along the Via Dolorosa were fixed over a period extending from the 13th to the 18th centuries; Map 33.

Villages of Jair, see HAVVOTH-JAIR.

Vulgate, n. applied, prob. since the 16th cent., to St Jerome's Lat. translation of the Bible; he revised the existing Lat. text of the N.T. *ca* A.D. 384, and, in A.D. 384–406, translated the O.T. from the Heb. text, taking into account the Gk. text of Origen. The Clementine Vulgate (first edition 1592) is the official text of the Roman Catholic Church. Vulgate means 'text for all and sundry'.

W

Watch Gate, Watch-tower Gate, see GUARD (Gate of the).

Water Gate, gate of Jerusalem, Neh 3:26, 12:37, cf. 8:1, 3, 16; localised S of the Temple; Map 24C. □

Well (Gate of the), see FOUNTAIN GATE.

Well of him that liveth and seeth me, Well of him who lives and looks on me, see BEER-LAHAI-ROI.

Western Sea, in Dt 11:24, 34:2, Jl 2:20, Zec 14:8 is the Mediterranean Sea, and is mentioned in the last two references with the EASTERN SEA, q.v.

Wilderness (River of the), see ARABAH (Brook of the).

Wilderness (Sea of the), see DEAD SEA.

Wild-goats' Rocks, ment. 1 S 24:2 (Heb. 3); near En-gedi; Map 15. □

Willows (Brook of the), torrent on the frontier of Moab, Is 15:7; doubtless the Zered. Cf. ZERED (Brook, Valley of).

Willows (Torrent, Vale of), see WILLOWS (Brook of the).

Wood (Fields of the), see JAAR (Fields of).

Woodland Vale, see SIDDIM (Valley of).

X

Xerxes, Gk. n. of AHASUERUS, q.v.

Y

Yahweh, Heb. n. of God, interpreted in Ex 3:14 as 'I am who I am'; the correct derivation is unk. The n. occurs as an element in many proper names, revealing the theocentric view of life of the Israelites. Cf. JEHOVAH.

Yarmuk, tributary flowing into the Jordan from the E; not ment. in the Bible; Map 2; p. 15.

Yehud, n. applied in the Aramaic text of Daniel and Ezra to Judaea as a subdivision of the Fifth Satrapy; Map 23.

Yiron, loc. of Naphtali, listed Jos 19:38; poss. mod. *Yarûn;* Map 11. □

Z

Zaanaim, see ZAANANNIM (2).

Zaanan, loc. ment. Mic 1:11; poss. identical with ZENAN, q.v.; Map 17. □

Zaanannim, n. of 2 loc., 1. on the boundary of Naphtali, Jos 19:33; sit. unk. □
2. loc. near Megiddo ment. Jg 4:11; poss. mod. *Khan Lejjûn;* Map 14. □

Zabulon, see ZEBULUN.

Zacchaeus, poss. an abb. of Zechariah; n. of the rich tax collector who climbed a tree to obtain a view of Jesus, Lk 19:2ff.; Map 34.

Zaccheus, see ZACCHAEUS.

Zachariah, see ZECHARIAH (1).

Zacharias, see ZECHARIAH.

Zachary, see ZECHARIAH (4).

Zadok, n. of several persons in the O.T., in particular the High Priest who lived in the reigns of David and Solomon; he remained faithful to David, 2 S 15:24ff., and anointed Solomon, 1 K 1:39.

Zair, loc. ment. 2 K 8:21; poss. identical with ZIOR, q.v. □

Zalmon (Mount), hill near Shechem, Jg 9:48, prob. the top of one of the slopes of Ebal or Gerizim; perhaps the same hill ment. in Ps 68:14 (Heb. 15). □

Zalmonah, a stopping-place on the Exodus after Kadesh-barnea, Nu 33:41f.; poss. mod. *Bir Madkhûr,* in the Arabah; Map 9. □

Zalmunna, n. of a Midianite king pursued and defeated by Gideon, Jg 8:5ff., cf. Ps 83:11 (Heb. 12). Cf. ZEBAH.

Zambri, see ZIMRI.

Zamzummim(s), see REPHAIM.

Zanoa, see ZANOAH (1).

Zanoah, 1. loc. of Judah, in the lowland, listed Jos 15:34; repopulated after the Exile, Neh 3:13, 11:30; cf. 1 Ch 4:18; mod. *Kh. Zanû'*; Maps 13, 19, 22. □
2. loc. of Judah, in the hill country, listed Jos 15:56; poss. mod. *Kh. Beit 'Amra;* Maps 13, 19. □

Zanoe, see ZANOAH.

Zaphon, 'village of the north' or 'look-out post'; loc. of Gad, listed Jos 13:27; prob. mod. *Tell el-Qôs,* in the Jordan Valley; Maps 11, 14. □

Zareah, see ZORAH.

Zared (Brook, Torrent, Valley of), see ZERED (Brook, Valley of).

Zarephath, city in Phoenicia where Elijah wrought miracles, 1 K 17:9f.; on the N frontier of Canaan, Ob 20; Lk 4:26 (where some versions have the G&L form, Sarepta) recalls the story of 1 K 17:9ff.; mod. *Sarafand,* between Tyre and Sidon; Maps 17, 23. □

Zaretan, see ZARETHAN.

Zarethan, loc. in the Jordan Valley, ment. Jos 3:16; facing Succoth, according to 1 K 7:46; in the obscure text of 1 K 4:12 it is apparently ment. in order to fix the direction of Abel-meholah; poss. mod. *Qarn es-Sartabeh,* on whose summit stand the ruins of the fortress of Alexandrium, in a commanding position W of *Dâmiyeh;* Maps 14, 17, 34. Cf. ZEREDAH (2). □

Zareth-shahar, see ZERETH-SHAHAR.

Zartanah, Zarthan, see ZARETHAN.

Zeb, see ZEEB.

Zebah, n. of a Midianite king pursued and defeated by Gideon, Jg 8:5ff., cf. Ps 83:11(Heb. 12). Cf. ZALMUNNA.

Zebedee, n. of the father of the Apostles John and James, Mt 4:21, 10:2 and parallel passages.

Zebee, see ZEBAH.

Zeboiim, city of the Pentapolis, Gn 14:2; cf. PENTAPOLIS (1).

Zeboim, 1. loc. inc. among the cities of Judah, Neh 11:34, and ment. with Lod (Lydda) and Hadid; sit. unk. □
2. valley NE of Jerusalem, 'valley of hyenas'; ment. 1 S 13:18; mod. *W. Abû Dabâ'*; Map 15. □

Zebulun, n. of the 6th son of Jacob and Leah, Gn 30:20; ancestor of the tribe whose territory is indicated in Jos 19:10–16; Map 11.

Zechariah, n. of more than 30 persons in the O.T., in particular 1. Zechariah, 14th king of Israel (743 B.C.), son of Jeroboam II, assassinated by Shallum, 2 K 15:8ff.
2. Zechariah son of Jehoiada, a prophet who was stoned to death at the command of Joash, 2 Ch 24:20ff.
3. Zechariah, 11th of the Minor Prophets, who gave his n. to the book of Zechariah.
4. in the N.T., Zechariah father of John the Baptist, Lk 1:5ff.

Zedad, loc. on the ideal N frontier of the Promised Land, Nu 34:8, Ezk 47:15; sit. unk. □

Zedekiah, n. of several persons, inc. the last king of Judah (598–586 B.C.), 2 K 24:17ff.; Map 19.

Zeeb, 'wolf'; n. of one of the Midianite princes defeated and killed by Gideon, Jg 7:25, 8:3, cf. Ps 83:11 (Heb. 12). Cf. OREB, with whom he is always associated.

Zela, loc. of Benjamin, listed Jos 18:28 (foll. the LXX, some scholars attach this word to that which follows and read Zela ha-eleph); the city where Saul and Jonathan were buried, 2 S 21:14; poss. mod. *Kh. Salah,* between Jerusalem and the high place of Gibeon. □

Zela ha-eleph, Zelah, see ZELA.

Zemar, see ZEMARITES.

Zemaraim, loc. of Benjamin, listed Jos 18:22; 2 Ch 13:4 (Mount Zemaraim); prob. mod. *Râs ez-Zeimara,* N of Jerusalem; Maps 11, 13, 17. □

Zemarites, one of the peoples of Canaan, listed between the Arvadites and the Hamathites in Gn 10:18 = 1 Ch 1:16; they lived in the city of Zemar, prob. mod. *Tell Kazel,* on the *Nahr el-Abrash,* N of the Lebanon; Map 4. □

Zenan, loc. of Judah, in the lowland, listed Jos 15:37; poss. mod. *'Arâq el-Kharba,* W of Lachish; Maps 13, 19. □

Zephaniah, 'whom Yahweh shelters'; n. of several persons, inc. the 9th of the Minor Prophets, who prophesied in Judah under Josiah before 622 B.C.

Zephath, city ment. Jg 1:17, where it is identified with HORMAH, q.v.; Map 14. □

Zephathah, valley near Mareshah, 2 Ch 14:10 (Heb. 9), unless we read with the Gk. text 'to the north of Mareshah'. □

Zephrona, see ZIPHRON.

Zer, loc. of Naphtali, listed Jos 19:35; poss. another n. for MADON, q.v., W of the Sea of Galilee; Map 11. □

Zered (Brook, Valley of), torrent in the S of Moab, Dt 2:13f., cf. Nu 21:12 (Valley of Zered); prob. the mod. *W. el-Hesa,* SE of the Dead Sea; Map 9. Cf. ARABAH (Brook of the), WILLOWS (Brook of the). □

Zereda, see ZEREDAH (1).

Zeredah, 1. city where Jeroboam was born, 1 K 11:26, in the mts of Ephraim; prob. mod. *Deir Ghassâneh;* Map 17.
2. the Zeredah of 2 Ch 4:17 is prob. an error for Zarethan which occurs in the parallel passage of 1 K 7:46; poss. identical with Zererah, Jg 7:22. □

Zeredathah, see ZEREDAH (2).

Zererah, loc. ment. Jg 7:22 (Heb.); cf. ZEREDAH (2).

Zererath, see ZERERAH, ZEREDAH (2).

Zereth-shahar, loc. of Reuben, listed Jos 13:19; poss. mod. *Zârat,* at the hot springs of Callirhoë, on the E shore of the Dead Sea; Map 11. □

Ziddim, loc. of Naphtali, listed Jos 19:35; sit. unk. □

Ziklag, loc. of Judah, in the Negeb, listed Jos 15:31; listed among the cities of Simeon, Jos 19:5, 1 Ch 4:30; given to David by the king of Gath, 1 S 27:6; David makes it his headquarters, 1 S 30:1, 14, 26, 2 S 1:1, 4:10, 1 Ch 12:1, 20; repopulated after the Exile, Neh 11:28; poss. mod. *Tell el-Khuweilifeh;* Maps 11, 13, 15; pp. 67f. □

Zimri, n. of the 5th king of Israel (*ca* 885 B.C.), 1 K 16:15ff.

Zin (Wilderness of), region in the extreme S of Canaan, ment. Nu 13:21, 20:1, 27:14, 33:36, 34:3, Dt 32:51, Jos 15:1; between the ascent of Akrabbim and Kadesh-barnea, Nu 34:4, Jos 15:3; not to be confused with the wilderness of Sin on the W side of the Sinai peninsula; Maps 9, 12. □

Zion, original n. of the Jebusite fortress captured by David, on the SE hill of Jerusalem, 2 S 5:7, 1 K 8:1; later applied particularly to this hill as the dwelling-place of Yahweh, and eventually extended to the whole city of Jerusalem; in the N.T., used chiefly in a symbolical sense. In Early Christian times the n. was applied to the 'upper room' on the SW hill, which came to be regarded as the original Zion and was even provided with a 'tomb of David'. Maps 24A, 33.

Zior, loc. of Judah, in the hill country, listed Jos 15:54; mod. *Si'ir,* NE of Hebron; Maps 13, 19, p. 105 no. 5; cf. ZAIR. □

Ziph, 1. loc. of Judah, in the Negeb, listed Jos 15:24; prob. mod. *Kh. ez-Zeifeh;* Map 11. □
2. loc. of Judah, in the hill country, listed Jos 15:55; cf. 1 S 23:14ff., 26:1f., 1 Ch 2:42, heading to Ps 54 (Ziphites); later fortified by Rehoboam, 2 Ch 11:8; mod. *Kh. ez-Zîf;* Maps 11, 13, 15, 17, 19. □

Ziph (Wilderness of), region around Ziph (2), 1 S 23:14ff., 26:2.

Ziphron, city on the ideal N frontier of the Promised Land, Nu 34:9; sit. unk. □

Ziz (Ascent of), theatre of the war between Jehoshaphat and the Edomites, 2 Ch 20:16; prob. in the mod. *W. el-Hasâsah,* SE of Bethlehem; Map 17. □

Zoan, city in Egypt, ment. Is 19:11, 13 (with Memphis), 30:4 (with Hanes), Ezk 30:14f. (with Pathros, Thebes, and Pelusium); in Ps 78:12, 43, 'the fields of Zoan' signify Egypt; cf. Nu 13:22; LXX has Tanis, the classical form of the n.; the ruins lie near *Sân el-Hagar,* in the NE of the Delta; Maps 7, 8, 9. Cf. AVARIS, RAMESES. □

Zoar, see PENTAPOLIS (1).

Zoba, see ZOBAH.

Zobah, an Aramaean state in the time of David, 2 S 10:6; Map 16. Cf. ARAM (2).

Zoheleth (Stone of), see SERPENT'S STONE.

Zophim (Field of), 'field of the watchers'; loc. near the summit of Pisgah, Nu 23:14. □

Zorah, city usually ment. with Eshtaol, on the boundary between Judah and Dan, Jos 15:33, 19:41; birthplace of Samson, Jg 13:2; ment. also Jg 13:25, 16:31; figures in the story of the Danites, Jg 18:2, 8, 11; fortified by Rehoboam, 2 Ch 11:10; repopulated after the Exile, Neh 11:29; mod. *Sar'ah;* Maps 13, 14, 17, 19. □

Zoreah, see ZORAH.

Zuph, n. of an ancestor of Elkanah, 1 S 1:1, 1 Ch 6:35 (Heb. 20); his clan inhabited the 'land of Zuph', a region of Ephraim, 1 S 9:5; sit. unk. □

Maps: 1 p. 9 / 2, 3 p. 10 / 4 p. 29 / 5, 6 p. 30 / 7, 8 p. 43 / 9, 10 p. 44 / 11, 12 p. 59 / 13 p. 60 / 14 p. 65 / 15, 16 p. 66 / 1 p. 81 / 18, 19 p. 82 / 20, 21 p. 95 / 22–24 p. 96 / 25–29 p. 103 / 30, 31 p. 104 / 32, 33 p. 115 / 34, 35 p. 116 / I, II end-

165

ACKNOWLEDGEMENTS

Alinari, Rome: 319–321, 323–325, 397, 406 – Anderson, Rome: 407 – Archives Photographiques, Paris: 81, 140, 169–171, 203, 218, 219, 246, 267, 282 – Benoit, Prof. P., o.p., Jerusalem: 349, 350, 395, 403 – Böhl, Prof. Th. de Liagre, Leiden: 87, 100, 106, 247b, 257 – British Museum, London: 86, 245, 258 – Consulate of Israel, Amsterdam: 151 – Cools, Prof. J., o.p., Nijmegen: 37, 157, 332 – Creten, Canon J., Louvain: 145, 146 – Department of Antiquities, 'Ammân (Jordan): 143, 144, 225, 311, 353 – Department of Antiquities, Baghdad (Iraq): 248 – Dunand, Maurice, Beirut (Lebanon): 208 – Dupont, J., o.s.b., Bruges: 250, 256, 297, 373, 380, 384 – École Biblique et Archéologique Française, Jerusalem: 92–94, 101, 149, 156, 385, 386 – Egyptian Museum, Cairo: 131 – Elia Photo Service, Jerusalem: 191 – Eyckeler, J., Druten: 228 – Galloway, Ewing, New York: 27, 356 – Giraudon, Paris: 74, 268, 318, 322 – Grollenberg, L. H., o.p., Nijmegen: 8, 11, 15, 18, 19, 21, 22, 28, 40, 45–48, 50–69, 79, 88–91, 96, 97, 122, 123, 133–139, 155, 158, 160, 174, 175, 178, 179, 185, 186, 189, 190, 204, 227, 254, 263, 264, 289–296, 299, 314, 329, 331, 335–345, 347–351, 363–365, 367, 372, 381, 391–394, 396, 401, 405 – Illustrated London News, London: 76, 107, 108, 124, 125, 168. – Institut Français d'Archéologie, Beirut (Lebanon): 3–5, 12, 13, 16, 17, 20, 35, 36, 43, 44, 334 – Israel Government Information Service and Press Division, New York: 188, 360, 370 – Jeep-Express (P. Pennarts and J. Glissenaar), Haarlem: 224, 352 – Keren Hayesod, Jerusalem: 368 – Koninklijk Kabinet van Munten, Penningen en gesneden Stenen, The Hague: 272–278, 283–288 – Kowadlo, Boris, Amsterdam: 378 – Lange, Kurt, Oberstdorff-Allgäu (Germany): 41, 42 – Laxague, H. D., o.p., Oullins (France): 152, 153, 159 – Lloyd, Dr Seton, Ankara: 83–85 – Louvre, Musée du, Paris: 167 – Maliepaard, Ir. C. H. J., The Hague: 78 – Mansell Collection, London: 230, 234, 237–243, 247a – Matson Photo Service, Los Angeles: 1, 2, 38, 82, 147, 148, 150, 180, 201, 251, 253, 327, 359, 371 – Oriental Institute, Chicago: 70, 75, 77, 183, 184, 198, 266, 269 – Palestine Archaeological Museum, Jerusalem: 33, 34, 161–166, 193, 195–197, 212–215, 217, 220–223, 312, 313, 315, 317 – Photopress, Paris: 130 – Picture Post Library, London: 298, 300 – Van der Ploeg, Prof. Mag. J., o.p., Nijmegen: 176, 255, 301, 316, 354, 355, 362, 374, 375, 377, 382, 383 – Van de Poll, Willem, Amsterdam: 14, 23, 29, 95, 141, 142, 177, 205, 206, 252, 308–310, 326, 330, 333, 358, 361, 387, 389, 390 – Popper, Paul, London: 25, 26, 366, 369, 379, 398–400 – †Reifenberg, Prof. A.: 209, 210, 231, 376 – Rijksmuseum voor Oudheden, Leiden: 126–128, 271 – Schweig, Jerusalem: 24, 32 – Spaarnestad, Messrs.,Haarlem: 9, 10, 30, 192, 207, 257 – Tel, Éditions, Paris: 80, 216, 235, 236, 244 – Times, The, London: 172 – Vaux, R. de, o.p., Jerusalem: 199, 200 – Van der Voort, A. J., s.c.j., Nijmegen: 49, 404 – Winkler Prins Encyclopaedias, Amsterdam: 39, 109–111, 226, 302, 303, 306, 307 – Zadoks-Josephus Jitta, Dr A. N., Amsterdam: 71–73.

ILLUSTRATIONS FROM BOOKS

6, 7: A. Poidebard, *La trace de Rome dans le désert de Syrie*, Paris 1934 – 102–105: O. Puchstein, *Boghasköi, die Bauwerke*, Leipzig 1912 – 112–120: A. Parrot, *Mari*, Neuchâtel 1953 – 121, 229: F. Vigouroux, *Dictionnaire de la Bible*, Paris 1895–1912 – 154: W. Wreszinsky, *Atlas zur altägyptischen Kulturgeschichte*, Leipzig 1923 – 173: A. Jacoby, *Das geographische Mosaik von Madaba*, Leipzig 1905 – 181, 182: U. Hölscher, *The Excavation of Medinet Habu*, Chicago 1934 – 187: *Epigraphic Survey of Medinet Habu*, 'Earlier Historical Records of Rameses III', Chicago 1934 – 194: W. Otto, *Handbuch der Archäologie*, Munich 1939 – 202: J. Vandier, *La sculpture égyptienne*, Paris 1951–211: F. Thureau-Dangin, A. Barrois, G. Dossin, and M. Dunand, *Arslân-Tash*, Paris 1931 – 233: T. Torczyner, L. Harding, and others, *Lachish I. – The Lachish Letters*, London 1938 – 249a, b: Gordon Loud and Ch. B. Altman, *Khorsabad*, Part II, Chicago 1938 – 259: E. Unger, *Babylon*, Leipzig 1931 – 261, 262: E. G. Kraeling, *The Brooklyn Museum Aramaic Papyri*, New Haven (U.S.A.) 1953 – 270: E. E. Herzfeld, *Iran and the Ancient East*, London 1941 – 280: A. Poidebard, *Tyr, un grand port disparu*, Paris 1939 – 346: *The Biblical Archaeologist*, New Haven (U.S.A.) 1948.

NIHIL OBSTAT:
Thomas Hanlon, L.S.S., S.T.L., Censor Deputatus
Die 13 Julii 1956

IMPRIMATUR:
✝ Gordon Joseph, Archbishop of St Andrews and Edinburgh
Die 13 Julii 1956

IMPRIMI POTEST:
fr. Hilarius Carpenter, O.P. Prior Provincialis Provinciae Angliae
Ord. Praed.
Die 13 Julii 1956

I T A L I

I L L Y R I A

ADRIATIC SEA

DALMATIA

MACEDONI

* Two years' imprisonment at Rome (A.D. 60-62):
'But the word of God is not fettered' (2 Ti 2:9)
Colossians, Philippians, Ephesians, and Philemon

○ ROME

○ Three Taverns

○ Forum of Appius

The brethren of Rome come to meet Paul:
'On seeing them, Paul thanked God and took
courage'

The Jews declare:
* These men who have
turned the world
upside down have come
here also

2 C
Phi

Beroea○

○ Thessalon

Puteoli * They find brethren here

I
T
A
L
Y

Nicopoliso
(Tit 3:12)

○ Rhegium

Sicily

Corintho ○ ○
Cenchreae

* Not the wisdom of
the Greeks, but the
folly of the cross
Paul before Gallio

ACHAIA

1 and 2 Thessalonians

○○ Syracuse   Paul stays here three days *

Stay of several months
Romans

* Mutiny of the crew is
suppressed by the soldiers;
the cargo of wheat is
jettisoned

* All hope is abandoned
Paul predicts shipwreck
on his account God will
save everyone on
board

Malta

* After drifting for fourteen days,
the ship founders. All aboard are saved
'They will pick up serpents...' (Mk 16:18)
After the winter of A.D. 59-60, the journey
is continued aboard the 'Twin Brothers'

* Violent ga
from reach
harbour of

II
THE TRAVELS OF SAINT PAUL
according to the Acts of the Apostles

* For fear of running on the Syrtis,
the sailors lower the gear
and begin to jettison the cargo

– – – – – – First journey (Chaps 13–14)
– · – · – · – Second journey (15:36–18:22)
– ·· – ·· – Third journey (18:23–23:35)
– – – – Journey to Rome (27–28)
⟨symbol⟩   Places where his addresses in synagogues
are mentioned
· · · · · · Journeys planned but thwarted
45   The dates of the beginning and end of the
journeys are not certain
Gal.   The Epistle thus indicated was
probably written at this place
☐   Roman Empire

The scanty data do not enable us to indicate
journeys of Paul after his release at Rome.
Possibly he realised his plans to visit Spain.
According to the Epistles to Timothy and Titus,
he worked again in Crete, in Asia, and in
Macedonia.

SYRTIS